SOCIAL
AND CULTURAL
FOUNDATIONS
OF GUIDANCE
A Sourcebook

SOCIAL
AND CULTURAL
FOUNDATIONS
OF GUIDANCE
A Sourcebook

Edited by

Esther M. Lloyd-Jones
Teachers College, Columbia University

and

Norah Rosenau

HOLT, RINEHART AND WINSTON, INC.
New York   Chicago   San Francisco   Atlanta
Dallas   Montreal   Toronto   London

ACKNOWLEDGMENTS

The project of which this book is one result was made possible by grants from the National Institutes of Health without whose support the materials assembled here could not have been developed and made available to the profession. This support and the permission to publish in book form the materials originated under the terms of NIH Contract PH43-64-93 is gratefully acknowledged.

The entire project has been throughout a demonstration of quite remarkable team work over a period of several years. Almost from the very beginning Esther Manning Westervelt worked with me closely. She helped plan seminars and conferences and contributed countless valuable ideas. After the masses of work I have seen her expedite with such apparent ease, she should have no trouble in moving any other mountains that ever get in her way.

The contributions of the illustrious Advisory Committee* are described in the introductory chapter. Let me record here that it was a delight to watch them take hold of problems and suggestions, shake the living daylights out of them, and come up with the most brilliant and compatible agreements. Our meetings were intellectual fun.

---

* See page 4 for the names of the members of the Advisory Committee.

To the many outstanding scholars who produced the ideas we have included here, and to their publishers who generously and graciously let us use these materials even in their drastically pruned forms, we give our humble and hearty thanks. It is our hope that those who meet the scholars in this book will want to pursue their acquaintance by reading much more fully from their extended writings.

We are indebted to the scholars who gathered together twice at Arden House to study and criticize the work we were doing and to make their own inspired and generous contributions to it.

But without the brilliant help of William Hollister, who, when he was Chief of the Child Mental Health Section of the National Institute of Mental Health back about 1961, literally took off his coat and went to work on my rather vague ideas, and then later risked his reputation with his higher-ups to get money for them, the project probably would have died aborning.

Later Caroline Chandler, who succeeded Dr. Hollister at the National Institute of Mental Health, gave the same kind of critical analysis, sustaining faith, and practical help that kept us moving forward.

Others who have worked on the team over the years are literally too numerous to mention; some of them will remember the times they worked almost all night to get the masses of materials mimeographed, assembled, and mailed—before the Arden House Conferences, for instance—and were still able to smile—at least feebly, as the dawn broke.

To all of these fine people, my friends to whom I am deeply indebted my grateful thanks.

Esther Lloyd-Jones

New York, N.Y.
August 1968

CONTENTS

INTRODUCTION

Why and how the project developed

Guidance-personnel workers—and all educators—as they adopt new theories and concepts, see their world and their work differently and relate to their world and work in changed ways. The project of which this book is a part and the preparation of this book were undertaken to build and strengthen the bridges between the social-cultural sciences and the practice of guidance-personnel work, in the belief that in a very real way concepts can change us and our world, and that the area of guidance and personnel work, and even of education as a whole, needs some new theories and concepts on which to base professional practice.

We have begun to wonder how the social environment, of which we are more and more aware, is affecting the individuals about whose welfare and development we are so greatly concerned. And we are especially concerned with the effects that an era of dynamic change may have on individuals. We have begun to wonder whether our social institutions might be changed radically enough to afford each individual his maximum potential for happiness, effective functioning, and complete development. It occurs to most guidance-personnel workers that it may be somewhat harder to bring about the Great Society than it would be for the school or college society to be transformed—the society in which he and the students (and the faculty and administration, of course) are living and working together. Those who are members of an institution not only perpetuate it and are acted upon by it, but also inevitably modify it either in random and unexamined or in purposive ways. At some point, if he is competent to do so, a guidance-personnel worker can become an analyst of human problems, not only in the counseling booth, but of human problems in the society that has helped to cause them and that exacerbates them. So he inevitably becomes involved with all kinds of problems for which his professional preparation as it is presently offered in universities, has not necessarily prepared him.

He realizes at about this point that he has no way of really understanding the social-cultural nature of his school or college. He has simply taken it for granted up to this point. It reminds one of Charles Darwin's description of a trip he took to Wales in 1830 to study strata. He studied strata diligently but did not even see the effects of glaciation. It was not until after Agassiz did his work on glaciation that Darwin saw the effects of glaciation and wondered that he could have been so blind before.

We have begun to realize that we have had no way of really understanding the social-cultural nature of our schools and colleges. We have simply taken "culture" for granted up to this point.

If the guidance-personnel worker were to learn in some depth about social systems and culture, he could understand his students and the context in which they live and grow and could have much more realistic and creative views as to whether and how a school or college can be purposively altered by those who are members of it.

What are some of the concepts that are dealt with most helpfully by sociology, anthropology and social psychology that guidance-personnel workers could well adopt? The concepts of society and culture are absolutely basic, of course. Culture is the inevitable product of men living in groups, not only in groups in the South Sea islands, but also in groups in the elementary school, or on a college campus. Culture includes purposeful activities and rules of conduct: ritual and habitual and expected ways of doing things, as well as guitars, football fields, Maypoles, styles of dress, public address systems, and beer bottles. Peer groups—subcultures— contribute to the quality of the overall culture, whether one be studying the overall culture of a primitive tribe, a town, or a school.

At the heart of a culture is a system of values. All too rarely do we attempt to look critically and analytically at the values that permeate the culture in which we live and of which we are a part. We tend to be aware of them only when they affect us adversely and when we disagree with them sharply. Some good work is now being done that aims to reveal the values that run through any and all of the educational institutions in which students live and learn, the values which they absorb into their life-view. Many situations can be better understood and dealt with as guidance-personnel workers know better how to get at value systems and can see where reinforcement is taking place, how value systems influence attitude and behavior, and where and why conflict occurs.

The concepts of status and role, position, achieved status, ascribed status, power structure, social classes, communication, social and cultural change all now have a good deal of substance. A thorough understanding of these concepts can be as useful to the guidance-personnel worker as can a thorough knowledge of personality theory. And, as the song says of love and marriage, a well-prepared guidance-personnel worker should not have one without the other or his training is one-sided, incomplete, and ineffective.

But it may be like crying for the moon to say that guidance-personnel workers need to be grounded in more than one discipline. It obviously is unrealistic and impossible to expect guidance-personnel workers to study in depth in all of the fields that have much to contribute to our practice. Any department of sociology or psychology or anthropology worth its place in the graduate school would insist on solid foundational courses in its own discipline and then sequential courses stacked at least two or three years high. The guardians of these disciplines are entirely right in not wanting half-baked sociologists, psychologists, or anthropologists at large bringing dishonor to the reputations of their fields. Furthermore, students who really do not wish to become sociologists, psychologists, or anthropologists find that the way the courses in these disciplines are organized and taught are impossibly time-consuming and far too detailed. Such courses at present make no attempt to focus on practice—at least not on the kind of practice and problems with which guidance-personnel workers are preparing to deal within school and college systems.

Is there any way out of this *cul de sac*? It just does not work to ask generous, well-disposed professors of sociology, anthropology, and social psychology to design and offer in their departments new courses in which the subject matter will relate directly to the problems faced by guidance-personnel workers. If professors undertook to do this then why not a lot of other new courses focused on many other specific practitioner fields as well? We asked some very distinguished professors of sociology, anthropology, and social psychology at a four-day conference in 1963 what they would teach from their fields if they undertook to tell us what we needed to know to help us deal with our problems. We got nowhere. They do not know what our problems are and they claimed that we were unable to explain the problems so they could understand them.[1]

How did medical educators persuade specialists from all the various life and natural sciences to identify knowledge from their fields that was pertinent to the practice of medicine? This has taken many decades and has been a herculean task.

---

[1]Jerry Godard, after the Arden House Conference of 1963, undertook from an analysis of textbooks to define what it is that leaders in the guidance-personnel field say they do. He also undertook cautiously to suggest the concepts and theories in the social-cultural sciences that relate to these functions. The results of his work are reported in "Toward a development of multi-disciplinary foundations for use in the preparation of guidance-personnel workers," an unpublished Ed.D. dissertation, Teachers College, Columbia University, 1966.

It appears to have been a cooperative job: specialists from the several fields have teamed with medical practitioners to identify problems and to invent ways of dealing with them. It has had to be a team job. Medical education and medical research have now built their bridges to the supporting sciences with truly miraculous results for medical practice.

Paul Lazarsfeld, distinguished sociologist, who has been studying research in the field of education, says that the quality of research conducted at graduate schools of education is of especially low quality when it is done without contact with the liberal arts faculty, and that some of the most advanced, complex, and promising research in departments of sociology is marred by too little knowledge of the realities which shape elementary, secondary, and higher education.

When the National Institute of Mental Health, the United States Office of Education, and the Ford Foundation cooperated to make it possible several years ago for the director of this project to attempt to bring the wisdom of leaders in the field of guidance-personnel work into conjunction with the knowledge of experts in the social-cultural sciences, it took a number of seminars before the social-cultural scientists could focus on burning interests that *they* had that seemed to the guidance-personnel workers to connect up closely with problems that confronted *them*.

After the opening skirmish in attempting to bring the social-cultural sciences and guidance-personnel practice closer together, the National Institute of Mental Health undertook to support this project that was focused on just this problem: the establishment of some multidisciplinary foundations for guidance. This volume reports one major phase of this project.

This phase has been carried out under the close guidance of a distinguished advisory committee drawn from the fields of anthropology, sociology, and social psychology. Solon Kimball, now University Professor at the University of Florida, who has worked with the project since 1962, and who is certainly one of the most brilliant of contemporary educational anthropologists, has served as chairman of the advisory committee. Other distinguished members of the advisory committee have included W. H. Cowley of Stanford University, whose scholarship permits him a broad and deep view of a good many fields, Everett Hughes of Brandeis University, Paul Lazarsfeld of Columbia University, Dorothy Lee, anthropologist at large, Anthony Wallace, Professor of Anthropology at the University of Pennsylvania, Goodwin Watson, well-known social psychologist, and E. G. Williamson of the University of Minnesota who has given unstintingly of his wisdom. This committee, after meeting and working together, drafted the outline for this volume and suggested promising sources from which to seek useful and authoritative statements of theory and concept, with special emphasis on sources that might provide reports of empirical research and substantive findings.

After the work had thus been mapped out, Dr. Norah Rosenau, research associate for the project, spent two years in libraries reading, organizing, cutting, arranging, and discarding. Periodically the advisory committee reviewed her work and reevaluated and further clarified the general level and direction of the endeavor. At the three-quarter stage of the project, a grant from the National Institute of Mental Health made it possible to bring to Arden House for four days about 30 professors from as many universities which offer professional training for guidance-personnel workers, and 30 professors, one from each of these same 30 universities, all of the latter 30 scholars in one of the social-cultural areas. These 60 people were supplemented by other especially invited guests each of whom had some special competency to contribute. A few of the guests were there simply to observe the behavior of such a mixture brought together for purposes which some of them decided on second thought were too new and unorthodox and not really related, after all, to their own individual scholarly interests.

The Arden House conference of 1965 is one of those experiences one is glad to have lived through. As the Social Science Research Council has pointed out in its *Items* of March, 1965: "Every interdisciplinary encounter by its nature involves tensions related to the differing values and expectations of the groups represented." Observers from the National Institute of Mental Health and others were apparently somewhat entertained by some of the encounters that took place at the Arden House conference, but they reassured us that the uncomfortable behavior was par for the course and unanimously rated the conference to have been a valuable and productive one.

In any event, some excellent suggestions for this book were made at the 1965 conference. On the whole, the conference scholars encouraged us to finish the work very much as we had planned. Since that conference, more work has been done on the reading selections: the final selection of the articles, their sequential arrangement, and the introductions to them that pinpoint the salient ideas, and the questions and implications appended to each selection that attempt to make clearer the relevancy of each article for the practice of guidance-personnel work and education generally.

There are, in all, 50 selections contained in Chapters 2-11. These chapters are preceded by this introductory chapter that describes why and how the project developed and by Chapter 1 on the way in which perceptions of educational systems effectually determine concepts of guidance. Most of the 50 selections are preceded by individual introductions, while Chapters 2-11, and Parts II and III, have, in addition, general introductions. Norah Rosenau, besides digging out and editing the excerpts, wrote these introductions, which had the admiring approval of the advisory committee.

After the advisory committee had disbanded, Esther Lloyd-Jones wrote the first two chapters of the book and the questions and implications for the excerpts in Chapters 3-11. She regrets that she could not have had the advantage of the suggestions and criticisms that the advisory committee might have given for this part of her work, but she appreciates the very substantial contributions they did make to the project over a period of time. Chapter 2 sets forth the social scientific approach to understanding human behavior from the standpoint of the social psychologist, the anthropologist, and the sociologist, and, with the introductory chapter and Chapter 1, is meant to form a background for the better use of the 50 excerpts or selections.

It is the hope of the advisory committee, of those on the staff of the National Institute of Mental Health who have supported the project, and of the initiator and director of the project that the work will prove useful to guidance-personnel workers who are searching for ways of improving the quality of their professional performance.

Elaborately selecting, arranging and trimming a set of materials, however, is only a first step in attempting to provide a sound multidisciplinary base for practice. The next problem, and it is a really big one, is to develop new ways of continuing collaboration between guidance-personnel educators and behavioral scientists.

Charles Fall, James Hansen, and Gilbert Moore have reported[2] an integrated foundations seminar that was developed at the State University of New York at Buffalo. They report that staff members representing sociology, anthropology, and educational philosophy were organized into a planning group with a specialist from the counselor education program. They agreed to make the functions and problems encountered by school counselors central and to focus their theoretical discussions on these problems. At the conclusions of two semesters of work, the instructors concluded that:

1. Precise evaluation of outcomes was impossible.
2. Learning activity in the social-cultural sciences was much more productive when it was organized around foci that had meaning for the individual—the functions and problems of school counselors, in this instance.
3. Areas of knowledge could not be seen as discrete in this seminar but rather became flowing, evolving, interacting elements which shed light upon an area of concern only when a unified approach was taken: There is no problem that is solely psychological or philosophical in its components, or that has solely sociological dimensions and anthropological elements.
4. Adequate preparation for personnel work should be organized to enhance conceptualization through an organization of learning activities in which the integration of knowledge elements is facilitated.

Fall, Hansen, and Moore report also that, although such collaborative efforts undoubtedly contribute valuably to the learnings of the students, there are, unfortunately, administrative problems. They remind us that university rewards are more often tied to specialization than to integration. They end their report by stating that in spite of this handicap the department heads and faculty involved in their experiment continue to be enthusiastic and that the spirit of enthusiasm thus far has helped solve the problems of load, remuneration, and so forth.

---

[2]Charles Fall, James Hansen, and Gilbert Moore, "A Behavior Science Seminar in Counselor Education," *Counselor Education and Supervision*, Vol. V, No. 1, Fall 1965, pp. 27-33.

It seems almost certain that the very need of it will ensure the success of other attempts at collaboration. After all, practitioners have challenging problems to work at on the growing edges of human affairs and development. As these problems are described and defined, scientists from the social-cultural fields will be challenged to help in the further definition and analysis of these problems, and then they cannot help but become deeply involved.

The director of the project has watched some of the most distinguished social scientists in the United States find intellectual stimulation and new perspectives as they have shared together in the challenge of attempting to understand and deal more effectively with educational possibilities and human problems that exist in schools and colleges, as these have been identified and described by guidance-personnel workers. It is not so much that they are flattered that their help is critically needed as it is that the problems themselves engage them. And, as they come to realize that practitioners work courageously—and even now often successfully— with such problems, perhaps their respect for the practitioners is also enhanced.

It may be that we can again take the analogy of the medical profession where pure scientists find inspiration and fulfillment in working with physicians in the development of new techniques, new knowledge, new drugs, new concepts.

If those in charge of the professional preparation of guidance-personnel workers can have the close collaboration of social-cultural scientists in teaching the introductory materials that have been selected and organized herein for textbook use, there would seem to be little danger that these excerpts from the social-cultural disciplines will be considered an adequate substitute for courses in the various social sciences. It is more reasonable to suppose, on the other hand, that more students from the applied field will be encouraged to explore further in one or more of the fields into which they will have had an intriguing glimpse.

Certainly, it is to be hoped that the collaboration suggested above will lead to the more frequent application of sociological and anthropological research methods to the problems of our field. It would seem reasonable to suppose, as Dr. Lazarsfeld has suggested, that teamwork in research on school and college guidance-personnel problems by social scientists and educators working together will produce more valuable research than could be produced by either group working alone. Those anthropologists and sociologists and those guidance-personnel workers who have begun to see the problems that need to be tackled and the new concepts and methods that could be brought to bear are stimulated and excited by new possibilities that now open up.

It may be that we should begin to think of postdoctoral training for "counselor educators" in social sciences other than psychology. (And maybe find a better title for them than "counselor educators"!) It may be that universities should attempt to set up faculty seminars of social scientists and "counselor educators" for the purposes of orienting the latter to the implications of such materials for professional education and guidance practice, and the former to the possibilities of research in guidance-personnel work.

Certainly we need a continuing dialogue and cooperative relationship between those who are experts in the fields of social-cultural knowledge and those who are faced with the kinds of problems that confront guidance-personnel workers. We need innovation in the professional preparation of guidance-personnel workers designed to strengthen the interdisciplinary foundations for their work.[3] We need to work collaboratively with our social-cultural colleagues in identifying problems that will lend themselves to our present research capabilities. We need to work together to discover how students majoring in sociology, for example, could get sound grounding in the context and operational processes of schools and colleges so that their research can be more fruitful. Similarly, we need the help of our colleagues in the social-cultural sciences in guiding our students in the guidance-personnel field and education generally to acquire the thorough knowledge and research skills that will enable them to contribute breakthroughs sadly needed in dealing with human problems in schools and colleges.

Certainly, guidance-personnel workers can test continuously the uses of scientific knowledge produced by sociologists and anthropologists; we can encourage the continuous scrutiny of the validity in practice of ideas selected from the social sciences, and we can more clearly identify areas in which new or further knowledge is needed.

Much remains to be done. A mere beginning has been made. Bigger and stronger bridges must continuously be built between knowledge from the behavioral sciences and professional practice if education is to contribute as it might and must to the development of every individual and so to a better world.

Esther Lloyd-Jones

New York, N.Y.
August 1968

---

[3] It is my own belief that attempting to try to give guidance-personnel workers adequate training for their work in departments of higher education, secondary education, or elementary education, as a few graduate schools are attempting to do, is as much of a mistake as to attempt to prepare them professionally within departments set up primarily to train psychologists.

PART I

RELEVANCE
OF THE
SOCIAL-CULTURAL
SCIENCES FOR
GUIDANCE-PERSONNEL
WORKERS

Chapter 1

Concepts of Guidance in Different Educational Contexts

Of books listing the areas and functions of a complete guidance-personnel program, and exactly how to perform these functions, there is no dearth. Such listings and descriptions are usually preceded by one or more chapters on general principles that the author thinks do or should underlie these programs and are often followed by one or more chapters that describe who should perform which functions and how these people should be related to each other in some kind of organizational plan.

The present book does not follow this pattern at all. Rather it attempts to open up new areas of knowledge that are drawn on inadequately in current texts about education and guidance-personnel work. In this chapter on concepts of guidance and its educational contexts, we shall attempt to show that agreement on principles, areas, functions, and who shall do what are not enough—that we are helped in making our work more effective only by having knowledge from more fields, but also by having a broader view of the educational contexts within which we do our work.

What is the nature of the educational system within which we work?

Back before the first industrial revolution a school or college was not thought of as a factory, but this is probably the perception that now most controls and determines the ways in which we work with students and each other within the educational context.

It was in 1916 that Cubberley of Stanford University, who was writing most influentially in that time about educational administration, first described the school as a factory. In this model of education, students are fed into the system as raw material and are molded by the various educational patterns the school provides for students. In this way the school intends to fit each student, when he is finished, into some vocational slot in the outside world. There is much concern with standardization so that more of the processes of the school and college can be automated in order to increase the efficiency of operation and get more dependable results. In this model, students move along on one of several or many conveying belts, or tracks, having standard things done to them, are removed if some imperfection appears, are subjected to extra heat or pressure or polishing, are put back on a conveying belt, and, desirably, emerge after a standard length of time as finished products meeting standard specifications as determined by tests.

Guidance-personnel workers in this day and age are as familiar with this model as they are with their own mothers. They easily adopt this view of the educational system and fit into it without any questions. This becomes their basic way of perceiving and they act out roles in accord with it. They then, of course, sort out the students when they first arrive at the school or college and put the units on the "right" tracks; they keep closely in touch with how each is doing by taking careful readings at regular intervals; they move individuals about to give them more or less heat or pressure or to remedy imperfections; they spend a great deal of energy in trying to find an outlet for their finished products: it may be a way into some other kind of "factory," a business, a college, a job of some sort. The expectation is that each of the units produced will eventually fit into some part of the great industrial machine that produces the goods that we enjoy in such abundance and that the unit will be fed and clothed and housed by that same great industrial machine which it will serve until it wears out.

But we can, if we but would and believed that we should, look at the context within which we do our work in quite a different way. We could, for instance, use an agricultural model. Each year the farmer plants new crops, but first he must prepare the soil for the kind of plants that are to grow in it. The farmer recognizes that the seed has a nature of its own and he needs to know a great deal about its nature and its needs—as well as about growing conditions generally—in order to help the seed achieve maximum growth. He cultivates the ground to help the plants to grow. He deals with matters of soil friability, soil erosion, irrigation, etc.

This model would perhaps place more emphasis on curriculum and its improvement than would the factory model. The role of the guidance-personnel worker would be to test by laboratory methods the "seed" to be planted, and the soil into which the seed is to go. Study would be made of the genetic nature of the seed. Careful attention would have to be paid to the potential markets for the "crops" and the effective marketing thereof.

I myself do not particularly like this model, because agriculture today is much like big industry. Cows on the modern-dairy farm are nothing more than machines which are maintained to turn out milk. Records are carefully kept and cows are retained or eliminated according to the quantity and quality of milk they produce.

One might perhaps use a garden model instead of a big farm model and cast guidance-personnel workers in the role of gardeners. After one does this, however, the model seems to fit more readily the private school or small, privately supported college than it does the big, publicly supported school or university. This model undoubtedly possesses potential stimulation for the thinking of guidance-personnel workers, but I doubt whether even hippies, who may identify more completely with flowers than the rest of us do, would want to be "cultivated" by "loving" guidance-personnel workers.

Nowadays one often hears educational systems called bureaucracies. Herbert Stroup, formerly Dean of Students at Brooklyn College, has written a book *Bureaucracy in Higher Education*.[1] If the education system is considered a bureaucracy, those within the bureaucratic system are forced into certain roles and patterns and, consequently, students in it are affected. In bureaucratic institutions, students are no longer thought of as boys and girls or men and women. This system pointedly minimizes their differences as much as possible. The students themselves try to minimize differences by the way they dress and by the way they cut (or mostly do not cut) their hair. Students are simply "students." The most essential aspect of their personalities—their sexuality—is officially ignored, insofar as possible. Bureaucracy seems to have to depersonalize in order to function efficiently and the surest way of doing this is to desex the student. Furthermore, anyone who regrets this desexing is labeled by those who perceive education as a bureaucracy not only as old-fashioned and quaint, but somehow also as a little bit indecent.

As evidence of this fact one could refer to statements by numerous Deans of "Students"—not of men or of women—stressing the *functions* to be performed by "my office," rather than the developmental needs of boys and girls and men and women students.

In a letter to the editor of *Journal of College Student Personnel* (January 1967), Richard S. Offenberg of Temple University inquires whether Deans of Women are necessary. He, like many others in the past few decades, would have a Dean of "Students" who would be assisted by an Associate and/or Assistant Dean of "Students." Job descriptions, Offenberg insists, "should not mention sex." Deans of Women, he declares, are as outmoded as are Deans of Men.

Guidance-personnel workers operating in bureaucracies are not human beings at all. The whole group of guidance-personnel people are encouraged to consider themselves "offices." In a large university the professional guidance-personnel worker works out of "The Office of the Dean of Students," and the Dean of

---

[1] Published by The Free Press, New York: 1966.

Students makes pronouncements as an "Office." The thing to do in this system is to hide behind the doors of one's office and expose oneself as little as possible as a person.

In the bureaucratic system each guidance-personnel worker is hired to perform a few specific functions; he is a specialist; he is not to intrude on the functions that other kinds of specialists have been hired to perform. Each person exists some place up or down or sidewise on a carefully prepared organizational chart: he knows to whom he should talk about what, and even how often and when he should do that talking.

One might well discuss further the legitimacy and the limitations of this model and develop its implications still further.

A sociologist has recently suggested, however, that schools and colleges are more like feudal systems than they are like bureaucracies. They have their principalities, their empires, their petty monarchs, peasants, and serfs. If we were to use this model as a way of looking at a situation in which we attempt to aid the development of girls and boys or men and women students, some interesting new understandings might result. There have been some clever and enlightening attempts to map a particular school or college, showing how it would look if one used the model of a feudal system.

Others see schools and colleges as vast Persian market places where each merchant spreads his wares in a bewildering panorama and hopes to sell. Students in such a model are largely at the mercy of the sellers: some merchants are more persuasive than others; know how to display their goods to better advantage; or may actually have excellent goods to sell, but do not know how to display them. Students differ in the size of their pocketbooks—to continue the analogy—and, certainly, each has his own individual interests at any given time as to what he wants to buy.

In terms of this model, guidance-personnel workers would have to be familiar with the operation of the market, what goods were being offered for sale, who the more reliable merchants were, where the cheaper goods and the goods of highest quality could be obtained. The guidance-personnel worker would undertake to guide each person in choosing wisely according to his interests, his needs, and the resources he possessed.

Certainly, the perception we have of the system within which we work is going to affect to a considerable degree the objectives that we have, the way we will perceive others in the situation, the kind of person each of us believes it is desirable and possible for him to be, and the way he will go about trying to help others in the situation develop their lives.

However viewed, we know—or anyway we hope—that schools and colleges are more than structures and organizations. They are potentially rich teaching and learning situations. Their structure and organization should exist for the purpose of facilitating and enriching teaching and learning. They are essentially communities of a unique and special sort. Furthermore, their number increases every day throughout the world and more hopes are centered on them in every country of the world because they, more than any other institution of modern society, have the ability to stimulate and guide human development and to transform society.

Schools and colleges viewed as special kinds of groups are held together by sentiments and common objectives, and have unique and well established patterns of human relationships and customs. This way of looking at the context in which we work is very different from the notion of working in a factory, on a farm, in a bureaucracy or a market. One begins to wonder whether a school or college might not be viewed as a kind of tribal group—or perhaps a collection of tribal groups. I do not remember that this model has been suggested previously, but it might have some genuine values, especially because the focal emphasis would be on students and faculty and their interactions rather than on the processes through which students are put or on faculty as machines that operate somehow to shape students to what they should become.

Schools and colleges, like tribes, are made up of several hundred or several thousand members all living together or coming together almost daily over years within a definite geographical area. These members have many similarities in terms of which they identify with each other. The members of the group develop countless patterns of interaction among themselves and with their elders. Each knows that he belongs to the tribal group, develops definite loyalties to certain aspects of it, and recognizes that he has an important life to learn to live in it for what may seem to him a very long time.

Neither in the school nor in the tribe does the individual have anything to say about whether or not he will be there; determinants quite outside of his own control usually have put him there, and he is required for many years to conduct his existence as well as he can within this group pretty much according to its time-honored, but more or less changing ways. He is set down as a "new" and innocent individual in a structured social situation in which he is required as fast as he can to adapt to pre-established norms, must learn and work for certain common objectives that he had little to do with setting up, and is stimulated to interact with others in the situation, to develop patterns and qualities of relationships within the group, to learn certain prescribed roles, and may be adroitly nudged—or relentlessly pushed—by methods which the group contrives, to move out of less mature patterns of relationships and behavior into greater responsibility and more maturity.

As Willard Waller[2] observed perceptively many years ago:

> Teachers have always known that it was not necessary for the students of strange customs to cross the seas to find material. Folklore and myth, tradition, taboo, magic rites, ceremonials of all sorts, collective representations, participation mystique, all abound in the front yard of every school, and occasionally they creep upstairs and are incorporated into the more formal portions of school life.

---

[2]*The Sociology of Teaching*, New York: John Wiley & Sons, Inc., 1932, pp. 20-21.

If one can transpose his perceptions of the school from those of a market place or a factory to that of a tribal system, then one can see people in a school or college in quite a different way, and the educational and guidance processes are also seen quite differently. Instead of seeing teachers as merchants trying to sell their wares, or as machines operating on raw material, teachers may be seen as members of the tribe, as the clever ones who have special knowledge to teach to the young ones growing up in the tribe.

Furthermore, every tribe has need not only of clever ones, but also of wise ones who are skillful in helping the tribe maintain its viable values, to help it realize its best interests.

None of the other models sketched above—the factory, the garden, the bureaucracy, the feudal community, or a market place—needs a "wise one." The factory and bureaucracy need administrators with underlings, each performing functions almost as though they were automated themselves. The farmer needs to know how to study the nature of his plants and provide conditions that will stimulate their growth; but the farmer nowadays is a kind of industrialist himself: he operates by formula and machinery; he treats his animals almost as though they were simply machines. He is not much like the wise one of the tribal model. The feudal system seems to need its fool, who often is extremely wise and helpful to the more constructive aspects of human life within the feudal system. The tribe, however, could not get along without at least one truly wise one to help it carry on its affairs as a tribe.

The wise ones help the tribe collectively to cultivate and maintain its wisdom. They are expected to guide the preservation and transmission of those traditions that have most value for the good life of the tribe. They preside over the plans and tribal ceremonies that help newcomers enter into tribal membership and that mark and assist transition from one emotional state to another. They help individuals and groups of individuals at critical times in their lives and, more importantly, they guide the members of the tribe in helping each other.

They also represent the group in meting out retribution when individuals or small groups defy the accepted mores and threaten the structure and orderly processes and the normal on-going life of the tribe as a whole.

I hold that deans and counselors—guidance-personnel workers—could quite appropriately be viewed as wise ones if the school or college were to be viewed as a kind of tribal group.

It might be the better part of valor—of course, particularly on the college level—to keep it a deep, dark secret from the students that the guidance-personnel workers regard themselves as wise ones! (Just as it would hardly be discreet to make too explicit the fact that students in the prevalent factory model are regarded only as raw material to be inexorably shaped or that they are seen as serfs in the feudal model!)

Nevertheless, to continue boldly with the analogy of the tribe, each tribe has its distinct ways of doing things and no one can qualify as a wise one who does not know the ways of his particular tribe. Certain ways of doing things, as every tribal member knows, are rated much more highly by the tribe than are other ways. From a sophisticated point of view, these preferences reveal—they are—the values of the tribe. New human beings, whom life's pressures force into the tribe, come in uncertainly, wanting more or less frantically to discover as instantly as possible, just how to live their lives so as not only to be accepted by the group, but even, indeed, to survive in it. We do not yet study the cultures that flourish in our schools and colleges as thoroughly as Beatrice Whiting[3] did, for instance, when she and her husband tried to find out the different ways used by six different groups in six different countries to rear their children. The Whitings were trying to discover, of course, how these different ways of rearing children reflected six quite different kinds of value systems in the tribes and resulted in six different general kinds of behavior among the children.

We are, however, beginning to know how to get at and understand the mores and values that are implicit in each school and college group and also in subgroups within those institutions. We know that, whether or not the person was attracted ecologically by his perception of a college to want to become a member of that college group or whether he was projected without choice into the group—as in the case of a public high school or elementary school—nevertheless real impact and change do take place as a result.

Besides becoming a student of culture, of group values, and of mores, what are a few of the many other things a wise one needs to know who attempts to operate in a school or college setting as though it were a kind of tribe? In his presidential address several years ago to the American Sociological Association, Howard Becker reviewed Durkheim's description of the destructive effects that anomie or normlessness in a society has on the personalities of those who live in that society. Dr. Becker also described a process which he called "sacralization." By this he meant a process that works in a society to avoid chaos by continuously revealing and helping the group restore norms that it as a whole can accept and live by.

A guidance-personnel worker in a school or college who recognizes the importance of sacralization and who attempts to reinforce the process, may expect opposition and obstacles. There are a number of professors and students in higher education who insist that the behavior and attitudes of students in college (except for certain sacred aspects of classroom behavior) are nobody's business except that of the students themselves. There are parents of secondary school youth, and even some educators and school board members, who argue that the business of the school is to teach subject matter, that that is its unique function and should be its only one, and that all else should be left to the family and to the church, as well, unavoidably then, to the police. How this unrealistic attitude and ignorance about the functioning of the peer society within the school or college manages to

---

[3]Beatrice Blyth Whiting, *Six Cultures, Studies of Child Rearing*, New York: John Wiley & Sons, 1963.

persist—or even to exist at all—is hard to understand. Maybe the wise ones have not been sufficiently active in representing to parents and other educators how powerfully membership in the school and college tribes determines the way students will learn to live their lives.

There are even those today who hold that almost any standards and norms are undesirably restrictive of individual development and are destructive of inalienable human liberties. This point of view is understandably attractive to those who want to live to themselves alone without regard for external law or standards—or even for the inalienable rights of others. This represents ultimate impersonality in that individuals are asked not to notice or care what others do. A great mystique seems to have grown up around this point of view in some communities: a profound belief that unfettered self-expression and individual freedom are good for personality and individual development. All of us undoubtedly would agree that self-expression and a sense of freedom—with responsibility—are essential to individual development, personality, and to a good society, but we would recognize that there are extremes that need to be guarded against because they are not good either for individual development and personality growth or for society.

The wise ones must care about the whole tribe and its welfare because they know that peers powerfully influence each other. They cannot stand aside too passively while every individual without regard for others attempts to express whatever he thinks he finds within himself. The wise one knows that this can quickly erode and destroy corporate life; obscure models of the good life; lead to anomie; disrupt avenues of understanding, concern, and mutual help; undermine the foundations of values in terms of which young people can learn something from examined social wisdom about how to live good lives; and plunge life in school and college back into what might be termed a jungle.

So the wise ones within each tribe, with the collaboration of the clever ones and other tribal members, work constantly, with purpose, integrity, and as much wisdom and artistic skill as they can command, at the process of sacralization. They work in multiple ways at the endless process of helping the tribe examine its ways of life, weigh its values, improve upon them, and then re-examine them. The wise ones keep steadily in mind, as they work at the sacralization process, the importance to the welfare of the tribe of maintaining and respecting diversity, of recognizing the dangers of totalitarianism, and avoiding the threats that anomie poses to human life.

The rather primitive notion about the virtues of maximum individual freedom with minimum accountability is only one of the notions that presently tends to enthrall the tribe. A vigorous advertising campaign has been under way for some time that extolls, not only the attractiveness and the wholesomeness, but also the actual necessity of wholesale intimacy. It is true that adolescents, in order to carry out subsequent life tasks and responsibilities and to learn to share deeply with other human beings and establish good homes for children, must develop their capacity for intimacy. We have seen the tragic consequences in homosexuality, frigidity, and a pathetic lack of full development—and even an inability to trust other human beings—that can result for those who do not progress normally in the development of their capacity for intimacy.

I listened recently to a woman wise in the ways of adolescents who discussed before a sound-movie camera with a group of adolescents the kind of intellectual and aesthetic life styles they thought they were developing. I was struck again during this discussion by the preoccupation of young people with what they referred to as their "shells." I played back the sound film and confirmed my impression that every one of the boys and girls kept referring to their shells, how hard it was to come out of them, and how they wished others would come out of *their* shells.

I suppose all of us know well the exquisite sensitivity that attends shell-coming-outs; the excessive amount of courage that it seems to take; and how difficult it is for an adolescent to practice self-disclosure and to relate more candidly and fully to other people. Most of this important process takes place during the long succession of school years, and more during the teen years within school and college communities than it does within the family. It needs desperately to be presided over by really wise ones who understand the phenomenon, who respect its importance, and who know how to help develop a social situation that will encourage and safeguard it as a process so that a capacity for intimacy does develop, and so that it develops naturally and as nearly as possible without trauma and disastrous consequences. Many schools and colleges at the present time as a matter of deliberate policy are trying to ignore in so far as possible this whole aspect of adolescent development as it now goes on quite haphazardly among the great congregations of young people in schools and colleges.

And, as we so often do in this country, we have carried the idea of intimacy in and for its own sake to ridiculous and dangerous extremes. If one, in order to mature, needs not only to come out of his shell, but also to develop the ability to be intimate and to disclose what are to him some of the most secret and important facts about himself, then he also needs to learn to do this with appropriateness. He must learn not to bestow his precious capacity for intimacy indiscriminately and thus eventually to render it cheap and relatively meaningless both to himself and to others.

Every group of people who have any continuing identity and relationships need norms to guide the way the individual members of the group will develop and will use their capacity for intimacy with other human beings. It would seem essential for people living and working together in schools and colleges to work at the basic facts and issues of independence, freedom, responsibility, and intimacy, with the help and guidance of their wise ones, and thus progressively to develop and learn to understand and use these qualities for better and more satisfying living.

How can the wise ones help individuals to understand and deal with these abstract qualities of life? Occasionally, certainly, by helping individuals separately confront their own problems as individuals, but continuously by helping groups work together toward greater understanding of these abstract concepts and principles that make life more or less good. These abstract qualities are confronted and take on meaning as they exist in endless form in concrete individual behavior and social situations within the group life that goes on incessantly in schools and colleges.

The wise ones continuously help the tribe examine its ways of life, its implicit values, and how they do or do not serve the best interests of learning to live well. The wise ones are, of course, concerned that accepted values not be violated and destroyed, but are more interested in keeping the tribal members at work on how the common values might be improved than in holding the norms frozen and inviolate. Working at improving them keeps them vital, while holding the norms frozen ultimately kills them.

The small substantive conference, which Margaret Mead calls a new social invention,[4] seems a more effective instrument for the purposes of the wise ones—the guidance-personnel workers—than a heavy reliance on individual or group counseling. Mead says that in conference the participants are concerned with an "invisible idea in the middle of the table." This process requires a faith in ideas on the part of the guidance-personnel worker. It also requires true sophistication on the part of the guidance-personnel workers about the nature of freedom and responsibility, far more than a superficial understanding of the need for and use of intimacy that every human being has at various stages of his life; skill in the use of conference technique, the encouragement of spontaneous and organized dialogue, and the vigorous use of inquiry. The guidance-personnel worker needs to know how to create situations in which "authentic communication"—freedom to express one's best and clearest understanding—about abstract ideas and values can take place with a resultant increase of every participant's understanding.

Someone has said that Western man was an animal and plant tender up to 1800. With the industrial revolution, man became a tender of machines. Now, in our age of cybernetics, man must learn to tend systems. We would seem to have built much of our present world—our thinking patterns as well as our institutions—in accord with concepts appropriate to a mechanical technology rather than to the new electronic technology. We may still be working in educational institutions, too, built according to models growing out of a mechanical technology. So, as we look at the educational contexts within which we work, we see predominantly such features as empires, hierarchy, centralization, specialization, and segmentation—all more or less characteristic of the straight-line thinking that is typical of mechanics.

If we learn to use a more constellational, multirelational type of thinking, we may be able to create new concepts and theories, enabling new institutional forms, procedures, and methods that are needed in education to be developed.

---

[4]Margaret Mead. "Conference Behavior," *The Columbia University Forum*, Vol. X, No. 2, Summer 1967, p. 15. See also *The Small Conference: An Innovation in Communication* by Margaret Mead and Paul Byers, New York: Mouton and Co., 1967.

Man now has access to enough knowledge so that he can be the prime influence on his own evolution. Whether he is wise enough in the aggregate to learn to guide his own development wisely is a moot question. Certainly, education is potentially one of man's most powerful means for influencing his own evolution. But whether educators are wise enough to help young people learn to guide their evolution in its most human aspects is still questionable.

Within the educational enterprise the development of the powers of each individual to form intelligent "good" purposes for his own life is an undertaking of crucial importance. Whether we are wise enough to help individuals do this fast enough is still another moot question—and a most important one.

Certainly, to undertake in schools and colleges to do this one by one in the fashion that many psychologists have said it must be done will be to miss the mark and to overlook the vast forces within the total group that can and must be enlisted in support of each individual's full development as a human being.

Danilo Dolci, an Italian social reformer who has been using western Sicily as a laboratory for his experimentation, has said recently:[5]

. . .even as each man must take stock of himself and learn to live according to his convictions, so the life of the group, community life, is an indispensable instrument for stocktaking and for individual and collective maturation. . . .one must work with the people to create new facts, at all levels, so that they can see through their own experience that things can be changed, and how this can be done, and to provide an opportunity for real communication between persons of many different backgrounds and walks of life.

The excerpts that follow in the succeeding chapters have been selected (1) to aid the process of establishing a broader foundation of knowledge for guidance-personnel practice, and (2) to enable educators to view in more critical and productive ways the institutional context that controls and obstructs or frees and enhances their efforts to stimulate the development of every student.

---

[5]"Tools for a New World," *Saturday Review*, July 29, 1967, p. 13.

Chapter 2

The
Social Scientific
Approach
to Human
Behavior

Having said that the aim of this volume is to introduce the reader to areas of social science relevant to the practice of guidance-personnel work in education, it is necessary to provide a more specific context for the materials to be presented. In this chapter, a leading member of each of the branches of social science represented in this book states his view of what that discipline is about. From these selections it is hoped that the reader will derive some understanding of what social scientists aim to do and of how they go about it. He should then be better able to assess the validity of their work as well as its practical relevance.

Such explanation and justification might, at first glance, seem unnecessary. If social scientists study people, should not anyone be able to examine their findings and conclusions, evaluate them, and put them to practical use? The answer is both yes and no. It is true that the subject matter of social science is closely related to most people's personal concerns and experiences, and thus it would seem that they could bring the necessary enlightenment and understanding to bear on their judgments. However, some of the assumptions and purposes of social science are at variance with the ordinary common sense views that people bring to their responses to social situations, and unless one is aware of these distinctions it is not possible to fully comprehend or evaluate social scientific products.

An example from a different area might help to clarify this point. If a botanist and a painter each studies a tree, we expect the results of their work to differ vastly from each other. The botanist starts from scientific premises and pursues scientific goals, while the painter bases his work on artistic notions and seeks to achieve artistic goals. Each will address himself to different questions about the same tree, seek to answer them with different methods, and be satisfied with different conclusions. As a result, the botanist's technical treatise and the artist's painting will bear little resemblance to each other and will be meaningful only in relation to their respective premises and goals.

In the area of human affairs, there are likewise a number of possible approaches to knowledge. Social science is only one of them, and it is based on the same premises and pursues the same goals as science in general. However, there are specific virtues and limitations in the application of the scientific approach to the understanding of human nature and human society and these are often unrecognized. Indeed, the free and widespread use of the label *social science* does not necessarily indicate a general acceptance of the implications of its second term, *science*, as applied to social phenomena. It is thus necessary to briefly discuss some of these implications before we can examine the differentiations among the subfields of social science represented in this volume.

There is, first, the matter of vocabulary. Any specialized study, whatever its orientation or topic, will develop special terms to refer to phenomena for which there are also commonplace words. For the outsider to understand the products of such study, he must not only learn the extensive terminology which may have evolved but he must also be willing to consider the subject matter in these new terms rather than in his own more familiar ones. This adjustment is likely to be especially difficult with respect to social science, whose subject matter encompasses our most personal experiences but which, like all science, attempts to maximize clarity and precision and to minimize ambiguous connotations. These goals tend to be incompatible with the emotional or evaluative reactions that the subject matter evokes, but, as we will elaborate below, they are for that very reason at the heart of the scientific enterprise.

What we are saying, in effect, is that the issue is more than one of mere vocabulary: the need for special terminology is only a reflection of a more basic feature of social science as an approach to the understanding of human behavior. This more fundamental quality is inherent in the term *science* and refers to an attitude of detachment and objectivity toward subject matter, regardless of its nature. Such an attitude is the defining characteristic of the scientific approach and it means that in observing, describing, and attempting to understand a piece of reality, the individual makes a deliberate effort to free his account of any preconceptions and judgments. To do this, he makes his assumptions about the subject matter, his methods of observation, and the logic of his inferences as explicit as possible. To the extent that he is successful, another individual can later retrace his steps and check on his findings and conclusions; and to the extent that this independent verification occurs, the facts which have been uncovered are scientifically true. They remain so until—and only until—they are shown to be false, or true only within certain limits, by the discovery of other facts.

Science, then, is one approach to knowledge, and social science is its application to human affairs. The primary feature of the scientific approach is that it is rooted in observables, and when it must deal with structures and events that are not observable, its statements are rigorously limited to what can logically be inferred from observation. A second distinctive feature of scientific knowledge is that it must be susceptible to being communicated: the scientist must be able to describe not only the content of his observations but also how he went about making them and by what intellectual processes he reached his conclusions. Thus, this type of knowledge is uniquely free of the idiosyncrasies of a single individual or situation and is continually susceptible to revision.

It follows that scientific knowledge is always tentative. This point can probably not be emphasized enough with respect to social science, which is still generally at a rudimentary stage. There are very few areas within it that have advanced to a point where general laws have been so widely verified that they can be asserted with certainty. Rather, the most important products that social science has to offer are analytic concepts and frameworks. These serve as incisive tools for describing and classifying reality in such a way that otherwise hidden relationships become evident and common features emerge among apparently disparate phenomena.

In sum, social science is a way of thinking about people, about their behavior, about society. It is a framework from which to derive questions and in terms of which to seek answers. It rests on the assumption, shared with all science, that natural phenomena are orderly and, at least in principle, capable of being understood. It is, in a sense, only a *method* for seeking knowledge about human events and, as such, it is by definition never complete but always dependent on continued empirical confirmation.

The selections that constitute this volume are drawn from three branches of social science—anthropology, sociology, and social psychology—and, with respect to most of the topics covered, there are relevant excerpts from each field. All three of them are social sciences, and it is important to remember that they have a fundamental commonality: the goal of furthering understanding of human phenomena. At the same time, there are differences among them in assumptions, methods, and specific objectives, and thus their insights into the same issues are complementary rather than identical.

In the first selection in this chapter, Robert Redfield identifies what he believes to be the contribution of anthropology to a science of man. He notes a variety of conflicting tendencies within the discipline, and sees these as reflecting two contradictory but basic connections of the anthropological approach—to the natural sciences on the one hand and to the humanities on the other. He considers this ambiguity to be not a handicap, but anthropology's uniqueness and strength. That is, while being rooted in an objective and empirical approach to knowledge, anthropology is at the same time deeply and firmly committed to "viewing the human reality 'holistically,' " that is, "in its entirety and as a whole," rather than in isolated segments and removed from its cultural context. As a result, it both curbs the other behavioral sciences from constructing a segmented and distorted view of man and adds new dimensions to the findings of their more narrowly focused investigations.

The second selection presents Alex Inkeles's statement of the "sociological perspective." He prefaces his attempt to define the subject matter of sociology with a pertinent and useful caveat against viewing the boundaries between related disciplines as absolute and unchanging. To the extent that sociology has a unique focus, however, he sees it to be the study of "systems of social action"—how they are organized, their continuity through time, and their change or dissolution. Anticipating some of the concepts that will recur in other selections throughout the book, he discusses the notion of "social system" as a complex set of interrelated social acts and points to the main problems that the sociologist studies in relation to such systems. In his view, these center around the issue of order and regularity in social life and behavior. He asserts the assumption, which, as we indicated above, is common to all science, that there *is* order in nature and he places sociology in this context as seeking to "discover, describe, and explain the order which characterizes the social life of man."

In his statement of "the characteristic point of view of social psychology," Theodore Newcomb spells out both its connection to and its distinctiveness from sociology and anthropology, which for his purposes he lumps together as one field. The similarity he sees mainly as one of subject matter and the uniqueness as one of viewpoint. All three fields study human individuals behaving in a sociocultural environment. The unique interest of the social psychologist, however, is in the *relationship* between the individual and the environment. Unlike other kinds of psychologists, he does not study individual processes as such, and, unlike the sociologist and anthropologist, he does not study the environment as such. His goal is to discern the systematic relationships in terms of which specific aspects of individual personality and behavior are influenced by specific aspects of the sociocultural environment. His statements thus refer both to society and culture and to organismic processes. The link between them is explained in terms of "intervening variables," which are mostly phenomena inferred to occur within the individual but which are carefully and explicitly associated with both ends of the organism-environment relationship they are said to mediate.

Newcomb's explication of why he sees social psychology as both a field in its own right and a meeting ground between individual psychology on the one hand and sociology and anthropology on the other serves as an effective summary for the fundamental point that this chapter should convey. This is that perspective rather than subject matter determines the nature and the products of an investigation, and thus that understanding of this perspective is an essential element in both the acquisition and the application of any kind of knowledge.

2.1 RELATIONS OF ANTHROPOLOGY TO THE SOCIAL SCIENCES AND TO THE HUMANITIES[1]

Robert Redfield

. . . .Considering the relations of anthropology to the natural sciences, on the one hand, and to the humanities, on the other, one may recognize the effects of both methodological and societal influences. The social relations of anthropology to the natural sciences are closer than they are to the humanities, and closer than are the relations of other social sciences to the natural sciences. . . .Both the degree of welcome given anthropology by the natural sciences and the relative weakness of anthropological connections with the humanities are undoubtedly in large part expressions of the fundamental conception which anthropology long ago formed of itself and still realizes in important degree: as a discipline interested in the phenomena and the forces of nature as they are, and how they have come to be, "without preconceptions and without primary ulterior motives of existing philosophy, theology, politics, or philanthropy" (Kroeber, 1948, p. 841).[2] At the same time, the orientation of anthropology toward the sciences rather than toward the humanities may be seen as an aspect of a general societal phenomenon: the arrangement of the disciplines in a hierarchy of status wherein the "harder" natural sciences occupy the uppermost positions and the humanist is the man farthest down. The point that will now be developed is that, while anthropology is pulled toward realization of a methodology like that of the natural sciences by both the attractiveness of superior status and its own fundamental conception of its nature, there is, nevertheless, in the very way of work which anthropology has developed, a strong check upon this pull, so that anthropology is held back from science toward a substantial, if not wholly recognized, connection with the humanities.

---

[1]Reprinted from *Anthropology Today*, Alfred L. Kroeber, ed., by permission of The University of Chicago Press. Copyright 1953 by the University of Chicago.

[2]The references in parentheses are to the bibliography at the end of the selection.

THE POLARITIES
OF THE
ANTHROPOLOGICAL FIELD
The existence, within anthropology, of two major centers of interest is simply apparent in the opposition of physical anthropology to cultural anthropology. Other separations made within the discipline are secondary to this one. . . .[A] statement of the two polarities of anthropology is, then, that anthropology is organized around an interest in man seen as something with the characteristics of all life, and around an interest in man seen as something human—a quality not shared, or very little shared, with other forms of life. The quality that induces the second polarity—humanity—is manifest in three basic forms: as it appears in individuals (personality), in persisting social groups or societies (culture), and in all socialized members of our species (human nature). It is this humanity, subject matter of that part of the anthropological field organized around the second polarity, that links anthropology, in spite of the powerful pulls toward natural science, with the disciplines which bear the name of that subject matter: "the humanities." . . .

THE "HOLISTIC" NATURE
OF HUMANITY
What is this relevant nature of the subject matter, humanity? It is the fact that it is the nature of humanity, in its three forms, to cease to be itself in so far as it is decomposed into parts or elements. What is in this respect true of stone or oyster is yet more true of culture, personality, and human nature. The effort of the scientific mind to reduce the reality to elements amenable to analysis, comparison, and even mensuration early results in a distortion or in the disappearance of the subject matter as common sense knows it. A culture or a personality is "known" in the first place and convincingly by an effort of comprehension which is not analytic, which insists on a view of the whole as a whole. When more is known of human nature, the same is likely to be said of that. The attempts of anthropological and other science to represent a culture by a list, a formula of structural relationships, or a single underlying pattern are resisted and corrected by the insistence of the reality itself which is so much more than any of these. This "more" is the whole apprehended without resolution into elements. The same assertion may be made of a personality.

EFFECTS OF
THE HUMAN REALITY
UPON ANTHROPOLOGY
Of all scientifically oriented students of man in society, the anthropologist is most accustomed to viewing the human reality "holistically." The small community of which he has characteristically been the sole responsible investigator has been seen by him in its entirety and as a whole. A complex community viewed in the same way is commonly identified as viewed "from the anthropological approach" (*Middletown*). So with respect to the more specialized social

sciences the influence of the anthropologist is to correct and enlarge the understanding achieved by more segmental and analytical approaches through consideration of the entirety. This entirety, seen as social structure, a system of social relations, or more commonly as culture, is again offered by the anthropologist in correction and amplification of the analytic, experimentally conceived science of psychology. And the more integrated view of the human personality taken by psychoanalysis is congenial to the anthropologist, while yet it, too, requires from him the context of culture which he supplies to these students of the human individual also. To that recent restatement of the more scientifically oriented study of man which now appears under the name of "the behavioral sciences," the anthropologist makes his contribution, but characteristically so as to demand that account be taken of culture and of personality seen as a whole. The very simplicity of the anthropologist's concepts, especially with regard to culture and particularly with regard to personality, leaves him free to return easily to the immediately apprehended real whole.

The complete identification of anthropology with "the behavioral sciences" is also checked by the necessity that the anthropologist, in understanding a culture or a personality, be guided by projection of his own human qualities into the situation to be understood. The anthropologist's own human nature is an instrument of work. In this respect the position of the anthropologist is like, on the one hand, that of the psychoanalyst; on the other, it is like that of the humanists of the Western tradition, at least since the Renaissance. A psychoanalyst, examining his science or his healing, has recently written: "We first give free rein to the imagination, in order to sense how the situation looks to the patient, and then we examine the situation carefully, to test the intuitive impressions thus gained" (French, p. 29). The psychoanalyst's intuitions and the anthropologist's also are provided with content by what each apprehends about his own and his neighbor's human qualities. And when Ruth Benedict wrote in her presidential address that the great tradition of the humanities "is distinguished by command of vast detail about men's thinking and acting in different periods and places, and in the sensitivities it has consequently fostered to the qualities of men's minds and emotions" (1948, p. 588), her words applied as well to anthropological students of culture, society, and personality.

THE VARIETY OF MODELS IN ANTHROPOLOGICAL THINKING[3] These ideas may be reviewed in terms of the conception of alternative models for achieving knowledge or for organizing knowledge so as to communicate understanding and to provide foresight. The models of overwhelming influence in our times are those provided by the natural sciences. As a pattern to follow in achieving new knowledge, the natural science model conceives of a

---

[3]The assistance of Milton Singer in connection with this section is acknowledged.

number of necessarily related steps: activities that begin with a problem seen and conclude with a theory tested. Such a model for work has been described recently by Donald G. Marquis (1948), who regards the social sciences as each separately developing one or a few of the steps necessary to make up a science; anthropology, by this view, already achieves careful observation and description but requires more effort in the direction of testable theory. Among models for the organization of achieved knowledge, the causal model is prominent in the natural sciences: in this model, classes of phenomena are arranged in the form of general causal laws which would make it possible for an ideal observer to predict all future states of a system from conditions at a given time. . . .The causal model may be developed by conceiving a system of universal relationships out of the observation of one or a few cases, . . .or it may, in a somewhat weaker form, be developed more inductively from statistical intercorrelations of traits and trait complexes, . . .A moderate statement of the causal model, contenting itself with "tendencies rather than universal principles," more characteristic of many anthropologists, is made by Firth (1944).

The other model, also in part derived from examples in the natural sciences, which influences anthropology, is the functional model. In this a culture or a society is seen as an organization of means designed to achieve certain ends. "The ends may be attributed to individuals, to associations of individuals, or, in some sense to the culture as a whole" (personal communication from Singer). These ends may be found in needs or impulses more or less biologically rooted or (as in art and religion as viewed by Malinowski) as acquired ends to some extent defined by culture. The means may be found in almost anything interior or exterior to the culture society. . . .[I]t may be possible to identify among models for the organization of conceptions of culture [another] model still farther away from the models of natural science and also identifiable with the arts: the symbolic model. In such a model a culture is conceived as represented in its characteristic properties as a whole by certain symbolic representations—epic, dance form, allegory, etc. The symbols may be transformations of the reality represented and of the impulses projected of perhaps quite fantastic nature: assumed is the capacity of symbol-creating and imaginative beings to frame meanings for themselves. . . .The dominance in anthropology of models associated with the natural sciences is not matched by corresponding success in executing studies based on these models. Anthropological formulations of knowledge do not serve as bases of prediction comparable with those provided for prediction in the natural sciences. The literature does not show competent general propositions applicable to all cases within precisely defined classes and allowing of exact predictive application. Though exceptions may be recognized (as in the prediction of linguistic change according to phonemic pattern), the success of anthropology in prediction takes place chiefly as a consequence of understanding gained of particular cases—the anthropologist studies the Indian tribe in transition, the social movement among

Japanese–Americans in confinement, the discontents of colonialized peoples—and foresees, more clearly than do most who lack his special knowledge, what will occur. Even where anthropological knowledge about the behavior of people and the expected consequences upon them of courses of action is framed in the form of general propositions, as in Leighton's *The Governing of Men*, the usefulness of the propositions suggests comparison rather with the formulated wisdom of a humane man than with the tables and formulas of the electrical engineer. Moreover, the validity of a characterization of a culture by any of the models employed, but especially those which approximate the aesthetic, logical, or symbolic models, is not today established (whatever may develop in the future) by experimental or any other precise proof such as is demanded in many fields of the natural sciences. Rather it may be said that the reader of an account of a culture or system of social institutions is satisfied as to the truth of what he reads only in part by the correspondences between the more comprehensive propositions and the documentation offered. In part the proof, if proof it be, seems to issue from the conviction brought upon the reader as to the congruence of the parts within a whole conceived. It is as if, in the establishment of "truth" about a culture or a personality, a part is played by an act of apprehension of the totality on the part of him who accepts the presentation as true. And such an act of apprehension is characteristic of the understanding of a work of art and plays a part also in humanistic activity.

ANTHROPOLOGY AS "FREEDOM IN TENSION" One might speak of anthropology as enjoying and also as suffering from the consequences of the polarities and ambiguities of its subject matter and its method. The coherence of the discipline is threatened by the variety of attachments which anthropologists make to problems and fields of inquiry that, though linked to anthropology, are far apart from one another. But the very tensions within anthropology, the disposition to become concerned with questions marginal to any sector of the immense and variegated study of man, make anthropology the freest and most explorative of the sciences.

Anthropology is thus provocatively undecided as to whether its subject matter is mankind *in toto* or man as a cultural being: "social anthropology" is taught in some places as a discipline by itself. It is unclear as to whether it moves toward the writing of a science (or perhaps separable sciences of social relations and of culture) or toward the writing of histories. Its views as to such histories as it does write vary from the more humanistic impressions of aboriginal history and of Indian personalities, as in the work of Radin, toward histories compared and reduced to generalizations about developments, cycles, transformations. It finds common cause with students of the behavior of rats in mazes, of human neuroses, of economic history, geography, geology, or the half-life of radioactive elements; and it also finds that it shares interests with Burckhardt, James Henry Breasted, Santayana, and the great works of Shakespearean criticism.

Experiencing such pulls toward disintegration, anthropology remains integrated by a number of centripetal forces. There is, first, the deeply established commitment toward viewing mankind, this creature both unique and yet one among all other creatures, objectively, completely, as all nature is looked at by all naturalists. This commitment holds together the two polarities of subject matter. It is helped to this end by the conception of the societal, for society, in the wide sense, may be and perhaps must be studied in all life-forms in which individuals maintain relations with one another from the Paramecia onward. It is helped also by the establishment of all societies on the land or on the sea; ecological problems are unifying. Both as history and as science, mankind may be viewed as one of many life-forms. And now anthropology, the years having established its university chairs, its associations, and its founding fathers, is helped to maintain its unity through the fact that it is itself a society, one of the societies of the greater society of scholars and scientists.

On the other hand, in so far as mankind is viewed as a unique realm of nature made up of persons and traditions, of moral life, self-consciousness, and creative activity directed by ideals, anthropology is not one thing but two: a science and history of that animal which is man; and a history and perhaps also a science or two of that special subject matter, humanity. In this direction anthropology becomes an influence upon the other social sciences to recognize, in their work, the holistic reality of humanity. And in this direction it is drawn toward interests shared with the humanities. . . .Finally, the developing explicit concern with values moves anthropology into developing relationship with the humanities. In the first place, there is the current anthropological interest in exploration of the concept of "value," as value is represented in those human beings who are the objects of anthropological study. Anthropologists have always studied values, for the attitudes of preference that are connected with acts and material objects are centrally characteristic of culture and personality; but now the conception is examined, its sources investigated, its varieties looked into, and its validations developed. This links the anthropologist with the philosopher. And also the anthropologist is drawn to value in another aspect: to value as it appears in the anthropologist himself. How do the anthropologist's own values affect his work? The earlier assumption that his own values are entirely removable as factors of consequence in anthropological research now comes to be questioned. The conception of anthropology as a purely theoretical part of natural history is now qualified by the recognition of applied anthropology, of "action anthropology," and of the responsibility of anthropologists in Point 4 and related programs. These engagements seem to make difficult or perhaps even impossible anthropology as a pure science alone. In

advising men of action, in participating in social change—indeed, in being themselves agents of social change in acculturated societies—anthropologists come to
entertain the question: What, then, is the good life?

BIBLIOGRAPHY

BENEDICT, RUTH, 1959, "Anthropology and the Humanities," *American Anthropologist*,
n.s., L, No. 4, Part I, pp. 585–593.
FIRTH, RAYMOND, 1944, "The Future of Social Anthropology," *Man*, XLIV, No. 8, pp.
19–22.
FRENCH, THOMAS M., 1952, *The Integration of Behavior*, Vol. 1, Chicago: University of
Chicago Press.
KROEBER, A. L., 1948, *Anthropology*, New York: Harcourt, Brace & World.
MARQUIS, DONALD G., 1948, "Scientific Methodology in Human Relations," *Proceedings
of the American Philosophical Society*, XCII, No. 6, pp. 411–416.

2.2 WHAT IS SOCIOLOGY: AN INTRODUCTION TO THE DISCIPLINE AND PROFESSION[1]

Alex Inkeles

THE SOCIOLOGICAL PERSPECTIVE . . . .Intellectual disciplines are so complex and
diverse that any brief effort to characterize
them must necessarily be full of arbitrary and
even distorted images. When we attempt to discriminate between the branches of
social study, the temptation is inevitably great to exaggerate differences rather
than to acknowledge similarities. Despite these grave risks, we clearly must offer
some map of the terrain to those who wish to orient themselves in the complex
realm of the social sciences. First, and necessarily superficial, impressions may be
altered as the novice becomes better oriented and deepens his understanding of
social science. And it is important to recognize that the differences in the perspective and practice of the several disciplines which treat man in society are often
fundamental and have endured for relatively long periods of time.

---

[1]From Alex Inkeles. *What is Sociology? An Introduction to the Discipline and Profession*, © 1964.
Reprinted by permission of Prentice-Hall Inc., Englewood Cliffs, N.J. Pp. 18-27.

Sociology and related disciplines

Sociology is a behavioral science. It seeks to explain contemporary or past human behavior as we experience it directly or encounter it embodied in artifacts, monuments, laws, and books. But in this sense history, economics, and even literary criticism are also behavioral sciences. Some grasp of what is distinctive about the sociological approach to these phenomena is necessary to our understanding of what sociology is.

The learned community is no tight ship all neatly divided into separate watertight compartments of knowledge. Any effort to distinguish sociology from other disciplines must be somewhat arbitrary and imprecise. As knowledge advances and trends of research change, currently adequate definitions of the several social sciences will be rendered inaccurate. Viewing the problem from a historical perspective, Professor Joseph J. Schwab, philosopher and historian of science, reports that "A mode of inquiry discredited by one scientist, dismissed at one time, discarded in one science, reappears and is fruitful in other hands and other times, or in other sciences."[2] Nevertheless, the branches of study concerned with man and his work do reveal numerous distinguishing features which, at the present time, fairly clearly mark off one discipline from another. Among the critical questions we ask as a basis for characterizing these disciplines is whether they are multidimensional or focus on only one aspect of social life, and if so which one; whether they are directly concerned with the observation of behavior or concentrate on data further removed from the realm of everyday action; whether they assign a prime role to abstract theory and generalization or emphasize description of the immediate and the concrete; and whether they stress measurement and mathematical manipulation of data or favor direct observation and a more "clinical" or "empathetic" mode of understanding human action. . . .

Disciplines, boundaries, and issues

Benjamin Kidd, writing about sociology in the 11th edition of *The Encyclopaedia Britannica*, said: "From the 17th century forward it may be said, strictly speaking, that all leading contributions to the general body of Western philosophy have been contributions to the science of society (sociology)." He went on to point out that over the years the following terms have been seriously proposed as substitutes for the word "sociology": politics, political science, social economy, social philosophy, and social science.[3] Under the circumstances, any novice in the field

---

[2]Joseph J. Schwab, "What Do Scientists Do?", *Behavioral Science, V, 1960, p. 1.*

[3]"Sociology," Vol. XXV, *Encyclopedia Britannica*, 1911, p. 322 *ff.*

must surely be forgiven if he expresses some bewilderment when faced with the task of distinguishing one social science from another. Maintaining these distinctions is made more difficult by the readiness of sociologists to accept responsibility for any institution which is not already the subject of an established discipline. To the degree that these subjects are important and would otherwise be neglected, sociologists deserve more to be praised than criticized. The scholarly world has shown a remarkable capacity to exclude from serious study enormous ranges of human activity, as if the common human nature expressed in family life, in stratification, in crime, made these vulgar studies unfit subjects for gentlemen scholars. For a new branch of study to win recognition in the university and the learned academies has been only slightly less difficult than for the camel to pass through that gate in Jerusalem known as "the needle's eye."

This open quality of sociology, its ready acceptance of new topical fields, stems from the sociologist's general concern with systems of social action and their interrelations. Inevitably this leads him to deal with all aspects of man's social life, whether or not the subject has already been marked out as the special province or preserve of some other discipline. . . .

Toward a definition of sociology:
Social order, disorder, and change

If you were to insist that the basic problem to which sociology addresses itself be described in a single phrase, we would reply: It seeks to explain the nature of social order and social disorder.

Sociology shares with all other essentially scientific perspectives the assumption that there is order in nature, and that it can be discovered, described, and understood. Just as the laws of physics describe the underlying order governing the relation of physical objects, astronomy the order of the planetary system, geology the order underlying the history and present structure of the earth, so sociology seeks to discover, describe, and explain the order which characterizes the social life of man.

When we speak of "order" we mean that events occur in a more-or-less regular sequence or pattern, so that we can make an empirically verifiable statement about the relation of one event to another at given points in time under specified conditions. Sociology deals with several such forms of order, varying greatly in scale but each having substantially the same character.

The problem is perhaps most evident at the level of the largest unit with which sociology usually deals, the nation-state or other form of large-scale society. Collectively, the members of a large society perform millions, or even billions, of social acts in the course of a single day. Yet the outcome is not bedlam, total confusion, and chaos, but rather a reasonable approximation of order. This order permits each individual to pursue his personal course without too seriously interfering with the pursuit by others of their purposes and goals. Indeed, this order generally assures that each can actually facilitate to some degree the attainment by others of their goals. The prime object of sociology is to explain how this comes about, how some reasonable degree of coordination of so many diverse individual actions yields the routine flow of social life. When we say that there is a social system, we refer to the coordination and integration of social acts which permit them to occur in a way that produces order rather than chaos.

Since our emphasis on order may be so easily misunderstood, we hasten to add early and emphatically that to delineate the nature of the social order is not necessarily to approve or justify it. A totalitarian government also develops a social order. A sociologist who studies it may explain the role of the monolithic party in monopolizing political power. He may show how the media of mass communication are used to mobilize public opinion and to manufacture the appearance of consensus, or expose the role which secret-police terror plays in permitting the elite to effect social control. In so doing, he obviously is not justifying, excusing, nor indeed in any necessary way judging the social order with which he deals. The sociologist may certainly be stimulated by his own values to explore and to emphasize one rather than another problem within such a system. In doing the job of analysis, he is also giving those of us not familiar with the system a basis on which we can form our own moral and political judgment. But such judgment should not be confused with the separate task of describing the basic order by which, for good or ill, a particular social system is kept in operation.

The sociologist's concern with the *problem* of order should not lead one to assume that he has no interest in or responsibility for studying manifestations of disorder. No social system functions flawlessly, regardless of the perspective from which it is viewed. Certainly no social system is perfect from the point of view of all its members. It is endemic in social life that some norms will not be met, some values not fulfilled, some goals not attained. Indeed, in any society, there may be some important realms in which the *majority* violate the socially or legally defined standard, and often at great cost of life. A trip along any of the highways of the United States during the Labor Day weekend will suffice to make the point. Almost all societies know periods, often long ones, of riot, civil war, mob violence, terror, crime, and general disorganization. Each of these manifestations is a departure from some social order already established or, as in case of counterrevolution, one seeking to establish itself. And even disorder is not necessarily chaos.

Within both individual and collective life there are "natural" forces making for order and stability and other equally "natural" forces making for disorder, conflict, and disruption. The balance between these forces may be very different at different times. It is a matter of preference, of personal inclination, or of philosophic orientation, whether you choose to see the world as a place inherently in a state of disorder struggling to achieve some order, or as normally in a condition of order but subject to constant disruption and the threat of disorder. For myself, I am quite satisfied that it fits the existing facts better, and is more conducive to effective analysis, to assume order as man's basic condition. To make this assumption is very far from passing on the importance of studying man's frequent and important plunges into a state of relative disorder. I stress "relative," because without some order, even within conditions of seeming general disorder, man would cease to survive. Some societies persistently failed to solve the problem of maintaining order, and have dissolved, their members scattered, absorbed elsewhere, or totally vanished. But always there has been another social system in which order prevailed and social man survived.

A sociology which completely ignores the manifestations of disorder in social life is clearly an incomplete and inadequate sociology. No less may be said of one which denies the basic facts of social order and turns its back on the mechanisms which insure it, concerning itself exclusively with the problems of social disorganization. The conflict between those who hold out for an "equilibrium theory" and those who urge us to adopt a "conflict theory" of society is sterile, since a complete sociology must include both the study of order and disorder, and also of orderly and disorderly *change*. . . .To delineate the social system by defining the underlying relationships among a complex set of social acts is perhaps the prime responsibility of the sociologist, but it is obviously only a beginning. Indeed, some sociologists argue that it is less important than another task, that of accounting for the persistence of social systems through time. The coordination, at a single point in time, of thousands and even millions of individual acts in a more or less stable system of social action is perhaps miraculous. Yet this short-term order is only a minor wonder compared to the grand miracle represented by the persistence of such systems of action over relatively long periods of time. Groups of animals, including dogs and elephants, can be trained to coordinate their behavior in very complex patterns of action. Without their trainer, however, these animals have no way of passing on to subsequent generations the tricks they have learned. The complex coordination of human action, which every social system represents, is almost always carried forward through time beyond the lives of any single set of participants. Such continuity is also found in colonies of social insects, but in their case we know that instinct insures the appropriate outcome. Since instinctive regulation of behavior is not equally important in man, the continuity of the social order must be explained by reference to other mechanisms.

Sociology, then, seeks to explain the continuity of social systems through time. Yet continuity must be recognized as relative. Its occurrence cannot be taken as assured, but rather must be acknowledged to be problematic. There is reason to believe that some unusually stable societies continued unchanged in all essential respects, often down to the smallest detail, generation after generation, for perhaps hundreds of years. Our impression of the relatively unchanging nature of these societies may be mainly an artifact of the inadequacy of the historical record. In any event, most of the societies which form part of the more recent history of man seem to have experienced an almost continuous, often pervasive, and sometimes highly accelerated process of change. Yet with change, as with continuity, the sociologist assumes that the sequence of events is inherently orderly. The process of change is not random, even though it may at times seem chaotic, and is often beyond the conscious control of individuals and of society as a whole. Sociology, therefore, also describes change in social systems, and seeks to uncover the basic processes by which, under specified conditions, one state of the system leads to another, including, potentially, the state of disorganization and dissolution.

In summary, then, we may say that sociology is the study of social order, meaning thereby the underlying regularity of human social behavior. The concept of order includes the efforts to attain it and departures from it. Sociology seeks to define the units of human social action and to discover the pattern in the relation of these units—that is, to learn how they are organized as systems of action. Working with such systems of action, sociology attempts to explain their continuity through time, and to understand how and why these units and their relations change or cease to exist.

2.3   SOCIAL PSYCHOLOGY[1]

Theodore M. Newcomb

THE CHARACTERISTIC POINT OF VIEW
OF SOCIAL PSYCHOLOGY

Borrowing from individual psychology

It is not the province of social psychologists to study protoplasm as such. Rather, they borrow from individual psychology, which, in turn, borrows from biochemistry and physiology. Individual psychology, building upon the data of biochemistry, physiology, and its own investigations, derives laws and principles concerning the behavior of an organism. The object of its study, however, is the organism not in a vacuum but as interdependent with its environment—*i.e.*, as it acts upon its environment and is acted upon by it. Individual psychology is thus:

---

[1]From Chapter One from *Social Psychology* by Theodore M. Newcomb. Copyright 1950 by Holt, Rinehart and Winston, Inc. Reprinted by permission of Holt, Rinehart and Winston, Inc.

. . . a science which treats of the inter-relationship between the stimulus world and the organism, a relation in which the stimulus world evokes the responses of the organism, thus changing the stimulus situation so that the organism is stimulated a moment later in a new way, and so on; the subject matter is *neither the world nor the organism in isolation, but the interaction of the two.* (Gardner Murphy, *General Psychology,* New York: Harper & Row, 1933, p. 10.)

Social psychologists adopt this point of view as to the interdependence of organism and environment. Like individual psychologists, they study individual behavior—especially as stimulus to or as response to the behavior of others. Unlike individual psychologists, they study individuals as members of groups. In fact, it is so characteristic of humans to behave as members of groups that the social psychologist finds it necessary to study the nature of groups in order to understand their individual members.

Social psychologists are not especially interested in how behavior changes with changing conditions of the organism. They do not deny anything the individual psychologist has to say about the organism's part in the relationship. Actually, they must rely heavily on certain psychological discoveries about the way in which the organism functions—especially in regard to motivation. It is the social aspects of the environment with which the organism is interrelated that most concerns the social psychologist. The behaviors of two individuals, or those of the same individual at different moments, may differ because of differences either in environment or in the state of the organisms. Social psychologists study primarily the former kind of variations—especially, of course, variations in social aspects of environment.

Tentatively, then, we may say that social psychology deals with the association of variations in the behavior of one or more individuals with variations in the social environment. Before accepting such a definition, however, we must note two important facts. First, differences in social environment do not automatically produce differences in behavior. It is a very important principle that (other things being equal) the same person will respond to two situations similarly or differently depending on whether he perceives them to be similar or different. Much of social psychology has to do with the conditions under which differences in social environment are actually experienced as differences or are not so experienced.

Secondly, differences in social environment and the way in which they are experienced are very largely determined by the way in which the individual's society is organized. People are born not into human-society-at-large but into a specific society with its own characteristic way of doing almost everything that human beings do. Each society, moreover, has its own way of organizing people into subgroups—by localities, by occupations, by classes, by blood-relatedness, by marriage ties, by political and religious affiliations, and in many other ways. Variations in social influence, and in ways in which influences are experienced, are not random but are closely associated with the culture of the whole society and with the common understandings of the groups and subgroups.

Borrowing from sociologists and anthropologists

Social psychologists do not study society as such any more than they study protoplasm as such. They borrow from sociology and cultural anthropology just as they do from individual psychology. . . . [T]he social psychologist accepts the general point of view and the principles established by anthropological and sociological investigations; indeed, he finds them indispensable. But his primary concern is with the influences which play upon individuals as members of various groups rather than with the fact that all members of those groups are subject to similar influences. (He wants to know, for example, precisely what influences play in what ways upon Edward Dodge, as a particular member of lower-lower-class Negro society, and not merely that most Negro boys of his class are subject to influences which tend to make them delinquent.) The effects of social (or any other) influences upon a person depend on the ways in which those influences are experienced by him as a unique organism. Two individuals, or the same individual at different times, may experience similar social influences in quite different ways and with quite different consequences. Hence, though the social psychologist can never afford to forget the ever-present facts of group membership, he is, unlike the sociologist and anthropologist, very much interested in resulting individual differences.

Social psychology as meeting-ground

Figure 1 illustrates the relationship among social psychology, individual psychology, and sociology-cultural anthropology. You will observe that between individual psychology and sociology (together with cultural anthropology) there is not much overlap. (According to some authorities, there is none at all). To a much greater degree social psychology overlaps both individual psychology and sociology-cultural anthropology. Many of the problems of the individual psychologist and of the sociologist and cultural anthropologist are actually social-psychological problems. Each of these two disciplines, however, treats such problems from its own point of view. In neither field does protoplasm "meet" society, for individual psychology has little or nothing to say about culture; and sociology and cultural anthropology have little or nothing to say about protoplasm as it functions in the human organism. It is social psychology which provides this meeting ground, by borrowing from both fields data upon which to build principles of its own.

This is not to say that social psychology is merely an attempt to bring closer together two other approaches to the study of human behavior. Much less is it an attempt to reconcile two "opposite" points of view, for insofar as the principles of either field are soundly established there can be no contradictions to be reconciled.

On the contrary, social psychology has a characteristic subject matter, a characteristic point of view, and its own set of principles. It "stands on its own feet" in the same sense that biochemistry does, though it owes as much to its neighboring disciplines as does biochemistry to biology and to chemistry.

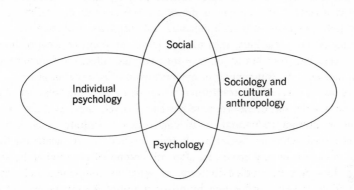

FIGURE 1.   THE RELATIONSHIP AMONG SOCIAL PSYCHOLOGY,
INDIVIDUAL PSYCHOLOGY, AND SOCIOLOGY-CULTURAL
ANTHROPOLOGY

Features of social psychology as meeting ground

This meeting ground, this area in which social psychology stands on its own feet, may be described as follows. Its subject matter is the interaction of human individuals with one another.[2] Its point of view is that of the scientist who investigates the ways in which the functioning of human organisms is modified by the fact that those organisms are members of a society.

THE ORGANISM IS RELATED TO SOCIAL INFLUENCES   These apparently simple statements of the subject matter and characteristic point of view of social psychology actually cover a vast amount of territory. For example, the social psychologist may find it necessary to study any aspect of the social environment. This includes, potentially, all those countless variations in customs, manners, and morals which have been noted by sociologists and anthropologists. The phrase "functioning of human organisms" includes, potentially, all functions of which the human organism is capable—and nearly all of them, incidentally, are subject to social influence, directly or indirectly. The territory covered by social psychology

---

[2]This includes, as we shall see later, not only direct face-to-face interaction but also symbolic interaction. For example, two widely separated friends, if they write to each other or even think of each other, are interacting symbolically. One person's behavior may be influenced by remembered or anticipated behavior of another. This is what is meant by symbolic interaction.

is thus very large and overlaps individual psychology as well as sociology and cultural anthropology at many points. But in spite of such overlappings, its viewpoint remains distinctive. For example, social psychologists deal with such problems of individual psychology as motivation and intelligence. But they study them always from the point of view of the social influences playing upon the behavior which is motivated in a certain way or which shows a certain degree of intelligence. When social psychologists deal with such cultural and sociological phenomena as family organization or race relations, it is always from the point of view of how social influences resulting from family or race membership affect the functioning of the organism, and how the functioning of one organism affects that of others.

Much of social psychology, traditionally, has dealt with the behavior of groups. You may be wondering, therefore, whether social psychology, as the study of "the interaction of human individuals with each other," includes such group phenomena as crowd behavior. Social psychology provides many means for the study of crowds. A crowd, or any group, is, after all, composed of individuals, and what the crowd does may be studied in terms of what its component individuals do. Each individual is being influenced by all or many of the others present (among other influences). And so social psychologists study the behavior of a crowd in terms of how each of its members is influenced in similar ways by other members. The study of what the crowd does as a group, however, without regard to influences upon individuals, is not a social-psychological but a sociological problem. Perhaps it is not necessary to add that neither approach is inherently better than the other—they are simply different. For some purposes one approach is more convenient or more efficient, and for other purposes the other is preferable.

Social-psychological data, in short, must be such as can be related to individuals, since, by definition, social psychology deals with the psychological functioning of individual organisms. But a statement about how an organism functions is not, in itself, a social-psychological statement. It becomes so *only if the functioning of the organism is related to a social influence.* But social influences, for two reasons, necessarily refer to the social environment within which they operate. First, the manner in which the influence is expressed (*e.g.,* spanking a child for his disobedience) varies from one social environment to another. Secondly, the manner in which the influence is experienced (*e.g.,* whether the spanking is regarded by the child as meaning that the parent does not love him) depends also upon the social environment. And so social-psychological data must refer not only to individuals but also, directly or indirectly, to the social environment in which they participate.

THE NATURE OF THE RELATIONSHIP IS SPECIFIED   Not all statements about individuals which relate them in some way to the social order are social psychological. For example, the statement that 80 percent of city boys of Edward Dodge's social class indulge in delinquent or criminal behavior is not a social-psychological statement. It is a sociological statement about a whole class of boys. It tells us nothing about any one boy except that his chances of becoming delinquent are rather high. And it tells us nothing about why some boys of this class do and others do not become delinquent. The statement that more city boys of Edward's social class than of the middle class become delinquent is also not a social-psychological one. It relates individual behaviors to certain aspects of the social environment, but it merely tells us that *there is* a relationship. It says nothing about the psychological factors involved in the relationship. It contains no information on the basis of which we can draw conclusions as to the processes by which different class memberships lead different organisms to behave differently. We can, of course, make certain guesses as to what these processes might be, but not without bringing in further information.

The [following examples] from the case history of Edward Dodge present a great deal of supplementary information of a social-psychological nature. We are told, for example, that Edward often feels that he must fight in self-defense, that he belongs to a group which takes fighting and stealing pretty much for granted, and that he is proud of his position as leader of this group. We are told, furthermore, that he feels that he can somehow wipe out the stigma of his birth by assuming leadership in fighting and stealing episodes.

From such evidence it becomes possible to make statements that are social-psychological. Such statements relate a person's behavior *both* to his social environment and to the functioning of his organism. We can see how certain aspects of Edward Dodge's social environment (slum conditions, irregular supervision by his mother, street-corner standards regarding violence and stealing, the social stigma placed on illegitimacy) lead him to *want* to behave as he does. When he sees an unguarded electric fan, for example, his body tenses as he anticipates the thrill of a successful theft and the threat of possible detection. When he is teased about his father, his body pulses with anger. These represent ways in which the functioning of his organism has literally been changed; and these changes in bodily function lead him in the one case to steal and in the other case to fight.

Any statement which links behavior to the functioning of an organism, which in turn is linked to the social environment, is a social-psychological one. "Edward lives in a social environment in which he has learned that his own illegitimate birth makes him a near-outcast, and in which he has learned that leadership in fighting and stealing can perhaps save him from this fate," is one example of such a statement. Such a statement provides a psychological link between behavior and social environment.

SPECIFIED KINDS OF "INTERVENING" CONDITIONS ARE NOTED The area in which social psychology has something to add to individual psychology on the one hand and to sociology and cultural anthropology on the other may be described as follows. The social psychologist not only observes behavior; he not only observes the social conditions under which it occurs; he also draws conclusions about the *manner* in which the one is related to the other. Such conclusions have to do with *something that happens within the individual between* (1) the impact of social conditions upon him and (2) his behaviors resulting from or reflecting this impact. These in-between processes are known as *intervening variables*, because they vary for different people and even for the same person at different times. They are usually not directly observable; no one has ever seen a motive, for example. It is inferred from what is observed. If, for example, we observe a man on a city street beckoning, gesturing, calling, and whistling at each passing taxicab, entering the first one that stops, and telling the driver to hurry to a certain address, we infer that he wants to get to that address. (Possibly, of course, circumstances have forced him to go to this address even though he would prefer not to, and in this sense he does not "want" to go there. It still remains true, however, that all things considered, he wants to. A more exact statement would be that he both wants to and wants not to, but the former motive is stronger.) We cannot tell *why* he wants to get there, of course, without more information about him; nevertheless his behavior becomes comprehensible to us when we infer that he has the motive of getting to this address.

Intervening variables help us to understand just how the *dependent* variable (the social behavior that we are trying to account for) is related to the *independent variable* (the social and/or biological influence which, hypothetically at least, helps to account for the dependent variable). . . . Figure 2 illustrates the relationships among these three kinds of variables.

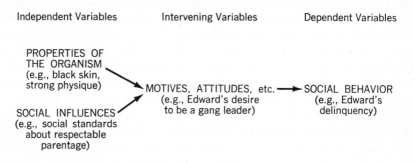

FIGURE 2.   RELATIONSHIPS AMONG THE THREE KINDS OF
VARIABLES

It is necessary to state many conclusions in terms of such intervening variables as motives, attitudes, values, group loyalties, and standards of judgment, because a given kind of social influence does not necessarily produce a given kind of behavior. Very often, however, a given kind of social influence does produce a given kind of behavior *provided a given intervening condition is present.* For example, the social influences which go with living in slum conditions in a city do not lead all boys into delinquent behavior. However, if these social influences lead some boys to form gangs, membership in which brings about the kind of attitudes, values, loyalties, and standards of judgment characteristic of Edward Dodge, those boys are very apt to become delinquent. Other boys who are not led by similar conditions into membership in such gangs, so that they do not form comparable attitudes and values, are very much less apt to become delinquent. It is in terms of such intervening variables that we can better understand the reasons why some boys do and others do not become delinquent.

Social psychologists are by no means alone among scientists in making use of intervening variables. No physicist ever saw an electron, although its existence was inferred long before its charge was measured. Protons and neutrons cannot be directly observed, but events which can be directly observed made it necessary to infer their existence, and the correctness of the inferences was confirmed in the investigations which led to the control of atomic energy. Individual as well as social psychologists make use of intervening variables. Even simple thought processes, which are often studied in the laboratory, can not be explained without assuming that an attitude, or "set," had been created in the experimental subject by reason of the instructions given to him. If, for example, subjects are presented with the printed symbols $\frac{6}{2}$ with no instructions other than to write the answer below the line, they are about equally likely to write 8, 4, or 12. But if a subject has previously been asked to add, he is almost certain to write 8. The inferred condition of "set" intervenes between stimulus and response in such a way as to determine the latter.

You must not draw the conclusion, however, that social psychology is concerned primarily with speculating about people's motives. A great deal of amateur social-psychologizing goes on at precisely this level—whether in the area of back-fence gossip or of international relations. But social psychologists, insofar as they are scientific, do not make use of intervening variables which they have created by speculation. Instead, they follow recognized rules of procedure. . . .The distinctive feature of social psychology lies not in its use of intervening variables but rather in the kind of intervening variables which it uses and in the way in which it relates them to protoplasm on the one hand and to society on the other.

The characteristic form which verified (or verifiable) answers to social-psychological questions usually take may be illustrated from the case of Edward Dodge. Edward holds certain positions (illegitimate son, gang leader) in certain groups and societies (lower-lower class of urban Negro society, delinquent gang). By virtue of these positions in these groups he is subject to certain influences (pressure to fight and steal, derision about his illegitimacy) just like any other boy in the same positions in the same groups. He is also subject to certain influences from his own body, some of which are common to all humans (hunger, for example), some of which are common to all boys of his age (need to use his arm and leg muscles, sexual urges), and others which are unique to himself (his particular physical and mental endowment, for example). Edward responds to all these influences (independent variables) by developing motives, attitudes, and ways of looking at things and feeling about them (intervening variables). Some of these motives and attitudes he shares with other members of his gang or with Negroes in general (*e.g.*, his attitudes toward fighting, or toward white people), and some are unique to himself (his feeling about gang leadership as a way of overcoming the handicap of his illegitimate birth). In either case, however, they represent not merely "mental states" but actual changes in the ways in which his body functions. His fighting, stealing, and truancy (the dependent variables) are responses to social influences and to influences from his own body *as those influences are mediated by his own motives, attitudes,* etc. His behavior cannot be accounted for in terms of the independent variables alone. It can be accounted for in terms of the intervening variables, but these in turn must be accounted for in terms of the independent variables.

A word of caution is needed, however. We cannot account for a given instance of behavior by an intervening variable which is inferred from that same behavior. That would be circular reasoning at its worst. In the case of Edward Dodge, for example, we cannot infer from his crying when asked about his father that he is ashamed of his delinquent status and then account for his crying by his attitude of shame. We observe, rather, other samples of Edward's behavior, relate these other behaviors to his social environment, and infer his attitude of shame. We can then account for his crying—and, incidentally, for a good many of his other behaviors, too—in terms of the inferred attitude. Thus a single intervening variable helps to account for a whole range of different behaviors which, superficially, have nothing to do with one another.

PART II

SCHOOLS

AND COLLEGES:

SOCIAL SYSTEMS

AND SOCIAL

INSTITUTIONS

In our attempt to bring new knowledge to bear on the tasks and concerns of the guidance-personnel worker, we turn our attention first to the immediate setting in which he works—the school and the college. Our goal is to increase the reader's awareness of the social phenomena that constitute the life of educational institutions and to provide him with a broader perspective from which to observe, evaluate, and respond to the events in his working environment. The materials selected for this purpose range from analyses of specific activities, to abstract discussions of broad patterns, to highly general theories about some of the processes and relationships that are at the core of an institution's pursuit of its goals.

Chapter 3 examines educational institutions from the inside, dealing with some of their characteristic activities and with the social relationships through which these are pursued. Chapter 4 takes an outside view, exploring some of the relationships that schools, colleges, and the process of education as a whole bear to their environment and some of the mutual pressures and demands by which they shape each other.

Chapter 3

The
Social System
of an
Educational
Institution

Any situation in which individuals behave and interact within the context of some general need, purpose, or goal can be viewed as comprising a social system. Thus we may consider any social group or organization which persists over time as a social system, whether it be a family, a friendship, a business firm, an orchestra, an army, or a factory. The advantages in doing so are that, on the one hand, many of the events that occur in such situations cannot be understood as fully or coherently from other perspectives and, on the other hand, new insights into the sources and consequences of what occurs, which would not otherwise be available, are thereby made possible. To consider any organized group as constituting a social system implies, first, that its activities and characteristics are ordered and interrelated in some coherent manner; second, that the nature of this order is primarily determined by the fact that its constituent elements and processes are social; and, third, that the patterns and regularities we discern are, in part, only instances of more general relationships, which occur among social variables in a large number of diverse situations. The selections presented illustrate and specify these points with respect to schools and colleges.

In certain respects, an educational organization resembles any system, such as the human body or a complex machine, whose overall purpose requires that a host of different activities be performed according to a given pattern. In the case of schools and colleges, this overall purpose is "education." For any system to maintain itself and make maximal progress toward the attainment of its goals, it is necessary that all its parts have specific tasks or responsibilities, that these be clearly defined and compatible with each other, and that there be some overall mechanism to regulate and coordinate them so that their total activity does in fact promote the purposes of the system as a whole. Some systems achieve these conditions spontaneously, through a natural process of evolution and change. Educational institutions, however, are formal social organizations, which means that they are deliberately created to accomplish a task which requires collective effort and that the arrangements by which their requirements are met are to a large extent calculated, explicit, and regulated, at any given point in time. These arrangements constitute what is usually referred to as the *formal* structure of an organization, and it consists of all the positions among which the task of pursuing educational objectives is divided and the prescribed pattern of relationships among them. Each position bears some logical relationship to the attainment of the desired goals, and this is expressed in the requirements to which its occupant is subject, which define the individual's formal role in the organization. The formal structure can thus be viewed as a system of roles, which organizes the behavior of their occupants so that, overall, the collective goals are pursued as intended. When changes in the formal structure occur, they are usually made explicit through statements and regulations.

As is true of any social system, the "parts" of an educational organization are human individuals. Although we can view it as a structure of positions whose requirements embody the purposes of the institution, the main point about these positions is that they are occupied by people, who must interpret the positions' requirements in order to perform the functions for which the positions were created. This fact introduces a whole set of additional factors between the structure and the activities of an educational organization, or of any other kind of social system, which importantly limit analogies between it and a non-social system. In the case of the latter, the sole purpose of each part of the system—whether it be the wheel of a car or a vital organ in the human body—is to perform the particular task which it is assigned within the system, and, generally speaking, it does not serve purposes of its own that are unrelated to the system in question. Human beings, on the other hand, bring to their participation in an organization a variety of needs, purposes, and predispositions, only a few of which are relevant to the organization's goals, but all of which are operative as the individuals go about fulfilling their formal roles.

As a result, the formal structure of an organization such as a school or college is only the bare skeleton onto which the life of the organization is attached. As the individuals go about fulfilling formal requirements, their behavior and interaction is a response to a wide range of other factors as well. Because people tend to react to each other as total individuals, rather than as narrow formal roles, the relationships that develop go far beyond, in both number and content, what an organizational chart might reveal. These other factors, however, although not formally prescribed, are by no means disorganized and random. It is an outstanding characteristic of human relations that they tend to fall into rather regular patterns, and thus it is possible to analyze the unofficial, or *informal*, aspects of organizational activity as if they too constituted a system or set of systems. As we will see, this informal ordering of activity in an organization is not independent of the formal structure, which serves as a basis and provides limits for the full range of interaction and relationships through which the work of the organization is carried out. Furthermore, changes in either one or the other of these systems—the formal or informal—may induce change in the other.

In the case of American schools and colleges, there are an almost endless number of aspects we could explore with respect to both their formal and informal structures. We are dealing with organizations which are frequently very large and also highly complex, both because of this factor of size and because of the multiplicity of specific purposes that are encompassed by the broad objective of education. With teachers, students, deans, college presidents, counselors, school superintendents, school boards, department chairmen, and still others as our elements, the number of actions, interactions, and relationships we could trace is staggering. The selections in this chapter do not provide such an exhaustive treatment. Instead, by applying theories and approaches from several disciplines that have proven useful in other contexts, they offer new insights into some of the major social processes within educational organizations. In each case, these insights affect understanding at two levels. On the one hand, they contain information about the concrete nature of specific phenomena. This contribution, however, is intimately dependent on the other level—the conceptual one. In exposing hidden patterns and pointing to factors and relationships that might otherwise not be taken into account, the selections that follow focus on some of the crucial features of schools and colleges and relate these to phenomena observed in a variety of other social situations. The concepts and generalizations that are thus conveyed should serve as new lenses, as it were, through which to observe the functioning of schools and colleges and of the people in them.

3.1   INTRODUCTION

Although written more than 30 years ago, when social science had yet to develop many of the concepts, theories, methods, and findings which make it what it is today, the excerpt that follows by Willard Waller is an example of sociological analysis at its most incisive. Most of the concepts and observations contained in the other selections in this chapter are implied and anticipated here, in Waller's analysis of the school's "political organization."

To the extent that Waller's analysis is valid, namely that the social relationships in the school are based on "some variant of the autocratic principle," it suggests a number of questions for those concerned with promoting the educational process. If, in fact, the school is a "despotism," and "self-government is rarely real," what do students learn about the nature of social relationships as they come to perceive and adjust to the discrepancy between the school's verbalized values and the facts of their experience? Is the degree to which a child becomes a "problem" or a "model student" a function of how well he assimilates this discrepancy and makes it the basis of his social interaction?

What are, typically, the interpersonal attitudes among individuals involved in authoritarian relationships: trust or suspicion, respect or exploitiveness, mutual concern or indifference, or hostility? If participating in a situation of unequal power fosters negative rather than positive beliefs and expectations, what are the consequences for the process of instruction and learning that is supposed to occur between teacher and student? If, as is likely, guidance-personnel workers are perceived by students as part of the "ruling class" rather than as one of them, why should the student believe that the counselor's purpose is to help him? What is there, or can there be, in the situation to make the student see the relationship as a cooperative one rather than an unequal struggle?

If the "despotic" structure is essential to the survival of the organization, are the independent and spontaneous ventures of students curbed at the most creative point, because they are then also most deviant?

Within such a social structure, which individuals are in the best position to influence the "culture" that develops in directions that are compatible with growth and learning? Do those whose interpersonal roles make them the most likely to succeed in such efforts also have the necessary prestige and power within the organization's "political" structure?

3.1   THE SCHOOL AS A SOCIAL ORGANISM[1]

Willard Waller

. . . .The characteristic mode of social interaction of the school, an interaction centered about the giving and receiving of instruction, determines the political order of the school. The instruction which is given consists largely of facts and skills, and of other matter for which the spontaneous interests of students do not usually furnish a sufficient motivation. Yet teachers wish students to attain a certain mastery of these

---

[1]From Willard Waller, "The School as a Social Organism," *The Sociology of Teaching,* New York: John Wiley & Sons, Inc., 1932, pp. 8–13.

subjects, a much higher degree of mastery than they would attain, it is thought, if they were quite free in their choices. And teachers are responsible to the community for the mastery of these subjects by their students. The political organization of the school, therefore, is one which makes the teacher dominant, and it is the business of the teacher to use his dominance to further the process of teaching and learning which is central in the social interaction of the school.

Typically the school is organized on some variant of the autocratic principle. Details of organization show the greatest diversity. Intrafaculty relations greatly affect the relations between teachers and students. Where there is a favorable rapport between the teachers and the administrative authorities, this autocracy becomes an oligarchy with the teacher group as a solid and well-organized ruling class. It appears that the best practice extends the membership in this oligarchy as much as possible without making it unwieldy or losing control of it. In the most happily conducted institutions all the teachers and some of the leading students feel that they have a very real voice in the conduct of school affairs.

Where there is not a cordial rapport between school executives and teachers, control becomes more autocratic. A despotic system apparently becomes necessary when the teaching staff has increased in size beyond a certain limit. Weakness of the school executive may lead him to become arbitrary, or it may in the extreme case lead some other person to assume his authority. The relationship between students and teachers is in part determined by intrafaculty relationships; the social necessity of subordination as a condition of student achievement, and the general tradition governing the attitudes of students and teachers toward each other, set the limits of variation. But this variation is never sufficient to destroy the fact that the schools are organized on the authority principle, with power theoretically vested in the school superintendent and radiating from him down to the lowest substitute teacher in the system. This authority which pervades the school furnishes the best practical means of distinguishing school from notschool. Where the authority of the faculty and school board extends is the school. If it covers children on the way to and from school, at school parties, and on trips, then those children are in school at such times.

The generalization that the schools have a despotic political structure seems to hold true for nearly all types of schools, and for all about equally, without very much difference in fact to correspond to radical differences in theory. Self-government is rarely real. Usually it is but a mask for the rule of the teacher oligarchy, in its most liberal form the rule of a student oligarchy carefully selected and supervised by the faculty. The experimental school which wishes to do away with authority continually finds that in order to maintain requisite standards of achievement in imparting certain basic skills it has to introduce some variant of the authority principle, or it finds that it must select and employ teachers who can be in fact despotic without seeming to be so. Experimental schools, too, have great difficulty in finding teachers who are quite free from the authoritarian bias of other schools and able to treat children as independent human beings. Military schools, standing apparently at the most rigid pole of authority, may learn to conceal their depotism, or, discipline established, may furnish moments of relaxation and intimate association between faculty and students, and they may delegate much power and responsibility to student officers; thus they may be not very much more arbitrary than schools quite differently organized, and sometimes they are very much less arbitrary than schools with a less rigid formal structure. The manifestations of the authority principle vary somewhat. The one-room country school must have a different social structure from the city high school with five thousand students, but the basic fact of authority, of dominance and subordination, remains a fact in both.

It is not enough to point out that the school is a despotism. It is a despotism in a state of perilous equilibrium. It is a despotism threatened from within and exposed to regulation and interference from without. It is a despotism capable of being overturned in a moment, exposed to the instant loss of its stability and its prestige. It is a despotism demanded by the community of parents, but specially limited by them as to the techniques which it may use for the maintenance of a stable social order. It is a despotism resting upon children, at once the most tractable and the most unstable members of the community.

There may be some who, seeing the solid brick of school buildings, the rows of nicely regimented children sitting stiff and well behaved in the classroom or marching briskly through the halls, will doubt that the school is in a state of unstable equilibrium. A school may in fact maintain a high morale through a period of years, so that its record in the eyes of the community is marred by no untoward incident. But how many schools are there with a teaching body of more than—let us say—ten teachers, in which there is not one teacher who is in imminent danger of losing his position because of poor discipline? How many such schools in which no teacher's discipline has broken down within the last three years? How many school executives would dare to plan a great mass meeting of students at which no teachers would be present or easily available in case of disorder?

To understand the political structure of the school we must know that the school is organized on the authority principle and that that authority is constantly threatened. The authority of the school executives and the teachers is in unremitting danger from: (1) The students. (2) Parents. (3) The school board. (4) Each other. (5) Hangers-on and marginal members of the group. (6) Alumni. The members of these groups, since they threaten his authority, are to some extent the natural enemies of the person who represents and lives by authority. The difficulties of the teacher or school executive in maintaining authority are greatly increased by the low social standing of the teaching profession and its general disrepute in the community at large. There is a constant interaction between the elements of the authoritative system; the school is continually threatened because it is autocratic, and it has to be autocratic because it is threatened. The antagonistic forces are balanced in that ever fickle equilibrium which is discipline.

Within the larger political order of the school are many subsidiary institutions designed to supplement, correct, or support the parent institution, drawing their life from it and contributing in turn to its continued existence. These institutions are less definitely a part of the political structure, and they mitigate somewhat the rigidity of that structure by furnishing to students an opportunity for a freer sort of social expression. These ancillary institutions are organizations of extracurricular activities, and comprise such groups as debating societies, glee clubs, choral societies, literary societies, theatrical groups, athletic teams, the staff of a school paper, social clubs, honorary societies, fraternities, etc. They are never entirely spontaneous social groupings but have rather the character of planned organizations for which the major impetus comes from the faculty, generally from some one member of the faculty delegated to act as "faculty adviser." These "activities" are part of that culture which springs up in the school from the life of students or is created by teachers for the edification of students. Such groups are often hardly less pervaded by faculty control than classroom activities, and there seems a tendency for the work of such institutions to be taken over by the larger social structure, made into courses and incorporated into the curriculum. Perhaps the worst that can happen to such organizations, if they are viewed as opportunities for the spontaneous self-expression of students, is that they shall be made over into classes. But the school administrator often thinks differently; from his point of view, the worst that can happen to such groups is that they shall become live and spontaneous groups, for such groups have a way of declaring their independence, much to the detriment of school discipline.

The political order of the school is characterized by control on three levels. Roughly, these are:

1. Theoretical. The control of the school by the school board, board of trustees, etc.
2. Actual. The control of school affairs by school executives as exerted through the teaching force or directly.
3. Ultimate. The control of school affairs by students, government resting upon the consent, mostly silent, of the governed.

The school is the meeting point of a large number of intertangled social relationships. These social relationships are the paths pursued by social interaction, the channels in which social influences run. The crisscrossing and interaction of these groups make the school what it is. The social relationships centering in the school may be analyzed in terms of the interacting groups in the school. The two most important groups are the teacher-group and the pupil-group, each of which has its own moral and ethical code and its customary attitudes toward members of the other groups. There is a marked tendency for these groups to turn into conflict groups. Within the teacher group are divisions according to rank and position, schismatic and conspirital groups, congenial groups, and cliques centering around different personalities. Within the student groups are various divisions representing groups in the larger community, unplanned primary groups stair-stepped according to age, cliques, political organizations, and specialized groups such as teams and gangs. The social influence of the school is a result of the action of such groups upon the individual and of the organization of individual lives out of the materials furnished by such groups.

A rough idea of some of the more important social relationships arising in the school may be derived from the following schema:

I. Community-School relationships.
   1. Relation of community to school in general. (Mediated through tradition and the political order of the community.)
   2. Relation of community to students individually and in groups. The parental relation and the general relation of the elders of the community to the young.
   3. Relation of community to teachers.
   4. Relation of special groups in the community to the school. (The school board, parent–teacher clubs, alumni, self-constituted advisory groups, etc.)
   5. Relation of special individuals to the school. (Patrons, ex-teachers, patriarchs, hangers-on, etc.)
II. Pupil to pupil relationships as not affected by the presence of teachers.
   1. Pupil to pupil relationships.
   2. Pupil to pupil-group relationships.
   3. Pupil-group to pupil-group relationships.
III. Teacher-pupil relationships. (Including also pupil to pupil relationships as affected by the presence of teachers.)
   1. Teacher to pupil-group relationship. (The customary classroom situation.)
   2. Teacher to pupil relationship.
   3. Pupil to pupil relationship as affected by the presence of the teacher.
IV. Teacher to teacher relationships.
   1. Relation of teacher to teacher.
      a. Teacher to teacher relationship as not affected by the presence of students.
      b. Teacher to teacher relationship as affected by the presence of students.
   2. Relation of teacher to teacher groups.
   3. Relation of teacher groups to teacher groups.
   4. Relation of teaching force to administrative officers.

NOTE: All these relationships are reciprocal.

The school is further marked off from the world that surrounds it by the spirit which pervades it. Feeling makes the school a social unity. The *we*-feeling of the school is in part a spontaneous creation in the minds of those who identify themselves with the school and in part a carefully nurtured and sensitive growth. In this latter aspect it is regarded as more or less the property of the department of athletics. Certainly the spirit of the group reaches its highest point in those ecstatic ceremonials which attend athletic spectacles. The group spirit extends itself also to parents and alumni.

A separate culture, we have indicated, grows up within the school. This is a culture which is in part the creation of children of different age levels, arising from the breakdown of adult culture into simpler configurations or from the survival of an older culture in the play group of children, and in part devised by teachers in order to canalize the activities of children passing through certain ages. The whole complex set of ceremonies centering around the school may be considered a part of the culture indigenous to the school. "Activities," which many youngsters consider by far the most important part of school life, are culture patterns. The specialized culture of the young is very real and satisfying for those who live within it. And this specialized culture is perhaps the agency most effective in binding personalities together to form a school.

3.2 INTRODUCTION

In this article, based on an extensive empirical study, C. Wayne Gordon points to some major dilemmas in which the teacher is inevitably caught because of his position in the school. His analysis makes particularly vivid the distinction and potential conflict between formal and informal demands. It seems intrinsically impossible for both to be met fully and thus stress is built in as part of the school's social structure.

Can we conceive of circumstances under which such structurally determined stress would be less pervasive? How possible is it for students' motivations and goals to be made more congruent, or at least less extremely discrepant, with the educational values that should ideally underlie the teacher's performance? Where is the key to the values of students: in the family, in the formal culture of their peers, in the pressures of the community, in the larger society?

There is no reason to expect that conflict and stress will be restricted to the role of the teacher. Students are subjected to the same types of incompatible pressures, and the situation is probably even more directly parallel for guidance-personnel workers. Gordon seems to suggest that, in the case of teachers, much of the stress would be relieved if they would come to perceive it as a general phenomenon that is part of the social structure rather than as a personal failing and a purely private problem. Under what conditions do social relationships permit the individuals involved in them to see themselves with detachment rather than narrowly and self-defensively? Would it be possible for the informal reward system within the school's social structure to give less emphasis to the personal implications of behavior and more to its educational outcomes?

3.2 THE ROLE OF THE TEACHER IN THE SOCIAL STRUCTURE OF THE HIGH SCHOOL[1]

C. *Wayne Gordon*

This paper will examine some of the complexities of the teachers' role in the social structure of the high school.[2] The analysis will be primarily concerned with those aspects of social organization which impinge directly on the teacher in the classroom.

This discussion will rely chiefly on a previously reported study of the social organization of a high school.[3] Wabash is a 4-year high school with a student population of 576 in a detached suburb of a midwestern metropolitan community. Lower middle-class members predominate, but all socioeconomic levels are significantly represented. There is diversity of socioeconomic levels to confront the teacher with a sufficient status range and power system to introduce maximum complexities related to social class which have been reported in other school and community studies.[4] The number of students is sufficiently small to permit the development of a social system in which the members interact sufficiently with one another to establish a clearly defined set of relationships which have a stable character.

Data on the teacher are from three major sources: (1) school records, (2) 200 personal documents written by upper grade students on their school careers with special reference to classroom performance, (3) the writer's field diary as a participant observer and classroom teacher in the Wabash school system for 10 years.

---

[1]C. Wayne Gordon, "The Role of the Teacher in the Social Structure of the High School," *Journal of Educational Sociology*, 27, 1955, pp. 21–29.

[2]The concept of a role used here is that of Talcott Parsons, and Edward A. Shils, with the assistance of James Olds, "Values, Motives and Systems of Action," Parsons and Shils, eds., *Toward a General Theory of Action*, Cambridge: Harvard University Press, 1951, p. 190; and Theodore M. Newcomb, "Role Concepts in Social Psychology." Paper delivered at the 1948 meetings of the American Psychological Association; Gross, Neal, and Ward S. Mason, "Role Conceptualization and Empirical Complexities." Paper delivered at the 1953 meeting of the American Sociological Society.

[3]C. Wayne Gordon, "The Social System of a High School." (Unpublished Ph.D. thesis, Washington University, St. Louis, Missouri, 1952). The complete study will be published by The Free Press, New York. A portion of this study was reported in a paper presented to the American Sociological Society, 1953.

[4]August B. Hollingshead, *Elmtown's Youth*, 1948. W. Lloyd Warner, Robert J. Havighurst and Martin B. Loeb. *Who Shall Be Educated?* Harper & Row, 1944.

THE STRUCTURAL CONTEXT OF THE TEACHERS' ROLE   The Wabash study revealed three major aspects of the high school organization to be relevant to an analysis of the teachers' role. Viewed as systems of expectations which define behavior they are: (1) the formal organization of the school which prescribes learning achievement, (2) the system of student organizations usually referred to as extracurricular activities, and (3) the network of interpersonal relationships defined by the friendship choice referred to here as the informal system.[5]

The chief general finding of the Wabash study was that the dominant motivation of the adolescent was to achieve and maintain a generalized social status within the organization of the school. General social status is regarded as the position held as a consequence of the various specific statuses he achieves throughout his high school career. At the action level, the dominant motivation of the adolescent will be to accept the roles of the informal group. This view suggests that the orientation of the individual is best understood and predicted given his position within the general system of action in the school-wide social system; for instance, the classroom behavior will be conditioned by his relation to his peers which introduces a general tendency to conflict with those performances which the teacher seeks to define. We are not proposing a simple dichotomy between the formal expectations and those of the informal group, rather two definitions of the situation compatible at times between teacher and students and having varying degrees of acceptability among students.

IMPLICATION FOR THE TEACHERS' ROLE: SOURCES OF STRAIN   The structural context of the school presents the incumbent of the teacher's role with the task of continuous integration and adjustment of conflicting expectations. There was a significant range of adaptation among teachers in their capacity to harmonize the conflicting tendencies. There also was a great range in the amount of personal anxiety teachers experienced in relation to their efforts to carry on the teaching function. It is further noted that some typical modes of adaptation are made by teachers over a period of years, as they routinized their functions in such a way as to minimize the amount of personal stress which they experience in a situation of endemic conflict.

The institutionally prescribed function of the teacher is to insure the enactment of roles related to learning achievement according to a specified range of standards. The range of standards defined by the grading system represents the instrumental goals of the system. . . . The task of the teacher is to insure the essential performances. By virtue of her adult status, her personal orientation to knowledge, and as custodian of the institutionally prescribed tasks, the teacher tends to seek performances from the students according to the standards somewhat higher than those which the adolescent group will set for itself. There results an incompatibility in the learning output norms which the teacher seeks to resolve.

---

[5]The formal-informal distinctions used here are those used by C. I. Barnard, *The Functions of the Executive*, Harvard University Press, 1948, p. 73.

In spite of the competitive-achievement orientation of the high school, the teacher is confronted with powerful ascriptive tendencies within the system. The Wabash study reveals the same ascriptive influences of the social class system which have been reported by Warner, Hollingshead, and others.[6] The drive for ascriptive rewards operates both at the value level which introduces subjective biases in the grading system and at the power level in which teachers assign rewards and punishments with the awareness that direct and indirect consequences may result from not doing so. Hollingshead demonstrated the tendency for teachers who originated from the local community to be able to ascribe success to members of the higher socioeconomic groups because they "understood" the backgrounds of the students.[7] The Wabash data show likewise that the longer a teacher worked in the community the more likely he was to accept the social class controls of the community in his assignment of rewards and punishments. The values of the teacher which define rewards in relation to achievement determine that consciously ascribed success usually is attended by personal conflict.

The clearly defined status system in the informal student group which coincides somewhat with the social class system and extends itself through differential participation also generates potent tendencies for the most prestigeful group to be ascribed success. . . .

THE AUTHORITY SYSTEM   Comment on the authority system will be confined to the role of the teacher as intermediate between students and principal. The duty of the teacher is to maintain order both as a condition for learning and because it symbolizes her competence. Teaching competence is difficult to assess, but disorder is taken as a visible sign of incompetence by colleagues, principal, parents, and students. In a situation of conflict the teacher has constant anxiety for his ability to control. A significant amount of conflict results from the requirements of the two sets of expectations which operate in the classroom, those presented by the teacher and those which the informal system defines.

Interaction within the student group is the most frequent cause of conflict between the authority of the teacher and the expectations of the informal group. The teachers' definition of order makes many of the actions within the student group a threat to authority. Teachers tend to accept noise, confusion, humor, and horseplay to a point where it becomes a challenge to authority. Consequently, talking, whispering, inattention, may be viewed as a challenge to authority. In one year there were 81 case of students being sent from the classroom to the principal's office for discipline. Of these 33 were for disturbance of the group, 27 were for talking without permission, and 14 for talking back to the teacher. The other 7 involved a variety of reasons. The reasons given by teachers are not necessarily the real cause for such action. They are rather symptoms of strain in teacher-individual student or teacher-group relationships. They are both an indication of a

---

[6]Warner, Hollingshead.
[7]Hollingshead.

mode of adaptation of teachers to the informal group structure and the adaptation of students to the teacher's definition of the expectations of the classroom.

Since eviction from class is a serious crisis in the relationships of students and teachers, eviction is a conservative index of the real conflict which occurs. The classroom situation may be characterized roughly as: (1) conflict of sufficient crisis proportion to result in eviction, with the enlistment of the principal's office to resolve it; (2) conflict of crisis proportions in which the teacher absorbs the conflict without resort to the principal; (3) conflict is minimized or nonexistent as a result of the way in which the teacher articulates the requirements of both the formal and informal groups.

Reasons for absorbing conflict in the classroom have been discussed by Howard Becker in connection with the tripartite relation to authority among students, teacher, and principal.[8] The extent to which the principal will support the formal expectations of the system by an exercise of authority will determine the kind of authority role the teacher may assume in the classroom. Students and teacher alike seek to avoid the crisis of eviction from the classroom. It affects both the status of the teacher and student in relation to the formal authority system. Student evictions affect student status because they become a factor in grading, establish a formal record of nonconformity, and may result in expulsion from the group. Teacher status is likewise adversely affected. When the burden of classroom control is shifted to the office of the principal, it calls attention to the problems which he usually prefers not to have made public beyond the classroom. Changes in the exercise of authority from the principal's office result in a greater diffusion of power throughout the school system among both teachers and pupils. In Wabash the number of classroom evictions over a 3-year period were for successive years respectively 160, 81, and 50. Reduction in the number of evictions was related to the dissemination of a rumor among the teachers that "the principal has a little black book in which he records the number of students which teachers send to the office. When he gets ready to rate your teaching he looks in the little black book and decides your salary increase for the next year." It appeared that the greater the support the principal gives the teachers' authority, the more likely the formal institutional role of the teacher will be utilized to coordinate the classroom. The less willing the principal is to support the teachers' institutional authority, the more likely that the teacher will absorb conflict in his classroom role, and the more likely he will be to resort to personalized leadership, and face a situation of endemic conflict. Waller has pointed out the hazards of personalized leadership because only the virtuoso can sustain it.[9] The personality of the teacher under such a situation will be exposed. An additional consequence is to shift a balance of

---

[8]Howard S. Becker, "The Teacher in the Authority System of the Public School," *The Journal of Educational Sociology,* November 1953.

[9]Willard Waller, *The Sociology of Teaching,* 1932.

power into the hands of the students. Here differentials in status among teachers will affect their ability to exercise power and their sense of adequacy since the ability to control is equated with the ability to teach. The Wabash study shows that least secure teachers in tenure are the ones least likely to be supported by colleagues, principal, parents, and the most likely to attack from students.

TEACHER ROLE AND THE INFORMAL SYSTEM   In Wabash the teacher role was conditioned by the fact that he faced in the classroom a system of student organization which was differentiated by grade rank, grade achievement, sex, social class, and prestige cliques which were value differentiated by their participation in both the formally organized and informal student culture. The system as mentioned above exercised a potent influence over behavior. The dominant motivation was to accept the role of the informal group or differentially defined roles within value differentiated cliques or simply the role of subordinate to an overwhelming status system by the unincorporated and incorporated members. There was a consequent muting of action in this direction of teacher-presented expectations. . . .

The informal system with its congeries of in-groups operates as a personalized system of relations significantly motivated by affective response. The teacher as the authority who controls the system seeks to control the system in the direction of affective neutrality. As the coordinator of the system, custodian of the formal sanctions, and dispenser of scarce rewards, he tends to increase or reduce the total anxiety of the incumbents of the system by the use of varying amounts of expressive affect in the communication process. The security and protection which students are afforded within the clique and congeniality groups may be adequate to the needs of the students. Furthermore, it may be disrupted by the way in which the teacher manipulates the reward system. The tension and anxiety is reduced by the manipulation of the symbols or gestures of varying and affective content by the teacher. Thus he will afford the maximum security to students if he expresses and bestows at least a minimum of esteem on every student. Evidence from social class and school studies suggests that teachers display a wide range in the amount of esteem and affective response for various categories of students. The Wabash dropout of 30 percent appeared to be directly related to the least esteemed and disesteemed students. We are suggesting that an adequate conception of motivation for the teacher is that which has been demonstrated in the studies in industrial sociology. The problem in the teacher's role is that he sometimes accepts the significance of affective response in maintaining student morale and motivation toward his objectives within an institutional framework based on a sanction and reward system of hedonistic psychology. The accompanying ambivalence constitutes a dilemma. He must define goals for students who are widely different in value orientation to his expectations. There is also a discrepancy between the values of the teacher and the students. The teacher will tend to present and express the values of the able minority without impunity from the formal authority system. However, the values of his professional role decree a 100 percent consensus on the goals he presents. If he cares for the consequences, he will have anxiety over the lack of interest on the part of the least motivated group. He will be led to strenuous efforts to sustain the interest of the group with the resulting charge on his physical and emotional resources and the necessity to reduce the stress may be considerable.

TEACHER ROLE IN RELATION TO STUDENT ORGANIZATIONS   We have mentioned the function of participation in student activities as a means for defining the general status of the student in the schoolwide informal system. The result is a status system with a powerful ascriptive tendency. The teacher may accept this system dominated by "big wheels" or she may insist on the achievement values of the institutional system with its narrow deference range admitted in the classroom among superior to failing students. To reject the status system of the students is to risk the sanctions of the informal group.

A second tendency of the system of student organizations which results from the extreme differentials in the amount of participation among most active and least active students is the differential association which is produced among most active students and teachers and least active students and teachers. The differential association results in diffuse affectively toned relationships with some students in contrast to specific affectively neutral relations with the nonparticipants. The result is to particularize with those he knows well in the distribution of rewards and apply universalistic standards with greater affective neutrality in the distribution of rewards and punishment to least active, least known students. For instance, freshmen make lower grades because teachers know them much less well in addition to the usually accepted fact that they are less sophisticated in the grade-getting culture. We seem to need a distinction between grade getting and grade achievement. By achievement we mean quality of performance and by grade getting the loss of objectivity which accompanies personalizing relationships as well as the student's manipulation of the teacher in the assignment of rewards which accompanies the process.

The more involved the teacher becomes in the student activity program, the more likely he is to be influenced by the particularistic tendencies. When he does he violates the standards of the universalistic or "fair" teacher defined by the institutional values and professional ethics of the teacher. He faces conflict with students in either case.

The teacher who is not involved in the student activity program will be less sensitive to the status differentiation of the informal system and therefore more universalistic with all members. Lacking the personal influence of association he may risk the conflict with the politically potent informal student group. He may likewise gain the esteem of the "underdog status" group.

More attention needs to be given to other than social-class factors in teacher-student relationships. For instance, in Wabash Miss Jones was generally regarded to be an able scholar who had high performance expectations of students. She was considered to be "fair", *i.e.* "just" in her grading by most students. But reputation of "fair" tended to be qualified by members of different groups. Upper middle-class members sometimes thought her "unfair" because she resisted social-class ascriptive tendencies. Lower class thought her very "fair" because she practiced a not too subtle form of "underdog" ascription. It should be noted that she was by origin of working-class background. Mr. Higby on the other hand who affected a manner of rigid universalism was thought by lower class members to be "unfair" and by all to particularize in favor of more attractive physically mature girls.

TEACHERS' ADAPTATIONS TO THE STRUCTURE   The foregoing discussion of the complexities of the teaching situation adds up to a situation of continuous stress in the teachers' role. An adaptation to the condition of the situation leads the teacher to seek to adjust the various pressures in order to protect his personality. Adjustments tend to be worked out privately or in intimate congeniality groups. The problems of the classroom are not shared on a colleague-wide basis due to the competitiveness of the status system among teachers. The success ideology of the school states that "successful teachers do not have problems," therefore the most disturbing problems of the teacher tend to be regarded as unique to his situation and therefore are private. His greatest anxieties are not expressed. The teacher perspective with its failure to incorporate the reality of the social structure in which he works prevents him from seeing problems as a consequence of this generic structure.

3.3 INTRODUCTION

James Coleman's depiction of the school in the next selection as more closely resembling an athletic club than an institution of learning brings some of the conflicts implied in the first article in this chapter, by Willard Waller, into sharper focus. Coleman identifies athletics as the core of the students' informal status system and demonstrates the strength and pervasiveness of its influence relative to scholastic achievement.

His analysis is disturbing, and it raises innumerable questions, even if one keeps certain reservations in mind in relation to the extent to which schools may be changing in these respects. A persistent question elicited by Coleman's article is: how do students learn these informal standards that are such potent regulators of school life? It is certainly likely that there is great variation among entering students in their concern for athletics. Thus, the potential for a variety of other dimensions to dominate the informal system is there, but it is apparently quickly extinguished. In terms of the concrete experiences of individuals, how does this occur? And why athletics? Is athletics merely the most efficient means for promoting institutional and community solidarity, or are deeper roots for this particular symptom to be found in much more general attitudes and values of our society?

If one views athletics from the broader perspective of the total culture, it is possible to evaluate its role quite differently from the way Coleman does. That is, it can be argued that football, for example, is an expression of and a training ground in basic American values having to do with the virtues of cooperative team activities and the necessity for the individual to subordinate his goals to those of the group. To the extent that such an interpretation of the function of high school athletics is valid, the emphasis placed on it can then be seen, not as pathological but, rather, as necessary and functional. In reading Coleman's critical views about the sources and consequences of the importance of athletics, it is important to keep in mind that athletics belongs to the larger realm of extracurricular activities and thus that it shares many of the values that the latter are generally considered to serve for the personal and social development of students.

Coleman suggests a purposiveness to the dominance of athletics, in that it counteracts the disintegrative effects of the competitive grading system upon loyalty and attachment to the institution. How valid and how useful, in terms of general applicability to organizational phenomena, is the logic inherent in the attribution of purposiveness? Moreover, Coleman's interpretation implies that such attachment is important or even necessary—presumably for the institution to be effective in its basic function of education. Does this then place the informal system of demands and rewards in a somewhat different perspective, as a potential tool rather than an obstacle?

3.3   ATHLETICS IN HIGH SCHOOL[1]

James S. Coleman

. . . .The amount of attention devoted to athletics would be most striking to an innocent visitor to a high school. A visitor entering a school would likely be confronted, first of all, with a trophy case. His examination of the trophies would reveal a curious fact: The gold and silver cups, with rare exception, symbolize victory in athletic contests, not scholastic ones. The figures adorning these trophies

[1]James S. Coleman, "Athletics in High School," *The Annals of the American Academy of Political and Social Science*, **338,** 1961, pp. 34–43.

represent men passing footballs, shooting basketballs, holding out batons; they are not replicas of "The Thinker." The concrete symbols of victory are old footballs, basketballs, and baseballs, not works of art or first editions of books won as literary prizes. Altogether, the trophy case would suggest to the innocent visitor that he was entering an athletic club, not an educational institution.

Walking further, this visitor would encounter teen-agers bursting from classrooms. Listening to their conversations, he would hear both casual and serious discussions of the Friday football game, confirming his initial impression. Attending a school assembly that morning, he would probably find a large segment of the program devoted to a practice of school yells for the athletic game and the announcement of a pep rally before the game. At lunch hour, he would be likely to find more boys shooting baskets in the gymnasium than reading in the library. Browsing through a school yearbook, he would be impressed, in his innocence, with the number of pages devoted to athletics.

Altogether, this visitor would find, wherever he turned, a great deal of attention devoted to athletics. As an impressionable stranger, this visitor might well suppose that more attention is paid to athletics by teen-agers, both as athletes and as spectators, than to scholastic matters. He might even conclude, with good reason, that the school was essentially organized around athletic contests and that scholastic matters were of lesser importance to all involved. . . .Considering his impressions, such a visitor to American high schools might ask himself two questions: First of all, why is it this way? He had assumed, naively, that schools were for learning, yet his impressions led to a different conclusion. . . .The visitor might ask another question: What are the consequences of the attention devoted to athletics? What are the consequences within the school itself, and what are the long-term consequences for these adolescents when they have become adults?

It is to these two questions, the question of consequences and the question of sources, that this paper is directed. The examination will be based upon evidence collected during a study of ten high schools in 1957–1958.[2] These high schools were located in the Middle West. Five were small-town schools with 500 or fewer students; one was a parochial school of 750 boys in a large city; there was a working class, suburban school of 1,000 students; two small-city comprehensive schools were included of 1,400 and 2,000 students respectively; there was an upper middle-class, suburban school of 2,000 students. Unless otherwise noted, the generalizations mentioned below apply to all schools.[3] In fact, a striking discovery in this study was the similarity of all schools in the importance attached to athletics. Greater similarity among schools was found in this than in any other dimension of the research.

---

[2]James S. Coleman, *The Adolescent Society*, New York: The Free Press, 1961, pp. 70–71, 88–90.
[3]In certain cases, random variation due to the small number of students in the smallest school prevents separate conclusions about it.

CONSEQUENCES   The more difficult question concerns the long-term consequences of attention to athletics. On this question, the study has no evidence, since adolescents were studied only during one year in high school, and there seems to be no systematic evidence on the matter available elsewhere. However, evidence from the research does show some of the short-term consequences, those manifest in the school itself.

Impact on freshmen

The attention focused upon athletics in high schools directly affects the impact of the schools upon their incoming freshmen. Football, which is played in the fall as school begins, is especially important. A major element in the impact of athletics is the visibility of athletic stars. A boy who achieves something, however creditable his achievement, can be a model to emulate only if that achievement is made visible by the structure of activities in the school.

Some idea of the relative visibility of scholastic achievement and athletic achievement can be gained through a finding from the survey of the ten schools. About six weeks after school opened in the fall, each boy in every school was asked to name the boy whom he saw as the best student in his grade and the boy who was the best athlete. This can be a difficult task for freshmen, but it is less difficult in those areas for which school activities focus attention on achievement. Thus, a comparison of the proportions of boys able to answer the questions provides some guide to the relative visibility of scholastic and athletic achievements in each of the four years of school.

Table 1 shows this comparison. The data indicate, in general, that the best athletes are more visible than the best scholars. The difference is greatest for the freshmen—the best athlete is known 10 percent more often than the best scholar in the small schools and 14 percent more often in the large schools. Only in the junior and senior years does the visibility of the best scholars catch up with that of the best athletes. Thus, for the impressionable freshmen, the achievements that stand out most are those of the athlete, not those of the scholar.[4]

Assuming adolescents desire to be successful, known, and recognized, one consequence of the visibility of achievement in athletics or scholarship would be the desire to achieve in these particular areas. Does the environment and climate of opinion in the school affect these desires? Boys were asked, in the fall shortly after school had started and again in the spring toward the end of the school year, how they would most like to be remembered at school—as a brilliant student, an

---

[4]Other areas of achievement were included in the questionnaire, for example, knowing about cars and being most attractive to the girls. The visibility for both of these was far below that for athletes or scholars.

TABLE 1   COMPARATIVE VISIBILITY OF BEST ATHLETES AND BEST

SCHOLARS TO THEIR CLASSMATES

	Freshmen	Sophomores	Juniors	Seniors
Small Schools				
Percent naming best athlete	68%	75%	88%	85%
Percent naming best scholar	58%	66%	83%	88%
Number of cases	317	292	214	205
Large Schools				
Percent naming best athlete	54%	56%	48%	72%
Percent naming best scholar	40%	47%	57%	68%
Number of cases	635	1,049	749	557

Note: Percentages are based on the nine public schools.

athletic star, or most popular. One would suppose, if schools focus attention on scholastic endeavors, that the effect of the school year would be to increase the strength of the brilliant-student image relative to that of the athletic-star image. Yet, for the freshmen and sophomores of the schools surveyed, matters are quite different. Of all those responding either "brilliant student" or "athletic star," 44 percent in each grade responded "brilliant student" in the fall and only 37 percent gave this response in the spring.[5] Rather than increasing in strength over the school year, the brilliant-student image declined in strength relative to that of the athlete. It appears, then, that the very functioning of the school itself tends to reduce the initial interest of the adolescent in being seen as a brilliant student, or tends differentially to increase his interest in being seen as an athletic star.

Another effect of athletics upon the incoming freshmen concerns the "leading crowd" in school. Most high schools, other than the very smallest, have a leading crowd in each grade, though schools larger than about 2,000 in enrollment may have more than one. This crowd is recognized by other students and by its own members, and most students can name members of the leading crowd in their grade. This, in fact, was what they were asked to do in the research discussed above. In addition, all boys were asked to name their friends, so that it was possible to reconstruct the actual crowds or cliques in the school. Then, by identifying which of the cliques had as members boys frequently named as members of the leading crowd, it was possible to identify objectively the leading clique or crowd in

---

[5]The number of cases was over 800 in each grade, so the difference reported is significant beyond the .001 level.

each grade of each school. Having done this, the question then was asked: What do these boys, who constitute the leading crowds in their grades, have in common?[6]

Among the freshmen in each of the four schools studied for leading cliques, the one attribute shared by every boy in every leading clique—23 boys in all—was being out for either football or basketball. Most of the 23 were out for both. No other attribute—in background, activities, or attitudes—so sharply distinguished the leading cliques. In the later years of school, the leading cliques were found to be less uniformly athletic, but, among freshmen, they were found to be totally so.

Athletic participation as a basis for membership in the leading clique is not, of course, characteristic of every freshman class in the country, but it seems likely that the general tendency is widespread. Athletic teams provide a basis for intensive and prolonged association, more than any other activity in school. Thus, the foundation is laid, from the very beginning of high school, for a cohesive, tightly knit group. This, together with the attention directed toward athletic contests and athletic stars in high school, makes it very likely that the athletes will constitute the leading crowd among freshmen. Later, when other activities develop in school and groups form on other bases, there is less dominance of the athletic crowd. But, in the crucial first year, when a boy's aims and aspirations in high school are established, the athletic crowd dominates.

Altogether, then, athletics is a particularly important factor in the impact of the high school upon its freshmen. Through the several mechanisms discussed above, the freshmen get a picture of the school focused even more toward athletic achievement than it actually is.

Athletics in the status system

One of the most important aspects of any social system is its distribution of status: the way status attaches to different persons and to different activities. The importance of the distribution of status lies partly in its effect as a motivating device, for it motivates people toward those activities which confer status upon them. To the extent that adolescents are concerned with status among their peers—and every indication suggests that the great majority of them are so motivated—their motivations and aspirations in various activities are shaped by the distribution of status.

It is important, then, in assessing the consequences of the attention to athletics in high schools, to examine the position of athletics in the adolescent status system. . . .

In this research, it was done by asking each boy to name another boy he would like to be like, one he would like to be friends with, and who were members of the leading crowd. The status of a boy was determined by the number of such choices

---

[6]This question was studied only in four of the five smallest schools; technical problems prevented it in the large schools, and the smallest school had no distinct crowds.

he received. Another question had made it possible to identify the boys seen as the best athletes and the best scholars. By comparing the likelihood of the best athletes to receive the status choices with the likelihood of the best scholars to receive such choices, it is possible to examine the objective status of athletic achievement. Table 2 shows the average number of choices on these criteria received by the best athletes, the best scholars, and all other boys in the schools studied.

As in various other tests, athletics scored higher than scholarship, although both athletes and scholars far outdistanced other boys. Stated another way, the star athletes, only 6.6 percent of the schools' male enrollment, received 47.4 percent of the "be friends with" and "be like" choices and 36.5 percent of all the leading crowd nominations.

According to all evidence, then, the status of athletic achievement in the schools surveyed is exceedingly high, considerably higher than that of scholastic achievement. Thus, the attention paid to athletics in American high schools, which would so puzzle an innocent visitor, is paralleled by the status of athletic achievement among adolescents. . . .

SOURCES Clearly, a part of the importance of athletics for adolescents lies in its compatibility with teen-age energy, enthusiasm, and explosive spirits. Were it not for this basic compatibility, the avidity with which teen-agers follow sports contests would be difficult to explain.

But the compatibility does not explain the special place that athletics holds in the activities of a school. As an innocent visitor might observe, the institution itself often seems more oriented toward athletic goals than academic ones. This can hardly be explained by the interests of teen-agers alone, for teen-agers are inter-

TABLE 2   AVERAGE NUMBERS OF CHOICES RECEIVED BY

ATHLETES, SCHOLARS, AND ALL OTHER BOYS ON STATUS CRITERIA

	Be Friends with or Be Like	Member of Leading Crowd	Number of Cases
Athletes	5.6	7.8	272
Scholars	3.4	4.9	278
All other boys	0.4	0.8	3,598

Note: "Athletes" and "scholars" are those named two or more times as best athlete or best scholar in their respective grades by other boys. Percentages are based on the nine public schools.

ested in many things—popular music, cars, dates—which have relatively little place in the high school structure of activities. Nor can the interests of teen-agers explain the fact that, in the ten schools surveyed, the strength of the athletic-star image increased during the school year and, apparently, decreased over the summer.[7]

Athletic contests in schools seem to serve an important function for the institution. Every institution depends for its survival upon capturing a certain portion of the energies of its members. In business organizations, this is done by pay, including incentive pay, and by opportunity for promotion. Among some members of an organization, identification with the achievements of the organization provides additional motivation. In unions, motivation derives from the common goals of the members, which can only be gained through concerted, collective effort.[8]

Schools, however, provide no comparable motivating devices for their students. Students are forced by family and by law to attend school, but this insures only their physical presence, not their involvement in school activities. The necessary motivation for the expenditure of effort in school arises naturally only for those students whose backgrounds and aspirations make good grades important for them. For some students, that is, grades are comparable to pay for workers in a factory. The crucial difference is that grades are important only for a part of the school population. For many adolescents, high school only delays their access to adult freedoms and pleasures and does not offer any unique and necessary benefits.

But, even for students with the right backgrounds, grades are a poor motivating mechanism, because they are unique to the school and useful only in comparison with grades of fellow students. This generates invidious comparisons, sets each student in competition with his fellows, and is a powerfully divisive force among the students. Direct incentive pay, or piece work, in factories produces the same effect and has sometimes been consciously used by employers to keep employees divided against each other.[9]

In the long run, this is a dangerous mechanism, as the history of incentive pay has shown. Under many conditions, it encourages informal norms restricting production—against the "rate-buster"—just as grade systems in high schools promote informal action against too much studiousness—against "the curve-breaker" or

---

[7]For further discussion of this point, see Coleman, p. 303.

[8]When a union becomes merely a business union, no longer actively fighting for collective worker benefits, it survives in name, but it can no longer depend upon its members for active support. This, in fact, is the fundamental problem of many unions at the present time.

[9]This can be illustrated by the story, perhaps apocryphal, of the employer who paid every second worker on an assembly line a higher rate, so that every worker's neighbors received rates different from his own. A similar mechanism has been documented in department stores, where clerks are given marginal differentiations in title and pay to keep them divided. See Carl Dreyfuss, "Prestige Grading: A Mechanism of Control," *Reader in Bureaucracy*, R. K. Merton *et al.*, New York: The Free Press, 1952, pp. 258–264.

the "D.A.R.," Damned Average Raiser. Finally, piece work systems in factories have led to organized collective activity against the companies, unless the workers feel strongly identified with their companies.[10]

A much more successful mechanism of control in an institution is one which generates strong positive identification with the institution. Churches employ such mechanisms with their revival meetings and special holy day services. Associations and groups of all sorts do the same with rallies and collective events. But schools—apart from their athletic contests and similar activities—are peculiar institutions. There are no collective goals which the students share, and the institution is lifeless. There are only individual goals, individual scholastic achievements, made largely at the expense of other students.

Athletic contests with other schools provide, for these otherwise lifeless institutions, the collective goals that they lack. The common goals shared by all makes the institution part of its members and them part of it, rather than an organization outside them and superimposed upon them. The results are evident to any observer: The adolescent social system is centered at the school, not at the drugstore; the name by which the teen-agers identify themselves is that of the school ("Those are East High kids; I'm from Tech."); the teen-agers think of the school, the team, and the student body as one and use the pronoun "we" in referring to this entity ("We're playing Parkville Friday."). . . .

Thus, the importance of athletic contests . . . lies, at least in part, in the way the contests solve a difficult problem for the institution—the problem of generating enthusiasm for and identification with the school and drawing the energies of adolescents into the school. . . .

Lack of common community goals

A force which strengthens the emphasis upon athletics in the high schools comes from outside the schools themselves. Except in the very largest cities, a high school is a community or neighborhood institution. Many communities have only a single high school, whose name is the name of the town. In those cities with several high schools, each school usually represents a community area within the city and often carries the name of that community.

Communities, like schools without interscholastic games, have few common goals. They fight no wars, seldom engage in community rallies, and are rarely faced with such crises as floods or tornadoes that can engender a communal spirit and make members feel close to one another by creating collective goals. One of the few mechanisms by means of which this can occur is that of games or contests

---

[10]One of the important reasons that incentive pay, in the form of commissions, has always worked well for salesmen is that their active work in selling the company products to doubtful customers generates in them a positive identification with the company. Another reason, of course, is that they are usually dispersed, not in contact with one another.

between communities. Sometimes these games are between professional teams representing the communities.[11] More often, there are high school games, and these contests serve the purpose admirably. The community supports the team, and the team rewards the community when it wins. The team is a community enterprise, and its successes are shared by the community, its losses mourned in concert.

The results of this are evident in many ways. One striking evidence is teacher salaries. The school board characteristically pays more to athletic coaches than to other teachers and, occasionally, to keep a winning coach, may pay more than to the principal. When a new principal is to be found among the ranks of teachers, the pattern is common for the athletic coach to be promoted to the job.[12]

Another indicator is buildings. It is often easier to obtain funds for a new gymnasium—especially in "basketball territory"—than for other buildings. In Paris, Illinois, for example, where the high school team won the state basketball tournament a few years ago, the community voted funds for a large new gymnasium, while the high school remained without a library. In one of the ten schools included in the survey, the author found, returning in 1961, that a new gymnasium and a new reading room had been built. Funds for the gymnasium had been donated by a member of the community; the reading room had been added by means of school building funds.

3.4   INTRODUCTION

The next article, from a much longer report of an empirical study, addresses the high school guidance counselor on his home ground. Although it concentrates on only a few among a counselor's total range of activities, its broader relevance is quite direct. In addition, it demonstrates the application of a most incisive approach to the understanding of what happens in an organization.

The authors show how a counselor's clinical orientation and vocabulary not only color but actually direct and limit his perception of a student, and how, because of the crucial position he is in, the counselor's perception has important consequences for a student's fate. There is a parallel here to some aspects of our discussion of social science in Chapter 2, where emphasis was placed on the central role of one's assumptions and objectives in determining the nature of the products of one's investigation. This is as true of the physicist studying the atom, as it is of the

---

[11]The sense of shock and disbelief in Brooklyn when the Dodgers moved to Los Angeles is a measure of Brooklynites' identification of the team with their community. On the other side, it has been said that Los Angeles ceased to be a collection of suburbs and became a city for the first time when "their" Dodgers won a pennant.

[12]This pattern is being replaced by a pattern of promoting assistant principals or guidance counselors, who have administrative training in schools of education. There is no evidence that they make better principals than coaches do.

sociologist observing a high school, as it is of the guidance counselor accumulating information about a student.

Given the complexity of human behavior, some part of the answer to one's questions is likely to be wherever one looks within the whole situation. The selection of where to look is based on one's assumptions. Therefore, the basis of the selection must be included as part of what is to be examined or one's assumptions will merely be confirmed and further search precluded.

As the authors suggest, the inclination to see student characteristics as the source of student problems directs attention away from the social structure as an equally likely source. This illustrates, then, a specific instance of the obstacles on the way to accomplishing the aspiration expressed in the selection by C. Wayne Gordon, that members of an organization should view problems as general and structural rather than individual. At least in the case cited here, but perhaps quite typically, these obstacles do not stem primarily from individual needs or personalities but are themselves an integral part of the organizational structure.

3.4 THE EDUCATIONAL DECISION-MAKERS[1]

Aaron Cicourel and John Kitsuse

. . . . In the following pages we present . . . [a] formulation that conceives of the differentiation of students as a consequence of the administrative organization and decisions of personnel in the high school. We shall contend that the distribution of students in such categories as college-qualified and noncollege-qualified is to a large extent characteristic of the administrative organization of the high school and therefore can be explained in terms of that organization. We shall be concerned primarily with the relation between the administrative organization of the high school and the ways in which the students are processed through it. More specifically, we wish to investigate how the routine decisions of the guidance and counseling personnel within the high school are related to the college/noncollege decisions and, by implication, to the occupational choices made by students.

Our more general concern with the allocation of personnel within the occupational structure of the larger society is similar to that of Parsons. We view as

---

[1]From *The Educational Decision-Makers: An Advanced Study in Sociology* by Aaron V. Cicourel and John I. Kitsuse, copyright © 1963 by The Bobbs-Merrill Company, Inc., reprinted by permission of the publishers.

problematic, however, his assumption that the "virtually ascribed" college-going expectation among the middle- and upper-class segments of the population *accounts for* the higher rate of students from those social classes who do in fact go to college.[2] Although he identifies the school and prior academic achievement as the institutional setting within which the college-going expectation is expressed, he does not systematically consider how the formal organization of the school affects the realization of those expectations. In stressing the class-ascribed character of the college aspiration, he assumes that the organizational processing of the aspiration is routine and nonproblematic. We wish to question this assumption in our study. . . .

Assuming that parents have college aspirations, to whatever quality of college, for their children, and assuming that their children have internalized those aspirations, whether or not such students do in fact became eligible for college entrance depends upon: (1) the communication by parents and/or the student to the school of the student's intention to prepare for college admission; (2) the enrollment of the student in high school courses that will qualify him for college—*i.e.,* courses that will meet college entrance requirements; (3) the satisfactory completion of such courses;[3] and (4), in some instances, the recommendation of high school authorities in support of the student's college applications, particularly in the case of applications to the "better" colleges. Organizational decisions and actions that affect these preconditions may occur at any point in the student's transition through the school system and may be quite independent of either his or his parents' aspirations.[4]

In stressing the significance of such organizational contingencies for the explanation of college/noncollege or "good"/"better"/"best" college distributions of the student population, we do not deny that the formal organization of the high school progressively implements the college and occupational goals of the majority of students. Such student goals, however, are processed and actualized through a system subject to the contingencies of organizational processes. Indeed, it is precisely the routine aspects of the organizational processing activity that are of interest and are revealed by the variety of "problems" that attend the movement of a cohort of students through the high school system.

---

[2]Talcott Parsons, "General Theory in Sociology," *Sociology Today,* R. K. Merton *et al.,* eds., New York: Basic Books, 1958, p. 27.

[3]"Satisfactory" in this context means that the student earned grades that were adequate for admission to the college of his choice.

[4]The consequences of such organizational activity may be unknown to the student or his parents until he seeks admission to a college, or indeed, they may never become known to him. The articulation of parental and/or student aspirations with the organizational processes that differentiate and channel students through the school system cannot, therefore, be assumed, for it requires a flow of information to, from, and within the family and school organizations.

THE CONCEPTUAL FRAMEWORK In his classic study of suicide,[5] Emile Durkheim underlined the central importance of rates of social phenomena for sociological theory and research. The sociological problem of rates may be stated simply as follows: How are the patterned variations in the rates of certain social phenomena to be accounted for as characteristics, not of individuals, but of the social and cultural organization of the groups, communities, and societies with which they are regularly associated? For example, how is it that rates of juvenile delinquency are higher among Negroes than whites, working class than middle class, urban than rural adolescents? . . .

If the rates of college-going students, underachievers, "academic problems," etc., are to be viewed sociologically as characteristics of the high school as a complex organization, then the explanation for such rates must be sought in the patterned activities of that organization and not in the behavior of students *per se*. The theoretical significance of student *behavior* for variations in the rates is dependent upon how the personnel of the high school interpret, type, and process that behavior. Thus, the problem was formulated as follows: If the rates of various student types are conceived to be products of the socially organized activities of the personnel, then the question is "How do these activities result in making a student a statistic in a given category?" . . .

The orientation that guided our research application of the problem of rates was drawn from the work of Alfred Schutz[6]—who takes the position that the perspectives of the actors (*i.e.,* the organizational personnel) whose actions produce the on-going social organization are of central importance for any investigation of how organizations come to define, record, and treat persons as instances of certain social categories. . . .

This theoretical orientation to the study of social organization may be applied to the present problem of explaining the variations in rates of college-going and other student types. Such rates, constructed by the sociologist from the various statistics of the high school, may be conceived as products of the socially organized activities of its personnel. Attention must therefore be directed to those definitions applied and procedures followed by the personnel whereby students are differentiated, labeled, and processed as "college material," "academic problems,"

---

[5]Emile Durkheim, *Suicide*, New York: The Free Press, 1951, pp. 41–53, 297–325.

[6]The following represent a selection from Schutz's writings: "On Multiple Realities," *Philosophy and Phenomenological Research*, 5, June 1945, pp. 533–575; "The Problem of Rationality in the Social World," *Economica*, 10, May 1943, pp. 130–149; "Common-Sense and Scientific Interpretation of Human Action," *Philosophy and Phenomenological Research*, 14, September 1953, pp. 1–37; "Concept and Theory Formation in the Social Sciences," *The Journal of Philosophy*, 51, April 1954, pp. 257–273. Harold Garfinkel's paper, "The Rational Properties of Scientific and Common Sense Activities," *Behavioral Science*, 5, January 1960, pp. 72–83, contains a detailed discussion of the present use of the notion of commonsense interpretations of social reality.

"trouble-makers," etc. The use of such definitions and their effects upon the interpretations of student behavior by the organizational personnel become the primary source of data for understanding how students come to be classified and distributed among the various categories of the high school's statistics. . . .

Thus, the first research task in our investigation of the rate-producing process was to explore the "vocabulary and syntax" of the language employed by the school personnel to identify the variety of student types recognized as significant in the day-to-day activities of the high school. Such types are the commonsense constructs by which the personnel interpret student behavior and classify them into organizationally provided categories.

The second task was to examine the consequences of these identification and classification processes for the direction and development of any given student's career within the high school. Our use of the term career follows Hughes' suggestive statement that a study of careers "may be expected to reveal the nature and 'working constitution' of a society."[7] As applied to our research, the day-to-day organizational activities of identifying and classifying student types may be conceived to produce a range of careers that lead to different outcomes for students processed through the system. Some careers may qualify students for entrance to accredited colleges and universities and lead to professional occupations. Others may lead to terminal junior college certificates and into the lower ranks of white collar positions, and still others to immediate entrance into the labor market. The concept of career provides us with a method of describing and charting the sequence of the organizational decisions made and actions taken toward students in their movement through the high school system.

In a current study of patient selection in a psychiatric outpatient clinic, Garfinkel and Brickman deal explicitly with the social processes by which a population is differentiated within a social organization. Their study is concerned with "the socially organized and socially controlled ways in which patients and clinic personnel make decisions that decide a patient's transfer from one clinic status to a succeeding one. We wish to study whether and how these ways account for the features of patient load and flow."[8] The design of their study provides us a method of investigating the processes by which different outcomes are produced in an organizational setting. The present formulation follows the framework of their study.

---

[7]Everett C. Hughes, "Institutional Office and the Person," *American Journal of Sociology*, 43, November 1937, pp. 404–413. For another related conception of career, see Erving Goffman, "The Moral Career of the Mental Patient," *Psychiatry*, 22, May 1959, pp. 123–142.

[8]Harold Garfinkel and Harry Brickman, "A Study of the Composition of the Clinic Patient Population of the Outpatient Department of the UCLA Neuropsychiatric Institute," unpublished manuscript, n.d., p. 16.

AN OVERVIEW OF THE SUBSTANTIVE ISSUES ...[W]e shall direct our attention to how the high school as a socially organized system of activities differentiates talented from average and low-ability students and college-going from noncollege-going students, and how such activities may affect the future occupational careers of the student population. . . .

In our study we wish to examine the thesis advanced in earlier studies that social class and organizational sponsorship, as opposed to capability, are critical for the manner in which students are processed through the school system. Since our student sample is drawn from an upper-income community, the students should, consistent with Parsons' hypothesis, be predominantly college-oriented. We seek also to show, however, that the notion of class-ascribed aspirations from which Parsons' hypothesis is derived must be articulated with a conception of organizational processes if we are to understand how effectively those aspirations are implemented for the majority of such students. We hope to shed light on how parental and student knowledge and activity regarding the college-going program influence the organizational processes of the high school.

The theory of social organization that orients our study leads us to conceive of a college-qualified high school senior as the product of the organizational actions of school personnel who record the college/noncollege declaration of freshmen students, classify them into ability groups, assign them to types of course programs, review and evaluate their performance, and define, interpret, and counsel them on their problems. We may ask, then: are students with college-going expectations automatically assigned to courses that will qualify them for college entrance at the end of their high school careers? Or, is such assignment subject throughout their high school years to specific organizational contingencies?

The "problems" that are attributed to students by school personnel should not be those which are widely, but generally, discussed as the so-called adolescent problem. The labels of "underachiever" and "overachiever" and the variety of social and psychological interpretations that are made of them—*e.g.*, "emotionally disturbed," "social isolate," "antisocial"—should be generated by the organizational activities of the school personnel. Our research formulation directs our attention to organizational factors for an explanation of how such students present problems for the high school.

We contend that the organizational production of various student problems is related to the bureaucratization of the counseling system and the professionalization of its personnel. Thus, the organization of the counseling system and the activities of its personnel have been a central focus of our study. Our interviews with counselors were designed to reveal that the clinical orientation of their professional training leads to the fusion of academic problems with personal problems of students. We suggest that among full-time counselors, and particularly among school social workers, the clinical interpretation of academic problems has become a means of explaining deviant cases of students who have capability but who fail to perform at their expected level.

Our study is indirectly tied to the larger question of whether and how the high school in American society operates to provide equal access to higher educational facilities to those of equal capability. The theoretical orientation we follow suggests that one of the major consequences of the current search for academic talent in the high school should be a limitation of access to future occupational opportunities by organizational decisions and actions that occur as early as the students' last year in junior high school. The activities of counseling personnel are of major importance in such organizational decisions and actions and therefore deserve close examination. . . .

THE BUREAUCRATIZATION OF THE SEARCH FOR TALENT   . . . .A major consequence of the policy of identifying talented students at an early stage in the educational process is that the high school tends to control the students' access to higher educational facilities and, in turn, their life chances. The practice of so-called ability grouping is an important structural feature of this control. The assignment of students to ability groups is primarily based on the interpretation of counselors and teaching personnel of the students' performance on aptitude tests. Since students classified as "low ability" in one or another section of the aptitude tests are not permitted to enroll in courses required for college entrance, ability grouping is significantly related to the distribution of educational opportunities among the student population. We wish to investigate the criteria employed by the school personnel to interpret test results as well as other, less objective measures of student performance in the processing of students through the system.

Our preliminary field investigations indicated that the counseling process provided for periodic reviews of student performance as the major method by which student problems were identified for investigation by counselors. The routinization of this counseling activity suggests that the academic as well as personal, emotional, and social "adjustment" of all students will be subjected to examination for evidence of difficulties. As specialists in the identification, interpretation, and treatment of student problems, counselors would occupy a strategic position in the network of communications concerning the general demeanor, conduct, association, activities, and performance of students both in and out of classrooms. Schools with highly bureaucratized counseling systems, therefore, may be expected to identify more students with problems.

Preliminary field work also revealed that students with discrepancies between their tested ability and achievement are particularly subject to counselor attention. Failure to achieve at the expected level alerts the counselor to investigate the "problem" for indications of "difficulties." An underachiever, for example, may reveal in a conference with the counselor that he simply failed to submit his homework in a course ("lacks motivation") or that his mother always expects him to do better than his brother ("sibling rivalry") or that he doesn't need any counseling ("reaction against dependency needs"). On the other hand, although students are expected to achieve up to their ability, evidence that a student has to work harder than he should for his grades may be considered prejudicial to his overall development.

The interpretation of such "problems" in psychological and clinical terms has important consequences for the degree to which the policies and methods of the school system remain open to evaluation of their effectiveness and to proposals for modifications. Our counselor interview schedule was constructed to focus investigation on the variety of academic problems that come to their attention. We sought to explore the extent to which some counselors seek explanations by use of a clinical vocabulary that would lead them to interpret those problems in terms of the student's "motivation," "family situation," "peer adjustment," etc.

The presence of social workers in the school we studied prompted us to ask if the failure of the student to respond to psychologically oriented treatment would tend to lead counselors and social workers to look for "deeper problems." We reasoned that, if the student is summoned by the counselor and encouraged to discuss his "difficulty," he may in the face of such solicitous treatment provide information to confirm the clinical interpretation of his "problem." Thus, the organizational efforts to "help" the student may redefine the initial basis of the student's "problem"—*i.e.,* the discrepancy between his capability and classroom performance. One consequence of such an orientation of "help" would be to deflect school administrators from examining the organization and methods of the school system, including the activities of counselors, as sources of academic problems.

Another consequence of this orientation would be the creation of a population of students organizationally differentiated as clinical cases in need of therapeutic treatment. Such a differentiation would presuppose some criteria of normal or healthy adjustment that counselors would presumably apply to identify and interpret problems. We asked, therefore, if there were consensus among school counselors and social workers concerning such criteria. If so, what are the empirical bases for their classifications? We sought also to determine whether and how such interpretations are communicated to the student and to his parents and teachers. When the student is defined as "emotionally disturbed," "anxious," or some similar term by counseling personnel, do the student, his parents, and his teachers accept the clinical labels, or do they propose alternative explanations of the academic problem?

Whether or not they accept the clinical labels, or indeed, even though they may be unaware that imputations concerning the student's "adjustment" have been made, his career within the school system and in later life may be significantly affected by the counselor's judgment. For the counselor's activities involve him in many aspects of the student's life. In addition to the personal counseling discussed above, his duties include vocational guidance, advising students on the programming of courses, certifying them as qualified to participate in extracurricular activities, writing letters of recommendation in support of college and job applications. Thus, we were interested to know when and how the counselor decides that a student with academic problems needs special guidance concerning the college to which he should apply, the occupational careers for which he is most suited, the extracurricular activities in which he should be allowed to participate. To what extent are decisions affected by the counselor's characterization of such students as "insecure," "emotionally unstable," or "aggressive and authoritarian?"

The introduction of clinical terminology and interpretations into the school system is one reflection of the increasing concern in American society for the maintenance of health, particularly mental health. . . .

In the context of this increasing stress upon good social and mental adjustment, our study examines the counselor's position of authority and power as a validating agent for the student's future occupational opportunities and careers. Many colleges and employers routinely request unofficial as well as official information in the form of recommendations from school personnel. In many schools such requests presumably would go to counselors as the personnel most intimately informed about the student's high school career. We are interested in knowing what information the counselor recalls about the student and how he recalls it, how these recollections inform his interpretation of the official records, and how the recommendation is phrased. In view of the trend toward the progressive coordination of records and information between the school and other agencies within the society, the student's school career, what is recorded about it, and the counselor's interpretation of it are of more than incidental significance for the processes of social mobility and stratification.

THE "ASCRIPTION" OF PARENTAL AND STUDENT COLLEGE ASPIRATIONS   In an educational system that is undergoing rapid change, a study of a "typical" high school would be out of date before the findings could be published. Our selection of a school for study, therefore, was not guided by a requirement that it be typical. We looked instead for a school that incorporates the most advanced developments in educational theory and practice. We selected a large, comprehensive high school, hereafter called "Lakeshore High School," with a national reputation for the excellence of its educational program and its student products.

How is Lakeshore High School atypical? First, there is considerable pressure for students to go to college, particularly to the "good" or "prestige" colleges and universities. The pressure is general as well as specific and is exerted by parents, peers, and school personnel. Further, at Lakeshore High, administrative decisions are crucial for the process by which students are qualified for college entrance. These decisions may be independent of the students' college-going aspirations, and they significantly control the flow of students through the several curricula of the high school. Such pressures and administrative decisions do not exist or are of minimal importance in most contemporary high schools, especially in those states where state colleges and universities automatically admit students on completion of a high school program of academic courses. In states where junior colleges exist there is virtually no barrier of any kind, since admission is not contingent upon administrative decisions or completion of an academic program, but on minimal test and course grade requirements.

What can be learned by studying an atypical high school like Lakeshore High? First, there are many high schools of its kind throughout the United States, located in the suburban areas of metropolitan regions and in the wealthier or middle- and upper-middle-class sections of large cities. Second, most American high schools have similar bureaucratic structures and organizational practices, so that the kinds of decisions that are routinely made about students at Lakeshore High are likely to appear with increasing frequency in schools throughout the country. The differentiation of students described in this book probably resembles that found in less "advanced" high schools, but the decisions (and the criteria employed in making them) that produce the differentiation are more important at Lakeshore High because of the strong emphasis placed not only upon going to college but upon attending one of a select group of "good" colleges.

The most important reason for studying this high school is that it has a highly developed counseling system and a curriculum notable for its range and quality. . . . The student-counselor ratio runs from 100 to 1 to 250 to 1, with the average case load 225 to 1. The program for ability-grouped classes at Lakeshore High and its counseling system (which includes social workers, psychiatrists, psychologists, and other specialists at all levels of the school system) reflect the general concern to differentiate students academically and to prepare them for college. Thus, although Lakeshore High is atypical among contemporary high schools, its curricular organization, administrative policies, and counseling system are likely to be adopted and developed more widely within the American school system. An understanding of the organizational practices and decisions whereby students are differentiated is important *per se*, but it is also likely that our study of an atypical high school can provide a preview of the future.

The social characteristics of Lakeshore High School

Lakeshore High School is located in a high-income suburb of a large metropolitan region. The 1960 Census reports show that the median income for local families was $9193 and the median educational level was 13.5 years for males and 12.6 for females. The occupations reported were in high proportion professional (24 percent), managerial (19 percent), and clerical and sales (26 percent). In the large city of which the community served by Lakeshore High is a suburb, median income for families is $7342, median education is 10.9 years for males and 10.8 years for females, and the occupational distributions shows 11 percent professional, 11 percent managerial, and 17 percent clerical and sales.

The percentage of Lakeshore High graduates who go on to college is high—from 70 to 75[9]. . . .

Of the Lakeshore class of 1959, 73.25 percent (N = 649) went to college. Although there have been some minor fluctuations, there have not been any major changes in the past 5 years in the percentage of college-attending seniors or in the geographic distribution of the colleges they have attended. Roughly 80 percent have gone to midwestern schools and 15 percent to eastern schools, while the remaining 5 percent have gone to southern and western colleges.

The organizational characteristics
of Lakeshore High School

Lakeshore High School currently enrolls approximately 3,600 students and employs about 200 administrative and academic personnel, excluding clerks and stenographers.[10] The general organization consists of four divisions with an equal number of students. Each division is headed by a division principal and three division assistants. The division principals report directly to the superintendent, but they handle all activities within their divisions. The superintendent delegates authority to both the assistant superintendent (who also is called the assistant principal because the superintendent is the principal as well as superintendent of the entire high school) and the administrative assistant. Division principals and other administrative officials are often instructed to channel their problems through the administrative assistant.

Within each division there are four counselors, a social worker, and three home rooms, which are managed by division assistants. There is at least one counselor for each grade level in the division (freshman, sophomore, junior, and senior), while the social worker covers the entire division. The counselors and social

---

[9]The college representative at Lakeshore High is in touch with representatives of various colleges, including the so-called prestige colleges in the East. Each year representatives from a wide variety of colleges visit Lakeshore High to interview students personally. The high school urges students to contact alumni of colleges that interest them and maintains for this purpose a list of such alumni in the metropolitan area.

[10]Lakeshore High is, by current educational standards, rather large. Its bureaucratic character, therefore, is probably enhanced by sheer scale.

workers report directly to the division principal, but they are also responsible, respectively, to the heads of the counseling group and of the social workers. These latter two officials report directly to the superintendent and his assistants. Finally, there are various department chairmen, such as those for business, art, combined studies (a combination of English and social studies), English, home economics, foreign languages, and the like, which cross-cut the four divisions. The division structure, then, is primarily an administrative device for handling a large student population under a decentralized system.

The students coming into the high school are randomly assigned to the four divisions, with some noteworthy exceptions. The first exception is that high-ability students are separated and distributed equally among the four divisions. This amounts to a planned separation along administrative lines. It is not clear why the randomizing procedure used for assigning all students would not accomplish the same objective for high-ability students. The second exception is the separation of Negro students and their equal distribution among the four divisions. Again, it is not clear why the randomizing device is not used. It appears that this administration has been concerned with an unknown amount of Negro-white dating. The subject is a touchy one around the high school and we were discouraged from asking questions about it.

THE CURRICULUMS   The basic division of curriculums within the school is that between college and noncollege courses. The students visit the school while in the eighth grade, take a battery of tests, and are asked to consider a choice between two plans—of which one prepares them for college and the other does not.

THE ORGANIZATIONAL DIFFERENTIATION OF INCOMING FRESHMEN   In this section we explore how the students in our sample are organizationally differentiated and processed by the admissions personnel of the high school. The general question we wish to address is: How are the college-going intentions of our students articulated with the organizational processes of the high school? In addressing this question, we shift our attention to the activities of the school personnel that structure and validate the movement of students toward or away from their stated goals and aspirations.

The college-going declaration

In principle, the student is entitled to exercise his right to choose either the college or noncollege curriculum independent of his capability, past performance, or personal and social characteristics, and the high school is committed to honor his choice by providing the conditions for the implementation of his educational goal.

In practice, however, the student's declaration of choice is not the only criterion of differentiation employed by the admissions personnel. The manner in which a student is processed as a "college-going" student is contingent not only upon those attributes that in principle he may consider irrelevant—*i.e.,* the above-mentioned capability, past performance, etc.—but also upon interpretations of those attributes by admissions personnel. Thus, a study of the distribution of college- and noncollege-going high school seniors that attends only to the individual's goals and the strategies he uses to achieve them does not reveal how the actualization of those goals is contingent upon the perceptions, decisions, and actions of the school personnel.

The first indication of how the student's declaration of college-going intention is translated into organizational terms may be seen in the student's freshman program of courses. The question may be asked: Are students who have chosen the college curriculum in fact enrolled in college-preparatory courses? Before we examine our materials with reference to this question, several features of the curriculums at Lakeshore High School should be noted.

First, most of the courses in the freshman program are prescribed for all students—English, history, mathematics, science, or a foreign language, an elective (which may be chosen from such courses as speech, chorus, mechanical drawing, or home economics), and physical education. Second, the freshman college-preparatory curriculum is distinguished from the noncollege curriculum by the *types* of mathematics and science courses included in the program and by the foreign language course. Three mathematics courses are offered: algebra, general mathematics, and basic mathematics. Of the three, algebra, a prerequisite for courses in higher mathematics, is the only college entrance course. General mathematics does not carry college entrance credit, but it does prepare the student for algebra. Basic mathematics is a course designed for students with low mathematical aptitude. Two types of science courses are open to freshmen—biology, which is classified as a laboratory science and thus carries college entrance credit, and general science, which does not. In the freshman year, the student may elect a foreign language instead of a science, thus working toward fulfilling the foreign language requirement for college entrance.

A third feature of the curriculums at Lakeshore High School is that enrollment in algebra, biology, and foreign language is not by the student's election alone. His election of the courses is reviewed by the admissions personnel, who may or may not approve his election. That is, the enrollment of a student in those courses which differentiate college preparatory from noncollege courses is by *assignment* based on the admissions personnel's assessment of his capability and performance. The formal criteria applied to assess capability will be discussed below. The point we wish to make here is that meeting college entrance requirements as a freshman is contingent upon the student's choice of the proper courses *and* his assignment to those courses by the admissions personnel.

ASSIGNMENT TO COURSES   The alternative combinations of courses that can be assigned may be classified as college-preparatory (*i.e.,* includes two college entrance credit courses), quasi-college-preparatory (includes one college credit course), and noncollege (includes no college credit courses) programs. We shall refer to the three combinations of courses as Type A, Type B, and Type C programs respectively. Table 1 presents the distribution of students who have declared college-going intentions among the three types of course programs. Of the 78 students who formally declared college-going intentions by their choice of Plan I, the majority (50 out of 78 or 64 percent) were enrolled in Type A, while 28 (36 percent) were placed in Types B and C. While assignment to Type B does not necessarily mean that the student will not eventually complete a college preparatory program, it does substantially lower the possibility of that outcome, and thus it represents a partial discrepancy between the formal declaration of college-going intentions and assignment to a college course program.

TABLE 1   ASSIGNMENT OF COLLEGE-DECLARED STUDENTS TO

TYPES OF PROGRAMS

Social Class	Course Type			
	A	*B*	*C*	*N*
Upper three	48	16	6	70
Lower two	2	3	3	8
N	50	19	9	78

TABLE 2   TYPES OF PROGRAMS* ASSIGNED TO COLLEGE-DECLARED

STUDENTS BY SCAT SCORES

SCAT Score	Upper Three Classes			Lower Two Classes			
	Type A	*Type B*	*Type C*	*Type A*	*Type B*	*Type C*	*N*
76-100	25	1	0	0	0	0	26
51-75	14	7	0	1	1	0	23
26-50	8	2	2	1	1	0	14
0-25	1	3	4	0	1	2	11
N	48	13	6	2	3	2	74†

* See text above for definitions of types.
† No information on four students.

TABLE 3   TYPES OF PROGRAMS* ASSIGNED TO COLLEGE-DECLARED
STUDENTS BY EIGHTH-GRADE POINT AVERAGE

Grade-Point Average	Upper Three Classes			Lower Two Classes			
	Type A	*Type B*	*Type C*	*Type A*	*Type B*	*Type C*	*N*
1.00-1.50	7	1	0	0	0	0	8
1.75-2.00	11	2	0	0	0	0	13
2.25-3.00	17	5	0	2	1	1	26
3.25-4.00	11	6	2	0	2	1	22
4.25-5.00	1	0	4	0	0	0	5
N	47	14	6	2	3	2	74†

*See p. 83 for definitions of types.
†No information on four students.

How is this discrepancy between the students' formal declaration of college-going intentions and their assignment to the three types of programs to be accounted for? If the distribution of students among the three types of programs is not a matter of election but rather of assignment, and if capability is the primary criterion of assignment, then we should expect a systematic relation between the students' SCAT scores and the types of programs to which they are assigned. Table 2 shows that 9 of the upper three social class students with SCAT scores between 0 and 50 are assigned to the Type A program, while 8 such students in SCAT categories 51 to 100 are assigned to Type B programs. This suggests that the assignment of a student to a program is not based solely on the declaration of college-going intention and a SCAT score within a given range.

If the SCAT score is not the primary criterion for distributing students among the types of programs, it might be suggested that actual performance as indicated by the students' past course grades might better account for the distribution. It might be argued that admissions personnel would be more strongly guided by past performance than by a single index of academic potential, of which the SCAT is presumably a measure. As a measure of past performance, we have computed a grade-point average from the students' course grades for their last semester in junior high school.[11] Table 3 presents the grade-point averages of college-declared students assigned to types of programs. If we arbitrarily take the 2.00 grade-point

[11]Only mathematics, social studies, general science, and English were considered. Letter grade *A* was scored one point, while letter grade *F* was scored five points. A simple average was computed.

average or higher (*i.e.*, B or better) as the cutting point for the assignment of students to the Type A program, the table shows that from the upper three social classes 63 percent (29 out of 46) of the students with grade-point averages below B are assigned to Type A programs and 37 percent (17 students) assigned to Types B (11) and C (6).

In view of the discrepancies that result when we apply the SCAT and grade-point criteria to account for the assignment of students to types of course programs, it appears that other, unknown judgments enter into the decisions by which the assignments are made and that the implementation of the student's declaration of college-going intention is far from a matter of course. Whatever the criteria of assignment to types of programs may be, the student's educational plans are subject to this organizational contingency at the very outset of his high school career. . . .

The evaluation of student performance

The significance of the differentiation of entering students discussed above may be seen by examination of the periodic evaluation of student performance that is routinely conducted by counseling personnel at Lakeshore High School. We wish, therefore, to investigate how student performances are evaluated by counselors, and how the organizational process of this evaluation further differentiates the student population.

Every student at Lakeshore High is assigned to a counselor who has access to his cumulative school records, containing medical, psychological, social, and personal as well as academic information. One of the duties of the counselor is to review at the end of each marking period the academic progress of the students assigned to him. Routinely the counselor's review consists primarily of checking the students' grades against their SCAT scores for evidence of "discrepancies." The nature of such discrepancies is noted—*e.g.*, students with high SCAT scores and average or low grades, or average SCAT scores and high grades—and an investigation is initiated by the counselor to determine the bases of the inconsistencies.

From an organizational point of view, the counselor's review of the students' performance constitutes a check upon the effectiveness of the school's program for identifying and developing talent. A large number of SCAT/grade-point discrepancies may be interpreted by the school administrator as evidence that (1) the criterion of "ability" employed is not efficient in differentiating students with different levels of ability, or (2) the "ability" identified by this criterion is not related to the courses that are presumably designed to develop it, or (3) teachers are not performing adequately in developing the ability of students assigned to their courses. Such interpretations of SCAT/grade-point discrepancies would direct the administrator to examine the system for possible methods of improving the "search for talent" program.

On the other hand, SCAT/grade-point discrepancies may be interpreted as *characteristics of students*. That is, the efficiency of the tests used to identify ability, the courses designed to develop it, and the teachers assigned to evaluate the degree of development is not questioned. Rather, what is questioned is the students' failure to perform "up to their ability." An interesting feature of our study is that references to inadequacies, defects, or failures of the "system" by organizational personnel were virtually absent. When such references were made, they were *ad hoc* or *ad hominem* comments concerning, for example, some student who was "mistakenly" assigned by "someone" to a higher or lower section than he should have been, or some student who is "really much better than those test results indicate," or some teacher who expects more or less of his students than he should. In short, the characteristic interpretation made by counselors and other school personnel of SCAT/grade-point discrepancies is that students perform below or above their tested ability as a consequence of motivational, personal, and social "problems," not methods of teaching, preparation (readiness), or aptitude.

In order to obtain information concerning the process of student evaluation as practiced by the counseling personnel, we systematically questioned the counselor to whom the students in our sample were assigned. We were particularly interested in the criteria used in categorizing student achievement and in how the achievement-type classification compares with the "objective" measures of student ability (SCAT) and performance (grade-point average in the freshman year). The materials obtained in our interviews with this counselor are presented below.

THE COUNSELOR'S ACHIEVEMENT TYPES   When we asked the counselor how she would classify each of the students in our sample,[12] she employed the following categories (which were widely used by the teaching as well as the counseling personnel at Lakeshore High) of classification: (1) "Excellent student," (2) "Average achiever," (3) "Underachiever," (4) "Overachiever," (5) "Opportunity student." Asked what she considered the most stable basis for her judgment of a student, she replied:

"Probably ability—that's the most specific and measurable."
Interviewer: "And how do you determine ability?"
Counselor: "By tests and performance, generally."

If we assume that the counselor's evaluation of student performance is to assess the students' progress in the courses to which they have been assigned, we would expect a systematic relationship between the achievement-type classification and the distribution of SCAT/grade-point discrepancies. In Table 4 we have included the SCAT scores and grade-point averages of each of the students classified by the counselor in order to show the relation between discrepancies and achievement types. An examination of the table will show the range of discrepancies classified

---

[12]The counselor did not classify seven students for various reasons, such as dropouts, transfers to another division, and no information.

TABLE 4   COUNSELOR'S ACHIEVEMENT TYPES BY SCAT SCORES
AND NINTH-GRADE POINT AVERAGE

Achievement Types	Ninth-Grade Point Average					
	1.00-1.50	*1.75-2.00*	*2.25-3.00*	*3.25-4.00*	*4.25-5.00*	*N*
Opportunity student			(15)	(06)(10) (12)(16)	(01)(02) (02)(13)	9
Overachiever		(42)	(27)	(16)		3
Underachiever		(68)	(68)(68) (73)(80)(84) (87)(90)(96)	(17)(39) (58)(75)(78) (80)(93)	(10)(39)	18
Average achiever		(47)(64) (64)(75)	(27)(32)(35) (39)(50)(64) (64)(68)(68) (68)(68)(73) (73)(78)(84) (87)(90)	(15)(20)(20) (35)(42)(42) (50)(52)(54) (75)	(28) (39)	33
Excellent student	(73)(73)(80) (84)(85)(94) (95)(97)	(75)(78) (84)(84) (90)(93) (95)(96)	(94)	(90)		18
N	8	14	28	23	9	81*

* No information for eight cases.

in the five achievement types by the counselor. (The range of discrepancies for each category of achievement types is summarized in Table 5.) For example, the "excellent student" category includes 9 students with SCAT scores of 90–95 and with grade-point averages ranging from 1.00 to 3.25. On the other hand, the 2.25–3.00 grade-point column shows that there are 4 students with SCAT scores of 90–95, but 2 are classified as "underachievers," another as an "average achiever," and the fourth as an "excellent student." These classifications are not a strict application of the SCAT/grade-point discrepancy criterion. The classification of other students (*e.g.,* the SCAT 68/1.75–2.00 "underachiever," the SCAT 17/3.25–4.00 "underachiever," the SCAT 47/1.75–2.00 "average achiever," etc.) provides added evidence that the criterion is not consistently applied and does not account for the distribution of achievement types. The table

TABLE 5   RANGE OF SCAT AND NINTH-GRADE POINT AVERAGE BY
COUNSELOR'S CLASSIFICATION OF ACHIEVEMENT TYPES

Achievement Types	SCAT Range	Grade-Point Range	N
Excellent student	73-97	1.00-3.25	18
Average achiever	15-90	1.75-4.25	33
Underachiever	10-96	2.00-4.66	18
Overachiever	16-42	2.00-3.75	3
Opportunity student	01-16	3.00-5.00	9
			81*

* No information for eight cases.

shows that neither SCAT nor grade point alone accounts for the achievement-type classifications.

The inconsistencies revealed in this classification of students are of more than passing interest, for the achievement types are not merely descriptive categories to the personnel who use them. The classification of students as achievement types in effect produces a distribution of students who are conceived by the organizational personnel to have "problems." With the exception of students classified, by whatever criteria, as "average achiever" and "excellent student," the achievement-type classification identifies those students who are performing below the level of their ability ("underachiever") or above it ("overachiever"), or who are lacking in both ability and performance ("opportunity student"). . . .

If the more or less "rational criterion" of SCAT/grade-point discrepancy does not account for the counselor's achievement-type classification of students, what are the bases of her judgments? What are the variables that might operate to produce the variations in the distribution discussed above? Social-class characteristics of the student population, commonly found by social researchers to influence the evaluations of students by school personnel, are variables that deserve examination. In our investigation of this possibility we were directed by our theoretical orientation, which emphasizes the vocabulary and syntax used by the organizational personnel, to obtain the social-class categories that *the counselor* used to differentiate the student population.

THE COUNSELOR'S SOCIAL TYPES   To explore the relation between the stratification system as perceived by the counselor and her classification of achievement types, we questioned her as follows:

a. How many social statuses, that is, social-class groups, would you say there are here at Lakeshore High School?

b. How would you describe, in general, each of the groups you mentioned?

c. How would you place each of the students named on these cards (handing her a set of cards with the names of all the students in our sample) into each of the groups you mentioned?

The phrasing of the questions assumes that social-status categories are recognized, if not employed, by the counselor as one dimension of her classification of students. The questions, however, allow the counselor to interpret "social status, that is, social-class groups" in her own terms. We would expect the counselor to base her evaluations on the same kind of commonsense criteria one would expect from persons in the general population—*i.e.*, the categories and criteria should be characteristically general, vaguely defined, and perhaps inconsistently applied.

When the counselor was asked question *a*, she offered without prompting from the interviewer a description of each group as she identified them. That is, the interviewer found it unnecessary to ask question *b*. The counselor's categories and comments were as follows:

1. First there's the main group—the in-group. This is the group that belongs to the "Y." They head this group, they're at the forefront of the activities in the school, they're the leaders. Most of them live in Lakeshore. They belong to the Presbyterian Church there, or is it a Methodist Church?

2. Then there's the group just below this group. They're trying to attain the [main] group. They're sometimes included in the activities of the first group, but they don't really belong. They might be the campaign managers for members of the first group if they're running for an office. This group will do almost anything to get into the other group.

3. There's the other element. These students would not at all consider getting into the first group. They get into a lot of trouble, they have difficulties with their studies. Most of the dropouts are from this group—they drop out at 16 or 17.

4. We can't deny that there's a Negro group here at Lakeshore. They have their own group, their own identification. In some instances there are those who cut across the line, but they don't participate in their "Y" activities. The "Y" seems to be the center of activities, and the "Y" is a segregated group.

5. Then there's the group that's left [not politically left, but left by subtraction]. This is not really a group. They don't have a group of their own. There are some strong individualists in this group.

6. We should make some note of those other students who are not in a group. They are noteworthy individuals. Because they are outstanding they are known to everybody. But they don't belong to any group. They're the kind that might wear black leotards or carry a guitar. They're a group, but not a group. They come to our attention in some way—they're outstanding

scholastically, or they're extremely sensitive, [the counselor smiled here, which was interpreted to mean that she did not want to be more explicit] or intelligent. Some of them are referred for psychiatric care. [The counselor cited the case of a student in our sample who would fit this group. She called this group "loners."]

7. [The counselor then mentioned another group who were "like loners" but she said they were "rebelling." This group dressed, she said, in extreme fashion.] They wear their skirts too short. [In our sample, this group consists of four or five girls who are described as being tightly banded together, but who are not thought to have the "nerve" to do anything as individuals.] They find it difficult to fit into things at Lakeshore High. Anything typical of teen-agers here is ridiculous for them. [The counselor stated that the "loner" described in the last group might wear leotards or braids or carry a guitar even if no one else were doing so.]

The counselor's response to question *a* indicates that she interpreted "social status, that is, social class" to mean different *social types* of students within the stratification system of the high school, and we shall refer to them hereafter by that term. With the exception of Social Types 1 and 2, and perhaps the "Negro group" (Social Type 4), her descriptions do not necessarily imply a strict hierarchical ranking in the conventional terms of social class. The pluralistic classification appears to be based on some combination of aspiration, rejection, or withdrawal of students from participation in school and out-of-school social activities.

In response to question *c*, the counselor classified the students in our sample into the categories that she enumerated and described. Table 6 shows the relation between her social-type and achievement-type classifications of students. Twelve of the 17 students classified as "excellent students" were also classified as Social Type 1. Conversely, all but 3 of the 15 Social Type 1 students were classified as "excellent students." In none of the remaining categories in which the frequencies are large enough to warrant consideration (*i.e.*, Social Types 2 and 5, and the achievement types of "average achiever" and "underachiever") is there a suggested relationship which approaches that between the "excellent student"— Social Type 1 classification.

It would appear that there is a fusion of academic and social-type criteria in the counselor's classification of the "excellent" Social Type 1 student. Table 7, which presents the distribution of social types with reference to the students' SCAT scores and grade-point averages, provides a clue to the nature of the academic criteria that may have been applied by the counselor in the social-type classification. With one exception (one student with SCAT of 68), all students in Social Type 1 have SCAT scores of 73 or higher, but their grade-point averages range from 1.00 to 4.00. The classification of the 94/2.25–3.00 student and the 90/3.25–4.00 student in Social Type 1 shows that these relatively large SCAT/-grade-point discrepancies (indicating underachievement) did not disqualify them

TABLE 6   COUNSELOR'S SOCIAL TYPES BY COUNSELOR'S

CLASSIFICATION OF ACHIEVEMENT DESIGNATIONS

Social Types	Achievement Types					
	Excel.	*Aver.*	*Under*	*Over*	*Oppor.*	*N*
7	0	1	0	1	1	3
6	1	0	0	0	0	1
5	0	10	7	1	4	22
4	0	1	0	0	2	3
3	0	2	4	0	1	7
2	4	16	6	1	2	29
1	12	2	1	0	0	15
N	17	32	18	3	10	80*

* No information on nine cases.

from inclusion in this category. We note, however, that although high SCAT appears to be a characteristic of Social Type 1 students, there is an equal number of students with scores of 73 or higher who were classified in other social-type categories.

The characterization of the "excellent" Social Type 1 student that may be made from Tables 6 and 7 is that of a student whom the counselor considers to be a "leader," who is in the "main group," and who has a relatively high SCAT score even if he does not have a high grade-point average. Table 7 also indicates that neither SCAT nor grade-point average separately nor the discrepancy between them is systematically related to the classification of social types. Our materials suggest that the counselor's social-type classification does not account for the majority of her achievement-type classification of students.

THE COUNSELOR'S SOCIAL-CLASS RATINGS   The counselor's response to question *a* raised the question of whether or not she differentiated students by social-class categories in the conventional sense. If so, would her classification of students in those terms better account for the achievement types than the social types? To obtain this information, we explained to the counselor that we would like her to classify our student sample into five strata of social classes. Using a fivefold classification, we presented these strata to her as: Class I, Upper; Class II, Lower Upper; Class III, Upper Middle; Class IV, Lower Middle; and Class V, Lower. No further criteria for the classification of students, except as indicated immediately below, were given to the counselor. When she was presented with these strata, the counselor asked:

What do you mean by "upper"? In Lakeshore that would have to be old-guard Lakeshore. There may be some with more money, but they wouldn't be old guard. For example, the ———boy's family has lots of money, but they don't make it on the old guard.

Interviewer: So, the ———boy would not be placed in the "upper" class if that's true.

Table 8 shows the social-class distribution that resulted from the counselor's classification of students by achievement-type categories. It should be noted that although the counselor indicated by her remark about the "old-guard Lakeshore" that she recognized the existence of an "upper" class, she did not assign any of the

TABLE 7   COUNSELOR'S SOCIAL TYPES BY SCAT SCORES AND

NINTH-GRADE POINT AVERAGE

Social Type	Ninth-Grade Point Average					
	1.00-1.50	*1.75-2.00*	*2.25-3.00*	*3.25-4.00*	*4.25-5.00*	*N*
7				(15)	(13)	2
6	(97)					1
5		(47)	(15)(27) (32)(39)(64) (68)(68)(73) (80)	(17)(20) (35)(52) (58)	(02)(07) (10)	18
4			(78)	(06)(50)	(01)	4
3				(10)(12) (39)(42) (54)(78)	(39)	7
2	(85)	(42)(64) (64)(75) (90)(93)	(27)(35)(50) (64)(68)(68) (84)(84)(87) (87)(90)(90) (96)	(16)(20) (42)(75) (93)	(02)	26
1	(73)(73) (80)(84) (94)(95)	(68)(75) (78)(84) (84)(95) (96)	(73)(73) (94)	(75)(90)		18
N	8	14	27	21	7	76*

* No information for 13 cases.

students in our sample to that social class. As in the case of Social Type 1, "excellent students" are predominantly from one category—all but one in Social Class II. The converse relationship, however, does not obtain: *i.e.,* only 40 percent (17 out of 42) Class II students are classified as "excellent students." Thus, although the social-class category adds the characteristic of Social Class II to the description of the "excellent student," it does no better than the social-type classification in suggesting the basis for the overall distribution of achievement types.

TABLE 8   DISTRIBUTION OF ACHIEVEMENT TYPES BY COUNSELOR'S

SOCIAL-CLASS RATINGS

Achievement Types	Counselor's Social-Class Ratings					
	I	*II*	*III*	*IV*	*V*	*N*
Opportunity		2	1	4	2	9
Overachiever		2	1			3
Underachiever		10	5	4		19
Average achiever		12	13	5	1	31
Excellent		17	1			18
N		42	21	13	3	80*

* No information on nine cases.

The bases of the counselor's judgments

In our discussion of the routine organizational evaluation of student performance at Lakeshore High School, we have focused our attention on the distribution of achievement types that is produced by the evaluation process. We have attempted to account for this distribution by a consideration of (1) the more or less "objective" criterion of SCAT/grade-point discrepancy which, given the method of assigning students to courses at this chool, is presumably applied in the evaluation process; (2) the counselor's social-type classification of students, on the assumption that more "subjective" factors enter into her evaluation of students; and (3) the counselor's social-class classification, to assess the importance of this often discussed variable. Our materials suggest that the counselor's achievement-type classification of students is a product of a subtle fusion of "rational" and commonsense judgments. Belonging to the "in-group" may be given greater weight than grade-point average in classifying a student as an "excellent student," or "getting into a lot of trouble" may be more important than "performing up to ability level" in deciding that a student is an "underachiever."

The tables that we have presented and discussed clearly do not reveal the subtleties that contribute to the counselor's assessment and interpretations of student performance. . . . We shall present here. . .a few of the counselor's comments concerning students in our sample in order to illustrate the variety of criteria that are implicitly or explicitly applied by the counselor in the evaluation process. These illustrative cases were selected from the counselor's response to our request that she tell us what she knew about each of the students in our sample.

CASE 10: SCAT 90/Grade Point 2.75, Social Class II, Social Type 2. "*Underachiever.*" His mother says he is a pleasant, outgoing boy. His teachers will say he's either a pleasant boy or that he's a pest. I think he's arrogant. He thinks he's handsome. He's nice-looking, but not handsome. He thinks he owns Lakeshore. He talks to his teachers as if they were stupid. He's a good student. He's in biology and algebra honors.
Interviewer: Is he going to college?
He plans college. I think he said he plans to go East like MIT, Harvard, etc. He wont' make it. He's a candidate for a middlewestern school. I think they'll all go to college. It's a matter of which one and for how long.

CASE 13: SCAT 90/Grade Point 3.25, Social Class II, Social Type 1. "*Excellent student.*" She's a very intelligent little girl. She's in all honors. They're an academic family. She's a mousy little girl. Maybe in time she'll develop socially. Her parents were concerned about her grade in English. They felt she could get a 1 instead of a 2. She got a 1 this time. And, of course, she'll go to college.

CASE 30: SCAT 93/Grade Point 2.00, Social Class II, Social Type 2. "*Excellent student.*" ———is a very able student. Kind of like an old man. Like he doesn't know how to have fun. He's always worried about doing the right thing. He came in and worried about which club to join because of how it would look for his college record, not for fun. I think he works after school in a store. It's as if he had to keep quiet all his life.

CASE 33: SCAT 75/Grade Point 2.00, Social Class III, Social Type 2. "*Average achiever.*" A very quiet girl. She doesn't come in very often. She'll go to college. She's in the highest honors in algebra but that's all. She's so quiet she probably goes unnoticed.

CASE 35: SCAT 20/Grade Point 4.00, Social Class II, Social Type 2. "*Average achiever.*" I just talked to her mother. A nice little girl. Not too bright. Her parents want her to go to college. She doesn't do too well. She's very enthusiastic about school. She'll probably go to ———, an expensive junior college in the East. It requires 4 years of English and graduation from high school. Her sister went there. Her mother is very realistic about this. ——— is like a finishing school.
Interviewer: Where is this college?

[The counselor looks it up.] Oh, it's in ———. I thought it was in the East. She comes in very often with small things that I can answer very quickly. She has troubles—she fails classes. She failed algebra, tutor and all, and had to switch to general math.

CASE 70: SCAT 10/Grade Point 4.66, Social Class II, Social Type 5. "*Underachiever.*" She's an opportunity student. She's a very conscientious girl. She tries hard, does neat work. She plans to go to college—she may get into some small junior college. She's very concerned at this point.

Interviewer: How do her parents feel?

I don't know—I haven't contacted them about it. I feel if her parents are concerned they will contact the school. Apparently they're not concerned. Or her parents might be concerned—some parents don't come in. She works hard—she'll probably benefit from some nonacademic college. [Looking at the record] Her father's senior vice president of ——— [a large corporation]—my, I didn't realize. He's been to college and her mother went to high school.

The discussion in this chapter may be summarized as follows:

1. Our examination of the ascription hypothesis . . . indicated that the relation between student and parental college-going aspirations and their implementation of those aspirations must be viewed as problematic. In the present chapter, we have stressed the point that, given the formal declaration of such aspirations, the implementation of the declaration is contingent upon the organizational procedures that launch freshmen students toward their educational goals. These contingencies are created by the educational doctrines of the school, the organization of its curriculums, and the routines of bureaucratic procedures in which "objective" and "subjective" criteria are combined in the processing of students through the system. The question we have explored is not how the school does or does not manage to process students independently of the students' declared educational aspirations. Rather, we have been concerned with how the school as a bureaucratic organization incorporates in its rules and procedures the processes by which the aspirations of students are recorded, their ability assessed, and their performance evaluated.

2. We have presented materials to illustrate the diffuse character of the criteria used in assigning students to types of programs and courses, and we have discussed the implications of this assignment procedure for the progress of students toward their declared educational goals. Our materials indicate also that the criteria used to evaluate the subsequent performance of students are equally diffuse and that the evaluation process makes the realization of those goals problematic. We have illustrated how the rationale of ability grouping organizationally produces and defines instances of SCAT/grade-point discrepancies as "problems" to be identified and classified by the counselor. In addition to the "objective" data of the SCAT/grade-point discrepancy, the counselor must somehow decide the rele-

vance of a variety of noncomparable factors for her evaluation of the students' performance. Such factors as the comments of teachers concerning students, the expressed concern of parents regarding the prospects of realizing their plans for sending their children to college, information about a student's "delinquent" activities, and the like may implicitly or explicitly enter into her evaluations. The limitations of resources and time do not allow the counselor to "objectively" weigh and give weightings to the variety of information considered relevant for the evaluation. The task of "objectifying" the bases of such decisions is clearly a difficult if not an impossible one.[13]

3. We have suggested that the differentiation of students produced by the evaluation process is directly related to the organizational effort to identify and develop talent, because the categories of differentiation are defined in terms of a presumed relationship between ability and performance. The classification of students differentiates those who are and are not "having trouble." The evaluation of student performance and the classification it produces has more than nominal significance for the future educational, occupational, and life careers of students. In a bureaucratically organized school such as Lakeshore High, the classification of students routinely initiates organizational actions that may progressively define and limit the development of such careers. From this perspective, the criteria employed in the evaluation process, the information considered relevant and recorded, the interpretations made of such information, and the organizationally defined categories by which students are classified are important for an understanding of how the school produces senior students who are or are not qualified for college entrance, "highly recommended" or "poor prospects," "well-rounded personalities" or "maladjusted."

3.5 INTRODUCTION

The article that follows summarizes one aspect of the findings of an extensive investigation conducted at Vassar College more than ten years ago into many features of the college experience. In the preceding selections in this chapter, a number of references have already been made to the "culture" of an educational organization, particularly the student culture. Here, Professor Freedman analyzes the various stages of adjustment to this culture that can be observed among

---

[13]This problem is not unique to the counselor but in various forms confronts other personnel at Lakeshore High School. For example, the official criteria presented to personnel to guide their placement of students in English honors sections states: "1. Have received a grade of *A* for their English work in the eighth grade. 2. Write well. 3. Appreciate good literature. 4. Read widely and well. 5. Are not 'grade-grubbers.' 6. Reason with logic in advance of their years. 7. Participate thoughtfully in class discussion. 8. Are emotionally and intellectually mature for their age. 9. Are intellectually curious. 10. Are well motivated and enjoy English." (Quoted from Lakeshore High placement criteria as developed by the English Department for selection of incoming freshmen for English honors advanced placement.)

students as they "pass through" it on their way from precollege to postcollege life in the larger society.

His discussion brings to the fore a theme that was initiated by Waller, Gordon, and Coleman (see selections 3.1, 3.2, and 3.3). This is that there is a basic incompatibility between the culture of students—the values, motivations, aspirations, and norms that shape and regulate their lives—and the educational values and goals that schools and colleges represent and that define the formal requirements to which both students and faculty are subject. The question of why this should be so thus becomes more insistent. One justification that might be deduced from Professor Freedman's analysis is that, if the culture of the larger society is taken into account as a third element in the situation, then the student culture may be said to protect students from, on the one hand, becoming maladjusted to the wider society by fully incorporating the academic goals and values of the faculty, or, on the other hand, being unable to survive the college experience due to overly strong commitments to conflicting extracollege norms. It may be, in other words, that the real opposition is between the values of the educational institution and those of its environment and that the student culture acts as a buffer against the full severity of the conflict that would result if this opposition were experienced directly.

If the student culture acts to ward off real educational impact, does this mean that individuals who are susceptible to real learning and change are also more likely to be somewhat maladjusted to the college environment? Is it likely that they are the very ones that will be perceived as "problems?" What might be the consequences of "helping" them?

At least in the college dealt with in this article, the leaders within the students informal social system were those in whom the college experience was least likely to induce change. To what extent might this have been a factor in determining the content of the student culture? In general, might the informal leadership group constitute an avenue for influencing student culture to those concerned with maximizing the educational consequences of student life?

3.5   THE PASSAGE THROUGH COLLEGE[1]

Mervin B. Freedman

This paper is an account of the major events or adjustments characteristic of each of the important stages of a college career in one institution, *i.e.*, entrance,

---

[1]Mervin B. Freedman, "The Passage Through College," *Journal of Social Issues*, 12, No. 4, 1956, pp. 13–28.

freshman, sophomore, junior, and senior years, graduation. It is based on information derived from interviews with students, discussions with teaching faculty and administrative officers, and general observations of the college "in action."

THE ENTERING The 400 odd freshmen who enter each year **FRESHMAN** are 17 or 18 years of age, chiefly upper middle or upper class in background. They have good academic records, and most have chosen the college with the expectation that it will be very demanding scholastically. Their knowledge of the institution varies somewhat with their backgrounds. About half of the freshmen come from private schools which prepare for eastern liberal arts residential colleges. Such students are likely to have considerable prior acquaintance with the college. Possibly they have visited it, have a relative who is an alumna or friends already among the students. We shall call these students Group A. The majority of the remaining students, Group B, are public school girls, a shade below Group A in social status. They are likely to have a fair amount of knowledge of the college although not so much as Group A. Group C consists of students for whom the college is a very new experience. This group is rather heterogeneous, containing girls from foreign countries and areas which do not ordinarily furnish students to the larger eastern women's colleges, a small number of students from lower middle-class origins who have been given scholarships, and some students from minority group families with limited educational backgrounds.

As one would expect, there tend to be different reactions or adjustments to the college characteristic of each of these groups. To understand these, some familiarity with the general functioning of the college is necessary. In describing the college we shall concentrate on institutional goals and procedures on the one hand and student culture on the other.

INSTITUTIONAL GOALS By institutional goals and procedures is meant **AND PROCEDURES** the major formal influences to which students are subjected through conferences with members of the administration and teaching faculty, lectures and assignments, and official writings and publications of the college. The major goal of the college is simple enough—the development of liberally educated individuals. Although a liberal education is not easily defined, there is general agreement as to the kinds of traits possessed by the liberally educated person, *e.g.*, knowledge of our cultural heritage, disciplined intelligence, responsible citizenship, curiosity, sense of reality, independence of judgment, interest in other cultures. As for the procedures by which the college attempts to attain its major goal, examination of the general curriculum seems to yield the most significant information. Study of the curriculum reveals first of all that the college is a "traditional" educational institution, not a "progressive" school.

"Traditional," in this context, does not mean inflexible, conservative, and the like; it means simply that adherence to certain formal curriculum requirements constitutes an important part of the academic program. This is in contrast with those educational programs in which such formal requirements are likely to be regarded as secondary to the needs of individual students. Thus, students must take a science and a language; in order to guard against overspecialization, they may not take more than a certain number of hours in their major field, and so on. Such regulations are by no means hard and fast; often they may be altered or waived, but by and large they serve as guideposts outlining the educational path for the student. These general academic requirements have administrative counterparts in regulations designed for the supervision of the student's social and recreational life. Students are not completely free to come and go as they please or to spend their time entirely as they see fit. For example, there are rules specifying the time by which students must return to their dormitories and the number of weekends permitted away from the campus. Upperclassmen are expected generally to behave more responsibly and to require less supervision, however, and consequently they are subjected to fewer social regulations.

THE STUDENT CULTURE We believe that a distinguishable student culture exists, one superordinate to the differences among students mentioned earlier or to be discussed later in this paper. The student body as an entity may be thought to possess characteristic qualities of personality, ways of interacting socially, types of values and beliefs, and the like, which are passed on from one "generation" of students to another and which like any culture provide a basic context in which individual learning takes place. We contend, in fact, that this culture is the prime educational force at work in the college, for, as we shall see, assimilation into the student society is the foremost concern of most new students. Suffice it to say now that in our opinion the scholastic and academic aims and processes of the college are in large measure transmitted to incoming students or mediated for them by the predominant student culture.

Although leadership in the student culture is likely to be provided by those students who are Group A on entrance, the general student climate is not one of snobbishness or exclusion. On the contrary the weight of the student or peer group culture is markedly in the direction of friendliness, acceptance, leveling of difference, and general ease of relationship. Participation in all activities on campus is open to almost every girl regardless of social background, race, or religion. All that is required for acceptance by fellow students is that one act pretty much like the rest—be cordial and friendly. Not that class or caste differences or distinctions of other kinds are completely obliterated. They appear on occasion in subtle ways, but as compared to American society at large, such distinctions are greatly minimized.

These qualities of agreeableness and cooperativeness are directed toward the faculty and administration as well as toward other students. Most students are dutiful, hard-working, and generally accepting of the college *status quo* and of the demands made upon them. Few girls, even those "snowed under" with academic work or subject to pressure of some other kind, are critical of the college structure or its procedures. When queried during interviews about the functioning of the college or about changes which might seem to be indicated on the basis of their own experiences, very few students believed that important changes should be made. Almost all felt that the way of life and the opportunities offered were nearly perfect. Where things were not going well, most students blamed themselves rather than the college structure, faculty, or administration.

Most students are interested, even enthusiastic, about at least some of their courses and academic achievements, particularly after they have chosen a major area and may pursue their own interests somewhat more freely. Many are attracted and excited by the rewards of intellectual activity as epitomized by certain faculty members. The student body in general can hardly be described as indifferent to academic work or as unaffected by it. However, except for a minority, the fundamental philosophy of the college and its academic and intellectual aims do not enter primarily into the formation of the central values and habits of life of the student body. Instead, for most students, educational experiences are assimilated to a central core of values and dispositions which is relatively independent of the more formal academic influences.

Marriage at graduation or within a few years thereafter is anticipated by almost all students; the percentage who state that they are not likely to marry, or who are quite uncertain about it, is negligible. Strong commitment to an activity or career other than that of housewife is rare. Many students, perhaps a third, are interested in graduate schooling and in careers, for example, teaching. Few, however, plan to continue with a career if it should conflict with family needs. Some report that they plan to forego careers when children are small and then resume them when children no longer require intensive care. As compared to previous periods, however, *e.g.*, the "feminist era," few students are interested in the pursuit of demanding careers, such as law or medicine, regardless of personal cost or social pressure. Similarly, one finds few instances of people like Edna St. Vincent Millay, individuals completely committed to their art by the time of adolescence and resistive to any attempts to "tamper" with it. Of course, strong interest in intellectual activities, careers, and forms of artistic expression is by no means lacking. The important fact is that such interests tend to be secondary in the lives of most students. The life goals of the students are, therefore, primarily to be wives and mothers, useful and intelligent members of communities. They wish to work, and often at some profession, but only when this does not interfere too much with family activities.

If the peer culture is relatively autonomous with respect to faculty, it is also relatively free from direct influence by the students' families. There are few instances of homesickness, even among freshmen, and the daily lives of most students seem little affected by thoughts of home or family. Moreover, influence from other extracollege sources, including young men, is not great. Of course, the values and expectations regarding their future wives which prevail among the young men whom the student knows must be considered. The important fact is, however, that these are interpreted for her and often pressed upon her by her own female peer culture.

Our observations on the role of young men in the lives of the students seem to run counter to what appears to be a rather universal campus "myth," namely, that most of the time not spent in academic pursuits is spent by students discussing dates, male friends, and weekend activities involving men. Our observation about the importance of early marriage as a life goal would appear to point in this direction. It must be kept in mind, however, that for a majority of students this interest in men, despite appearances, is really quite limited. Thus, most dating and concern with men is based less on interest in the men involved than on desire to maintain prestige among fellow students by doing what is expected. Since successful participation in student culture calls for some dating and interest in men, students engage in such activities, often in fairly routine fashion. Student society frowns upon "too much" dating or interest in men, a degree of interest that might interfere with adequate academic work and campus friendships. It is interesting to observe that sophomores and juniors commonly report that they dated more as freshmen, that somehow at the time it seemed "expected of them" but that now they "can relax" and not feel obligated to go out with men, when they really do not wish to. Interest in men is revived among upperclassmen, particularly in seniors as graduation and an end to the security of student days approach.

The influence of the student culture would not be so great or pervasive were it not characteristic of American society in general, of adolescence in particular, that status and security depend in large measure upon relationships with one's peers. The student culture provides order and comfort. It instructs in how to behave in various social situations, in what to think about all manner of issues, in how to deal with common problems and troublesome external influences. It even offers instruction in how to keep the faculty at a distance, how to bring pressure that will insure that the faculty behaves in expected and therefore manageable ways. It permits pleasant association with faculty members but discourages genuine relationships of a kind that might challenge the basic values of students. Although many students say that they would like greater opportunity to associate with the faculty, what they often have in mind is aid in the solution of practical problems rather than relationship on an adult basis.

Whereas for most of the students involved the peer culture provides merely a convenient and comfortable means for dealing with a fairly complex social situation and valuable preparation for the social world that they will enter after graduation, for others it is necessary to the maintenance of stability of personality. There are students who have been unable to develop internal agencies of control, who consequently have depended for a long time upon the direction of their peers. Separation from the peer group would put them under a very severe strain. This is a source of that rigid adherence to peer values which we sometimes see in individual students and is also a factor making for resistance to change in the culture itself.

THE FRESHMAN YEAR   ENTRANCE   Most freshmen arrive enveloped by an air of eager expectancy. Those who are familiar with the college may be relaxed, those with little first hand knowledge of it may feel some trepidation about what will happen, but by and large most freshmen arrive anticipating new and different experience and ready and willing to meet it. Getting into the college represents a real accomplishment for most of them; they are proud to be members of the college community and are eager to live up to the honor of having been admitted.

The prime concern of most entering freshmen, although often not a matter of explicit or conscious knowledge, is with acceptance by their fellow students. Not that entering freshmen are unconcerned about educational or intellectual matters. These constitute, in fact, their greatest conscious anxiety. When queried concerning the areas in which they anticipated their chief problems and difficulties, in thinking ahead to college life, most freshmen reply with some expression of uncertainty about intellectual competition with other students, the difficulty of the courses, and the like. Such considerations are real and important, but in our view they are, for the majority of students, secondary to often less conscious but more pressing social concerns.

In considering the earliest adjustments to the college we may focus on the differential adjustments of the three groups of entering students described earlier. Of the largest, Group A, no great academic adjustments are required. They have been well prepared both in terms of course content and in work habits for the demands that will be made upon them. To be sure, the courses they take as freshmen are likely to be more difficult than any in preparatory school, and greater individual responsibility in planning work is expected, but by and large important academic readjustments are not necessary. Similarly, these students are not likely to be faced by novel or truly pressing demands of social adjustment. The student culture tends to be in many ways a continuation of the kind of social life with which these students are already accustomed. Moreover, students of this group are likely to have friends and acquaintances in the college.

So it is that college entrance makes few demands upon these students in the sense of requiring major changes in their established ways of perceiving or doing things. Or at least it may be said that the way is open for this kind of *status quo* adjustment to the new environment of the college. Of course, all students of this group need not and do not choose this path of least resistance; but it is our impression that most do, perhaps because inertia and resistance to change are strong forces in most people. If one important function of a college is to induce students to re-examine their established ways and accepted habits of thought, it appears that the difficulties in the way of carrying out this function with the present group of students are great.

The initial situation is different for the second group of students, Group B, those who are similar to Group A in social or geographic background but who are graduates of public schools. Most of these students do not enter the college with the basic knowledge or habits of work that permit a relatively easy transition to the academic life of the college. Their secondary education has usually been neither so good nor so thorough. Some of the most able of the students in this group can effect the necessary academic readjustments with a minimum of effort, but for the majority the initial academic impact of the college is very great. For a good part of the freshman year many of these students are under great pressure; they work long hours, often get poor grades, and feel generally incompetent intellectually and academically.

Such involvement with academic problems tends to obscure the social adjustment of this group, which is for them a more subtle process. There are no clearly defined social distinctions analogous to the educational differences between this group and the previous one. Prior to entrance the members of this group are likely to be concerned about the social fate awaiting them. They wonder if they will be liked and if they possess the requisite qualities of personality and attractiveness to enable them to enter into the general social scheme of things. Above all they do not wish to be excluded by their peers or to be "out of things." Although these concerns loom large, they are not likely to be so explicit or clear as the matter of academic adjustment. This is so because qualities like social ease and poise facilitate the desired social adjustment; and in order to maintain these qualities at as high a level as possible, one is likely to play down concern or anxieties of this nature, to hide them from others or even to deny them to oneself, when this is necessary for the maintenance of self-esteem.

The initial social impact of the college on these students is a gratifying one. They are happy to find the student culture so friendly and agreeable, and they are pleased to learn that entrance into the prevalent student society makes few demands upon them for change of accepted thoughts or ways. By behaving pretty much as they always have or by modifying their behavior only slightly, they can get on well socially. So almost without giving these matters "a second thought" this group of students is absorbed into the main stream of student culture. They are happy to relax and let this happen, to find that their social fears are so easily allayed. Thus, while attention is centered on academic adjustments, these students implicitly and quietly slip into the student society which is to play so large a role in molding the values they will live by.

Things are different again for the third and smallest group of entering students described earlier, Group C, the one containing the more atypical students. The educational adjustments of the students in this group are similar to those of the second group in that they find themselves to be not quite prepared for the academic demands made upon them and consequently find the academic going rather rough at first. They differ from the second group, however, in that social adjustment is also a demanding process. These students, like those in the previous group, enter with considerable concern about how they will be received by other students, and they are similarly gratified to discover the agreeableness, the openness, the friendliness of the prevalent student society. Unlike the previous group, however, they are sufficiently different from the major peer culture in social background, habit, and custom so that they cannot subtly adjust to it almost automatically or unthinkingly. Some greater effort is required. Not that participation in the general student society is in any way barred to this group: most of these students who so desire can enter into it, depending, of course, to some extent upon their qualities of general attractiveness. For these students adjustment to the student culture is much more a matter of explicit or conscious decision. They do not enter into it as a matter of course, like the first group, or unconsciously through subtle adjustments, like the second. Standing somewhat apart from the student culture to begin with, these students must make some explicit decisions concerning the degree to which they wish to participate in it and the methods by which they wish to do so. They are thereby forced to consider alternative modes of behavior and alternative values.

THE REMAINDER OF THE FRESHMAN YEAR Within a short time, several weeks or months after entrance, most students have settled into a relatively characteristic student role; that is to say, certain patterns of student behavior and attitude may be identified (they may be thought of as subcultures within the predominating student culture), and most students may be characterized quite early in their college careers as exhibiting one or another of these patterns. These educational patterns bear some systematic relationships to the groups of entering students described above, [but] we shall concentrate [here] on overall characteristics of the student or general college community at various stages, ignoring for the time being variations from one type of student to another.

The freshman year determines the basic orientation to the college and goes a long way toward either establishing or reaffirming certain enduring habits and values of life. For the great majority of students it is a happy year. Almost all adjust successfully to the peer society and find appropriate companionship, at least one or several students, if not many, with whom they can share thoughts and feelings, in whom they can find support. Those who are not quite prepared on arrival for the high level of work expected of them may have a difficult time academically, but social satisfactions often offset this strain. Within a short time freshmen are caught up in the relatively self-sufficient student culture; family ties are attenuated, extracollege pressures are minimal, real faculty influence is yet to come.

There is, however, a small group of students whose general adjustment to the college runs rather counter to the predominant student culture. These are the students who are already faculty-oriented or, better possibly, "adult-oriented." They are interested in establishing personal relationships with members of the faculty. Often the attempt is to reconstitute some family or parental situation with the faculty member, to establish, for example, a mother-daughter or father-daughter kind of relationship. These students, often, are very promising. Since they are not encapsulated within the student culture, the possibility exists of "reaching" them intellectually and hence of coming closer to attaining the goals of the college. The "trick" in achieving this end is for the faculty member to place the emotional force of the relationship behind striving for academic or intellectual goals. The student learns, in short, that the road to adult or faculty approval and to mature adult relationship is real scholarship.

One other small group of students should be considered here, because it comprises many of those who withdraw from the college in the freshman or sophomore year, particularly in the freshman year. This group of students is not cooperative, dutiful, agreeable, and the like. Rather these students tend to be assertive, somewhat rebellious toward authority, unconventional; in short, quite the opposite of the majority of students. They tend to be resentful of college regulations or prescriptions, social or academic, and so they find adjustment to the college community very trying, if not impossible. When such students leave the college, it is often to attend other schools which they think will place less restraint upon them. It is interesting to note that these students, who are rebellious toward authority and unusually independent, tend to seek out one another and to find support thereby for their rather deviant attitudes or behavior.

The phenomenon of withdrawal from college before graduation merits some attention as a problem in its own right, since the percentage of students who withdraw from liberal arts colleges has risen in recent years. What seems to be reflected in this increase in withdrawals is a conception of a college or of a college education as some sort of marketable product, as something one purchases essentially, as something one can obtain at one institution just as readily as at another. Thus, a student considers it quite in the scheme of things to "shop around" from one college to another. Prior to World War II, however, entrance into a college probably implied much greater commitment to it. It is interesting to note that in England, if a student leaves a university, it is assumed that he has done so because of academic failure. There is seldom any other reason.

THE SOPHOMORE YEAR   By the sophomore year the basic processes of adjustment to the college which were started in the freshman year have reduced many if not most of the marked differences among freshmen. The predominant student culture and the subcultures within it now stand out clearly; pre- and extracollege influences and forces seem to shrink even more into the background. So it is that the importance of the quality of secondary schooling now becomes a negligible factor. By sophomore year those students who were handicapped in the beginning by deficiencies of secondary schooling have had opportunity to overcome them, and the level of a student's work is now pretty much a function of her intrinsic ability, interest, and motivation. As we have observed earlier, many sophomores display less interest in young men. Those students who were interested in men chiefly because of external social pressure no longer yield so readily to this pressure. The chief energies of most students are now concentrated on the campus, in academic work and in associations with fellow students.

The sophomore year is the one in which a major field of concentration must be selected, and by the second semester of the year most students have made a choice. Often, of course, the choice of major is one based on real awareness and evaluation of the potentialities involved and the meanings of such a choice in one's general life plan; and thus, it represents a real commitment to a field or discipline. Sometimes choice of a major is a function of deep unconscious motivational forces in the personality which tend unduly to influence the contemporary scene or more purely educational considerations. In a large number of cases, choice is based not so much upon either one of these factors as upon conditions relatively peripheral to the student and her real needs for growth and development, for example, reasons of convenience or expediency. As one would expect, there are certain majors which are more "fashionable" than others, which have more prestige value among students. On occasion students select a major field or turn away from one because of feelings of liking or dislike, often temporary, for students or faculty in that field. But perhaps most common of all is choice of an area of concentration which is calculated not to upset one, to allow one to go along with a minimum of change in fundamental values or beliefs. It is not surprising that expressions of dissatisfaction with choice of major in college are common among alumnae. When asked if they would choose another major were they again to be students, from a third to more than a half of the alumnae in various samples say that they would do so.

Academically things are likely to go rather smoothly in the sophomore year. Where there were handicaps of inadequate secondary schooling, they have often been overcome, and those students who have been lacking in direction tend to become better oriented. On the whole sophomores are industrious and enthusiastic about academic work. They enjoy most of their classes and look forward to being upperclassmen, anticipating that they will have the privilege of greater freedom in choice of courses and in work performance. Evidences of what has been called "sophomore slump" are rare. Rather it appears that the inertia or disorganization implied by this term are more likely to occur in the second semester of the freshman year.

If academic industry and enthusiasm are common among sophomores, they are, as we have observed, also characteristic of the student culture at large. It might be said, then, that in these respects students are sharing in both the explicit goals of the college and in the general value system of student society. The influence of the student culture is, however, rather a leveling or moderating one from the point of view of scholastic motivation and aims. On the one hand, it pulls in the direction of serious scholarship for those students whose academic motivations are dubious. Often a student learns the excitement and enjoyment of intellectual pursuit from another student before she does so from any particular book or class. On the other hand the student culture may soften or blunt strong intellectual or career drive. For example, students who enter college with the aim of achieving high artistic or intellectual goals often find themselves tempted to "relax and take things easier."

Often such ambitiousness is associated with factors like the desire to rise socially in the world, and students learn that they can do this merely by being pleasant, nice, agreeable. In fact being "too outstanding" might interfere with one's acceptance by certain groups. Or again it may be suggested by one student to another that some great or noble aim may be merely a "cover-up" for certain unfortunate personal characteristics, such as competitiveness with men.

In summary, the lives of sophomores are centered in the college community, in the enjoyment of friendships and associations with fellow students and in academic work which is highly demanding of their time and effort but which nevertheless provides much satisfaction. Before going on to the junior year, we should comment on a number of students who are rather exceptions to the general type of sophomore. These are students who are interested in men in a serious way, and whose interests are therefore not centered primarily or almost solely in the college community.

These students are of two rather different kinds. The first kind seems to be primarily socially oriented. They do not share in the explicit aims of the college or in the predominant student culture. They have come to college to make a good marriage or to acquire a smattering of a liberal education for its usefulness in social situations, and they are quite resistive to real intellectual development. This group of students finds the academic demands of the college very onerous, and many are likely to withdraw at the end of the sophomore year. Two years is sufficient for most of these students to get what they think they want out of college. This group plus the rebellious type referred to earlier who remain beyond the freshman year comprise most of the withdrawals during the sophomore year.

The second kind of student with strong interest in men is quite different, because this interest is not accompanied by a paucity of academic or intellectual interests. Rather these students tend to be superior scholars. They are girls who are engaged to be married or are seriously involved with men but who do not feel any need to sacrifice their own individuality or intellectual, professional, or career aims in the process. Thus, these students tend to have rather clear notions concerning the place of their current educational interests or esthetic or intellectual pursuits in their future lives. One gets the impression that in these cases the interest in men is a meaningful expression, that it is not, as it is with many students in the former group, some kind of defense against intellectual development. In not every case is a deep interest in men indicative of an educational loss.

THE JUNIOR YEAR   The junior year may be thought of as the year of maximum solidarity in the college community both educationally and socially. Many of the more deviant kinds of students have withdrawn. Those who remain comprise a student body held together by such strong bonds as shared experiences and common values. The forces of socialization within the student culture have in a sense achieved their maximum effect in the junior year, and it is the juniors who seem to be the chief heirs and transmitters of student culture. They are the torchbearers in this process, the individuals who serve as the chief models upon which lower classmen will pattern themselves. Seniors, to be sure, are the acknowledged campus leaders in the sense of filling the highest offices of student government and the like, but they already have one foot outside the college, and, as compared to juniors, they are moving away from the center of student culture.

In some ways the junior year contains elements which make of it a unique social experience, one not likely to be repeated again in the lives of most students. It is unlikely that a student will find herself at some future date in a society which offers so great an opportunity for differentiation of role and function and at the same time such a high degree of order and security. The junior class exhibits this great social solidarity despite the fact that subgroups within the junior culture display a considerable degree of variation. There are groups of juniors who may be identified by their common interest in political affairs, there are a few Bohemians and esthetes, there are the girls whose lives are centered on more purely intellectual activities, and so on. Yet the bonds of cohesiveness are such that these differences may be tolerated without detracting from the unity and identity of the class as a whole.

Educationally the junior year is likely to be the most satisfying. There is the gratification of being an upperclassman, of having required courses out of the way, of being able to take elective courses in one's chosen field of concentration. Intellectually or academically, the juniors may be thought of as the group most identified with the college, with both its explicit and implicit values. The juniors participate most in the general college culture which exists over and beyond the student culture. Thus, it is likely that the differences in values and general outlook between seniors and freshmen. . .already exist among juniors. As observed earlier these changes are a compromise between the explicit goals of the college and its faculty and the defenses of the student culture against too radical an encroachment upon their habits and mores; but nevertheless, as compared to freshmen, the juniors have been "liberated" in the direction of the aims of a liberal education. In short, juniors, more than any other class, share in the general value system of the faculty and administration. Not that seniors do not share in this, but, as we shall see, the imminence of graduation and future changes complicates their participation in this aspect of the life of the college.

Juniors have a fairly stable sense of identity as liberal arts students and as members of the college community. For most students this is somehow a broader, a more differentiated or complex identity than the one possessed as a freshman. Consequently such an identity usually represents an advance on the road to self-development. There is some danger, of course, that this identity may be too satisfying, that too many students will wish to return to it in the face of the difficulties and anxieties of subsequent periods of life. From this point of view one may think of the "perennial junior" rather than the "perennial sophomore." Such a person would not have grown beyond the secure, stable, and satisfying identity of her junior year and would like to return to it.

THE SENIOR YEAR The senior year is climaxed by graduation and highlighted by the imminence of the "after-life," as it is called by some of the students. No longer is the student's life largely circumscribed by the college, and no longer is her major task that of adjusting to the college community. The processes of the past three years must suddenly be reversed, as it were. We have seen that the first three years are characterized by increased adjustment, increased solidarity within the college structure, this process reaching its apex in the junior year. Now suddenly a student must respond to very different pressures, one external to the college community. Many students are on the verge of losing their chief emotional support, the friendship of fellow students. Many are likely soon to find themselves in environments emphasizing values and a general orientation to life quite different from their own. Despite these new and pressing concerns, however, there is really no let-up in current demands. However much seniors may be oriented to the larger community, they must deal with the pressures, academic and social, of the college. Small wonder then that seniors often feel tense, frustrated, confused.

One way of looking at the situation of the senior is to consider that as a freshman she entered with a fairly stable and integrated notion of what she was and where she belonged, with some real sense of identity based on her place in the family and home community. Certain religious, social, and political convictions were accepted almost as given in the nature of things. The process of education brought about changes in this identity, as the student shared more in the general values and outlook of the college community, as she took on the identity of a liberal arts student. These changes could occur fairly smoothly, without a great deal of anxiety and difficulty, however, because the weight of the college environment supported them. The changes did not place a student in a situation of actual or potential confusion or conflict, at least not to a marked degree. The situation of the senior, however, is different. She has lost the identity with which she entered college and fears that her new one, that of the student and liberally educated woman, will not be adequate to the demands of the "after-life." As we have elsewhere put it, "Many seniors are in a situation of having thrown off traditional values without having fully established others of their own, of having loosened long-standing inner controls at a time when new experiences have to be integrated, of having rejected old identities at the very time when important decisions have to be made. We should not be surprised, then, if they tend to be rebellious rather than autonomous, dominating rather than self-assured, cynical rather than realistic, hungry for sensations rather than able to enjoy them in a relaxed way."

Since an essential element of the senior experience is preoccupation with one's future role and identity, let us examine some of the possibilities open to seniors after graduation and the ways in which the college experience is related to them. The most common expectation is that students will marry and thus have as their prime identity that of wife and mother. Usually this concept of wife and mother or housewife is broadened by notions of contributing to the community, *i.e.*, to the

Red Cross, the League of Women Voters, and the like. Now how is one's college experience related to this future goal? The college, of course, does not prepare a student for being a wife and mother in the same way that it may prepare her for certain professional careers, such as teaching or law. Rather, the relationship is somewhat less close, the reasoning being somewhat as follows. A liberal education, regardless of field of concentration, enables one to function more creatively and efficiently, to live more fully, no matter what one's specific life situation. The emphasis is not so much on doing something then as on being something, a person who can think rationally and logically, who can appreciate and understand another person, another culture, a book, play, political discussion, and so on. The aim of a liberal education is to produce a free person, one who is liberated from prejudice and blind adherence to convention and tradition, free to apply herself as reason and morality seem to dictate.

In effect, though, a stumbling block often arises in the transition from the role of liberally educated student to that of the liberally educated member of society at large. Particularly in the senior year, the translation from the one to the other may well become quite obscure. The reason for this appears to be the absence in our society of a real place for the liberally educated individual who is not identified with some accomplishment or activity. The emphasis in our society is, in short, on doing, not being; and unfortunately, the doing involved in being a wife and mother often brings little recognition, no matter how demanding the tasks involved, no matter how creative the participation.

Many seniors, then, experience a sense of conflict between what they have been educated for and what awaits them. They seldom can define this conflict for themselves or elaborate its details; but it is present nevertheless, and it often contributes considerably to the perturbations and doubts of the senior year. One has but to question a number of college alumnae on the subject of what meaning their college education has had in their lives in order to realize the extent of this feeling, for often from the housewives among them comes a kind of half-hearted response to the effect that their education has enabled them to appreciate a play more fully, to understand a newspaper editorial better, or to participate more effectively in an intellectual conversation. Implicit in their replies is often a note of apology. Somehow they feel that they have let their college down and have not lived up to what has been expected of its graduates. They seem to feel that accomplishments within the home and family are hardly worthy of mention.

So it is that many seniors, when considering marriage, find that their intellectual and academic pursuits and accomplishments lose much of their luster. Marriage and commitment to a certain discipline or body of knowledge are often seen as mutually incompatible, and to the extent that marriage is seriously considered, a senior is likely to question the value or relevance to her future life of her current intellectual activities. Unfortunately, this conflict is likely to be strongest for the more serious students, since those not strongly committed to a discipline can more readily abandon it. Indeed, anticipation of this type of conflict is a major reason why many students avoid any serious commitments throughout their college careers.

In this area, it should be noted that students with professional ambitions often fare better. As we have pointed out earlier, most of these students plan to marry and to forego their careers or at least interrupt them in accord with family needs. These students, however, are not faced by what seems to be the all or none conception of marriage of the foregoing group of students. Rather, marriage is more an activity in which they voluntarily choose to participate and is not one which determines their entire sense of identity. They are not wives and mothers solely but are also actual or potential teachers, scientists, business or professional women, and the like. What appears to be evident in this group of students is a measure of sucess in combining career and marriage in their anticipations. Indeed, one may well wonder if a more equal admixture of professional and liberal schooling may not at the present time, given the current status of the housewife in our society, be more effective in "liberating" women than is the current liberal arts philosophy with its secondary emphasis on professional training. One might argue, in short, that an important contribution to the "freeing" of a woman would be to give her the feeling she could do something of importance, if she wished to, besides being a housewife. Voluntary choice of a housewife's career would then make of it less a secondary avocation into which one "sank" out of lack of ability or inertia.

The foregoing leads directly into the general meaning, or meanings, of marriage for seniors. In keeping with the general tenor of the times, most students marry fairly young. Many are engaged by graduation and marry shortly thereafter. The majority of the remaining students work at something, usually something well below the level of their ability, or else they attend school for one or a few years, marking time, as it were, until "the right man" comes along. For many students, of course, marriage is the natural outcome of a meaningful relationship. They know the man well and are ready for the demands of married life. For many, however, early marriage represents in essence an attempt at solution of seemingly insurmountable problems. Thus, many seniors rush into marriage, hardly knowing the man involved, as a way of resolving the dilemmas thrust upon them by graduation. It often seems to be an inviting resolution of difficulty to a student unaccustomed to choice who must now make many choices, to a student facing the prospect of working at something which has but little intrinsic meaning for her, or to a student who feels somehow abandoned in the face of loss of the emotional support of her classmates.

It seems that the most characteristic feature of the senior year is the sense of uncertainty, of strain, of confusion in the face of the need to make choices or decisions. Unfortunately, in many cases, seniors have had little practice in making meaningful decisions. They come to college as freshmen almost automatically, as another step in an orderly life progression. They enter a college community which, led by the predominant student culture, is well calculated to protect students from uncertainty and strain, from experiences of failure and defeat, from the need for making difficult decisions. (As we have seen, often even the very important matter of choice of major rests upon peripheral factors and does not deeply involve students).

One would hope, of course, that seniors would rise to the demands of the occasion; that faced by the loss of the protective environment of the college and by the need to deal with complex issues of life in society at large, they would carry out the examination of their position, the "soul-searching" necessary to the charting of their future courses. Many do so, of course. Militating against this process, however, is the general pressure of other forces during senior year. It is, after all, only one academic year of some nine months duration, and during this brief time a senior is subject to much academic pressure. She may recognize some of the issues involved and desire to do something about them but still be blocked from doing so by lack of time and energy. Under such circumstances one would hope that at the least a process could be begun in the senior year which would be carried over into the "after-life" and continued there. From this point of view postponement of major decisions for a time after graduation through such means as additional schooling or working is preferable to an attempt at premature solution, for example, a marriage for which the student is really not prepared. The former provides opportunity for further growth, while the latter may place one in a situation that makes further development difficult if not impossible.

The difficulties faced by seniors would seem to argue for some sort of college environment which does not shield students from experience with complexity, difficulty, even failure, and from the necessity for making meaningful decisions. This might mean an attempt to "challenge" the predominant student culture in some way so that most students can not get along well simply by being what "they have always been." Probably the earlier in a student's career that this can be done the better. It may be that many students, when they achieve the intellectual heights desired for them in the senior year, find that there is not time enough to exercise these functions adequately; and as we have seen, for many, intellectual growth stops with the senior year.

3.6   INTRODUCTION

The article that follows brings into sharp focus a number of points about student culture that have been noted or implied in the preceding selections. In particular, this discussion emphasizes the basic interdependence between this informal culture and the formal process of education. Indeed, the authors believe that a major aspect of the student culture, that which consists of common solutions to educational problems, enables students to "make what they will of their education."

The case of the medical student is an extreme example of the frequent discrepancy between, on the one hand, faculty expectations about what and how much students should study and, on the other, what students perceive to be necessary, important, and possible. Students are concerned not only with learning but also with getting through the institution. The faculty, however, are likely to acknowledge the relevance only of learning the subject matter of their course, and strict adherence to their demands may actually be ineffective as a way of obtaining the institutionalized symbols of achievement. Thus, that the students filter and reinterpret these instructions need not be due primarily to anti-academic values on their part. It may, rather, be at least partially understood as a rational adaptation to the realities of academic institutions.

It is quite possible, of course, that both faculty members and others concerned with tending to the students' overall experience will perceive the students' informal norms as reflecting characteristics only of the students rather than also of the situation. As we saw in the selections by Gordon (Selection 3.2) and by Cicourel and Kitsuse (Selection 3.4), this is likely to occur for both personal and structural reasons. As a result, the responses of such individuals may be such as to actually reinforce the very patterns they want to alter, as might occur, for example, if academic demands are further intensified in order to compensate for what is defined as students' insufficient motivation.

3.6   STUDENT CULTURE IN MEDICAL SCHOOL[1]

Howard Becker and Blanche Geer

Although students may interpret and respond to their educational experiences in an individual and idiosyncratic way, this is neither necessarily or usually the case. More typically, as they come to know one another in the course of their school activities they develop common understandings about those interests and activities they share as students and working agreements as to what constitutes proper and reasonable behavior in this role. Many of the professional educator's dilemmas arise from the fact that his students do not respond "properly" to programs and procedures based on the notion that students will react as individuals. The unanticipated consequences of the existence of an *organized* student body show up in significant redirections of educational aim and effort.

---

[1]Howard Becker and Blanche Geer, "Student Culture in Medical School," *Harvard Educational Review*, **28**, 1958, pp. 70–80.

When we speak of *student culture*[2] we refer to this body of understandings and agreements among students about matters related to their roles as students. We do not mean simply anything which is a matter of consensus among students, for there may be consensus about many things by virtue of other similarities among them. For instance, a suburban high school may, because of residential homogeneity, have a student body which agrees on such things as the proper way to dress, the correct kinds of relations between the sexes, and so on. We have in mind, rather, such issues as arise within the educational activity proper—why one goes to school and what he expects to get out of it, how one should behave toward a teacher, what things are worth learning and why, how to pass examinations, how to avoid punishment.

Our discussion is based on the study we have been making of a large state medical school,[3] but we believe that the major points we make—the existence of student culture and its consequences for the educational enterprise—are worth examining in educational institutions generally. (Medical students acquire two cultures during their years in school: student culture and the rudiments of the culture of the medical profession; this paper discusses only the acquisition of student culture.)

---

[2] The notion of student culture has appeared in the literature previously (Davie and Hart, 1956; Hartshorne, 1943). These authors, however, use the idea to refer to the body of custom and tradition characteristic of the residential college, encompassing both educational and extracurricular interests. We restrict the term to the consensus among students on purely educational matters.

[3] This study is sponsored by Community Studies, Inc., of Kansas City, Missouri, and is being carried out at the University of Kansas Medical Center, to whose dean, staff, and students we are indebted for their wholehearted cooperation. Professor Everett C. Hughes of the University of Chicago is director of the project. The material on which this paper is based consists of two years of participant observation among students and a series of interviews with a random sample of 62 students.

Participant observation is a technique in which data are gathered by an observer from the vantage point of a participant in the action under study. We went with students to lectures and to the laboratories in which they studied the basic sciences, watching their activities and engaging in casual conversation with them. We followed students to their fraternity houses and sat around while they discussed their school experiences. We accompanied students on rounds with attending physicians, watched them examine patients in the wards and in the clinics, sat in on discussion groups and oral exams. We had meals with students and took night call with them. We stayed with one small group of students on each service in the curriculum for periods ranging from a week to two months, spending many full days with them. The observational situations allowed time for conversation and we took advantage of this to quiz those we observed about things that had happened and were about to happen, and about their own backgrounds and aspirations. We have discussed some of the problems of this method in more detail elsewhere (Becker and Geer, 1956, and "Participant Observation..."). A general discussion of the method can be found in (White, 1951).

This paper is a preliminary statement of one portion of our analysis of the medical school. The entire study will be reported in a forthcoming volume by the authors of this paper in collaboration with Everett C. Hughes and Anselm L. Strauss.

CONDITIONS FOR THE DEVELOPMENT OF SUBCULTURES Subcultures of the kind we are discussing develop best where a number of people are faced with common problems and interact both intensively and extensively in the effort to find solutions for them, where people who face the same contingencies and exigencies in everyday life have an opportunity to deal with these communally.[4] Medical school is an ideal hothouse for such a plant.

Medical students live with a number of pressing and chronic problems, the most important stemming from the fact that they are continuously presented with an enormous and, in any practical sense, unlimited amount of material to learn. Though students and faculty agree that the criterion for choosing what to learn should be relevance for medical practice, there is enough disagreement and uncertainty among the faculty as to what is relevant that the student is never presented with a clear directive to guide him in his own studies. Students worry together over this problem, in one or another of its many transformations, during their four years of school.

Similarly, medical school provides extremely propitious conditions—intensive interaction and isolation from outside influence—for the development of common solutions to these problems. Students usually spend eight or more hours in school every weekday, working and studying together in the labs and on the wards, and are likely to spend many evenings and weekends together in similar activity as well. Much of their work is carried on in groups of from four to twelve students, and these are arranged so differently from course to course that the students come to know many of their fellows with the intimacy that arises from close, continuous association at work. The students are insulated from contact with others, both by reason of their crowded schedules and because they find it difficult to talk with people who are not suffering the same things they are. Even those students who have friends or brothers only a year or two ahead of them in school report that they get little help with their immediate problems from these people. Each class of approximately one hundred students goes through school as a unit, meeting the problems posed together.

This intensive interaction in an isolated group produces the understandings and agreements we call student culture—a set of provisional solutions and guidelines for activity. One set of understandings specifies goals and values, telling the students that they are in school to learn those things relevant to their prospective professional futures. In the school we studied, students came to believe that they were in school to acquire the knowledge and clinical experience one must have before he can assume the responsibility of the physician for the lives of his patients, a responsibility they intended and expected to have once they finished school. They based their interpretations of the worth of various school activities on

[4] For a discussion of the origins of subcultures see (Sumner, 1907, paragraphs 1 and 3), and (Cohen, 1955).

the criterion of how well this function was served in each. Another set of understandings suggested modes of cooperation designed to meet examinations and other crises, and such recurrent problems as sharing loads of clinical work assigned to groups.

The student's interpretation of specific events and issues tends to be made in categories which are part of the student culture, because these events and issues are new and unfamiliar and do not fit easily into categories provided by his earlier experiences. These cultural understandings coerce his behavior though not, at least in medical school, by methods as crude as punishment by fellow-participants in the subculture (characteristic of subcultures in the underworld or industrial work groups). It is not that the student *must* abide by these informal, hardly conscious, agreements, but rather that they constrain his thinking and perspective almost without his being aware of it (though a rare exception consciously feels the tension between what he might like to do and what the group norms specify as correct).

THE ACADEMIC YEARS Perhaps the most important factor in the development of student culture during the freshman year is the formation of a group in which all or nearly all members have opportunities for interaction with each other. When the freshmen arrive in medical school, although they come with the common intention of becoming physicians, they are not a group in any but the nominal sense that all are in the first year class. They begin to get to know some of their fellow students right away, but this takes place not in the class at large but within small groups. The small groups are of two types. First to form are friendship groups consisting of students similar in social status who have opportunities for leisure interaction because they live near or with each other. . . .The second type of group forms in the anatomy laboratory. As the faculty assigns students in groups of four to a dissection tank, members of different friendship groups get to know each other under the intimate conditions that dissection of the same cadaver imposes. The intersection of work and friendship groups makes it possible for each student to learn the attitudes current in other groups toward student problems, and, at the same time, carry back to his own friends solutions he and his lab partners have tried out in the course of their work together.[5]

The spread of common understandings among the freshmen is also promoted by their isolation. Unlike most graduate students, all members of the medical school class are taught together. They spend an eight-to-five day in one building. Each morning and afternoon, lectures lasting as long as the instructors wish are followed immediately by laboratory periods. Review and preparation is done at night, usually at home (for there is little or no library work) or once again in the

---

[5]On intersecting groups, see Simmel, 1955, pp. 149–50.

laboratory. On a schedule like this there is little opportunity for interaction with groups outside the class, nor do the students turn to the faculty with problems except about details of daily work. For as they begin to draw together and get a sense of themselves as a group, they think of the faculty as a group opposed to their own. To ask faculty advice is to break student ranks. Thus, the students come to an understanding among themselves of what the study of medicine is and how it should be accomplished. Their notions are derived from what the faculty says and does (which are sometimes quite different), from the future they envision for themselves as physicians, and from their past experience in getting through school and college.

The student concept of what medicine is develops first. They believe it is a great body of known facts, some of which will be imparted to them in the first year for eventual use when they become physicians. The idea that everything is important soon gets them into a dilemma, for there are more facts than they have time to learn. They are told this by the faculty, and prove it to themselves when, after studying four and five hours a night and on weekends as well, they have not mastered the material to their own satisfaction.

As they realize they can't learn everything, all but the most self-exacting students see that they must study only important things and let the rest go. But what is important? This question becomes the chief subject of discussion in student groups shortly before the first major examinations. Two points of view predominate. One group of students believes the important facts are those they will use in medical practice. (Selection of these facts is a matter a student feels quite competent about even if he has only been in school a few weeks.) A second group of students, most of them fraternity members, takes into account the necessity of passing examinations to stay in school. On this basis, the important facts are those the faculty thinks important. Students who believe this develop various systems for finding out what the faculty wants them to know.

Although taking the examinations brings the issue of what to study to a head, it does not settle it. Rightly or wrongly, students consider some questions "impractical", unrelated, that is, to the practice of medicine. These questions lead students of the group that believes in studying things important for medical practice to begin thinking more about what the faculty thinks these are. In preparation for the next examinations these students pool their knowledge, make use of files of old tests, and consult members of the class who already study in this way. But the examinations also contain questions students consider "unfair"— points not emphasized in lectures or texts. Students who follow some system for learning what the faculty wants are unable to predict such questions. The faculty has not been "playing the game". As a result of their difficulties with the examinations, both groups of students begin to have doubts about the faculty. The practice-minded group wonders whether the faculty teaching first year subjects (most of whom are Ph.D.'s) knows much about practice. The system-minded group wonders whether the faculty is agreed about what is important; if not, perhaps it is impossible to predict what will show up on an examination. Both groups consider briefly whether the faculty is "out to get them." The significance of all this for the development of student culture is that in their bewilderment, students draw closer together and finally settle their problem in a way acceptable to all but a few.

They agree that they ought to study the "basic medical facts." These are the only ones they have time for, as there is so much to learn. These are the facts important for practice, certain to be on examinations if the faculty is reasonable. To this central proposition the students add a number of other understandings which they apply to their daily activities. (1) Basic facts are most economically learned from textbooks. This means that lectures which do not follow the text are a waste of student time, and a faculty member who strays from the text is a poor lecturer who probably has some scientific ax to grind in connection with his own research which does not concern medical students. (2) Demonstrations and lab work which repeat classical experiments are a waste of time; the results are more easily learned in the text and students can't do them well enough to learn much anyway. (3) Theoretical material, concepts (except those which help to organize facts), and research findings not yet in clinical use are not facts and are not useful to medical students.

These understandings of the student culture can be summed up in the student phrase "give it to us straight," which has its counterpart in the derogatory faculty phrase "spoon feeding." A student will say that he does not want to be spoon fed, but points out that there is so much to learn he hasn't time to think or worry about "minutiae" (details) and "all that academic crud" (nonfactual material). Once they have decided the question of what and how to study, the students settle down to hard work. They are no longer worried about how to select the important things to read because "you just go by the black type." In the same way, they learn to get through their lab work by various shortcuts which are both approved by student culture and not penalized in examinations by the faculty. The following incident shows how such a shortcut became widely used in the class.

Each anatomy student is given a dissecting guide with explicit directions on what to do, in what order, and what to look for during the lab session. Reflection of skin is the first step in dissection of each part of the cadaver. The lab guide calls for great care in reflecting so as not to pull off the underlying layer of fat which adheres to the skin. Imbedded in this subcutaneous fat are tough, threadlike fibers—the peripheral nerves. These are to be traced to their origins and identified. It is a slow, exasperating task; virtually impossible if reflecting is not cleanly done.

When the class began dissection of the lower leg, we noticed one group had taken off skin and fat together leaving the nerves undissected. A student at the tank said, "You see, it's easier this way. I think it saves a lot of time because you really can't get those nerves anyway." His partner agreed, saying, "It's much better to get the nerves from the book." Another student, speaking for himself and his tank partners, said, "We knew we couldn't do the nerves because they are all different on every body. It doesn't make any difference if you do the nerves or a lot of other things." By the third week of dissection, most groups observed were stripping off skin and fat together; identification of the peripheral nerves was omitted.

Collective behavior of this sort does not mean students do not work hard. They continue to work very hard on the things they think important. One reason for their neglect of peripheral nerves, for instance, is their haste to get to the next layer down which contains the larger structures, muscles, and blood vessels, that every doctor must know about. It does mean that where the faculty fails to "give it to them straight" in accordance with student concepts of why they are in school and what and how they ought to study, various shortcuts are devised in more or less open defiance of faculty instructions, and students who have deviant interests outside the student culture keep them increasingly to themselves.[6]

THE CLINICAL YEARS   During the last two years of medical school— the clinical years—the student's work consists largely of taking medical histories from and performing physical examinations on patients, in order that he may develop these skills and use the information so gained in learning how to diagnose and treat various diseases. While he continues to be tested on his knowledge through formal examinations, he is told in various ways and believes that the crucial decisions about his future in school—whether he passes or fails, for example—are based largely on the faculty's evaluation of his clinical work. Furthermore, he believes that, having got this far, it is very unlikely that he will be flunked out of school; few such cases are known to have occurred.

The major problems requiring collective solution no longer lie in the realm of examinations. Rather, students focus their attention on how to deal with the continuous pressure of a heavy load of clinical work and how to get the most out of that work in terms of the future one envisions for himself in medicine. Student culture develops as a set of perspectives on and solutions for these problems.

The view that the function of medical school is, among other things, to train students to recognize and deal with diseases that are commonly run across in a general medical practice constitutes one such perspective, shared by almost all students, even those who do not contemplate becoming general practitioners themselves. This basic proposition itself derives in part from statements by the school's faculty and administration and in part from the inability of most students to visualize anything but general practice for themselves before they have had clinical

---

[6]The sophomore year is very largely a repetition of the academic laboratory work of the first year, although students do have a small amount of contact with patients in their physical diagnosis course. The major themes of student culture remain those developed in the first year but this contact with patients produces intimations of those new themes which come into view in the clinical years.

contact with other medical specialties.[7] Once formed, the proposition continues as a more or less unquestioned premise even after the students know more about specialized kinds of practices.

The students draw several more specific conclusions about their school work from this proposition, in the course of conversations and discussions of specific incidents. These specific items of student culture may be summarized as follows. (1) The patients whom it is really important to study thoroughly are those who have common diseases — whether simple or complicated — for which there are available treatments a general practitioner could utilize. (2) All those kinds of clinical work which they cannot imagine themselves doing in a general practice are regarded as a waste of time. (3) Courses in which they are not given practice in techniques they regard as important for the practitioner to know tend to be disliked. Matters of this kind are widely discussed among the students and have important consequences for the way they interpret their experience in school and distribute their effort and time among their many competing interests.

The following incident, one among many observed, provides a nice example of the way students collectively draw inferences from the basic proposition stated above and use these to guide their behavior in school.

In one of the third year courses students are required, at the end of the course, to turn in elaborate summaries of each case assigned to them during their time on the service. These summaries must include the important findings of their own examination, important laboratory findings, a discussion of all the possible causes for these findings, references to relevant literature, and a discussion of modes of possible treatment. They are long and require a great deal of time to prepare.

The students in one group we observed established an informal norm specifying the number of such summaries they would turn in, although they were definitely directed to turn in one on every patient they had been assigned. Over a period of several days preceding the date the summaries were due, the six students in this group discussed the matter at length and decided that they would all hand in no more than a certain number. Further, they agreed on the criteria for selecting those to be turned in, and on the premise that the real purpose for these summaries was to provide material for the faculty to quiz them on during oral exams, so that the actual number was unimportant (in spite of the definite order that all cases were to be so summarized).

---

[7]Most students are aware of the model of the general practitioner when they enter medical school; it is a common enough model in the society generally. Some few are aware of the nature of some kinds of specialized medical practice. But the issue of general vs. specialized medical practice is not a salient one during the first two years, being overshadowed by the more immediate issue of whether. the lectures, reading, and laboratory work are relevant to any kind of medical practice. In consequence, elements of student culture based on this issue are not of much importance in the early years of school.

The criteria for selection of cases derived from the premises of student culture. The cases discarded were those which it was agreed provided them with no knowledge they did not already have of treating common medical problems, or where the work involved in preparing the summary would not add to such knowledge. Thus, patients with fractures or simple infections, whose treatment was more or less standard and afforded the students no chance to participate were not summarized, and "crocks" were not summarized. ("Crocks" are patients who have no physical pathology, but only vague and untreatable psychosomatic complaints, thus patients from whom nothing can be learned that might prove of use in general medical practice.)

The decision that these criteria were the relevant ones was reached in discussions between the students in the group and in discussions with students who had been through the course previously who confirmed this interpretation.

A similar set of attitudes has grown up around the routine laboratory work—blood counts and urinalyses—the students must do on incoming patients assigned to them. They greatly resent this work because, among other reasons, it wastes their time since they themselves will not do these procedures, they think, when they are in practice.

This general frame of mind, as we have said, coerces the students' thinking to a striking degree. . . . [C]ourses are judged with reference to the amount of training they provide for the exigencies of general practice. . . .

CONSEQUENCES OF STUDENT CULTURE   Student culture affects the larger social system in which it is embedded—the medical school—in two ways. On the one hand, it provides the basis for a modus vivendi between the students and their superiors, providing a perspective from which students can build consistent patterns of response enabling them to fit into the activities of the school and hospital. In this respect student culture is an accommodation on the part of the students to the facts of life of the school. On the other hand, student culture provides the students with the social support that allows them, in individual instances and as a group, independently to assess faculty statements and demands so that they can significantly reinterpret faculty emphasis and, in a meaningful sense, make what they will of their education. In this sense, student culture is a mechanism which creates the conditions for considerable deviance from formally stated institutional rules.

When students first enter school their emphasis on medical practice—their belief that they are in school to learn to save lives (Becker and Geer, 1957)—leads them to rebel against laboratory work, essentially nonmedical, and against the drudgery of studying for intensive academic examinations. Later, they must deal with the same problem of an overload of work in a clinical setting in which examinations are not so important although the possibility of being tested and found wanting is always present. The understandings and agreements which make up student culture, by solving these problems in one way or another, allow the students to fit into the system without being constantly so upset as to be unable to function. In this way, student culture is a mode of accommodation to what the students find expected of them in school.

At the same time student culture affects the level and direction of effort students expend while in school. Everett Hughes has called attention to the way the effort of any group of participants in an enterprise can vary, with regard both to its intensity and to the directions in which it is expended (Hughes, unpublished). The amount of effort may be collectively restricted (as in industrial work groups) or it may be intensified. Similarly, though less frequently noted, the amount of effort may remain constant but it may be applied in varying directions, and there may be disagreement between categories of participants as to the proper direction.

Student culture in medical school provides the students with a rationale for restricting the theoretically infinite amount of time and effort they might devote to their school work. More importantly, it provides them with sufficient collective support to allow them to direct their effort in quite different directions than those suggested by the faculty, considered either as a unit or even with regard for the divisions of opinion within the faculty itself. Though members of a given department may feel that their course is really designed to put across such-and-such a brand of knowledge for this-and-that purpose, the students may remain relatively immune, drawing the strength to ignore the faculty's otherwise authoritative notions from the lore which makes up student culture. (Student culture is thus the cornerstone of many faculty difficulties with students, one of the facts of life to which teachers must, in their turn, make some accommodation).

As we have said earlier, medical school represents an extreme case of the development and operation of student culture. We would not necessarily expect it to play so important a role in other educational institutions. But we do believe that it is likely to exist in such places and that it will likely be found to have a least the two functions we have discussed for the medical instance, that of providing a means of accommodation for the students to the difficulties of school life, and that of providing the basis for redirection of effort on the students' part, possibly in defiance of faculty standards and ideals.

BIBLIOGRAPHY

BECKER, HOWARD S., 1956, "Interviewing Medical Students," *American Journal of Sociology*, 62, pp. 199–201.

BECKER, HOWARD S., AND BLANCHE GEER, forthcoming, "The Fate of Idealism in Medical School," *American Sociological Review*. (Paper read at the meetings of the Midwest Sociological Society, April 5, 1957, Des Moines, Iowa.)

BECKER, HOWARD S. AND BLANCHE GEER, forthcoming, "Participant Observation and Interviewing: A Comparison," *Human Organization*.

COHEN, ALBERT K., 1955, *Delinquent Boys: The Culture of the Gang*, New York: The Free Press.

DAVIE, JAMES S., AND A. PAUL HART, 1956, "Button-down Collar Culture: A Study of Undergraduate Life at a Men's College," *Human Organization*, 14, pp. 13–20.

HARTSHORNE, EDWARD Y., 1943, "Undergraduate Society and the College Culture," *American Sociological Review*, 8, pp. 321–332.

HUGHES, EVERETT C., unpublished manuscript, *Direction and Style of Effort in Schools and Colleges*.

SIMMEL, GEORG, 1955, *The Web of Group Affiliation*, Reinhard Bendix, trans., New York: The Free Press.

SUMNER, WILLIAM GRAHAM, 1907, *Folkways*, Boston: Ginn.

WHYTE, WILLIAM FOOTE, 1951, "Observational Field-Work Methods," *Research Methods in the Social Sciences*, Marie Jahoda, Morton Deutsch, and Stuart W. Cook, eds., New York: Holt, Rinehart and Winston, Vol. 2, pp. 393–514.

3.7 INTRODUCTION

The final selection in this chapter represents an attempt to apply some general social scientific conceptions about social systems to the school in order to get a more objective view of what it is like and how it differs from other types of social systems. In doing this, the ensuing selection serves both to integrate many of the notions that have been presented or implied in this chapter and also to preface much of what will follow in subsequent chapters. That is, Miles deals with the school both as an organization and as a unit serving societal functions and he is thus led to touch on many issues that are themselves explored in greater depth later in this book—the relationship of educational institutions to their communities and to the society, the process of socialization, the sociocultural factors that affect education and learning, role expectations and conflict, interpersonal and group processes.

One of Miles's major underlying concerns is that of finding ways to improve schools. Thus his focus is always, at least implicitly, on the potentialities for change of different aspects of the school as a social system, making his analysis directly relevant to the activities and concerns of guidance-personnel workers. Of particular interest also is his attempt to view phenomena through the eyes of both the social scientist and the child. This approach enables him to probe situations more fully and to much greater depth than is possible from more limited viewpoints.

It might appear that the relevance of this article is limited, since it deals with elementary and secondary schools but not with colleges. The analytic approach used and the problems discussed, however, actually concern any educational institution and thus, even if certain aspects unique to higher education are not dealt with directly, this essay provides a solid base on which to build systematic understanding of any educational social system.

3.7 SOME PROPERTIES OF SCHOOLS AS SOCIAL SYSTEMS[1]

Matthew B. Miles

Responsible efforts to improve schools ought presumably to rest on an analysis of their actual, contemporary properties as social systems. Even if we take the Lewinian route to understanding a system by trying to change it, it remains true that we must at least know which structures and processes are, on the face of it, most promising as an entry point for change efforts. We need some mapping of the territory called "the school"; otherwise disproportionate amounts of energy may go into change efforts which are ultimately self-defeating, or perhaps only irrelevant.

In spite of the current wave of interest in educational innovation, there do not appear to have been very many analyses of schools or school systems which would help us discriminate them from systems of other sorts (agricultural, medical, industrial—all of which are frequently used as analogical models when someone wishes to make his favorite point). Speculative analyses have been made by Campbell (1958), Miles (1964), Wayland (1964), and Buchanan (1965). The present discussion is an attempt to extend and integrate these discussions, and is a development of comments made from working notes and discussion at a seminar of the Cooperative Project on Educational Development (August 8–10, 1965).[2]

The effort throughout is to see schools as we think they are, minus ideology, conventional "wisdom," and polemics. This is no easier for the author than for anyone else; one of the severe problems of any analysis of this sort is that all adults have had experience with schools, some of which has usually been negative in one way or another. Thus the feeling of wanting to "get back"—in both the retaliatory and conservative sense—tends to cloud vision, and to induce a tendency toward normative prescription.

The discussion includes four sections. The first section discusses five general features of the American school which have come to be central to it, largely because of historical precedent. The second section suggests some presently existing properties of the American public school seen as a coherent social system; the aim

---

[1]This material will appear in a forthcoming publication by the Cooperative Project on Educational Development (COPED), and is used by permission.

[2]Critical comments and suggestions were made on an early draft of this paper by Paula Holzman, Dale Lake, Goodwin Watson, Betty Miles, and Paul Buchanan. Donald C. Klein in particular supplied detailed suggestions, along with the preliminary draft of the final section covering implications and conclusions.

here is to look at the genotypical level as far as possible. The third section moves to the phenotypical level, and examines the resulting "symptoms" or problems with which anyone planning to carry out school improvement efforts in America is faced. This mode of presentation obviously suggests the belief that dealing directly with symptoms will be unproductive, unless diagnosis and change efforts are constantly informed by genotypical notions. The fourth section of the paper discusses some of the research and action implications of this analysis.

GENERAL FEATURES OF THE SCHOOL

Children-changing emphasis

Probably the only really essential feature of any elementary or secondary school is that it is a social arrangement which exists for the purpose of bringing about desirable changes in children. This bare-bones definition has at least two implicit features hidden within it. First, the children involved are ordinarily considered to be normal rather than ill or severely retarded. Second, the children are not the exclusive property of the school, but are lent to it for varying periods of time by their parents, who compose part of the "sponsoring public" for the school. Some problems and derivations can immediately be seen (for example,[3] *what* changes are seen as desirable? and by whom? what kinds of overlapping group memberships and role conflicts are children likely to have as between school and home? etc.), but these will be developed in the next section. Here, it is sufficient to point out that the school, like the church, the clinic, and the Scout troop, is basically a system aimed at bringing about desirable changes in children.[4]

"Local" public control

Schools can, obviously, be organized in a wide variety of ways. In America certain historical precedents have grown up, and have become deeply ingrained in the schools as we now know them.

One of these is the idea that the schools "should" be locally financed, and controlled by the general public. In principle, this is usually carried out by the appointment or election of a supposedly policy-making board of local citizens, and by the raising of funds from the local community, usually by taxes on real property.

---

[3]In some senses, the parents themselves may also be seen as a "target" public—the school seeks to influence them in ways beyond those necessary to seek support and sponsorship.

[4]Change induction in children is the manifest function; many semilatent functions (*e.g.*, preservation of certain academic traditions) and some clearly latent functions (*e.g.*, baby-sitting, the provision of a dating facility for adolescents, the enhancement of community pride in its public buildings) also exist. These will be explored more fully in the following section in the discussion of goals.

In fact, the average American public school receives about half its support from state rather than local funds. And there exist (as we shall see), a wide variety of constraints, from national examination systems and nationally marketed books and equipment to the existence of a nationally mobile (hence interchangeable) teacher and student population. Beyond this, there is some doubt whether local boards do in fact exert policy control; the superintendent may well be the main source of influence on all but gross matters (for a case, see Kerr, 1965). However, in spite of all this, most Americans operate from the belief that schools not only "ought" to be, but *are* locally controlled. For this reason, school problems usually turn out to be deeply political in nature, and involve a fair amount of lay participation. Most school decisions are made on a community-by-community basis— often in response to similar national pressures—rather than at the state or national levels directly. There are about 30,000 local school districts, and for many purposes they can be regarded as meaningful units, whether seen from a social-psychological, a financial, or a legal point of view. They are not, however, genuinely locally controlled.

Nonvoluntarism

The American public schools—like those in all industrialized countries—are compulsory up to a certain age. More precisely: every child must be in *some* school, and the chances in America are about six to one that it will be a public one. The compulsory aspect of the school makes for problems in both learner motivation and teacher attitude. The brute fact to keep in mind, however, is that about 48 million children are required to be in elementary and secondary schools in America each day during the school year. Taking care of these bodies necessitates the training and regular replenishment of a work force of about 1.8 million teachers, along with about 100,000 superintendents, principals, and supervisory personnel. With numbers of this sort, there must inevitably be an enormous range of variability among persons holding educational positions. Thus it becomes difficult to assert that teachers and administrators are professionals in any meaningful sense of that word (which usually implies a body of practice grounded in one or more basic disciplines, reference-group control over entry to the profession, and a widely accepted code of ethics regulating contacts with clients and others). As Wayland (1964) has pointed out with clarity, teachers and administrators are actually semiprofessionals operating in a bureaucratic structure.[5]

---

[5]These professionals, by the way, all fall into the age category "adult." With the exception of the work on peer teaching by Lippitt (1965), institutional arrangements in schools always seem to assume that stronger, more powerful, more educated persons occupying adult status are the only legitimate educative agents.

Isolation from other socializing agencies

The school in America, as now arranged, appears to be disconnected from other institutions which also have the function of bringing about changes in children. These include the church (for historical reasons of separation of church and state); the family (in any systematic sense); and the entire range of rehabilitative, recreational, therapeutic, and protective agencies (courts, police); employers; and various political groups. There are strong legal supports for this disconnection, of course, in the form of certification requirements, specifications for legitimate sources of funds, and the like. If we examine the situation from the point of view of the child, however, these socializing agencies are not emotionally separate at all: each is making demands on him, each supplying gratifications and rewards of particular sorts. He may, in fact, find himself in considerable conflict as he copes with varying demands from different socializing agencies. The general point being made here is that local "horizontal" *institutional* linkages, other than open school nights, report cards, and the P.T.A. are not well developed (see Lippitt, 1965).

Linkage to larger systems

The American school is tied by more or less tacit "vertical" linkages to a number of other institutions and organizations in the larger society. These include colleges and graduate schools, who are able to make and enforce certain demands as to curricular offerings; the general occupational structure of the society and the requirements of the occupational roles as they develop; accreditation agencies; state departments of education; and—increasingly—the federal government. In addition, a wide variety of commercial structures form a part of the environment: materials vendors, equipment manufacturers, the mass media, and research and consulting organizations. So too, do a variety of nonprofit structures, including foundations, testing organizations, special interest groups, and voluntary and professional organizations, along with special innovative groups like those represented in national curriculum programs. The general point is perhaps obvious; it only must be emphasized that the so-called locally controlled school district does, in fact, exist in a complex environment, some aspects of which exert close legal and financial constraints. There are, in effect, a large number of relevant publics for any particular school district—or school building.

This section, then, has stressed five general features of the American public school: its children-changing emphasis; the notion of apparent local control; the nonvoluntary nature of the undertaking for children and adults alike; relative isolation from other socialization agencies in the local community; and tacit or explicit linkages to a wide variety of subsystems in the larger environment, some of which exert clear constraints.

GENOTYPICAL PROPERTIES OF TODAY'S SCHOOL   To distinguish genotypes from phenotypes is always difficult. The intent here is to focus on properties of the school which seem—partly because they flow from the general features just discussed—somehow more basic, more underlying, more *essential* properties of the school as we now know it than are statements of symptoms and recurring "problems." The ideas in this section have been organized under four general headings: properties relating to the organization's goal; those dealing with its task accomplishment methods; those relating to its integrative or internal maintenance efforts; and those properties dealing with its adaptation skills in relation to the broader environment. For each of these general headings, there will be an attempt to discuss the problems as seen from the point of view of the organization, *qua* organization,[6] and from the point of view of the child as inhabitant of the organization.

Wherever possible, these genotypical properties will be linked back to the general features described earlier; the reader will undoubtedly be able to make many sorts of connections which go unspecified in the text.

Goal specification properties

DIVERSITY AND CONFLICT   Since the public schools are supposed to bring about desirable changes in children, and exist in an environment of so-called local control amid a host of other subsystems, all with expectations for the school, educational goals are usually (1) vaguely stated; (2) multiple in nature, such that the school is expected to do many different things to meet the wishes of its many publics; (3) conflictful, in the sense that different publics may want mutually incompatible things. For example, the school is expected to cause children to "achieve" mastery of academic subject matter, *and* to develop and maintain

---

[6]Controversy as to whether the American public school is "really" an organization is probably unprofitable. If by "organization" we mean a hierarchically organized assemblage of persons and groups aimed at the accomplishment of some task, then the school clearly qualifies. If we have an image of organization which implies a tightly organized "line and staff" model drawn from military or industrial experience, the appellation is less appropriate.

It does seem extremely clear that schools are—because of some of the features discussed in the preceding section—rather unlike organizations devoted to producing physical things and selling them at a profit, or even unlike organizations devoted to making knowledge.

The fact that the child exists not only as a "member" of the school as an organization, but also as a member of his family, for example, means that the school and the community it is located in form a kind of complex intersystem, and cannot be thought of as isolated, closed, or as determined primarily by forces within the system as such. This is not different in kind, of course, from the problems faced by an industrial firm, which must also engage in meaningful commerce with its environment; the point being made here is that the school is perhaps more like one component of a community's life than it is like a factory, a university, or a government agency. It is possible that the intersystem properties of the school are among its most crucial features. (See also the discussion of adaptation properties below.)

physical and emotional health in children, *and* to socialize children (compare Parsons, 1959) into industrial society (*e.g.*, make them neat, obedient, prompt, achievement-oriented). There are many circumstances under which these goals may prove mutually interfering.

As if this goal diversity were not enough, the school is also faced with tremendous input variability, in terms of the learners who are expected to achieve these goals. The compulsory nature of the public school means that children occupying a very wide range of ability and motivation to learn must be accepted. The wide variability in personnel competence which is a function of mass schooling has already been discussed above.

Given goal diversity, and the variability in children and personnel, one natural response is to create a hierarchy of goals. One's impressions are that "subject matter" outcomes—whether in terms of basic skills or retained information and principles—tend to be most highly valued, with socialization goals nominally second in line.[7] Custodial-care goals (baby-sitting, keeping teen-agers off the streets) seem generally to be taken for granted, treated as latent functions of the school.

---

[7]The *content* of socialization goals undoubtedly shifts as different age levels of students are considered. For young children, the development of achievement motivation, a sense of membership in the classroom group, and a certain degree of neatness, obedience to authority, etc., seem central; for adolescents, the management of sex and aggression seem more on center stage.

One feels a need for more empirical data on goals. Consider, for example, a phenomenon which might be characterized as The Case of the Beatle Haircut. Adolescents and school administrators increasingly are in conflict over matters of personal dress, appearance, and so on, with administrators imposing a wide variety of sanctions in this area. Some alternative interpretations which have been offered to the author to explain this are :

1. Beatle haircuts (also eye make-up, sloppy clothes, short skirts, etc.) destroy the image of the school which the administrator wants to create in the public's eye.
2. The school legitimately stands *in loco parentis*, but this position is being challenged (hence is reactively asserted by administrators).
3. Adults feel jealous of (or guilty about) adolescents' management of sex between puberty and marriage.
4. Intergenerational value conflicts are at work.
5. Presentations of self which are erotic or violent interfere with the learning process.
6. The school is expected to be a bastion of morality, strengthening superegos as much as possible.
7. Being neat, formal, etc., must be taught to children if they are to take their place in society; casual clothing also implies that no serious attention to learning is taking place.
8. A competitive, win-lose, negotiative relationship has developed, rather than a cooperative, problem-solving one.
9. School administrators are playing Delilah to the teen-agers' Samson.

All of these proposed explanations have a certain plausible charm, but in the absence of clearer conceptualization and data collection, it is difficult to know what is at work.

EMOTIONAL LOADING   System goal specifications are also emotionally loaded, in the sense that children are valuable property—property with which the parent has already had varying degrees of success and failure.[8]

PRODUCT MEASUREMENT PROBLEMS   Since stated goals for schools are vague, multiple, conflicting, emotionally laden—and constitute changes in persons which occur slowly and over an extended period of time—most schools experience a good deal of difficulty in evaluating outcomes in any systematic way. Measures of socialization outcomes, other than teacher marks for classroom behavior (if they are given) are practically nonexistent, except in terms of the incidence of deviant behavior (fighting, truancy, etc.). And even the existing measures of intellectual mastery of subject fields tend to be limited to factual recall rather than internalization of the relevant methods of inquiry.[9] While product evaluation is technically difficult in schools, it is not impossible; the fact that it is done so rarely in any satisfying way (Miles, 1964, 657–659) may be an indicator of organizational defense against the conflicts and problems that would be inevitably laid bare if systematic evaluation were to be carried out.

FROM THE CHILD'S VIEWPOINT   The idea of interviewing a sample of children of various age levels about educational goals is an attractive one. Discussion with three close relatives of the author (in third, sixth, and eighth grades respectively) turned up responses to the question, "What is school for?" like, "It's to learn, it's to teach us stuff—you know, school stuff, like reading, arithmetic, writing, social studies." A little probing and a query: "Is the school supposed to teach you manners?" evoked items like, "Yes, not to talk in halls, not to run, raise your hand if you want to talk, be good, wait for your turn." The eighth grader, when asked, "Is school supposed to help you learn to get along better with other kids?" said, "Yes, it's supposed to, but it doesn't really work out that way, because they don't have any classes in it." The third grader said, "It's supposed to keep you physically fit." None of these children mentioned socialization goals spontaneously, nor did they mention custodial goals ("taking care of us while we are at school"), as might have been expected. The material supplied under socialization goals ("take your turn, don't run in the halls", etc.) suggests that for

---

[8]This comes out most strikingly, perhaps, in relation to the socialization goals of the school. If the child succeeds in both this and academic areas, it is often felt to be to the school's credit. If he fails in terms of socialization goals (*i.e.,* is aggressive, drops out, or whatever), this is seen as being a failure of the socializing efforts of the parent. At any rate, it seems quite clear that parents do have expectations that the school will, or should, specify goals in the socialization area, many of them inconsistent with each other (not fighting versus being aggressive and standing up for yourself, being cooperative, but not conforming; being disciplined versus being creative, etc.).

[9]See the charming fable, "The Year the Schools Began Teaching the Telephone Directory," (Harmin & Simon, 1965).

the child (as perhaps for the adult) socialization as such is less central than sheer control of large numbers of exuberant young bodies. The comments by these children also suggest that both they and their teachers tended to share relatively static assumptions about learning (*i.e.*, transmission of subject matter as a major mode of learning) as contrasted with discovery-type methods, the encouragement of independence, support of critical thinking, and the like).

Task accomplishment mechanisms

In any system, the school included, there are various activities, procedures, behaviors which the members of the system believe will cause movement toward system goals.

AGE-GRADED COHORTS   For one thing, it is assumed that age-grading is essential if subject matter appropriate for a particular level of child is to be communicated adequately; by and large, students are organized in cohorts of a particular age range, rather than being in learning units composed on other bases ("readiness," sophistication about the subject matter, preferred learning style, etc.). The ungraded classroom, the interage group, the "teachable group" (Thelen, 1961) are not typical of the American school. This may have arisen historically from the idea of the core value of "fairness" in an equalitarian culture, or from realistic, intuitive ideas about when children are developmentally ready to cope with a particular learning content. It is possible, too, that age-grading (and moving the children onward to new teachers each year) serves to reduce the intensity of the emotional relationship to the teacher and enable *Gesellschaftlich* orientation to take hold (compare Parsons, 1959).

ROLE PERFORMANCE INVISIBILITY   The basic role performance in the school— teaching—takes place out of sight of adult contact or supervision for perhaps 90 percent of the time. Role performance is accordingly judged on formal, or once-removed, criteria such as the children's interest, or number of graduate courses taken by the teacher (regardless of content), rather than on direct observation and monitoring of performance. Thus, it is difficult to get feedback—to know whether a particular teaching behavior does encourage movement toward particular goals (compare Lippitt, 1965, 48). The present role structure of schools tends to discourage data collection along these lines. Informal norms also grow up supporting "autonomy" and prohibiting "interference" (Lortie, 1961). Under these circumstances, teachers who wish for support find it difficult to get; administrators who are concerned about inadequate teaching behavior find it difficult to get enough data to be helpful; and parents exert erratic pressure based on children's reports of "what the teacher did."

LOW DEGREE OF ROLE DIFFERENTIATION   In the elementary school in particular, there appears to be little division of labor in carrying out work operations.

A teacher is a teacher is a teacher; this tends to mean that upward mobility within the teacher role is relatively infrequent (and, for other reasons, that mobility out of it to the administrative role is frequent only for males).

This lack of role differentiation seems connected with a kind of role stereotypy (children as young as three can play the teacher role in games with ease). Teacher mobility across school systems may encourage this standardization still further. So does the fact that the "sponsoring public" of schools is composed of adults who were socialized into the learner role, and developed a clear set of expectations for the teacher role 20 to 30 years ago. Researchers differ on whether wide teacher behavior differences can be discovered across classrooms. If gross indices, such as the proportion of interaction occupied by the teacher, are considered, the variability is not large: most teachers talk from 60 to 80 percent of the time (Flanders, 1960). The physical arrangements of the classroom may encourage this further, but the presence of a body of subject matter, an adult, and some children tends to create role pressures toward "explaining," asking for recitation, etc., relatively independently of the personality of the particular incumbent at hand. Biddle, after extensive research on teacher role behavior (See Biddle and Rosencranz, 1964) suggested that "the teacher is on rails"[10]; almost nothing can be done to alter the role performance short of radical structural change, such as that involved in team teaching.

LOW KNOWLEDGE COMPONENT   It may seem paradoxical to say that schools are organizations which use organized knowledge minimally, since they presumably deal centrally with the dissemination of knowledge. But when it comes to knowledge bearing on the efficacy of the *work processes* being used by schools, it seems clear that awareness and direct use of relevant areas of knowledge (learning psychology, social psychology, sociology of the community), is limited. This may stem in part from the fact that policy decisions are made by a board of lay persons; this in combination with teachers' semiprofessional role definition means that the distance between lay and professional persons is relatively smaller than in most other organizations.

The absence of concrete evaluation methods and criteria may also contribute to the use of ritualism and tradition, rather than the results of inquiry, as a basis for work-flow decisions.

In addition, schools as we now know them organize the work flow mainly through persons as agents of the organization, placing a low amount of total investment into physical technology; this too seems a connected point.

DIFFICULTY IN PRACTICE DIFFUSION   One last comment might be made about work-flow activities in schools. As Lippitt (1965) points out, the adoption of educational innovations often turns out to be relatively difficult, since the innovations involve human interaction, and often require active learning or retraining of the

---

[10]Personal communication.

operative, so to speak. The diffusion of behavioral innovations is a much more difficult matter than in systems in which physical technology is the item being diffused.

FROM THE CHILD'S POINT OF VIEW　It is difficult to know what the child makes of all this; like the fish in the water, he may be the last to question the way in which work operations in schools are organized. Some things do seem relatively clear, however.

For the child, the question of whether or not his new teacher is "nice" becomes a question of very high priority. A person with such power over one is, hopefully, benevolent; if not, the task is to learn what behaviors on one's part will please the teacher, stimulate benevolence, or at least stave off malevolent behavior. The child, in one sense, may initially put more energy in on learning the teacher, than the subject matter as such.

Heavy subject-matter orientation probably becomes internalized relatively rapidly in children; along with many teachers, they too conceive that education is the process of transferring information from one person's head to another's. As the new curricula develop further, inductive knowledge-testing, knowledge-making modes may become more salient. But one suspects that this may be a long time coming.

As children grow older and become more and more able to verbalize their feelings about teachers (when they talk to friends, parents—anyone but the teacher himself), and as they encounter more and more different teachers, one suspects that they become more able to understand that variability in teacher competence is at least as great as the variability of child learning ability. In this sense, the notion of invisibility of role performance is inapplicable as far as the child is concerned; he can observe very closely and acutely—and can report to trusted others—his judgments of the adequacy of the role taking involved.[11]

But children have relatively little legitimate power over adults. Many available modes of influence seem ultimately self-defeating: rebellion, refusal to learn (one suspects that for many "difficult," "disadvantaged" children, nonlearning is an active stance, aimed at "getting back" at the teacher). Other influence modes are demeaning: begging, wheedling, cunningly giving the teacher the desired response in order to gain a point.

So, as the raw material of the organization around which work flow is presumably organized, it is hard for children not to become passive recipients of task accomplishment efforts on the part of teachers and other adults. However, a major untapped resource in any school is the ideas and reactions of children about the efficacy of the educational procedures in which they are involved, the role behaviors which are being presented to them, and possible innovations which would

---

[11]Yale University proposed using judgments of teaching competence made by students after their graduation as one factor in faculty tenure decisions (*The New York Times*, October 15, 1965).

improve task accomplishment and emotional climate.[12] Direct feedback channels, from this point of view, are much needed.

Internal integration

Another cluster of properties centers around the degree to which school systems are able to coordinate their different subparts, effectively, to evoke the vigorous support of members for organizational goal achievement efforts, and to make sure that the informal "contract" which the individual makes with the organization is a mutually satisfying one.

LOW INTERDEPENDENCE   Generally speaking, it seems accurate to say that the different parts of school systems do not lock together as closely and sensitively as those (for example) of an industrial firm built around the construction and marketing of physical objects. Schools as they are now organized in America maintain adults in relative isolation from each other during the working day. Perhaps because of the vagueness involved in change induction in persons, most teachers do not appear to have a genuine common fate, in the sense that one person's role performance crucially links with that of another. This tends to be true not only at any given point in time, but sequentially as well: as children move from one classroom to another, and from one school unit to another (elementary to junior high school), there seems not to be active, interdependent work contact between the adults in the different parts of the system. In some school systems, the principal is a central exhibit of noninterdependence; he operates his building as a "king," avoiding or ignoring central office demands, *and* spends little time working with teachers on the improvement of their role performance.

It is important to note that a low degree of interdependence ordinarily makes a system much more difficult to alter, since if changes occur in one part (*i.e.*, in one teacher's practices), there are no meaningful channels or linkages by which they can travel to other parts of the system. This state of affairs may lead to internal integration problems centering around teacher morale, feelings of isolation, depression, and nonconfirmation by peers.

MOBILITY LIMITATIONS   Another source of morale problems centers around career paths and mobility routes in schools. It has already been suggested that

---

[12]As in other hierarchical settings, it seems quite likely that subordinates (children) will stress emotional climate and consideration factors more than sheer task factors on the part of the superior (teacher). A simple experiment which the author has replicated a number of times with groups of adults goes as follows. Half the group lists the most important characteristics which they feel they should have as teachers. The other half lists the most important characteristics which their own best teacher had (themselves in the student role). When discussing own teaching behavior, the dominant theme tends to be mastery of subject matter, ability to "put it across," and organization of learning situations. From the point of view of the learner, at least as recollected, great teachers nearly always have high consideration, warmth, and attention to the learner as a person.

mobility within the teacher role[13] tends to be relatively difficult (or at least will remain so until differentiated roles like those of master teachers and team leaders become much more widespread than at present). This has historically meant in American public schools that, for women, school teaching was a job entered as a temporary position between college completion and marriage, *or* a relatively stable role entered by people without active ambitions for upward mobility. For men, on the other hand, the teacher role has classically served as a stepping stone to administrative jobs. Thus, there are at least two sources of potential nonoptimization of the psychological contract between the teacher and the organization: the job is often a means to something else, not intrinsically satisfying; and it is usually not easy to become radically more skilled or developed in the job, and to receive added recognition and rank increments for this.

ACCOUNTABILITY AND COMPULSION   A third source of integration problems stems from the facts that children *must* be at school,[14] and *must*, custodially speaking, be taken care of. If schools are minimally staffed, as often seems to be the case, teachers often have little or no time during the day for peer work, personal development, teaching preparation, or rest. Thus principals worry about ways of "motivating" teachers to learn, grow, and develop—but usually do little to alter the basic constraints which limit the effectiveness of the teacher.

FROM THE POINT OF VIEW OF THE CHILD   Compulsion probably looms fairly large to the child; he *must* come to school whether he likes it or not, unless he can occupy the magical sick role. Teachers' efforts to "motivate" him are probably appreciated, but continued compulsion, as Goodman (1964) implies, may well wither the inner motivation to grow and develop which is present in all infants. Compulsion communicates: We do not think you want to learn.

If the child sees the teacher role as a not particularly desirable one for adults (*i.e.*, perceives the mobility limitations in it), one might expect teachers to be chosen less frequently as role models, or consulted less frequently about decisions that matter. Coleman (1961) did find that when high school students were asked whose disapproval would be hardest to take, their nominations were for parents (54 percent), peers (43 percent)—and teachers (3 percent).

Low interdependence among teachers and other personnel probably encourages the child to concentrate on pleasing or reacting to the individual teacher with whom he happens to be interacting at the moment. Attempts to change or improve the organization (*e.g.*, the operations of high-powered student councils) do occur, but not frequently.

---

[13]Though mobility from less desirable to more desirable *buildings* or systems (Becker, 1952) does occur frequently. Average system turnover annually is about 13 percent.

[14]Except in Mississippi and South Carolina.

Adaptation problems

Many different system properties seem to center around the mutual adaptation of school and community, seen as a special case of the organization in its environment.

VULNERABILITY AND DEFENSIVENESS Perhaps the most central of these is the notion that the "skin" of schools feels almost unbearably thin for many of its inhabitants. Insiders feel that demands, criticism, and control can come into the system at almost any point. This flows not only from the definition of the schools as public and "locally" controlled, but from the fact that children return to their parents each night with news of how they have been treated. Yet many parents seem to feel hesitant, powerless, unable to complain if they hear of teacher behavior or a curriculum item of which they disapprove, and sure that teachers or principals will react defensively. These paradoxically differing sides of the coin suggest that manageable means for accepting influence from the environment may be underdeveloped in many school systems.

Of course, it is reasonable that a system which not only must accept all the (child) input which comes to it, but also has a "nonquitting" clause attached to the child's participation should remain open to inspection. In this sense, openness to influence from the environment is a functional property of a school system. However, as suggested in the next section, this genotypical property can also lead to symptoms on the order of organization passivity and willingness to be "run by the environment", deceptive stances toward the environment, or (given a conservative surrounding) reinforcement of safe, traditional practices.

NONCOMPETITIVE POSITION The American public school is defined as essentially noncompetitive with other schools in its environment. It must take all comers who apply: it has difficulty in extruding even the most severely disturbed or retarded child. And there are few ways, because of school district boundaries, in which a school district can enter the market and actively bid for particularly capable and interesting learners—in the same way that private schools and colleges can.[15] In short, regardless of its performance level, the American public school will continue to exist. There is little interschool competitive pressure for excellence. Locating and attracting a superior staff usually seems to be accomplished primarily by financial means, rather than by allusions to the quality of the educational experiences offered in the system.

RADICAL ENVIRONMENTAL CHANGE The American public school today is in the midst of an environment changing more rapidly than at any time in the history of the common school. The changes include the numbers and social class membership of students appearing at any particular school; the attitudes, information, and

---

[15]This pattern has exceptions, of course. In New York, specialized high schools (Music and Art, Bronx Science, Performing Arts) compete with general high schools for talented students. And the swim club at the Santa Clara, California, high school has produced enough Olympic champions so that families move to that community for just that purpose.

values they bring to the school program; the explosion of knowledge underlying school subject matter; and the political, social, and economic structures surrounding the school. So, whatever the adaptation problems of schools may be, we can be quite sure that in the immediate period ahead, they will be accentuated radically. Indeed, it may not be too much to say that adaptation failures are the most serious problem area for almost any school district in America today.

FROM THE CHILD'S VIEWPOINT   While parents may feel a sense of frustration at not being able to influence the school, and teachers may feel vulnerable and overinfluenced by parents, the child probably experiences the vulnerability/defensiveness of the school primarily in terms of role conflict and his membership in overlapping groups. He becomes the focus or arena of conflicting forces, and is likely to respond in a variety of familiar ways: compartmentalizing and separating "school" from "life" (often with the school's encouragement); giving one set of demands primacy at a given point of time and slighting the other; becoming immobilized; trying to meet both sets of goals and norms with resulting high tension; or playing off one set of demands against the other.

The noncompetitive nature of the American public school may also have motivational effects for the child. Since the school is not a scarce resource in the child's environment, and since public schools in America are apparently not that radically differentiated from each other, the psychological dropout who is an apparent stay-in may be more frequent than we think. Though strong deviant behavior is controlled by various familiar means, the child can easily become a hidden deviant from school system norms by withdrawing, remaining passive, or accepting "side payments" in the form of athletic participation, friendship, or sexual activity.

What do school children think of the "explosion of knowledge?" One's impression is that they welcome it. This is simply the way the world is—curiouser and curiouser. Though the child is not really the noble savage some polemicists paint him, he is certainly less likely than adults to have investment in old frameworks, or to chew up his self-esteem in the problems of unlearning; he can simply begin discussing satellite orbits immediately—because that's the way the world is. It has already been suggested that the child's major weapon is the threat or action of refusing to learn (at least in the school's terms); it may be that a matter of fact confrontation with the complexity of the modern world is almost as successful and upsetting a defense against "the old folks."

SYMPTOMS OF   The intent in this section is not to produce an
DIFFICULTY IN   exhaustive category of ailments with which
one might expect school systems to present a
TODAY'S SCHOOLS   diagnostician. Rather, the attempt is to label a
number of behaviors or problems which can be
seen as symptomatic resultants of the genotypical properties of the school, in interaction with the present demands it is facing.

Most of the symptoms and problems specified here are as seen by an outside diagnostician with social scientific interests. Some of them would not be seen as problems by practicing administrators (and have in fact been denied as central by some the author has talked to). One ought, optimally, to collect a large sample of diagnostic statements from practitioners, then look at their relevance to the analysis above. In the absence of anything like empirical data, however, the statements of problems which follow have flowed from some relatively limited experience with school systems, as well as from the analysis as such.

As before, the problems are organized around the four general categories of goal, task functioning, internal integration, and adaptation.

Goal problems

MORALISM   Outside observers often comment that people working in schools tend to invoke ideological, judgmental, or moralistic bases for making decisions. "Should" and "ought" seem to outweigh "is" and "can".[16] School people too complain of this, saying that they "do things by the seat of our pants" rather than relying on research or inquiry. Statements of intention (*e.g.*, "make better citizens") more often than not outnumber actual goal-directed efforts.

This general tendency may be connected with the problem of goal ambiguity and the fact that few hard data are available to guide decisions anyway.

In addition, because the schools are an avenue which can permit later mobility of students, there are strong forces toward parents' perceiving the school as a "judgmental agency," which categorizes one's child along important dimensions, (achievement, middle-class value orientation), and compares him with other children in the neighborhood.

VALUE CONFLICT   Vulnerability, and "local" control, in conjunction with the socializing function of the school, may mean that latent or explicit value conflict is a frequent problem area. The Case of the Beatle Haircut can be called moralistic repressiveness if one happens to be on the side of adolescents (see Friedenberg, 1965) and disruptive exhibitionism if one happens to be on the side of administrators. One gets the impression that the school tends to lag considerably behind community sentiments, perhaps because of its traditionally conserving role, and because of the perceived vulnerability problem. The school's role as a transmitter of ideal culture means, in Linton's terms, that it can not tolerate attacks on the ideal, even though ideal-actual discrepancies are visible and acknowledged.

FINANCIAL EMPHASIS   In the absence of clear output criteria (and, in the absence of capable internal data collection mechanisms) considerable energy in schools goes into money-raising efforts of one kind and another. Also, educational programs seem to be justified either in terms of the amount of money which is

---

[16]Compare Ojemann's (Muuss, 1960) focus on developing causal orientation in teachers to offset the moral-evaluative stance.

eing spent (we care about our children, and we want to spend as much as we ossibly can, within reason, to get them the best possible education)—or by laking a virtue of thriftiness (we are providing the same adequate services as efore at a reduced cost). In either event, the criteria tend to become primarily *nancial*, rather than directly goal-connected and output-based.

ask functioning

PROCEDURAL RIGIDITY   It does seem difficult to change the way in which eachers and administrators do things. In the absence of clear output criteria, there s little motivation to shift procedures. And, it is true that in a system open to nfluence from the outside, some aspects of the system need to be kept firm (*i.e.*, enure systems, predictable scheduling, etc.) as a kind of hedge against the inroads f the environment. Nevertheless, both outsiders—and many insiders—seem to vish that schools could change their practices somewhat more expeditiously than .t present.

LACK OF R & D FUNCTION   Out of 30,000 school districts, there may be 100 or o (usually large city systems) which have a research function built in, in any sysematic way. (One's impression is that even these few tend to become "educational ookkeeping" and administrative data-gathering devices.) It is very doubtful if nore than a dozen school systems in America (1965) have anything that might be .alled a systematic research and development unit to develop new practices, test hem for feasibility and efficacy, and aid in diffusing them to various parts of the ystem. In addition, institutionalized change-agent roles analogous to the engineer, he field tester, or the county agent seem to be underdeveloped or lacking in the raditional American system.

Lippitt has suggested[17] that in a relatively low-interdependent system such as he teachers in a particular school building, or a school district among other school listricts, scattered adoptions of innovations is a fairly easy matter—but systematic liffusion across subsystems is much more difficult. The converse has been sug-;ested to be true for the educational system of the Soviet Union, in which the gross umber of innovations is relatively smaller than the total here. But—in such a iigh-interdependent system—adoptions of what *is* invented and tested take place nore rapidly and on a wider scale.

ADMINISTRATIVE OVERLOAD   Life being what it is and aspirations what they ire, almost any executive will complain that he has too much to do. This pre-enting symptom, however, is perhaps more frequently encountered in schools han in other types of organizations. This problem is perhaps primarily a function)f high system vulnerability. Beyond this, certain notions about role boundaries nay be at work—such as the unshakable idea that a superintendent of schools nust work capably with the board, *and* be an educational statesman in the com-

---

[17]At COPED Seminar, August 5–9, 1965.

munity, the state, and the nation, *and* attract funds from federal and state sources, *and* be an instructional leader within the system—all with only seven days and nights a week available in which to work.

TEACHER-QUALITY PROBLEMS   Self-selective processes appear to occur in the recruitment of teachers for the American public school; persons who are less verbally able, more passive, more deferent, and less competitive than other professionals tend to enter teaching jobs. Some of these traits are congruent with nurturing, supporting behavioral styles, and are thus role-appropriate. However, persons with lower verbal ability (and less informational content, as some studies of teachers have discovered) can only be seen as limited in their capacity for effective teaching. This problem, when combined with the fact that thoroughgoing tenure regulations exist in most school districts, seem to cause many administrators to feel despair and helplessness, or to resort to variously Machiavellian styles of persuasion in "motivating" teachers to learn, grow, and develop.

CONFLICTS OF EXPERTISE   Connected with this is another problem: many internal school decision issues involve administrators and teachers, or teachers and teachers, in latent struggles over who is more competent to decide the particular issue at hand. This is a more subtle version of the lay-professional problems which plague superintendents, boards, citizens—or almost any school role occupant. This may be one of the reasons why both administrators and teachers seem to be particularly anxious about the problem of teacher performance improvement. Managers are always panicked by the thought of having to be helpful to subordinates and to aid their development in any systematic and serious way. It seems likely, however, that in educational systems, such anxieties are enhanced by disagreements over the legitimacy of one's expertise, particularly in a setting in which one's immediate superior may know considerably less about the problem at hand than oneself.

Integration and maintenance

MORALE   As in other types of systems, this label covers a multitude of strains. In the case of the school, frustration stemming from expertise conflicts, the sense that one's work is not intrinsically satisfying, and hopelessness about one's career future may all tinge one's day-to-day sentiments negatively.

INTERGROUP CONFLICTS   Because the school is age-graded, and divided into elementary and secondary building groups, conflicts between elementary, junior high, and high school teachers seem to arise routinely, and are accentuated by conflict between each of these groups and "the central office" in any system of more than moderate size. These conflicts seem sharpest at points of articulation between the various levels. As in any intergroup conflict, there are problems of inflated group self-image, negative stereotyping of the other, and so on. In the case of teacher-central office conflicts, the main issues may well center around the use of power (compare Fischer, 1964).

LOW PERSONNEL DEVELOPMENT INVESTMENT   In comparison with most other types of organizations, little money is expended by school systems on the development of system members. Such learning is conceived of as an individual matter, or is regarded as a violation of norms of academic freedom, autonomy, (etc.) if engaged in at all seriously. Yet, it seems true that serious innovation in many school systems has only come about when rather vigorous personnel development efforts—often with outside funds and facilities (*e.g.*, National Science Foundation institutes) have been developed as a routine part of organizational life.

Adaptation failures

PASSIVITY   In many school systems, the main stance of the chief administrator in the face of system vulnerability and varying demands from the environment is a withdrawing, passive one; the school is seen as the dependent variable, as "the Other," to borrow from Simone de Beauvoir. The tacit view of the school is that it has little power to initiate, develop, grow, push things, or be disagreeable to anyone or anything.

DEFENSIVENESS   Setting up barriers of various kinds, withdrawing into ritualistic use of existing procedures, justifications of existing policy, etc., also seem to appear relatively frequently as a response to pressure from outside. Here, too, the passive stance seems part of the implicit assumptions held by the administrator.

"PROBLEMS WITH PARENTS"   Several years ago in a training group composed of elementary school principals, the author asked the members individually to jot down topics for a role playing scene they would like to do. Thirteen of fourteen principals, after brief reflection, came up with "an interview with an irate parent." Rage over the treatment of one's child is sometimes legitimate, one supposes—but presumably nonrational factors are at work too.

The young child's departure to the school can induce family disequilibrium and a strong sense of loss in parents. And if the school is actually successful with the child, reactions of envy and hostility often set in. Parental fear and mistrust can also develop because of the school's power to make judgments about the child's competence. Some parents feel they may be stereotyped as inadequate in their previous socialization efforts—and feel little expectation that they will be praised if the child turns out to achieve well in school.

DECISION-MAKING PROBLEMS   Many superintendents report severe difficulty in coping with boards of education, not because boards are an overselection of particularly cantankerous people, but presumably because the board represents a kind of arena of conflicting influences in the local community. It is in such decision-making sessions—whether closed or open to the public—that one sees very clearly that the school is part of a large intersystem; it acts more like a subsystem of a community than a classical, isolated bureaucracy. Thus diffuse, conflictful, mistrustful, value-laden interaction is likely, and good decisions are hard to get.

IMPLICATIONS FOR RESEARCH AND ACTION   This section[18] attempts some derivations from the foregoing analysis which may guide efforts—like those being launched in the COPED project—to derive valid knowledge about the process of improving schools. It is intended to be stimulative and questioning rather than exhaustive, and covers general implications; broad change goals; and some concluding commentary on types of social inventions needed.

General implications

It seems that many aspects of schools as organizations, and the value orientations of their inhabitants, are founded on history, and on what feel like genotypical properties. These appear to be important to the schools; they help maintain continuity and balance in the face of the school's ambiguous mission, and its vulnerability to external pressures from parents and others. Therefore, it may be that, while rapid shifts in specific school practices are relatively more possible, changes touching on the central core of assumptions and structures will be far more difficult to achieve.

Present properties of school systems have current utility. Change efforts must be prepared to acknowledge and respect the functionality of those properties which achieve such objectives as the following: (1) softening or bridging class distinctions; (2) maintaining a "thing" orientation deemed necessary to an industrial society; (3) controlling large numbers of children in situations of high population density; (4) maintaining the job security of school personnel. Whether or not change agents' values square with these objectives, they are held, explicitly or implicitly, by many in our society. To the extent that current properties of schools serve these objectives, the properties will be more immune to change efforts. . . .A further implication of the foregoing analysis is that one must be prepared to consider whether the changes being worked on at any point represent attempts to modify essential properties, or are only attacks on symptoms. . . .

Even if it is clear that genotypes *are* being worked on, the question of the degree of modifiability remains. For example, consider the essentially involuntary nature of the school-client relationship. Would it be possible for change-agent teams to modify this aspect of the schools? With only a little imagination it is possible to suggest ways in which families could have more freedom in choosing their children's teachers, (compare open enrollment plans, Project Exodus in Boston, etc.) and vice versa. No doubt any such change would add to the cost of education. However, the increased cost would probably be compensated for by increased efficiencies following from the elimination of some of the control mechanisms established to protect both parties against unduly arbitrary behavior on the other's

---

[18]Co-authored with Donald C. Klein.

part. But even so, strong resistance could be expected toward any effort to alter such a central characteristic of schools. . . .

Finally, and most crucially, many of the very properties discussed here—resistance to evaluation, concern about vulnerability, adaptation failures—may make a responsible field research design difficult to plan and hard to execute. Demonstrating that the change-agent teams' interventions have in fact caused noted changes, *and* explaining why they occurred, may well be much more difficult than in (for example) industrial settings. . . .

Change goals

The analysis in this paper suggests four major change goals for school systems. These are: (1) increased internal interdependence and collaboration; (2) added adaptation mechanisms and skills; (3) stronger data-based, inquiring stances toward change; (4) continuing commitment to organizational and personal growth and development.

INTERDEPENDENCE   It has been suggested that isolation of individual educators within a system probably has defensive function. It also makes it very difficult for school personnel to secure help and support from one another, to develop adequate solutions to educational problems—and to diffuse these inventions to others. Thus it seems useful for change-agent teams to identify and reinforce existing interdependencies within each school system, and to build additional ones as indicated.

A collaborative approach to change presumably involves an interplay between parties who relate to each other on a reasonably equal-status basis. The analysis earlier suggested that each status occupant in the school (*i.e.*, child, parent, teacher, administrator, school board, citizen) feels relatively powerless to affect the schools, at least in certain significant areas. Thus power equalization becomes an important aspect of facilitating interdependence.

ADAPTATION   This paper has asserted that the major problem of school systems today seems to be that of keeping pace with rapid and radical changes in their environments, the communities served by the schools, as well as state-level and federal-level government, foundations, materials producers, and a host of other systems. A major function of an effective change program should probably be that of attempting to help the schools develop, test, and institutionalize the adaptive mechanisms they must have in order to cope effectively with accelerated change.

For example, though it is clear that school officials labor under a tremendous overload, in terms of time, emotional investment in the problems which confront them, and the impossible multiplicity of functions—it is not wholly clear what maintains this state of affairs. It has clearly been the function of the superintendent to act, virtually singlehandedly, as the linking pin between school personnel and the public, while giving hopefully inspired leadership to both groups. Perhaps because of the uneasiness with which communities grant autonomy to the professionals in education, it is difficult for superintendents to share the linking and leadership functions. We should be seeking a better understanding of this situation, and helping school systems invent alternative coping mechanisms.

It would appear that most change-agents are committed to strengthening school-community ties; they tend to accept the value of participative models of teaching, planning, and decision-making. However, organizations, like persons, need defenses. The adaptation problem is perhaps not so much that of shutting out the environment vs. admitting it in a rush, as specifying more clearly what the *quality* of the organization-environment transaction should be.

DATA-BASED INQUIRY   Much of the analysis above stressed the inadequacy of available data in school systems (as a guide for both short-run operations and longer-term change). Both at the classroom and the system level, it seems quite likely that building in new feedback loops is a basic change goal.

COMMITMENT TO SELF-RENEWAL   Perhaps it is tautological to say so, but one feels a need to be explicit about the goal of starting self-developmental, continuing change processes in school systems. The orientation is not toward specific change projects alone, but to the *institutionalization* of change functions: research, system development, personal development. The growing availability of federal funds for such purposes is an encouraging support for work toward this goal. . . .

Needed social inventions

A seriously self-renewing school system would presumably, with collaborative help from outside change agents, be able to invent and install a wide variety of structures—mechanisms for correcting dysfunctional aspects of schools. Lists of needed inventions are always fun; herewith the author's.

1. METHODS FOR GOAL CLARIFICATION   Instruments and work methods for specifying areas of goal vagueness and dissensus, and for increasing goal clarity via dialogue would aid life in schools a good deal.

2. GOAL MOVEMENT ASSESSMENT TOOLS   It would be nice to have instruments which could help teachers assess precisely, from day to day, what the real, short-run consequences of their work have been.

3. IMPROVED MECHANISMS FOR FEEDBACK FROM CHILDREN   Not only instruments, but simple work structures which would permit more child influence on the classroom   and the school building are much needed. The requirement is: how can adults hear, and use, what children have to say?

4. EASY-TO-USE ADULT BEHAVIORAL MEASURES   If the effects of changes in the school as an organization are to be monitored well, we need simpler and better measures of variables such as role definition, morale, perceived norms, conflict management. As in industrial settings, as Likert (1961) has pointed out, we need routine behavioral data as much as we do information on budgets, scheduling, and staffing.

5. FREE SPACE FOR PERSONAL AND ORGANIZATIONAL DEVELOPMENT   More

inventions on the order of flexible scheduling, staff load reduction, released time, sabbaticals, and early dismissal seem crucial if serious effort is to be devoted to improving, rather than just running, the educational shop.

6. CHANGE-MANAGING UNITS   The idea of an R & D council for a school system (involving special project teams, a genuine research director, a couple of natural strategists, the superintendent, etc.) seems attractive. Other types of stimulative and planning subsystems should undoubtedly be designed.

7. INTERAGENCY LINKING MECHANISMS   How about a confederation of child socialization agencies and roles which meets recurrently in work conferences to diagnose and remedy the articulation problems they are facing? Child and parent members would be included.

8. PERSONNEL DEVELOPMENT UNITS AND PROGRAMS   Most school systems could use a powerful and legitimated role (or group) devoted to the growth, development, and career planning of individuals in the system. Creative adaptations of management development schemes used in voluntary agencies, government, and (even) industry could undoubtedly be made. For example, job rotation within local systems seems like a useful (and so far undeveloped) tool.

9. ROLE SUPPORTS FOR THE SUPERINTENDENT   Unleashing some innovative thought on the question of "The Superintendency: an Unworkable Role" might turn up new ways of using other administrators (and teachers) in work with the board; the creation of a grant-getting role; and the development of a panel of school system speakers for community groups.

10. CONFLICT MANAGEMENT EDUCATION   Adaptation of methods already in use by National Training Laboratories for increasing awareness of and skill in conflict-handling would undoubtedly be helpful.

11. INTERROLE AND INTERGROUP CONFRONTATION MECHANISMS   We need schemes which will permit distantiated and conflicting roles (central office people and principals; elementary and junior high faculties) to engage each other in mutually profitable confrontation and work. Or how about the parents from one district coming to the principals of another district to explore "what principals and parents do to each other?"

12. ENVIRONMENTAL SCANNING ROLES   There could be explicit roles in school systems devoted to scanning certain aspects of the environment (*e.g.,* U.S. Office of Education programs; new developments in behavioral science; the local political structure and climate; State Education Department developments) and to feeding the resulting information to appropriate groups and roles within the system.

13. BOARD DEVELOPMENT MECHANISMS   Why not coopt and professionalize boards of education even more than now happens? Team development work sessions; the use of data collection, process analysis and feedback; and the redesign of public meetings are all possible, as is anything, in principle.

In practice, schools are less innovative than many people think they could be. The crucial issue underlying this paper is: do we understand the essential properties of schools well enough to start improvement programs that have a reasonable chance of becoming self-operative and self-developmental? That remains to be seen.

BIBLIOGRAPHY

BECKER, H. S., 1952, "The Career of the Chicago Public Schoolteacher," *American Journal of Sociology, 57,* pp. 470–477.

BIDDLE, B., AND H. A. ROSENCRANZ, 1964, "The Role Approach to Teacher Competence," *Contemporary Research on Teacher Effectiveness,* B. J. Biddle and W. J. Ellena, eds., New York: Holt, Rinehart and Winston, pp. 232–263.

BUCHANAN, P., "Innovation in Education," *FGSE Newsletter, 4* (3), Ferkauf Graduate School of Education, Yeshiva University, pp. 2, 5.

CAMPBELL, R. T., 1958, "What Peculiarities in Educational Administration Make It a Special Case?" *Administrative Theory in Education,* A. W. Halpin, ed., Chicago: Midwest Administration Center, University of Chicago Press, pp. 166–186.

COLEMAN, J. S., 1961, *The Adolescent Society,* New York: The Free Press.

FISCHER, J., 1964, "Changes in American Education in the Next Decade: Some Predictions," *Innovation in Education,* M. B. Miles, ed., New York: Teachers College Press, pp. 622–625.

FLANDERS, N. A., 1960, *Teacher Influence, Pupil Attitudes and Achievement,* Minneapolis: University of Minnesota, USOE Coop. Res. Project No. 397.

FRIEDENBERG, E. Z., 1965, *Coming of Age in America,* New York: Random House.

GOODMAN, P., 1964, *Compulsory Mis-Education,* New York: Horizon Press.

HARMIN, M., AND S. SIMON, 1965, "The Year the Schools Began Teaching the Telephone Directory," *Harvard Educational Review, 35* (3), pp. 326–331.

KERR, N. D., 1964, "The School Board as an Agency of Legitimation," *Sociology of Education, 38* (1). Also available as Bureau of Applied Social Research Reprint No. 404.

LIKERT, R., 1961, *New Patterns of Management,* New York: McGraw-Hill.

LIPPITT, P., AND J. F. LOHMAN, 1965, "Cross-Age Relationships—An Educational Resource," *Children, 12* (3), Children's Bureau, Department of Health, Education and Welfare.

LIPPITT, R., mimeographed, 1965, "Improving the Socialization Process," *Socialization and Society,* Chapter 7, forthcoming.

LORTIE, D. C., 1961, "Craftsmen and Colleagueship: A Frame for the Investigation of Work Values among Public School Teachers." Paper read at ASA meetings.

MILES, M. B., ed., 1964, *Innovation in Education,* New York: Teachers College Press.

MUUSS, R. E., 1960, "The Relationship between 'Causal' Orientation, Anxiety, and Insecurity in Elementary School Children," *Journal of Educational Psychology, 51,* pp. 122–129.

PARSONS, T., 1959, "The School Class as a Social System: Some of Its Functions in American Society," *Harvard Educational Review, 29,* pp. 297–318.

THELEN, H. A., 1961, *Teachability Grouping.* Chicago: Department of Education, University of Chicago, USOE Coop. Res. Project No. 428.

WAYLAND, S. R., 1962, "The Teacher as Decision-Maker," *Curriculum Crossroads,* A. H. Passow, ed., New York: Teachers College Press, pp. 41–52.

WAYLAND, S. R., 1964, "Structural Features of American Education as Basic Factors in Innovation," *Innovation in Education,* M. B. Miles, ed., New York: Teachers College Press, pp. 587–613.

Questions and Implications For Practice

3.1 WILLARD WALLER

1. Do you agree that a school or college must *necessarily* be organized on *some variant of* the autocratic principle? If you agree, then what options does the counselor (the guidance-personnel worker) have in relation to this system?

   a. Can he be in, but operate apart from, the system?
   b. Should he, as a matter of principle, seek to destroy the system?
   c. Should he be openly "on the side of the students?"
   d. Should he aim to be passive, neutral, and permissive in relation to the system, and hope to "get away with it?"
   e. Should he attempt to contribute to the communication and understanding between executives and teachers and thus diminish the autocracy?
   f. Can he "improve" the situation by which the system operates and enhance its educational benefits for the students by facilitating continuous interaction and feedback from students to administrators, administrators to students, students to teachers, teachers to students, and students to students, etc.?
   g. Should he try to encourage extracurricular activities within which students can have more freedom?

2. Can you give instances of how students have seriously disturbed, or even destroyed a school or university?

3. Do you know of cases in which protest and conflict have had constructive results?

4. Discuss the place the guidance-personnel worker occupies, or should occupy, in the schema of reciprocal relationships that Waller presents. Should the guidance-personnel worker have a special place in this schema to represent his relationships? Would his relationships be to students only, and to individual students only? Or might guidance-personnel workers, if there had been more of them when Waller wrote his book 30 years ago, have been given multilateral relationships in his schema?

5. Are there any implications in Waller's writings that guidance-personnel workers should have knowledge of group development and the skills of small conference method?

6. Can ceremonials, ritual, and tradition be used to increase feelings of social unity within a social system to the end that autocracy (and despotism) are diminished? If so, how? Might it be well for the guidance-personnel worker to understand something of these dynamics, or are they in no way within his area of concern?

7. Can—should—a guidance-personnel worker help students understand and cope with their feelings of hostility that naturally tend to arise in a meshwork of authoritarian relationships, and thus perhaps dissipate their hostile feelings?

8. Is it desirable for students to learn to understand and accept authority? What are some of the ways in which this can be done that are apt to have undesirable outcomes or that may positively improve the insights, strengths, and the mental health of all concerned?

3.2   C. WAYNE GORDON

1. What are the relative advantages and disadvantages for the effectiveness of work of (a) the counselor and the director of guidance in the elementary school or the high school, or (b) a personnel worker in a college (be specific as to the kind of personnel worker) who attempts to rely on personalized leadership to develop and maintain a role for himself in the school or college in which he works? Many of those who write concerning the role of the counselor maintain that the counselor must rely on personalized leadership if he is to "help" his "client." However, such writers frequently are not writing for counselors in school or college settings. Also, in considering the extent to which the guidance-personnel worker can rely on personalized leadership, students cannot accurately be described as "clients." How do the roles and statuses that students occupy differ from those of a "client?"

2. In what ways does the situation of a guidance-personnel worker differ from that of the teacher which Gordon describes? What advantages and what disadvantages might this guidance-personnel worker find in *not* attempting to evade the responsibility of membership in the authority system?

3. Does the guidance-personnel worker find it helpful to understand the status system within which students find themselves required to operate? Can you think of any advantages he might find in trying to remain aloof or in deliberately adopting and maintaining an attitude of naivete toward the schoolwide social system and the student system in particular?

4. Can a counselor who understands the status system of the students communicate with students more meaningfully? Or is it, perhaps, enough for the counselor to be highly sophisticated in personality theory?

5. Where a counselor or other guidance-personnel worker fails the failure is often ascribed to personality weaknesses. Could a counselor or other guidance-personnel worker fail because he did not understand the reality of the social structure in which he was attempting to work?

6. What research methods might one use to make more explicit the goals and values that always exist implicitly in the formal organization of a given school? How might one attempt to get at the goals and values that inhere in the extracurricular program as a whole, or in specific parts of it? Could the same methods be used to study the common expectations and values that inhere in and influence the patterning and operation of interpersonal relationships in a class in a school, for instance, or in a residence hall in a college, or in an in-group of teachers? Be specific.

3.3   JAMES S. COLEMAN

1. Coleman vividly describes the way the student society distributes status thereby affecting the aspirations and decisions of students. How might the counseling of a skilled counselor have some effect on the student society's norms and rewards?

2. What are the implications in the situation which Coleman sets forth for the role of the guidance-personnel worker who wishes to influence beneficially the aspirations and decisions of a maximum number of students?

3. Can groups of students and their leaders be helped to examine the way status is being distributed in the student society? Might this perhaps result indirectly in modifying the goals and aspirations of more students than can now be reached effectively by individual counseling?

4. If the guidance-personnel worker were to help student groups understand their status systems, what sort of knowledge and skills would he have to have?

3.4   CICOUREL AND KITSUSE

1. Discuss pro and con the ideal set forth by Cicourel and Kitsuse that "the rates of certain social phenomena are to be accounted for as characteristics, not of individuals, but of the social and cultural organization of the groups, communities, and societies with which they are regularly associated."

Does this concept agree with the "principles" found in most guidance-personnel text books? What basic principles and beliefs does it seem to contradict?

2. If rates of certain social phenomena are not to be accounted for as characteristics of individuals, what happens to our concepts of free will, individual responsibility, and the importance of individual counseling?

3. Do you agree that clinical labels, as Cicourel and Kitsuse suggest, may powerfully affect the attitudes formed toward a student, as well as that student's evaluation of himself, and so powerfully determine his life? Why or why not?

4. Is there convincing evidence in this study that the counselor's view of the appropriateness of a boy's or girl's objectives will be the factor that decides whether or not he or she will get a chance to try for them?

5. Are the general hypotheses and conclusions of this study substantially those that the minority groups in our society are voicing ever more articulately?

6. What implications for counselors and teachers do you see in the study? Or would you prefer to discount the study, perhaps on the basis that Cicourel and Kitsuse are prejudiced against counselors? In all fairness, can you do this?

7. Should guidance-personnel workers and teachers be more concerned than many are with the characteristics of the social and cultural organizations of which both they and students are members?

8. "Although they did not realize it, Lakeshore High to the counselors is very much like a factory. The role of the counselors essentially is to classify the raw

material and get it on the proper conveying belts. Certainly Lakeshore High is not seen as a society in which teachers and students, teachers and teachers, teachers and administrators, and students and students, etc., are endlessly interacting in a myriad of ways as a result of which attitudes are made manifest, and are confirmed or modified." Criticize this statement and, using the models set forth in Chapter 1, try to write a better one of the way the Lakeshore counselors unconsciously perceive the institution in which they carry out their roles.

3.5   MERVIN B. FREEDMAN

1. Do you agree that "the scholastic and academic aims and processes of the college are in large measure transmitted to incoming students or mediated for them by the predominant student culture?" How does this influence the guidance-personnel worker (in elementary school, in secondary school, or in college) who wants to help each student progressively to develop his own academic purposes? What, for instance, might this mean for the child-guidance consultant in his concerns for elementary school children who come from homes that are impoverished economically and socially? How must it be taken into account by a secondary school guidance-personnel worker who is committed to helping each student develop all of his abilities through the use of school resources? By the assistant dean who is in charge of the orientation program?

2. How can the guidance-personnel worker increase his competence to understand the "predominant student culture?"

3. How are new students assimilated into the society of a particular school or college, or a home-room or student club or fraternity? Cultural anthropology suggests more studies of this sort.

4. What chance do you think a counselor, who believes everyone should have an occupation, has of changing the ideas of girls whose career goals are feeble? Which will have more influence on the girl's motivation and planning: the values of the peer culture or the values of the counselor? How much effect do you think the expectations of the girl's family will have on the girl's planning for her future?

5. In adolescence, when boys and girls are trying to become more independent of adults, is it likely, as Freedman suggests, that faculty members and counselors do not have any central or dramatic importance in students' lives? What, then, can the guidance-personnel worker do if he wishes to enhance the value of the education experiences of young people and wishes to help them make informed and wise decisions?

6. Does the peer culture in the school or college you know best help students deal with complex social situations in the school or college, educate them to deal successfully with social problems after graduation, and also help some of them who especially need such help to maintain stable personalities and emotional life while in the school or college?

7. How important is the peer culture in determining the mental health of students? Is it more important for guidance-personnel workers to help individual

students understand the effect of the peer culture on them as individuals, or to attempt to work with students in groups to help them learn how to assess the culture, of which they all are a part, and to change it in desirable directions?

8. Who is to determine what "desirable" directions would be? Or this question might perhaps better be asked: "By what process or processes may it be possible to ascertain what 'desirable' directions would be?"

3.6 BECKER AND GEER

Research is revealing ways of getting at an understanding of "student culture." Such studies as those of Martin Trow, Robert Pace, and George Stern have thrown light on the ingredients of student culture and the wide variations that exist among institutions. Margaret Berry at the University of Texas has attempted to get at the components of student culture in that institution by comparing the themes followed by student editors in the student publications of that institution over a period of 50 years. The Educational Testing Service of Princeton, New Jersey, has set up a division that will attempt to help institutions study the characteristics of their own cultures.

1. How important is it for a guidance-personnel worker to know how to study the student culture of the institution in which he works? Do you agree with Becker and Geer that the student culture gives the students a way to accommodate to the difficulties of their school? Does the student culture also redirect the efforts of the students? If you agree that this is so, then should a guidance-personnel worker know how to assess the operation of the student culture in relation to its student members?

2. How can he learn how to do this? Many professors who are developing the curriculum for the preparation of student guidance-personnel workers presently believe that the heart of training should consist of practicum training in the face-to-face counseling of individuals. This involves many hours spent closeted with one other individual in a relationship, characteristics of which are being spelled out in more and more detail. When one considers that the verbal exchange that takes place in this dyadic relationship is tape-recorded, transcribed, and then studied and criticized in detail, it leaves little time in the typical program of professional training to learn how to assess and work with students in the understanding and modifying of their student culture. And yet it can be conceded that the norms that lie at the heart of social systems powerfully influence the norms and aspirations of students, that the culture of an elementary school, high school or a college tends to be perpetuated and transmitted unchanged from one student generation to another, and that it is the student culture that students tend to rely on to help them accommodate to the difficulties of a school or college. Therefore, it seems that at present the emphasis in preparing a guidance-personnel worker is too one-sided.

3. Examine programs designed to prepare guidance-personnel workers for elementary or secondary school, junior colleges, colleges, or adult education. Do

these programs provide the understanding that might well come from the social cultural sciences? How might they be improved?

3.7 MATTHEW B. MILES

1. To what extent does Miles demonstrate a constellational rather than a linear way of thinking as he attempts to analyze schools as social systems?

2. Note the way he looks at aspects of the system from the points of view of the various groups involved and elaborate further on his descriptions of various destructive features and problems of the school as these are viewed by (a) the students; (b) teachers; (c) parents; (d) tax payers; (e) top management; and (f) guidance-personnel workers in the system.

Chapter 4

The School in the Community and Society

In the previous chapter we examined educational institutions in America from the point of view of the school or college as a self-contained social system. Implicit in all the discussions, however, was the fact that schools and colleges are not isolated but are themselves part of the larger system of American society. To an important extent, in other words, the goals and activities of a school or a college derive both their content and their significance from the institution's relationships to factors outside the individual organization. The selections in this chapter explore a few of these relationships to the outside world.

In examining schools and colleges from the outside, we can assume a number of different perspectives, since there are many larger systems to which educational institutions can be considered to belong and to whose purposes their activities are relevant. From the viewpoint of society at large, schools and colleges are instruments for accomplishing tasks which are considered socially essential. The continuity and stability of the society require that new members learn its culture and acquire the knowledge and skills that will enable them to play useful social roles as adults, and it is this broad function which we call "education." Because of the basic and crucial nature of this societal requirement, it is to be expected that there should be intense and widespread concern about educational results and, indirectly but inevitably, about the means used to achieve them. Given the size and diversity of our society and the breadth and complexity of what constitutes its culture, however, such concern does not have a single voice. Indeed, there are as many viewpoints about what education should accomplish, and how, as there are identifiable points on the many dimensions in terms of which the society can be viewed—political, economic, religious, philosophic, ethnic.

Education, in other words, is not a clear and unambiguous goal. People differ widely and vigorously both about what it should be and about the means for achieving it. Moreover, every individual and every group has some stake in the promotion of certain social values and practices and in the eradication of others. Since education is viewed as the natural instrument for inculcation and training, schools and colleges become the foci, or targets, for all the interests, concerns, and conflicts within and among diverse segments of the society. Stated more generally, whatever trends and forces are operative in the external environment of the educational organization will somehow be reflected in pressures for the latter to modify its activities. At any point in time and in any particular place, the content of education will thus reflect the social structure and the culture in which it is set, while it also responds (and contributes) to conflicts and changes in that environment. Viewed over time and across wide distances, American education reflects both the constancies and variations of American society: there are the dominant cultural themes, the variations in form and emphasis attributable to different regions or subcultures, and the shifts due to gradual social change or to sudden responses to major national or world developments.

If we were to compare elementary and secondary school curricula across the country between 1955 and 1965, for example, we would probably find a significant increase in emphasis on the natural sciences. Tracing the timing of the changes more precisely, we would probably be able to date them as following upon the Russian launching of Sputnik in 1957. It would undoubtedly be possible to find many other changes and innovations in many aspects of education dating from the same period—changes in college entrance requirements, changes in the content of standardized examinations, increases in the number of research grants awarded to academies in the natural sciences, increases in the number of laboratories built in schools and colleges as compared to other facilities. We are suggesting that these changes are both the indirect reflection and the deliberately brought about result of the alarm that shook Americans in 1957. The widespread response throughout the society was a resolve to strengthen its ability to compete successfully with the Russians, and the heightened emphasis on scientific education was one of the steps considered to be necessary.

This was a rather dramatic incident, and most changes in education are not directly attributable to such single and sudden events. Over the last 30 or 40 years there have been many changes in curricula, course content, and organization at all levels of education, reflecting, to cite but a few examples, the increased awareness and involvement with the rest of the world, altered values about what schools and colleges should teach, the growth and acceptance of psychology and social science as significant disciplines, and, especially during the last decade, increasing public demand for and concern with guidance services.

In addition to changes over time, there are also geographic and subcultural variations, which result from differences in the values and concerns of different segments of the population. Such variations might be different emphases or interpretations, say, in the teaching of American history in the South than in the North. Or they may be differences in the nature of courses given to girls and boys separately (homemaking, carpentry, health and hygiene, "family living," etc.) between rural and urban areas or between the East and the Midwest, reflecting the general patterns and judgments with respect to sex-role differentiation dominant in the local population. Or they may be differences in the goals the community perceives as most important for guidance programs in the schools—getting children into college, or reducing the number of dropouts, or relieving emotional problems, or vocational counseling. Such variations reflect the distinctive features of the immediate social and cultural environments and also contribute to the perpetuation of these differences. It is important to keep in mind that the relationship between education and its social environment is not one-way and each is both source and consequence of the other.

Over and above changes and variations, however, the content of education and the behavior of those involved in it would show many uniformities across time and space, reflecting basic and enduring themes in American culture. The competition inherent in the grading system, the relatively free and democratic relationship between teachers and students, the strong pressures against any form of unfairness or favoritism in dealing with others—these and many other phenomena would be readily apparent if we were to examine the behavior of those involved in education. Such patterns are so basic to our culture that they go unnoticed, but the contrasts would emerge sharply if we were to analyze comparable situations and activities in other countries.

The processes by which education is affected by its social context are many and varied, and occur at several levels. As we have suggested, because education is a matter of widespread public concern, it is subject to pressures stemming from the society and will reflect the particular state of quiet, change, or conflict that prevails. Because education involves individuals who are also a part of other systems in the society, they are the carriers of the influences that give education its shape and content by introducing into the educational organization those norms which generally guide their behavior. Thus, the manner in which they carry out their educational roles and the specific objectives they promote and pursue as their interpretation of education are at least broadly directed and limited by the major cultural norms. Similarly, individual members of an educational institution are caught up in the social, political, philosophical, and technological trends and changes which occur in the society at large and they tend to exert pressure, directly and indirectly, for educational practices and content to respond to those developments which they endorse. Less widespread values and regional or temporal variations on the dominant themes are introduced in much the same manner, as individuals bring to their educational roles the effects wrought upon them by all the events in their life and environment.

Stated differently, what individuals "are," and thus the manner in which they participate as members of a school or college system, is a product of the sum total of their current and past experiences and relationships. Every individual is a member of many systems, and at least partially subscribes to the goals and values of each of them. To the extent that this range of values becomes his own, what motivates him in his behavior in the context of one system will carry over into his performance of other roles. In this manner, general norms, specific objectives, or concrete practices of one system may come to be reflected in the activities of another system. Moreover, individuals do more than internalize the values of the groups and organizations with which they are affiliated. All social systems require, as a basic condition for their survival, some degree of loyalty on the part of their members. For groups, families, organizations, and societies to endure, their members must not only conform to the appropriate norms but they must also be committed to making the system continue and to pursuing its goals. Such commitments are more or less explicit depending on the system involved, but for any system to persist its members must to some extent see its interests as their own and direct their actions accordingly.

We have been speaking very generally, but the issues are even clearer when viewed in more concrete terms. When we say an individual is a member of many systems, we mean to denote a wide range of possibilities: his family, his circle of friends, his club, other organizations with which he is affiliated, the system constituted by him and his wife, by him and one particular friend, by him and one working associate, his profession, his business firm, his church, his political party, his ethnic group. Each of these systems may define meaningful roles for a single individual and impose requirements which he feels a strong obligation to fulfill. To a large extent, an individual's life is so organized that his multiple affiliations do not exert conflicting pressures, and he can thus derive satisfaction from his actions while remaining a "member in good standing" in many systems. But it is often the case that an individual will be committed to two or more groups or organizations whose goals are incompatible, or who at least put pressure on him to act in ways that are necessary from the viewpoint of one of them and detrimental from that of another. The norms of a student's peer group, for example, may conflict with those of the school and with those of the student's family. Such conflicts may be overt or they may be subtle and mostly unconscious. The opposing pressures may be very one-sided, making the resolution of the conflict rather clear-cut, but they may be virtually equal, making the individual's conflict more acute, and acceptable but satisfying resolutions less readily accomplished.

In considering the specific content of the relationships between an educational institution and its environment, it is easy to see that those with the immediate community are likely to be particularly significant in affecting behavior within the organization. The students of elementary and secondary schools and of certain types of colleges live in the community, and the institution is thus directly responsible to local families as a provider of the public service of education. Whether it be only a few members of the faculty or the entire student body, schools and colleges bring people from out of town to live in the community and thus provide additional consumers for the goods and services sold by local businessmen. Members of the educational organization are likely to share other affiliations, activities, and responsibilities within the limits of the community, and thus their formal relationships are likely to be heavily interwoven with informal expectations, loyalties, and conflicts that are directly related to the community's social, economic, and political structure.

The interdependence between education and society, between the school and its community, is, in sum, fundamental, thorough, and complex. There is the fact that education is carried out by people whose needs, values, purposes, attitudes, and habits are derived from their multiple statuses and relationships in the society at large and in their immediate community. In addition, because of its important function for the society, education is the continuing object of public attention and concern and its content is shaped and modified by the impact of social, economic, and political pressures at all levels. Finally, and because of its basic role as the transmitter of culture, education reflects the dominant needs, moods, and orientations of the society as it also both reinforces and modifies them.

4.1   INTRODUCTION

With the breadth of perspective characteristic of the anthropologist, the author of this article looks to American culture as a whole for both the sources and the particular nature of the controversy that has centered on education in our society. There he finds two contrary sets of basic values which he believes account for two major opposing outlooks on education. He calls one set "traditional" and the other "emergent" and sees our culture as in the process of shifting away from the former toward the latter. Because the change is incomplete, however, both value systems still exert their pull within single situations and even single individuals, and much of the stress, dissension, and inconsistency which has become increasingly evident can be understood in terms of the particular effects of this ambivalence in education.

In describing the content of the two sets of values and identifying various educational roles with particular positions between the traditional and emergent extremes, Spindler suggests a number of issues that are of central relevance to a guidance counselor's concerns, objectives, and behavior. Most basically, what effect is the counselor's own value position likely to have on his reactions to those with whom he interacts? Will his professional perceptions and judgments, as well as his sympathy and understanding, of two students be different depending on where their respective values fall in relation to his? If, for example, the guidance counselor's values are primarily emergent (as Spindler defines this type), is he as likely to look to the student who generally goes along with the group for symptoms of "problems" as to the loner who pursues his own interests in his own style? How strongly is the guidance counselor committed to emergent values as part of his professional self-image, as Spindler suggests most educators are? What are likely to be the consequences of such commitment for his relationships with more traditionally oriented others (some parents, older teachers, students from certain ethnic groups, etc.)? Will they perceive him as understanding their needs and aspirations or as trying to impose his alien preferences? Will he be free not only to recognize or understand the former but also to consider them valid?

4.1   EDUCATION IN A TRANSFORMING AMERICAN CULTURE[1]

George D. Spindler

The American public school system, and the professional educators who operate it, have been subjected to increasingly strident attacks from the public and from within its own ranks. My premise is that these attacks can best be understood as symptoms of an American culture that is undergoing transformation—a transformation that produces serious conflict. I shall discuss this transformation as a problem in culture change that directly affects all of education and everyone identified with it.

The notion of social and cultural change is used persuasively, if carelessly, by too many writers to explain too much. Generalized allusions to technological change, cultural lag, the atomic age, the mass society, are more suggestive than clarifying. We must strike to the core of the change. My argument is that this core can best be conceived as a radical shift in values. . . .

The statements to be made now about American values, their shift, and the effect on education, are based upon the varying responses of different age groups in the sample,[2] upon person-to-person variation in responses, and upon variations in response and particularly contradictions of response within single individual protocols (the total set of responses for a single individual). On the basis of these

---

[1]From George D. Spindler, "Education in a Transforming American Culture," *Education and Culture*, George D. Spindler, ed., New York: Holt, Rinehart and Winston, 1963, pp. 132–133, 136–147. Reprinted, with revision, from *The Harvard Educational Review*, XXV, 1955, 145–156, with permission. Copyright©1955 by President and Fellows of Harvard College.

[2][Editor's note: The reference is to the study on which the ensuing discussion is based, whose aim the author describes earlier as that of finding out "what features of social character (. . .those personality elements that are most relevant to social action)" are held "as being valuable." The subjects of the study were "several hundred students, ranging in age from 19 to 57 years, mainly participants in professional education courses, and representing socioeconomic strata describable as lower-middle to upper-middle class."]

kinds of data, in the context of wider observations on institutions and culture patterns in the United States, it appears that a major shift in American values is taking place.[3] I find it convenient to label this shift as being from *traditional* to *emergent*, though no basic cultural change of this kind is actually linear. The values thus dichotomized are listed under their respective headings. . .[in the table below], with explanatory statements in parentheses.

American culture seems to be undergoing a confused transformation, producing many disjunctions and conflicts, from the traditional to the emergent value systems

Traditional Values	Emergent Values
Puritan morality	*Sociability*
(Respectability, thrift, self-denial, sexual constraint; a puritan is someone who can have anything he wants, as long as he doesn't enjoy it!)	(As described above. One should like people and get along well with them. Suspicion of solitary activities is characteristic.)
Work-Success ethic	*Relativistic moral attitude*
(Successful people worked hard to become so. Anyone can get to the top if he tries hard enough. So people who are not successful are lazy, or stupid, or both. People must work desperately and continuously to convince themselves of their worth.)	(Absolutes in right and wrong are questionable. Morality is what the group thinks is right. Shame, rather than guilt is appropriate.)
Individualism	*Consideration for others*
(The individual is sacred, and always more important than the group. In one extreme form, the value sanctions egocentricity, expediency, and disregard for other people's rights. In its healthier form the value sanctions independence and originality.)	(Everything one does should be done with regard for others and their feelings. The individual has a built-in radar that alerts him to others' feelings. Tolerance for the other person's point of view and behaviors is regarded as desirable, so long as the harmony of the group is not disrupted.)
Achievement orientation	*Hedonistic, present-time orientation*
(Success is a constant goal. There is no resting on past glories. If one makes $9,000 this year he must make $10,000 next year. Coupled with the work-success ethic, this value keeps people moving, and tense.)	(No one can tell what the future will hold, therefore one should enjoy the present—but within the limits of the well-rounded, balanced personality and group.)
Future-time orientation	*Conformity to the group*
(The future, not the past, or even the present, is most important. Time is valuable, and cannot be wasted. Present needs must be denied for satisfactions to be gained in the future.)	(Implied in the other emergent values. Everything is relative to the group. Group harmony is the ultimate goal. Leadership consists of group-machinery lubrication.)

[3] In my formulation of value trends and the interpretation of my data I have been particularly influenced by the writings of David Riesman.

outlined above. It is probable that both value systems have been present and operating in American culture for some time. But recently, and under the impetus of World Wars, the pressures exerted by the "radical right" and the "radical left," the external communist threat, atomic insecurities, and a past history of "boom and bust," the tendencies in the emergent direction have gathered strength and appear to be on the way towards becoming the dominant value system of American culture. At the same time, there is a minority resurgence of extreme versions of the traditional values as some people reaffirm allegiance to them as a reaction to the threat of rapid culture change.

Like all major shifts and schisms in culture, this one has consequences for people. Culturally transitional populations, as anthropologists know from their studies of acculturating Indian tribes, Hindu villages, and Samoan communities (among others), are characterized by conflict, and in most severe form—demoralization and disorganization. Institutions and people are in a state of flux. Contradictory views of life are held by different groups and persons within the society. Hostilities are displaced, attacks are made on one group by another. And this applies as well to the condition of American culture—the context of American education.

The traditionalist may view the emergentist as "socialistic," "communistic," "spineless and soft-headed," or "downright immoral." The emergentist may regard the traditionalist as "hidebound," "reactionary," "selfish," or "authoritarian."[4] Most of what representatives of either viewpoint do may be regarded as insidious and destructive from the point of view of the other. The conflict goes beyond groups or institutions, because individuals in our transitional society are likely to hold elements of both value systems concomitantly. This is characteristic, as a matter of fact, of most students included in the sample described previously. There are few "pure" types. The social character of most is split, calling for different responses in different situations, and with respect to different symbols. So an ingredient of personal confusion is added that intensifies social and institutional conflict.

I hypothesize that the attacks upon education, which were our starting point, and the confusion and failure of nerve characterizing many educators today, can be seen in clear and helpful perspective in the light of the conflict of traditional and emergent values, and particularly in the extremes of both forms that have been described. It is the heart of the matter. The task then becomes one of placing groups, institutions, and persons on a continuum of transformation from the one value system to the other. A simple diagram will aid comprehension of what is meant.

The diagram conveys the information that different groups operating in the context of relations between school and community, educator and public, occupy

---

[4]Irrespective of this kind of name-calling, the dichotomy of values employed in this analysis is not the same as "conservative" and "liberal" or politically "left" and "right." It is certainly very probable, for example, that some political liberals are traditionalists in respect to core cultural values.

different positions on the value continuum, with varying degrees and mixtures of traditional and emergent orientations. It should be understood that the placements indicate hypothecated tendencies, that no one group representing any particular institution ever consists of "pure" value types, but that there is probably a modal tendency for the groups indicated to place on the transformation, or continuum line, in the way expressed in the diagram.

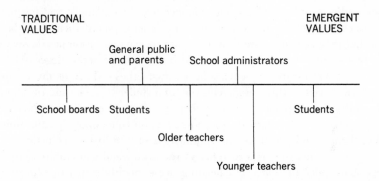

FIGURE 1.

School boards are placed nearest the *traditional* end of the continuum because such boards are usually composed of persons representing the power, *status-quo*, elements of the community, and of persons in the higher age ranges. They are therefore people who have a stake in keeping things as they are, who gained their successes within the framework of the traditional value system and consequently believe it to be good, and who, by virtue of their age, grew up and acquired their value sets during a period of time when American culture was presumably more tradition-oriented than it is today. They may be driven to extreme forms of traditionalism as a response to the pressures mentioned previously.

The general public and parent group, of course, contains many elements of varying value predilection. It is therefore unrealistic to place this public at any particular point in the value continuum. But I hypothesize that the public *tends* to be more conservative in its social philosophy than professional educators are. The placement to the left of center of the continuum takes on further validity if it is seen as a placement of that part of the public that is most vocal in its criticism of educators and education—since many of the criticisms made appear to spring out of value conflicts between traditionalist and emergentist positions. Parents complain that their children are not being taught the "three R's" (even when they are), that educators want to "socialize" the competitive system by eliminating report cards, that children are not taught the meaning of hard work. These all sound, irrespective of the question of their justification or lack of it, like traditionalist responses to change in an "emergent" direction.

Students are placed at two points on the transformation line because it is clear that those coming from traditionalist family environments will tend to hold traditionalistic values, but hold them less securely than will their parents (if our hypothesis for overall change is¹ valid), while other students who come from emergent-oriented families will tend to place even further, as a function of their age and peer groups, towards the emergent end of the line than their parents would. This is only partially true, indeed, for such a rationale does not account for the fact that offspring in revolt (and many American children from 6 to 16 are in a state of revolt against parental dictums) may go to extremes in either direction.

School administrators, older, and younger teachers, place at varying points on the emergent half of the transformation line. I have placed them there because I believe that the professional education culture (every institution has its own way of life, in this sense) that they have acquired in the schools and colleges of education has a clear bias towards an emergent-oriented ethos. Many of my educationist collegues will reject this interpretation, and indeed, such interpretations are always guilty of overgeneralization. Others will welcome such a characterization, but still question its validity. My case must rest on contemporary educational philosophy, theory, and practice. The emphasis is on the "social adjustment" of the individual, upon his role as a member of the group and community. Most of the values listed under the *emergent* heading are explicitly stated in educational literature as goals. Some of them, such as conformity to the group, are implicit. This value, in particular, grows out of the others, is more or less unintended, and constitutes a *covert* or *latent* value, by definition. This is, admittedly, a little like accusing a man of hating his mother, but not knowing it, and such accusations are usually rejected, or rationalized out of existence. But I believe that it is literally impossible to hold the other values in this system and avoid placing a strong emphasis on group harmony, and group control of the individual. My data, at least, gathered largely from students in professional education courses, indicate that this is the case.

But educators and schools do not all come off the same shelf in the supermarket. Older teachers will tend, I hypothesize, to hold relatively traditionalist views by virtue of their age, and time of their childhood training (when they acquired their basic values)—a period in American culture when the traditionalist values were relatively more certain and supported than they are at present. Younger teachers were not only children and acquired their personal culture during a relatively more emergent-oriented period of American history, but they have been (I hypothesize) exposed to a professional education culture that has become emergent-oriented in its value position. They are therefore placed near the extreme of the transformation line in the emergent direction.

School administrators came from a different shelf in the same section of the supermarket. They, to be sure, range in age from young to old, come from different family backgrounds, and have been exposed in varying degrees to the professional education culture. But sociological and anthropological studies of the influence of status and role on behavior and perception indicate that these factors tend to override others, and produce certain uniformities of outlook. The school administrator's role is a precarious one—as any school principal or superintendent knows.

He faces towards several different audiences, each with different sets of demands—school boards, parents, power groups, teachers, and students—as well as other administrators. He has to play his role appropriately in the light of all these demands. The fact that many cannot, accounts for the increasingly short tenure of personages like school superintendents. But to the extent that he plays *across the board* he will place somewhere towards the center of the line of transformation. Furthermore, his dependence upon the school board, and the power groups in the community, in many cases will tend to make his outlook relatively more conservative, and probably more traditionalistic, than that of his teachers—at least the younger ones. There are many exceptions, of course. I am only claiming *tendencies*.

My thesis, I hope, is clear by now. I am attempting to explain, or help explain, the increasingly bitter and strident attacks on schools and educators, and the conflict and confusion within the ranks. I have claimed that this situation can better be understood in the context of conflicts in core values. And I have tried to show the direction of the values shift in American culture and place the various actors in the drama upon a transformation line within this shift.

In this perspective, many conflicts between parents and teachers, school boards and educators, parents and children, and between the various personages and groups within the school system (teachers against teachers, administrators against teachers, and so on) can be understood as conflicts that grow out of sharp differences in values that mirror social and cultural transformation of tremendous scope—and for which none of the actors in the situation can be held personally accountable. This is the real, and perhaps only contribution of this analysis. If these conflicts can be seen as emerging out of great sociocultural shifts—out of a veritable transformation of a way of life—they will lose some of their sting. To understand, the psychiatrist says, is to forgive.

But now, though it seems indeed improper at this point, permit me to add another complication to an already complicated picture. I have tried to make it clear that not only are there variations in values held by groups and different parts of the social body and school institutions, but that there are also various values, some of them contradictory, held by single individuals as diverse streams of influence in their own systems. This is always true in rapid culture-change situations, as the anthropologist and philosopher know.

This means that the situation is not only confused by groups battling each other, but that individuals are fighting themselves. This has certain predictable results, if the anthropological studies of personal adaptation to culture change have any validity. And I believe that those results can be detected in the behaviors of most, if not all, of the actors in the scene. Let me try to clarify this.

I will deal only with teachers, as one of the most important sets of actors on this particular stage. I hypothesize that the child training of most of the people who become teachers has been more tradition than emergent value-oriented. They are drawn largely from middle to lower-middle social class groups in American society, and this segment of the class structure is the stronghold of the work-success ethic and moral respectability values in our culture (even in a culture that is shifting away from these values). Furthermore, it seems probable that a selective process is operating to draw a relatively puritanistic element into the public school teaching as an occupation. Self-denial, altruism, a moralistic self-concept, seem to be functional prerequisites for the historically-derived role of school teacher in American society (I might have said "school-marm").

If this can be granted, then only one other ingredient needs to be added to explain several persistent types of personal adaptation to value conflicts observable among school teachers. That ingredient is one already spelled out—the relatively heavy emphasis, within the professional education culture, on the emergent-oriented value system. Teachers-to-be acquire their personal culture in a more tradition-oriented family environment, but they encounter a new kind of culture when in training to become school teachers—in the teacher-training institutions. This is a particular kind of culture-conflict situation that anthropologists have recently begun to study, but mostly in non-Western societies undergoing acculturation under the impact of the western way of life.[5] . . .

In conclusion to this incomplete analysis, let me make it clear that I am not attacking either the emergentists, or the traditionalists. Value systems must always be functional in terms of the demands of the social and economic structure of a people. The traditional mode has been functional in our society, and there is a staunchness, and a vitality in it that many of us view with considerable nostalgia. But rugged individualism (in its expedient, ego-centered form), and rigid moralism (with its capacity for displaced hate) become dysfunctional in a society where people are rubbing shoulders in polyglot masses, and playing with a technology that may destroy everything with a pushing of buttons. The emergentist position seems to be growing in strength. Social adaptability, relativistic outlooks, sensitivity to the needs and opinions of others, and of the group, seem functional in this new age. We need, as citizens, educators, anthropologists, and parents, to examine our premises more closely. The emergentist can become a group conformist—an average man proud of his well-rounded averageness—without really meaning to at all.

And lastly. I would like to reiterate the basic theme of this article. Conflicts between groups centering on issues of educational relevance, and confusions within the rank and file of educators, can be understood best, I believe, in the perspective of the transformation of American culture that proceeds without regard for personal fortune or institutional survival. This transformation, it is true, can be guided and shaped to a considerable degree by the human actors on the scene. But they cannot guide and shape their destiny within this transformation if their energies are expended in knifing attacks on each other in such a central arena as education, or if their energies are dissipated in personal confusions. I am arguing, therefore, for the functional utility of understanding, and of insight into the all-

---

[5] *Acculturation* is used here to refer to the changes brought about in the culture of groups or individuals as adaptation to a culture different from their own takes place.

encompassing transformation of American culture and its educational-social resultants.

4.2, 4.3, 4.4   INTRODUCTION

The three selections that follow differ sharply from each other in the particular observations and insights they present about the relationships between schools and their communities, but, taken together, they strongly underline the closeness of such relationships. Thus, each of the excerpts should be studied for itself, but their contents should also be treated as a unit and their similarities and contrasts linked to the more general relationships they jointly reflect.

All three selections discuss the place of the school in relation to the social, economic, and political life of the immediate community. Vidich and Bensman give a vivid picture of both the unity and divisiveness of a rural town, documenting the pervasive and intricate manner in which educational issues tap economic rivalries, political competition, and value differences, and thus serve as a focus for broader issues in the community. The implication of other interests in the resolution of school problems is quite overt in this small town and the promotion of educational values depends on whether the more powerful political faction can be made to see them as not dangerous to the *status quo*. In contrast, Wood and Dahl find that in both the suburbs and in the city, education is viewed as "above" politics, which means only that politics enters more subtly, often at the level of values rather than of crude interests.

Because a school is part of a community, the nature of the education that it provides is determined not only by the training, competence, and educational philosophy of its faculty and staff, but very importantly by what the community expects to get out of "education." In the rural town agricultural training dominates the curriculum although it no longer serves the needs of the youth and despite the contrary preferences of an otherwise highly effective principal. In the more "advanced" city and suburbs, the school is perceived to be, in effect, responsible for the total individual. The result of such a broad and necessarily ambiguous goal, combined with the norm that education is a nonpolitical issue, is that the pressures on school policies are much more diffuse—but equally real and pervasive.

The guidance counselor working in a school is a part of the complex network of relationships that exist between that school and its particular community and his activities are no less subject to pressures and demands than were those of the principals, board members, and superintendents in the cases described in the ensuing selections. Every individual with whom he interacts or who is in some way affected by the guidance counselor's actions is part of a number of other social systems in the community and has both overt and implicit commitments to a variety of outside norms, values, interests, and persons. These commitments are in themselves unrelated to the school, but they are part of the context of school-related activities. Thus, for example, a guidance counselor who attempts to institute courses in sex education in a high school must anticipate the possibility of opposition and criticism from, say, church groups or from segments of parents of particular ethnic backgrounds.

Depending on the size, socioeconomic composition, and political structure of the community, such opposition may be expressed by parents speaking privately to the school principal and putting pressure on him to curb the counselor, or by the PTA taking a stand, or by individuals and groups pressing members of the school board to act, or even by newspaper editorials on the issue. Whatever the issue (changing the emphasis of the school curriculum, creating new extracurricular activities, advising certain students to take college rather than vocational courses, attempting to improve race relations in the school), every action taken by the guidance counselor in the performance of what he defines as his responsibilities will be perceived and responded to by a variety of people beyond those whom he might see as directly involved. Whether his actions accomplish their objectives or not will to a large extent depend on the nature of these reactions. Moreover, each incident will build expectations on the part of relevant others as to the guidance counselor's behavior and outlook and thus generalized attitudes of opposition *or* support may develop and prevent or facilitate the success of all his efforts.

The conclusion to be drawn from an understanding of such complexity need by no means be that innovation and change are impossible or that no action can be adequately planned and calculated because there are too many contingencies and ramifications to be considered. On the contrary, the greater the guidance counselor's recognition of the particular features of a school-community situation and of the range of values and beliefs held by all the people who in one way or another will react to his activities, the more able will he be to avoid misperceptions of his goals and to anticipate and optimize the consequences of his behavior.

4.2   THE CLASH OF CLASS INTERESTS IN SCHOOL POLITICS[1]

Arthur J. Vidich and Joseph Bensman

ORGANIZATION AND CHARACTER OF
THE SCHOOL BOARD

The institutional setting

The school board is composed of five elected board members, each elected for a five-year term on successive years. The board itself elects one of its members as

[1]Arthur J. Vidich and Joseph Bensman, "The Clash of Class Interests in School Politics," *Small Town in Mass Society: Class, Power and Religion in a Rural Community*, Princeton, N. J.: Princeton University Press, 1960, pp. 174–207. Reprinted by permission of Princeton University Press, Copyright©1960 by Princeton University Press.

chairman. In addition to these board members, who alone possess the voting privilege, an appointed clerk, an appointed legal counsel, and the principal and district superintendent (who are *ex-officio* members) attend the board meeting. Meetings are held monthly except during the summer months when school is recessed.

The geographical boundaries of the centralized school district approximately coincide with the legal boundaries of the township. The school is located in the village and has an attendance of approximately 600 students in grades 1 through 12 from all sections of the township.

A budget of a quarter of a million dollars makes the school the major "industry" of the village, a major purchaser of goods and services and the source of a substantial section of purchasing power. Every family with school-age children has a daily contact with it for nine and one-half months of the year. School buses cover the township roads twice a day. Most of the major social, cultural, and athletic events of the community take place within its halls.

In contrast to the village and town boards, the school board is faced with making important decisions on issues which have far-reaching consequences in the community at large. Politically it is the area in which most community issues, interest, activities, and discussion are present. The decisions of the school board focus on the following problems:

1. The budget, specifically as related to school buses, expanded curriculum, and expanded plant facilities, which together determine the school tax rate.
2. The proportioning of the agricultural curriculum as against college preparatory and industrial and business crafts curricula.
3. Appointments and reappointments of teachers, and granting tenure.
4. The appointment of janitors, bus drivers, and motor repairmen.
5. School food and supply purchases.

All these are crucial issues in the community and decisions made in connection with them have extensions into many other sectors of community life. The reappointment of a teacher determines his continued residence in the community. School buying affects the volume of local business. Curricula offerings determine the type of education children receive.

The decisions of the school board are highly visible in their consequences to the entire community, not alone through the direct contact which adults have with school affairs, but particularly through reports they receive directly from their children. The consequences of decisions of the school board are almost as visible as the actions of the teacher in the classroom. This situation makes it difficult for the board to maintain secrecy with respect to its decisions, and results in greater efforts at concealment. The greater efforts to conceal result in a more strict adherence to the principle of unanimity of decision.

The school board, like the other governing boards, reaches its decisions through a process of discussion which results in an inchoately arrived-at unanimous decision in which no vote, or only a perfunctory one, is taken. Agreement becomes apparent to all present or dissenting opinion silences itself and the final vote is recorded as unanimous. In the ordinary routine meeting (all meetings are open to the public but not attended) business is conducted on this basis with little apparent friction or difference of opinion. When it appears that differences exist and that several sides must be heard or when a major item of new business is to be discussed, the board adjourns to executive session from which the public is excluded.

Concealment and crisis

Any one of the problem areas mentioned above can easily become the focal point around which a public crisis can develop, and no year passes without the occurrence of a crisis. Because of this susceptibility it becomes central to the psychology of the members of the board to attempt to minimize or avoid crises, and this leads to further demands for unanimity and concealment. Research protocols reveal this process in a major crisis which developed in connection with the dismissal of a principal. The reasons for the dismissal of the principal were not given to the public. The P.T.A., which supported the principal, invited the board to attend a P.T.A. meeting to explain the reasons for the dismissal. Two hundred citizens attended the meeting which, to insure impartiality, was chaired by a minister from another town. After three hours of wrangling, no answer was given to the central question of *why* the principal was dismissed. The meeting was reported as follows:

"The main question asked by three or four people was, 'What were the specific reasons for Marsh's dismissal?' The board refused to answer this question. The following was the sequence of events:

1. Rev. Vicker read the question stated somewhat differently from four to five papers. He said he would not read the questioner's names although all the questions were signed. . . .
2. Holden (chairman of the board) stood up, faced the audience. He said that the board was elected to decide about school matters and they thought that it was for the best interests of the school that Marsh's contract not be renewed. Holden said he would need to have the names of the questioners so he would know better how to answer the question. Vicker than got the approval of Mrs. Regner for reading these names and read the names, . . .
3. Rev. Vicker repeated the question and said he felt it had not been answered. He understood that the board didn't want to but that they should be explicit about their decision not to answer or should answer the question. (He was applauded by the audience.)
4. After what seemed to be a long pause Holden said he didn't feel that this was the proper body to receive the answer to the question, that the matter concerned the whole school district and that if and when the board decided to give its reasons for Marsh's dismissal the board would call its own meeting. . . ."

Three days later the board at a special open meeting of its own, attended by 250 individuals, still refused to answer any specific questions in connection with the dismissal and remained unanimous in their agreement not to divulge any information, in spite of the fact that one member of the board was known to be opposed to the dismissal. Once the action had been taken and intense interest and pressure had been aroused, the iron laws of unanimity and concealment remained intact even in the face of the opposition of the member.

Due to the high visibility of the consequences of decisions, to the *necessity* of making decisions in order to keep a large institution going and to efforts to conceal the locus of decisions from a highly interested public, the school board and school policies become the focal point of public crisis. Almost every major decision of the board carries within it the seed of crisis. In the past five years these crises, half of which have resulted in mass protest meetings, have centered on the following issues: a school construction program, a businessmen's protest against the school administration for permitting "socialism in the school," the dismissal of the principal and the dismissals of popular teachers. Yet, in spite of these crises, the decisions of the board stand and the social composition of the board remains the same from year to year.

SELECTION AND SOCIAL COMPOSITION OF BOARD MEMBERS Elections of board members take place at the annual school board meeting which is usually attended by 30–90 individuals, depending upon the intensity of previous crises. Candidates must be nominated by a petition containing at least 25 signatures. Typically one candidate is nominated in this manner and is elected to office by a near unanimous vote of all those present at the meeting. Candidates may not be nominated from the floor, but there are usually one or two write-in votes. Those who attend the annual meeting vary from year to year but in any one year the majority of those in attendance are made up of relatives and friends of the nominee. The board hires a clerk, a counsel, and a principal who then attend board meetings. The superintendent of schools is appointed by outside agencies.[2]

The central fact of the social composition of the school board is the dominance of rural over village interests. The board is always made up of four rural members

---

[2]The position of district superintendent of schools in rural areas is a hangover from the days of precentralization, which in Springdale occurred in 1937. He then acted to coordinate and maintain standards for all one-room schoolhouses in the district, and an area comprising a large part of the county. Centralization and consolidation have reduced his duties to "form filling and administrative detail." The principal, by virtue of his close and daily contact with school affairs, has necessarily taken over a large part of his functions and duties. Hence superintendents are generally unfamiliar and unacquainted with the problems of any one central school and have no voice in policy as it is made and executed day-by-day. Since superintendents are powerless except as members of the board,

and one village member. Historically this dominance stems from informal political agreements made at the time of centralization in 1937. In an effort to insure passage of the centralization referendum, which was opposed by rural interests, village interests at that time "agreed" to a school board composed of four members from the old rural districts and one from the old village district. This agreement has been respected up to the present time.

The rural members have traditionally been "respectable" prosperous farmers who have been residents of the township for all or most of their lives. The fifth member has always fulfilled the requirement of residence in the village, but this has not in itself insured a representation of village interests. Prior to centralization, the village district was dominated by "retired farmers." For 20 continuous years prior to centralization, Hilton, a partner in the Jones and Hilton firm, sat as a member of the board. After centralization, Hilton continued to sit as the village representative of the new centralized board. When Hilton retired from the board, he was replaced by Ralph Jones, son of Howard Jones and junior partner in the firm of Jones and Hilton. It is reasonable to affirm that the village position on the school board has traditionally been held by the Jones and Hilton feed mill. The interests represented on the school board are overwhelmingly rural and, moreover, are the interests of the prosperous farmers.

The school principal is always a nonresident outside expert. The clerk of the board is usually a white-collar worker who is capable of acting as scribe and record keeper. . . .The legal counsel since centralization has been Flint, whose connections, as noted previously, are to the village board and the Republican committee.

The Republican committee as such plays no legal function in school affairs. At this point politics are separated from education. Political parties do not support school board candidates and do not formally meet to nominate them. . . .

THE CONSEQUENCES OF RURAL DOMINANCE   Rural dominance has its consequences in the overall administration and character of the school.

Although farmers represent only one-third of the population, a heavy emphasis in the school curriculum is placed on home economics and agricultural training.

---

where they do not possess necessary and sufficient information they are generally regarded as incompetent. The president of the school board, sitting in the same room with the superintendent at the public meeting of the board mentioned in the test above, referred to Springdale's superintendent in the following manner: "As noted earlier, Holden had stated that the school superintendent was of no value to the board—'He was as much value to the board as three wheels are to a bicycle.' Then Holden was interrupted by Vicker for making personal comments. Holden said that Anderson (school superintendent) was present and could speak for himself. This was not quite so, as no one was allowed to speak from the audience."

Between 1945 and 1951, 21 out of a total of 57 male graduates took the agricultural course, yet only 4 of the 21 were engaged in farming in 1951. The major opportunities for the school's graduates lie in industry, business, and college. The business course, a relatively recent addition taught by one person, consists of business accounting and secretarial training; its inclusion in the curriculum represents a concession to businessmen. The industrial arts program consists of a mechanics course which is geared to tractor and automobile repairs. No provision is made for industrial training to qualify students for employment in industry, where the large majority seek jobs. As a consequence most graduates take unskilled jobs since regional industries do not hire them as apprentices. The college preparatory course, the other major offering, meets minimum state requirements and on the whole qualifies students for admission to state teacher's colleges, where three or four go each year. Agricultural training is overemphasized and perpetuates a tradition of what has largely become useless training.

The school bus service, which represents an annual budget item of $25,000 and a capital investment of $100,000, is provided for rural children only. The dozen jobs connected with operating this transportation system constitute the major political plums which the board has to offer and these jobs, except for two or three, are given to farmers.

The appointment of teachers has far-reaching consequences not only for education but also for the social composition of the community. Preference is shown for native daughters who return to the community from college. Three of four teachers are the wives of farmers, and several more represent village families. The great proportion of teachers, however, must be hired from the "outside," which usually means the importation of 30–35 families into the village; the school chooses these carefully. One of the primary criteria used in selecting teachers is their social origin—whether they were "reared" in a city or in the country. The applicant who comes from a farm or a small town is uniformly appointed if a choice between two candidates is available; by and large the staff is composed of teachers who have a rural background. Through such processes of teacher selection an attempt is made to perpetuate the rural tradition and to minimize innovative tendencies which might run counter to it.

The business conditions of the community can be affected by school purchasing policies, particularly by purchases of food for the cafeteria. Traditionally the school board has supported local groceries by purchasing food supplies equally from all five groceries on a rotating weekly basis. It once offended local merchants during a major construction program by not following a policy of local buying. This can happen because local prices are not competitive and because state construction requirements set minimum standards and prices.

Businessmen are the only group in the community who take a direct and organized interest in school policy. Since the board is controlled by rural interests, the relations between businessmen and the school board constitute an important segment of school politics.

RURAL DOMINANCE AND THE BUSINESSMEN   Business interests and farm interests coincide in the low-tax, low-expenditure ideology and at this level a *modus vivendi* in school policy exists between the two sets of interests. Beyond this, business interests, because they are narrow, are accommodated easily by the board in the interests of local "peace and harmony." When it is necessary for the businessmen to make their voices heard, they express themselves through the business bureau. They are generally interested in two things: the maintenance of law and order for the protection of property, and the effects of school policy on the level of local business.

In concrete terms the maintenance of law and order means receiving cooperation from the school to insure an orderly and disciplined adolescent population on the village streets. The central school accounts for the daily concentration of 500–600 children who represent a daily threat to the "peace and order" of the village. By virtue of the school bus service a large percentage of these children safely bypass the village on their way to and from school. The major problem is the noon hour, which in response to business interest is taken up with a program of movies and other forms of organized recreation. That this interest is respected by school policy is shown by the following excerpt from the school principal's newspaper column:

Noon Hour Program

We are scheduling a noon-hour program that will give all children some good healthy activity of their own choosing during their free time. We do this for two reasons: *the first, to keep them under supervision to cover our legal liability and our moral obligation to you*; the second, to develop their leadership ability and their skills in organization and activity.

This program will include such things as intramural sports, publishing a school paper, publishing a school annual, Future Farmers of America, Future Homemakers of America, other clubs and hobby activities. . . .

Where school policy affects local business, however, conflicts arise and businessmen bring pressure to bear on the school administration in an effort to protect their business. Since members of the school board are prosperous farmers they tend to think in terms of buying where it is cheapest. In their personal affairs they are accustomed to mail-order purchases, to shopping around, and to hunting for bargains. They are psychologically capable of bypassing village tradesmen when it is to their economic advantage. They bring this attitude with them to the board of education and hence it happens that the largest part of school expenditures are made with outside firms. This is a source of constant irritation to the businessmen and it leads to resentment against those who administrate the board's policies: the principal and his assistants. Since the businessmen are powerless to change the board's purchasing policies, their resentments must find expression in other channels. The classic businessmen's issue rests on the sales competition of student money-raising enterprises, which are supervised by the administration rather than by the school board.

On one occasion this issue of sales competition was broadly debated in the business bureau as one of "socialism in the school." High school seniors were raising money for an annual trip to Washington, D.C., by selling ice cream to each other. Lee, attacking the school as a threat to business interests, wrote an editorial entitled "Socialism in the School"; following this, the matter was brought up for official consideration at a meeting of the business bureau. . . .

The protest was effective and ice-cream sales along with a junior class popcorn-vending venture were terminated by the administration. This, in turn, aroused the resentment of farm families whose children's trip to Washington, D.C., was at stake. The school board, however, remained aloof from the issue, thus permitting the administration to absorb the resentment and guaranteeing the continuation of rural dominance on the board in exchange for a minor concession to business interests at the cost of the administration's program.

All other groups in the community who may be said to have special interests in school policy are given no direct or indirect political representation except as they express themselves in the P.T.A., discussed below. These include the professionals, industrial workers, traditional farmers, shack people and the marginal middle class, all of whom fall beyond the purview of educational politics.

THE PRINCIPAL AS AN ALIEN EXPERT

The role of the principal

The role of the principal represents a unique and unusual factor in local politics. He expresses himself politically through his specialized interests in education. Although his primary interest is in education, he must deal with and through political forces to accomplish his ends. His position is the focal point around which a large segment of politics takes place and his ability to evade, bypass, and manipulate invisible government determines his success as a principal and the continuance of his appointment. The dismissed principal alluded to earlier, Marsh, was unsuccessful in this task and in spite of a large unorganized body of supporting opinion lost out to the forces desiring his removal. The case of his successor, Peabody, incumbent since 1951, epitomizes the process and reality of the principal's political role.

Peabody, a man in his mid-thirties, and his wife live in a "self-imposed" isolation from the rest of the community, including the community of teachers. His private as well as his social life is almost unknown to the community. All of his contacts with the community result from his position as principal, a position to which he devotes almost all his time and energy and which he fills with a high degree of technical competence.

The school principal, always known as "The Professor," is central to the life of the community, but he is known to it almost exclusively through his professional activities and for this reason he can be treated as a public figure only as the community knows him in the following of his capacities: (1) Through school children who see him in his day-to-day role as the authority of the school. (2) Through his activities in the P.T.A. and its various committees in which he takes an active interest. (3) As the author of a weekly column in the newspaper on school policy and affairs. (4) As an ex-officio, nonvoting member of the school board. In each of these capacities his central interest is in promoting education for the community. Together these activities constitute his job, make him the personal embodiment of education and draw him into the political scene as a central figure.

The principal and the public

Through his newspaper column and daily supervision of the school, the principal has mechanisms for distributing information and an image of himself to the public. At this level Peabody has established a reputation for being a good disciplinarian, a trait highly valued by the community, but not a harsh disciplinarian (he recommended dismissal of a teacher regarded as too harsh). He has raised the standards of classroom work (more homework for students), but has not increased the number of failures (everyone's child is still getting educated). He has supported a modern approach to sex education, but not in a radical manner (abrupt dismissal of a teacher who discussed sex in a classroom not connected with hygiene). In his newspaper column he discusses a great variety of school facts and problems, such as school board meetings, teachers meetings, the budget, curriculum problems, and occasionally he suggests methods for improving the school. . . .

The principal and the parent-teacher association

While the newspaper column appeals to local pride and prejudice, the principal's actions in the P.T.A. are oriented to introducing his educational philosophy and other innovations to a specialized segment of the community which is interested in education as such. The P.T.A. membership is composed of the teachers, wives of professional and industrial workers, and the wives of a handful of prosperous farmers. The attending membership, excluding the teachers, adds up to 30–40 persons who are interested in P.T.A. activities because they have school-age children. Their interest in the school, moreover, is apt to be most intense at those points where school problems impinge directly on their child's grade; the membership's interests tend to be atomized. More than this, however, the group as a whole is not organized on an independent basis; they meet under the auspices of the school and revert to congeries of atomized individuals outside of meetings. One of the reasons for this is that historically the local P.T.A. has never been well organized or active. Peabody has taken a direct interest in organizing P.T.A. activities and plays a decisive role in its affairs.

Through a step-by-step progression in the course of his administration, Peabody has introduced a variety of modern educational practices and methods to the P.T.A. Health (sex) education, a new reading program for the elementary grades (reading "readiness"), new curriculum additions (driver training, vocational education), new plant expansion plans–all such innovations are first introduced in the P.T.A. Through his control over teachers and his requirement that they attend P.T.A. meetings (on alternating years a teacher is president of the P.T.A.), and due to his ability to secure special speakers and programs, the principal plays a dominating and controlling role in this organization. He uses his dominant position for the purpose of gaining acceptance for his educational programs. However, at no point in this procedure does it appear that the P.T.A. has been forced to accept the principal's ideas. For, through the process of committees and agendas, it appears publicly that P.T.A. members themselves, when making their reports, have originated the ideas which have been given them by the principal. Through the complexities of this procedure, the P.T.A. voices the policies of the principal and, in turn, the principal uses the P.T.A. as an informal political instrument against those interests in the village and town which oppose his program. While doing this, however, he is careful to restrain the P.T.A. if it gets overly ambitious. He is careful, moreover, to report in his column P.T.A. activities as P.T.A. activities and not as his own policies.

The P.T.A., however, is most important in concrete policy matters as these are brought before the board of education. Here the P.T.A. does not act directly, but rather acts through the principal. At this point the function of the P.T.A. is to create the issues and define the problems necessary to carrying out the educational policies of the principal. The principal mediates between the P.T.A. and the school board and presents the P.T.A. educational program to the board as the program of a pressure group.

In his relations with the P.T.A. the principal is able to pretest his ideas before a segment of the community which is interested in education and which represents groups otherwise not heard. When it appears that the P.T.A. is ready to support his views, a resolution is passed for presentation to the board. Since the principal prepares the agenda for board meetings, the resolution is assured a hearing.

At times the principal must restrain the enthusiasms of the P.T.A. Since he is generally aware of the thinking of the board members, he knows in advance what constitutes a reasonable request and what measures will arouse antagonism and be rejected. When he cannot kill "unreasonable" P.T.A. requests within the P.T.A.—a rare circumstance—the P.T.A. officers themselves present the issue to the board. Thus the principal dissociates himself from unpopular causes and does not jeopardize his relations with the board. In some circumstances he kills or dissociates himself from ideas which he himself first introduced to the P.T.A., a fact which leads to the development of resentments against him within the P.T.A.

However, through the operation of such intricate processes, Peabody has succeeded in instituting a number of his ideas: hiring a professional cafeteria manager to replace a local person and introducing several new courses. More significant, through these processes he has managed to create an independent group of lay advisors. These lay advisors are organized into committees (school expansion committee, agricultural advisory committee, vocational advisory committee) which are composed of *individuals* who do not otherwise participate in school affairs. Each committee contains a mixture of farmers, businessmen, professionals, and industrial workers, while Peabody is an ex-officio member of each committee and coordinates their combined activities. What is interesting about the lay advisory committees is that they do not involve any new *groups* in school affairs: they extend and broaden the base of participation of those groups already involved in P.T.A. affairs. Moreover, by mixing up members of different classes on each committee, the principal seems deliberately to be atomizing the classes. He handles these committees in the same manner as he handles the P.T.A., the committees report to the school board and also to the P.T.A. and hence have the effect of giving the voice of the P.T.A. a broader base. Thus the principal involves a broader segment of the community in his program and brings himself to the school board with public support for his program.

The principal and the board of education

The principal comes to the board meeting as a technical expert and as the administrator of board policies. As the day-to-day administrator of policy and as an expert, he enjoys a tactical advantage over the board members who are concerned with education only once a month. He has a thoroughgoing knowledge of state legal and administrative requirements and he understands the problems of school curricula and daily administration in detail. While the principal possesses the powers of the expert in relation to amateurs, the amateurs, in this case, control the budget and are responsible for hiring the expert. It is in this context that the relations between the principal and the board are worked out. This relationship, as reported by an observer of board meetings, may be described as follows:

> First, there are the minor problems of administrative detail which Peabody presents at school board meetings. In most cases he has already reached a solution to the problem and action has been taken. He may be doing this merely to keep the board informed on such matters. There is the possibility that he wants the board to be aware of the fact that he is handling these things efficiently.
>
> Secondly, there are problems of a strictly professional nature which Peabody feels quite capable of solving and which he is, in fact, quite capable of handling. He, nevertheless, presents these problems to the board for their "advice," since he is "new here and not acquainted with past policy." Invariably, the board responds in a specific way when these problems are presented. Holden and Tafe quickly draw the line, indicating that such problems are the business of Peabody and that they choose to rely on his judgment and discretion. Ralph Jones is more inclined to want to air these matters. He apparently feels better equipped to discuss professional matters. But, nine times out of ten, Peabody has solved the problem and made a decision previous to the meeting and is well armed with supportive material to back his stand. His strategy is approximately as follows:
>
> 1. Become aware of all the facts of the case.
> 2. On the basis of these facts, paying special attention to the reactions of the significant people involved, reach a decision.

3. Formulate a definite plan of action based on the decision, implementing every step of the action in detail.
4. Come to the board meeting fully prepared with the detailed solution of the problem and then present the problem as though you just realized the problem existed and "could the board help you with some advice since you are new and inexperienced in Springdale and they are familiar with the precedent."
5. Let the board knock it about for awhile while you sit back and size up their individual stands on the issue.
6. Present the facts and the carefully worked out solution, countering every argument with a better one, being, of course, very tactful.
7. Wait for Jones to make the motion that your plan be adopted.

Thirdly, there are problems which involve mostly matters which are of direct concern to the board because they involve finances or public relations between the school and the community. Here again, Peabody ascertains as many of the facts in advance as is possible. He decides for himself what course of action he would prefer. But here the board stands firm on its right to decide the course of action. In this general area Peabody uses his influence and whatever methods of persuasion he knows in order to gain his own ends, but he is extremely careful to do it in a subtle way. He does not run headlong into the board, because he is aware that they want and need some area in which they can feel that they know better than he. For example, when Peabody proposed the buying of the P.A. system with the surplus money from the budget, he was met with abrupt and almost reprimanding resistance from all the board members.

The board respects Peabody and his knowledge of his profession. They feel that their own actions are constantly under his scrutiny and are careful not to go out on a limb with respect to educational practices and principles. But where they have the edge, where they hold the purse-strings, they try to exercise their power.

On the whole, Peabody seems to have taken much of the power from the board. They are ambivalent about this. They are pleased, on one hand, to have a principal to whom they can turn over an immense amount of responsibility with complete confidence. But at the same time they don't want to lose the upper hand in the bargain. Holden has foreseen this and fears it. The others have sensed it to a lesser degree. The board cannot attack the very thing in Peabody that has put him in the position he is in now, so they will keep trying in other ways to keep him in check.

It is in and through the school board, in this manner, that the principal as an expert has an opportunity to achieve his educational program. As an expert his powers are based on administrative and manipulative skills and these skills must be coordinated with the political philosophy of the school board. Hence, the principal is able to institute most easily those elements of his program which coincide with the sentiments of the school board as he finds it or as he is able to change it. The board and Peabody have discontinued cafeteria food purchases from local groceries and instead now make these purchases more efficiently and at less cost through wholesalers. Both the principal and the board were psychologically capable of alienating local businessmen in this way. The addition of a professional cafeteria manager was justified on the basis of greater efficiency and cost savings "in the long run." The principal can, however, receive no concessions for his teaching staff. Teachers are expected to work "full time," to be on call at all times and generally to devote themselves to the school and its activities while leading exemplary lives in the community. The principal defers to the board in its expectations of teachers and, in consequence, he is disliked by the teachers since they have no spokesman to represent their interests on the board of education. When it comes to such complex issues as school expansion and curriculum changes, the principal restructures the position of the board in relation to the community. The lay advisory committees are an effort to create an independent organization which will give the principal's position public support. In addition, he has for the first time in Springdale history succeeded in placing a rural nonfarm resident on the board. Through this process of joining with the board while at the same time altering its composition and its position in the community, the principal promotes his educational program.

The internal contradictions of the
principal's role

In these terms, then, the school principal is an alien expert who knows the ways and laws of the world and who uses this knowledge to shape the community as it bears on him and his ends, which are necessarily in the selfish interests of education. However, in dealing with the various segments of the community with which he comes in direct contact, he must recognize differences of power. He must recognize the interests of the farmers, professionals, industrial workers, party politics, the generalized desire for low taxes, and he must give each of these elements their due weight in his educational calculations. To the extent that he makes an accurate assessment of local power relations and acts on this assessment he has a chance, at least in the short run, to succeed with his program.

While giving due weight to these various interests he must at the same time try not to alienate any one of them. As a result he publicly tends to try to agree with everyone and his public statements are of sufficient generality as to be satisfactory to almost all groups. However, when pressed, he agrees most, in terms of his rhetoric, with the rural interests since this is the dominant group within and through whom he must work.

This he must do even though his underlying educational program is against a lopsided, farm-dominated school system. Vocational training, college preparation, a guidance program and modern methods are central to his educational philosophy. But in order to accomplish his program, he must constantly make concessions to the dominant interests behind school policy and attempt to implement his program through more indirect and subtle means. As a consequence of this, it frequently happens that he is forced to dissociate himself from his own ideas in the P.T.A. and to take public positions which are inconsistent with his long-range program.

However, in making these concessions, and sometimes being overly subtle in his approach, he alienates the village by being overly affirmative to the town interests, even though his ideas correspond to village interests—a fact which only a few recognize. After one year of Peabody's incumbency, Flint recognized this sufficiently to resign his position as legal counsel to the board in the sure knowledge that "the school's in good hands now. They don't need me around anymore." But others, who are not in a position to observe the principal's acts at close range and who must form their opinions from his public statements, begin to form into nuclei of opposition.

In addition, it remains as a fact that the political maneuverings of the principal are resented by those groups before and against whom he displays his knowledge and technique. He remains an alien expert who cannot conceal the rationality of his calculations and operations. At this point, particularly with respect to budgetary considerations, the school board acts as a watchdog agency and always jealously guards this prerogative. Moreover, the board is always in a position to create an issue which will lead to the removal or resignation of the principal. One member of invisible government, in agreement with the principal's educational policy, has remarked that "He's a little too inhuman—has never got into anything in the town. He's good for Springdale until he gets things straightened out. Then we'll have to get rid of him." But this cannot be done as easily now as in the past. Recent state laws designed to protect the security of teachers now include an automatic tenure provision upon completion of five years of continuous teaching in the school. Thus the principal's position is supported by state law. The board's position in relation to the principal, particularly in view of Peabody's ability to prevent organized opposition to himself, has been considerably weakened. In fact, for the first time in the history of the community, the principal is a permanent part of local politics until he elects to resign or is forced to resign in response to extralegal pressures.

4.3   LEADERS IN PUBLIC EDUCATION[1]

Robert Dahl

Though leadership in the public school system has many of the characteristics of leadership in the political parties and in urban redevelopment, there are also significant differences. Like the parties but unlike urban redevelopment, the school system has existed for a long time. Policy-making in the schools is far more routinized than in redevelopment; it is far more professionalized—one might say bureaucratized—than in the parties, in the sense that almost all of the people who

[1]From Robert Dahl, "Leaders in Public Education," *Who Governs? Democracy and Power in an American City*, New Haven and London: Yale University Press, 1961, pp. 141–147, 150–159.

make day-to-day decisions about the schools meet certain professional standards and have a strong sense of their own professionalism. The schools are more insulated from electoral politics than are the parties, of course; as with redevelopment, leaders in the schools maintain an aura of nonpartisanship.

As in urban redevelopment and party nominations, there are a number of diverse elements in the political stratum whose educational wants and concerns the leaders attempt to conciliate, anticipate, and satisfy. In so far as they are organized into self-conscious associations, these elements, the public school interests, are somewhat like the subleaders in the political parties. As in redevelopment, the public school interests possess a strong concentration of purpose. Moreover, most of the associations active in school affairs are specialized around the politics of the public schools and play a minor part in the political parties and in urban redevelopment. . . .

The public schools are a large operation. Annual outlays for the public school system run from a quarter to a third of all city expenditures and constitute far and away the biggest item in the budget. (By comparison the police and fire departments together amount to only one-fifth of total city expenditures; health and welfare are between one-twentieth and one-tenth.) In 1959 the regular school system employed about 1,250 people, including 924 teachers, 98 administrators, 43 clerks, and 184 janitors, repairmen, etc. In addition, programs in adult education and summer recreation employed over 200 persons. Altogether one out of every two persons employed by the city government worked in the school system.

The responsibilities placed on the public schools by law, custom, and popular expectations are heavy. The schools are, of course, expected to provide a minimum level of knowledge for all except the mentally retarded and a much higher level for the increasing proportion of students who aspire to higher education. The schools are, and from the time of their establishment have been, expected to prepare the student for a useful calling. In addition, the schools have always been assigned a heavy responsibility for helping to form the character, moral sensibilities, and civic attitudes of the student. In a city of immigrants like New Haven, the last task has necessarily assumed a position of key importance.

Considering the nature of the tasks assigned to the public schools, it is hardly surprising that control over the schools is seen as worth fighting for by leaders of many different groups.

THE SPLIT: PUBLIC VERSUS PRIVATE   One factor that bears heavily on local decisions about the public schools and on the nature of leadership in school affairs is that a large number of parents send their children to Catholic parochial schools, to private nonsectarian day schools in the greater New Haven area, or to boarding schools. This separation between public and private school population, which is common in other cities along the eastern seaboard and almost unknown in the Middle West and Far West, is highly significant in New Haven, where about one child out of five attends a private school. . . .

Unfortunately for the public school leader, some of the private schools draw off the students from the more prosperous and better educated elements in the community, as James S. Davie showed in a study of children 16 or 17 years old in 1949 whose parents were legal residents of New Haven. Using a 6-fold classification of residential areas (based on income, nationality, occupation, delinquency, dependency, social club membership, and inclusion in the social register), Davie found that only about 1 child out of 10 in the 3 lower residential categories was sent to a private school. In the 2 intermediate residential categories, one out of 5 went to a private school. But in the highest category—children from "Class I" neighborhoods—4 out of 10 children were in private schools.[2]. . .

Among private school children, however, there is a marked difference between those who go to Catholic parochial schools and those who go to nonsectarian private schools. Children in "Class I" neighborhoods go overwhelmingly to nonparochial schools; in the three lowest ranking neighborhoods, on the other hand, a child who does not attend a public school is almost certain to go to a parochial school. . . .It follows that the private nonparochial schools consist mostly of students from only the better neighborhoods; in 1949, Davie's data show, threefourths of the students in private secondary schools came from Class I and Class II neighborhoods. By contrast, nearly three-fourths of the students in the parochial secondary schools lived in the three lowest ranking neighborhoods. . . .

The split between private and public schools in New Haven has two consequences. It reduces the concern among the better educated elements in New Haven for standards of excellence in the public schools, and it creates among about a fifth of the parents a double load of costs for education—local taxes and private tuition—that generates latent opposition to increasing the outlays on public schools.

As to the first point, when an educational leader in New Haven tries to mobilize parents to press for better public schools, he finds that his own standards of adequacy—not to say of excellence—are likely to be higher than those of the average parent with children in public schools. To meet his own standards, then, a leader must push for better educational facilities and services than many parents would insist on if left to themselves. It is not so much that parents make demands on leaders for better schools as that leaders try to win the support of parents.

Of course the standards of excellence used by any professional group are frequently higher than those satisfactory to a layman. To meet the standards articulated by the various professional groups in any modern community would exhaust the total available resources many times over. But in the field of public education

---

[2]James S. Davie, "Education and Social Stratification" (Doctoral dissertation, Yale University, 1951). See also his article "Social Class Factors and School Attendance," *Harvard Educational Review, 23,* 1953, pp. 175–185.

in New Haven the discrepancy between standards is particularly acute because the average parent of a public school child has had considerably less formal education than is now compulsory. In 1950 half the people 25 years of age or over in New Haven had not gone beyond the ninth grade. Only a little more than a third had completed high school. In 18 wards, or more than half, the average (median) person had stopped just short of the ninth grade. In 7 more wards, the average person had gone beyond the ninth grade but had not finished high school. In only 8 wards, or not quite one-fourth, had the average adult completed high school. Many of the better educated parents, who might normally be expected to support high standards in the public schools, are likely to give their attention instead to the private schools where their own children are enrolled.

As to the second point, parents bearing a double load of costs for education are joined in latent opposition to increasing expenditures on public schools by the business firms, corporations, and individuals with extensive property holdings who pay a large share of the taxes. But they represent a relatively small proportion of the voters and are greatly outnumbered by the parents of public school children.

The net effect of the private schools, parochial and nonparochial, is to reduce enthusiasm for expenditures on the public schools among various strata in the population whose interests would not ordinarily coalesce. In contrast to a community located in the Middle West or the Far West where a leader concerned with excellence in the public schools can often count on the support of the better educated and more prosperous people in the city, in New Haven he has to seek support elsewhere. Because the standards of educational excellence accepted by the great bulk of the population are low, and because the parochial schools in any case draw off some of the enthusiasm that might otherwise be generated among the less educated and less well-to-do, any effective educational coalition is likely to be composed for the most part of the better educated people in the middling strata of the community, with a tiny sprinkling of Social and Economic Notables who for various reasons feel a commitment to a good public school system even though they may send their own children to private schools. . . .

THE DISTRIBUTION OF INFLUENCE: THE LEADERS   An examination of eight different sets of decisions taken between 1953 and 1959 indicates that there are three main centers for initiating or vetoing policies involving the public schools. These are the mayor, the board of education, and the superintendent of schools.

In New Haven, the seven members of the board of education are appointed for four-year terms by the mayor, who is *ex officio* an eighth member. Appointments are staggered; hence by the end of his first term in office a mayor will usually have had the opportunity to appoint a majority of the members to the board.

Because the local norms prescribe that the schools should be insulated from politics, a mayor who attempted to press his own policies directly on the school
system through the board or the superintendent would antagonize the segments of
the political stratum most keenly interested in the schools. Consequently, the
mayor ordinarily influences school policy only indirectly through his appointments
to the board. Even then, the mayor does not have a free hand. By tradition,
members are reappointed as long as they are willing to serve; because of this
tradition, it is not always simple to ease out a board member whom the mayor
would prefer not to reappoint. Moreover, some ethnic, religious, and professional
distribution is assumed to be necessary. In recent years, the board's appointive
members have included three Catholics, two Protestants, and two Jews. Among
the Catholics were one man of Irish stock and another of Italian stock. Mayor Lee
appointed the state head of the AFL-CIO to the board; fear of trade union resentment may henceforth require a trade union man on the board. In response to
rising demands from Negroes, Lee also appointed a Negro; probably no future
mayor will fail to follow his lead.

Once the mayor has appointed his members, his direct influence is limited. The
board members are unpaid. They have careers, goals, and standards of their own.
Membership on the board is time-consuming and even onerous. Board members
do not feel particularly beholden to the mayor. Hence the most a mayor can do is
to choose people in whom he has confidence and then give them his strong backing
when they call for help.

The superintendent of schools is a major official. In 1960 his annual salary of
$16,300 was the highest of any official in the city except for the mayor himself.
Once appointed, a superintendent is difficult to remove, not only because he builds
up his own following among the public school interests but because he can invoke
the support of national professional groups if his removal does not seem to be
based on considerations of professional adequacy.

Because of all the constraints on the mayor and the board of education, a superintendent in whom they have confidence can be expected to acquire a major,
perhaps even decisive, influence on policies relating to essentially internal school
matters—that is, policies that do not require extensive negotiations with elements
in the political stratum not primarily concerned with the public schools. If the
mayor and the board lack confidence in the superintendent, then the direct influence of board members on decisions is likely to increase, as board members
substitute their own judgment for his. Finally, if the situation of the schools generates a series of proposals and decisions that require extensive negotiations
outside the public school system, then the direct influence of the mayor is likely to
increase. Consequently the relative influence of the mayor, the board, and the superintendent tends to be different at different times and with different kinds of
decisions.

Consider now the following scoreboard. In 8 different sets of decisions between
1953 and 1959, there were 27 instances in which the initiation or veto of a policy

alternative could be attributed to a particular individual, group, or agency. The successful actors included 8 individuals, a group of 3 members of the board of education, 3 official agencies (in cases where the action could not be attributed to any particular individual), and the Teachers' League. Of the 27 instances of successful action on policy, all except 3 were traceable to participants officially and publicly involved in the school system. Fifteen, or more than half, were traceable to the mayor or officials who were members of his educational coalition. All the rest were scattered among a variety of individuals and agencies, from the Board of Finance and the Board of Park Commissioners to the superintendent of schools and the president of Yale.

One might suspect the validity of crude measures of this sort, but the conclusions they suggest fit with the qualitative evidence. Taken together, the qualitative and quantitative evidence seems to support three propositions. First, the number of citizens who participate directly in important decisions bearing on the public schools is small—just as it is in the other areas of public life we have examined. Second, direct influence over decisions in public education seems to be exerted almost entirely by public officials. Third, in recent years the chief center of direct influence has been the mayor and his appointees on the board of education, rather than the superintendent.

As with urban redevelopment and political nominations, however, it would be a serious error to assume that the individuals and groups with the greatest *direct* influence on decisions are autonomous. On the contrary, they consider the reactions of a number of different public school interests who can, if aroused, make themselves felt in various ways—not least through elections. . . .

DEMOCRATIC RITUAL: The greatest ambiguity in the relations of
THE FOLLOWINGS leaders and constituents stems from the fact
that individuals who seem to have the greatest direct influence on decisions are themselves influenced in their choices by the need to gain and retain popular support. This ambiguity is further compounded by the fact that leaders do not merely respond to demands; they also help to generate them. In public education, as we have noted, differences in the objectives of leaders and parents induce leaders to develop methods of generating new demands among parents and other citizens. One of these methods is the creation of special associations. Just as the numerous action committees provide a democratic façade and a body of subleaders and followings for leaders in redevelopment and renewal, and the party functionaries and convention delegates furnish auxiliaries for party leaders, so certain citizen organizations provide subleaders and followings for leaders in public education. The P.T.A.'s fit most obviously into this role.

Ostensibly, of course, a Parent-Teachers' Association is a democratic organization of parents and teachers associated with a particular school, brought into being and sustained by their joint interests. In practice, a P.T.A. is usually an instrument of the school administrator. Indeed, an ambitious principal will ordinarily regard an active P.T.A. as an indispensable means to his success. If no P.T.A. exists, he will create one; if one exists he will try to maintain it at a high level of activity.

The functions of the P.T.A. are rather like those of party subleaders. The P.T.A. supplies a group of people whose loyalty and enthusiasm can occasionally be mobilized for educational purposes important to the leaders. Thus an energetic principal of a New Haven school in a low-income neighborhood described how he had organized a P.T.A. in order to improve the facilities of the school. He went to an important neighborhood leader, he said, and persuaded her that "the kids in the neighborhood needed help." Together they started a P.T.A. In order to involve the parents even more heavily, they then induced the P.T.A. to endorse a hot lunch program; this required P.T.A. members to raise funds and even to hire kitchen help. As participation in the P.T.A. increased, the principal began to work for a new school to replace the old one. When obstacles were raised by the city administration, the principal called a meeting of P.T.A. members and other neighborhood leaders and "gave them a rousing speech asking for their help. Within 24 hours they were on the phone and in other ways bringing pressure on the administration. The problem was solved."

It is a rare P.T.A. that ever opposes the wishes of a principal, and its mere existence helps to give a certain legitimacy to the otherwise hierarchical structure of the school system. As long as the principal keeps the active P.T.A. members moderately satisfied, he will appear to have the "backing of the parents" for his programs and policies.

But a P.T.A. is also useful to head off or settle conflicts between parents and the school system. A shrewd principal often uses the P.T.A. to find out what problems are in the parents' minds; he then brings about some adjustments in the school's program or perhaps allays the concern of parents simply by discussing the problem with them. P.T.A. meetings also create an atmosphere of friendliness and conviviality that blunts criticism. For many women, in fact, the P.T.A. is obviously an outlet for social needs; P.T.A. meetings furnish opportunities to escape from the home for a few hours, meet neighbors, make new friends, gossip, talk about children, partake of coffee and pastry, and achieve a fugitive sense of social purpose. Some female Machiavellians even look upon P.T.A. activity as a way of assuring favorable treatment for their own children. And they may be right, for the experienced principal or teacher learns from P.T.A. meetings who the most interested parents are, who the "trouble-makers" might be, who makes demands on the school system, and who does not. If he is politically sensitive, the principal is likely to conclude that it is safer to ignore the difficulties of a child whose parents are not interested enough to participate in the P.T.A. than the problems of a child whose mother is a P.T.A. activist.

The P.T.A. is also a legitimate channel through which potential leaders may enter into the school system, test themselves, gain experience, and pass into the ranks of the leaders. It is a remarkable fact that three recent appointees to the New Haven board of education all became involved in the politics of the public schools via the P.T.A. To be sure, each of these men had already possessed a strong prior interest in education. But it was when the education of their own children was at stake that they became active in their P.T.A. . . .

Ordinarily a P.T.A. president is a housewife who lacks the time, experience, interest, and drive to move into the real centers of educational influence. Moreover, the focus of the individual P.T.A. is narrow, since parents are more interested in the current education of their own children than in enduring problems of the educational system as a whole. It is probably for these reasons that the individual P.T.A.'s and the New Haven Council of Parent Teachers' Associations have not played a prominent role in important decisions.

It was because of the limitations of the P.T.A.'s that Mayor Lee created the Citizens Advisory Committee on Education (CACE) in 1954. The CACE was originally outside the framework of the CAC [Citizens Advisory Committee], largely because many business leaders felt that redevelopment ought to be kept distinct from education, but at Lee's insistence the CACE was finally incorporated into the CAC as a special subcommittee. Thus the CACE furnished a new corps of auxiliaries in the field of public education.

The CACE illustrates nicely the way·many citizen committees fit the needs of leaders. The first chairman, John Braslin, was an educator who worked in New York and lived in New Haven; he had been chairman of the P.T.A. at a school located in one of the best residential areas of New Haven. Before World War II, he had taught French at Hillhouse High; he was an old friend of the Mayor— they had even been in the same platoon in basic training during the Mayor's brief stint in the army—and the Mayor turned the task of organizing the committee over to him. Braslin said later,

> What I did was to make a list of about 150 names of people. . .many of whom I knew through Junior Chamber work, through work prior to the war. . .air raid wardens, and activities of that sort. And then I asked representatives of various organizations like the labor unions and the merchants downtown, the League of Women Voters, the P.T.A. council, to recommend names to me who would be members of the CACE and act as liaison with these various civic, social, and service groups in the city. . . .I whittled the list down to 100 names. . .I wanted a large representative group that would really cover a broad section of the city.

The first task of the CACE and probably its most important one was to help arouse support for new public high schools. But it had other jobs to do, too. Braslin said,

> In order to keep this large committee as a functioning group, what I did was to break it down into 7 subcommittees and I first appointed a governing board as an executive board composed of 15 members. . . . I figured . . . I'll pick these people because these are the ones that I will have to work with, that I will be openly responsible for, and on whom I

will depend to lead and encourage and arouse the other members of the overall committee. So from among these 15 I was able to draw a chairmanship for each of the seven subcommittees. Then, the executive board first decided on and we picked 7 areas of study: personnel, finance, building, school population, and publicity, public relations, and the like.

The leaders then sent out a note to the members asking them to indicate the area each was most interested in; they placed the members on subcommittees according to their interests.

From its inception, then, the CACE was an instrument of its leaders for generating support for schools. How effective it was it is difficult to say. There is little doubt that it helped to generate support for new high schools at a time when the mayor badly needed support. It pressed for higher teachers' salaries. It sponsored an improved program for testing the vision of school children that was finally adopted by the board of education. . . .

4.4   THE SPECIAL ISSUE OF THE
PUBLIC SCHOOLS[1]

Robert C. Wood

A sketch of suburban politics as the power relations of a relatively large number of personalities and of relatively few and generally harmonious interest groups operating under the cover of nonpartisanship needs to be qualified in at least one important respect. The program and expenditures of suburban schools are quite likely to engender a brand of active, if not frenzied, political behavior that stands in stark contrast to the more controlled decision-making in other parts of suburban government. Part of the pattern of school politics is explicable in universal terms and is likely to be found in all types and sizes of American communities; part seems to be peculiar to the suburbs. Regardless of its source and motivations, however, the operation of the public schools results in more extensive public participation in political affairs, more heat, and not infrequently less light than any other function.

The quantitative magnitude of the school problem is one aspect of school politics. Since the suburbs represent the growing edge of the American population,

[1]From *Suburbia: Its People and Their Politics*, pp. 186–194. Copyright©1958 by Robert C. Wood. Reprinted by permission of the publisher, Houghton Mifflin Company.

the provision of school facilities is their major public problem. The central cities wrestle with deteriorating land values, slums, and blight, and concentrate on renewal and redevelopment programs to restore physical and fiscal soundness. Rural areas find highways perhaps the most persistent and politically sensitive public function. But the suburbs grapple with the growing tide of children who invade their borders. Following the Pied Piper lure of better schools, family after family lists consideration of their young as a primary cause for the suburban trek, and they tumble over one another to find governments with "good school systems."

In this context, the relative youth of the suburban population, the social acceptability of large families in the growing middle class, the almost universal practice of the present generation to complete at least a high school education, all combine to raise enormous quantitative demands on public education. In all local American governments, educational expenditures account for almost one half of the total budget; for suburban governments it is frequently a good deal more. Metropolitan school systems spend considerably more per pupil, adopt advanced techniques in instruction more quickly, and expand curricula more readily. Because the schools have the largest bureaucracy, take the greatest part of the tax dollar, and represent the most rapidly growing public demand, they are the most important function suburban governments perform.

Viewed in these terms simply of quantitative pressures, the school problem exaggerates whatever conflicts and disagreements already exist. Cleavages between established residents and new, commuters and stay-at-homes, young residents and old, industrial and residential taxpayers, are naturally intensified. And new dimensions in the power pattern are likely to come to the fore, expressed by the sharply different attitudes of Catholics, Protestants, and Jews toward the proper role of public education. The conflicting pressures of population and finance are likely, in and of themselves, to ignite public debate.

Yet quantitative pressures alone do not generate the suburban school battles which are so evident at the present time. Americans, and particularly suburbanites, care deeply about the qualitative aspects of public education—how "good" the additional teachers and the expanded curricula are. In part, this strong popular interest results from the suburban preoccupation with family and children. In part, it arises from the demands for literary and technical skills in our highly developed economy. In part, too, it stems from the social responsibility education now provides.

But the qualitative aspect of school politics stretches back beyond the values of our contemporary culture. A full explanation of school politics, its emotionalism and agitation, lies buried in the American political tradition as it is interpreted in educational philosophy. The national commitment to education began with the eighteenth century belief in man's reason as a prerequisite for popular government. Given that conviction, it follows that the development of the power to reason deserves the most careful attention any democracy can manage. If man is perfectible, in the sense of becoming progressively more reasonable, then the schools are the critical force in guiding and shaping his advance.

The twentieth century emphasis on irrational and emotional factors in human nature—the discounting of pure reason as a major determinant in human affairs—does not diminish the importance of the school. On the contrary, as the educator interprets the new philosophies, they extend its responsibilities. No longer does the cultivation of rationally acquired skills suffice; the proper qualities of attitude and outlook, psychological balance and social poise, need also to be instilled. To reading, writing, arithmetic, and vocational training, modern educational doctrine adds instruction in social skills and group behavior, to ensure the development of the well-rounded personality. The "whole" child has to be considered, and his orderly adjustment to the world around him becomes a major function of the school. Even the techniques of teaching traditional subjects must be altered to ensure proper motivation and incentive for the student. In a curiously distorted way, the liberalism of Dewey has fused with the liberalism of Locke and the function of public education becomes no longer "schooling" in the restricted sense of imparting definite skills and knowledge. Now its responsibility is even greater: it is nothing less than the successful ordering of man's relationship to man, the happy adjustment of the individual to society.

Take the outright quantitative pressures on schools, add the requirements of modern culture, and mix philosophical assertions that raise fundamental issues about human nature, and an explosion is inevitable. A special type of politics emerges, and focuses on the suburb: the "politics of the particularists," a pattern isolated and divorced from other local public duties. Since education is of such unparalleled importance in making money, in the achievement of success, and especially in the well-being of a democratic society, it is a "unique" function. If it is unique, it has priority above all other governmental responsibilities. If it has such priority, it deserves special institutional arrangements and a special decision-making process. So the major public activity of suburbia is carefully set apart from the rest of suburban political life and wrapped in a shell peculiarly its own. The politics of the schools, rooted essentially in the educator's assertion of primacy, intensifies and exaggerates—almost to the point of burlesque—the features of suburban political behavior. . . .

Because the function is of such importance, it should demand the special attention of every resident in town. Further, it is not enough that school systems be local public institutions; they must be a particular type of local government. Since education is so vital a public activity, ordinary officialdom cannot be trusted with its management, and a special form of grass roots administration must be installed to isolate education from the more humdrum problems of land use, welfare, highways, police and fire protection.

Therefore, except in New England, an entirely separate government is provided for school management; and even in New England, the school board shares the limelight with the selectmen. Independent, popularly elected school boards and, quite frequently, elected school superintendents, take their places alongside—but apart from—other local officials. A separate tax levy is set aside for the school; generally, independent control of the budget is granted to the school government. Separate qualifications for the recruitment and advancement of the school bureaucracy are established; special arrangements are made with the state for financial aid.

Not only is the government divided once again but the political man of suburbia is himself subdivided. He is already partly partisan and partly nonpartisan. Now the suburbanite must become a "school nonpartisan" as well. Education is too important to be left to ordinary political attitudes and actions; it must be "taken out of politics," and the last vestiges of group dissension and compromise must be erased. The all-wise, objective citizen assumes another burden. Responsibility and objective inquisitiveness are no longer sufficient for good citizenship; for the schools, positive support, open dedication and unquestioned allegiance are required. Patronage and favoritism cannot be allowed to enter the classroom in the way in which they are acceptable in granting highway contracts. No real debate can take place about the comparative needs of schools and other functions for no one can seriously argue that the building of a new fire station should be made possible by cutting the school budget. The essence of politics—compromise among competing needs, majority decisions between competing values—is ruled out. The school citizen must talk only about school.

Yet if politics is barred, who makes the decisions? Here an important shift in the relationship between expert and interest group takes place. In the case of the city manager, the professional might actively solicit support, but when he crossed over the line from administration to policy, he still had to convince his audience of the correctness of his views. In the schools, the expert looms even larger; the interest group exists to support the professional, almost without regard to his policies. The Parent-Teachers Association unites bureaucracy and the school public to work continually—if vaguely—for school "betterment," and in rapidly growing, predominantly Protestant suburbs, the P.T.A. quite frequently can deliver a majority of the electorate.

The critical figure is the school superintendent. He has, in the words of Herold Hunt, the obligation not to defend his policies, as is the case with other professionals, but to "explain" them. Standards of administration and personnel performance have become the almost exclusive prerogative of the professional along with the substance of the school program, the curriculum. Even the school construction program may be put into the hands of the educators instead of into those of architects or builders, since each physical detail of the classroom intimately affects the attitude of the child. The "lobby of the good," the professional teacher mobilized to defend the basic principle of American education and their lay disciples, frequently becomes the most powerful force operative in the public affairs of the locality.

Of course, the declaration that schools must be above politics and that the professional's judgment must be accepted as the determining one is not an accurate summary of the actual state of affairs. It is too much to expect a public activity, equipped with a popular decision-making process that includes elections, to operate without politics. The school board and the superintendent are subjected, as numerous case studies testify, to all kinds of pressures and demands. Some are of the ordinary, garden-variety type of political action: petty intrigue on the part of school architects, connivance in the adoption of textbooks, building and equipment awards. More frequently the focus is on the philosophy of education adopted by the given school system. Is the program excessively "modern" or too old-fashioned? Should progressive techniques be encouraged or would a return to the discipline of vocational training be more appropriate?

On the critical issue of philosophy—of what the schools should do—the school officials are often curiously silent, except for defending the development of the curriculum as a professional matter. Generally, they concentrate solely on the quantitative aspects of the problem. They make a "bricks and mortar" defense: more buildings, more teachers and more money. When pressed, they exhibit the uncertainty in beliefs and the capacity to change dogmas in midstream which the investigators of Crestwood Heights discovered when they studied the objectives of school experts. As a rule, however, the educators strive either to keep the problem to themselves or to avoid participating in its public debate.

In terms of political realism, this position makes more sense than the Crestwood Heights analysis supposed. It is not so much a commentary on the unsettled doctrines of the educational profession as it is a tribute to that profession's recognition of the Pandora's box which is unlocked when the bricks-and-mortar position is abandoned. For when the slogan "betterment of schools" is directly examined, it becomes nothing less than a debate on fundamental principles—on the validity of the underlying assumption which makes education a prerequisite not just for democracy but, in modern dress, for the reform of society itself. There is nothing else really left to debate since the divorce of school government from other government removes the opportunity to compare the values received from other public services. The demands for school expenditures become insatiable, for the goal of the school system is as unspecific as the citizen's individual prescription for the ills of all mankind.

Thus the school electorate finds itself at the extreme end of the road that the logic of nonpartisanship has built. The conscientious citizen is called upon to determine not only ways and means, to decide not just between competing priorities in functions. He is required to define, year after year, the goals of government itself, and to resolve persistent philosophical disputes. School politics take on the color of a constitutional convention that is continually in session, always discussing the fundamentals of its political order. It operates, moreover, in the open atmosphere that prevailed in France after the Revolution rather than in the closeted, protected circumstances in which the American Constitution was prepared. The participants are asked to dig up their first premises by the roots and examine them anew, while constantly under public scrutiny. When debate of this nature occurs, it is violent; ardent Deweyites are asked to defend their prophet, and sometimes they may be forced to read him. The "Americanist" strand of liberalism thunders that current school philosophy is nothing less than subversion. The dwindling ranks of Horatio Algers call out for a return to practical education without frills and fads. Lay Catholics are brought again to the question of defining the boundaries between Church and State, in an atmosphere in which even Jesuits find an orderly discussion difficult.

Once the politics of the school particularists become really politics, one of Jefferson's least promising injunctions is pushed to an extreme that even he never intended. There is no longer just a revolution every generation, there is a revolution going on constantly. Divorced from the rest of the political process, suburban school government may avoid some of the unpalatable by-products of partisan politics, but it exposes itself to the dangers of ideological politics where no holds are barred, common beliefs rarely recognized, and where opponents can constantly hurl charges of infidelity to basic principles. In school politics, grass roots democracy attains its ultimate promise: the citizens not only fully participate as individuals, but participate by laying bare their most fundamental convictions. And, since the goals of prevailing educational philosophy are open-ended, even agreement reached at one time in any one locality is unrewarding. The schools remain unsatisfactory, and the constitutional convention goes on unendingly.

4.5   INTRODUCTION

The final selection in this chapter takes the reader away from the concrete details of formal education and views them from a perspective no less encompassing than that of all cultures and across history. Analyzing the contents of schooling in general as a composite of intellect, technic, and morality and the orientation of any society as revolutionary, conservative, or reactionary, the author presents a theory of how these two classifications are related in actuality. Thus his essay is an attempt to specify with respect to education the basic anthropological premise that any social process is a derivative of its cultural setting. He reasserts the mutuality of the relationship between education and the larger culture, viewing each in turn from the perspective of the other: Given the state of a society, what do its occurrence and maintenance require of education? And, conversely, given what a society's educational institutions actually do, what will be the consequences for the direction of the society's development?

As Wallace points out, no society is purely one type or another. Moreover, especially in a complex society such as ours, "schooling" is not a unitary phenomenon and the ordering of values that it embodies is not uniform across its various levels and over the range of subcultural differences that the whole of American culture subsumes. The preceding selections by Vidich and Bensman, Wood, and Dahl have made it clear that what goes on in a particular school is the result of the various cultural emphases that, as expressed in political, economic, and social interaction, come together and give that situation its shape and content. Thus it is through the behavior of the individuals who participate in the concrete process of education—teachers, parents, deans, principals, students, board members, etc.—that the relative emphases on intellect, technic, or morality are established, maintained, or altered, and, as a result, that revolutionary, conservative, or reactionary orientations are fostered or weakened.

Whether or not one agrees with Wallace's recommended ordering of values, it could well be argued that a guidance counselor is in an unique position of potential influence with respect to what happens to the ordering that is reflected in the activities and policies of his particular school. His judgments and actions are important determinants of the choices students make and, more basically, of the alternatives open to them. Not only do they affect the direction of a student's educational career, but a guidance counselor's behavior is an important element in defining a school's *operating* (*i.e.,* actual rather than ideal) values and goals. The latter are not to be found in formal statements, but are more validly inferred from such things as the relative number of awards, honors, and celebrations involving academic and nonacademic matters; the manner in which students are assigned to different classes and programs; how deficient students are handled; the relatedness or separateness between extracurricular and academic activities; the aspects of academic performance that are used as the basis for special rewards. All of these are features which guidance-personnel workers can, and typically do, influence. In doing so, they must choose, whether or not they do so deliberately, to support one or another educational orientation—toward intellect, technic, or morality. Their actions may be erratic or consistent, skillful or ineffectual, but, whatever their quality, they will affect the nature of education and ultimately the nature of society.

4.5 SCHOOLS IN REVOLUTIONARY AND CONSERVATIVE SOCIETIES[1]

Anthony F. C. Wallace

It is convenient to arrange the circumstances of human learning in the form of a scale of generality, each category of which is contained in, and implied by, its succeeding category. If we take *schooling* as the initial category it is followed by *education*, then *enculturation*, then *learning* itself. Schooling is the learning that is

---

[1]From Anthony F. C. Wallace, "Schools in Revolutionary and Conservative Societies," *Anthropology and Education*, Frederick Gruber, ed., Philadelphia: University of Pennsylvania Press, 1961, pp. 29–54.

done in a school; and a school, as before, is an institution which deliberately and systematically, by the presentation of symbols in reading matter, lectures, or ritual, attempts to transform from a condition of ignorance to one of enlightenment, the intellect, the morality, and the technical knowledge and skills of an attentive group of persons assembled in a definite place at a definite time. Education is all learning (including but not confined to schooling) obtained from reading or from listening to formally prepared symbolic presentations. Enculturation is all learning enjoined on the person with a particular status as a member of a particular culture-bearing society, and thus includes, in addition to schooling and education, such homely but essential skills as knowing a language or two; observing the proper times, places, and techniques for the execution of such malleable bodily processes as urination, defecation, breathing, walking, eating, sleeping, and sexual intercourse; the securing and effective use of clothing, shelter, transport, weapons, and help; even the manner of communicating emotion and other information by facial expression, body posture, and other kinesic devices. Learning, of course, is the cover term, embracing all of the foregoing, and also those idiosyncratic learnings which every person accumulates throughout his lifetime and which may or may not be transmitted to others.

Let us now classify learning in a different way, by matter rather than by position on a scale of circumstance. In any situation of learning, three matters can be learned. These are the matters of *technic*, of *morality*, and of *intellect*. And since the bulk of this essay will concern the content and priority of these matters under various conditions, we shall now discuss these three matters of learning in some detail.

Technic is the most conspicuous matter of learning. And it is the teaching of technic which has been the subject of the most intensive analysis by psychologists and educationists. The most widely used paradigm for the learning of technic has been the stimulus → cue → response → reinforcement structure (the so-called S-R type of learning). This paradigm describes an animal which acts after it has been "stimulated" (*i.e.*, after an environmental process has produced a change in its internal state). It has an opportunity to do various things, but at least one of these things will be followed by a "reinforcing" (*i.e.*, punishing or rewarding) change of the organism's internal state. Furthermore, each action is performed in a context containing perceptible "cues." Experience shows that for almost any species it is possible to select some combination of stimuli, cues, and reinforcements in the matrix of which the animal will with increasing reliability perform some one action. The process of reliability increase is called "learning" because the observer feels that he too, if he were in the same spot, would perform that act as soon as he discovered that it was more frequently followed by a reward, or at least by the negation of punishment, than any other alternative. In naïve language, the animal "learns how" (*i.e.*, learns the technique) to secure reward and/or to avoid punishment. It is easy to infer from this what corresponds to common belief, namely that people, dogs, and rats all learn best when they are "motivated." It is also easy—but not necessarily valid—to infer that people, dogs, and rats will learn best what *is* reinforced, directly, personally, and materially.

Technic, therefore, is "how to" learning by reinforcement. It includes such things as learning how to talk, how to extract the square root of a number, how to dance, how to harpoon a walrus, how to play a piano, how to decorate an apartment, how to cook a meal, how to balance a budget, how to identify a witch, how to get to heaven. From this standpoint, even the rote learning of information—dates, names, events, formulas, art work, institutional structures, store prices, fashions, and the like—is "how to" learning, for the motive lies not in the acquisition of the information but in the use to which it may be put, whether to impress the neighbors, to win prizes, to fill out the image of the "intellectual," or whatever. And even values—such as standards of beauty, tastes in music, concepts of the good life—may be learned, both by rote, as when one learns first the symbols for the rewarded values, and later, by performing the act that earns the reward.

Morality, on the other hand deals not so much with "how to" as with "what." Furthermore, in my usage here, morality concerns, not just positive and negative goals, not just values, not even all socially approved values, but one particular kind of socially approved value. This kind of value is the conception that one's own behavior, as well as the behavior of others, should not merely take into consideration the attitude of the community, but should actively advance, or at least not retard, its welfare. *Morality* is thus to be sharply distinguished from mere propriety, conformity, and respectability, although it is not necessarily nonconformist. *Morality,* in this sense, is most *conspicuously* exemplified by such heroic actions as the soldier's who throws himself on a hand grenade in order to smother the blast and save his buddies; as the statesman's who suffers political oblivion rather than betray his country's interests; as the tribesman's who gives himself up to the enemy for punishment in order to prevent retaliation upon his whole people. It is also most *commonly* practiced in the humble endurance of discomfort, protracted over decades, by inconspicuous people in positions of responsibility. . . .

The third of our matters of learning is *intellect.* By intellect I do not mean intelligence, nor do I mean intellectualism. As Jacques Barzun has lucidly and at considerable length explained, intelligence is not necessarily governed by intellect, nor is the intellectual, as a social type, necessarily a custodian of the "House of Intellect." Intellect is, as he puts it, an "establishment":

> That part of the world I call the House of Intellect embraces at least three groups of subjects: the persons who consciously and methodically employ the mind; the forms and habits governing the activities in which the mind is so employed; and the conditions under which these people and activities exist. . . .
>
> Intellect is community property and can be handed down. . . .
>
> From the image of a house and its economy, one can see what an inquiry into the institution of Intellect must include. The main topics are: the state of the language, the system of schooling, the means and objects of communication, the supplies of money for

thought and learning, and the code of feeling and conduct that goes with them. When the general tendency of these arrangements makes for order, logic, clarity, and speed of communication, one may say that a tradition of Intellect exists. (Barzun, 1959, pp. 3–6)

Intellect thus is, to begin with, a social tradition, an aspect of culture, if you please. The core of this tradition is the proposition that if a subject is worthy of consideration at all, it should be considered in a particular cognitive form. That particular way of proper consideration may vary considerably from one society to the next, and, in a complex society, from one group to the next. . . .

We may make a schema to represent the divisions of learning which we have so far discussed. In Figure 1 are shown the three matters of learning and the scale of the circumstances of learning:

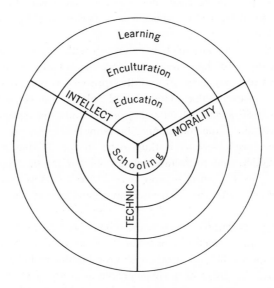

FIGURE 1.   THE DIVISIONS OF LEARNING

WHAT SHOULD A MAN LEARN?   The obvious answer to the question of what a man should learn has already been taught us by the anthropologists. Manifestly, what it is needful to learn in one society is not necessarily needful in another. Cultural differences demonstrate that there is no absolute set of things to be learned; what a man should learn is a function of his culture.

But concealed behind this principle lies a corollary: in order that noticeable cultural differences shall exist at all, there must be a significant degree of conformity to norm within each society. And this prevents us from going on to assert that what a man should learn is a matter for him alone to decide. There is, in fact, no human society on the face of the earth which concedes to *any* individual the right to learn anything he chooses. And furthermore, it is the school which is established by the community—not, be it noted, by the family—to ensure that the individual learns what he must know.

The values which guide the group in its choice of what learnings to impress on the individual are legion, and they may be described on many levels of complexity; but for our purposes three contrasting value orientations are most significant: the revolutionary, or utopian, orientation; the conservative, or ideological, orientation; and the reactionary orientation. What a man is expected to do in his life will, in part, depend on whether he lives in a revolutionary, conservative, or reactionary society. And what he is expected to do determines what he is expected to learn. Furthermore, not merely what a man should learn, but whether he should learn it in a school, or from his parents, or from his peers, or by casual reading, conversation, and attendance at entertainments, will be in part determined by whether he lives in a revolutionary or a conservative or a reactionary society.

We are asserting, in other words, that the value orientation of the society—in the tripartite sense given above—will determine not only the content of what a man is expected to learn, but whether he is expected to learn it in a school or under some other circumstances.

Now the utility of the three value orientations as a means of classifying each of several contemporaneous societies is unquestionable. Without much difficulty one could, for instance, label China and Cuba today as revolutionary societies; the United States and Great Britain as conservative; and Portugal and the Union of South Africa as reactionary. China and Cuba are deliberately and forcibly replacing old institutions with new ones organized in a new way according to a plan. The United States and Great Britain are, in regard to domestic policy, conservative in the sense that the existing institutions are considered to be adequate, not perfect but perfectible, and hence in need not of replacement but of repair. Portugal and the Union of South Africa are reactionary in the sense that their leaders' internal policies have been warped by an intention to ward off internal attack from groups which threaten to replace existing institutions with new ones. While no society can be wholly one thing or another, everywhere, in all of its aspects, at any one time, it seems reasonable to consider one value orientation or another as predominant in a given group, such as the political, economic, or religious leadership, during a stated period. The precise content of these values, of course, will vary: thus a revolutionary society may be communistic, capitalistic, Muslim, nativistic, or whatever, depending on local circumstances; and a comparable variety of conservatisms and reactions are also available.

But we may also use this tripartite classification for different time periods in the same society. Here one may expect that the orientations will change in a definite order: a society which is now revolutionary will, if it changes, become conservative, next reactionary, and again most probably revolutionary. Thus, over centuries or millennia, any one society is apt to follow a roughly cyclical path through revolution, conservatism, and reaction, over and over again. This subject has been approached by scholars and scientists in various ways and is one of the classic problems of the social sciences. My own approach to it has been via the study of what I call revitalization movements, particularly of a religious variety.

Thus one may, with regard to any one society, expect to find that the content and circumstances of learning will vary with the varying predominance of its value orientation. And now we may go to the crux of the matter. It would appear that with each of the major value orientations there is associated a philosophy of schooling which characteristically assigns priorities to the matters of learning in schools. It is to the elucidation of the association between these priorities and the value orientations that the remainder of this essay will be devoted.

THE REVOLUTIONARY SOCIETY Let us consider first the dynamics of a revolutionary society. A revolutionary society is a society dominated by a revitalization movement, which may be defined as a deliberate, organized, conscious effort by members of a society to construct a more satisfying culture. It may in the extreme be either religious or political, but is usually a combination of both. The code of the movement defines the previous state of society as inadequate, perverse, even evil, and depicts a more or less utopian image of the better society as the goal culture toward which the *ad hoc* and temporary social arrangements of the present transfer culture is carrying the society. . . .

The present world, no less than past human history, affords numerous examples of revolutionary societies. We have already cited China and Cuba as examples. Communist nations form a large class of revolutionary societies today, but many other kinds exist: for example, a revitalization movement among the Manus, off the coast of New Guinea, described at length in Margaret Mead's book, *New Lives for Old*; the numerous "cargo cult" and "marching rule" movements delineated in Peter Worsley's study of Melanesian cults. *The Trumpet Shall Sound*; the nationalisms, Egyptian, Algerian, and contemporary African; the new India and Indonesia; and so on. Much of contemporary world history can best be understood in terms of revitalization theory.

With respect to schools and schooling, one inference is paramount: that in a revolutionary society (*i.e.*, a society in the process of cultural transformation under the leadership of a revitalization movement) the primary concern of schools must be the *moral* transformation of the population. Next in order of priority will be intellect; and last of all, technic (despite the often critical need for technically trained personnel to carry out the program of the transfer culture). The reason for this priority list—morality, intellect, and technic—is that the moral rebirth of the

population and development of a cadre of morally reliable and intellectually re-
sourceful individuals to take over executive positions throughout the society is the
immediately necessary task. This is a capital investment, so to speak, from which
interest in the form of technical skills will ultimately be generated. The moral
intellectuals produced by revolutionary schools may, to conservative eyes, appear
to be fanatics and theoreticians who fumble badly on technical tasks. But they are
necessary, during the temporary period of revolution, in order to do the work of
converting the populace, developing large plans, and adapting the code to local
and temporal circumstances. If they do their work well, they will develop a base
upon which later expansions of technic can build without fear of counterrevolution, apathy, and lack of foresight. . . .

THE CONSERVATIVE
SOCIETY
A conservative society is a society in which a
revitalization movement has won its battle
with reaction and has established a successful
new culture. This new culture may, in terms of the revitalization code, be only a
transfer culture, but since the process of transfer may, even in theory, take a long
time, it can become a stable way of life. Being secure and successful, the old
movement does not need to preoccupy itself with combat against reaction or
against new revitalization movements. The problem is to keep the machine going
as efficiently as possible, with occasional improvements, and possibly with
smoothly programmed shifts from one stage to another on the path toward the
goal culture.

With respect to morality, the transformation of the society is sufficiently complete for severe moral nonconformists to be treated as delinquents, criminals, or
victims of mental illness. The reform, rehabilitation, or control of these people can
be safely left to the police, the courts, the medical profession, and (most importantly) to the informal sanctions of the family and the community itself. All communication media are saturated with applications of the new code. Society as a
whole can therefore communicate the moral values necessary to the maintenance
of the transfer culture, and thus to the achievement of the goal culture, through
multiple channels of communication as part of the general process of education
and without extreme dependence on schools. It is even possible to permit a degree
of open nonconformity, of a less severe kind, to be sure, in order to avoid the
inconvenience of exercising close surveillance over individuals and the expense of
deliberate schooling. A conservative society is, paradoxically, also a liberal society,
precisely because the elite is secure enough that it can afford to learn from its
critics and even to absorb them into the ranks of conservatism as a "loyal
opposition."

With respect to intellect the conservative society is tolerant, but since the work
of code formulation and its application has been largely accomplished, the skilled
practitioner of intellect is not necessary to the regime. Intellect becomes a rather

special tradition, relatively free from constraint, but without access to power because, in a political sense, it has little power to offer. Thus the schools see relatively little need to force intellect even upon the intelligent. Intellect becomes a career in itself, self-sought and guild-protected, with the members of the guild practicing partly for the fun of it and partly as professional men selling their services to the highest bidder (and not necessarily, alas, for a high price). Under such circumstances, remarkably "pure" intellect can develop, producing vastly significant contributions to knowledge, and ultimately perhaps exerting considerable social power. But this power is exerted in an amoral manner, as in the creation of new weapons and technologies, new philosophies of the mind, new mathematics, and so forth. The *morally* concerned "intellectual" is apt (in a statistical sense) to be no intellectual at all, but a taker of unconventional moral and aesthetic stands in a stereotyped conventional way, a snob, a *poseur* who pretends that what is different from mass behavior must be based on superior values. The "intellectuals" and the practitioners of intellect are generally rather distinct groups in conservative societies, the true practitioner of intellect being a professional, ruthlessly severe in competence, and relatively indifferent to the moral implications of his work, even though his life as citizen, parent, and friend may be highly moral. Indeed, for some professionals of this type, the work of intellect is in itself morally good, provided it is competent work: this the scientist, if not the humanist, maintains. The "intellectual," by contrast, is likely to be an amateur, a dilettante, a poor painter, a sloppy writer, and an incompetent musician, whose noisy revolt against conventional morality and technical materialism is supported for its entertainment value by materialists, condemned by moralists, and largely ignored by practitioners of intellect.

But the divorce of intellect from morality, ending a marriage which was consummated in revolution, makes the house of intellect itself appear to the outsider to be merely a specialized machine shop of technic, and transforms the orientation of the school toward it. The school now emphasizes technic as its primary mission. It first of all trains people to do jobs. The jobs may be closely defined: bookkeeping, automobile driving, jousting with a lance, praying correctly; or they may be vaguely defined: being able to vote intelligently in elections, handling human relations smoothly. The demands of morality come next, for morality is considered, in a negative sort of way, to be necessary to keep society from falling apart. (In the revolutionary society, morality was supremely necessary, both to prompt the destruction of the old society and to guide the building of the new one.) Intellect is respected, but it is also recurrently confused with native intelligence, with the pseudo-intellectualism to which we alluded earlier, with some sort of impotent disloyalty, with stuffiness, with an inhuman lack of concern for human values, or even with immorality and cruelty. As such, it may be allowed to develop spontaneously but will not be supported by the state, for fear of developing something dangerous at the expense of undeniably useful technic and unquestionably desirable morality.

THE REACTIONARY The reactionary society is a post-conservative
SOCIETY society. The conservative order, having been
challenged by a budding revitalization
movement (*i.e.*, by what it regards as a treasonable, heretical conspiracy imported
from abroad), adjusts its posture to minimize the effectiveness of its competitor's
propaganda and to mobilize counterattacks. In the interest of preserving the same
values that an earlier revitalization movement established in pain and sweat, and
which the conservative society cherished and elaborated, the reactionary society
subverts its own way of life in order to deliver telling blows against the enemy
within. In so doing it may destroy the very social structure which it is defending;
and it becomes, because of the growing discrepancy between ideal and practice,
and because popular confidence in its values begins to erode, rapidly moribund, an
eminent subject for revitalization.

The reactionary society thus, in the area of learning generally, has two paramount concerns: first, to combat the alien heresies by revealing the inadequacy of
their values and the poverty of their practice; and second, to recapture the moral
enthusiasm of its earlier, revitalization phase. Consequently, the reactionary society shares with the revolutionary society a supreme concern with *morality:* a
paradox of social history which is apt to puzzle the sophisticated conservative in
the middle, who finds it difficult to understand the extremists, who seem to understand each other very well. This concern with morality is reflected in a re-empha-
sized religiosity, a refurbished political ritualism, repressive laws, an oppressive
police, and—in the schools—a conviction that the moral education of the young
must take precedence over all else. This anxiety lest the young can be morally
seduced requires, as in revolutionary societies, the schools to take over from the
family, from industry, and from other social groups the responsibility for the
moral development of the young, and to place extreme emphasis on the human
environment of the school child. The moral purity of his teachers and his school-
mates comes to be more important than the content of instruction, or even than
school itself, and if either knowledge or rectitude must be sacrificed, it is knowledge whose immolation is certain.

Although they share a preoccupation with morality, the reactionary and the
truly revolutionary society differ in their evaluation of intellect. In the logic of
revolution, morality and intellect are believed to be linked in a pact with the
future. Hence, as we have suggested, the revolutionary society will place intellect
before technic in its scale of priority: the cultivation of intellect becomes a kind of
capital investment in people. In the reactionary society, by contrast, intellect is
feared as a potential enemy because, in the preceding conservative phase, it has
acted as endowed critic of the conventional wisdom, charged with responsibility
for pointing out pathways to improvement; and because, in the competing contemporary revolutionary organization, students and mature intellectuals are conspicuously influential. Thus the reactionary society will favor technic over intellect, will
redefine tasks which previously were regarded as intellectual in order to make

them technical, and will redefine relatively harmless aesthetic diversions as "intellectual." The cost of this scholastic reorganization, however, is apt to be very great, since the derogation of intellect will reduce the number of persons in the reactionary society who are capable of thinking coherently, purposefully, and creatively on matters of public concern. The ultimate consequence to a reactionary society of neglecting the cultivation of intellect is collapse before the onslaught of a revitalization movement which is guided by intellect.

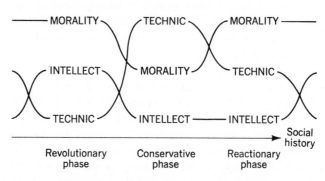

FIGURE 2.   THE MATTERS OF LEARNING

CURRENT APPLICATIONS   Today our society here in the United States is conservative. We went through our major revitalization movement nearly two hundred years ago; we have elaborated and refined the principles established during our revolutionary period—principles thought out by men of intellect and codified in the Declaration of Independence and the federal Constitution—and have since that time worked to preserve and perfect a way of life guided by these principles. Under the pressure of internal strains and foreign wars, cold and hot, we have so far avoided becoming truly reactionary.

There is a clear danger, however, that the external pressure of a revolutionary Communist philosophy, even though its internal influence is very small, may provoke the unwary into adopting a reactionary posture. Nowhere is this danger more present than in regard to the schools. Our schools have traditionally been, as must be the case with any conservative society, less interested in intellect than in technic, but nonetheless more interested in intellect than in morality. Elaborate precautions have been taken to prevent the excessive intrusion of overt religious or political interests into the public and private schools. But by placing control of schools in the hands of all too often technically, rather than intellectually, committed educators and practical business and professional men, equally elaborate efforts are made to ensure that technic takes precedence over intellect. . . .

Thus, in the view taken in this essay, the school problem of the contemporary United States does not arise from some inexplicable deterioration of moral and intellectual stamina, related to a Spenglerian decline of the West. Nor is it the consequence of any particularly perverse philosophy of education. The progressive schoolman and the fundamentalist in education—neither of whom wants precisely what I want, but who are nonetheless likely to be skilled, devoted, and self-sacrificing public servants—are both at the mercy of innumerable semieducated electorates and their politically affiliated school boards, of state and federal educational bodies, of legislatures, of boards of trustees, of colleges and foundations, all of whom are exquisitely sensitive to dangers to the conservative position, and many of whom will soon be all too ready to insist that the school's first duty is to develop moral and well-trained citizens and soldiers, and that its last duty is to discipline the mind.

Let me suggest what, in a conservative society intending to survive in a revolutionary world by refusing to freeze into the reactionary posture, the value hierarchy of the schools should be. The cultivation of intellect should come first, technic second, and morality last. Intellect should be cultivated in all persons, to the limit of their abilities, and those whose abilities are least should learn to respect and admire the achievements and the rewards of those more fortunate. (This is not a psychological impossibility, nor need it be traumatic: athletic sports are not prohibited as mentally unhygienic simply because ability and hard work are conspicuously rewarded, while the vast majority are left to watch delightedly the feats of the stars.) Far from supinely assuming that the rigor of logic and mathematics and of language studies does not generalize to anything but itself, such rigor should be required in work on all other subjects, both humane and scientific. The goal should be a citizenry who feel an obligation to be rational in their thinking on personal or public affairs as well as in their technical work. . . .

Now this, to my mind, is the kind of thing that intellect is all about. Intellect is a cultural matter; it must be learned; and, for survival, it must be used. Our country's survival as a conservative society—or, indeed, as any kind of society—depends radically upon maintaining a system of schools which teaches the tradition of intellect as its primary obligation.

BIBLIOGRAPHY

BARZUN, JACQUES, 1959, *The House of Intellect*, New York: Harper & Row.
MEAD, MARGARET, 1956, *New Lives for Old*, New York: William Morrow.
OPPENHEIMER, J. ROBERT, 1954, *Science and the Common Understanding*, New York: Simon and Schuster.
WALLACE, ANTHONY F. C., 1956, "Revitalization Movements," *American Anthropologist*, Vol. 58, pp. 264–281.
WORSLEY, PETER, 1957, *The Trumpet Shall Sound*, London: Macgibbon & Kee.

Questions and Implications for Practice

4.1 GEORGE D. SPINDLER

1. Does guidance-personnel work in its stress on the individual tend to reinforce traditional values? Defend your point of view.

2. Is it desirable or perhaps inescapable for the guidance-personnel worker to understand and to take a position in terms of these conflicting values? Would it be preferable for the counselor to profess agnosticism, to try to maintain a tolerant, neutral position? Is this possible?

3. Where, in your opinion, should guidance-personnel workers be placed on the continuum on which Spindler places other groups involved with education?

4. How can the guidance-personnel worker attempt to deal with the tensions caused by the transformation apparently going on in American society?

4.2 VIDICH AND BENSMAN

1. Does the guidance worker in Peabody's school need the kind of sophistication Peabody possesses, or is it enough for him just to counsel students? Is it, perhaps, possible for the counselor to avoid visibility and thus also avoid criticism, conflict, and opposition that could obstruct his work? Could his insistence on confidentiality reduce his visibility and thus increase the scope within which he can work without friction from other elements? Can his very effort to operate in relation to only one person at a time get him into complications? How and why?

2. "Wouldn't it be asking a good deal to expect that teachers, guidance counselors, Deans of Women, Deans of Men, and college professors should care about and try to understand their school board or their board of trustees and the community in which their school or college is located? After all, most guidance-personnel workers, for instance, are trained to be experts in individual psychology and dyadic counseling. Why shouldn't they simply trust the principal or president to deal with politics and ask him to protect them from having to waste their time on such matters?" Do you agree or disagree with the point of view expressed in the above statement? Why?

4.3 ROBERT DAHL

1. In what way would the guidance-personnel program benefit by a study of the distribution of influence in some school or college situation that you know well?

2. On higher education levels do you think students themselves might well be involved in such a study? Why or why not? If so, just how might their interest be enlisted? What roles should they have? What sort of structure might be used?

How might students be given help to make their work of good quality? How could the process be safeguarded so that students will not feel they are being exploited or overdirected?

3. What kind of training, knowledge, and skills would be useful in attempting to produce a true, fair, and revealing picture of the power structure and distribution of influence in any situation?

4.4 ROBERT C. WOOD

1. Most, but not all, educators and a large majority of citizens, would agree that "the function of public education [is] no longer 'schooling' in the restricted sense of imparting definite skills and knowledge. Now its responsibility is even greater: it is nothing less than the successful ordering of man's relationship to man, the happy adjustment of the individual to society."

If you agree with this statement of Wood's, it might make an interesting exercise to project yourself into a specific role in some school or college you know well and try to think of all the appropriate and effective ways in which you as a professional worker might try to contribute to your students learning how to order their relationships successfully with others, and how to adjust happily to society.

2. Wood also says the goal of the school system is as unspecific as the citizen's individual prescription for the ills of all mankind. Would your ability to relate "appropriate and effective ways in which you as a professional worker might try to contribute to students learning how to order their relationships with others and how to adjust happily to society" tend to contribute to the specificity of educational goals? Why or why not?

Would you, for instance, be able, and would you think it appropriate—if invited to do so—to discuss with a Kiwanis Club (or some other community group) why the cultivation of rationally acquired skills is no longer a sufficient objective for the school?

4.5 ANTHONY F. C. WALLACE

1. To what extent do you agree with Wallace's brilliant analysis of schools in various types of societies? Is your own view of the relative importance of intellect, technic, and morality basic to the way you practice your profession?

2. If the bulk of guidance-personnel workers in United States' schools and colleges were to assign supreme importance to technic as being of most value in our technological age, to morality as being essential to community peace and comfort, and to intellect as of third importance, what effect, according to Wallace, might this have on moving us into another type of society?

3. Compare the broad frame of reference within which Wallace views the values of our society with the more specific view that Spindler takes with regard to traditional and emerging values.

PART III

THE INDIVIDUAL,

SOCIETY,

AND CULTURE

Having examined individuals and groups behaving and interacting in the complex situations that constitute the guidance counselor's immediate working environment, we now take a closer look at the individual—what he is and how he gets that way. The various analyses and discussions that are presented in the next seven chapters approach this general problem from several points of view, the overall purpose of the selections being to examine the individual as a product of, and existing in the context of, a social environment. The relevance of the materials included here is less direct than that of the selections in Chapters 3 and 4, which focused directly on education. It should become clear, however, that the relevance is nonetheless there and, although more indirect, it is also more basic.

Chapter 5 deals with the relationship between the individual and his social environment at the broadest level: Which aspects of a person are derived from the fact that he lives in society? Which aspects of a society and its culture significantly affect the development of its members? Chapter 6 approaches the problem from a different direction, examining some of the major groups, situations, and interactions through which the relationship between the individual and his social context is created and nurtured. Chapter 7 elaborates on Chapters 5 and 6 in that it deals with particular features of the social structure, the nature of their effects, and the cultural variations and segmentation associated with them. Chapter 8 is concerned quite exclusively with the crucial element of the educational process—learning. The selections in this chapter bring many of the ideas and findings dealt with in earlier ones, as well as some new ones, into a common focus, both specifying and elaborating their relevance to what and how individuals learn.

In Chapter 9, the individual's social self is broken down further into parts, called roles, which are used as units in analyzing a number of situations and behaviors. Chapter 10 deals with some of the patterned relationships among individual, social, and cultural factors which shape and direct the behavior of the individual so that a "working" relationship between him and his social environment is maintained. Finally, Chapter 11 considers the phenomenon of change in social systems and, mostly through concrete illustrations, shows the complexity of both causes and effects that are associated with even the simplest social alterations.

Chapter 5

Cultural Dimensions of Personality and Behavior

The association between what people are like and their membership in particular societies and cultures was a part of men's thinking long before social scientists made it the target of their attention and inquiry. People from a particular region or nation are sometimes characterized as friendly, lazy, stingy, hard-working, trusting, warm, hospitable, re-served, etc. Whether such descriptions are accurate or not, implicit in their usage is the notion that a common origin will produce similarities in traits and behavior—that "where one comes from" helps to de-termine what one is like.

Once these hidden assumptions are exposed, certain questions follow quite directly. Which aspects of a person's background are crucial? Precisely how do they have their effects? Having accounted for similarities among people, how do we account for differences? The selections that follow in this chapter aim to examine these questions and the many issues and problems they subsume.

Even without any formal training in social science, most people today are familiar with that part of its general approach which con-siders, in the first place, that man can be understood only in terms of his environment and, secondly, that perhaps the most significant as-pects of that environment are those which are, in effect, "man made"—societies and their culture. Such a conclusion, easily and widely accepted today, is the result of lengthy and intensive thought and empirical investigation concerning the sources of man's character and behavior. Yet, the careful sorting out of what is given in man's biology and what he has come by through other processes for which physical structure is only one of the necessary conditions is an enterprise which has by no means been completed.

As we know him, man is a phenomenon existing only in the context of a culture. The concept has meaning for us only as it implies the existence of social arrangements and shared symbols of some kind, however rudimentary. These are the products of the unique intellectual capacities that are made possible by man's physical structure. As such they are an inherent part of what man is and he cannot be described except in terms of them. Nevertheless, for purposes of scientific understanding, it is necessary to break down this unity into its basic elements and trace the manner in which they are interrelated.

From one point of view, culture may be said to be the result of man's struggle with the physical environment and his attempts to understand both the nature and the meaning of that struggle. The outstanding finding of social science in this respect, however, is that men in different places and at different times have used a virtually innumerable variety of methods to solve the problems posed by the fact of living and have developed a comparable range of symbols and meanings to make their world and their life comprehensible.

Comparisons among societies at different stages of development and in different physical settings have freed our perspective and made it clear that the social and cultural phenomena that constitute our own life experience are only a very limited segment from a wide range of possible variation. Such study has gradually revealed the intricate relationship between the content of people's lives and the way they themselves define and perceive it. As individuals have been observed, analyzed, and compared over a variety of physical, social and cultural conditions, the realization has emerged that an individual's sociocultural environment is an integral part of his personality and behavior. These are the complex products of the human organism's striving to obtain satisfaction for its needs from the environment, and therefore their form and content depend importantly on which aspects of the environment the culture makes available, how different satisfactions are defined and evaluated, and the means for obtaining the satisfactions to which the individual is culturally directed.

Societies and cultures are not merely aggregates of structures and symbols that cope with the problems of collective life. They are, rather, coherent systems, by which we mean that their content and functioning are dependent on and partly determine the nature of each of their elements. The elements of a sociocultural system include its individual members; the arrangements by which their relationships are organized and regulated so that the tasks necessitated by group life are accomplished; and the beliefs, goals, values, and other symbols which give rise to and direct individual and group behavior. All systems strive to maintain their own stability and continuity by ensuring the integration of the component parts. In the case of a sociocultural system, this means that the system strives to mold its individual members in a manner compatible with the structure of the system as a whole. More specifically, the system tends to motivate individuals toward those goals which are available within the system and it fosters conceptions of what is necessary, desirable, and valuable that are compatible with the conditions that the system seeks to maintain. Or, to state it in yet another way, the personalities of members of a well-integrated society would be such that individuals would derive satisfaction from its culture and would not, generally or predominantly, behave in a manner contrary to its major themes. To the extent that a sociocultural system approaches such conditions, personality dimensions will reflect cultural ones and, at the same time, the persistence of dominant cultural themes will be fostered by the personality patterns with which they are congruent. Such conditions, however, are only theoretical possibilities and not to be found in any real society. They do not constitute actual situations, but, rather, indicate the direction in which social and cultural pressures operate. To the extent that the system falls short of such integration, strains and conflicts arise, both for the individual and for the society, making other forms of adjustment or compensation necessary and increasing the likelihood of change.

Over and beyond such considerations, however, not all members of a society have the same personality. Together with his physical endowment, the events of each individual's life history shape his personality. These events, to be sure, are culturally patterned, but within those limits a wide variety of configurations are possible, involving both common and unique aspects and situations, and producing personalities which will likewise have similar as well as different elements and combinations of elements. Having recognized that individual personalities both reflect culture and shape, reinforce, and perpetuate it, the problem of specifying this reciprocal relationship and identifying the events and processes through which it becomes established still remains. The selections presented in this chapter suggest some of the directions which social science inquiry has pursued in its attack on this problem.

5.1 INTRODUCTION

In this selection, Ralph Linton, an anthropologist, defines the concept of culture and places personality in relation to it. He distinguishes the role of the person as a social unit, produced by and integrated with the culture, from the concurrent role of the person as an individual, reflecting but also deviating from standard patterns. In presenting this dual view of the individual, this selection serves as an introduction to the other materials in this chapter as well as to the subsequent chapters in Part III.

Linton contests the rather common tendency to consider all of a person's actions and qualities as a product of his individual characteristics, pointing out that most of what a person is and does is better explained in terms of cultural patterns. Thus Linton makes a distinction between the personality, by which he means the unique features of the person, and the total individual, by which he means the personality plus the culturally predictable features. Linton's approach to this issue represents that of a major segment within the field of anthropology, but it should be noted here that there are other anthropologists who work with different conceptions of the relationship between culture and personality and thus Linton's views should not be thought of as *the* anthropological approach.

When we speak of "culture" in our society, of course, the term does not refer to a single homogeneous system to which all individuals are uniformly linked. The particular aspects of culture which constitute an individual's reality may be a composite of ethnic, minority group, social class, or regional elements operating in relation to more general themes from the overall culture of the society. If we could know all the relevant cultural influences, most of an individual's behavior would be seen to "fit," indeed to be rather predictable. But, in actuality, our understanding tends to be much more limited, not only because such thorough information is unlikely, but primarily because our perceptions are shaped by our own particular pattern of cultural influences. As a result, we look at the products of a different culture and respond to them as if they should fit into ours.

This creates a basic problem for the practitioner who deals with individuals from a variety of cultural backgrounds, and who must interact with them as a basic part of his role. Social interaction presumes, if it is to continue and be even minimally smooth, a common framework of symbols and meanings, behavioral as well as verbal. Such similarity, however, will not necessarily be the typical situation for, say, the middle-class guidance counselor working in a slum school, or for the white counselor explaining a Negro child's learning problems to the child's parents, or for any guidance counselor attempting to justify certain prohibitions to a deviant teenager. In any of these cases, the guidance counselor's help may be resisted, not because the individual is neurotically defensive, or deliberately obstructive, or unintelligent, but quite possibly because the whole concept of "help" and of the relationships and situations in which it is appropriate is so different in his culture than in the one which defines the counselor's role.

The materials in subsequent selections will add much substance, of specific relevance to the work of a guidance counselor, to the notion presented below of the embeddedness of personality and culture in each other. Here, however, the goal is to confront this fact fully and at its most general level, initiating a shift in the reader's focus from the self-contained individual to the larger system of the individual-in-the-culture (or, indeed, the culture-in-the-individual) as the source of behavior and personality.

5.1   THE INDIVIDUAL, CULTURE, AND SOCIETY[1]

Ralph Linton

For the present it is sufficient to define a culture as the way of life of any society. This way of life includes innumerable details of behavior but all of these have certain factors in common. They all represent the normal, anticipated response of any of the society's members to a particular situation. Thus, in spite of the infinite number of minor variations which can be found in the responses of various individuals, or even in those of the same individual at different times, it will be found that most of the people in a society will respond to a given situation in much the same way. In our own society, for example, nearly everybody eats three times a day and takes one of these meals approximately at noon. Moreover, individuals who do not follow this routine are regarded as queer. Such a consensus of behavior and opinion constitutes a culture pattern; the culture as a whole is a more or less organized aggregate of such patterns.

The culture as a whole provides the members of any society with an indispensable guide in all the affairs of life. It would be impossible either for them or for the society to function effectively without it. The fact that most members of the society will react to a given situation in a given way makes it possible for anyone to predict their behavior with a high degree of probability, even though never with absolute certainty. This predictability is a prerequisite for any sort of organized social living. If the individual is going to do things for others, he must have assurance that he will get a return. The presence of culture patterns, with their background of social approval and consequent potentialities for social pressure upon those who do not adhere to them, provides him with that assurance. Moreover, through long experience and largely by the use of the trial-and-error method, the culture patterns which are characteristic of any society have usually come to be closely adjusted to one another. The individual can get good results if he adheres to them, poor or even negative ones if he does not. The old proverb, "When in Rome do as the Romans do," is based on sound observation. In Rome or in any

---

[1]From: *The Cultural Background of Personality*, by Ralph Linton. Copyright, 1945, by D. Appleton-Century Company, Inc. Reprinted by permission of Appleton-Century-Crofts. Pp. 12–17, 28–29, 81–85, 90–98.

other society things are organized in terms of the local culture patterns and make few provisions for departure from them. The difficulties of an Englishman in quest of his tea in a small Middle Western American town would be a case in point.

If the presence of culture patterns is necessary to the functioning of any society, it is equally necessary to its perpetuation. The structure, that is, system of organization, of a society is itself a matter of culture. Although for purposes of description we can turn to spatial analogies and plot such a system in terms of positions, such positions cannot be defined adequately except in terms of the behavior expected of their occupants. Certain characteristics of age, sex, or biological relationship may be prerequisites for the occupation of particular positions by the individual, but even the designation of such prerequisites is a cultural matter. Thus the positions of father and son in our own social system cannot be made clear by any statement of the biological relationship existing between the two. It is necessary to give an account of the culturally patterned behavior of the occupants of these positions towards each other. When it comes to such positions as those of employer and employee, we find it impossible to define them except in terms of what the occupants of these two positions are expected to do for (or possibly to) each other. A position in a social system, as distinct from the individual or individuals who may occupy it at a particular point in time, is actually a configuration of culture patterns. Similarly, the social system as a whole is a still more extensive configuration of culture patterns. This configuration provides the individual with techniques for group living and social interaction in much the same way that other pattern configurations, also within the total culture, provide him with techniques for exploiting the natural environment or protecting himself from supernatural dangers. Societies perpetuate themselves by teaching the individuals in each generation the culture patterns which belong with the positions in the society which they are expected to occupy. The new recruits to the society learn how to behave as husbands or chiefs or craftsmen and by so doing perpetuate these positions and with them the social system as a whole. Without culture there could be neither social systems of the human sort nor the possibility of adjusting new members of the group to them.

I realize that in the foregoing discussion of society and culture emphasis has been laid mainly upon the passive role of the individual and upon the way in which he is shaped by cultural and social factors. It is time now to present the other side of the picture. No matter how carefully the individual has been trained or how successful his conditioning has been, he remains a distinct organism with his own needs and with capacities for independent thought, feeling, and action. Moreover, he retains a considerable degree of individuality. His integration into society and culture goes no deeper than his learned responses, and although in the adult these include the greater part of what we call the personality, there is still a good deal of the individual left over. Even in the most closely integrated societies and cultures no two people are ever exactly alike.

Actually, the role of the individual with respect to society is a double one. Under ordinary circumstances, the more perfect his conditioning and consequent integration into the social structure, the more effective his contribution to the smooth functioning of the whole and the surer his rewards. However, societies have to exist and function in an everchanging world. The unparalleled ability of our species to adjust to changing conditions and to develop ever more effective responses to familiar ones rests upon the residue of individuality which survives in every one of us after society and culture have done their utmost. As a simple unit in the social organism, the individual perpetuates the *status quo*. As an individual he helps to change the *status quo* when the need arises. Since no environment is ever completely static, no society can survive without the occasional inventor and his ability to find solutions for new problems. Although he frequently invents in response to pressures which he shares with other members of his society, it is his own needs which spur him on to invention. The first man who wrapped a skin about him or fed a fire did this not because he was conscious that his society needed these innovations but because he felt cold. To pass to a higher level of culture complexity, no matter how injurious an existing institution may be to a society in the face of changing conditions, the stimulus to change or abandon it never comes from the individual upon whom it entails no hardship. New social inventions are made by those who suffer from the current conditions, not by those who profit from them.

An understanding of the double role of individuals as individuals and as units in society will provide a key to many of the problems which trouble students of human behavior. In order to function successfully as a unit in society, the individual must assume certain stereotyped forms of behavior, that is, culture patterns. A great many of these culture patterns are oriented towards the maintenance of society rather than the satisfaction of individual needs. Societies are organisms of a sort, and it has become common practice to speak of their having needs of their own as distinct from those of the individuals who compose them. Such usage carries unfortunate implications, since the qualities of societies are quite different from those of living organisms. It is safer to express the necessities implicit in the social situation by saying that a society can neither endure through time nor function successfully at any point in time unless the associated culture fulfills certain conditions. It must include techniques for indoctrinating new individuals in the society's system of values and for training them to occupy particular places in its structure. It must also include techniques for rewarding socially desirable behavior and discouraging that which is socially undesirable. Lastly, the behavior patterns which compose the culture must be adjusted to one another in such a way as to avoid conflict and prevent the results of one pattern of behavior from negating those of another. All societies have developed cultures which fulfill these conditions, although the processes involved in their development are still obscure.

The culture patterns upon which any society depends for its survival must be established as patterns of habitual response on the part of its members. This is rendered possible by man's extraordinary ability to absorb teaching. Teaching is used advisedly since something more than mere learning from accidental and unorganized experience is involved. All human beings receive deliberate and purposeful instruction from their elders. Complex patterns of behavior are transferred from generation to generation in this way. The individual's incentive for assuming these patterns lies in the satisfaction which they afford to his personal needs, especially his need for favorable response from others. However, from the point of view of his society such satisfactions are important mainly as bait. He learns the patterns as wholes, and these wholes subtend the necessities of social living quite as much as they subtend his own needs. He takes the bait of immediate personal satisfaction and is caught upon the hook of socialization. He would learn to eat in response to his own hunger drive, but his elders teach him to "eat like a gentleman." Thus, in later years, his hunger drive elicits a response which will not only satisfy it but do so in a way acceptable to his society and compatible with its other culture patterns. Through instruction and imitation the individual develops habits which cause him to perform his social role not only effectively but largely unconsciously. This ability to integrate into a single configuration elements of behavior some of which serve to meet individual needs, others to satisfy social necessities, and to learn and transmit such configurations as wholes is the thing that makes human societies possible. By assuming such configurations and establishing them as habits the individual is adjusted to occupy a particular position in society and to perform the role associated with that position.

The fact that most human behavior is taught in the form of organized configurations rather than simply developed by the individual on the basis of experience, is of the utmost importance to personality studies. It means that the way in which a person responds to a particular situation often provides a better clue to what his teaching has been than to what his personality is. In general, all the individuals who occupy a given position in the structure of a particular society will respond to many situations in very much the same way. That any one individual of such a group manifests this response proves nothing about his personality except that he has normal learning ability. His personal predispositions will be revealed not by his culturally patterned responses but by his deviations from the culture pattern. It is not the main theme of his behavior but the overtones which are significant for understanding him as an individual. In this fact lies the great importance of cultural studies for personality psychology. Until the psychologist knows what the norms of behavior imposed by a particular society are and can discount them as indicators of personality he will be unable to penetrate behind the façade of social conformity and cultural uniformity to reach the authentic individual. . . .

The real culture of any society consists of the actual behavior, and so on, of its members. It includes a vast number of elements, no two of which are identical. No two persons ever react to a given stimulus in exactly the same way, and even the same person will react to such a stimulus differently at different times. Every individual bit of behavior differs in some particular from every other bit. To increase the complexity, no two stimuli are ever identical, either. However, the individual is able to develop successful and more or less automatic adjustments to his environment in spite of this intrinsic variability. He generalizes with respect to stimuli of a particular sort, lumping them together on the basis of their similarities and ignoring their differences. Thus a student learns that the ringing of a bell in the classroom means that the hour is up and ignores the minor day-to-day differences in the tone and duration of the signal. Similarly, his response to such a signal, although never twice exactly the same, will be much the same on all occasions. Passing from the individual to groups of individuals having a common background of knowledge and experience, we find a very similar situation. To revert to the classroom, all the experienced students will prepare to leave the room when they hear the bell ring. Although their individual preparations will differ in detail, the differences will normally fall within a rather narrow range of variation. Thus the students are fairly certain to close their notebooks and gather up whatever objects they have brought to class with them but exceedingly unlikely to take off their overcoats or rubbers.

It follows that the innumerable items of behavior which constitute a real culture can be sorted out on the basis of the situations which normally evoke them. Each generalized situation will be linked with a particular series of behaviors all of which have numerous features in common. Moreover, the variations in such a series will ordinarily be found to fall within certain easily recognizable limits. These limits may be set by purely practical considerations; thus there are only a few ways in which coiled baskets can be made. They may also be established by social sanctions. Thus every society has certain recognized techniques for getting married or for approaching a superior to ask a favor. In either case, behaviors which fall outside the normal range simply do not bring the desired results. This fact will be tacitly recognized by the members of the society themselves. Behaviors which fall within the effective range will be considered normal, while those which fall outside it will be regarded as queer and, frequently, as reprehensible.

Such a range of normal responses to a particular situation may be designated as a pattern within the real culture. Conversely, the real culture may be conceived of as a configuration composed of a great number of such patterns all of which are, in greater or less degree, mutually adjusted and functionally interrelated. The important thing to remember is that each of the *real culture patterns* is not a single item of behavior but a series of behaviors varying within certain limits. . . .

THE ROLE OF CULTURE IN PERSONALITY FORMATION One of the most important scientific developments of modern times has been the recognition of culture. It has been said that the last thing which a dweller in the deep sea would be likely to discover would be water. He would become conscious of its existence only if some accident brought him to the surface and introduced him to air. Man, throughout most of his history, has been only vaguely conscious of the existence of culture and has owed even this consciousness to contrasts between the customs of his own society and those of some other with which he happened to be brought into contact. The ability to see the culture of one's own society as a whole, to evaluate its patterns and appreciate their implications, calls for a degree of objectivity which is rarely if ever achieved. It is no accident that the modern scientists's understanding of culture has been derived so largely from the study of non-European cultures where observation could be aided by contrast. Those who know no culture other than their own cannot know their own. Until very recent times even psychologists have failed to appreciate that all human beings, themselves included, develop and function in an environment which is, for the most part, culturally determined. As long as they limited their investigations to individuals reared within the frame of a single culture they could not fail to arrive at concepts of human nature which were far from the truth. Even such a master as Freud frequently posited instincts to account for reactions which we now see as directly referable to cultural conditioning. With the store of knowledge of other societies and cultures which is now available, it is possible to approach the study of personality with fewer preconceptions and to reach a closer approximation to the truth.

It must be admitted at once that the observation and recording of data on personality in non-European societies is still fraught with great difficulty. It is hard enough to get reliable material in our own. . . .

In spite of this frank recognition of difficulties and limitations which only time can remove, certain facts seem to be well established. All anthropologists who have come to know the members of non-European societies intimately are in substantial agreement on certain points. These are: (1) Personality norms differ in different societies. (2) The members of any society will always show considerable individual variation in personality. (3) Much of the same range of variation and much the same personality types are to be found in all societies. Although anthropologists base these conclusions on informal observations, they seem to be substantiated by the results of certain objective tests. Thus Rorschach series from different societies reveal different norms for such series as wholes. They also reveal a wide range of individual variation within each series and much overlapping between series. Even without this evidence, the consensus of opinion on the part of those who should be in a position to know cannot be dismissed lightly. In the absence of more complete and accurate information it seems justifiable to accept these conclusions as facts and to take them as the starting point for our investigation of the role of culture in personality formation.

That the norms for personality differ in different societies will scarcely be doubted by anyone who has had experience of societies other than his own. In fact the average individual tends to exaggerate rather than minimize such differences. The only question likely to be raised in this connection is whether a given society should be thought of as having a single personality norm or as having a series of different personality norms each of which is associated with a particular status group within the society. Any difficulty in reconciling these two points of view will disappear when one sees them in proper perspective. The members of any society will always be found to have a long series of personality elements in common. These elements may be of any degree of specificity, ranging from simple overt responses of the sort involved in "table manners" to highly generalized attitudes. Responses of the latter type may underlie a wide range of more specific responses in the individual. Similarly, value-attitude systems which are shared by the members of a society may be reflected in several different forms of status-linked overt behavior. Thus the men and women within a society may share the same attitudes with respect to feminine modesty or masculine courage, although the behavior linked with these attitudes will necessarily be different for each sex. For the women the common modesty attitudes will be expressed in particular patterns of dress or conduct, for the men in more generalized responses of approval or disapproval for particular costumes or conduct. These common personality elements together form a fairly well-integrated configuration which may be called the *Basic Personality Type* for the society as a whole. The existence of this configuration provides the members of the society with common understandings and values and makes possible the unified emotional response of the society's members to situations in which their common values are involved.

It will also be found that in every society there are additional configurations of responses which are linked with certain socially delimited groups within the society. Thus, in practically all cases, different response configurations are characteristic for men and for women, for adolescents and for adults, and so on. In a stratified society similar differences may be observed between the responses characteristic of individuals from different social levels, as nobles, commoners, and slaves. These status-linked response configurations may be termed *Status Personalities*. They are of the utmost importance to the successful functioning of the society, since they make it possible for its members to interact successfully on the basis of status cues alone. Thus even in dealings between complete strangers, simple recognition of the social positions of the two individuals involved makes it possible for each to predict how the other will respond to most situations.

The status personalities recognized by any society are superimposed upon its basic personality type and are thoroughly integrated with the latter. However, they differ from the basic personality type in being heavily weighted on the side of specific overt responses. The weighting is so pronounced that it might even be questioned whether status personalities can be said to include any value-attitude systems distinct from those included in the basic personality. However, I feel that it is legitimate to distinguish between *knowledge* of a particular value-attitude system and *participation* in such a system. A status personality will rarely include any value-attitude system which is unknown to the members of other status groups, although it might come to do so under conditions of extreme intergroup hostility. On the other hand, it may very well include value-attitude systems in which the members of other status groups do not participate. Thus free men may know and allow for the attitudes of slaves without actually sharing them. In any case, it is the specific, overt responses which give status personalities most of their social significance. As long as the individual develops these responses, he can function successfully in the status whether he shares the associated value-attitude systems or not. Informal observation leads us to believe that such cases are fairly numerous in all societies. The specific response patterns of a status personality are presented to the individual in simple, concrete terms which make it easy to learn them. Social pressure towards their assumption is constant, and adherence to them is socially rewarded and deviation from them punished. Even the internal conflicts which may arise during the assumption of a specific response pattern which is at variance with one of the individual's value-attitude systems are not too disturbing. Although they may be vigorous at first, they tend to diminish and finally disappear as the response becomes automatized and unconscious. . . .

✓The influences which culture exerts on the developing personality are of two quite different sorts. On the one hand we have those influences which derive from the culturally patterned behavior of other individuals *towards* the child. These begin to operate from the moment of birth and are of paramount importance during infancy. On the other hand we have those influences which derive from the individual's observation of, or instruction in, the patterns of behavior characteristic of his society. Many of these patterns do not affect him directly, but they provide him with models for the development of his own habitual responses to various situations. These influences are unimportant in early infancy but continue to affect him throughout life. The failure to distinguish between these two types of cultural influence has led to a good deal of confusion.

It must be admitted at once that the two types of influence overlap at certain points. Culturally patterned behavior directed towards the child may serve as a model for the development of some of his own behavior patterns. This factor becomes operative as soon as the child is old enough to observe and remember what other people are doing. When, as an adult, he finds himself confronted by the innumerable problems involved in rearing his own children, he turns to these childhood memories for guidance. Thus in almost any American community we find parents sending their children to Sunday School because they themselves were sent to Sunday School. The fact that, as adults, they greatly prefer golf to church attendance does little to weaken the pattern. However, this aspect of any society's patterns for child-rearing is rather incidental to the influence which such patterns exert upon personality formation. At most it ensures that children born into a particular society will be reared in much the same way generation after generation. The real importance of the patterns for early care and child-training lies in their effects upon the deeper levels of the personalities of individuals reared according to them.

It is generally accepted that the first few years of the individual's life are crucial for the establishment of the highly generalized value-attitude systems which form the deeper levels of personality content. The first realization of this fact came from the study of atypical individuals in our own society and the discovery that certain of their peculiarities seemed to be rather consistently linked with certain sorts of atypical childhood experiences. The extension of personality studies to other societies in which both the normal patterns of child-rearing and the normal personality configurations for adults were different from our own only served to emphasize the importance of very early conditioning. Many of the "normal" aspects of European personalities which were accepted at first as due to instinctive factors are now recognized as results of our own particular patterns of child care. Although study of the relations between various societies' techniques for child-rearing and the basic personality types for adults in these societies has barely begun, we have already reached a point where certain correlations seem to be recognizable. Although a listing of all these correlations is impossible in a discussion as brief as the present one, a few examples may serve for illustration.

In societies in which the culture pattern prescribes absolute obedience from the child to the parent as a prerequisite for rewards of any sort, the normal adult will tend to be a submissive individual, dependent, and lacking in initiative. Even though he has largely forgotten the childhood experiences which led to the establishment of these attitudes, his first reaction to any new situation will be to look to someone in authority for support and direction. It is worth noting in this connection that there are many societies in which the patterns of child-rearing are so effective in producing adult personalities of this type that special techniques have been developed for training a few selected individuals for leadership. Thus, among the Tanala of Madagascar, eldest sons are given differential treatment from birth, this treatment being designed to develop initiative and willingness to assume responsibility, while other children are systematically disciplined and repressed. Again, individuals who are reared in very small family groups of our own type have a tendency to focus their emotions and their anticipations of reward or punishment on a few other individuals. In this they are harking back unconsciously to a childhood in which all satisfactions and frustrations derived from their own fathers and mothers. In societies where the child is reared in an extended family environment, with numerous adults about, any one of whom may either reward or punish, the normal personality will tend in the opposite direction. In such societies the average individual is incapable of strong or lasting attachments or hatreds towards particular persons. All personal interactions embody an unconscious attitude of: "Oh, well, another will be along presently." It is difficult to conceive of such a society embodying in its culture such patterns as our concepts of romantic love, or of the necessity for finding the one and only partner without whom life will be meaningless.

Such examples could be multiplied indefinitely, but the above will serve to show the sort of correlations which are now emerging from studies of personality and culture. These correlations reflect linkages of a simple and obvious sort, and it is already plain that such one-to-one relationships between cause and effect are in the minority. In most cases we have to deal with complex configurations of child-training patterns which, as a whole, produce complex personality configurations in the adult. Nevertheless, no one who is familiar with the results which have already been obtained can doubt that here lies the key to most of the differences in basic personality type which have hitherto been ascribed to hereditary factors. The "normal" members of different societies owe their varying personality configurations much less to their genes than to their nurseries.

While the culture of any society determines the deeper levels of its members' personalities through the particular techniques of child-rearing to which it subjects them, its influence does not end with this. It goes on to shape the rest of their personalities by providing models for their specific responses as well. This latter process continues throughout life. As the individual matures and then ages, he constantly has to unlearn patterns of response which have ceased to be effective and to learn new ones more appropriate to his current place in the society. At every step in this process, culture serves as a guide. It not only provides him with models for his changing roles but also ensures that these roles shall be, on the whole, compatible with his deep-seated value-attitude systems. All the patterns within a single culture tend to show a sort of psychological coherence quite aside from their functional interrelations. With rare exceptions, the "normal" individual who adheres to them will not be required to do anything which is incompatible with the deeper levels of his personality structure. Even when one society borrows patterns of behavior from another, these patterns will usually be modified and reworked until they become congruous with the basic personality type of the borrowers. Culture may compel the atypical individual to adhere to forms of behavior which are repugnant to him, but when such behavior is repugnant to the bulk of a society's members, it is culture which has to give way.

Turning to the other side of the picture, the acquisition of new behavior patterns which are congruous with the individual's generalized value-attitude systems tends to reinforce these systems and to establish them more firmly as time passes. The individual who spends his life in any society with a fairly stable culture finds his personality becoming more firmly integrated as he grows older. His adolescent doubts and questionings with respect to the attitudes implicit in his culture disappear as he reaffirms them in his adherence to the overt behavior which his culture prescribes. In time he emerges as a pillar of society, unable to understand how anyone can entertain such doubts. While this process may not make for progress, it certainly makes for individual contentment. The state of such a person is infinitely happier than that of one who finds himself compelled to adhere to patterns of overt behavior which are not congruous with the value-attitude systems established by his earliest experiences. The result of such incongruities can be seen in many individuals who have had to adapt to rapidly changing culture conditions such as those which obtain in our own society. It is even more evident in the case of those who, having begun life in one culture, are attempting to adjust to another. These are the "marginal men" whose plight is recognized by all who have worked with the phenomenon of acculturation. Lacking the reinforcement derived from constant expression in overt behavior, the early-established value-attitude systems of such individuals are weakened and overlaid. At the same time, it seems that they are rarely if ever eliminated, still less replaced by new systems congruous with the cultural milieu in which the individual has to operate. The acculturated individual can learn to act and even to think in terms of his new society's culture, but he cannot learn to feel in these terms. At each point where decision is required he finds himself adrift with no fixed points of reference.

In summary, the fact that personality norms differ for different societies can be explained on the basis of the different experience which the members of such societies acquire from contact with their cultures. In the case of a few small societies whose members have a homogeneous heredity, the influence of physiological factors in determining the psychological potentialities of the majority of these members cannot be ruled out, but the number of such cases is certainly small. Even when common hereditary factors may be present, they can affect only potentialities for response. They are never enough in themselves to account for the differing content and organization which we find in the basic personality types for different societies. . . .

Similarities in the ability levels of members of different societies are not difficult to explain. All human beings are, after all, members of a single species, and the potential range of variations in this respect must be much the same for all societies. Similarities in the generalized value-attitude systems of individuals reared in different cultural environments are more difficult to account for, but there can be no question that they do occur. In the light of our present knowledge the most probable explanation seems to be that they are primarily a result of similar family situations operating upon individuals with similar levels of ability. It has already been noted that culture patterns for the interactions of family members always permit a considerable range of individual variation. In all societies the personalities involved in family situations tend to arrange themselves in much the same orders of dominance and to develop much the same patterns of private, informal interaction. Thus even in the most strongly patriarchal societies one encounters a surprising number of families in which the wife and mother is the dominant member. She may accord her husband exaggerated respect in public, but neither he nor the children will have any doubt as to where real power lies. Again, there are a whole series of biologically conditioned situations which repeat themselves irrespective of the cultural setting. In every society there will be eldest children and youngest children, only children and those reared as members of a large sibling group, feeble, sickly children and strong, vigorous ones. The same thing holds for various sorts of parent-child relationships. There are favorite children, wanted or unwanted children, good sons and black sheep who are constantly subject to suspicion and discipline. Even while operating within the culturally established limits of parental authority, various parents may be affectionate and permissive or take a sadistic delight in exercising their disciplinary functions to the full. Each of these situations will result in a particular sort of early experience for the individual. When essentially similar individuals in different societies are exposed to similar family situations, the result will be a marked similarity in the deeper levels of their personality configurations.

Although the family situations just discussed operate at what might be termed a subcultural level, the frequency with which a particular situation arises in a particular society will be influenced by cultural factors. Thus it is much more difficult for a wife to establish control in a strongly patriarchal society than in a matriarchal one. In the former case she has to work counter to the accepted rules for the marital relationship and to brave all sorts of social pressures. Only a woman of very strong character, or one with a very weak husband, will be able to establish dominance. In the latter case any woman with ordinary strength of character can dominate her household with the aid of social pressures. In every society the bulk of the families will approximate to the culturally established norms in their members' interpersonal relationships. It follows that most of the children reared in a particular society will be exposed to similar family situations and will emerge with many elements of even the deeper levels of their personalities in common. This conclusion seems to be borne out by the study of a wide range of societies. In every case numerous correlations can be established between the culture patterns for family organization and child-rearing and the basic personality type for adult members of the society.

In summary, culture must be considered the dominant factor in establishing the basic personality types for various societies and also in establishing the series of status personalities which are characteristic for each society. It must be remembered that basic personality types and status personalities, like culture construct patterns, represent the modes within certain ranges of variation. It is doubtful whether the actual personality of any individual will ever agree at all points with either of these abstractions. With respect to the formation of individual personalities, culture operates as one of a series of factors which also includes the physiologically determined potentialities of the individual and his relations with other individuals. There can be little doubt that in certain cases factors other than the cultural ones are primarily responsible for producing a particular personality configuration. However, it seems that in a majority of cases the cultural factors are dominant. We find that in all societies the personalities of the "average," "normal" individuals who keep the society operating in its accustomed ways can be accounted for in cultural terms. At the same time we find that all societies include atypical individuals whose personalities fall outside the normal range of variation for the society. The causes of such aberrant personalities are still imperfectly understood. They unquestionably derive in part from accidents of early environment and experience. In how far still other, genetically determined factors may be involved we are still unable to say. . . .

5.2   INTRODUCTION

The second selection in this chapter deals with one aspect of the social structure, kinship, which the author views as the main link between the individual and his culture. It is an individual's "primary web of relationships," he asserts, that connects him to others and thus to the overall way of life of his society. The nature of the kinship system must therefore be intimately related to the society's characteristic patterns and values, and it is the validity of this hypothesis that Hsu's essay aims to demonstrate.

Hsu posits four types of kinship systems, distinguished in terms of the primary relationship which is given most emphasis by the culture (father-son, husband-wife, mother-son, brother-brother). He then goes on to document the relationships between the psychological consequences of being reared in each system and the general features of societies in which it prevails. His analysis is provocative and persuasive, although he is careful to emphasize its exploratory and tentative nature.

Our own kinship system and its relationship to our cultural values and emphases fall under a different light when analyzed in these terms, some nonobvious features emerging more clearly and some apparently simple ones being shown to be less so. The essential characteristic of Hsu's approach is its comparative orientation which, in examining the similarities and differences among particular cultures, does so from a single perspective that is more general than any one of them and leads to understanding that is more basic than that possible from a more limited approach.

Although Hsu identifies each type of kinship system with particular sets of foreign cultures, it is important to note again that there are many different cultural emphases within our own society, stemming from religious, ethnic, and regional differences, and there are also correlated differences in the nature of kinship systems. Although the husband-wife relationship may receive the greatest emphasis throughout, due to the pressure of our society's overall structure and culture, there are nonetheless important variations in the relative importance of other relationships and thus in the prevalence of the psychological variables associated with them. Except for those working in colleges, where foreign students are becoming increasingly numerous, most guidance counselors are not likely to come in contact with non-Western youngsters in the course of their work. However, they will deal with children and adolescents from a wide range of subcultural groupings, and it would seem that Hsu's analysis would be no less relevant in such cases.

Depending in part upon the nature of his kinship relations, for example, a child or adolescent will be more or less receptive to help from an outsider, or more or less willing to discuss his difficulties. More basically, Hsu's analysis implies that such broad cultural values as individualism and self-reliance are not automatically absorbed merely as a result of membership in the society but depend on transmission through the family. Thus, for any particular child, they may or may not be part of his make-up, and, if they are not, they cannot be made so by mere exposure or even direct instruction. Such individuals often become problems that the guidance-personnel worker must handle, and recognition of the complexity and variability of what is involved would seem to be an important prerequisite for sympathetic and effective action.

5.2   KINSHIP AND WAYS OF LIFE: AN EXPLORATION[1]*

Francis L. K. Hsu

To the individual in all societies the importance of other human beings, as compared with that of nonhuman elements in his environment, is supreme. This factor can even overshadow his basic desire for self-preservation, for it is not hard to find individuals in any culture who will give their lives because of their parents, spouses, tribe, or nation. Whether the custom is head-hunting or potlatch, whether the economic activity is agriculture, nomadism, or mechanized industries, and whatever the individual's status or interest, the prime mover of the individual's behavior lies in the nature of his relationship with other members of his society. The extent to which he will exert himself is in direct ratio to the degree to which he feels he has attained a proper place among his fellow men. That is to say, he tends to experience a greater urge to strive toward improvement of his position if he pictures himself to be in a wrong or lower place from where he ought to be, whereas he tends to be more satisfied with the *status quo* if he feels the reverse. The specific methods he resorts to are, of course, as varied as they are culturally given, but the basic objects he strives for may be summarized into three categories: sociability, security, and status. The meanings of these basic social needs of the individual, and how they compare with needs postulated by other scholars, have been discussed elsewhere (Hsu, 1963, Chap. VIII). Suffice it to

[1]Reprinted from Francis L. K. Hsu, "Kinship and Ways of Life: An Exploration," in Francis L. K. Hsu, (ed.), *Psychological Anthropology* (Homewood, Ill.: The Dorsey Press) 1961, pp. 400–456.
*In preparing this [material], I am particularly indebted to Dr. Paul J. Bohannan for going over the entire manuscript and making many valuable comments and suggestions, especially with reference to the relationship between kinship structure and kinship content. I am also indebted to Dr. G. P. Murdock for his constructive comments when the basic ideas of the paper were first presented at the annual American Anthropological Association meetings at Tucson, Arizona, in 1953 and to Drs. W. R. Bascom and Fred Eggan for going over the early version of the manuscript and materially helping its birth.[F.L.K.H.]

point out here that whether the individual has achieved his proper place among his fellow human beings is measured by two interrelated yardsticks: on the one hand, by what Mead, Sullivan, and others, describe as the *attitudes toward himself* (M. H. Kuhn, 1954); on the other hand, the attitudes toward him on the part of those fellow men to whom he is bound or with whom he is identified.

Thus, whether the individual attempts to improve himself by getting married, by conquest of air and sea, by acquisition of wealth, or by elaboration of the imaginary, his primary concern is his place among fellow men. The place of the individual among his fellow men refers, of course, not only to the present. It could be keyed to the past, so that this concern is chiefly centered in his elders and, by extension, his departed ancestral spirits; or it could be keyed to the future, so that this concern is primarily aimed at his descendants, and, by extension, those yet to be born; or it could be keyed to both past and future.

Nor is the place of the individual among his fellow men static. It is subject to the changing circumstances in which the individual finds himself. For example, in spite of the most serene childhood experiences, a majority of individuals will not feel secure when faced by later economic, social, or political uncertainty. Regardless of early histories, a majority of human beings in any crowd escaping from a fire will become panicky and trample one another.

The relative importance of early versus later experiences is immaterial to the arguments of this chapter. The crucial point here is the great importance of kinship as the primary web of relationships connecting every new-born individual with his fellow men and through them, with the overall pattern of thought and action prevailing in the society of which he forms a part.

The connection between a kinship system and the overall pattern of thought and action of a people may be seen from two angles. On the one hand, some kinship systems enable the individuals reared in them to achieve their appropriate places in terms of sociability, security, and status with greater ease than do other kinship systems. The inference is that the individuals who grow up and live in the former type of kinship system may be expected to bestir themselves far less than those who grow up and live in the latter type of kinship systems. Hence, the societies with the former type of kinship systems are likely to be more dynamic than those with the latter type.

On the other hand, the individual can be expected to strive more not only when his self-attitude is higher than accorded it by his fellow human beings but also when the people related to him cause him to feel that he has some chance of success and much to gain after his success. Conversely, he is unlikely to strive very hard when the people related to him give him reason to believe that he has little chance of success or little to gain even with success. Therefore, the individual's tendency to adventure, conquest, and expansion no less than his tenacity to face terrible disasters like epidemic, drought, or foreign conquest depends greatly, in the first place, on whether or not his society demands such heroic actions on his part in order for him to keep his membership in it as a self-respecting man, and in the second place, on whether or not his group provides him with social-psychological support for prolonged efforts and concerted action. This hypothesis makes no assumption on the uniformity of behavior in any society. A few individuals may be aggressive where most others in the same society are docile; a few may fight a last-ditch battle where most others have given up; but the behavior of the majority is strongly affected by the forces just described.

The hypothesis

However, existing results of kinship studies would seem to show that varieties of kinship have no connection with the diverse ways of life in different societies.[2] There does not seem to be any way of avoiding this conclusion when we note that the Eskimo "type" of "kinship organization" is also characteristic of the highly industrialized Yankees of New England, the peasant Ruthenians of eastern Europe, the simple agriculturalists of Taos Pueblo in the southwestern United States, and the Andamese pygmies of the tropical forest as well as many others (Murdock, 1949, pp. 226–228); and that the Dakota type of kinship organization is also characteristic of such diverse peoples as the Fijians, the Tallensi, the Manchus, and the Chinese (Murdock, 1949, pp. 236–238). For in spite of the similarity or even the identity of the kinship structures in question, the ways of life of the diverse societies in which they are found bear no resemblance one to another.

What has happened so far is that most students of kinship from Murdock (1949), Spoehr (1947), Goldschmidt (1948) to Levi-Strauss (1949), Eggan (1950), Leach (1952), and others have concentrated on certain aspects of kinship structure. They attempt to answer in one way or another the following questions: What factors are correlated with the development of kinship groups such as clan, phratry, dual organization, or their shift from one emphasis to another? What factors affect the change of kinship usages such as relationship terms, mother-in-law avoidance, and forms of marriage? But there has been little or no serious attempt to deal with kinship content which can go far to help us with another question: What effects do certain types of kinship organization have on the pattern of thought and behavior of individuals reared in them?

Answers bearing on such a question have been sought by some students of psychological anthropology with the central focus on child-rearing practices (see Whiting, 1961) some students of kinship have not been completely oblivious of this question. . . .

---

[2]The term "way of life" is used to denote the characteristic manner in which the people of a given society look at things and express their outlook in concrete actions. It is, therefore, the same as "national character," . . . except that "national character," by custom, is applicable to large and literate societies, while "way of life" here applies to all societies. For a fuller exposition of what the "way of life" means, see Hsu, 1953, pp. 2–17.

However, armed by an untenable antithesis between psychological and sociological explanations, students of kinship have not only seen no necessary connection between their work and the culture-and-personality studies but often reacted to them with frank hostility. The task of a systematic exploration of the exact relationship between kinship variation and specific ways of life in different societies remains to be attempted. This line of inquiry seems imperative if the study of kinship is to attain a truly significant place in the total perspective of the science of man. For if kinship is the web through which human beings are woven together from birth to death, it most certainly must, *a priori*, be related not only to matters such as kinship terms or mother-in-law avoidance but also to the formation, organization, and operation of the most essential patterns of thought and behavior.

The purpose of this chapter is to show that a very real correlation exists between kinship and ways of life. This hypothesis is based on three interrelated propositions: (1) The failure to perceive this correlation thus far is due to concentration on structure to the neglect of content, (2) kinship structure is less clearly related to the thought and action patterns of the individual than kinship content, and (3) kinship content is, in the last analysis, rooted in kinship structure.

Kinship structure and kinship content differentiated

Kinship structure describes those features which govern the formal patterns of arrangement among individuals standing in reciprocal categories of kinship. It comprehends rules of descent, residence, inheritance; in-law avoidances; conjugal or joint families; and so forth. Kinship content pertains to the characteristics which govern the tenacity, intensity, or quality of interaction among individuals related through kinship. It crystallizes itself into such values as individualism and self-reliance, romantic love in marriage, emphasis on youth, or on the importance of ancestors.

To illustrate, a new-born infant may have coming early into his life only his parents or mother and mother's brothers plus a few siblings and an occasional contact with others; or he may have coming early into his life relatives including not only his parents or mother and mother's brothers as well as siblings, but also a vast array of other relatives and nonrelatives. These are matters of kinship structure. They spell the differences between the conjugal family and some larger unit, or between patrilocal or matrilocal residence.

However, two infants who have the same number and kind of individuals come into their respective lives may be affected differently because these individuals may act as though they each possess them and can order their lives separately; or these individuals may act as though they are mere spectators and that their own mothers are the real powers that lay down all laws. These are matters of kinship content. They are rooted in the difference between mutual dependence and individualism, both terms to be explained below.

The differences between structure and content have been explored in another publication (Hsu, 1959). What needs to be pointed out here, however, is that the content of a kinship system is to a great extent determined by the emphasis given one or another particular primary relationship in the kinship structure.

Eight basic relationships are to be found in every kinship system. They are those of husband-wife, father-son, mother-son, mother-daughter, father-daughter, sister-sister, brother-brother, and brother-sister. No matter how much more extensive the kinship system is, the relationships between more remotely situated individuals in it (designated in this chapter as secondary relationships) are, with few exceptions, extensions of one or another of these primary relationships. However, these eight primary relationships are not given the same emphasis by different societies. Furthermore, when a kinship system gives emphasis to one of these relationships, it does so not only by reducing the importance of other relationships, but also by modifying their contents, so that the resulting kinship systems vary greatly in attributes and in their influences on the individuals reared in them.

To pursue this hypothesis I propose to examine, in the balance of this chapter, four types of kinship systems, each dominated by one structural relationship, and see how they may be related to many outstanding characteristics in thought and behavior among the peoples living in them. The hypothesis presupposes that each structural relationship possesses inherent and distinctive attributes. When one relationship is elevated over other relationships in a given kinship system, the attributes of the dominating relationship tend to modify, eliminate, or at least reduce the importance of the attributes of other structural relationships. The hypothesis further presumes that the total effect of the dominance of the attributes of one structural relationship leads to a particular kind of kinship content which in turn strongly conditions the pattern of thought and behavior of the individual reared in it. The four types of kinship content and their structural connections are given below:

A. Mutual dependence among members of kin and community, which is rooted in the emphasis on father-son axis at the expense of all other relationships.
B. Self-reliance on the part of the individual which is rooted in the supremacy of husband-wife axis at the expense of all other relationships.
C. Supernatural reliance which is found where the mother-son axis tends to have more primary importance over other relationships.
D. A degree of mutual dependence together with the emphasis on brother-brother axis and practically no worship of the ancestors.

It is understood, of course, that no typology covers all the facts or puts all of them into perfectly neat compartments (J. H. Steward, 1954). First, every typology is a matter of abstraction, and the level of abstraction determines what facts must be included and what must be excluded. Second, even the facts covered by any one statement are never as uniform as the statement would indicate. Consider such an observation as "American society is founded on the ideas of equality, freedom, and fair play." Surely any reader can find many historical and contemporary facts as well as the outlook of individual Americans which obviously negate the high-sounding principles. Yet, to conclude that the American society is not founded on these ideas is to be blind to the fundamental trend of development of American society and culture and, therefore, to be very wide of the mark. Even a statement such as "Universal education prevails in American society" is not without exception. In World War II, at least 2 percent of American males were rejected because of illiteracy. Yet, no one can dispute the fact that universal education is firmly established in this society both as a matter of conviction and as a matter of practice. Third, every type enumerated below contains internal variations which, in more elaborate treatments, may merit description as subtypes.

With these qualifications in mind let us, then, examine in some detail the characteristics of behavior in the four types of societies that are associated with the four different kinds of kinship content.[3]

TYPE A SOCIETIES Included in this group are those of a majority of the Far Eastern peoples, including Chinese, Japanese, Koreans, Siamese, and others, but excluding the major inhabitants of India: the Hindus and the Moslems.

Kinship

The structural characteristics of these kinship systems are simple: they are patrilineal, patrilocal, and by and large patriarchal. The basic unit in which the infant finds himself is generally the patrilineal extended family. Among the lower classes this unit is smaller, approximating the individual family of parents and unmarried children, but in higher classes, it is sometimes enormous. However, even among the poor, the child's grandparents and in-laws are likely to be much in evidence.

The structural relationship most elevated is that of the father-son. All other relationships are either extensions of this central axis, or are subordinated to and modified by it. The boldest example of this type is found among the Chinese and the weakest among the Siamese. The first attribute of the father-son relationship is inclusiveness. There is only one father but there are usually many sons. In fact, even when there is only one son the parents as a rule hope for more. The other

---

[3]The sequence of A, B, C, and D given the four types of society discussed in this chapter has no ranking significance. It really follows the sequence of my academic acquaintance with these societies. I began my studies of the Chinese culture as a student in 1934; then came my introduction to English culture in 1937; this was followed by my residence and work in the United States since 1945; and a period of 18 months' field work in India from 1955 to 1957. My serious reading and reflection on Africa had only begun in 1959. I have since worked in Japan, 1964–1965.

attribute of it is continuity. Every father-son relationship is a link in an endless chain of father-son relationships. For every father is a son and every son, in the normal course of events, will be a father.

The characteristic kinship content correlated with the emphasis on father-son axis is mutual dependence. Enmeshed in a network of continuous relationships, the individual is conditioned to orient himself lineally, and, in a secondary way, laterally within a well-defined group; he is naturally the product of his forebears before him as he is automatically the progenitor of his descendants yet to come. His place in that line is specific and inalienable. Superficially the relationship seems to be one sided, namely, sons owe much more to their fathers than their fathers do to them. The obligations are actually quite mutual. The son owes his father all services as desired, unquestioned obedience, extreme respect, and complete support in life as in death. But the father owes to the son marital arrangement, protection, and all his inheritance. (In Japan the inheritance rules are governed by primogeniture.) The ideal son is sensitive to every whim on the part of his father. The father's every wish is his command. But the ideal father takes every precaution to see that his sons are well married, well educated, well connected, and well provided for. Death and torture are often endured willingly by sons and fathers in fulfilling some of these obligations. The mother, by virtue of her marriage to the father, her assumption of his clan membership, and the biological relationship with the son, is an integral part of this core relationship: whatever is due to the father is equally due to the mother, except that she is not expected to have the means to support her son.

Starting from this basic father-son axis, similar relationships extend both vertically and horizontally. Vertically each father-son axis is a necessary link in a chain connecting one's lineal forebears, living or dead, with one's lineal descendants already born or yet to be born. Horizontally it is the model against which are measured one's attitudes, duties, and obligations toward all agnatic male kinsmen and their wives in the ascending or the descending generations.

In this web of kinship the individual has no freedom; he is hedged in on all sides. But he also has little fear of being left out, for he can count on help from all sides just as he is expected to give help. This is at the root of the well-known Oriental nepotism, except in Japan (Hsu, 1954). Symptomatic of this solidarity is the fact that ancestor worship, going back for many generations, is the rule among them. The living descendants have the duty of providing for the ancestors who have departed and of glorifying them. In turn, the departed members of the family as a matter of course look after the interests of the living descendants. So great is this sense of solidarity that, unlike the ancestor cult found in any other part of the world, these peoples do not believe that the departed ancestors will do them harm as spirits. There does not seem to be any Oriental society in which ancestral spirits are prayed to for forgiveness during emergencies such as sickness, floods, or epidemics.

The great importance given to the father-son axis reduces, modifies, or dominates all other relationships, including that between husband and wife. Indeed the married woman's primary duties are not those to her husband but to her husband's parents or her sons. Similarly the married man's duties to his parents and to his sons take precedence over those to others. For this reason romantic love as an ideal is absent and public expressions of intimacy, whether by a man and his wife before his parents or by a man and his wife before their children, are taboo. A son can be required by parents to divorce his wife if she fails to please them, just as he is duty-bound to take a concubine if his wife fails to provide a son. The need for vertical continuity and horizontal solidarity within the kinship group practically eliminates individual privacy. Consequently, children are raised to enter into the adult world as soon as they are physically and mentally capable to do so. In fact, mutual dependence requires that children share the vicissitudes of the adult world from infancy onward. Discipline (punishment, reward, rules) tends to be inconsistent for it is never exclusively in the hands of mother or parents. For not only grandparents, but in-laws, neighbors, and friends can actively interfere with it.

The clan is seen as an extension of the father-son axis to all male agnates. Clan is usually present among most of these peoples. This clan is not a mere device to regulate marriage. It is usually an organized body which regulates the members' behavior, settles their disputes, and defends them against outside oppressors or enemies. So strong is the patrilineal emphasis in the clan that all women married into it assume its identity, a trait not found elsewhere so far except among the Gusii of Kenya (Mayer, 1949).

General characteristics

People living in this type of kinship pattern will be satisfied with the status quo and are conservative. There is no urge within the society toward fission. On the contrary, there are deep-seated centripetal tendencies. Since the place of the individual in the web of kinship is inalienable and perpetual, his need for striving to prove himself is not great. And since the individual's growing up experiences are multiple-centered, he tends to view the world not in absolute terms of black and white but in relativistic fashion with many compromises. Consequently, there are fewer chances for men to be pulled asunder by abstract issues or by the desire for all or none. Even faced with famine, they tend to tighten their belts and eat less instead of moving to new lands. The small minority of them who do emigrate tend to make up an elaborate duplication of the way of life that they had known before, and/or maintain their solidarity with the home society and/or return physically to the home society at some later date. With few exceptions, they wish to die at the places of their birth and to be buried in their ancestral graveyards. Most of them do so.

From this point of view we may see the relation between language and culture in a new light. Some scholars have tended, as did Whorf later, to conclude that the Chinese had not developed science because Chinese thought would have been incongruous with Western logic based upon Indo-European grammar (Granet, 1934 and Chang, 1939). Our analysis here makes it clear that the Chinese lack an interest in abstraction because their anchorage in the web of human relations fore-doomed the development of any scientific spirit and inquiry, in spite of an early history of science and invention. Elsewhere I have already detailed this point (Hsu, 1953). What we need to point out here is that the Chinese language, especially the written version, instead of being the cause of Chinese lack of science, was probably shaped by the same restraining forces which limited the development of Chinese science. Chinese is the only completely nonalphabetical language in the modern world; it is more difficult to learn and use than the alphabetical ones. What is more, while Japan, Korea, and Annam of Indo-China (until the French conquest) each has its own separate set of alphabet, all have tenaciously retained the Chinese characters which they borrowed before they acquired their alphabets, to be concurrently used with their own alphabetically derived words, even though this is not only unnecessary, but also a source of great inconvenience. Their conservatism is, therefore, great. A final fact indicating that language does not limit the development of science is that Japan, after her Meiji Restoration which propelled her to a position of world prominence, did not even attempt to eliminate the parallel use of Chinese language. After World War II the teaching of Chinese in Japanese schools was suspended on order of General MacArthur, but was resumed after the end of the American occupation.

Their literature is voluminous. And their art works, especially those of China and Japan, are regarded as among the best in the world. But because of the individual's security and submersion among fellow human beings, their literature and art delve very little into emotion or into the unseen. Their music is characterized by melodious elaboration of a simple nature, albeit they have many more kinds of musical instruments than most nonliterate peoples. Yet no matter how many instruments are played together, the result is unison, not harmony of different chords or melodies. The music is often functional, to be played on social, ceremonial, and religious occasions and is at best tied to acting such as in operas. . . .

Impetus to change

The individual tends to be highly competitive for traditional goals. A man can, and is in fact encouraged to, exhibit initiative in getting up more costly and pompous funerals for his parents, or in going to some extreme to please his parents in filial piety, to glorify his ancestry, or, in Japan, to show devotion to the emperor. But he is unlikely to exercise his imagination by doing things which are not traditionally given, such as for a scholar to go into business. Internal impetus to change within these societies is generally lacking. For the individual can, in the main, reach his proper station among fellow men through the kinship framework. But forces limiting change have a snowballing effect on the aggrandizement of tradition. Thus, a tradition, whether it be footbinding or the contempt for soldiers, tends to become stronger and even goes to extremes as time goes on. Footbinding in China began as a frivolity among some court dancers who wrapped their bare feet with white satin to please the emperor. By the early twentieth century, many women deformed their feet into such small points that they could hardly walk. The higher the social class, the greater the competitive tendency and the smaller the feet.

Most individuals are automatically assured of honorable places in the social organization, in life as well as after death. Ancestor worship provides a complete continuity between the dead and the living, the past and the present. Therefore while the tendency to excel in glorification of the lineage and ancestry is great, the tendency to preserve everything traditional, from duties and obligations to mores and customs, is also great. The very close and permanent human ties serve as a drag on initiative so that people are prevented from venturing out into untrodden paths, intellectually, emotionally, and physically (except Japan; see Hsu, 1954). The social organization is such as softly but unremittingly to nip in the bud a majority if not all internal efforts to change the scheme of things. There is a general lack of interest in associations other than those based on kinship, marriage, locality, and occupation. For the vast majority there are not even age groups or hunting organizations and rarely any sort of sport which requires the competition between two organized bodies. Overthrow of the ruling dynasty was reported (except Japan), but revolution was unknown before impact of the West. Since they have little urge to elaborate the unseen, their utopias, never numerous, tend to be close copies of the actual worlds in which they live, minus such disturbing elements as war, banditry, and dishonesty. There may be different indigenous philosophies, but these have never become bases for contending factions in any irreconcilable way for the simple reason that the majority of peoples in this type of society have a tendency not to get actively involved in ideologies which are abstract and remote from the immediately accepted reality.

Over long periods of time there seem to be only two conditions which are the mainsprings for change in these societies. One condition is the increase of population which precipitates some inevitable expansion, even though the peoples entertain no great dream about new frontiers. But, as pointed out before, the expansion is slow and is not accompanied by any noticeable desire to cultural, political, or economic independence of the newly acquired territory. The other condition for change is external pressure or invasion. Such societies have successfully withstood external forces, military or cultural, by their basic cohesion. But they may be overrun, although they seem to have the ability to modify ultimately the alien forces in their midst, and they usually recover by achieving new syntheses between their traditional and the alien elements. They tend to render the alien-imposed programs ineffective not by armed opposition (though this occasionally occurs) but chiefly by emasculating them through unobtrusive persistence. The strength of their way of life lies in its permanent solidarity between the dead, the living, and the unborn. This kinship relationship provides the individual with great resilience toward environmental problems so that he is not easily given to despair or loss of heart.

In the process of their persistence, they cannot but change a little. But such changes, especially the more spectacular and speedier ones, do not easily take deep root. It has been said that while China had successfully absorbed her foreign conquerors in the past, she may not be able to do it with Western powers. This remains to be seen. From this analysis, it seems certain that neither China nor Japan will be basically threatened or altered very easily by the West, even though the West, including the Communist West, certainly has caused them great disturbances.

No society in this type is likely either to die out physically through conquest or loss of resources or even to lose the continuation of its way of life such as is found in many parts of the nonliterate world or the West.

TYPE B SOCIETIES   Type B includes the societies of a majority of the Western peoples—Europeans and the peoples of European origin throughout the world.

Kinship

The kinship structure of these peoples is usually patrilineal, patrilocal or neo-local, and in many instances, nominally patriarchal. The basic unit in which the infant finds himself is the individual family, consisting of parents and unmarried children. In some parts of Europe, especially in premodern times, the joint family prevailed more than the individual family, and even in modern times some of these peoples have more affines living under the same roof than others. Among the lower and upper classes, the number of children is generally larger, while among the middle classes, the trend is in reverse.

The structural relationship most elevated is that of the husband-wife axis. All other relationships are either subordinated to this central axis or are patterned after and modified by it. The strongest example of this type is found among modern Americans of the United States, and the weakest, among the eastern Europeans.

Unlike those of the father-son axis, the attributes of the husband-wife axis are exclusiveness and discontinuity. It is discontinuous over the generations because each husband-wife relationship is ended when one or both of the partners die. It is exclusive of other individuals because each husband-wife relationship is not only complete by itself but is intolerant of intrusion by any third party. It must, therefore, insist on monogamy as an absolute ideal. Among the peoples constituting Type B there is, of course, variation in the nature of the husband-wife axis. In Eastern Europe the husband-wife axis is unquestionably husband-dominated, and in the United States the wife so equals her husband in nearly every way that it gives the impression of being wife-dominated. But whichever case we refer to, the central and dominating position of the husband-wife axis over all others in this type of kinship system is obvious. In contrast to Type A societies, the husband-wife union is the only relationship which is expressly and elaborately sanctioned, guaranteed and safeguarded by the church as well as by the law. It is so elevated above all other relationships and so freed from their encumbrances, that it is glorified by, and only supposed to be founded, on romantic love, an expression which embodies unaccountableness of the choice, exclusive possession between the partners of each other, freedom from interference by other human beings, and complete lack of definite ties with other relationships whether they be parent-child or fraternal. In Type A societies the father-son axis symbolizes all that is "forever." In Type B the husband-wife axis is the only relationship which is "forever."

Given this central emphasis it is easy to see how the other relationships in this type of system are either subordinate or thoroughly unimportant. The parent-child relationship is given great importance only before the son or daughter reaches majority. Even during this period, once the parental consent for marriage is given the parents no longer have control over anything. Support of children by parents is limited by the same factor. Support of parents by children is, even where the law insists on it, highly conditional and no child has to keep a parent under the same roof with his or her spouse. Generally speaking, parents have complete freedom in bequest.

Polygamy of any variety is incongruous with the emphasis on husband-wife axis. Mistresses and gigolos may be kept on the side by men and women who have the means. They may be connived by the public and in the church, but these relationships have never been made truly legitimate as they have in Types A, C, and D. Divorce rested at first with the church and has gradually been shifted into the hands of the two married partners, but at no time has it been a matter of the authority of the parents. Sibling relationships, uncle-niece relationships, uncle-nephew relationships, mother-in-law and daughter-in-law relationships all are reduced more or less to matters of friendship. If the parties concerned like each other, they may develop very great solidarity with each other. But if they do not happen to enjoy the sight of each other, one can die without knowing where the others live. They have no definite legal and social obligations to each other. Their economic relationships are limited to voluntary gift making or certain claims on assets left by the intestate dead. This is the only type of kinship system in which all sorts of public display of erotic expressions between lovers and spouses is encouraged, pictorialized, glorified as though they could be separated from physical sex, and played up so that they can almost stop traffic in the busiest thoroughfare.

While emphasis on the father-son axis leads naturally to the social importance of extended relationships along the male line and the formation of the clan, the emphasis on husband-wife axis cuts each married couple adrift to itself. The family starts with a man and a woman. They beget children and the family may be enlarged to a size of 10 or even 15 or more, but as the youngsters are married and move away, the family shrinks back to where it began. In contrast to the child in Type A, that in Type B grows up under the monolithic hands of the parents, usually the mother. Right and wrong, reward and punishment, tend to be absolute and clear-cut. Before reaching majority children are the exclusive charges of the parents. Any interference in discipline of the child from any source (even grand-parents) is resented unless the parents ask for it. At the same time the value of individual privacy leads the parents to foster in their children a childhood world of their own, divorced from that of their elders. The tendency is to make this childhood as simple as possible, as consistent as possible, as angelic as possible, so that the little ones will be free from frustration. Since parents tend not to divulge their own affairs to their children and since children's activities have little or no reference to the adult world (such as making a living), the youngsters are likely to be unaware of the inconsistencies in adult life, in which honor and dishonesty, triumph and tragedy may occur simultaneously or intermixed, sometimes without rhyme or reason. On the contrary, the children tend to be conditioned to a black or white picture of life, in which all good men are rewarded and all bad ones punished.

The kinship content most commensurate with the emphasis on husband-wife axis is individualism or self-reliance. Having to seek a mate on his or her own merits or demerits, and having to establish and nurture such a new relationship by cutting himself adrift from those who have been so dear and so close, the indi-vidual is conditioned to think in terms of the first person singular, here and now; his own rights, his own pleasures, and his own privacy; his own status, and his own chances for advancement or dangers of regression. For he is trained to regard the human world around him as impermanent. He has no inalienable place in the scheme of things except that scheme he himself initiates and constructs.

Here one must enter a note of caution about the use of the term "individu-alism." This term has been used so loosely to describe the pattern of behavior of many nonliterate societies (see, for example, Mead, 1937) that it has lost all signifi-cance. Individualism is neither the same as individual differences nor as self-in-terest or egotism. Individual differences exist in all societies, as demonstrated by Gillin years ago (1939) and reiterated by Hart more recently (1954). Self-interest is never absent even among peoples who are said to value "giving for the sake of giving" (Hsu, 1943), and self-interest can certainly vary in degree from society to society. But individualism is that conception of each human being as unique and as possessing God-given rights which cannot be taken away from him by men, society, or tradition. To express this uniqueness he must have freedom and, to safeguard his right, his due is equality. Individualism so defined was only initiated and exemplified by occidental peoples of our Type B and was unknown among all other peoples before the impact of the West. Self-reliance is the American variety of individualism where it has reached its widest and most extreme expression so far (Hsu, 1953).

The peculiarity of this kinship content is the primary emphasis given to the uniqueness of the individual rather than relationships between individuals, and to

he likes and aspirations of the individual rather than the duties and obligations of
ne individual to another—for parents and children tend to be equal before the
aw and certainly before the supernatural. There is therefore an inherent tendency
o conflict between the generations not known in other types of kinship systems.
On the one hand parents view their children as their exclusive possession, since
hey are given unbridled authority to order the youngsters' lives. On the other
nand, privacy and self-reliance keep parents and children apart even before the
atter reaches majority in ownership of property, correspondence, relationship
vith friends, romance, and in the choice of life partners. Therefore parents often
ind it hard to let their children go their own way as the youngsters advance in
ge, while children often find it necessary to reject their parents as the most important sign of maturity and independence. As a result the parent-child tie is not
nly terminated legally upon the youngster's reaching majority, it may be socially
nd psychologically broken long before.

Ancestor "worship," even when present, is never more than the mere pride in a
distinguished genealogy and is never calculated to benefit the dead. In fact, death
evers the relationship among men, for the spirits of the dead have no more in-
erest in the living, while the living remember the dead only if there is individual
affection. Clán is generally not an active organization, and wherever present, as in
Scotland or Ireland today, of little more than nominal value.

General characteristics

The emphasis on the uniqueness and independence of each individual cannot
out encourage creativity (that is, change and deviation from the established norms)
n general. Given a blackest black or whitest white pattern of approach, these
annot but cause those who desire change to champion their ends as absolute and
with finality. Such individuals at once threaten those who do not see eye to eye
with them and who are committed to other positions with equal absoluteness and
inality.

There is an eternal struggle. Those who desire to change what has so far been
held as true will be vehement about their intentions and often violent in their techniques. Others who think they have the truth already will inevitably feel compelled to defend themselves as vehemently and violently. Consequently, in this
ype of society, we obtain ultraconservatives and ultraradicals, arch-racists and
arch-lovers-of-all-mankind, extreme isolationists and extreme one-worlders, each,
being armed by the absolute truth, bent on a showdown with and complete conquest of the other. The net result is a type of society full of exuberance. It is
characterized, on the one hand, by convulsions, purges, and revolutions, and, on
the other, by initiative, emigration, science and technology, idealism, and new
frontiers. Even without significant internal turmoil, the tendency of the individual
in this type of society is centrifugal. Many of them cannot wait to move out to
somewhere else or to move up the social or economic ladder. In any event, the
desire to change may come about as a means of climbing the social ladder or be

precipitated by the need to better the older generation or by the differences of opinion within the primary groups. And when there is significant failure in the natural resources, such as the failure of Irish potatoes in the late eighteenth century, or when there is a significant strife between those who entertain different beliefs, such as that which underlay the tensions between the early American pioneers and their other Anglican brethren, emigration tends to be on a large scale. Moses led the Jews out of Egypt, and the White Russians dispersed all over the world after 1917. It is interesting to note that even where there was still an unlimited frontier nearer to home, a considerable number of Southerners moved from the United States to Brazil and elsewhere as a result of the Civil War.

When peoples from this type of society move to a new area, their intrinsic tendency is to set up a new society that is independent from their old. This tendency is founded on two factors. One is that, lacking permanent kinship ties, they will as a whole have little urge to return to their home society. Second, they are likely to be fired by an idealism that is not often present among peoples from societies of other types. Children who are raised apart from the vicissitudes of adult life tend to be freer with their imagination. But since the children are at the same time under the complete control of their parents, they are likely often to use their fantasy world as a reaction against the elders. Personal independence is often inextricably interwoven with the idea of doing something different. This was why all the independent immigrant republics were formed by Westerners, from Australia to the New World. Conversely, no Chinese immigrant groups in historical times and no Japanese colonizers in modern times have ever even suggested a separatist movement from their respective home countries (except for one Chinese group in Borneo for a few years). Under conquest, people of this type of society will tend to resist with violence either in open rebellion or in underground movement. Many of them would rather die than conform to the new rule. And the population is likely to be sharply divided between those who accommodate to the conquerors and those who do not. The ultimate result is likely to be either that the conquerors are overthrown by force or that the resistors are overcome and driven out by force. This does not mean that the ways of life of the conquerors or the conquered will not in the end become intermixed, but there will be persistent efforts to root out the suppressed elements.

They all have alphabetical languages of probably the same origin. Their written languages have changed from society to society and from period to period. Both of these changes tend to be much more pronounced than with the Oriental people belonging to Type A. The archaic form of Chinese writing found inscribed on oracle bones over 3,700 years ago has more in common with modern Chinese writing than does Latin with French or even Chaucerian English with modern English.

Part of the reason may, of course, be that the Indo-European written languages are phonemic while the Chinese written language is ideographic, but that is cer-

ainly not the whole story. As we noted earlier, the Japanese and Koreans are
unwilling to give up the more inconvenient Chinese ideographs even after
adoption of the alphabet. The conservatism of Japanese and Koreans with reference to their written languages is obviously based on other reasons than the
relative ease with which their written languages can or cannot change.

Their literature is more voluminous than that found in the societies of Type A
in spite of the fact that they came upon printing much later than the Chinese.
Their literature is infinitely richer in the imaginative and emotional qualities than
the Orientals or nonliterate peoples, but not peoples of Type C such as the
Hindus. Their art is great for the same reason. Since the uniqueness of the individual is best displayed in creativity, art for art's sake has developed to an extent
unknown elsewhere. Their music is truly one of the greatest gifts bestowed upon
mankind; even the great music of the Hindus and Indian Moslems cannot surpass
it. They have developed harmony systematically and intensively; they have a
wider variety of instruments, more precise instruments, and instruments which are
able to cover a wider musical range than all other peoples except, perhaps, the
Hindus. Unlike the peoples of Type A, they have much music that is played
simply as music, not as accompaniment to some thematic plot or dance. With their
urge to explore the unseen and the unknown, these peoples have advanced science
both qualitatively and quantitatively to a height undreamed of by the rest of the
world. . . .

Impetus to change

Over any period of time, this type of society tends to propel itself toward in-
cessant change. There will be, as pointed out above, extreme conservatives and
extreme radicals. But since those who do not wish to change do not hesitate to
force a showdown with those who desire extremely to change, the result is usually
a major or minor explosion. And when the remains of an explosion are gathered
and reintegrated together, they are never the same as before. In any case, the average individual in this type of society is encouraged to show initiative or he will
lose his self-respect. This is the psychological background of free enterprise as a
way of life. This is the reason why associations of all descriptions, based on both
abstract and concrete goals, are countless. This is the crucial force giving societies
of this type a degree of internal impetus to change undreamed of by all other
types.

In one sense, the technological development and changes are most noticeable
and are usually described as being most characteristic of this type of society. But
changes in other areas of life are no less colossal. Thus, in religion, this type of
society has changed from early polytheism to Catholicism, and from Catholicism
to Protestantism; or from polytheism to Mohammedanism and then branching out
into such creeds as Bahaism. The family has changed from being extremely authoritarian in form through being equalitarian to that of America in which the

family ties even between parents and children are based on ideals of friendship There are drastic changes in laws, in the treatment of criminals, and so forth Most prominent of all are the revolutions which are unique to this type of society The revolutions, though primarily directed to a change in the form of government always have had much wider effects, partly because Western forms of government affect the people's way of life much more than do the Oriental ones, and partly because each revolution is always based on some ideology which envisages a new society that it hopes to realize. Utopias are numerous and most of them very different in form from existing reality.

Such societies tend to be able to develop strong internal solidarity to withstand external pressure, military or cultural. But because of their strong solidarity and of the solidarity of those who hope to conquer or are opposed to them, the resulting conflagration and destruction are sometimes irreparable. In addition to the more severe nature of the explosion, many, perhaps most, individuals in this type of society tend to be brittle psychologically and lack elasticity to deal with ambiguity, having been trained in a kinship pattern to insist on all or none, black or white, completely right or completely wrong. They will be hilarious in their triumphs and extremely depressed in their failures. They may go on to greater achievements and greater glories, but they may also sicken at heart and die out, in the Toynbeean sense.

TYPE C SOCIETIES   Societies in this group include those of the Hindus in India and possibly the Moslems of this subcontinent as well.

Kinship

The center of the kinship structure of the Hindus is the joint family ideal like that in China and Japan. It is patrilineal, patrilocal, and generally patriarchal. It has a nominal clan (Gotra, etc.) that is mainly a negative means of regulating marriage, but is not organized as a whole and not based on blood (genetic) relationships.

In one respect the kinship pattern is similar to that in Type A. Children tend to live in the adult world and are actively initiated into adult roles as soon as they are physically and mentally capable of doing so without waiting for the official age of majority (Mandelbaum, 1949 and Murphy, 1953). But the most important structural relationship is that of mother-son. The mother-son axis distinguishes itself from both the father-son and husband-wife relationships by several attributes. Like the father-son axis but not the husband-wife axis it is inclusive. There is usually more than one son, and there is the perpetual desire on the part of the parents for more than one son. In the Orient and in India, high infant mortality is especially conducive to the usually conscious feeling that there is security in numbers. Unlike the father-son axis, but like the husband-wife axis, the mother-son relationship is discontinuous. No mother is a son and no son is a mother. A mother-son relationship is not, therefore, a link in a chain of a continuous mother-son line.

A third attribute of the mother-son relationship makes it totally dissimilar to both of the other axes. It is more one-sidedly dependent, and more all-inclusively so, than either of the other two. An infant after birth is undifferentiated in its reaction to its surroundings, whether human, animal, or material. Watson, reporting the studies of Bridges, states that the emotional differentiations in the infant begin at about three weeks of age "when distress characterized by muscular tension, trembling, crying, and checked breathing can be distinguished from excitement" in general (Watson, 1959, pp. 199–201). The mother-son relationship begins essentially with complete emotional and physical dependence on the part of the son upon the mother. As the infant grows in years he learns more and more to differentiate between persons, things, and ideas, as well as between different persons, different things, and different ideas. Paralleling with these processes the infant experiences another process: while external stimuli are undifferentiated, all things are translatable into all things. But with differentiation of them into categories, he finds that some categories are translatable, or more nearly so, into each other while others are absolutely immutable into each other. For example, a toy dog and a toy duck are far more easily translatable into each other, from the point of view of the child, while a toy dog and an actual dog are far less translatable into each other. For some time a toy dog and an actual dog may be the same to a child, but as he matures, he is going to perceive a greater immutability between inanimate and animate things. Similarly, as he grows in his power of perception he is likely to become aware of the differences between a toy dog and a toy duck even though this pair will remain more translatable into each other than the other pair. Later on baby sitters are usually translatable into each other. As the child is more used to one baby sitter than another, he may develop a higher degree of preference for one over the other, thus developing a feeling that some baby sitters are not translatable into others. But in the majority of cases, the younger the infant the more dependent he is upon his mother, since she is the answer to all his troubles and needs, and the more all categories of stimuli which come to him are translatable into each other (or undifferentiable).

In the father-son axis, the son does not come into close relationship with the father at first,[4] but is more likely to do so from one year of age or when he is weaned upon the birth of the next sibling. In the husband-wife axis, the son may come into close relationship with both parents at the same time, though his relationship with the mother is likely to be more intense at first. His possibly close

---

[4]The picture may be different in societies where the custom of *couvade* prevails. But what is said here certainly applies to the Type A peoples specified in this chapter.

contacts with both parents from the beginning of life may enable him to have from the start a greater experience of differentiated stimuli than in the case of the father-son axis. In the mother-son axis, since the son retains a close contact with the mother till he is much older than in the case of the father-son axis or the husband-wife axis, the individual is conditioned to retain more of the thought pattern of mutability between all categories of stimuli than would be the case in the other two types of kinship system.

The characteristic kinship content correlated with the emphasis on mother-son axis is what may be described as supernatural dependence. The most basic quality of the content of supernatural dependence is that, instead of solving life's problems by self-reliance, external safeguards, and conquests as in Type B, and instead of looking to mutual dependence with other human beings as is the case with Type A, the individual is encouraged to seek supernatural help either by passivity or by active elaboration of rituals to control or at least influence the gods. Passivity often leads to reduction and even the elimination of many or all of the individual's desires and wants. (Popularly this pattern has been associated with Buddhism. What is less well known is that Buddhism is merely a protestant movement of Hinduism and that self-negation has always been part of the essence of traditional Hinduism as well.)

The importance of the mother-son axis is not rooted in the cultural design. It is not the traditional ideal. Wherever mentioned in the scriptures, the father-son and mother-son relationships are given nearly equal importance, with a slight edge in favor of the former. However, the actual pattern of life in the Hindu kinship system is such as to produce the unintended effect of increasing the importance of the mother-son axis and of decreasing the importance of the father-son axis.

The Hindu culture, even more so than the cultures in Type A, is male-oriented. For example, where the Hindu scriptures and ritual practices are concerned, the males are the primary beneficiaries or sufferers. Females are mentioned sometimes. They may suffer in the other world as a result of certain things; but if and when they benefit somewhere, such benefit primarily comes through men. Otherwise they seem to have the role of accumulating spiritual merits for men. They observe fasting days for their husbands and sons; they practice austerities so that their deceased husbands can fare better in the nether world; and they jump on their husband's funeral pyres so that all members of their husband's families in many generations can go up to heaven. They have no part in the major rituals of any worship. They cannot wear the sacred thread except in a modified form among smaller protestant sects such as the Lingayats.

The clearest statement of the male-centered nature of Hindu culture is to be found in the four stages (ashramas) of life which every individual should *ideally* pass through: brahmacharya (studentship), grhastha (life of a married man), vana-prastha (life of disinterested hermit, in which familial ties and social relations are renounced) and samnyasa (life of the ascetic). I am not aware of any Hindu scripture or even its modern expositions which attempts to apply this or any similar scheme to women. It is simply designed for men.

Despite the male-centered nature of Hindu kinship and culture, the mother-son axis exerts far greater influences on the Hindu individual for a variety of reasons. In the first place, the Hindu household is one in which adult males and females are much more segregated from each other than in Type A and Type B societies. The higher the caste and the socioeconomic status, the closer the family tends to approximate complete segregation. Male children, before puberty or adolescence, tend, therefore, to be under the protective and guiding hands more of females such as mothers and grandmothers than of males such as fathers and grandfathers. . . .

In the second place, the relationship between Hindu fathers and their sons is less close than that between their Oriental or Occidental counterparts. Mrs. Murphy observes in her chapter on "Roots of Tolerance and Tensions in Indian Child Development" that Hindu children "are carried easily, first in cradled arms which do not grasp them possessively. . .later they straddle a hip of a sister or a brother, father or mother, balancing comfortably." (Murphy, 1953, p. 49). In different parts of India, from Punjab to Cape Comorin, Bengal to U.P., a child may be carried in this way most frequently by a mother, or sister, less frequently by a young brother, but rarely by a father. I think part of the reason is the Hindu male's strong aversion against pollution by the bodily functions of infants and children. But another part of the reason is that the Hindu fathers are also likely to be more preoccupied with some aspect of the ritual activities, such as pilgrimage, designed to bring them closer to their deities or the Truth. . . .

One other fact is worth noting. While the father-son relationship in Type A societies is, as in the Hindu scene, also marked by greater formality than the mother-son relationship, it is far more continuous in nature than the latter. The Hindu father-son relationship does not seem to go much beyond life since ancestor worship is of no great importance. The overall tendency of the people is to look to the ultimate station of reaching oneness with the universe through religious devotion rather than the maintenance of entities of individual ancestors and lineages. Thus, while each father-son axis in the Chinese kinship system is one link in a perpetual line of ancestors and descendants fortified by an organized clan, the Hindu father-son relationship has no such significance and is not so fortified. The Hindus tend to keep no genealogical records except in Rajasthan and, as we noted earlier, have no organized clan (Hsu, 1963), though the recognized circles of relatives are greater than in Type B. At the same time the absence of individualism does not encourage the Hindu children to any great desire for independence from their parents which, under the circumstances, means their mothers more than their fathers. Hindu mothers, in contrast to American mothers, do not have to worry about resentment on the part of their grown sons, because Hindu sons, in contrast to American sons, do not have to regard acceptance of their mothers' affection and control as signs of immaturity or weakness. The result is a closer mother-son tie than is found in either of the other two types of kinship systems analyzed before.

It is, of course, difficult to determine whether the kinship content of supernatural dependence or the structural elevation of mother-son relationship came first. That is not a scientifically profitable question to be dealt with. But given the cultural tradition of supernatural dependence, the influence of mother-son relationship generates the appropriate psychological material in the individual for it. Ramakrishna, the greatest Hindu saint in modern times, asked: "Why does the God lover find such pleasure in addressing the deity as Mother?"

And he answered himself: "Because the child is more free with its mother, and consequently she is more dearer to the child than anyone else." (Muller, 1898, No. 89 as quoted in Payne, 1933, p. 128). . . .

Undoubtedly Mother Goddess worship is one of the most prevalent forms of worship in India, but there is no need to restrict our consideration to it. The complete dependence of the child upon the mother is a universal human fact. To the child, the mother is the magical source of all power, gratification, and punishment. This is the psychology that makes the widespread appeal of the creation story in Genesis or other forms possible. In Type A societies this mother dependence is soon tempered by the authority of the father and later altered by the individual's integration into a network of human relationships, with specific duties, responsibilities, and privileges with reference to ascendants including deceased ancestors and descendants both born and unborn. The adult individual's place in the scheme of things is measured by concrete points of reference, and no longer submerged under the unexplainable power of the mother. In Type B societies growing up means independence not only from the mother but also from the father, self-reliance in food and sex quest, and ability to make decisions and bear consequences. It is not surprising to find that Type A peoples are close only to their ancestral spirits and make offerings to other gods primarily for ulterior motives, while Type B peoples believe that God only helps him who helps himself.

The mother-dependence relationship of Type C peoples generates the psychological material which feeds a cultural orientation of supernatural dependence, continued and elaborated generation after generation. The difference between supernatural dependence and self-reliance is obvious, but the difference between supernatural dependence and mutual dependence is equally significant. For one thing, in contrast to mutual dependence, it is one-sided. The worshipper-dependent expects much more from the gods than they give to the gods, just as the child does with the mother. For another thing it is all demanding and, therefore, the objective realities tend to be less differentiated and more mutable. The worshipper-dependent expects simple boons to solve all problems however difficult, just as the child demands of his mother. And finally, unlike mutual dependence, it is loaded with diffuse sexuality. Type A peoples relegate sex into a few social compartments and see sex as having no relevance to their relationship with the supernatural. Type B peoples repress sex so that they must have a God-child who is born without sex. Type C peoples neither relegate sex into separate compartments nor eradicate it. As a whole, they approach the supernatural through sexuality, an element which is at times blatant, and at other times thinly veiled, but at all times more or less present. When demands or supplication fails, the strongest step on the part of the worshipper-dependent is extreme passivity, fasting, abstention, and other forms of austerity, just as many a child can, or thinks he can, bring his mother to her knees by refusing to eat or to get up. . . . .The Hindu way in penance and austerity to achieve power has been made famous by Gandhi in India's long history of struggle against British colonialism, but also by the martyrs and would-be martyrs in many an internal struggle (for example, the struggle for linguistic states) since Independence.

General characteristics

There will be more emigration from this type of society than from those of Type A because the people will not only be propelled by hunger, but also motivated by pilgrimage. However, Type C peoples disperse less easily than Type B because the Hindu society has no inherent tendency to explosion as has its Western counterparts. When peoples from this type of society move to a new area, they tend not to set up a new society that is completely independent from their old. On the other hand, there is also no such great urge as exhibited by the Chinese and the Japanese to return to their homeland for retirement or death. Under conquest peoples in this type of society tend to act like those of Type A, except that, because of the centrifugal tendencies inherent in their supernatural orientation, the conquerors will find them more difficult to administer than Type A peoples.

At home they will show more dissatisfaction with the *status quo* than the Chinese or Japanese, and will be more vociferous about their dissatisfaction. Most religions embody contradictions, but the Hindus see little or no necessity to reconcile highly obvious incongruities in their religious beliefs as well as in their secular life which is governed by religion. Hence, historical changes in their society due to internal impetus are as insignificant as among Type A peoples.

Their art and literature tends to be richer than that of China or Japan in the imaginative and emotive qualities, but poorer than those of the Occidental societies in the logical and rationalistic qualities. Their music is neither Oriental nor Occidental, being based on the most refined and complicated rhythmic patterns and tonal elaborations the world has ever seen. Unlike the Chinese music, all Hindu music, like Hindu art and literature, is religious. In science the Hindus made more theoretical contributions than the Chinese or Japanese, but the volume is not great and the practical application of it is insignificant. . . .

Impetus to change

To the extent that there is more internal dissatisfaction with the *status quo* in such societies than in Types A and D, there should have been more internal tendency toward change. But this pressure for change is greatly undercut by the diffuseness of its direction and objectives. Over a long period of time, there tend to be changes in appearance but not in substance. This is probably a partial explanation for the fact that of all the large status-oriented societies of the East and West, only India built up a caste system, the numerous princely states, and the highly differentiated nature of the endogamic circles within each caste. The Hindu caste system is an accommodation between the two opposites: change and no change (Hsu, 1963). There have always been many centrifugal tendencies but there have never been any revolutions and/or utopias which aimed at achieving a new way of life on this earth. These types of societies are less likely to die out than the Western variety, either from loss of resources or from external conquest. The peoples of this type of societies have a similar ability to endure suffering as those of Type A, even though they may appear more unhappy about it because of their tendency to voice their dissatisfaction with the *status quo*. The peoples in this type of societies are somewhat more likely to take to changes than their brethren in Type A, once they are under the pressure of, and given direction by, the West, though the permanency of the new changes is questionable.

TYPE D SOCIETIES   In type D societies are to be found the majority of the Africans south of the Sahara.

Kinship

The kinship structures are varied and the basic unit in which the infant finds himself may be large or small. There is no ideal of individualism or supernatural dependence as a road to personal salvation. The structural element in systems of kinship which seems to have a great deal of dominance over others is brother-brother axis, across lines of descent, inheritance, and succession. Their kinship content may be described as fraternal equivalence.

Similar to the father-son and mother-son axes, brother-brother relationship is inclusive. But similar to the husband-wife and mother-son axes, it is discontinuous. There is always more than one brother, but the brothers of each generation have no intrinsic relationship with the brothers of another generation. To the extent that the individual tends to be oriented little toward the past and the future but much toward the present, the brother-brother axis is similar to the husband-wife axis. And to the extent that the individual is conditioned to be mutually dependent among the peers, the brother-brother axis is similar to the father-son axis. But the feature which distinguishes the brother-brother relationship from all other axes, including the husband-wife axis, is its inherent competitiveness. Where there is acknowledged unequalness between the parties of a relationship, there is little potential source of competitiveness. This is the situation of the father-son and mother-son axes. The father and the son or the mother and the son are not equal. In the husband-wife axis the relationship may be equal in conception but never really equal in reality, for men and women are different and they are bound to perform different roles, however such differences are minimized by other factors. The brother-brother axis is one in which the parties to the relationship are more equal and more similar than the parties to any of the other three axes and, therefore, more competitive with each other.

The kinship content correlated with the brother-brother relationship is fraternal equivalence. But before I go into the characteristics of fraternal equivalence I must enter a word of caution for my readers.

In the analysis of the African situation I am on far less certain ground than in what has gone before. My views on the previous systems are based on my own field observations as well as extensive acquaintance with works of my colleagues. I have had no field experience in Africa, having visited parts of it for only short periods of time; and my acquaintance with anthropological works on Africa is far more limited. Nevertheless, what I have read so far has emboldened me to make this exploration, following the same trend of analysis which I have pursued so far, and to hope that the results will stimulate further works in this direction.

In analyzing Types A, B, and C peoples, I have first examined the characteristics of a particular structural relationship which dominates the kinship system; then proceeded to relate those characteristics to the kinship content; and finally extended the latter characteristics to the attitudes and ideas underlying the wider culture as a whole. In analyzing Africa I shall reverse the first two, by discussing first content of the kinship system and then stating my case for expecting the dominance of the particular structural relationship in question.

Like Type A and C societies, Type D peoples raise their children to enter into adult worlds as soon as they are physically and mentally capable of doing so. They do not attribute great value to individual privacy. These two facts favor a community of interest between the generations. But in spite of such resemblances to Type A societies, the kinship content is one in which the ties between generations are overshadowed by those between males of the same generation.

First, the claims to dependence between parents and their children seem to require constant reiteration or open gestures to meet with satisfaction. The fear against overclaim and against nonfulfillment of expected claims is indicated by the almost universal belief in sorcery or witchcraft among close family members, especially between parents and children (between mother's brother and sister's son in matrilineal systems), and between other individuals, who are related as seniors and juniors, but almost none between brothers and others, who are related as equals.

Secondly, though some African societies—Dahomey, Yoruba, many Bantu tribes, and others—maintain rites designed to deal with the dead, they and their ancestral spirits do not have unquestioned reliance upon one another. The living may regard the dead as possible sources of benevolence but more constantly suspect them as possible sources of harm; while the dead always enforce their demand on the living for sacrifices and offerings by means of disasters such as epidemics and personal accidents imposed on their descendants.

Thirdly, in many instances the African word translated into English as ancestors simply means spirit or god. In most cases there is a tendency for ancestral spirits to lose their identity and connection with their own descendants, so that ancestral spirits are simply one of the several mechanisms (equally important) for human beings to reach the supernatural, or the connection with the past is simply a means for vindicating the status of the present.

Fourthly, strong age-grading customs prevail in most parts of Africa except among people like Dahomean and Bantu of North Kavirondo (Wagner, 1949) so that the youngsters, after reaching a certain age, leave their parental houses for their own separate quarters and/or by the well-known phenomenon of secret societies in which members maintain strong bonds outside of kinship. The children may or may not be directly dependent upon initiatory rites, but such rites are undoubtedly as important in Africa as they are insignificant in Asia. The relationship among the youngsters so separated from their parents may range from that of intimate friends, such as the "best friend" institution in Dahomey (Herskovits, 1938), to what has been described as a kind of "Communist" order such as found among the Umbundu (Childs, 1949, pp. 114–115).[5]

Fifth, although parents and other elders can exercise an authoritative hand over members of the younger generation, the latter seem to exhibit much more independence of thought and action than in Type A societies. In some African societies the pattern is even described as "respect" for the personality of the children (Childs, 1949, pp. 120–121). In practically all known African societies the young tend to have to work for the establishment of their own homes and their own marriages, as well as to exercise rather decisive influences over the choice of their own spouses. In addition there is much evidence indicating a linkage in the marriage payments and obligations between brothers and sisters (Radcliffe-Brown, 1950, pp. 52–53).

Sixth, while the institution of blood-brotherhood (that is, a group of unrelated men usually of similar age swearing themselves into a brotherhood by rites involving letting or exchanging of blood) is found sporadically in diverse parts of the world including Europe and Asia, its prevalence in Africa south of the Sahara and outside of Ethiopia is well known. It is said that a blood brother is a "much better friend than a real brother" (Tegnaeus, 1952, pp. 13ff.).

Finally, while the problem of royal succession is nowhere on earth near a perfect solution, it seems to assume extraordinary proportions in many parts of Africa. Tor Irstam of the Ethnographical Museum of Sweden has made a study of

---

[5]In a comprehensive treatise on age groups all over the world Eisenstadt's examples from the "Primitive" and "Semihistorical" societies are all taken from Africa (over 40 tribes and groups of tribes) except for ancient Sparta, five of the Plain Indian groups in North America, Irish peasants, some tribes in India, and some vague allusions to ancient Inca and Aztec empires (Eisenstadt, 1956).

the sacral kingship in Africa in which he surveys many traits (he calls them "institutions") connected with the coronation, life, and death of the king in 103 tribes from existing ethnographic reports. Four of the traits are particularly relevant to the question of succession: (1) "The announcement of the king's death was followed by a period of anarchy"; (2) "the king's death was kept secret for a certain time"; (3) "the king's brothers were killed"; and (4) the king was challenged to a "ritual combat" (Irstam, 1944, pp. 78–166).

We have, of course, to exercise much caution in ascertaining the meanings given to each fact by the particular people among whom it occurs. Thus, among the Ganda the king's ritual combat sometimes led to actual fighting which was "continued until only one of the rival princes was left alive," but among the Nyoro, as far as the ethnographer was able to determine, "only actual fighting for the throne occurred" (Irstam, 1944, p. 62). Again, the custom of the newly crowned king going into a certain period of solitude was practiced "to avoid his brothers' envy and conspiring" but the same sentiment was not reported for the other tribes with a similar custom. For this reason, this last-mentioned usage is not included in our list of traits considered as supporting our contention that the problem of royal succession seems extraordinary, and the magnitude of this problem is related to the importance of the kinship content of fraternal equivalence which undermines the vertical continuity.

From Irstam's study we have 62 tribes (or over 60 percent of his total) in which at least one of the 4 traits or customs indicating succession difficulties was found. Trait No. 2 ("The king's death was kept secret for a certain time") was found among the largest number of tribes (32). Trait No. 1 ("The announcement of the king's death was followed by a period of anarchy") was found among the second largest number of tribes (19). The other two traits are found among 7 (Trait No. 3) and 10 (Trait No. 4) tribes, respectively. From the logical point of view the 4 traits are obviously interrelated. The fraternal contention for the throne will lead to suppression of the news of the king's death, which when released leads to a period of anarchy, and for both of which the killing of the king's brothers seems to be a reasonable solution. The ritual combat to which the king is challenged could be considered a formalized version of the actual fight which frequently occurs among the contenders.

A tabulation of the occurrence of these traits shows a high degree of correlation among them and indeed supports this thesis. The correlation is less pronounced between Trait No. 2 and others (out of 51, 19 are correlated with one or more other traits) than between Trait No. 1 and others (out of 19, 17 are so correlated). (See Table 1.)

It is on the basis of the foregoing facts that I expect the dominance of the brother-brother relationship in a majority of African kinship structures over other relationships. I frankly admit that I have as yet insufficient direct data except in a few African societies, such as the Nyakyusa age-set villages as reported by Monica Wilson (Radcliffe-Brown and Forde, ed., 1950, pp. 111–138). However, I feel strongly that if future students of African tribes will explore this hypothesis, their

TABLE 1   DISTRIBUTION OF TRAITS AMONG TRIBES*

Trait or Trait Combination	Tribe	Total Number of Tribes in Category
No. 1	Kabinda, Ha	2
Nos. 1 & 2	Dahomey, Konde, Kuba, Luba, Lunda, Mbundu, Nyamwezi, Pare, Shambala	9
Nos. 1 & 3	Wydah (Wadai) (?)	1
Nos. 1, 2, & 3	Abyssinia	1
Nos. 1, 2, & 4	Congo, Loango, Ruanda, Shilluk	4
Nos. 1, 2, 3 & 4	Ganda, Nyoro	2
No. 2	Ashante, Bena, Camba, Comendi, Daka, Djaga, Gbande, Gissi, Gogo, Hona, Igara, Yoruba, Jukun, Kam, Kanakuru, Kimbu, Konongo, Kpelle, Mbum, Ngoni, Safwa, Sango, Saramo, Shona, Soga, Sove, Temne, Tikai, Toma, Vende, Zeguha, Zulu	32
Nos. 2 & 3	Kaffitsho	1
Nos. 2 & 4	Tonga, Nkole	2
No. 3	Limmu, Koki, Benin	3
Nos. 3 & 4	Rundi	1
No. 4	Umundri, Mossi, Ziba, Toro	4
	Total	62

*Greater statistical sophistication is not attempted at this stage of the analysis. This will be done in a later paper when more precise data may be obtained from the literature and field work.

chances of being rewarded are likely to be good. Furthermore, the theory of tribal and lineage segmentation developed by Africanists like Evans-Pritchard and Fortes in which the peoples are said to live in "ordered anarchy" (Evans-Pritchard, 1940, p. 181) and in which corresponding segments oppose each other, suggests that horizontal or fraternal solidarity and opposition are actually far more important in African kinship system than are parent-child and other relationships.

General characteristics

In contrast to Type B societies the individual here will have less urge to leave home because there is no need to prove his worth elsewhere. But in contrast to Type A societies the individual here will also be more easily forced to do so by nature (population pressure, epidemics, and so forth), or by human enemies (war, conquest, and so forth), because of lack of strong anchorage with the past. The kinship content of fraternal equivalence makes possible larger expansion of human relationships than in Type A. That is to say, whereas in Type A societies the individual is encouraged to think lineally and to regard himself as a link in an endless chain connecting the past with the future, in Type D societies he is encouraged to think horizontally and to gravitate toward contemporaries far and near. Therefore, once forced to move they tend to be more ready than Type A peoples to give up much of the past and make *new* adjustments on *new* bases. . . .

Compared with Type A peoples, they have less determination to resist external cultural pressures or to absorb the invaders and to restore their past glory; but compared with other nonliterate peoples they are much more indomitable because of their tendency to group themselves horizontally. They do not easily give up the struggle for political independence. However, their fraternal solidarity is undermined by much opposition which some psychoanalysts could easily designate as a sort of "sibling" rivalry. The Type B peoples form many effective nonkinship groups to revolt against the past. Type A peoples form few effective nonkinship groups because they have solidarity with the past. But the most important attributes of Type D peoples' kinship content is rooted in the fact that the brother-brother relationship is discontinuous with both past and future at the same time that it is internally competitive. The difficulties of the horizontal groupings of Type D peoples are due, outside of foreign domination, primarily to the fact that they are their own worst enemies.

As a rule they have no written languages even though they must have at one time or another come into contact with either the Egyptian hieroglyphics or the Indo-European alphabets. My inference is that the assumption of a written language, even though its elements may have been borrowed, as were those of a majority of mankind who have written languages, depends upon a strong need for a wide circle of communication and for a permanent preservation of the relationships with the past, and requires a concerted and continuous group exertion. Most peoples of Type D obviously did not feel the need and were not willing or prepared to make the necessary efforts. . . .

Impetus to change

Because the individual can more or less reach his proper station among fellow men through the kinship framework, there is, as in Type A, little internal impetus to change. But since the solidarity within the kinship groups is far less than that in Type A, there is not the same centripetal force to resist deviation. In fact, there is evidence that a daring member of the society, if he is really determined, can actually break some of the traditional rules by personal initiative. Witness the way in which incest taboos can be and are actually broken in spite of the threat of death penalty, which is rarely carried out to the extent that they are formally threatened (Hsu, 1940). But although they tend to have more nonkinship groupings than in Type A societies, such as age-grade villages and secret societies, which seriously claim the individual's allegiance and attention, such ties remain concrete but not idealistic in nature. Therefore, customs, whether considered by the West as good or evil, tend to perpetuate themselves since no individuals or groups will take it upon themselves to eradicate them. Too, although they have many more revolts against their rulers than would be the case among Type A societies, they also know no such thing as revolution of an internal origin, which aims at not only changing the ruler but also the social order. Having no written languages, their opportunities for accumulation of knowledge and ideas from the past and for stimulation within the society are much more limited than among Type A, B, and C peoples. This fact actually gives such societies, in spite of their greater instability, fewer internal chances for cultural evolution than Type A societies.

Concluding remarks

This chapter is no more than a preliminary exploration of the hypothesis. It is offered in the spirit of a Chinese proverb: "Throw the bricks to lead in the jade." In the first place, there are, of course, many facts which cannot be squeezed into the categories postulated, although as pointed out before, no scientific classification covers all the facts. In the second place, many differences do exist within each of the types postulated. Take prejudice for example. Obviously, not all societies in Type B are equally prejudiced. The pattern of variation in prejudice coincides roughly with that of variation in individualism. In Europe, racial prejudice is more pronounced in Britain and Germany, where individualism is stronger, than in Spain and Italy where it is weaker. This difference becomes magnified when European peoples settle in colonies. As a matter of fact, there is almost a complete dichotomy with Protestant colonies, including the United States, Canada (the word "colony" is applied to these independent countries in a historical and cultural sense), Union of South Africa, East Africa, and Australia, showing more racial prejudice than Catholic colonies from French Equatorial Africa, Portuguese East Africa, to Mexico and all South American republics.[6]

The differences between China and Japan (both being Type B) are perhaps even more spectacular. Elsewhere I have advanced one reason why Japan had ac-

---

[6]New Zealand is a possible exception so far. There the relationship between the Protestant whites and the Maoris shows greater harmony than that between the indigenous populations and white settlers elsewhere. There are some peculiar but complex reasons for this which are not as yet systematically explored. One of these reasons is that the Europeans never scored decisive victories over the Maoris in battle. Another reason is that Maori values seem to have a great deal of affinity to those of the European settlers. Judging by the white New Zealanders' prejudicial attitude toward other nonwhites, the significance of the nature of their relationship with the Maoris remains inconclusive. According to recent reports, the situation in Angola seems to be one other exception. But the usual defect in such reports is their failure to distinguish politically and militarily oppressive actions from the continued and tenacious prejudice in day-to-day life. A truer picture must await more intensive researches.

tively and successfully met the modern challenge of the West while China remained politically, economically, and militarily prostrate for a whole century. I found the presence of the kinship usage of primogeniture in Japan and the absence of it in China to be one of the most relevant factors (Hsu, 1954). The diversity in patterns of life among nonliterate tribes, even of one in sub-Sahara Africa, is both great and obvious.

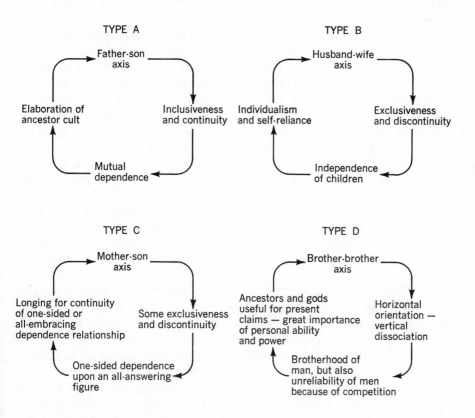

FIGURE 1.

The relationship between kinship structure, kinship content, and way of life postulated in this chapter must be seen as circular or spiral, with all variables boosting or limiting each other in time, rather than in the manner of a straight line, with one variable being the ultimate cause of another. The circular or spiral relationship in the four types of societies may be crudely represented in the . . . diagrams [in Figure 1].

The peoples belonging to each of the four types of kinship systems presented here enjoy some obvious advantages and suffer from some obvious drawbacks.

Continuity in Type A is an advantage because it provides the individual with psychological security, but it also can be a drawback because it restrains the individual's initiative. With reference to the discontinuity of Type B, the order of advantage versus disadvantage is exactly the reverse. Type C peoples may be more diffused in outlook than others but among them we find more individuals reaching great heights of spirituality than among others. Type D peoples may fight more among themselves, but their kinship content is the only one of the four which seems truly consistent with universal brotherhood of man.

Finally, the kinship structure and content of a people obviously form only one of the variables, though a most important one, affecting its development. The physical facts of size of population and ecology may have a great deal to do with it. Firth's description of Tikopian family, clan, and ancestor cult (Firth, 1936) bears great resemblance to what we find in China, but factors other than kinship (for example, life on isolated islands as compared with that on a vast continent) obviously have some important bearing on why the Tikopia did not develop vast empires such as those of the Chinese. Other important factors in the development of peoples are the presence or absence of external threats of conquest, of intertribal or international communication and stimulation, and perhaps even climatic conditions and biological compositions.

The error of some students lies in their attempt to produce final explanations for all by one factor. But the error of some others lies in reluctance to explore any hypothesis to its logical conclusion for fear of the accusation of being biased. Neither of these approaches, if carried to the extreme, is likely to be fruitful in the long run.

What I have tried to do in this chapter is probably to raise many more questions to be settled by further research than I have answered. My purpose is to show that the patterns of kinship content, which have been neglected in systematic kinship studies, are demonstrably rooted in those of kinship structures, and that both have strong bearing on the patterns of personality and culture in different societies. In the preliminary results, I plead guilty to having lumped numerous peoples together whom many will certainly regard as being incongruous. But I am no more guilty than the zoologist who puts fish, chickens, crocodiles, monkeys, and humans together into the single category of vertebrata and attributes to all of them a number of common characteristics. If differences alone are stressed, I am positive that no two human societies are identical. For that matter we can go further and note that no two individuals are completely alike. At a certain level, it is important to ascertain the exact cultural differences between two particular tribes just as at a certain other level it is relevant to see the mental differences between two individual leaders. But before those who are interested in diamonds attempt to ascertain the differences between diamonds and pebbles, they must first make sure that they know what separates, on the one hand, the diamonds and pebbles (which are both stones), and, on the other, cabbages and turnips (which are both vegetables). For further refinement and exploration of this hypothesis see Hsu, 1965.

BIBLIOGRAPHY

CHANG, TUNG-SUN, 1939, "A Chinese Philosopher's Theory of Knowledge," *Yenching Journal of Social Studies,* I. (Reprinted in *ETC,* 1952, 9, pp. 203–226.)

CHILDS, GLADWYN M., 1949, *Umbundu Kinship and Character,* London: Oxford University Press.

EGGAN, FRED, 1950, *Social Organization of the Western Pueblos,* Chicago: University of Chicago Press.

EISENSTADT, S. N., 1956, *From Generation to Generation: Age Groups and Social Structure,* New York: The Free Press.

EVANS-PRITCHARD, E. E., 1940, *The Nuer,* London: Oxford University Press.

FIRTH, R., 1936, *We the Tikopia,* London: Routledge & Kegan Paul.

GILLIN, J., 1939, "Personality in Pre-Literate Societies," *American Sociological Review,* 4, pp. 681–702.

GOLDSCHMIDT, WALTER, 1948, "Social Organization in Native California and the Origin of Clans," *American Anthropologist,* 50, pp. 444–456.

GRANET, MARCEL, 1934, *La pensée chinoise.* Paris: La Renaissance du Livre.

HART, C. W. M., 1954, "The Sons of Turimpi," *American Anthropologist,* 56, pp. 242–261.

HERSKOVITS, M. J., 1938, *Dahomey,* 2 vols., New York: J. J. Augustin.

HSU, FRANCIS L. K., 1940, "The Problem of Incest Tabu in a North China Village," *American Anthropologist,* 42, pp. 122–135.

HSU, FRANCIS L. K., 1943, "Incentives to Work in Primitive Communities," *American Sociological Review,* 8, pp. 638–642.

HSU, FRANCIS L. K., 1953, *Americans and Chinese: Two Ways of Life,* New York: Abelard-Schuman.

HSU, FRANCIS L. K., 1954, "Cultural Factors," *Economic Development,* Williamson and Buttrick, eds., Englewood Cliffs, N.J.: Prentice-Hall.

HSU, FRANCIS L. K., 1959, "Structure, Function, Content, and Process," *American Anthropologist,* Part I, 61, pp. 790–805.

HSU, FRANCIS L. K., 1963, *Clan, Caste and Club: A Comparative Study of Chinese, Hindu and American Ways of Life,* Princeton, N.J.: Van Nostrand.

HSU, FRANCIS L. K., 1965, "The Effect of Dominant Kinship Relationships on Kin & Non-Kin Behavior: A Hypothesis," *American Anthropologist,* 67, pp. 638–661.

IRSTAM, TOR, 1944, "The King of Ganda," *Studies in the Institutions of Sacral Kingship in Africa,* Stockholm: The Ethnological Museum of Sweden, New Series, Publication 8.

KUHN, MANFORD H., 1954, "Factors in Personality: Socio-Cultural Determinants as Seen Through the Amish," *Aspects of Culture and Personality,* Francis L. K. Hsu, ed., New York: Abelard-Schuman, pp. 43–45.

LEACH, E. R., 1952, "The Structural Implications of Matrilateral Cross-Cousin Marriage," *Journal of the Royal Anthropological Institute of Great Britain,* Parts I & II, 81, pp. 23–55.

LEVI-STRAUSS, CLAUDE, 1949, *Les structures élémentaires de la parente,* Paris: Presses Universitaires de France.

MANDELBAUM, DAVID G., 1949, "The Family in India," *The Family, Its Function and Destiny,* R. N. Anshen, ed., New York: Harper & Row.

MAYER, PHILIP, 1949, "Lineage Principle in Gusii Society," *Memorandum XXIV,* London: International African Institute.

MEAD, MARGARET, ed., 1937, *Cooperation and Competition among Primitive Peoples,* New York: McGraw-Hill.

MULLER, F. MAX, 1898, *Ramakrishna, His Life and Sayings,* London: Unwin.

MURDOCK, GEORGE PETER, 1949, *Social Structure,* New York: Macmillan.

MURPHY, GARDNER, 1953, *In the Minds of Men*, New York: Basic Books.
PAYNE, ERNEST A., 1933, *The Saktas*, Calcutta and London: Oxford University Press.
RADCLIFFE-BROWN, A. R., and DARYLL FORDE, eds., 1950, *African systems of kinship and marriage*, London: Oxford University Press.
SPOEHR, ALEXANDER, 1947, "Changing kinship systems," *Anthropological Series*, Field Museum of Natural History, Vol. 33, No. 4.
STEWARD, JULIAN, 1954, "Types of Types," "Discussion of Ford: The Type Concept Revisited," *American Anthropologist*, 56, pp. 42–54, 55–57.
TEGNAEUS, HARRY, 1952, *Blood Brothers*, Stockholm: The Ethnological Museum of Sweden, New Series, Publication 10.
WAGNER, G., 1949, *The Bantu of North Kavirondo*, London: Oxford University Press.
WATSON, R. I., 1959, *Psychology of the Child*, New York: John Wiley & Sons.
WHITING, JOHN W. M., 1961, "Socialization process and personality," *Psychological Anthropology*, Francis L. K. Hsu, ed., Homewood, Ill.: The Dorsey Press, pp. 355–380.

5.3 INTRODUCTION

This excerpt from the report of a study of recently arrived Indian students vividly illustrates many of the implications of the preceding selections by Linton and Hsu. The picture of our culture that is apparently conveyed to these students is one which will strike the reader, at different points, as accurate, distorted, incomplete, or totally erroneous, and his response may vary from agreement, to reluctant acknowledgement, to annoyance and anger. He will also recognize the inevitability of much of this picture and the difficulties involved in any attempt to alter it.

The single feature that is most outstanding throughout the findings is the individual's use of his own culture as the standard in assessing all new experiences. The authors call this a "mechanism of cultural reference" and believe it to have been the major determinant of what these Indian students "saw" when they looked at America. What this illustrates is that we never merely look at people and situations, we also evaluate them; and evaluation implies a standard of comparison. Unless we deliberately choose to impose a different one, this standard will be drawn from our own cultural experience and, as a result, our perceptions of another culture are likely to be primarily reflections of our own.

Indians and Americans are geographically, as well as culturally, remote, but the attitudinal and perceptual phenomena observed in this study also characterize relations among subgroups within a single society and, generally, among any groups with their own practices and norms. For the guidance counselor, whose effectiveness depends on the validity of his perceptions and on the response that he in turn evokes, the importance of recognizing these cultural pulls on himself and on those he deals with can hardly be overemphasized. His work brings him in contact with a variety of different cultures—that of adolescents, of faculty members, of particular ethnic groups, of various organizations. Not only must he bridge such "cross-cultural" gaps himself, but he may often find himself attempting to mediate between cultures. In these terms, a number of points made in this selection are especially suggestive: that we are most impressed in others by that which is most different from ourselves, that what we select from our culture as the standards for evaluating another culture are our ideals rather than our actual practices, that in interacting with a "foreigner" our behavior may adjust to what we think his expectations will be so he is in fact not exposed to new information, that we are likely to structure our overall view of people in terms of our perception of a single aspect. How will such tendencies, in himself and in others, affect a guidance counselor's ability to help, to introduce changes, to persuade, to provide information? What are the possibilities of preventing or at least compensating for such tendencies?

5.3   INDIAN STUDENTS AND THE UNITED STATES: CROSS CULTURAL IMAGES[1]*

Richard D. Lambert and Marvin Bressler

The emergence of India as a major world power, sympathetic but uncommitted to the West, has created a measure of self-conscious curiosity, sometimes anxiety, in many Americans concerning the reactions of Indian leadership and public opinion to the United States. It is inevitable that the image of the United States conveyed to the Indian public should be somewhat selective and distorted, inasmuch as the Indian media of mass communication concern themselves largely with American foreign policy and neglect broader sociocultural aspects of the American scene. Such information on the United States as is exported characteristically fails to provide a substantial corrective—neither the superficial frivolities emanating from Hollywood nor the excessively grim realities of the protest novel are capable of transmitting a representative picture of the United States.

The nature of this picture formed at a distance is illustrated by the preconceptions entertained by Indian students upon arrival in the United States—a stereotypical, indistinct, and limited image composed of uncorrelated fragments. They had

---
[1]From Richard D. Lambert and Marvin Bressler, "Indian Students and the United States: Cross-Cultural Images," *The Annals of the American Academy of Political and Social Science*, 295, 1954, pp. 62–67.

*This project is part of a program sponsored by the Committee on Cross-Cultural Education of the Social Science Research Council and supported by grants to the Council from the Carnegie Corporation, the Ford Foundation, and the Rockefeller Foundation.

anticipated that the United States would be a land endowed with abundant natural resources and wealth, whose inhabitants worked feverishly and constantly to command a whole host of mechanized wonders, whose cities were dominated by skyscrapers, whose ethos was scientific and rationalistic to the neglect of the spiritual, whose social relations were marked by casualness, rudeness, and violence, frequently institutionalized in the person of the gangster, whose social system was equalitarian except for discriminatory practices directed against colored peoples; and whose labor force contained a disproportionate number of cowboys. The students were aware that some of these images were oversimplified, bordering on caricature, but in essence these grotesqueries constituted almost the whole of their expectations.

One expression of official concern with this naïve and unflattering stereotype takes the form of encouraging Indian students to attend American institutions of higher learning with the expectation that these foreign visitors, having observed the "American way of life," will return to their home country prepared to convey a more favorable image of the United States. The exchange-of-persons program reflects a basic confidence in the capacity of American institutions to arouse admiration: there seems to be some assumption that the sustained and intimate scrutiny implied in the process of guided culture contact will foster accurate perceptions which confirm the excellence of American institutions and thereby create the basis for favorable attitudes to the United States.

The actual mechanism of image formation and the development of favorable attitudes toward the United States appear to be considerably more complex. It is quite obvious that at the very minimum the student's personality, life history, preconceptions, experiences en route and in the United States, and anticipation of return all contribute to the content of his perceptions and to a generally favorable or unfavorable appraisal of the United States. However, our data indicate that the primary determinant of image formation involves a process by which American institutional areas are perceived and interpreted in the context of their relevance to Indian culture, history, and aspirations. This mechanism of cultural reference is operative among all students and is applicable to all institutional areas over all points of time, whether or not images of American life are derived from the media of mass communication or from direct observation. Other personality and behavior dimensions not specific to the Indian culture usually assumed their chief significance as superimpositions on this basic process. The emphasis of this article, therefore, is upon cross-cultural links; how the "Indianness" of the student affects his image of the United States. . . .

THE FAMILY   The comments of the Indian student about the American family system tended to cluster around three areas: (1) the family's restricted function and interaction; (2) the role and status of its various members; and (3) family emphasis upon the gratification of personality needs rather than societal ends, with a resulting general orientation of capriciousness and frivolity in family institutional practices.

Restricted function and interaction

The Indian joint family is a unit comprising several degrees of kinship and several generations organized communally and usually living in the same household. It is an economic unit, a graduated status system with clearly defined roles, a vehicle for ritual and the observance of religious practices, a common commensal unit, a dormitory arrangement, and a sphere of relationships within which primary psychological needs are met.

Family roles are hierarchically stable, clearly defined, and reciprocal duties and obligations take precedence over individual motives. The effect of any act on other members of the family may be anticipated and therefore conflicts can be kept to a minimum. To be sure, intrafamily clashes do occur, but many of these are institutionalized, culturally acceptable, and thus do not constitute a serious disruptive force. For instance, quarrels between the sisters-in-law and between mother-in-law and daughter-in-law are a culturally required part of joint family living, even though the outcome is predictable and the victors never vary. These and other sporadic conflicts can be resolved by a final arbiter, the patriarchial figure. The individual spends his life in some joint family. If for any reason a joint family splinters it breaks into segments, but seldom involves the departure of isolated individuals. The occasional mobile member, not essential to the family welfare at the moment, can leave to pursue his own ends, but the price of his freedom is a willingness to return in the event of family need.

The joint family so described was widely admired among the Indian students for ensuring stability and performing most of the functions necessary to individual members, and for providing a satisfactory, conflict-free psychological setting. The admiration persisted in spite of the fact that none of the students identified his own family as fulfilling all the requirements of the ideal type.

In contrast to the satisfying and benevolent despotism of the joint family the Indian students perceived in America a loosely knit structure providing for limited interactions and restricted functions. The simple quantitative fact of a three-, four-, or five-person household limited to two generations provides striking contrast to the emphasis on the intimate relationships among the members of the joint family. While several commented that the complexity inherent in large numbers is reduced in the American small family, the net effect is diminution of the responsibility, warmth, and serenity associated with the orderly relationship of the extended group. From the standpoint of the Indian student, there is ample evidence of the lesser importance of the home in American life. For example, lack of elaborate family ritual at meal time, restrained rather than demonstrative greetings at family reunions, the brittle casualness of the chic middle-class mother in dealing with her children, ready divorce, serial monogamy, and the increasing vogue of the psychiatric couch and the marriage clinic.

Role and status

The Indian student is not likely to become sufficiently intimate with any one American family to observe the subtle interplay of "real" family relationships. Few American families can resist the temptation to display the "typical American family at home," a dramatization which frequently results in an exaggerated caricature of the official norms. Consequently, the perceptions of Indian students tend to be influenced by consistently overplayed family roles. The specific roles which impress themselves most upon Indian students are the role of women and the role of the aged—those most markedly different from the Indian pattern. The traditional literature, current folklore, songs, and moving pictures depict a vast number of heroines who embody an ideal role for women which is widely accepted by all segments of Indian society. She is to be docile, patient, submissive, a paragon of housewifely virtues, but at the same time full of charm, a companion, and wise in the ways of beauty. Above all, she should be modest and show continued awareness of the double standard by observing rituals of inferior status, and by exhibiting proper embarrassemnt and constraint in interactions with men. While in actual practice, of course, woman's role is considerably more complex and ambivalent, nevertheless this ideal image served as one standard by which all women, and consequently American women, could be judged.

In addition, the Western liberal-humanitarian system of values which is opposed to all immutable status distinctions, including those pertaining to women, has been internalized to a varying extent by all of the Indian students. In general the inferior role assigned to women jars against the Western ideals of equality of individuals and greater emphasis on achieved rather than ascribed status. Indians apply the emancipation ethics fully to certain isolated women—brilliant women in the professions, arts, and politics—and favor such lesser commitments to emancipation as disapproval of "cruelties to women" such as suttee, prohibition of remarriage, complete dependence upon males.

In view of these contradictory philosophies—the Indian ideal woman and the Western emancipation ethic—the student sometimes finds himself in favor of the role-status structure of the American family when he perceives it in equalitarian terms, but opposed to the same characteristics when he views them in the context of the ideal role assigned to Indian women. However, American family life is presumably characterized by so much of this allegiance to the humanitarian individualistic ethic that it excludes cherished values still present in the Indian social framework and still held by our subjects. It would be possible to marshal an impressive array of quotations to illustrate this feeling among the students, but the following passage will suffice to show the attempt to reconcile the contradictory philosophies.

> I might say something regarding the social life of the people, absolute equality among the two sexes and how the women also help the family by supplementing the income, how these ladies are also educated, they can talk on public affairs. . . .

I mean it has its advantages to some extent, I thought, that the woman is independent and she can look after herself. If she has some work or something important and if the husband is not at home or nobody is at home, she could do it herself. Now in our society she wouldn't know what to do because she wouldn't have been taught.

I should say the freedom you allow your women, I was very much struck by it. I should say that in my experience it is more than what the woman deserves. Women we consider to be something delicate and feminine. She must distinguish herself in dress, manners, and everything, which is not the case here. She wears blue jeans and walks like a tractor truck. In that case I can't appreciate the femininity of women.

Old people

There were considerably fewer data indicating contradictory feelings concerning the role of the aged in the American family. All Indian students who had occasion to speak to this subject disapprovingly noted the comparatively inferior status of old people. As they recalled India, it seemed to them that:

... there is greater affection and love between father and son, because there there they regard that it is the sacred duty of the father to look after his son during his infancy and it is the sacred duty of the son to look after their older parents.

By contrast:

Here we find that people have greater individuality, and they will not like the fathers or grandfathers to live with them because that interferes with the development of individual personality.

There was very little disposition to dismiss this particular status pattern as one of those inevitable cultural differences which are likely to distinguish one nation from another. Characteristically, the student felt obliged to determine the causes of the relegation of the aged to an inferior status—it was seldom mentioned without accompanying analysis. Those students who were troubled by this question, but whose tact or approval of the United States forbade wholesale condemnation, struggled to explain it by appealing to the authority of some larger, more acceptable value, such as individual responsibility. More commonly, so fundamental a violation of what they consider to be a basic and universal ethical imperative implied deeper revelations about the spiritual basis of the entire social structure. The lack of respect for age sometimes confirmed latent suspicions that the student was observing a culture which was devoid of real ethical principles and which was dominated by a complete and all-embracing utilitarian complex.

Self-gratification and capriciousness

The supremacy of group values as a governing principle in Indian family life leads the Indian students to consider American emphasis on individual gratification and sexual compatibility to be misguided. They perceive in the American institutional pattern an acceptance of hedonistic pursuits unrestrained by the "higher ideals" which alone are capable of ennobling the marriage relationship.

Critical statements included not only disparagement of American family values but also the paradoxical assertion that even individual happiness is not so well achieved as by the Indian model, whose social arrangements provide personal satisfactions only as a peripheral by-product. So even though in India

> the marriage takes place before you are independent enough to think of selecting your own partner. . . . I think I am very happy, and these marriages are generally happier than the marriages which are by choice of the partner.

Closely related to the contention that there were defects both in the dominant value system and in the familial institutional structure is a less clearly defined, but apparently intense feeling that Americans as individuals have a common failing; namely, they lack the proper high moral seriousness in their approach to family life. The Indian students discerned an element of lightheaded frivolity and capriciousness in courtship and family behavior. This view was sometimes expressed in the sternest moralistic terms as in "embracing and kissing and these things I take to be just the road for going into debauchery or the lack of morals." At other times it was contained in the assertion that the slightest irritation or weariness was apt to be accompanied by divorce in contrast with the Hindu practice where, in the higher castes, divorce is forbidden, and where in fact it is largely unnecessary, "because the girl who marries a boy is very much faithful to the boy. . . she is always so much devoted to the husband and the husband to the wife." On still other occasions this feeling is implied in the discovery of such terms as "boy friend," which is not as one might expect, "that one whom she would actually marry, but she would at any time drop him too. . . if she comes across a better or someone whom she likes later much more, she would drop." Or to summarize the complex more explicitly, "I mean, to me it is not bad at all to go with a girl, but the only thing is that I think to go you must be serious. It shouldn't be just one of those things."

The impression should not be conveyed that the Indian students perceive American family life as entirely uniform or that their reactions were wholly unfavorable. The "what were your first impressions" or "what struck you most" type of question which is inevitably present even in the most nondirective interviews tends to bias responses toward generalizations emphasizing perceived differences rather than toward those elements mutually present and approved in both cultures. The interviews indicate that the students are sometimes aware that although there may be customary patterns and practices which tend to distinguish the entire social structure, various social strata and groups in the United States exhibit pronounced differentials in their behavior. Thus there were some comments on the greater simplicity, refinement, and spirituality of family life in religious homes, especially among the Society of Friends. There was also some recognition of rural-urban and regional differences. Nevertheless, the differences were perceived as minor variations on a common pattern, and it was the common pattern which figured in comparisons with India. . . .

5.4 INTRODUCTION

The selection that follows traces the relationships between psychological and sociocultural patterns, revealing the complex manner in which such patterns reflect and support each other's consistencies and paradoxes. It is drawn from an extensive study of the life and culture in a suburb of Toronto, Canada, carried out shortly after World War II. Although this suburban setting will probably seem more familiar to the reader than the far-flung cultures encompassed in the previous selections by Hsu, the authors' thorough unevaluative analysis goes far beyond the familiar and locates their findings within a general framework applicable to the study of any community.

The main theme that runs through all their data on the beliefs of the people of Crestwood Heights is one of cleavage, of opposites existing simultaneously, pervasively identified with the single distinction of sex. At every level and in every area of experience, men and women were found to have opposite orientations. (It is of interest to note, in this respect, that the content of these differences is consistent with the mass of converging data that is accumulating from many directions on the differences between men and women in a wide range of psychological and social aspects.) Despite the sharp differences, however, the social system survived, most children did not become psychotic as a result of being reared in such a divided world, and the relations between men and women were not characterized by overt dissension and conflict. The outstanding feature of the analysis in this excerpt is its success in identifying the intricate psychological, social, and cultural arrangements that accounted for the cleavage, reflected it, sustained it, partly compensated for its undesirable consequences, and systematically perpetuated it. The authors express surprise at the cleavage, because the community was, overall, a stable one. Yet one could argue that a sociocultural system requires heterogeneity in order to remain alive as well as stable and thus that differences, even sharp ones, should have been expected. From this point of view, the orientations of the men and women of Crestwood Heights can be seen as complementary, rather than contrary, and thus as a striking illustration of both the diversity of a dynamic system and its concurrent stabilizing tendencies.

It becomes an interesting exercise to imagine a guidance counselor from some other cultural context working in a Crestwood Heights school. It seems likely that the counselor's professional orientation would coincide more closely with the feminine side of the cleavage than with the men's. If so, then a male and a female counselor would undoubtedly evoke different reactions and develop different kinds of relationships with both children and adults and would elicit predictably different reactions from men and women in all their roles—as parents, P.T.A. members, school board members, politicians, civic leaders, etc. To what extent would the counselor's effectiveness be hindered if he or she conformed to the appropriate expectations for his or her behavior in terms, say, of concern for emotional problems, or of attitudes toward discipline? On the other hand, what kind of repercussions might result if the counselor exposed children to other expectations and definitions of themselves and of others than those consistent with the community's culture?

5.4   CRESTWOOD HEIGHTS: BELIEFS[1]

John R. Seeley, R. Alexander Sim, and
Elizabeth W. Loosley

The beliefs of men both relate them to objects, to one another, and to themselves and express the relations in which they actually find themselves. Beliefs influence behavior—albeit, frequently, in devious and obscure ways—and are also themselves an attempt to give form and expression to behavior existing temporally in advance of beliefs. . . .

BELIEF
IN CRESTWOOD
HEIGHTS

The first impression made by the expressed beliefs of the population of Crestwood Heights upon any observer-listener might well be that pure chaos reigns within and between persons. A man who is a good and devoted, not to say passionate, Calvinist, an enthusiastic proponent of original sin and predestination, also believes in, and practices as far as he is able, a psychotherapy which can only be rationalized on the basis of utterly contrary premises. One informant is with equal fervor a devotee of Marxist dogma (and the program of those who presently call themselves Marxists), of Zionist nationalism, and of the detached and objective viewpoints of the cautious, sober social scientist. A religious leader can at one and the same time believe, and urge others to believe, that his parishioners are "in no way different from anybody else," *and* that they have a special history and a particular ethical and religious mission; that what is needed for his parish is

---

[1]From *Crestwood Heights: A Study of the Culture of Suburban Life*, by John R. Seeley, R. Alexander Sim, and Elizabeth W. Loosley, Copyright©1956, by Basic Books, Inc., New York.
World rights, excluding the United States, by permission of University of Toronto Press.

much greater intimacy between his followers and those outside the fold, *and* that what is needed is "cultural pluralism," a situation of sufficient mutual isolation to allow each group to develop its own culture and its difference within a merely political or politicoeconomic framework. Instance could be piled upon instance. A great and good friend of children, who understands most of them intuitively and most of the rest out of his psychological learning, has concluded that corporal punishment is no aid to learning, indeed that it militates against the kind of learning which he wishes to secure. So he uses it, as a policy, "only as a last resort"—that is, precisely in those cases where his knowledge should have led him to conclude that something was seriously amiss and the most gentle, careful treatment was required, and precisely at those points where violence would have the greatest (*i.e.*, from his own viewpoint, worst) effect.

The internal contradiction which was true for the same person was found to be *a fortiori* true between people who thought themselves likeminded—and in the respects in which they thought themselves likeminded. Verbal agreement as to the desirability of "discipline," "maturity," "responsibility," "democracy," "freedom," "autonomy," etc., joined together those who, on even slight probing or on the evidence of their behavior, differed about as much as conflicting ideologists in global war, hot or cold.

So marked were these internal contradictions that the possibility of writing a chapter on the system of beliefs of Crestwood Heights seemed virtually to be nil. The search for some system or order in the beliefs found was rendered doubly difficult by the false clues offered: particularly the clues that people would differ categorically in their beliefs principally according to class, ethnic, religious, and professional classifications. There were indeed such differences, but they can be disposed of in a few paragraphs. The only important discoverable difference in beliefs lay precisely in that area in which "informed people" informed us no real differences lay: there *was* a difference in the belief systems of the two sexes. . . .

MEN AND WOMEN, AND BELIEF   The deepest cleavage[1]* in the belief system of Crestwood Heights—more basic and deeper (we feel) than differences in age, ethnic group, or status—is created by the striking divergence in the belief systems of men and of women[2]. The differences, the polarities, the selective, unlike, and emphatic emphases exist not merely at the level of detail, but, more important, at the very core of belief.

This cleavage, which seems on the basis of our experience to appear in connection with virtually every important conviction, is obscured and covered over by another difference between men and women: as to whether, indeed, such im-

---

[1]*[This reference and those that follow are to the notes at the end of this selection. Because of the length of the explanatory footnotes, the original format has been retained. Eds.]

portant differences between them exist. Perhaps as a function of the conflict involved in the progressive emancipation of women in the last century or half-
century, perhaps for other reasons,[3] the ideology of the women tends to minimize
the differences between the sexes. The "without regard to race, creed or color"
pronouncement, the "people are people" view, the individualistic approach which
tends to regard any categorization of people as wicked: these are used with
perhaps even greater warmth and emphasis to play down or deny differences
between men and women, other than those unblinkably given by anatomy.[4] The
women are thus—and here again they are in league with the experts—the pro-
moters of an ideology of identity at the ideological level: men and women should
(they feel) and would, except for irrational accidents of history, share a single
value-system: the "maturity," individual-oriented values for which they themselves stand.

The men, on the contrary, tend to exaggerate the cleavage, and even, ideologically, to regard it as an impassable gulf to be accepted with good-humored tolerance. "Weaker sex," "inferior species" is now forbidden terminology, but the
classification of "women and children" is more than a separation of convenience.
Women are alleged to be unalterably sentimental, nonlogical, and incapable of the
heroic efforts needed for substantial accomplishment. This is supposed to be so
much the case that the case cannot—in spite of all the evidence—be demonstrated
to women. They must be "handled," like children, with careful concealment of the
definition by which they are defined.

That the differences in ideology exist would be denied by one side (the women);
that they ought to be examined as having validity, as possessing equal biological
and social importance, as being complementary and mutually necessary in the division of labor, social and evolutionary, would be denied by the other side (the
men).

An exhaustive treatment is not possible here, but some illustrations of such differences may be useful.

Ideology and action

INDIVIDUAL AND GROUP   One such striking difference, perhaps the most important in its effects on the formation of character and on human relations, is
found in the estimate of the moral value and operational importance of "the individual" and "the group." For the women (and their allies among the experts,
male and female) the supreme value is the happiness and well-being of the individual, which taken in its immediacy determines day-to-day policy. Does a general
rule press heavily on a given child? Then the child ought to have special support
or an exception to the rule should be made, or the rule should be amended or
abolished. The particular, the unique, the special, the case, the individual is both
the focus of concern and the touchstone of policy. The institutional regularities are
seen rather as obstacles than as aids to the achievement of the good life. Mores,

folkways, laws, norms are considered to function as obstructions to the development of those unique characteristics, configurations, and activities which are the height of value, if not its very meaning. Individuals so reared and freed will, it is felt, produce the minimum of order which may be required—if any is—for concerted action where that is necessary.

The men have a firm hold on the other horn of what is cast by both sides as a dilemma. For them generally, the organization, the business, the institution, the activity, the group, the club, the rules, the law are the focus of loyalty. True, they have a supplementary or supporting belief, that the stability and persistence of the group accrue to the good of the individual; but the "army" comes clearly before "the soldier" and indeed without it there will be no soldier. If the individual will learn to fit into the going institutions he will find therein whatever field of expression and achievement it is proper and permissible for him to have. . . .

These primary orientations which lie at the level of thought and feeling and expression, are, curiously, contradicted by each sex in its role as "operator." The men, who allege the supremacy of the organization, the collective, are the practitioners of skills which rest, consciously or not, upon contrary beliefs. They bring to rare perfection and are secretly (within or between themselves) proud of those arts of interpersonal manipulation that are intended to make the organization work to the benefit of a particular individual. They have the "know-how": they know "who's who" and "what's what."[5] Business is thus chiefly an interpersonal operation in which the ostensibly worshipped collective and its norms are *felt* to function (as the women *say* they do) as obstacles to be dealt with or circumvented as far as prudence will permit. The appeal is taken by the individual to the individual for the sake of the individual, although the best cover for action is reference back to the welfare of the organization as the apparent ground.

The women, on the contrary, who allege the supremacy of the individual notably act in groups to persuade or coerce individuals into making changes in the conditions of group life, for example, a change in a norm system or activity. It is they who, instead of taking direct individual-to-individual action, organize, work in concert, know and use the techniques of group pressure, and so secure alteration in the circumstances of the group. . . .

What might be said, summarily, after due allowance for exceptional individuals or for ordinary individuals acting under exceptional circumstances, is that men tend to use a psychology of individual differences in the name of the institutions, quite commonly for an individual, competitive object; the women tend to use a social psychology in the name of individual autonomy, quite frequently to secure collective and cooperative alteration in the ways of groups.

VOLUNTARISM AND DETERMINISM   Logically subordinate, perhaps, but psychologically prior to the individual-group polarity is a polarity that, for want of a better name, might perhaps be called "voluntaristic-deterministic."

Ideologically, the women are great determinists of various schools of determinism, particularly, but not exclusively, psychological.[6] For them, the school psychologist's reiterated statement that "we should remember that behavior is caused" has the ring of the self-evident as well as sufficient statement. They, together with the majority of the experts, are concerned with the discovery of just those regularities in human behavior which will permit an expanding science of known laws or determinacies in reference to it.

The men, ideologically, find themselves very nearly at the opposite pole. They tend towards a Great Man theory of history, both ancient and everyday. They see and feel an active agency; the underlying theory of the free will is dominant; they are great voluntarists and, therefore, moralists. What a man can do depends largely on the strength of his desire or his will to do it, and the success-stories which they admire demonstrate the soundness of this view very nearly as well as the success-stories which they *are*.

What is true for each sex as a routine of thought and feeling is again contradicted for each, at the level of both goal and activity. The men believe that sufficient effort on their part as free agents will so order the world, human and nonhuman, that good results human and nonhuman will thenceforward and thereby be determined. The women believe that a sufficient exploration of and recognition of and adaptation to the determinacies in human and nonhuman affairs will lead towards an increase in autonomy, in freedom, in objective, effective agency.[7]

IMMUTABILITY AND PERFECTIBILITY   The same kind of double contradiction between the sexes, and on the levels of both ideology and action, obtains with respect to attitudes towards human perfectibility.

The women incline ideologically towards the view of human perfectibility, taking their point of departure in the known plasticities of human nature, the established variations (throughout history and across contemporary cultures) in the culturally sanctioned ways of doing things. If this variety is possible, it is argued, so presumably is any amount of variation, which includes everbetter constellations. This bare possibility is further supported, as a matter of morale, by a rather vague inheritance from religious or evolutionary ideology or both, which is given the interpretation that, since things *may* get better, the universal process ensures that they *will* do so.

The men incline more to the recognition of invariances in human behavior, to a definition either that human nature is unchanging or, with more sophistication, *plus ça change, plus c'est la même chose.* Elevated or exalted views of human nature as it exists are dismissed as naïve; similar views about potentialities, as "utopian," in a pejorative sense.

Both sexes reverse themselves in action. It is the women who, by and large, in action take count of the intractabilities and unchangeableness in human beings, as given, and who "realistically" adapt themselves to these facts and operate quietly in their context. It is the men who demand a process of continuous perfecting in their operations, and who rail loudly against anyone sufficiently implastic to be incapable of constant improvement.

It is this differing attitude to perfectibility generally that in the first place underlies and in the second is a consequence of differing involvement with the psychological, human relations, or social science expert.

The feeling among women is widespread that since human nature and social life both *are* perfectible and *ought* rapidly to be perfected, the answer to any given human problem from how to be happy in marriage to how to age gracefully either is or ought to be readily available and can be learned from the right expert, and, having been learned, will be put into practice either automatically or with a modicum of effort.[8] The men, who have long employed and subordinated the expert-in-reference-to-things, confront the expert-in-reference-to-people with, first, a deep and sometimes inveterate scepticism, and even where this is weakened, with a demand for his aid in the achievement of ends which they (the men) have already defined. Where this can be done, they can employ such experts also, but in a subordinate capacity as facilitators, *i.e.* they can use the "intelligence-testers" in the Selective Service system in wartime. Where the orientation of the expert raises questions about the ends, however—as, at the moment, in most cases it must—the tendency is to return to scepticism if not to move on to irritation or anger.[9]

EMOTIONALISM AND RATIONALISM   Not unrelated to, but not wholly included logically or psychologically in, the voluntarism-determinism polarity is another which may be called "rationality-emotionality" or "thought-feeling."

The orientations for the two sexes are again dissimilar both as to fact and as to ideal: as to what is and what ought to be supreme, ultimate, decisive, or determinative. Again, the women, at the ideological level, give greatest weight to the feeling or emotional process, and indeed take the view that this both is and ought to be the final determinant of behavior. Rationality is to be at the service of emotion, and first place must be given to emotional considerations. It is an easy step from "the child cannot learn unless he is happy" (happiness is a necessary condition) to "the child will learn if he is happy" (happiness is a sufficient condition) and, while the two positions are rarely clearly separated, the women tend towards the second. Typically, however, in action and especially for themselves, they adopt practices that would be thought logical consequences of the ideological position of the men: "one cannot be happy unless one learns" (a necessary condition) or "by learning one will be made happy" (a sufficient condition).

The position of the men ideologically and their actions, are, as might now be expected, the point-for-point opposite. They cleave ideologically to the view that feeling is or ought to be subordinate to thought; they act on the assumption that feeling, or the distillate of experience which is intuition, is sufficient for their practices. There is very nearly the acting out of a conviction as to the "Divine Right of Men"; they act on the assumption that, without the study and thought so necessary to the women, they will know decisively at any given point what is right, or at least best or most suitable. It is to women that they attribute intuitive powers; but it is to themselves that they arrogate exclusive right of intuition-based action.[10]

What has been said so far might be represented in a table, in which it may be observed that the ideological tendency of each sex is "counter-balanced" by its own habits of action and by the prevailing ideology of the opposite sex: there is thus an inner and an outer check.[11]

TABLE 1   DIFFERENCES IN IDEOLOGY AND ACTION

ACCORDING TO SEX

Sex	Sphere of Ideology	Sphere of Action
Male	Collectivist	Individualist
	Voluntarist	Determinist
	Immutabilist	Perfectibilist
	Rationalist	Emotionalist
Female	Individualist	Collectivist
	Determinist	Voluntarist
	Perfectionist	Immutabilist
	Emotionalist	Rationalist

Habits of thought and action

Not quite identical with the ideology-action distinction between the sexes, is a similar distinction between characteristic habits or modes of thought and action.[11]

SPAN OF MATTER   It is most notable that in the realm of thought itself it is the women who are the great system-builders and system-seekers; and the men who notably invent or accept innumerable little islands of unconnected—indeed often incompatible—belief. The urge to "philosophize,"[12] to integrate experience in an intellectually consistent, comprehensive fashion is quite markedly a female characteristic; the urge to leave experience as an enjoyable muddle, or, at most, to organize small areas of it intellectually *ad hoc* by crude rule-of-thumb, is quite definitely male.

In contrast, it is the women who are in action the great improvisers, inventors, and demonstrators and devotees of the value of spontaneity. It is they, and those influenced by them, who in an endless flow of minute-to-minute adaptations and improvisations fit action to unforeseen possibility or opportunity—to the point where men feel that directed movement is lost in the confusions of "tacking." For the man, any sense of direction in action, lies in habit, system, routine, rule, and institution to the point where, for the woman, his constancy of direction under shifting circumstance is a permanent or recurrent threat to arrival at the goal originally intended.

SPAN OF TIME   Similar in its effects,[13] and perhaps necessary to the maintenance of the foregoing difference, is a difference with respect to the time-span habitually taken for granted in thought or action. The women predominantly think in the long range, almost *sub specie aeternitatis*, in terms of ultimate effects, just as they do in terms of logical conclusions. Their thinking attaches less to the immediacies of time and place, and tends to take into imaginative consideration not only the here and now, but the new generation, the "children yet unborn," altered circumstance, and perhaps even a new society as yet only vaguely envisioned. The men, on the contrary, much more earthbound and datum-driven, take into consideration an evanescent present or, at most, a very short-run future, in which things will be much as they are now and have always been. It is perhaps not a contradiction—on the assumption of changelessness—that the men, in action, are the makers of long-term plans and the builders of persistent material and social edifices. They, predominantly, are the authors of enduring buildings, indestructible dams, business and social organizations that are intended to and do have an immortality transcending their own lives. The women, again, adapt old buildings to new uses—homes as adult-education centers, schools as community recreation centers—and create the multiplicity of cliques, alignments, groups, temporary committees which they intend to be as short-lived as the purposes for which they were brought into being. . . .

Means and ends

The relation of ends and means is, of course, not given in nature, but only in the nature of man. There are no things that are "naturally" means and others that are "naturally" ends. Objects are given an ends-means relation by the place they occupy in the schemes of a purposing and conscious being. Needless to say, such relations, then, tell us about purposes—and not about the natural order independent of human purpose.[14]

The differences between men and women as to ends and means seem again to run through nearly every important category or modality of experience, and only some of the most striking will be touched on here.[15]

BASIC LOCATION   More fundamental perhaps than any following distinction is a difference between men and women as difficult to define in a single term as it is psychologically impressive and significant. We have called it one of "basic location" because it has to do with a fundamental feeling which each sex expresses as to where it is most comfortable, most secure, most "at home": the women among ends and ultimate or long-term purposes (about the means to which they are relatively uncertain and unclear); the men among a proliferation and elaboration of means (as to the ends or purposes which these are to serve, they are less sure, more uneasy, and less interested). It is to this difference that each sex points when it reports the difficulty of getting the other into "serious" discussion: for the men, this represents an accusation that the women's discussion of ends is irresponsible, relatively divorced as it is from the close consideration of means; for the women, the men's interminable discussion of mere means has, in the absence of clarified purposes, a futility so potent as to disbar any possible claim to seriousness.[16]

POINT AND DURATION   The fundamental orientation of the two sexes towards two aspects of time seems to provide the ground for a whole series of related distinctions in valuation. Both sexes, needless to say, experience time in all its modalities or significances especially both as a series of discrete points (a sum of evanescent presents) and as a continuum, an unbroken (in one sense, timeless) flow or duration. For the men, quite dominantly, duration has to be accepted for the sake of point, the spaces between for the sake of the crises that punctuate and enliven them, the states of being for the sake of the events that may be counted upon to follow and render them meaningful. For the women, with equal clarity, events are engineered for the sake of the states that are to follow, the points accepted for the sake of the durations they seem to prelude or promise. It is as though in a system that flows while it pulses and pulses while it flows, the men felt the pulse of experience and valued it, while the women felt and valued the flow.[17]. . .

HAPPINESS AND ACHIEVEMENT   Here for the first time, in the analysis of the written and spoken material, we seem to run into a psychological inconsistency.[18] Men seem to be telling one another and their children and such others as their propaganda may reach: "To be happy you must achieve." Women say: "To achieve, you must be happy." The first proclamation seems to look upon happiness as the end, achievement as the means; the second, to look the other way Surely this is on both sides "out of character."

Indeed it is, for what has here been intercepted in the propaganda war of the sexes is a "message to the enemy" couched by each side in the vocabulary of the other in order to get inside his psychological defenses. What the men are saying really is: "Even if you believe (mistakenly) that happiness is the end of life, it makes no difference; you can only get there by putting our first value, achievement, first. Then you may get happiness and not otherwise; and, if you don't, you will have achieved and that is what matters." Similarly the women are saying "Even the (mistakenly) achievement-oriented must know that happiness is indispensable to their aim, so they had better seek it first in the first place.". . .

Summary

An attempt to summarize the difference in the belief systems of men and women in Crestwood Heights, without judging between or evaluating the issues, might justly conclude that the fundamental difference is in their basic orientation to two complementary aspects of living.

The men seem primarily concerned about the preservation of life against destruction, and they feel and believe accordingly. The women seem concerned about the creative and elaborative processes, and they believe and feel accordingly. The men attend to the *necessary* conditions for living; the women to the conditions that would make life *sufficing*. The men are oriented to the biological and social sub-stratum, to minima; the women to the social and psychological superstratum, to maxima. The men are concerned with the prevention of positive "evils"; the women with the procurement of positive "goods." The men live psychologically in an emotional climate of scarcity requiring the close and calculated adaptation of means to ends; the women, correspondingly, live in a climate of abundance requiring the wise selection and utilization of the riches available. The men are for prevision—and provision accordingly; the women for vision—and enjoyment as of now. The men are sensitized to necessity: the women to choice. Compulsion, the *vis a tergo*, the drive from the past press with more weight on the men and order their behavior; yearning, "final cause," the pull of the future, lure or govern the women. Rousseau speaks more nearly for the women; Hobbes for the men.

The disappearance of the patriarchal family from practice as impossible and from ideology as immoral has, seemingly, left untouched in the men the more general orientations which it bespoke, and to which under the then-existing conditions of life it was probably the best answer.

The functional utility of this strong representation by male and female of the defense and the elaboration of life, respectively, is evident. In terms of material goods, it is not unlikely that we are now in North America at a transition point between the stages where a logic of scarcity was, and a logic of abundance is, an appropriate adaptation.[19] What is true of material goods is probably no less true of the new knowledge, of emerging art forms, of new modes of human relating, of developing possibilities in the formation of character and the structure of personality. Perhaps this transition is—or seems to be—eternal, or at least coextensive in time with human life. In such situations there appears invariably to be a party that would outrun the possibilities of change, go "too fast," and a party that would outwait these possibilities, go "too slow." These parties usually see one another as enemies, frequently as mortal ones. Where the parties are, as in the present instance, divided largely on sex lines, and where the life-conserving or life-defending and the life-enriching or life-developing impulses are pitted against one another in the area of greatest intimacy and cooperation, it might seem that the possibility of fruitful juncture had been sacrificed to the necessity of adequate representation.

This would indeed appear to be the case. To the degree that the picture represented is a true one, every child is assured of the experience of being pulled in two different directions with respect to all important matters. He must not only achieve an integration that will permit him to function adequately at each stage in the presence of two such opposed parent-figures, but he must further "choose" to make dominant the orientation appropriate to his sex unless he is to become or feel a social and occupational misfit. This he is quite generally able to do, but the task is rendered no easier by the playing down of social and psychological sex-differences that has accompanied the twentieth century's recognition and rewarding of anatomical and physiological ones.

DISORDER If the picture of confusion, internal contra-
AND OPERABILITY diction, and incompatibility in belief within
persons and between them has any veracity, it
may well be asked how it is possible in Crestwood Heights for individual human
beings to operate as personalities at all, for families to remain visibly intact as
families, or, more generally, for action to be concerted in any social act. On the
basis of the situation described, one might expect very high rates of psychopathology and social disorganization—much higher than any actually found or even
suggested.[20] What countervails against the production of the expected results?

It is probably not sufficient to say, in awe and wonder, that man can sustain an
incredible degree of confusion, pain, and disorganization without becoming radically disorganized. Nor is it sufficient to point to the fact that—short of pathologic-
ally recognizable disorganization—a great deal of distress is borne, felt, and
talked about as opportunity occurs by Crestwood Heights folk.[21] Even the
widespread nature of this distress, recognized as such by its victims or not,[22] is
lower, one senses, than the situation would lead one to expect.

In striving to account for the *relative* lack of disorganization, personal and
social, one is driven to observe more closely the effects of habit and inertia, the
viability of specific solutions in the face of disappearing general supports, the protective nature of the social structure as a guard against the full impact of confused
beliefs.

A culture of specific solutions

In contrast with the confusion, uncertainty, and turmoil, chronic for many if not
most in the realm of general beliefs, there is a marked sense of predictability for
any one person or institution at the level of response to specific acts. No matter
how wide the swing may be in the realm of belief from Watsonian "conditioning"
of the child to "unconditional love," the Crestwood child who consistently brings
mud into the broadloomed house *will* be met by fairly consistent disapproval. He
may at one time be shouted at—"conditioned" by startle. He may at another be
made to clean it up—the unnaturally "natural consequence of his own act." He
may be offered material reward or approval or love on a conditional basis—"se-
duction." He may be invited to consider the inner meaning to himself of his act—
"insight therapy." He may be urged to consider its objective consequences—"reality orientation." He may be made competitive or ashamed, or given positive incentive. The act may be ignored as being a "stage"—and such evident, studious
ignoring is a pressure that the child knows about. But, however done, and
however varied, the teaching that mud in unreasonable amounts is not to be
brought into the house will be effected, and mud in diminishing amounts will be
brought in. The psychological theory will change, the feelings on both sides permitted release and expression will change, the rationalizations will change, the
talk will change in volume and content, but finally, in view of the persistent realities of the mother's increasing work-load and diminishing access to sources of
domestic aid, the volume of mud will diminish. Necessary tasks, close to brute

compulsion, natural or social, will be carried out. Necessity is perhaps the mother of invariance rather than invention!

What is true for the perhaps objectively trifling problem of mud is true for such germane areas as personal cleanliness and sexual patterns and control. The meaning of mudpie-making or "messing" with fingerpaints or other substitutes may at one period not be evident and at another quite evident to the latter-day parent. But necessity will drive her in both cases equally to find ways of reducing the child's messing to acceptable forms in acceptable places within the range of time she thinks public opinion, or the opinion of the figures significant to her, will tolerate. The action-lesson learned by the child of the former- and latter-day parent will not differ too much; *how* it is learned and what it means psychodynamically to child and parent may vary a great deal.[23] Similarly, in psychosexual matters, children of homes that express the maximum degree of sexual permissiveness[24] will enter upon a period of sexual latency, and in steadiness and duration it will not differ from the similar period in a less progressive or permissive home.[25]

What might be called "behavioral lag" (since the behavior continues long after the support in belief or justification for it is gone)[26] thus introduces or maintains in conduct that would otherwise be chaotic, a sensible degree of order, indeed of behavior which is markedly similar to what it would have been if the belief system still stood intact. The props furnished by belief are gone, but *mirabile dictu*, the building made in action stands not visibly affected. The analogy perhaps fails, since there may be not only a behavioral invariance under changing belief; there may well be, as the foregoing material suggests, a compensating movement of behavior in opposition to belief or, to use the terms introduced above, of beliefs "action-expressed" in opposition to beliefs "ideology-expressed." If this is the case, the discrepancy constantly found between ideology and action would be accounted for, and its utility in providing a measure of stability in an unstable world would be manifest. Perhaps if anything is to be inveighed against or deplored, it is less this inconsistency than the demand for consistency—individual consistency—where the price of it may be stability—social stability.

A second countervailing mechanism to the swings in behavior that might otherwise be produced by the swings of belief lies in the relatively stable socioeconomic structure, which local opinion cannot hope in the short run to affect.

It is possible, for instance, for the belief in the "dignity of the individual" and the "sacredness of personality," in the valuation of people "for what they are instead of what they have," to be widespread and genuinely and passionately held without untoward consequences for social arrangements that actually separate men largely according to what they have. In Crestwood Heights, particularly but not exclusively among the women, such views are indeed so held, and they come to their ultimate expression and test in the "romantic" view of how marriages of their children ought to be founded: on "love," sympathy, compatibility, and personality characteristics, "without regard to race, creed or color" or, above all— ugly word!—money. Despite these deeply held and pervasive views, the marriages that do occur are not notably different from those that might have been arranged in a caste system based on race, creed, color, and—above all—money. Marriages between Jew and Gentile, Protestant and Catholic, rich and poor,[27] are almost as rare as "marriages out" in any group that punishes them by formal expulsion (for example, the Quakers until recently).

These beliefs and these practices (which would be the objective outcome of the contradictory beliefs) can coexist without sensible strain at the crudest level simply because the socioeconomic structure has already separated out all or most of the persons from the circle of interaction who could possibly put the beliefs to the test of action. A Crestwooder does not meet in his club people from a lower class-level;[28] or, if he does, he changes the club for a "better." Crestwooders do not meet, at the summer resort, people from what is felt to be a different religious faith—or, if they do, when the children are small, they do so on the basis of a conscious tolerance which is about as firm a basis for exclusion from intimacy as law would be. Private schools are notably unmixed, and not only or primarily in reference to sex.[29] The sheer statistical probability of meeting "unsuitable" candidates for marriage or other intimacy is thus notably small, and the further probability of such meetings ripening into a commitment to further intimacy is still smaller.[30] Even in such large, public institutions as the university where the religious and economic range is much greater and the period of ostensible mutual exposure much longer, and where a transcendent basis for intimacy in a common dedication to scholarship is provided for, a whole set of countervailing institutions exists to reseparate the improper mixtures.[31] The long and careful indoctrination of the child in favor of personality alone as the basis for intimacy may be seen very largely as careful provision for a contingency which is rarely or never allowed to arise. . . .

Several more mechanisms in addition to those already mentioned above (behavioral lag, unconscious communication, and socioeconomic rigidity) serve to restore to the social system a measure of stability. Four of these have to do with a division of labor in which someone other than the progressive parent teaches the child the reactionary views which the parent cannot on moral and ideological grounds pass on to him. These divisions of labor take place: (1) within the family informally, (2) in a kind of barter of the function between similarly situated adults (friends of the family), and (3) in a trading of function either up to a special group of specialists or (4) down to the child's peers and age mates.

In the division of labor within the Crestwood family,. . .broadly speaking, the father supplies more than a touch of short-run realism, as he sees it, to offset the mother's long-term idealism. There can be—and in a few families is—a feeling that these views need to be joined, that they complement one another, that both report valid conclusions about real experiences which the child needs to understand in order to orient himself adequately in his world. In a few other families also, these are the grounds for and provide the weapons of an open struggle, in which now one side now the other dominates, and in which the child's emerging picture of reality is alternately built up and fractured while he is simultaneously buffeted in his relationships and torn in his loyalties. Mostly, however, what goes on is neither alliance and peace nor enmity and war, but a kind of antagonistic cooperation in which, without every coming to a clear struggle, a kind of gentle, guerillalike action is carried on, intermittently and for limited gains—indeed without total victory even as an objective. The parents appear to show each other and each other's views a great deal of respect and tolerance,[32] and the commentary on each other's views is carried on very largely at the level of gesture—set lip, raised eyebrow, flared or narrowed nostril, caught breath, fleeting smile, or short laugh. This division of labor within the family is only possible where father and mother can and do take opposite views, and where, moreover, they are not so strongly attached to these views that the difference becomes the ground for open war.

In most cases where both parents share in progressive views, the services of third parties must necessarily be employed if the child is not to take these views too seriously. Such third parties offer themselves in the shape of friends and relatives, specialists, and peers.

The commonest use of the third-party intervention occurs in what is virtually a straight barter deal. Parents who cannot bring themselves to describe to their own children the somewhat harsh facts of life—whether these facts are more obvious, as in the necessarily competitive character of many present social relationships, or less obvious, as in the mixed motivation of even the "best" acts—will be found somewhat if not considerably more free to tell these facts to other children. They will with fair freeness communicate not only hidden fact, but ideologically disapproved attitude and even forbidden action, for example, the offering of bribes for "good" conduct. That these things would happen almost anywhere, and that in the bygone days of the large family, grandparents largely performed this function is true. What is perhaps remarkable here is a substitution for the grandparental brake on parental acceleration in the production of social change, of a situation in which the same parent acts as accelerator in reference to his or her own children and brake to those of her friends. (More rarely, but nevertheless not infrequently, is the opposite effect seen: provision of progressive ideas to the children of conservative or reactionary parents.) This is striking enough, but what is most illuminating is what occurs when these corrective influences are exerted by friends in the presence of the original parents. A smile of genuine pleasure (with a little of the air of a secret, hugely enjoyed) is visible from the original parent and not the expected strained smile of tolerance—indicating that, ideology or no, a substantial and needed gratification is being had. In contrast with the situation within the family, where a covert gentle war is being carried on under cover of a nominal alliance, here a covert cooperation is being carried on under the guise of a seeming gentle war. Indeed, when all the parents in the friendship-group are seen as a system, it is clear that for each pair, the others are taking in the psychological washing that that pair cannot itself perform; and so for each pair in turn. What is nonsensical economics may be necessary psychology and sociology.

In spheres so taboo that no friend and neighbor can be found to take on the unpleasant task—for example, when the use of large doses of calculated ("dispassionate") violence is required—an outside, paid expert in the shape of the private schoolmaster may have to be employed.[33]. . .

Similarly in areas which the foregoing arrangements either fail or refuse to cover, the peer group, also unpaid,[34] may be invoked as a compensator or regulator. Crestwood parents who would deem it morally wrong and psychologically destructive to regulate the expression of their children's tastes, after self-examination realized and stated that they were able to afford these views because and only because in these areas the peer group performed a satisfactory policing function for them. . . .

By these various mechanisms (and perhaps others unnoted) relative invariance in action can be maintained despite tremendous variation in ideology, and immense constancy in concrete or proximate ends with extreme variety of means.

Costs

In spite of these stabilizing mechanisms which do tend to reduce the unpredictability of action, it should not be assumed too readily that the creation of effects in one sphere (belief) and their defeat or cancellation in another (action) is a "cost-free" process socially or psychologically.

Where the countervailing mechanism set up to abort aspiration or protect from the consequences of belief, depends on an interpersonal division of labor, as described, the sense of dependency for achievement, personal integration, and social safety on a host of others, ideologically defined as "opponents," creates a situation of markedly heightened tension. Perhaps quite generally, but certainly in a culture highly valuing self-sufficiency and independence, dependency is felt as "bad enough." But when the dependency must be upon those who are by definition and by the situation ideologically and emotionally distant and opposed, the capacity of the relation to produce anxiety and hostility is sensibly magnified.

Some of the statements about the expert and his Messianic role might now be better appreciated. There can hardly help but be, in people so situated, a continuous latent hope, impervious to all experience, that someone somewhere has sufficient knowledge and good will to resolve these intolerable relations of hostile dependency. That someone must be "someone who understands these things"—social relations and human affections. If he would but come, and render those dependencies unnecessary, the prospective dependency on him might be relatively tolerable—even where foreseen.

Where, in contrast, the countervailing mechanism depends not on a division of labor between people, but on one within them; where their action systematically negates their ideology, or their unconscious communication contradicts their conscious speech, it will seem that circumstances defeat honest intentions. Such continuous frustration, apparently coming from the outside, might be expected to lead eventually to an adjustment on the basis of a philosophy of resignation. That it rarely does so,[35] depends on two considerations, one cultural and one psychological. Culturally, resignation and acknowledgment of defeat are heavily disvalued; they belong with the complex of characteristics identified with the hated and feared old age, indeed are taken as symptoms of termination of the career, and are hence hardly emotionally possible solutions. Psychologically, the real source of the difficulty, in the self, and the real attitude to the defeat, partial gratification, cannot easily be held out of awareness. The threat that they might break into awareness can be counteracted in part by stepping up the rate of activity oriented towards others, and this in turn may raise sufficient resistance and hostility on their part to give ground—for the time being—to the belief that the difficulty is really outside.

Where, therefore, the countervailing mechanism is social—the interpersonal division of labor—the consequences are likely to be felt psychologically: an unexplained feeling of hostile dependency. Where the mechanism is psychological—self-counteraction in either of the forms described—the consequences are likely to be felt socially: an unexplained hostility in many human relationships. . . .

NOTES

1. The word "cleavage" may be ill chosen, since it implies that there ought to be (as perhaps there ought not) or that there was expected to be (as indeed there was) a substantial degree of unity, at least among adults, and at least with reference to basic beliefs.

2. There is evidence from Human Relations class material that these sex differences are established or emerge early, for example at age 10 or 11, and perhaps earlier.

3. The differences in orientation between the sexes must derive from a multiplicity of sources. The social history of men compared with that of women in the Western world must be of significance, as must the current differences in status, social definitions, and occupational tasks. Occupations have their preoccupations, and the basic division between child-rearing and family-tending, on one side, and all other occupations, on the other, cannot be excluded. Whether the Oedipal drama is regarded as a function in whole or in part of the foregoing or not, it is scarcely credible that the differences in role and mode of resolution between the sexes could fail to affect deeplying feelings and modify basic attitudes accordingly. If behind all these and fundamental to them are biological differences both structural and functional at every level from the cell up, the existence of the radical differences which appear at the ideological level might be less an occasion for surprise than a confirmation of expectation. Cross-cultural studies give as yet no unambiguous answer as to what is (so far) culturally general and universally valid in the distribution of attitudes between the sexes; we only know that the distribution by sex of tasks, status, and social definition differs over almost the whole range of possibility from society to society.

4. The extension of knowledge as to the role that difference in sex, as biologically given and socially defined, plays in every sphere of activity has been paralleled by the seeming denial that the difference makes any difference. The freedom to discuss sex freely, and the disappearance of the taboo against exchanging information on sexual activity (in its narrowest connotation), has been accompanied, for the women, by another taboo against discussing the proposition that men and women may have, on biogenic or sociogenic grounds or both, radically differing orientations towards critical issues and aspects of life.

5. Knowing "who's who" does not mean merely the memorizing of a table of organization, nor having for every person a knowledge of his functional properties, *i.e.*, the characteristics attributed to him because of the role he plays or the office he occupies. It

means, on the contrary, knowing those psychological idiosyncrasies, those chinks in the armor which will permit him to be used in ways additional to or other than those which the mere discharge of his duty requires.

6. This statement applies with one noteworthy exception—as to the role of biological heredity. The women lay much greater stress on the effects of environment, and the men proportionately greater stress on the effects of heredity. In actual mating behavior, however, the women pay careful attention to biological characteristics dispassionately considered; the men respond more impulsively to the immediate environment.

7. This may account, for example, for Lionel Trilling's observation that: "Educated people more and more accounted for human action by the influence of environment and the necessities and habits imposed by society. Yet innocence and guilt were more earnestly spoken of than ever before." L. Trilling, *The Middle of the Journey*, New York: The Viking Press, 1947, p. 145.

8. *Cf.* R. de Roussy de Sales, "Love in America," *Atlantic Monthly*, May, 1938, pp. 645–651, where he observes this attitude in reference to love as "a national problem," but mistakenly, we think, attributes to the people generally what is a characteristic, dominantly middleclass and feminine. That he should do so, moving in intellectual circles of "experts," themselves representative of the "feminine" view, is understandable.

9. On the basis of this material on perfectibility and on attitude to the expert, which indicates a tendency for males to maintain ego and institution intact while strains mount unnoted, and for females to sacrifice ego and institution to the attempt to maintain continuous adjustment, one might expect, in the field of mental health phenomena: (1) continuous strain and gradualness of onset of trouble in the women; and (2) crisis (personal and institutional) and suddenness of onset in the men. Whether this expectation could be confirmed or not, we do not *know*. We have a strong impression (where there *is* pathology) of long-sustained harried tension in women and of eruptive phenomena (for example, sudden neurotic breakthrough, ulcers, etc.) in men; but it is no more than an impression.

10. Among the minor pieces of systematic evidence of general sex differences in hope or expectation or demand systems was some material cast up as a by-product of a Human Relations class in Grade XII. The topic selected by the students had been "popularity" and they had already recognized that their demand for this commodity was unlimited and that they had no way of ever knowing when they had achieved it, or sufficient of it; it therefore presented an inescapable focus for continued concern and a permanent source of anxiety.

   After about a month's discussion in which the character of their demand had been somewhat clarified, it occurred to the students to ask whether indeed such universal, unlimited popularity was within the realm of logical and psychological possibility. One avenue of exploration that suggested itself was for each student to secure from (a) peers of each sex, (b) teachers of each sex, and (c) *their own two parents separately*, lists of the three chief qualities "that would make a girl and a boy of my age rate tops with you." These "demands" on boys and girls were than tabulated by source and target. There was pooling to the maximum extent of qualities that might be similar, though called by different names, for example "grace" and "ladylikeness." Even after such pooling, however, the boys discovered that they would have to have 72 different (and many mutually incompatible) traits to "rate" with this small sample; and the girls would have to have at least 91.

   What is of consequence, however, for this discussion is the distribution of most-demanded traits by parents according to the sex of the child. If a separation along general lines can be roughly made and the traits demanded grouped accordingly, the following picture emerges:

TABLE 2   DOMINANT DEMANDS BY PARENTS

ON GRADE XII STUDENTS

Sex of Child	Sex of Parent	
	male	*female*
Male	Utilitarian	Decorative
	Active	Passive
	Differentiative	Conformative
	Aggressive	Controlled
Female	Decorative	Utilitarian
	Passive	Active
	Conformative	Differentiative
	Controlled	Aggressive

What was true for parents was also true, but less markedly, for teachers and peers.

Fathers wanted in their sons the "male" virtues which mothers wanted in their daughters; and fathers wanted in their daughters the "female" virtues that mothers wanted in their sons. This female support of *animus* in the daughter and *anima* in the son must be related to what has been said previously about the ideology of women in relation to impulse as against control. The suggestion can hardly be avoided that the women, themselves socially suppressed historically, are on the side of the psychologically suppressed (or repressed); the men on the side of suppression.

11. The ideology-action distinction presupposes a conscious argument, an ideology, logically and otherwise elaborated, pursued as a program of thought, and "recommended." What we subsequently call "thought-ways," are mere ways of thinking, which are mostly not conscious, do not constitute a "program," and would not be recommended by either party. How—if at all—they are related to ideology, it is difficult to say.

12. Note, in contrast, the coexisting male belief that women are "illogical," not only in general, but most particularly those known to any male speaker. The jokes, direct and indirect, on the topic are innumerable. Somewhat similar is the male allegation that they have "no organization," *i.e.* cannot organize their personal lives or concert action with others. The facts seem to run directly to the contrary.

13. Similar in the sense that philosophic "system" implies a large span of matter, and "long-range," a large span of events. . . .

14. It is, moreover, true—whatever philosophers may posit as ideal in the interests of neat systems—that, psychologically, ends do not fall into a stately hierarchy, nor is the distinction between ends and means categorical, clear, or constant. Variations occur in time and context so that X, a fellow human, may be now a means and later an end, or a means in this situation and an end in that, or even more characteristically, now and in this situation, a means in some respects and an end in others.

Having, however, paid this tribute to the necessary and perhaps not unprofitable disorder in any existent or perhaps possible means-ends schema, one can still make observations about recurrent or dominant patterns about relative "ultimacy" of ends or "irreducibility" of preferences. Though these relative invariances do not correspond to the absolutes postulated by philosophers, it is no more necessary to abandon the terms than it is to abandon the concept of circularity because no circle is ever found in nature; indeed, we know the first to be foolish and the second (even conceptually) impossible. Thus the means-ends terminology is used here, though with due reservations as to exception and variation.

15. It is taken for granted that the reader will understand throughout that it is a relation of value, not of cause and effect, that is spoken of. The question is which is "for the sake of" what. Religion may or may not contribute to "peace of mind," but those who value it for the sake of peace make it, for themselves, a means to peace as an end. Whether or not it is an efficient means is a quite separate question, and one for psychology to determine; though one would suppose that here as elsewhere the perception of the behavior would also affect the effect of what is perceived.

16. Again, the ethnic minority follows the pattern of the domestic one; among them was noted a pronounced tendency to clear ultimate purposes first, indeed to proceed from whole to part, from generalization to particular.

17. The possible basis for such a view, once recognized as having support in actuality, suggests itself all too obviously in the biology of the sexes; and such a possibility, the authors feel, can hardly be blinked. It must be recalled, however, that they came to their material with no preconception of this possibility, but indeed with the sociologists' professional bias against such biological explanation. The sociologist must still reserve judgment; he is not *driven* to a biological explanation, since the occupations and roles of the mother, as socially defined, would equally well account for the data. What is hard to resist is the conclusion that the socially ascribed roles are here a good fit to underlying biological tendency—or necessity!

18. Not to be confused with a logical inconsistency. By a psychological inconsistency is understood here what would be felt as emotionally (or aesthetically) inharmonious or clashing: something that prevents the formation of *Gestalt* in the personality. A logical inconsistency may do so—for logical people—but there is little, if any, necessary relation.

19. *Cf.* D. Riesman, (in collaboration with R. Denney and N. Glazer), *The Lonely Crowd: A Study of the Changing American Character*, New Haven: Yale University Press, 1950, pp. 6–25.

20. We still have no way of estimating incidence or prevalence of various categories of psychological disturbance in Crestwood Heights. Even for the subpopulation of school-age children actually in the Crestwood Heights public schools, where a psychiatric clinic was operated for five years for the benefit of these children, only a *minimum* rate can be estimated, since the clinic was always busy and could only accept a few of the cases proffered. On the basis of that experience, a least estimate of children needing and given aid would be 5 percent of that population at any one time. Impression suggests that something more than twice this number were in need of expert aid; at any one time, probably 5 percent or more of that child population acutely so. But these are low figures in the light of the situation as described. If *somehow* 18 or more out of every 20 children can manage to get through childhood without direct psychiatric intervention, one would also have to regard the system as considerably less than wholly pathogenic. See also L. F. Maltby, "Report on Work of the Clinical Team, Crestwood Heights Schools' Child Guidance Services," Typewritten report, submitted to the Department of Psychiatry, University of Big City, 1953. . . .

21. As has already been stated, at least one of the authors—and to some degree all of them—received throughout the period of the study a steady flow of direct requests for direct aid, or direct requests for help in securing aid (mostly psychiatric). This occurred

despite the provision of the clinic for children already referred to, despite the authors' insistent disclaimers of therapeutic competence, and despite widespread knowledge that they were too busy to act as a referral agency. By a "steady flow" is meant a flow that involved, on the average, 5–10 percent of a work-week—without any attempt to *treat* any case.

22. Manifest cases of disturbance, not defined as such by the victim, are those where marked signs or symptoms were put in evidence or claimed, without being referred by the claimant to any more general emotional problem.

23. Even here, however, variation will be much less than one might think, since the child learns more than the ostensible lessons mediated by the consciously chosen words and methods of his parents. He learns also, more importantly, from minimal cues which stem from the parents' unconscious mental processes, and which in turn give him the vital clues as to what they "really" want. These latter wants—for better or for worse—remain extremely persistent, forceful, and invariant despite enormous swings in belief.

24. The maximum permissiveness is not, of course, a permissiveness of commission but one of omission. In such a home, the child's infantile exhibitionisms, sexual "advances" or experiments will not be criticized, *i.e.* suppressive acts by the parents are *omitted*. In no case, will increased activity be encouraged, or the activity indulged in meet with its sought response from adult or sibling: there will be no *commission* of acts that would permit the child to secure the gratification he is seeking. (A few pathological stimulations of the child are found: pathological in the sense that they spring from the parent's repressions. But these are relatively rare.)

25. Parents permissive in this area are frequently amazed and sometimes (happily) surprised at the emergence of behavior which they could not help but be pleased by, though they would not openly demand it; for example, the spontaneous appearance of "modesty." There is no ground for invoking biological (instinctive) explanations, since such behavior obviously does not occur in all cultures. The learning is frequently from other adult relatives, teachers, Sunday school personnel, athletic coaches, friends, peers, or by reading, radio, TV, or direct observation of how others behave. These sources furnish models, but their binding force and intensity of attraction are difficult to account for without the supposition that the child senses the relation of the models to the "real" and unconscious wishes of the parents.

26. Note how much of a contrast this description provides to accepted theories of "cultural lag," which maintain that technology changes first and most easily, institutional (*e.g.*, family) patterns with some time-lag and greater resistance, beliefs with great difficulty and huge delay. Here, belief swings nearly free in the shifting winds from expert opinion; institutions (*e.g.*, the school) are relatively adaptive; concrete personal habits, particularly at or near the technological level, change hardly and slowly, if at all. As the Dean of a well-known medical school said: "Among doctors, there is no learning [of new techniques], only biological replacement." *Cf.*, against this view, W. F. Ogburn, *Social Change, with Respect to Culture and Original Nature*, New York: The Viking Press, 1938, pp. 200 ff.

27. Marriages between Jew and Gentile are very rare, even in the synagogue of a liberal rabbi, who solemnizes reluctantly but "without making obstacles." Those between Protestant and Catholic are exceedingly rare, partly owing to the very small Roman Catholic population in Crestwood Heights (less than 5 percent). Marriages between rich and poor are negligible; one such case came to attention in the five-year life of the Project.

28. They must be there in the shape of club managers and service personnel, but these are not so much "met" as people as "encountered" as furniture. The very American gestures of pseudo-intimacy—mostly in the form of badinage—function as a barrier, not a channel, to mutual awareness.

29. Indeed, it seems that coeducation has only been sacrificed—like the mixture of religious and economic levels—so that the twin tasks of academic learning and social (*i.e.*, class and ethnic and "religious") orientation may the more singlemindedly be pursued.

30. On the one side, no institution that would provide for such extended contact exists; on the other, the culture requires that the commitment be made only after extended contact. The last is rather curious, given the element in the romantic tradition that believes compatibility is recognized intuitively, recognition coming indeed at once in a moment of fulminating insight.

31. These countervailing institutions may be formal ones, administration-operated, such as the "Colleges" which not only largely separate Protestant from Catholic (and these from "the rest") but, within the former, one denomination from another; or formal ones, student-operated and administration-blessed, such as sororities and fraternities, clubs, and the like; or informal ones, wholly student-operated, such as friendship groups and cliques.

32. "Tolerance" here as elsewhere (for example, in interethnic relations) takes the state of war as a premise and seeks merely to domesticate it in reality, or preferably, in appearance. It is a highly valued virtue in Crestwood Heights which simultaneously, however, values relationships in which tolerance is not merely unnecessary but offensive. It is not that one (tolerance) is, even mistakenly, viewed as a step to the other (peace); both are uncritically, simultaneously, and equally valued.

33. The cram-school teacher also performs a paid, unreputable function.

34. Except in terms of privilege (such as access to the rumpus-room, kitchen, or house generally) or affection.

35. Two such cases of adjustment turned up in the five-year period of intimacy with this community.

5.5   INTRODUCTION

The final selection in this chapter takes a rather different view of the relationship between personality and the sociocultural environment and serves to complement and clarify many of the insights of the previous selections. The author points out that culture consists of a wide range of expectations and norms, so that a personality "consistent" with a culture is one that is in fact adapted to a variety of situations, many inconsistent with each other. The theory to explain such a complex relationship deals with personality as a system of "learned roles and role components" that develops in response to the vast system of role demands that constitute a society's culture.

As Brim notes, his theory upends many traditional notions with respect to personality, and it will be equally clear to the reader that Brim's approach differs greatly from those represented in the earlier selections in this chapter. Taken as a whole, this variety is an important illustration of the diverse viewpoints within social science regarding the same problems. As such, it should also serve as an example of the broadening and deepening effects of such diversity upon our developing knowledge.

The most important feature of this essay is the manner in which it directs attention to the social situation as a major source of an individual's behavior, making motives, habits, values, and other individual processes relevant only as aspects of the roles that situations evoke. In other words, this theory considers that an individual is always in a role in a particular situation and that his behavior is generally a response to what he perceives to be the demands for the performance of that role. Understanding an individual's behavior is thus a matter of identifying the role he is playing, the prescriptions he perceives for it, and what his experience has taught him about proper performance. Similarly, changing behavior in a given situation becomes a matter of teaching the individual a new role, correcting his perceptions of the role's demands, or altering the actual demands to which the role is subject in a particular situation.

As presented here, this viewpoint is quite abstract, and considerable translation is needed in order to arrive at notions that are directly applicable to the problems of a practitioner. What it provides is a view of consistency and variation in behavior which attempts to account for specific aspects of generalized relationships. It thus makes the interdependence of personality and culture a matter to be observed and understood in terms of concrete individuals and situations and, conversely, places the everyday observations of practice in the same framework with all cultural phenomena.

5.5   PERSONALITY DEVELOPMENT AS ROLE LEARNING[1]

Orville G. Brim, Jr.

It is our contention that the traditional approaches to personality which either assume, or seek to find and measure, "general characteristics," "source traits," "genotypes," "life styles," "basic factors," and the rest have taken the wrong road to understanding the person, and are in error in their fundamental premise that there are such general styles, characteristics, or traits. In contrast to this is a general theory of personality development, presented here in outline, which draws heavily on sociological concepts.

This theory sets forth the view that personality differences consist of interindividual differences in characteristics as expressed in social roles, and of little else. It holds that the proper explanatory variables include not only motivation, but also knowledge of the role demands and ability to perform. It maintains that variations in individual motivation, knowledge, and ability are produced not merely by cul-

[1]From Orville G. Brim, Jr., "Personality Development as Role-Learning," *Personality Development in Children*, Ira Iscoe and Harold W. Stevenson, eds., Austin: University of Texas Press, 1960, pp. 127–133, 137–149, 152–159.

tural or idiosyncratic differences in background, but in addition by the types of social structure in which one has participated—the latter regulating, so to speak, which aspects of the culture one will learn.

A few observations are in order to clear the way. First, socialization is defined as a process of learning through which an individual is prepared, with varying degrees of success, to meet the requirements laid down by other members of society for his behavior in a variety of situations. These requirements are always attached to one or another of the recognized positions or statuses in this society such as husband, son, employee, and adult male. The behavior required of a person in a given position or status is considered to be his prescribed role, and the requirements themselves can be called role-prescriptions. In addition, the individual holding a given position has prescriptions concerning how people in other positions should behave toward him, as well as an understanding of what the others expect of him. Thus, between individuals in two social positions there are sets of reciprocal requirements or prescriptions, regulating the individuals' behavior towards each other.

If socialization is role-learning, it follows that socialization occurs throughout an individual's life. The new student, the army recruit, the young honeymooners—all become socialized as they enter their new statuses. It is fair to say that during the past decade probably the bulk of sociological research on socialization has not dealt with the process during childhood, but rather with entrance into roles during the adult period of life (Becker and Carper, 1956; Merton, Reader, and Kendall, 1957). This work is often unrecognized by the persons engaged in it, or by students of personality development, as being systematically related to the study of socialization during childhood.

In any event, the concern in this essay is with personality development in children. That is, after all, the fundamental process. . . .

What is presented here builds upon the theories of personality presented by James (1904), by the symbolic interactionists of an earlier day such as Cooley (1902) and Mead (Strauss, 1956), and by the latter-day protagonists of role-theories of personality such as Cottrell (1942), Parsons (1959; 1955, Chap. 2), and Sullivan (Mullahy, 1952). . . .

No detailed exploration of this approach can be made in this essay. Instead, there is a quick journey down the main road to see where it leads. To anticipate what follows: through an expansion of some earlier ideas and by the judicious addition of some concepts, this approach to personality development does in fact lead to new things. For one, it points to research operations on some classes of variables that up to now have been related to personality development only in unorganized ways. In addition, the general theoretical position advanced here seems to have the possibility of integrating some of the different interests of sociologists and psychologists in personality. . . .

THE DEPENDENT VARIABLES   . . .[L]et us turn directly to the task of presenting the analysis of personality development as role-learning. The first step is to indicate the kinds of dependent variables with which the theory is concerned. These dependent variables involve differences between individuals in some characteristics, whether of motives, ideas, behavior, or effects of their actions. In this, traditional personality theory and the approach to personality through role-learning are identical. The critical difference, however, between the two is in the level of specificity at which such personality characteristics are to be studied.

Traditional personality theories deal with personal characteristics at a most general level; the analysis of the situation in which high or low amounts of a given trait will be displayed has received some theoretical attention, of course, but the empirical work has dealt with the effects of electric shock, of simulated hostility in experimental small-group settings, and others, none of which remotely approach the degree of influence of the many different social-stimulus situations. . . .

This. . .theory would view personality as composed of learned roles and role components, rather than of general traits descriptive of behavior across situations. It would be heartening to be able to refer to a large body of research, rather than the few studies (*e.g.*, Goffman, 1956) that we have, showing how the characteristics of personality vary depending on the role one is in. But the work has not yet been done, and in lieu of it one must appeal to one's own familiar observations.

When one looks at what is actually going on around him, he finds striking the great variation in the individual's behavior from one situation to another during the course of the day: as the individual moves, for example, from his occupational role, to his various family roles, to his roles with the neighbors in the community, and so on. Recall the familiar example of the German adult male who is meek and subservient to his superiors in his occupational role, but who changes into a domineering, hostile, and aggressive father upon returning to his home. Consider the modern executive, who in his occupational role is autonomous, creative, and decisive but who upon going home and taking up his status as husband may become docile and dependent in family matters. What should capture the interest of the student of personality, therefore, is not the consistency of individual differences as he looks upon behavior. Rather it is the great adaptability, the truly impressive variation in response to situational demands, which characterizes man as he moves from one situation to another. The question becomes not "What is his life style?" but instead, "How can it be that his character is continually transformed to accord with the social demands of his life?"

The case could hardly be otherwise; obviously roles demand quite different responses from individuals at different times. The not-so-obvious conclusion that follows is that the function of the socialization process is not to produce for society something such as the "dominant" individual or "dependent" person; socialization instead is aimed at producing individuals equipped to meet the variety of demands placed upon them by life in a society. Socialization is successful to the extent that it prepares individuals to perform adequately the many roles that will be expected of them in the normal course of their careers throughout society. It does this by increasing a person's repertoire of behavior; extending the range and increasing the complexity of responses which he has at his command; freeing him from a limited series of stereotyped responses; providing him with a richer set of discriminations between various social situations; and proliferating the specific motives which can be switched into action by appropriate social stimuli.

Especially one sees that socialization must develop the individual's potential responses along the whole range of variation of some given characteristic; for example, given the fact that different social situations require varying degrees of dominance, from high dominance in one to extreme submission in another, it follows that the successfully socialized individual must have acquired the ability to make responses with all different degrees of dominance. Nor is this true alone of dominance. This applies to all dimensional characteristics of behavior, whether they be achievement, nurturance, hostility, or whatever. Here, also, socialization to be successful must equip the individual to respond, when appropriate, with any given amount of a characteristic. One has to know how to get ahead in life, as well as how to relax. One has to know how to be kind to people, and how to be demanding of them. One has to know how to get angry, as well as how to be friendly.

The fact that research is able to find any consistency at all in individual responses across situations reflects several things. . . .Consistency in the behavior of some individuals in varied social situations probably reflects the degree to which their socialization was unsuccessful and left them unable to meet the contrasting role demands. Perhaps one has not had experience in dealing with certain kinds of interaction situations and therefore generalizes from his limited repertoire of roles. Or, he may have had little training in discriminating between different roles, so that he appears socially crude and clumsy in his behavior by treating everybody alike. Thus traditional personality theory might be viewed as studying the waste materials, so to speak, of the socialization process, rather than the standard product itself.

Consistency may indicate only that the situations in which it is found have similar prescriptions for the individual's behavior. The consistency comes not from some unyielding trait of the individual, but from just the opposite source, his ability to meet the similar demands of similar social situations.

Some traits may show more consistency than others. These would tend to be functionally unimportant characteristics, their greater consistency arising because the expression of these characteristics is less regulated by situational norms. This reduced regulation in turn arises because these traits are less important to the success of the interaction.

Finally, some individuals may show consistency in some characteristics but not in others. Here a straightforward process of generalization of response from one highly salient role to others would seem to be the explanation. For example, the business executive whose major rewards are derived from his occupational role, and the bulk of whose time is spent in this social situation, may find the responses acquired in this role to remain relatively high in his response hierarchy, and continually to spill over, as it were, in response to the stimulus conditions of other roles; *e.g.,* he begins to treat his wife as if she were his secretary and needs to be reminded of the fact that he is no longer at the office. . . .

It is about this time that one might ask, "But what has become of the personality itself?". . .The answer is that the learned repertoire of roles is the personality. There is nothing else. There is no "core" personality underneath the behavior and feelings; there is no "central" monolithic self which lies beneath its various external manifestations.

But, one says, what then of the self? The answer is that the "self" is a composite of many selves, each of them consisting of a set of self-perceptions which are specific to one or another major role, specific to the expectations of one or another significant reference group. The self-perceptions are of how one measures up to these expectations with respect to behaving adequately, possessing the right motives, producing the right results. The individual says, bringing together his many selves, "I am the person who is a husband, a father, a steam-fitter, an Elk, a Democrat, and a Scout troop leader." The work by Kuhn and his associates at Iowa (Kuhn and McPartland, 1954) shows that when a person is asked, "Who are you?" he responds by saying, "I am a Catholic, I am a student, I am a man," and so on. Note that he does not respond by saying, "I am strong," "I am dominant," "I am dependent." When these responses do occur in the Iowa data it is almost without exception after production of the status names which mark the role conceptions of the self. . . .

Where one does in fact view his "self" as co-extensive with one particular role, then there has occurred the elevation of one particular segment of the self to a dominant position. To some extent this occurs with all persons. There will be roles in which the rewards and punishments to the individual are much greater than in others, and which demand his continuing concern with their performance. Thus, for one individual most of his waking thoughts may be concerned with his performance and achievement in his occupational role; it is himself in this particular role which he tends to think of as his "real" self. This elliptical manner of speaking, however, is misleading and it would be wiser to speak of the one or two selves of most significance to the individual.

It follows, too, that evaluation of the self as being good or bad must proceed in terms of evaluations of one's behavior along certain dimensions within specific roles; one says, "I am a person who is a good husband," "a sometimes too cross father," "a successful businessman," and the like. Self-evaluation means that the individual compares his own performance in the role with the expectations he perceives others to hold for him, or which he holds for himself because of earlier learning of what his parents or others would have expected.

One's self-evaluation can be realistic or not, depending primarily on two factors. The first is whether one's own evaluation of his role-performance is similar to that made by other people. Another is the correctness of his appraisal of others' expectations of him so that his evaluation of his role-performance is made according to valid standards. . . .

THE INTERVENING VARIABLES   The problem has been defined as the explanation of individual differences in behavior in specific social situations. What intervening variables will be useful in explaining such individual differences?

The intervening variables must pertain to what has been learned, for differences between persons arise in greatest part from differences in the content of prior experiences, that is, their socialization. Two questions thus arise: how one learns, and how this learning is to be described. Regarding the first, . . .[i]t is necessary only to assume that the child learns from experience, and that the fundamental processes such as generalization and discrimination regulate this learning process.

The second appears as the critical question. . . .Here a role-theory of personality can make a contribution through its derivation from the more general analysis of conformity and deviance in role-performance.

The reference points for appraising the amount of individual variation are either the social norms (role-prescriptions) which regulate the social situation, or the median performance of persons in the role, which must reflect the social norms. Given this point of reference, then, in order to conform to such demands, an individual must know what is expected of him in a situation; he must have the ability to fulfill its demands upon him; and he must be motivated to do so. These three variables of awareness and knowledge of role demands, of ability to meet them, and of motivation to do so will serve in this theory as the intervening variables. They describe the learning that has accrued to the individual regarding a role. The major sources of variation between individuals in roles thus involve different degrees of ignorance of what is expected, different degrees of ability to learn and perform that which is expected, and different degrees of role-appropriate motivation. . . .

First, to a large extent an individual is aware of and conforms to others' expectations. Hence, where the individual varies from some prescribed standard the deviation may be because he is ignorant of this prescription, meanwhile endeavoring to conform to some other prescription that he perceives applies to the role. This causes him to differ from others in the same role, who are oriented to a set of prescriptions different from those he sees as applying to him. . . .

Second, the variations which occur in the performance of. . .individuals may, in contrast to the above, arise instead from their inability to behave in the expected way, even though they know what this is and they wish to do it. One source of such inability is genetic. Another is acquired through physical handicap. Inability also results from failures in training for these roles. . . .

Third, it may be that. . .these persons know what is expected of them and are able to conform to such demands, but that their difference from others in these situations is that they are unmotivated to behave in the expected ways. Differences in appropriate role motivation on the part of individuals indicate variation in, or in extreme cases failure of, earlier socialization. It is easily seen that variations between individuals in role-appropriate motivation may range from hostility towards and rejection of the role-performance through an affectively neutral position, to one of a high level of positive motivation in the role because of its considerable rewards for the individual. In like manner, the motives of a given individual vary between his many roles and may be substantially stronger in one role than another because of differential rewards. Thus, some individuals have a substantial preference for performance in their occupational in contrast to their familial roles, whereas for others the reverse is true. . . .

THE INDEPENDENT VARIABLES   We have stated that it is the differences in learning related to knowledge, ability, and motivation which underlie the situationally specific differences in personality. The next question, therefore, must be that of how such differences in learning occur.

Consider that in the society where a child matures there are always a great number of discriminably different social situations, each with its own norms, its specification of motives and behavior. We have argued that the acquisition of knowledge, ability, and motivation is always situationally specific. With respect to knowledge, as one observes the course of the child's day one is impressed by the time and effort directed to identifying and discriminating new situations; to gaining understanding of the precise combination of responses which is called for; to exploring the degree to which this new situation is similar to ones previously identified and from which prior behavior might be generalized. Regarding ability, one sees him trying new responses; seeking to develop his abilities to discharge successfully his role in some given situation; appraising his performance after the fact and discovering those parts of his behavior which require improvement. Last, although not observable directly, one views the child acquiring situationally appropriate motives; learning that it is a desirable thing for him to behave in way x in situation y, in other words, developing the motive to perform x in situation y.

There are two major types of variation, two fundamental classes of events, which one can discern in this vast and complicated socialization of the child. These two classes of events are the independent variables of the theory and serve to organize and describe systematically the sources of variation in learning that can accrue to children.

The first fundamental class of events pertains to the social-structural aspects of the child's environment, the network of related statuses in which he can be involved. The culture acquired by the child in socialization is associated with these specific interpersonal situations. The social structure through which he matures thus regulates in large degree which aspects of the culture the child will be exposed to and which he will learn. If certain statuses are not present in this social structure, it follows that the aspects of culture learned through interaction with individuals in such statuses are missed by the child, and that he remains deficient in learning in this respect, undeveloped in this potential aspect of his personality. Straightforward examples of these variations in social structure are the presence or absence of the father, the presence or absence of sibs of the same or opposite sex in the family, or the presence or absence of peers for the adolescent living upon the isolated farm. One can even conceive of differences in the overall "richness" of the social-structural environment of different children. Some children will grow up in a structure involving perhaps only one or both parents and themselves. Others will grow up in a crowded community with a large and extended family, where they are forced to differentiate between people in a complex social structure, and to acquire a wide response repertoire. . . .

The second fundamental class of events which regulates what is learned is the familiar one of cultural content. . . .We have stated above that the cultural content which the child learns in socialization is always attached to some specific interactional context, and that variations in the kinds of statuses he faces determine what is learned. Now, the second point is that the actual content associated with any particular role relationship—the characteristics of the interaction itself—will vary according to the particular culture or subculture in which it occurs. In different cultures, the conception of the desirable adult may differ and different ends may be sought in socialization. Or, there may be similarity in the values of different cultures, but disagreement on the means, *i.e.,* on the ways children should be raised to produce the desired results. Thus in different cultures children interacting with some specific person in their social environment, for example, two boys interacting with their respective fathers, may be confronted with somewhat different experiences.

Another source of variation in the content of interaction is the expression of personal characteristics by the specific individuals actually occupying a given status with whom the child interacts. Every society allows individual variation in role-performance within certain prescribed limits. Thus there is always some amount of idiosyncratic difference in the experiences two boys will have in interacting with their fathers, even though the boys' cultural background is the same. The differences arise, of course, as each parent adapts his role (within the allowed range of variation) to better fit his own abilities and desires. The differences become then personality differences attributable to the parents' own socialization experiences. . . .

SOME IMPLICATIONS . . . .The concepts presented in this essay suggest some different approaches to familiar problems. For example, the appraisal of child-rearing practices (probably the major source of variation in personality in later life) should give more attention to the ways in which parents teach children to be aware of different roles. What of the differences between parents in how they actually perceive the social structure, and in the discriminations which they pass on to the child? Which areas of differentiation do they see as the most important? Which ones do they insist that the child learn? Conversely, which are those areas of social structure that a particular set of parents fails to emphasize? Consider common cultural distinctions such as those between male and female and the possible differences among parental couples in their emphasis upon these. Certainly there are parents for whom the male-female role differentiation is substantially less than for other couples. The same is true of the differentiation of power and authority between generations. Parents must differ markedly in the degree to which they insist the child distinguish between various age levels as statuses. These degrees of insistence must have significant effects upon the child's ability to discriminate different role situations and also upon his ability to understand what is expected of him, and should take their rightful place beside modes of discipline and other child-rearing variables.

As another instance, consider the situation where a wife is described as acting toward her husband as if he were her father; that is, she treats him as a father figure. Rather than consider this characteristic to be the expression of unconscious motives on her part, why not explore the alternative hypothesis which is that her behavior is the only kind of intimate, female-to-male interaction pattern that she knows? Then one looks for causes of this deficiency in her repertoire of action both in the content of the child-rearing experiences which she had and in the social-structural aspects of her early environment. Did she have the opportunity to interact, in a continuing and important relationship, with any man besides her father? Perhaps she never learned to discriminate between the different male-female status relations and never learned the behavior appropriate to each. A hypothesis is that wives who behave in this way come most frequently from families in which they were an only child; or, in any event, in which they had no brothers.

Something closely related to the preceding hypothesis is presented in an analysis (Brim, 1958) of a set of data originally collected by Helen Koch. These data consisted of teachers' ratings of children on many personality traits. All children had one sib. One finding was that boys with sisters had fewer masculine and more feminine traits than did boys with brothers. This was interpreted as the result of the necessary process of "taking the role of the other" in interaction, which in this case would lead to a dilution of the boy's own masculine responses. Now an additional and not incompatible interpretation is available with the concepts advanced here. Where the boy has only one sister, he learns peer level interaction patterns appropriate to a male-female relation. Certainly the expectations of his sister, and those of his parents for him toward her, include less aggression, less anger, and so on, than if another male (a brother) were involved. In the first-grade classroom he would tend, through generalization, to respond to his peers as he did to his sister, and hence would receive a lower rating on aggression and similar traits. As a firmer differentiation of male and female peers is learned, and the responses appropriate to interaction with both are acquired, these effects of sex of siblings should diminish. . . .

BIBLIOGRAPHY

1. BECKER, H. S., and J. W. CARPER, 1956, "The Development of Identification with an Occupation," *American Journal of Sociology*, LXI, January, pp. 289–298.
2. BRIM, O. G., JR., 1958, "Family Structure and Sex Role Learning by Children: A Further Analysis of Helen Koch's Data," *Sociometry*, XXI, March, pp. 1–16.
3. COOLEY, C. H., 1902, *Human Nature and the Social Order*, New York: Charles Scribner's Sons.
4. COTTRELL, L. S., 1942, "The Analysis of Situational Fields in Social Psychology," *American Sociological Review*, VII, June, pp. 105–117.
5. GOFFMAN, E., 1956, *The Presentation of Self in Everyday Life*, Edinburgh: University of Edinburgh Social Science Research Center.
6. JAMES, W., 1904, *Psychology*, New York: Holt, Rinehart and Winston.
7. KUHN, M. H., and T. S. McPARTLAND, 1954, "An Empirical Investigation of Self-Attitudes," *American Sociological Review*, XIX, January, pp. 68–76.
8. MERTON, R. K., G. G. READER, and P. L. KENDALL, eds., 1957, *The Student Physician: Introductory Series in the Sociology of Medical Education*, Cambridge: Harvard University Press.
9. MULLAHY, P., ed., 1952, *The Contributions of Harry Stack Sullivan*, New York: Hermitage House.
10. PARSONS, T., 1959, *The Social System*, New York: The Free Press, Chaps. 3, 6, 7.
11. PARSONS, T. and R. F. BALES, 1955, *Family, Socialization and Interaction Process*, New York: The Free Press.
12. STRAUSS, A., 1956, *The Social Psychology of George Herbert Mead*, Chicago: University of Chicago Press.

Questions and Implications for Practice

5.1 RALPH LINTON

1. How would a keener appreciation of culture require guidance-personnel workers to modify their roles and their practices?

2. Why is the guidance field so late in discovering culture and in seeing its implications for the practices and roles of guidance-personnel workers?

3. Barry and Wolf in *Motives, Values and Realities*[1] have summarized some of the theory as set forth by Linton and have illustrated by numerous case studies the fact that personality does in fact have a cultural background. Should a guidance-personnel worker limit his practice to understanding the varieties of personality that emerge from culture, and concentrate on a more effective style of verbal interaction with individuals he is assigned to help rather than to arrive at decisions compatible with the strains and tensions their culture imposes upon them? Do Linton's theories persuade you to modify this view? Why or why not? If so, in what ways?

4. Can a school or college be said to have a culture and subcultures? If so, how is interaction between the personalities of students and this culture or these subcultures similar to or dissimilar from the kind of interaction process Linton describes? Should the guidance-personnel worker limit participation to verbal interaction between himself and a student or should he also be concerned with the interaction that takes place constantly between students and their school or campus culture and subcultures?

5.2 FRANCIS L. K. HSU

1. In Hsu's analysis of four types of kinship systems, girls—until they become wives and mothers—are completely unnoticed. And yet only half of those we deal with in our schools are sons and brothers. The other half, of course, are daughters and sisters.

Using Hsu's approach, in so far as you can, look at the general pattern of kinship relationships in this country as these affect and are affected by daughters and sisters. Compare your views with others who may also have attempted to do this. In what respects do you agree and disagree? How might your findings modify your own attitudes and program with relation to the students you deal with who are girls? Why?

---

[1]Ruth Barry and Beverly Wolf, *Motives, Values and Realities*, New York: Teachers College Bureau of Publications, 1965.

2. Why do you think there are so very few studies and so few pieces of fiction about girls who are growing up in the less advantaged segments of our country? Try to find at least one that focuses on one or more girls and compare the kinship pattern depicted there with the pattern (or patterns) revealed in one or more studies or stories about a boy or boys in this same segment of society.

3. Do you perhaps agree that girls can properly remain invisible until they take on the roles of wife and mother? If you agree, or if you do not, what are the implications for guidance practice?

4. Identify as objectively as you can some other group in our multicultural country which does not look at things or do things in the same way that you and the group of which you are a member looks at them or does them. (You may be a New Englander, or a product of The Deep South, or from a big city in the Middle West, or from some other section that has left its imprint upon you; a male or female; middle-aged or under thirty; educated; the recipient of an annual guaranteed wage; black or white; a fundamentalist, a liberal, a conservative, a radical; etc.) What are some of these "things" that are important, as suggested by Hsu? How does the other group look at them or do them?

5. What does the other group think of the way you look at "things" and do them? Which of you is more nearly "right"?

6. Is there perhaps some advantage for the guidance-personnel worker to try to maintain some kind of transcendent position over and beyond his culture? Is this possible?

5.3 LAMBERT AND BRESSLER

1. Do the Indians studying in this country, on whose views Lambert and Bressler report, see accurately some of the features of our family life? How would you describe some of these features in a sharply different way?

2. Is it possible for an outsider to see a culture more clearly than those who have grown up in it and are immersed in it?

3. In what directions would you like to see family life in this country change?

4. Are you, having been raised in the particular culture in which you grew up, and immersed as you inescapably are in its belief and behavior system, able to understand and appreciate the belief and behavior systems even of groups different than your own who live in this country?

5.4 SEELEY, SIM, AND LOOSLEY

Coeducation has played down the social and psychological differences between girls and boys and men and women. To be sure, research has demonstrated no sex differences in I.Q. and no significant differences in learning abilities. Men's and women's brains, however, are packaged in bodies that have many real and important functional differences. There is also much evidence that their outlooks on life and their belief systems are quite different.

1. Would it be desirable to try to eliminate sex differences in belief systems in education and counseling? If you believe it would be desirable, how could this elimination of differences be accomplished more surely and quickly?

2. If you believe it is neither desirable nor possible to eliminate sex differences in belief systems, what differences would you seek to retain? What means might be used to establish or perpetuate the differences you think desirable?

3. In what ways do the roles the power structure assigns to men and women administrators and to men and women guidance-personnel workers both reflect and affect the differences that develop in the belief systems of men and women?

4. Try to make explicit—at least to yourself—how you really feel about your own sex and about the opposite sex. Are people who do not agree with you abnormal in some way? Are their "distorted ideas" the result of deficiencies in their own family experiences or of other unfortunate life experiences? Why are your beliefs superior to those of others with whom you do not agree?

5. Looking toward the year 2000, what would be a really good belief system that either does or does not provide for differences in the sexes?

5.5 ORVILLE G. BRIM, JR.

1. How does the theory of personality development as outlined by Brim differ from the theories of Freud?

2. If personality development is role-learning, as Brim says, how useful then are personality tests on which psychologists and some counselors rely for their understanding of personality? Is it possible that test results are in the nature of "judgments" or labels, while an understanding of the processes of role-learning opens up more avenues for guidance-personnel workers to stimulate individual development? What, specifically, are some of these avenues? How do the possibilities for the guidance-personnel worker to use this theory extend beyond the typical verbal interaction between counselor and student as the main instrument for change?

3. Does the classroom, the school, the dormitory, the club, the clique give each individual the opportunity to learn roles that affect his personality positively or adversely? Do teachers and guidance-personnel workers know how to look at situations from the standpoint of the roles individual students are to play? How and why do teachers and guidance-personnel workers expand or limit these roles for different individuals? Is this always done thoughtfully and consciously?

4. Is there any evidence that this country (and other countries as well) is reinterpreting the meaning of "feminine" and "masculine" roles? What seem to be some of the main causes of this reinterpretation of sex roles? What are some of the processes by means of which the reinterpretation is being made?

Chapter 6

The Family, Peer Groups, and Socialization

Our examination of the relationship between culture and the indi-vidual has dealt, so far, with the general nature of this relationship and in the next chapter, we will examine some of its specific manifesta tions and variations in American society. In this chapter, the analysis is directed at the general question of *how* the interdependence between concrete individuals and particular cultures is established and main tained. That is, what social structures and cultural mechanisms ac count for this interdependence? When and by whom are the pressures exerted that give the individual his cultural shape?

The human being at birth is quite undeveloped and helpless in re lation to his eventual fully mature state. This discrepancy is greater than it is for any other organism and, combined with the complexity o what the human individual must learn in order to live within the context of his culture, it leads to a long period during which he is not ready to participate as a full-fledged member of society. Instead, he must wait for the process of physical maturation to be completed, and at the same time undergo the lengthy training necessary to the late fulfillment of adult social roles. The more complex the culture, the more there is to learn, the longer the period of growth and learning and the greater the gap between its early stages and the finished product.

From the viewpoint of the society, this period of preparation presents a twofold problem. On the one hand, although not yet fully socialized, young individuals must nonetheless be taken into account by the social structure and their roles in the various systems with which they are involved must be defined. Whether it is explicitly assigned and recognized or not, everyone in effect has a status, or a number of statuses, simply by virtue of being a member of the society and participating in social interaction. The societal problem is to make the status of a young person consistent with the stage of his physiological and social development, while also compatible with the society's socialization goals. On the other hand, the main societal perspective toward each stage is that the individual should leave it behind and move on toward full-fledged status. Such steady progress must be made possible, and indeed must be fostered and supported.

From the individual's viewpoint, what the society must provide during the period of socialization is a current meaning and structure for the experiences at each stage and, at the same time, incentives that will motivate him to effect the necessary changes and transitions until he is ready to fulfill the requirements of adult participation. Age, in other words, has both an absolute and a relative meaning, and both types of consideration are relevant to the expectations to which the individual is subject at any point.

Before raising some of the specific problems encompassed by this dual perspective, it is important to clarify the sense in which the word "must" has been used in the previous paragraphs. Implicit in statements about what a society *must* do and what individuals *must* have has been the assumption that societies strive to maintain their stability and that such a goal requires that certain internal conditions be maximized. In other words, certain things must be done or instability and disintegration are likely to follow. It is in this context that we draw attention to the processes and mechanisms through which a society molds its members and directs the course of their experiences.

The most general and basic question to be asked about a society's training of its young is: How adequate is it in relation to the actual demands which adult individuals in the society must meet? This question can be specified in a number of ways. For example, are the motives which it fosters relevant and useful or inappropriate and counterproductive for the assumption and successful performance of adult roles? Stated differently, how are these motives related to the rewards associated with adult roles: do they tend to make the latter intrinsically satisfying or are they likely to require substitute outlets and gratifications? Similarly, are the interpersonal attitudes and expectations developed during preadult socialization consistent or incompatible with those that are appropriate and necessary in adult situations? If there are differences, do they require minor variations or radical reversals of the earlier learning? Are certain emotional needs and involvements encouraged early which later must be suppressed or eliminated? Conversely, are there areas of emotional experience that will be significant later that are not developed at earlier stages?

Closely related to the adequacy of the socialization process is the problem of how the transitions from one state to the next are handled. Such shifts involve the assumption of new roles and the learning of new skills, adjustments, and attitudes, none of which are easy accomplishments. Societies vary widely in their acknowledgment of the potential difficulties contained in these changes and in the extent to which aspects of their structure exist which serve to ease or aggravate them. Whether the transitions are inherently difficult or not, the amount of stress which they produce is probably due mostly to the manner in which they are handled by various aspects of the social structure—what kind of specific preparation is provided, what supports exist during the period of change, what rewards and punishments are given for success and failure, what allowances are made for individual differences.

In pointing to these issues about the socialization process, we are suggesting some of the major problems which a society must face in order to maintain its integration. In doing so, we are also indicating possible sources of strain and conflict both for the society and for its individual members. No society is free of conflict, but stability can nevertheless be maintained through compensatory mechanisms and structures. Both the conflicts and their resolutions are culturally determined and patterned phenomena, and thus knowledge of the culture is necessary to fully understand their sources and their consequences. At the same time, such understanding feeds back into our general knowledge of the culture, deepening and extending it.

6.1   INTRODUCTION

The initial steps in the individual's socialization are taken in the family and the basic learnings that occur in this early setting are the foundation on which all later experience builds. Thus, in order to understand the nature of socialization, it is necessary to understand the family itself as an aspect of society and culture. The first two selections in this chapter place the family in such a perspective and, in doing so, also point to the dimensions of social and cultural organization in general that are significant determinants of individual experience.

In the selection that follows, anthropology as both a viewpoint and a body of findings is brought to bear on the American family, transforming it from the "natural" phenomenon it is in our experience into something quite unique in relation to the patterns that are actually most frequent. Like all cultural developments, our small family pattern can be understood in terms of our history and it is consistent with our dominant economic, political, and social values and institutions. As Arensberg points out, however, the pattern is still more of an ideal than an actuality, both because there are major groups in the society of whom it is not characteristic and because, even where it prevails, many individual and social problems remain to be resolved. These reasons make this analysis of our family system of central relevance for guidance theory and practice.

The groups for whom the isolated small family system is alien or untypical constitute a substantial proportion of American society and, for a variety of related reasons, individuals from these groups are particularly likely to become the targets of a guidance counselor's concern. Negroes, Puerto Ricans, Italians, Spanish-Americans, some Jews, many lower-class Americans—these are all categories of individuals whose family ties tend not to conform to the American "ideal pattern." Since, as subsequent selections will show, an individual's values, attitudes, goals, and even perceptions are fundamentally dependent on his family environment and experience, these individuals also fall outside of a number of other dominant patterns. They are thus particularly vulnerable to becoming "problems," but, at the same time, they are particularly invulnerable to rewards, incentives, appeals, or "logic" that presume the dominant value.

For example, a young child from a lower-class Italian family may be getting poor grades because he is afraid to "bother" the teacher with questions when he does not understand. Reassurances that the teacher wants him to bother her will be difficult for him to believe, however, because, in his world, this is not a typical adult attitude. Moreover, even if he were reassured, it would still be discrepant with his own personality, which in response to his family environment, consists of quite different needs and attitudes toward adults.

Innumerable illustrations, not all as simple as this one, could be cited of the problems of interaction and communication that follow when the products of different family patterns come together. The ensuing essay examines the universal dimensions to which all such problems can be referred, highlighting the characteristics of the American pattern in relation to the entire spectrum of cultural possibilities.

6.1 THE AMERICAN FAMILY IN THE PERSPECTIVE OF OTHER CULTURES[1]

Conrad M. Arensberg

That the family is part of the universal experience of mankind we know to be true. It is also true, however, that the family experience of the modern United States has very special features. In considering American families and their effect upon children at home and in society, it is necessary to be clear as to universal characteristics of the American family and as to its special or unique features.

---

[1]From Conrad M. Arensberg, "The American Family in the Perspective of Other Cultures," *The Nation's Children*, Eli Ginzberg, ed., Vol. 1, New York: Columbia University Press, 1960, pp. 50–71, 74–75.

In part, of course, the special features of the American family, in comparison with the family of other parts of the world, are twentieth century products. In far greater part, however, they are enduring particularities of American culture, built upon American inheritances from Europe. This specificity of the cultural tradition which has shaped the American culture and its characteristic family life is quite striking when we match American family experience against that of most of the extra-European world of both today and yesterday. The family traditions of Europe, like other aspects of European civilization, have been reworked and reshaped here, rather than those of Asian, African, or other civilizations, in the succeeding stages of our national development and amalgamation. Much American custom, modern and self-evident as it may seem to us, is both unique in the world and old and special in kind because it happened to have the particular special European beginnings on which it was built.

In world perspective, then, we must first note that the American family, seen generally, shares many aspects of family life and organization, first of all and very deeply, with Great Britain and the other European countries, particularly the northern and western ones. Some of these European roots are very ancient. The United States has been and is still a great mixture of peoples and conditions. Seen comparatively, its culture is new, recently unified from an assemblage of diverse regions, classes, and ethnic groups. Majority and minority ethnic strains, yielding American subcultures, have evolved an American family life, perhaps not yet completely unified but making a fairly well-understood common ideal pattern which continues to show variations dependent upon different social traditions and different past and present circumstances of economic, religious, and social life.

The common or generally perceived ideal pattern of family life in the United States today shapes our formal institutions and our legal system, lends its values to popular culture and public education, and influences strongly many of the national characteristics of our people. Nevertheless,. . .one must also recognize and cope with many deviations from this general majority culture pattern, anchored in the variant ethnic, regional, and class traditions and circumstances. In discussing the American family as it compares with those of other lands and civilizations both the general pattern and the exceptions to it must be presented. . . .

In taking the worldwide, fully anthropological perspective, we can trace the American family's evolution to its own maturity from its European origins and see more fully the cultural continuities involved. We can avoid thus the temptation to think of our own American family experience as much like others in kind but somehow different chiefly because it is luckier, more progressive, and more modern than that of the rest of mankind. Modern anthropological science, indeed, has come to reveal how very rich, complex, and diverse have been the differing forms of family life and organization of human beings round the world, in cultures both primitive and civilized. This complexity and diversity, indeed, continues to exist even in the "one world" of modern communication. . . .

In comparing the families of the cultures of the world, it is possible to distinguish between the immediate family and household, surrounding children from their births through their maturation and until they establish families of their own, on the one hand, and the larger "kinship system," uniting immediate families in larger, extended relationships and groupings, on the other. This "kinship system," as the anthropologists call the circle of relatives about each person, obviously unites families across the generations and through marriages, weaving a network of associations and obligations, perhaps even forming a community of succor, cooperation, or defense among the relatives of his own and of his spouse which nearly every man possesses.

THE IMMEDIATE HOUSEHOLD It is, of course, the universal experience of mankind, in every culture, that a person has a family in which he is born and grows up, providing him for good or ill with a father, a mother, perhaps with brothers and sisters. If this group of parents and siblings fails to exist, we of course take special note that the man is an orphan or product of a "broken" family, an unusual, fateful case. It is equally universal that many if not most of the adults, but not all, in a society, whether primitive tribe or modern civilization, come to head similar families in which they in their turn are parents of children of their own and thus create the next generation. The two families most persons experience have been aptly called the family of orientation (the one in which a person grows up and is oriented toward his world), and the family of procreation (the one in which he is a parent in his turn). The names, naturally, reflect subjective experience; seen more objectively the two families are merely two in a repetitive succession of like social organisms, families, endlessly transmitting cultural and social experience. . . .

Yet they are not always alike. It is difficult to believe the evidence that has now been amassed as to how various, underneath this universality, the particularities of organization and experience are from country to country and culture to culture and how special is modern American experience. Roles of the sexes, duties of parents, definitions of father, mother, brother, sister, sizes of the household, durations of the obligations and the affections, longevity of the family grouping, any and all of the behaviors, attitudes, and relationships so universal to human experience leave us little more certainty than that some kind of family life is to be counted on in every human community. The details telling us what kind are much more variable than we expect them to be.

THE KINSHIP SYSTEM Equally universal is the existence of some sort of kinship system, as we have called the circle of relatives beyond the immediate family. In normal social life. . .most of mankind have been and still are born into a web of relationships uniting other families to their own. Through their parents they are brought into a circle of secondary relatives large or small, alive or dead but remembered, giving them their grandparents, uncles, aunts, cousins, and so on. . . . Later on most persons who marry spouses not orphans or isolates acquire upon marrying another such circle or "family" of in-laws, technically called affinal relatives, as opposed to the first set, their "blood" kin or consanguinal relatives, now relatives who are in turn relatives of their children.

The existence of both types of relatives, consanguinal and affinal, still "family" in the larger sense of relationships of familial and kinship sort, is another universal of human culture. Groupings of such sort mark the social organization and the customary moralities of every culture and society and always have. . . .and it is only recently in political evolution that law and civil right have come to strip them of legal and political force over individuals as in our modern civil codes. Here again, if modern conditions seem to have diminished the importance of such kindreds for Americans, to the point where American discussion of the family tends to omit them altogether, and if modern life seems sometimes to weaken the customs of kinship obligation and responsibility almost to nothing, and even to increase markedly the number of persons in society who are without such relatives or think themselves free of them, then these facts of change away from the usual expectancies of human social life are unusual and deserve special comment.

Today social scientists, moralists, reformers, social workers, and persons concerned with the welfare of dependent persons, old people, women, as well as children, all note alike the decay of kinship in modern life. They all alike note the growing isolation of the immediate family and the small household, not only from ties of neighborhood and residential community but also from those of kinship with other families, from parents and relatives of any sort. The decay of kinship ties is not always regretted. It seems to have been specially marked under American historical conditions calling for great mobility, for free movement from place to place, occupation to occupation, the prerequisites of an "open" society such as ours. American moral and ethical imperatives of personal and small-family self-reliance seem also to have supported the man who could "go it alone," "make a fresh start," "make his own way," free of entangling kindred. But here again the special American accent on kinship does not exempt American family experience from participation in the universality of kinship organization in human cultures; it merely shows us the radical character of the American treatment of kindreds.

Here again, however, the universality of some type of kinship extending beyond the immediate family is merely the first comparative fact we must note. The types of kinship system and the groupings, obligations, the moral imperatives upon persons, the reliances and entanglements to which they put most people in the many and varied societies of the world, past and present, are unbelievably varied and differing. Modern anthropological science has revealed, here too, how strong and ruling kinship customs still are in the world of today, and how various they continue to be in their not yet relaxed hold upon the nationals of country after country in the world nowadays, not only in the underdeveloped areas where pre-modern conditions still persist but into the upper ranks of civilized persons everywhere, despite the attacks of every kind of modern doctrine, from Communism to democratic idealism, upon such remnants of a pre-individualist order. . . .

THE INSTITUTION OF MARRIAGE Another universal of human organization we must mention in order to place the American family in proper comparative perspective is the existence of some sort of marriage in every recorded human society. Every culture anthropology has studied carries some sort of customary legal or moral sanction upon the recognized near-exclusive association of particular male and female human beings. Usually but not necessarily always these are mates, partners in the procreating of and the caring for the children of an immediate household or small family. Thus, we can speak of a "biological" family man shares in some ways even with the higher animals. This serves to unite sex partners at least for the years when children require care and extends sexual association into parental association and cooperation.

But here again we must be careful not to mistake American custom and morality for universalities of human experience and social organization. In many cultures and civilizations the conjugal relation and the cooperation of married partners may well not be the central family relationship at all. Filial and fraternal relationships may be stronger; grandmothers and aunts may have more to do with bringing up children than mothers; mothers' brothers, not fathers, may discipline children, transmit inheritances, represent the family before the community, etc. The immediate equation we make between a married couple and a family, when we think instinctively of the family as a small group dominated by immediate parents of minor children, betrays us into error. Especially, our notion that each married couple lives by itself and by itself constitutes a family, so that we can even speak of a childless married pair as a "family without children" or call a wife or a husband "my family," fails us in many parts even of the modern world.

The anthropological facts are simply that marriages and families always exist, but they differ from ours quite often and interconnect in different ways from ours. While all cultures show some sort of marriage, in the sense of a sanctioned preferential right of association, sexual, economic, proprietary, between one or more men and one or more women, in many parts of the world still today and in many civilizations in history marital unions have not necessarily been nor are they now monogamous, nor even theoretically permanent, nor need husband and wife always live together, nor do necessarily they "cleave together and forsake all others," nor need they be the main source of either their own livelihood or the care, protection, discipline, and legal identification of their children. Other family systems than ours can and do assign all these functions to other relatives and groupings of relatives than the father and mother as husband and wife in a small family. Our American assumptions, equating marrying, setting up an independent household, and supporting a spouse and children as coincident responsibilities of a family life, take our custom for granted and mistake it for an inevitable and universal fact of human life. But once again we must see American family experience, particularly where it makes a successful marital partnership a principal, if not the sole source of love and security for children and of happiness and self-esteem for adults, as in some ways a special product of a highly particular and limited European and American social and legal evolution.

Indeed, in some ways our equation of family stability and successful marital partnership, which American ideals urge upon us, is almost a world extreme both in the reduction of the family in size as a social unit and in central emphasis upon the conjugal tie, with its interspouse adjustment and cooperation, as a basis for family living. Our democratic and individualist traditions and our feminine revolution have brought us costs as well as victories. The imperatives of our family system, basing the small household on the conjugal pair, isolating that pair to free them to command their own destinies and satisfactions and to confer on them nearly complete and untrammeled authority over minor children (except where the state and community limit them), are not easy ones. Nor is the task our educational ideal assumes a simple one: to prepare each and every man and woman to be in adulthood spouse, parent, householder, and family head all at once. These imperatives of our present small, conjugal type of family, with its minimum of kinship entanglement and support, ideally require each person to find a mate for himself, to love that spouse, to share the upbringing of children with him or her, to maintain a household with him, to find chief emotional identification in the little family growing up around this spouse and partner freely chosen and freely retained. To carry all these roles is not easy and to put so many eggs in one basket is certainly risky; few other family customs or national cultures seem to require such concentration of emotional effort in individual responsibility for self-directed personal adjustment and for unaided child-training. Here again, American family custom has special features, imperatives, and problems, arising out of a special past and responding, perhaps, to special present conditions.

These, then, are the universalities. Families, marital unions, kinship systems are present in every human society and culture. But they are shaped differently; they interconnect in many various ways; they assume different relative importances in the functions of support of every kind, from livelihood to affection, they perform for human beings, both the grown-up ones and the children. Let us see more closely where American family, marriage, and kinship, with their special American interconnections, fit in.

THE MIDDLE-CLASS IDEAL   First, the American family is distinguished by the great importance, emphasis upon, and independence of the small, immediate or "biological" family of father and mother and minor children. American custom attempts to generalize this small unit, free it, trains most persons for roles heading it in adult life, delegates societal and legal authority over and responsibility for children almost exclusively to immediate parents in it. In spite of some recent increases in the birth rate this unit is small; on an average households are four and five persons at most; they begin with a marriage of two potential parents, the spouses, who are urged to take up residence, ideally, by themselves and away from others, "undoubling" the larger households of larger, three-generation families still common in many of our recent European immigrant and even our Southern populations; they swell for some years while minor children appear and grow to young adulthood; they contract thereafter as children leave for an existence and a family life of their own.

The unit is not only small, so that households are small and mobile, the family following the husband as he moves from job to job, position to position, or town to town, increasing its isolation not only from kindred but from neighbors and fellows of the community, in the great fluidity of American occupational and residential life, but it is often very short-lived. Not only are divorces common, contributing the major cause of family dissolution (rather than war deaths or famine or emigration of husbands, as in less fortunate countries) but the termination of family life in a period of "the empty nest," with the spouses returned to a life together without children, is a standard, approved, and even planned-for regularity of American social life. Just as the children are trained for the day when they will "leave home" and "have a family of their own," so old people are (ideally) expected to live apart and alone, visited perhaps by adult children but not sharing a household with them, an eventuality perfectly natural in most parts of the world, where gaffers and dowagers may even rule the roost and certainly more often continue in it than leave it as here. But here even the small family endures, in an American's life time, only 20 years or so, especially when the parents ideally have all their children in their younger married years.

All this custom, most of it ideal middle-class American family life whose real prevalence in our mixed and varied population we can only guess at, reflects, obviously, the individual and equalitarian ideals of our country's social and political life, the spread of a wage-earning and money-and-credit consuming way of economic life among most of our people as well as the already mentioned traditional cultural emphasis upon the small family, with its connections to the free choice of mate and residence and occupation and to the open mobility between places and statuses of our society. . . . [T]he special traditional cultural descent of this kind of family custom which present American conditions continue to deepen and generalize should be noted. . . .

THE JOINT-FAMILY   The best anthropological classification of the families of mankind treats them first as they vary in progressive size of the family unit, particularly as that unit forms the usual households of a society. Largest are the joint-families of India, the patriarchal families of the Chinese gentry of yesterday, the large households of the Middle East countries, of much of Africa where they may be also polygynous, the *zadrugas* and other patriarchal households of the peasant lands which in the remote Balkans still today practice a household economy like that of ancient Rome. Here a founder, his sons, his sons' sons, and all their wives, children, grandchildren, dependents, and servants or slaves live their lives out in a house or compound of many rooms with common fields, gardens, and larder under central authority and in common defense for a lifetime. Eventually such a family usually splits to make more like it; the common lands or joint economy make greater size of household equivalent to strength and security; and the continually splitting households often retain ties of common defense, including even blood vengeance, to form far-flung clans of common unilineal descent.

We tend to forget how widespread even today, especially in the underdeveloped countries, are such great families and how common such clans, with the security and the trammels they bring, still are in the world. . . . Some of our American ethnic groups, both immigrant and native, have strong and recent memories of joint households and clan ties, so different from the individuation of the small family of our majority tradition. . . .

THE STEM-FAMILY   Our small-family tradition is based, of course, on quite other cultural antecedents than the joint-family and the clan uniting forever all the sons and grandsons of so-and-so. The next classification of families and households common in many parts of the world bases them on a size intermediate between the great households of the joint families and our own small ones. American experience, indeed American social science, does not recognize this classification and fails to note that it is very widespread in the world, particularly in Europe, but also in Asian peasant lands, especially where small proprietorship has fostered the growth and transmission of inherited family farms. In the European countries, especially in those of small peasant holdings. . .but also in Japan, the Philippines. . .and in parts of peasant India and China both, an intermediate size of family and household, living for generation after generation on a family holding, has often become standard and customary. This counted in the homestead in each generation the peasant holder, his wife, his minor children, his unmarried brothers or sisters, living as unpaid farm laborers and helping him until they should move away or marry off, his father and mother, perhaps retired from active work but still influential and assisting. . . .

This kind of family organization became and is still standard in most of the European countries, whence its name coined by the great French family sociologist LePlay comes: the *famille-souche* or the stem-family (*Stammfamilie*, in German). . . .

So deeply is it ingrained in European tradition, whether peasant or of higher class, that many discussions between Anglo-Saxons and Europeans founder on the unrecognized adherence of Anglo-Saxon tradition to the small-family and the usual European to the stem-family. Where an American, and an Englishman, in the small-family tradition, may be enjoined by his own desires, his wife, and his columnist of manners and personal problems, such as a Mary Hayworth, to set his old mother up to live alone and think it a hardship to have her under the same roof with his wife and children, a Frenchman may define the *foyer* (intimate family) to include her and regard it as unthinkable that grand'mere live anywhere else. Much of the "Americanization" of modern Americans involves undoubling of such stem-family households today, the dissolution of family kitties which pool the incomes and the salaries of even adult children, a usual and expectable Euopean practice in many countries—indeed even necessary where "family allowances" and state pensions do not even presume individual wage equalities or reckon a living wage to include a family livelihood as with us. Countless thousands of Americans of second-generation or third-generation immigrant origin or even of American Southern and Southern Hill background are new and transitional to the small-family, individualizing family tradition, moving toward it from the other moralities of the stem-family tradition. . . .

FAMILY TRANSFORMATIONS The general European movement of family organization during the Middle Ages seems to have been much that of Yugoslavia in recent decades, a movement from joint-family and clan protection for individuals and great-household economy, even for peasants, to smaller peasant subsistence holdings, of stem-family kind, with proprietorship passed down the line of family heirs. . . . [L]et us see what kind of kinship evolution took place as stem-families, if not conjugal small ones like ours, succeeded, at least in Europe, joint-families, and great-households.

One change was certainly the spread of bilateral as opposed to unilateral kinship units, a shift from exclusive clans of the kind we have mentioned, to diffuse and general kindreds of the sort we know today, in which all the blood descendants of the same grandparents and great-grandparents as our own, are our cousins, regardless of whether they come through the male or through the female lines. We still reckon as relatives upon whom we have some claim, if only a bed in emergencies, the whole diffuse circle of such natural kin; no longer can the world be divided into the sons of my fathers, whom I must defend to the death, and the sons of my mother's clan, who may have to shoot me on sight. Only the family name still, with us as with other Europeans, descends down the paternal line, as a vague identifier. We can trace through European history, as we can trace it still in the spread of the national state today, the shift over to such stem-names, giving each man a family name. . . . We can likewise trace the dissolution of clans and phratries. . .with the shift to the kind of bilateral, diffuse, cousin-counting kinship we ourselves know. In this shift to diffuse, relative reckoning of significant kinship, from a former counting instead of exclusive and corporate groups of special legal and moral force, we can still see a background to the individuation and the liberation from status and adherence prescribed at birth that has gone so far, as we have pointed out, in our own American treatment of kinship.

Let us at last return to that part of the European tradition in which, as with our own Anglo-Saxon heritage, neither the stem-family of the peasantries nor the fixities of joint-family and clan figured. Other parts of the world, as we said, have been found by social anthropologists to possess small-family organization. Notably these are some of the hunting peoples organized for a subsistence requiring great movement and fluidity among small bands of persons and, oddly enough, many of the civilized peoples of South East Asia; Malays, Thai, Burmese, etc. There is some evidence, too, that in periods of rapid urbanization, as in ancient Roman days, great movement and migration of persons and extreme fluidity of occupational life and easy social mobility have tended more than once to dissolve kinship rigidities, to isolate and free individuals, and generalize small families, just as in recent British and American history.

A great argument of social science can be waged today whether pecuniary civilization, industrialization, the factory system in themselves do not force a generalization of small families, and indeed the European practice is to treat the small family, which we call the "democratic" type of family organization, as the "proletarian" or the "disorganized" one. But the argument is better left to one side, the more so as Japan, India, the Middle East, and even such countries as Belgium and Germany seem to be able to undergo industrialization without a wholesale or even a widespread adoption of American and British small-family social patterns. The only causative argument or association we can advance for the distribution in the world of small families as the standard family system of a culture is that any pattern of economic subsistence requiring fluid movement of persons and alternate sources of hands for impermanent productive units, whether bands of gatherers or hunters, or crews of fishing boats, or short-lived reindeer herds, or new factories recruiting temporary labor forces, seems to favor small-family generalization. . . .

The special features of American family experience. . .have legitimate origins in the cultural history of the country as well as in the special economic, legal, and political historical conditions of the country's growth. These special features pose special problems, psychological or other, for Americans. They pose such problems for Americans both in their own persons as sharers and movers of the American customs of family life and in their special difficulties of child welfare and child care. . . .

Most of these problems, social, legal, and psychological, seem to flow from the continuing evolution of our particular traditions, with the attendant individuation and dissolution of stabilizing and assisting personal contacts in our lives and their replacement by professional and community services. The trend is one that our long evolution of small-family independence and diffusion of kinship and other fixed-status ties long ago began. It is certainly irreversible, even if we wished to reverse it, which our people do not seem to wish to do. But if some information about its special historical character, its special place in the alternate ways of family and community organization in the history of mankind, and its special demands upon ourselves can help us manage better the trends and currents of social change in which we are caught, then perhaps this brief summary of the place of American family life in the perspective of other cultures will have served a purpose.

6.2   INTRODUCTION

The ensuing excerpt explores further several of the issues already raised in this chapter about the nature of the American family and its two-fold contribution to the socialization of the individual and the needs of society. The authors address themselves to the contrast discussed in our introduction to the previous selection between the emotional intensity that prevails in the family and the autonomy that is necessary in the occupational realm. The main gist of their complex argument is that the early emotionality is actually necessary for the later independence. In their view, the emotional intensity of the home makes it possible for parents to train children without too many clear expectations. Thus, the child is motivated to achieve at higher and higher levels not because he has internalized a well-structured general system of norms, but because of his intense commitment to the family as a unit. He must later free himself from this emotional commitment to the family as a unit and acquire other commitments (to his job, his organization, his profession, etc.). The shift, however, is only to a different object: the quality of commitment is the same. According to Parsons and White the dissociation of adult occupational commitments from external normative criteria—such as family or friendship—is essentially similar to the isolated intensity of the earlier family attachments.

The main emphasis in this selection is thus on the continuity of American socialization. In response to pressures exerted primarily by the school, children and adolescents gradually move toward the culturally required achievement and autonomy. As part of this process, the focus of the individual's emotional dependence shifts from the family to the peer group and the latter both compensates for the psychological strains produced by the new demands and acts as a crucial agent of socialization in itself.

If this general view of "growing up" in America is valid, it has major implications for virtually every aspect of educational guidance. Most basically, it contends that emotional dependence, first on parents and then on peers, is not a necessary evil but merely necessary. In this light, deviant cliques and exaggerated attachments between children or adolescents are only undesirable versions of a necessary and desirable tendency, calling for redirection rather than suppression. Moreover, if such "problems" are viewed as being at least in part compensations for pressures from the environment, then the latter becomes an important aspect of any solution, along with whatever individual measures are also deemed appropriate.

However, because of the generality of Parsons's and White's observations, caution is important in their application. As noted earlier, there are major distinctions in family structure and relationships associated with subcultural variations in our society, and the particular emotional and interpersonal aspects discussed here may be less or not at all relevant to certain groups.

Perhaps the most fundamental question this excerpt raises for both the practice of guidance and its underlying theory and philosophy concerns the meaning of "autonomy" and "independence" as the goals toward which individuals should be helped. Do these terms have some absolute meaning or do they merely refer to the particular type of dependence, which is culturally prescribed? Where does a guidance counselor's definition of his role fit in relation to these two alternatives?

6.2   THE LINK BETWEEN CHARACTER AND SOCIETY[1]

Talcott Parsons and Winston White

TRENDS IN THE AMERICAN FAMILY   Before approaching the problem of the role of the peer group in socialization. . .we must say something about the family. Our general view is that. . .the American family has been undergoing an important process of restructuring, which is part of the more general process of differentiation. . . . It has first become a much more differentiated unit than before, and hence its functions relative to those of other units have become more specialized. In the process, as always and necessarily happens, there has been a "loss of function" to other units, which include, at the childhood level, the school and peer group and to some extent the mass media, and at the adult level, above all economic organization and other occupationally organized types of units, such as hospitals, but also certain voluntary associations.

[1]Reprinted with permission of The Macmillan Company from *Culture and Social Character,* Seymour M. Lipset and Leo Lowenthal, eds., pp. 115–122.©The Free Press of Glencoe, 1961.

The most conspicuous change is the one already alluded to, where functions of economic production have been transferred to other units. Also, however, through private and social insurance and other agencies, even important parts of the older responsibility for financial security have been transferred. The broad result has been to concentrate family functions on what, in certain respects, may be called the highly personal relations of its members to each other.

Associated with this is the increasing structural "isolation" of the nuclear family. Seen in comparative terms, this is particularly conspicuous in the setting of kinship as such—relative, that is, to "extended" kinship relations. The new marriage establishes a unit, which in residence, economic support, and a wide variety of relationships, is independent of the families of orientation of both partners. This isolation is strongly reinforced by geographical mobility, since in a decreasing proportion of cases are the parents of either marriage partner resident in the same local community, especially at the neighborhood level. Isolation, however, in this sense, has the further aspect that there is far less continuity of neighborhood relations over long periods, to say nothing of that of generations, than in other societies or in our own past. It is the nuclear family that is the primary unit of our processes of social mobility in both the geographical and status senses.

These changes, which we interpret as primarily processes of structural differentiation, have not led to any general tendency to "dissolution" of the family; rather, we think, the contrary. Of this there are such evidences as, first, that the proportion of the population married and living with their spouses has increased rather than decreased; it now stands at the highest level in the history of census data. Second, the divorce rate, after reaching a peak after the war, has considerably receded. Third, home ownership of single-family dwellings is at an all-time high, with an immense relative as well as absolute increase since the war. Finally, fourth, the postdepression revival of the birth rate has persisted, so that it is no longer possible to interpret it as simply an economic recovery phenomenon. Indeed, the general "familistic" trend has gone so far that some of our ideological bellwethers are coming to view it with alarm, as evidence that interest in occupational concerns is declining. In this connection, whatever the masculine role, it is interesting, and in line with our general view, that this process of reinforcement of the nuclear family has coincided with a very large increase in the participation of married women in the labor force.[2]

Our view, then, is that the family has become substantially further differentiated from other agencies in the social structure than previously. Its primary societal functions are now much more sharply defined than before: the socialization of children and the psychological or personality "tension-management" of its adult

---

[2]*Cf.* Manpower Commission Report. The broad data on the family situation were summarized in Talcott Parsons and R. F. Bales, *Family, Socialization and Interaction Process,* New York: The Free Press, 1955, Chap. 1. The trend since these data were brought together has been somewhat further in the same direction.

members. On this new structural basis, after a considerable period of crisis, it has now begun at least to be stabilized.

This restructuring of the relation of the family to the wider society has been accompanied by important internal changes, which involve the fundamental roles of the sexes and the generations in relation to each other and have an important bearing on the socialization function. The first of these is a shift in the balance of the sex roles, which is often, with only partial accuracy, described as a decline of masculine "authority." Our interpretation of the shift is that, broadly speaking, as the family has become a more specialized agency in terms of societal function, the "managerial" responsibility for the implementation of its functions has tended to become increasingly concentrated in the wife-mother role, whereas the husband-father has tended to assume more of a "fiduciary"—"chairman of the board"—type of role, concentrating his primary commitments more in the field of extrafamilial functions, particularly through his occupational role. This shift naturally appears to some as an "abdication" of masculine prerogative, but we think of it rather as an aspect of the "loss of function" which *always* accompanies processes of structural differentiation. Essentially, this is to say that the "average" woman is trained to be more of a specialist in "human relations" and the management of motivationally subtle psychological problems than is the average man (discounting of course the senses in which men on occupational bases can become higher-level experts in certain of these fields). The more that functions other than this type of management are dissociated from the family, the more a differentiated specifically feminine role comes into its own, and the more it is emancipated from an authority that was grounded in other functional imperatives, such as the maintenance of family property through business enterprise.

The related shift in the generation roles is, we feel, intimately connected with this. Essentially it is that the child is no longer to the same extent placed in a situation to which he has to "adapt" in the sense of "conforming"; but *his* "problems" are more explicitly taken into account and made the object of more or less deliberate management. This is connected with the sex-role shift in that the average woman, both by virtue of her own socialization and by virtue of her actual role-responsibilities in the family, which include far more continual and intimate contact with the children, is better fitted than her husband to undertake the active management of these problems, so far as it is undertaken at all.

One aspect of the generation shift is, necessarily, greater permissiveness to children, more concern with them as persons. The crucial question is whether the essential feature of this aspect is the abdication of parental authority, and still more of responsibility, in the interest of letting children do anything they want, or is rather a new way of "leading" the child, rather than "forcing" him, to higher levels of growth through the internalization of social object-systems and patterns of normative culture. It is definitely our view that the latter is the main trend, though of course on the way there are many actual failures of responsibility.

If our interpretation is correct, then a very important apparent paradox must be faced. As a condition of building up motivation to the higher levels of autonomous and independent achievement, it is necessary to cultivate *dependency* in the relation of child to parent, at the appropriate stage. We feel that the greater and more explicit emotional intensity of American family relations, particularly between mother and preoedipal child, is directly linked with the greater requirements that the child has to face later on in developing capacity for independent achievement without the guidance of specific parental role-models that could be presumed, in an earlier type of social situation, to be more nearly adequate.

Thus on the one hand, by cultivating intense attachments, the American family deprives the young child of the emotionally "cool" early independence conspicuous above all in the English family. But this dependency in turn is the psychological foundation on which is built a later autonomy that helps to equip him for facing situations that are specifically *unstructured* by comparison with our own earlier and other social systems. What seems to many foreigners to be the incredible leeway given to American latency-period and adolescent children is thus linked with the intensive concern of parents, particularly mothers, with the children's attachment to them, especially in the earlier periods. To us this is an instance of the increasing mobility of resources constituting one of the central conditions of the development of an industrial society.

Look, now, at the structural situation facing the child in these terms. In the preoedipal period within his own family he has been very intensively "enveloped" in a "closed emotional corporation." The condition of such envelopment is the existence of a group, the members of which are bound to each other by essentially ascriptive ties, and who do not compete with one another. Then, first in the immediate neighborhood, the child is exposed to relations to others, with whom his parents have no ascriptive ties at all—most definitely his playmates are not cousins, or even the children of close family friends, but are likely to be the children of relative strangers. Then, on entering school, he is exposed to a highly formalized process in which, regardless of sex and family relation, he must strive to achieve in a context where the judge is an impersonal teacher. It is crucial here that his achievement in the first few years of schooling will become the primary basis of his occupational future, which, in the American system, is *the* primary aspect of his total future as a person.[3]

Seen in this perspective, the recent changes in the American family may be said to be adjustments to the requirements of the type of society we have sketched

---

[3]Seen in this context, the nursery school is an interesting phenomenon. It may be regarded as a response primarily to two complementary pressures. One is the difficulty faced by the child in unregulated peer relations in the neighborhood. The other is the parents', above all the mother's, drive to get him started on independence, which we believe is only secondarily motivated by her understandable desire to "get him off her hands" for part of the time. Essentially what the nursery school does is to provide an opportunity for working out relationships to age-mates to whom the ascribed relation of siblings does not apply, but under adult supervision and without the process of formal evaluation of performance that is the crucial feature of the regular school. It fits very directly into the analysis put forward by S. N. Eisenstadt (*From Generation to Generation*, New York: The Free Press, 1956) concerning the mechanisms that must operate in mediating between the particularism of family involvements and the universalism of an achievement-oriented adult status system.

above, as those requirements apply to the earlier stages of the socialization process for adult roles in that society. There has indeed been quantitative expansion in the newer type of family function—witness the proportion married and with children. But most important for our purposes, there has been both differentiation and upgrading. Differentiation in the present context applies above all to the functions of the family relative to other agencies in the socialization process, notably after the early period: the school and the peer group. This we will take up presently. But the most important point to make here is that, in relation to its function in the socialization process, the American family has been subject to a quite definite upgrading process, not, as is so frequently suggested, a downgrading process. The requirement of preparing the child for high levels of independence, competence, and responsibility means that as socializing agent the family cannot do its job unless it emancipates its children from dependence on the parents, an emancipation that precludes parents from being too definite role-models for the child's own life course. What Riesman interprets as the abdication of the parents from their socializing responsibility can therefore be interpreted in exactly the opposite way. If parents attempted to impose their role-patterns in a detailed way on their children, they would be failing in their responsibilities in the light of the American value system.

THE CONTINUITY OF THE AMERICAN SOCIALIZATION PATTERN   Particular attention should be called to the *continuity* of the main features of the socialization situation, from the preoedipal stages within the nuclear family to postgraduate professional training. The central keynote is training for achievement, conceived. . .in the first instance as contribution to the good society. . . . This contribution is to be made within an occupational system that has been coming to be progressively more widely expanded, more highly differentiated, and in general upgraded. Furthermore, as a result of this process, and of the attendant social mobility, the average time-interval between the laying of the motivational foundations of this achievement-orientation in the family and the actual commitment to occupational roles has been increasing, thereby decreasing the detailed and specific influence of parents in determining the commitment pattern.

. . . [T]he primary keynotes of the adult occupational role, so far as these can be generalized relative to the immensely differentiated variety, are, besides the commitment to achievement as such, "independence," responsibility, and competence. Independence in the present sense refers above all to capacity to "alienate" the orientation of labor from undue attachment to functionally diffuse contexts of attachment, in the first instance delineating commitment to the job context independently of family, friendship, and the like. The meaning of competence would seem to be clear enough without further elaboration. By responsibility we mean, in the occupational context itself, psychological capacity to make decisions in accord with the relevant normative criteria as distinguished from undue vulnerability to the various internal and external pressures to evasion by the "easy" way.[4]

. . . [T]he development of the personality structure in which these motivational patterns are highly developed requires the temporary cultivation of high levels of emotional dependency. The most conspicuous and best-documented case of this is the early dependency on the mother. This is associated with the motivational capacity necessary for the earlier phases of performance-learning, in the preoedipal period starting with the very basic motor and communication skills exemplified by walking and talking and their subsequent elaborations. The "dialectical" relation between dependency on the one hand, independence and achievement on the other, we believe does not cease with the oedipal period.

To be sure, the child becomes "emancipated" from his parents, through several stages, but most conspicuously in the early latency period and again in adolescence. We suggest that the very compulsiveness of his attachments to his peer groups at those stages is an indirect expression of the severe psychological strains that the process entails. More broadly, we suggest that the school, with the performance-learning expectations associated with it, is the primary focus—in the structure of socialization agencies—of the pressure to learn independence and achievement; whereas the peer group tends to replace the parents, or more broadly the family of orientation, as the primary focus of the emotional support that is necessary if the effort exerted in competitive achievement is not to be too severely disorganizing to the developing personality.

On these grounds we would expect that, as a consequence of the general process of differentiation and upgrading in the occupational and education spheres, there would appear. . .a more prominent and more differentiated set of peer group expectations and interactions than was characteristic of an earlier type of social system. Broadly, from the psychological point of view, this peer group structure tends to fulfill one set of needs that are prominently involved in the socialization process, and is in this respect the primary successor of the more supportive and nurturant aspects of the family functions, which of course tend to be centered primarily in the maternal role. Furthermore, as noted, we think that these phenomena are most prominent at two different phases. The first is the early latency

---

[4]We have chosen to stress the occupational role as the goal of the socialization process because of its strategic place in our social structure. Clearly not even for the most committed male is this exhaustive of his role-obligations, and it does not explicitly take account of the predominant factor in the feminine role. With respect to the latter it is undoubtedly significant that a larger and larger proportion of women in increasing proportions of the life cycle are indeed assuming occupational roles—as well as becoming more highly educated. But in addition to this, as an aspect of the differentiation of the family from other structures, there has been a change in the direction of "occupationalizing" familial roles, particularly for the adult woman. We feel that the concern for psychology, the "rationalizing" of child training and the like, fit into this pattern, as do the more "material" aspects of home management. Similar considerations apply to other roles that have not become formally occupational, such as much "volunteer" community service.

period, in which the crucial phenomenon is the one-sex peer group. This may be regarded as a mechanism of reinforcement of the ascription of sex-role, the primary structuring of which was a central aspect of the oedipal period itself; one might say it was a mechanism for carrying over this structure from the familial to the extrafamilial context, thereby generalizing sex-role commitment. The second is the adolescent peer group, where the primary pattern of independence from the family has already become established, and the "problem" is that of mobilization of motivational resources for the decisive phase in which both occupational role and marriage commitment are to be worked out, notably, by contrast both with our own past and with most other societies, *independently* of the family of orientation.

It is our main contention that the phenomena of peer groups in our society should not be treated in isolation but should be seen in the context of their relation to the educational and occupational systems on the one hand, to the family on the other. In interpreting them it should be remembered that the child who is a peer group member is at the same time in school as well as typically living at home and economically dependent on his family; and that he is, with increasing self-consciousness, looking forward to a place in the adult world—for the boy, above all his own position, for the girl, partly her own but more decisively that of her prospective husband. Furthermore the family lies not only *behind* him in the form of his family of orientation but also *ahead* of him as his own prospective family of procreation. His "job" is not only to internalize the values and orientations of his family of orientation, but to adapt himself to the exigencies of the educational system and to treat these, by both conscious and unconscious mechanisms, in relation to his future in both occupational and familial terms. . . .

6.3 INTRODUCTION

The following excerpt presents some of the conclusions and generalizations drawn from an extensive study of adolescent groups, and it serves to complement and extend the discussion in the previous selection. In particular, it emphasizes the role of the peer group in defining the individual's conception of himself in relation to the norms and values of his social environment. Thus, like Parsons and White, the Sherifs view the importance of the peer group as an aspect to which it is particularly difficult for adults to make a positive contribution, since its very function is partly anti-adult.

Another way of stating this view is to say that peer relationships constitute a learning experience. In the course of his intense involvement with them, the individual clarifies his conception of himself as a social being, as one who responds to others' expectations, and has expectations of his own for himself and for them. In order to do this, the individual must free himself from his acquiescence to his parents, and, since they have been the main adults in his world, this turning away

ill tend to include the adult world as a whole. The individual can then develop his
wn norms and learn to apply them. It is only if this stage runs its full course that
he next one is possible, namely, the integration of individual norms with those of
dult society.

Because of this element of rejection of adults inherent in the peer group, as this
election points out, adult pressures on a group tend only to strengthen its soli-
arity and heighten its significance for its members. Thus, for example, if a delinquent clique is subjected to threats and punishments by adults in positions of au-
hority, the most likely result is that its members will become more and more com-
nitted to the group. The group's delinquency will probably increase even further
nd there is the very real possibility that the dependence of the individual members
n the group will become so intense, and their rejection of adult values so
ntrenched, that they will be unable to accomplish the subsequent shift to full adult
tatus. The relevance of these phenomena to the concerns of a guidance counselor
eems self-evident.

5.3   ADOLESCENT REFERENCE GROUPS AND ADOLESCENT CONSCIENCE[1]

Muzafer Sherif and Carolyn W. Sherif

In recent years, the concept of "reference group" has shown its usefulness as a
ool for distinguishing the individual's psychological relatedness to groups, on the
ne hand, and the other groups in which he moves and acts in daily life. Those
groups in which he wants to be counted as an individual, which include the individuals whose opinions make a difference for him, whose standards and goals are
his, are his reference groups (Sherif and Cantril, 1947; Sherif, 1948; Sherif and
Sherif, 1953, 1956). Quite evidently, a person can and does have more than one
reference group, especially in modern urban life. An adolescent, for example,
usually has a family and perhaps school and church groups, as well as groups of
peers of which he considers himself a part.

The puzzle in the growing contemporary literature on adolescent conformity,
adolescent morality, and adolescent conscience seems to be why adolescents fre-

[1]Pp. 180–183, 239–244, *Reference Groups: Exploration into Conformity and Deviation in Adolescents* by Muzafer Sherif and Carolyn W. Sherif. Copyright©1964 by Muzafer Sherif and Carolyn
Sherif. Reprinted by permission of Harper & Row, Publishers.

quently do not reflect the moral values and prescriptions to which they have been exposed in the family, church, or at least in the schools which they have attended for over half a dozen years before reaching adolescence. Aside from traditional conceptions of morality and conscience in religious dogmas, the source of this puzzle lies largely in the predominance of Freudian psychoanalytic conceptions of development and of conscience. In the Freudian conception, the significant events in psychological development occur in childhood, well before adolescence is attained. Socialization is accomplished through acceptance of the prescriptions of society regulating one's instinctive impulses, particularly the prohibitions and dictums of parents. These societal prescriptions, especially those of his family become his conscience, and he feels guilty when he violates them—hence the self regulating character of moral behavior.

As Sears (1960) pointed out recently, this classic conception of conscience is almost wholly a negative one—applicable to problems of "resistance to temptation" and "guilt" but not at all to those "positive qualities which become ideal to be attained in their own right" (p. 96). Sears notes that the Freudian conception of conscience was developed to deal with severely disturbed individuals who "resist temptation too little or too much, and who are in trouble one way or another with their feelings of guilt" (p. 96).

If discussions of adolescent morality and conscience are to square with the facts two lines of factual evidence have to be considered in addition to the obvious fact that life is not wholly made up of avoiding temptation or feeling guilty.

First, there is ample evidence, contrary to Freudian notions, that psychological development continues throughout life and that, in particular, the adolescent period is characteristically a period of change (*cf.* Sherif and Cantril, 1947, Chaps 8 and 9; Ausubel, 1954; Horrocks, 1962).

Second, the individual's standards of right and wrong behavior are not derived simply from representatives of adult society (parents, teachers, church, mass media of communication), and even these are filtered, reinforced, or contradicted in interactions among those of his peers who count for him. Thus, "conscience" is not a set of prescriptions divorced from his continuing psychological development. It is the warp and woof of his very conception of himself in relation to others who *count* in his eyes, woven in the course of interactions with them—whether the source of its values is parents, school, church, mass media, or peers (Sherif, 1962).

This is the feasible explanation for the fact that an individual may know perfectly well what his parents, teachers, and preacher say is right and wrong, and *yet violate this without feelings of guilt if his fellows do not condemn him.* The term "conscience" ceases to be useful as a *psychological* concept when applied only to those prescriptions which adult and legal authority uphold. It becomes psychologically meaningful when used to refer to those standards which the individual *does* uphold and relative to which he *does* experience remorse when he violates them. Such standards are those of his reference groups, whether these be his family, his school, his church, a tightly knit group of his peers, or the charmed world of television and motion picture celebrities.

By specifying the source of the values which actually do regulate the individual's behavior, in terms of his reference groups, it becomes operationally possible to specify why his behaviors are in harmony with the prescriptions of adult society or some part of it, on the one hand, or why his behavior is "immoral," using adult prescriptions as a standard. Such specification of *source* will show us that conscience is a typically human product, even though the particular behaviors which arouse pangs of conscience differ considerably. The boy who defies major values of society without regrets may feel profound guilt if he betrays fellow members of his group. . . .

The adolescent period in modern industrial societies is, as we have seen, marked by shifts in the relative importance of family, school, and other adult groups, on the one hand, and agemates, on the other. W. M. Prado (1958) demonstrated this shift for boys between 8 and 11 years old and in adolescence. He deliberately selected boys who *preferred* their fathers and who felt that their fathers understood them. Then he had each boy with his father and his best friend (agemate) take part in a simple game in which the outcome was not self-evident to the subjects, but which he could score objectively. He asked the boy to estimate the performance of his father and his best friend.

The outcome was that 20 of the 25 children appraised their fathers' performances as superior to their friends', but 19 out of the 25 adolescents judged their friends' performances to be superior. (The average sizes of these differences were statistically significant.) In 16 cases, the adolescents judged their friends' performances as better than their fathers', when in fact the father had done equally well or better (as measured by the experimenter). Thus even adolescents who love their fathers and prefer them tend to overvalue the achievements of friends, which is not the case among younger children.

The shift in the significance of agemate reference groups in adolescence is accompanied by spending more time with peers, engaging in more activities with them, and turning more and more toward their evaluations of one's own qualities and behavior. Pleasure and satisfaction of engaging in desired activities apart from adults, a sense of being someone with a clear-cut place in some scheme of things, interactions in activities reflecting that scheme, contribute to the adolescent's willing participation with others and his willing regulation of his own behavior within the group's shared expectations for member behavior and other norms of the group. For the time, the peer group is his most important reference group. Its values or norms are the ones that count for him. . . .

Failures of parents and the family have frequently been given exclusive blame for youths' fierce attachments to their fellows. It is true that those adolescents who faced extremely unpleasant home situations were eager to get out of them whether the unpleasantness stemmed from conflict between parents or from the crowded quarters. But this condition was not an isolated element in the most secretive, exclusive, well-coordinated (in short, solidary) groups studied in low-rank neighborhoods. In these groups, the striking fact was the convergence of conditions at home, at school, and in the neighborhood which presented the adolescent with a picture of himself as someone thwarted, unwanted, looked down upon.

In short, the highest solidarity was found in groups where conditions were most conducive to the members' finding their only locus of pleasurable activity, their only source of personal recognition, their only web of stable relationships, and their only clear personal identity in a group of their peers. For example, members of Group B IIIs 2b had withdrawn or been expelled from school by ages 14–16 for "antisocial" behavior and classroom failure. To them, school had been an unpleasant situation, not an avenue to achievement or a place to be comfortably engaged in extracurricular pursuits. Less than a third of the boys had fathers supporting the family. The mothers of these boys worked hard at poorly paid jobs to support younger children. Life in their crowded homes was far from regular. In most cases, the father had left the constantly growing family after failing to support it. A social worker in the neighborhood tried to help some of these boys find work when they left school. He concluded that their complaints of not being able to find work were entirely realistic. His efforts with business acquaintances succeeded no better than theirs. As a result, the only possible source of money for these boys was stealing, which they did. Some of them even tried to sell the observer a stolen tire, which he declined. The boys spent most of their waking hours together; most of their activities were in company with some members of the group. Their chief source of personal satisfaction was accomplishment in these activities and its recognition by members. . . .

GROUP SOLIDARITY, Whatever the motives bringing adolescent boys **SPREAD OF** together and making membership important to them initially, the actual interactions of **MEMBERS' DWELLINGS,** members from day to day in their environment **AND PERSONAL SACRIFICE** produce conditions affecting the importance of the group to individual members. . . .[O]ne of these conditions is the relationships with other social units. Competition or threat from other groups and adult authorities particularly draws individuals closer together and generates heightened significance of the group to them. In adolescent groups, threat or opposition from the outside is immediate whenever their activities are socially defined as deviant and are subject to sanctions. . . .

Individuals finding a sense of personal identity and recognition almost exclusively within the bounds of a tightly knit group of peers are less responsive to the rewards, enticements, and threats from outside the group, whether these come from parents, other grownups, or are the more distant possibilities of future achievement through neglecting the group and concentrating on school and work. . . .

The fact that an adolescent group may weigh more heavily than ties with family, school, and community should come as no surprise in the light of the following generalizations from the findings reported in this book and by other investigators:

1. Individuals do not form groups of their own choosing just to be, mechanically, one of a set, or because of any inherent tendency to conformity, or because they want to regulate their behavior in this or that direction. They come together and interact with strongly felt urges and with desires experienced as their own, whether these be desires to be accepted as a person in one's own right, desires to gain social distinction, sexual urges, wishes for desirable objects and instrumentalities, desires for exciting leisure-time activities, searches for recognition, or desires to prove themselves apart from adult supervision. No matter what the specific content of their goals, no matter whether the aims are socially desirable or not, individuals come together in informal association and stay together because they experience *some* strong motivational basis which is not effectively fulfilled by themselves, individually, or through other existing social channels.

2. No matter what the initial bases of coming together, the interaction among individuals over a period of time becomes the source of satisfactions and frustrations for the individual members, experienced in highly personal terms. The process of interacting with others and developing mutual expectations for behavior is not a coldly intellectual affair, but has direct bearing on the most intimate personal conceptions of oneself. Through the patterned and reciprocal expectations for himself and for others, the individual looks to fellow members for acceptance and recognition in some capacity. The verdicts of others are not just one among a number of alternative evaluations. They are evaluation which *count* for him. It is through the dynamics of patterned interaction with others that he comes to regulate his behavior voluntarily in line with their expectations of him and with other norms shared by all members. . . .

BIBLIOGRAPHY

AUSUBEL, D. P., 1954, *Theory and Problems of Adolescent Development*, New York: Grune and Stratton.

HORROCKS, J. E., 1962, *The Psychology of Adolescence: Behavior and Development*, second edition, Boston: Houghton Mifflin.

PRADO, W. M., "Appraisal of Performance as a Function of the Relative Ego-Involvement of Children and Adolescents," Ph.D. thesis, University of Oklahoma, 1958.

SEARS, R. R., 1960, "The Growth of Conscience," *Personality Development in Children*, I. Iscoe and H. W. Stevenson, eds., Austin: University of Texas Press.

SHERIF, M., 1948, *An Outline of Social Psychology*, New York: Harper & Row.

SHERIF, M., 1962, "The Self and Reference Groups: Meeting Ground of Individual and Group Approaches," *Annals of New York Academy of Science*, 96, pp. 797–813.

SHERIF, M., and H. CANTRIL, 1947, *The Psychology of Ego-Involvements*, New York: John Wiley & Sons.

SHERIF, M., and CAROLYN W. SHERIF, 1953, *Groups in Harmony and Tension. An Integration of Studies on Intergroup Relations*, New York: Harper & Row.
SHERIF, M., and CAROLYN W. SHERIF, 1956, *An Outline of Social Psychology*, revised edition, New York: Harper & Row.

6.4   INTRODUCTION

The ensuing selection by a noted anthropologist deals with one of the universal aspects of socialization—the learning of sex roles—and explores both its regularities and its variabilities across cultures. Margaret Mead relates the regularities to certain constancies of human biology and development, but emphasizes the extent to which even these are dependent on cultural support and are thus potentially susceptible to almost unlimited variation.

A number of points in her discussion seem especially significant for all those who deal with young people and are involved in their development. For example, the observation that in any culture there are likely to be many individuals who find the cultural ideal for their sex alien to their own temperament certainly seems relevant to American society. Our emphasis on sexual adequacy and distinctiveness, coupled with the increasing ambiguity and overlap of sex-role requirements, should make such individual reactions particularly probable. If, as Parsons and White suggested in Selection 6.2, a major function of the peer-group attachments of late childhood and adolescence is the clarification of sex roles, feelings of inadequacy and confusion should be particularly salient during that period. In this light, it does not seem unreasonable to interpret much of the behavior of this age group as an attempt to prove, to themselves and to others that they really are male or female (for example, boys' intense involvement with sports and cars, girls' overconcern with clothes and appearance, the exaggerated styles of girls' dress, their mutual competitiveness and more or less friendly downgrading).

Mead's discussion of female sex-role development also raises a number of questions when applied to our own society. She considers that this development, unlike that of the male, is continuous and self-completing: the girl starts out as an infant identifying with her mother and moves steadily to the culmination of her femaleness when she becomes a mother herself. Thus, for women to seek other goals beyond child-bearing, they have to be taught to want such goals. This would seem to be what American culture does, placing girls in the same achievement-oriented educational system as boys and rewarding, within that context, the same kinds of motivations and behavior. The question which arises, however, is whether this training is compatible with the dominant cultural image of what a woman should be and do. Or, if it is not, whether there is an acceptable substitute image with which a girl can identify.

The lack of sexual differentiation in our educational system raises another question. If, as Mead suggests, maleness is defined primarily as that which is not female, what happens to the male role as more women begin to participate in pre-viously male activities? To what extent does our socialization process make the boy's self-image dependent on such traditional distinctions? Does the fading of dis-tinctions imply that both sexes are developing a wider or a narrower range of human characteristics?

6.4   MALE AND FEMALE[1]

Margaret Mead

The growing child in any society is confronted then by individuals—adults and adolescents and children—who are classified by his society into two groups, males and females, in terms of their most conspicuous primary sex characters, but who actually show great range and variety both in physique and in behavior. Because primary sex differences are of such enormous importance, shaping so determinative-ly the child's experience of the world through its own body and the responses of others to its sex membership, most children take maleness or femaleness as their first identification of themselves. But once this identification is made, the growing child then begins to compare itself not only in physique, but even more impor-tantly in impulse and interest, with those about it. Are all of its interests those of its own sex? "I am a boy," but "I love color, and color is something that interests only women." "I am a girl," but "I am fleet of foot and love to run and leap. Running and leaping, and shooting arrows, are for boys, not girls." "I am a boy," but "I love to run soft materials through my fingers; an interest in touch is femi-nine, and will unsex me." "I am a girl," but "My fingers are clumsy, better at handling an axe-handle than at stringing beads; axe-handles are for men." So the child, experiencing itself, is forced to reject such parts of its particular biological inheritance as conflict sharply with the sex stereotype of its culture.

Moreover, a sex stereotype that decrees the interests and occupations of each sex is usually not completely without a basis. The idea of the male in a given society may conform very closely to the temperament of some one type of male. The idea of the female *may* conform to the female who belongs to the same type, or instead to the female of some other type. For the children who do not belong to these preferred types, only the primary sex characters will be definitive in helping them to classify themselves. Their impulses, their preferences, and later much of their physique will be aberrant. They will be doomed throughout life to sit among the

---

[1]From Margaret Mead, *Male and Female: A Study of the Sexes in a Changing World*, New York: William Morrow, 1949, pp. 108–126. This is an abridgment of the full text.

other members of their sex feeling less a man, or less a woman, simply because the cultural ideal is based on a different set of clues, a set of clues no less valid, but different. And the small rabbit man sits sadly, comparing himself with a lionlike male beside whom he is surely not male, and perhaps for that reason alone yearning forever after the lioness woman. Meanwhile the lioness woman, convicted in her inmost soul of lack of femininity when she compares herself with the rabbity little women about her, may in reverse despair decide that she might as well go the whole way and take a rabbity husband. Or the little rabbity man who would have been so gently fierce and definitely masculine if he had been bred in a culture that recognized him as fully male, and quite able to take a mate and fight for her and keep her, may give up altogether and dub himself a female and become a true invert, attaching himself to some male who possesses the magnificent qualities that have been denied him.

Sometimes one has the opportunity to observe two men of comparable physique and behavior, both artists or musicians, one of whom has placed himself as fully male, and with brightly shining hair and gleaming eye can make a roomful of women feel more feminine because he has entered the room. The other has identified himself as a lover of men, and his eye contains no gleam and his step no sureness, but instead an apologetic adaptation when he enters a group of women. And yet, in physical measurement, in tastes, in quality of mind, the two men may be almost interchangeable. One, however, has been presented, for example, with a frontier setting, the other with a cosmopolitan European one; one with a world where a man never handles anything except a gun, a hunting-knife, or a riding-whip, the other with a world where men play the most delicate musical instruments. When one studies a pair such as this, it seems much more fruitful to look not at some possible endocrine difference, but rather at the discrepancy, so much more manifest to one than to the other, between his own life preferences and those which his society thinks appropriate for males. . . .

So in each of the societies I have studied it has been possible to distinguish those who deviated most sharply from the expected physique and behavior, and who made different sorts of adjustment, dependent upon the relationship between their own constitutional type and cultural ideal. The boy who will grow up into a tall, proud, restive man whose very pride makes him sensitive and liable to confusion suffers a very different fate in Bali, Samoa, Arapesh, and Manus. In Manus, he takes refuge in the vestiges of rank the Manus retain, takes more interest in ceremonial than in trading, mixes the polemics of acceptable trading invectives with much deeper anger. In Samoa such a man is regarded as too violent to be trusted with the headship of a family for many, many years; the village waits until his capacity for anger and intense feeling has been worn down by years of erosive soft resistance to his unseemly overemphases. In Bali, such a man may take more initiative than his fellows only to be thrown back into sulkiness and confusion, unable to carry it through. Among the Maori of New Zealand, it is probable that he would have been the cultural ideal, his capacity for pride matched by the demand for pride, his violence by the demand for violence, and his capacity for fierce gentleness also given perfect expression, since the ideal woman was as proud and fiercely gentle as himself.

But in complex modern societies, there are no such clear expectations, no such perfectly paired expectancies, even for one class or occupational group or rural region. The stereotyped roles for men and for women do not necessarily correspond, and whatever type of man is the ideal, there is little likelihood that the corresponding female type will also be the ideal. Accidents of migration, of cross-class marriage, of frontier conditions, may take the clues for the female ideal from quite another type from which the male ideal is taken. The stereotype may itself be blurred and confused by several different expectations, and then split again, so that the ideal lover is not the ideal brother or husband. The pattern of inter-relationships between the sexes, of reserve or intimacy, advance or retreat, initiative and response, may be a blend of several biologically congruent types of behavior instead of clearly related to one.

. . . [W]e must conceive of children as continuously reinterpreting experience as their own bodies develop among the developing and developed and involuting bodies of members of both sexes. And when we do so, when we think always of a two-sex world, always of human beings of different ages and sizes, we find that there are certain biological regularities that cannot fail to play a part in these interpretations.

The first of these regularities is that both boys and girls are nursed by the mother, which means that one sex receives a picture of muted complementary behavior within its own sex, and the other—the male—initially encounters a complementary relationship with the opposite sex. However much or little the three-month-old infant may be capable of realizing alone the difference between the sexes, the mother is fully capable, and her smile, her arm, the whole position of her body, are conscious—albeit in different ways in different societies, and for different temperaments—of that contrast. The little female is a small replica of herself. "As she feels now, so I once felt" is an introspective comment by the mother that is easily enough communicated to the child. It lays the basis in a girl for an identification with her own sex that is simple and uncomplicated, something that exists, requires no elaboration, can be accepted simply. But for the boy, the mother's comment must inevitably be, "This is different for him." Inception is not the same for the male as for the female. Transmuted into adult terms, this is a reversal of the male and female roles, in which "I insert, and he receives. Before he is a man he will have to accomplish a change from this passive inception." So the female child's earliest experience is one of closeness to her own nature. Mother and female child together fit one pattern, the mother's assumption that their pulses beat to the same rhythm provides an immediacy to the child's development. The little girl learns "I am." The little boy, however, learns that he must begin to differentiate himself from this person closest to him; that unless he does so, he will never be at all; that he must find out—says his mother's smile, the slight coquettishness or perhaps aggressive tightening in her arms, or the extra passivity with which she yields her breast—who he is, that he is male, that he is *not* female. So at the very start of life, effort, an attempt at greater self-differentiation, is suggested to the boy, while a relaxed acceptance of herself is suggested to the girl.

The discussion that has gone before has suggested some of the ways in which different societies have twisted and distorted and overemphasized, overvalued or devalued, membership in one sex or the other. In this chapter, however, I am emphasizing the biological regularities that underlie these enormous diversities. Whether women like being women or deeply resent it, they will teach their girl-children that they belong to the same sex, whether that sex is regarded as fortunate or unfortunate, and their boys that they belong to a different one. This fundamental regularity is of course tied up with lactation, and with the carry-over into social patterns that because women breast-feed children, they are also the ones to care for them. If breast feeding were completely superseded as a form of feeding infants—always a possibility in our mechanically oriented society—and fathers and brothers were to take over an equal responsibility for the child, this biological regularity would disappear. Instead of girls learning that they simply were, and boys that they must become, emphasis would shift to such matters as relative size and strength; the preoccupations of the developing child would alter, and so might the whole psychology of the sexes. At present, the by-products of lactation still hold universally, for in all societies the care of infants is believed to be more women's work than men's, and we have therefore no way of telling whether or not the male drive towards assertion of maleness by differentiation from females through achievement has any other base beyond this earliest one. Cultures like the Arapesh show how easily, where parents do not discriminate strongly between the sexes of their children and men take over a nurturing role, this drive in the male may be muted. But this muting on the whole seems expensive enough so that it makes one question whether there are not a number of other, perhaps more phylogenetically determined, roots for assertiveness in the human male. However that may be, the mother-child situation at present provides a perfect learning context in which girls learn to be and boys learn the need to act.

At the next step in development, the stage at which the relationship to the breast becomes an active one, the child seeking, the mother according or withholding the breast, the learning situation is to a degree reversed. The mother may interpret as male behavior the active seeking of her male baby and reinforce him in this seeking, demanding attitude, or she may still be sufficiently preoccupied with the reversal to feel that his seeking is rapaciousness, emptying her rather than replenishing her femininity. The girl-baby may similarly be treated as if her eagerness is unseemly in a female, or as if it is merely a phase of natural female receptivity. This period, then, when the infant shifts from passive receptivity to active, eager pursuit of the breast, is one in which there is a possible confusion, in terms of the basic relationships between developing mouth and offered breast. It is not surprising that here many elaborations of mother-child relationships, many complications of attitudes towards others, seem to develop, and that a detailed exploration of the nursing situation from the second half-year of life to weaning is always rewarding.

Then comes weaning, always somewhat loaded with emotion, whether it comes while the child is still majorly preoccupied with intake, too young to walk, or after the child can walk and talk and fend for itself. When the break comes, the girl leaves her mother-child relationship, although she will some day repeat it. The boy leaves it forever, reliving it only inasmuch as intercourse may express symbolically re-entry into the womb. . . . Among the Arapesh, little girls share their mothers' extreme valuation of nursing, and are as unwilling as little boys to be weaned. In Manus, mothers have already communicated their lack of enthusiasm for the maternal role to their small daughters, and the girl-child on the point of weaning treats the mothers's breast in a slightly jeering cavalier fashion. But whatever the nuance, for the boy it means the end of a type of relationship, while for the girl it means the end of one side of a complementary pattern and the beginning of preparedness for the other.

The period when small children are learning to regulate their elimination again provides a natural basis for interpreting sex membership. . . . If the child has already learned in the period of nursing definite attitudes towards taking in, towards defending his mouth from attack by persons or things, or habits of holding food in the mouth and refusing to swallow, these in turn may be reinterpreted into his eliminative behavior. . . .

In any discussion of the way attitudes towards elimination pattern attitudes towards sex, much more than in the discussion of nursing behavior, it is necessary to qualify the discussion in terms of different culturally allowed possibilities. The whole operation of eating, digesting, and eliminating is very complex, and may be interpreted in many different ways. The difference in structure between boy and girl can be very heavily muted by cultural convention, and there is no one clear and simple way in which this stage of childhood can be said to contribute to a sense of maleness and femaleness, although some important contribution may always be expected.

However, it is important to emphasize that the gastro-intestinal system as a whole is the system by which the body is related to objects rather than to persons, in which food is taken in and absorbed, and waste products are given out. On the other hand, the child's first feeding relationships are primarily relationships to a person, although the child's discrimination between itself and its mother's breast may be as dim as many students of infancy believe it to be. Where the mother gives the child food as well as nursing it, the relationship of child to object and child to person will have one character; where she nurses it without supplementary feeding it will have a different one. . . .

Whatever the transition, the distinction between mother's body and the own body, as satisfying or dissatisfying in interpersonal terms, and in person-object terms, is an important one. Where the nursing situation is not emphasized and the whole process of eating and elimination is the center of adult-child communication, the child may form a picture of the world in which things are more important than people, in which relations with others are seen primarily as interchange or reciprocity, in which the production of children is equated with the production of any other object, so that birth itself becomes a sort of externalization. In the imagery of our industrial society, the human body becomes a factory that manufactures human beings rather than the factory's becoming an imperfect model of a human body itself. The products of the body become identified as nonpersonal, and the orientation of the individual to the outside world is made more predominant as the relationship to the own body shrinks. This is the Manus character structure, as well as being a character that develops in modern society rather frequently, but its occurrence at such a primitive level as among the Stone Age, ghost-guarded, pile-dwelling Manus people of the Admiralties suggests that while it is congruent with the machine and the factory, the dynamics lie deep in the relationship of individuals to their own bodies. . . .

So to the interpretation of its own sex through its own sex organs the child brings these earlier experiences through which interrelationships with others have reinforced the cues of its own body. If the adults have differentiated, and differentiated happily, between the two sexes, the boy will be able to take pride in his realization that he is a male, and will find the structure of his body impressive, worthy of exhibitionism and boasting. The girl will be considerably less sure that the immediate structure of her body is something to be proud of. . . . The more biologically accurate the earlier stages have been, the more the mother has made her male child feel his maleness and the female child her femaleness, the more this period is likely to be one of assurance for boys and uncertainty for girls. . . .

Here again the phrasing that growing-up receives reverses the position of boys and girls. The boy learns that he must make an effort to enter the world of men, that his first act of differentiating himself from his mother, of realizing his own body as his and different from hers, must be continued into long years of effort—which may not succeed. He still carries his knowledge of childbirth as something that women can do, that his sister will be able to do, as a latent goad to some other type of achievement. He embarks on a long course of growth and practice, the outcome of which, if he sees it as not only being able to possess a woman but to become a father, is very uncertain.

But the little girl meets no such challenge. The taboos and the etiquette enjoined upon her are ways of protecting her already budding femininity from adult males. She learns to cross her legs, or tuck her heels under her, or sit with her legs parallel and close in. She is dressed to enclose her further against attack, against premature defloration. Implicit in the abundant rules that are laid upon her, the prohibitions against the freedom, the exhibitionism, the roaming and marauding, permitted to her brother, is the message "It might happen too soon. Wait." And this comes at the very time when her brother is permitted far more exposure in public, when he may go about naked, unkempt, uncared-for, the very negligence of the adult world proclaiming aloud that nothing is going to happen *from him* yet that can possibly matter to any one. So in Iatmul, in Arapesh, in Mundugumor, in Tchambuli, the little boy puts on a G-string when he feels like it, but the girl has a grass skirt carefully tucked around her diminutive waist. And as adolescence approaches the prescient signs that surround the girl increase: chaperonage will increase in those societies which value virginity, approaches from older men will increase in boldness in those societies which do not. Upon the initial uncertainty of her final maternal role is built a rising curve of sureness, which is finally crowned—in primitive and simple societies, in which every woman marries—with child-bearing, with an experience that is so real and so valid that only very few and very sick women who are bred in societies that have devalued maternity are able wholly to disavow it. So the life of the female starts and ends with sureness, first with the simple identification with her mother, last with the sureness that that identification is true, and that she has made another human being. The period of doubt, of envy of her brother, is brief, and comes early, followed by the long years of sureness.

For the male, however, the gradient is reversed. His earliest experience of self is one in which he is forced, in the relationship to his mother, to realize himself as different, as a creature unlike the mother, as a creature unlike the human beings who make babies in a direct, intelligible way by using their own bodies to make them. Instead he must turn out from himself, enter and explore and produce in the outside world, find his expression through the bodies of others. His brief period of simple sureness that he is fully armed for the fray—seen as simple copulation or as simple feats of strength and power—is brought to naught by the awareness that he himself is not ready to act. This imposed uncertainty, this period of striving and effort, never really end. He may grow up, take a head, or collect for himself a bride-price; he may marry, and his wife may have a child, but the child his wife bears is probably never the absolute assurance to him that it is to her. Possibly cultures like the Arapesh, which associate the creation of a child with arduous and continuous work on the part of both parents as the child is built up of steady accretions of semen from the father and blood from the mother, come the closest to giving the male who has fathered a child a sense that he has accomplished something in his own right. But the Arapesh version of paternity is after all a myth, a myth congruent with the great value set on parenthood by the Arapesh. At the simplest level of human society, men have had no way of estimating the relationship between copulation and paternity; as the habit of making correlated and exact observations has increased, his own role has been specified as a single copulatory act that was successful. While modern genetic theory has again dignified the paternal role to a genetic contribution equal to the maternal, it has not increased our ability to prove that a given man is, in fact, the father of a given child. Genetic theory has simply increased our capacity to prove that a given man could *not* be the father of a given child. It may protect a man against a lawsuit and help him verify his suspicions of his wife's infidelity, but it does not increase his certainty of his paternity. Paternity remains, with all our modern biological knowledge, as inferential as it ever was, and considerably less ascertainable than it has seemed to be in some periods of history. So while in the end the female in societies in which every woman marries is practically certain of resolving all the doubts about her own sex membership that were implanted in her in the natural course of her long infancy and childhood, the male needs to reassert, to reattempt to redefine his maleness.

In every known human society, the male's need for achievement can be recognized. Men may cook, or weave or dress dolls or hunt humming-birds, but if such activities are appropriate occupations of men, then the whole society, men and women alike, votes them as important. When the same occupations are performed by women, they are regarded as less important. In a great number of human societies men's sureness of their sex role is tied up with their right, or ability, to practice some activity that women are not allowed to practice. Their maleness, in fact, has to be underwritten by preventing women from entering some field or performing some feat. Here may be found the relationship between maleness and pride; that is, a need for prestige that will outstrip the prestige which is accorded to any woman. There seems no evidence that it is necessary for men to surpass women in any specific way, but rather that men do need to find reassurance in achievement, and because of this connection, cultures frequently phrase achievement as something that women do not or cannot do, rather than directly as something which men do well.

The recurrent problem of civilization is to define the male role satisfactorily enough—whether it be to build gardens or raise cattle, kill game or kill enemies, build bridges or handle bank-shares—so that the male may in the course of his life reach a solid sense of irreversible achievement, of which his childhood knowledge of the satisfactions of childbearing have given him a glimpse. In the case of women, it is only necessary that they be permitted by the given social arrangements to fulfill their biological role, to attain this sense of irreversible achievement. If women are to be restless and questing, even in the face of child-bearing, they must be made so through education. If men are ever to be at peace, ever certain that their lives have been lived as they were meant to be, they must have, in addition to paternity, culturally elaborated forms of expression that are lasting and sure. Each culture—in its own way—has developed forms that will make men satisfied in their constructive activities without distorting their sure sense of their masculinity. Fewer cultures have yet found ways in which to give women a divine discontent that will demand other satisfactions than those of child-bearing.

6.5 INTRODUCTION

The following selection concludes this chapter by looking at the process of socialization from the perspectives of both its objects and its agents, drawing together many of the issues raised up to this point. Kimball summarizes the nature and purpose of socialization succinctly in his statement that "the fundamental role of the child is to become an adult." To complement this, the major role of the adult is to guide, lead, instruct, and support this transformation, relentlessly and without exception. Kimball goes on to examine the specific learnings which the adult American world imposes on its children, identifying some of their unique features and special problems.

The view of the child-adult relationship presented in this essay poses a dilemma with respect to the values of self-fulfillment, identified here as central to the American way of life. This is that the child must internalize this value but must also perceive the fulfillment to which it refers as that of his future adulthood, and not his present childish self. In other words, the child must learn to value his individuality while rejecting its present form. It is not difficult to see that this necessary duality in what he is taught may often be perceived by the child as mainly duplicity and that such a perception might have serious consequences for his concept of the adult self and his progress toward its attainment.

The guidance counselor's role, with its emphasis both on the needs of the individual and on the adequacy of his relationship to the social environment would seem to exaggerate both elements of the paradox. While his aim is to help the child or adolescent through the stresses of socialization, he is at the same time, and inevitably, an agent of socialization himself. Indeed, to the extent that the child perceives himself as being helped, to that extent is the guidance counselor's potential influence increased. On the other hand, if the child perceives the guidance counselor as having a stake in promoting particular outcomes, he is likely to become protective of the self he is learning to value, severely limiting the counselor's opportunities to make a positive contribution. The inevitability of this dilemma should be kept in mind as the reader ponders the questions raised in this selection, about the nature of the pressures on the child and the barriers on the way to achieving maturity, and relates these to the practice of guidance.

6.5   CULTURAL INFLUENCES SHAPING
THE ROLE OF THE CHILD[1]

Solon T. Kimball

FORCED ABANDONMENT   Although it is seldom stated in this way, the
OF CHILDHOOD   major role of the child *qua* child is to submit
                              to and assist in the activities and processes
which prepare him for adult status. The extreme dependency of early infancy permits no choice in the selection of the external environment in which the initial

---

[1]From Solon T. Kimball, "Cultural Influences Shaping the Role of the Child," *The National Elementary Principal*, XL, No. 1, September, 1960, pp. 20–31.

learning occurs. Later when, presumably, the child has developed some rational discrimination in his response to demands placed upon him, it is too late for him to make effective protest. He has already internalized the emotional set of a system which requires that he eventually abandon the thought and habit ways of children and substitute those of the adult world.

However rewarding the culture of childhood, that of the grown-up world is continuously and persistently presented as more rewarding and desirable, and childhood is defined as a transitory and to-be-abandoned stage of life. No matter how entrancing, the never-never world of Peter Pan turns out to be just that, a fantasy in which childhood is forever threatened by pirates symbolizing demanding adults who must eventually win in the age-old struggle between old and young. Although James Barrie allows the illusion of a different solution, both child and adult know that his ending is founded in the realm of dreams.

This forced abandonment of childhood in which, if it is successful, the child is a willing participant, represents the first of a sequential series of tragedies which each individual encounters on the road of life. No matter how sentimental or protective adults may be, the gradual and sometimes forcible destruction of the innocence of childhood is a necessary function of the relationship between adult and child. The latter is not the only one who suffers in this nearly abrupt destruction of childhood certainties. The transition also demands its costs of the adult. The mother's mixed emotion of anguish and pride when her "baby" first enters school is repeated later when her child, turned young adult, leaves home for marriage, college, or the world of work. She may also carry a sense of guilt because of the contradictory desire to both hold and eject, and guilt because there can never be assurance that one has done enough or that what one has done has been right. There is solace in believing that one has done the best he could, but doubt may also nag the conscience.

The male response to these crises is different only in degree, and both parents share the knowledge that they have been parties to a failure, concealment, or perhaps even deception in communicating to the growing child what the world is really like. This conspiracy of silence is in part a function of the inability to articulate the realities; in part, it is an attempt to continue the protective role assumed during infancy; and, in part, it is a result of the parents' own unwillingness or incapacity to face the realities of their own lives. The delusion they have perpetuated, the illusion they have lived under and passed on to their children, should not be assessed as deliberate. Not that adults and parents are blameless, for they are not. The offense with which they may be charged is the same one as that which they first permitted and then prohibited, that of innocence.

The adult world is no more free of fantasy and illusion than is that of the child. The Walter Mittys are everywhere among us. Shaw's *Pygmalion* expresses a contemporary version of the Cinderella story. Our devoted adherence to romantic love as a necessary prerequisite to marriage and adult responsibilities of family and parenthood is real enough, but do we not deceive ourselves when we act as if erotic love is the panacea for the tough job of cementing relations between men and women in domestic functions?

These beliefs, and similar ones in other spheres of life, sustain us through bitterness, tragedy, and boredom. They are undoubtedly a necessary aspect in our kind of cultural world and as such should not, even were it possible, be either dispelled or destroyed. Our sin is that we let them delude us, that we insist upon maintaining an innocence of realities. Perhaps there is no simple way to explain why this is so, but probably these tendencies are linked with the generalized guilt which our culture so successfully inculcates during that period of defenseless infancy. . . .

STANDARDS OF ADULTHOOD The course which begins in infancy inevitably leads through childhood and adolescence into adulthood. This progression can be viewed in part as the result of natural processes, in part as the consequence of training received from parents, peers, and teachers, but in even larger measure as directed, purposeful, and at times aggressive activity of the child himself. If the question were asked, "Is not this the universal process of acquiring adulthood in all cultures?" the answer given could not be an unqualified affirmative. The major difference is found in the early inculcation in the American child of certain standards of self-performance, the full realization of which will be achieved simultaneously with maturity. Later on we shall show that this expectancy proves to be an illusion which is, nonetheless, also transmitted to each succeeding generation.

First, however, the problem of what these standards are and how they become internalized and are maintained should be examined. Simple observation establishes that a parent comforting a hurt child often urges that he behave like a little man and stop his crying. In hundreds of other instances in the life relationship of parent and child, each time the former holds up adult behavior as superior there is implicit in the action a denigration of child behavior and an affirmation of superior adult standards. When boys are told, "Done like a man!" the implications of the praise for the action performed are quite explicit. Has anyone ever intended praise when he explained, "You act like a child!"? And when older people do childish things, we call them senile or foolish.

Just when and where do we, in our multifaceted relations with children, ever really judge their behavior except against the measure of progress they exhibit in the acquisition of adult standards? Irrespective of the steps by which the process is initiated, it is not difficult to observe the relentless insistence upon acquiring adult standards. If, by chance or intention, parents and teachers should abandon this aspect of their role, they would then have, to this extent, abandoned their function as adults.

The other part of the problem posed earlier, the question of what should be included under any listing of adult standards, was answered in large measure by Arensberg* in his enumeration of the imperatives of our family system. Within this framework, however, there are certain specificities that need to be mentioned and their relevance elaborated if we are to grasp the role of the child.

It is generally accepted that family, school, and church transmit a greater portion of the cultural heritage to the child than do other agencies. What, then, among the many things which adults expect the child to learn, may we count as significant? The broad categories include skills for handling, knowledge for understanding, and feelings for evaluating the things, persons, and ideas which are encountered in the business of living. These requirements are so universal, however, that their generality does not help us much. If we look at some of the requirements imposed upon the individual in the American cultural system and then examine these in their relation to the family and respective roles within it, we shall encounter those specific traits which have been idealized for all members of the society.

COMMITMENT TO CHANGE   The central and perhaps most crucial commitment of American civilization is to the inevitability and, in most instances, the desirability of change. The activities and events of everyday life are interpreted through such terms as "progress," "advancement," and "development" within the context of the never-constant environment in which we live. If the individual is to be successful in this type of society, and the promise of success is one of the imperatives which moves him, he must at least keep up with the times. Even those not motivated by promises of success know that stagnation is penalized. For the individual, this imperative means that he must be continuously poised to take advantage of opportunities for advancement. In fact, he must actively seek and, if possible, modify the environment to insure that situations favorable to him present themselves. Favorable chances and maneuvering avail nothing if there is resistance to working in new surroundings with new people and possibly learning new skills for new activities.

The successful meeting of new demands requires, first of all, readiness to abandon the present whether it be locality, associations, or activity. Under such circumstances, it is unwise to invest too deeply either emotionally, professionally, or financially, for the wrench which change demands may require a sacrifice too great to make. The easy fashion in which Americans establish and abandon new relationships disconcerts Europeans who accuse us of emotional superficiality. Their projection of values hardly explains the situation, nor are they likely to understand the necessity of such behavior as a function of our commitment. And the more deeply imbedded guilt with its corollary of tragedy they utterly fail to comprehend.

---

*[See Selection 6.1.]

SELF-FULFILLMENT   These imperatives of mobility, independence, adaptability, and the capacity for continued growth represent, in one sense, subsidiary aspects of a more central requirement, that of self-fulfillment. Implied in the objective of adulthood achieved is the acquisition of competence, wisdom, and maturity. But fulfillment in the context of perpetual change contains a contradiction incapable of resolution. Final achievement is impossible because the objectives themselves are not fixed. They expand, recede, or are modified as the conditions within the system are changed, changes to which the individual in his progression also contributes. There can be no ultimate in the world view of those who adhere to the concept of an ever expanding system. One might suppose that these circumstances would breed frustration and defeat but apparently this occurs rarely since one is taught to accept striving as a lifelong necessity.

PERPETUAL OPTIMISM   Finally, the role must be performed in a mood of perpetual hopefulness, a trait which has also been set by the culture. The extent to which this mood has been integrated into the events of daily life may be met in many contexts. The language of salutation reveals the extraordinary extent to which we have carried our insistence upon a positive and optimistic approach to the world. No matter how we really feel, we are obligated to meet the world with a sunny disposition. Our conventional "Good day" has no relation to the actual state of the weather nor do our replies to inquiries about our well-being have relation to the actual situation. The response of "Fine," or one of its many variations, expresses how we ought to be. Any other admission is incorrect. The child learns this ritual language and the accompanying values in his earliest years. He is taught to condemn whining, complaining, crybabies, and pessimists. We should also like to deny that pain, evil, and death exist, and although we are forced to recognize them we assign them only marginal status. We would like to believe that all beings are basically good and should be trusted, a character quality which sometimes causes others to accuse us of being naïve. These optimistic and positive traits found expression in the 1920's in the ringing slogan of Coué, "Day by day in every way I am getting better and better!"

Our culture demands that we maintain this euphoric façade in our own perception of the world and our place in it. Furthermore, we demand that our children acquire and exhibit the same psychological posture. Obviously, at times, this optimistic perceptual screen through which we interpret the events of the world must lead to some distortions in our apperception of reality. The truth is that, on occasions, the situation we find ourselves in, individually or collectively, is damned bad. But our "natural" optimism carries us through with the belief that tomorrow or next year will be better, that all things work out for the best, it's always darkest before the dawn, and so on through the dozens of aphorisms which give expression to the same point of view. The fact that events usually do turn toward the better lends credence to the belief.

It is my contention that the configuration of beliefs that we have been examining is a necessary corollary to the central value of self-fulfillment. To deny, in any degree, that societal conditions are not improving (through change) or that individual incapacitation prevents further growth is to admit that this keystone (self-fulfillment) upon which the structural unity of purpose in life has been erected is faulty—denies, then, the very basis of the American's conception of himself in his life role.

It should be apparent now why it has been necessary to examine these interconnections before we could turn to the direct study of the role of the child. The American small family, relatively isolated in its activities from other communal institutions, with the insistence upon the capacity for independence and mobility of its members, building and maintaining in each person the psychological posture of perpetual optimism with its corollary of self-fulfillment, taken as a whole and as functionally interdependent with other cultural systems, provides the conditions within which the role of the individual is defined.

Under such circumstances, the role of the child is as much central to the continued functioning of the whole as is the role of any other family member. A mutual dependence exists between children and their parents since the latter seek some portion of their own fulfillment through their children. In part, they fulfill themselves by providing a sheltering environment which expresses and enforces a temporary dependence. The dependency relationship, however, contains both contradiction and conflict for eventually, as both child and parent know, the independent and mobile condition must be claimed by or forced upon the child since adulthood is a necessary step for continued growth. This brings us to the point where we can more adequately conceptualize the child's role.

PROGRESSION INTO ADULTHOOD   Those who propose two alternative ways of viewing the child, namely, either as a miniature adult or as an undeveloped person but possessing the capacities for achieving maturity, may come to conclusions that distort reality. There is no intention to pose a conundrum by saying that the child is neither and both. For example, most children by the time they have reached the age of three or four have already learned a number of important adult skills. They walk, talk, control the elimination of bodily wastes in socially acceptable ways, and have developed habits, points of view, and skills around sleeping, eating, and their relations to a limited number of other persons. Childish ways may still adhere to some of their activities, but any realistic appraisal of the contrast between behavior in the first year of life with that of the fourth must grant that in some directions adult standards have been successfully transmitted. By six or seven, some children are judged precociously mature. For most children, however, the period of development coincides with physical growth, except that in our society the dependence is maintained for a much longer period because of the requirement for formal training through postadolescent years.

Thus, at a very early age the child acquires some of the requisite skills of an independent individual. To this extent, he has cleared some hurdles which test for adult competency. In other areas, he remains dependent, undeveloped, and not yet capable of unguided mobility. We again restate the point made earlier that the fundamental role of the child is to become an adult. All his activities are either contributory or incidental to this end. The progression is partly a function of physical and neural growth, partly a function of the social and cultural environment within which the child learns, but it is continuous although uneven.

PRESSURES ON CHILDREN TO BE ADULT   The responsibility parents feel for converting their children into adults is so great that they impose a rigorous regime upon them during their dependent years. The intensity of parental concern reaches into every aspect of child behavior. It is expressed by an overconcern and overdirection of the child's activities. All types of special "opportunities" for developing skills are sought out. One manifestation has been the downward extension of formal schooling to pre-kindergarten classes.

The reality eventually became sloganized in the phrase "child-centered." Whatever excesses have been committed in home or school by adults who abdicated responsibility because of this doctrine, their behavior never violated the fundamental principle that children must be turned into adults. The freedoms given the child in activity or temperament were never justified on the grounds that these would permit him to remain a child; it was because this freedom ensured a healthier, better-adjusted adult. In effect, child-centered dogma was an unwitting device for putting ever greater pressures upon the child. In its rationale, the adults deluded both themselves and the children they tended because it was never explained that this was a long-term transaction with an expected profitable payoff at the end.

Perhaps we should be more explicit about the pressures to which the child is subject. The cultural context within which these appear is, of course, that children cannot just be allowed to grow up; they must be wisely directed. The justification is based upon the great latent "potential" in the unformed young which is waiting to be realized. Only as the potential is realized can the child fulfill himself and fulfillment is a function of adulthood, not childhood. What is not made explicit to the child and is probably perceived by only a few parents and teachers is that their own role is dependent upon child accomplishments. Under these conditions, the child carries a heavier burden of responsibility in the proper performance of his role than that placed upon the young in any other society.

The child is expected to grow not only into an adult but into a successful one. The definition of the latter is, of course, adult determined. Success must be found in career, in marriage, in family, in community, and in one's personal life. The adult believes and the child comes to accept early that the route to these objectives can be reached through training. The apparatus through which much of this training is transmitted is the formal educational system. It is here that performance is judged by agreed-upon standards and a preliminary preview of the future seen. Hence, the parental pressures on the child for academic striving.

BARRIERS TO ADULTHOOD   Unfortunately, there are several conditions which inhibit and limit the child's efforts in acquiring that experience necessary for adulthood. The culturally isolating centripetence of metropolitan life reduces enormously the opportunities for significant cross-group experience. The capacity to make social adaptations cannot be learned in the severely limited urban enclave or homogeneous suburb. Emphasis upon personal adjustment is probably related to the narrow range of interpersonal experiences and the ultimate necessity to rely upon oneself. The poverty of cultural variation must have a serious distorting effect on capacities for comparative perception. Vicarious experiences provided by fantasy or documentary in television, cinema, drama, or literature are no substitute and cannot be truly comprehended unless there is a substantial comparative understanding from which these can be interpreted. Situations portraying romantic love, the vicissitudes of family life, or the struggle for power may be dramatized in African, Asian, or American settings but the meaning is reduced to horizons found in Scarsdale, Plainville, or Little Rock.

In spite of our insistence upon cultural pluralism and the tolerance of deviancy, the danger of cultural diversity remains a powerful threat. Is it possible that the social isolation of the American small family intensifies the internalization of its values, manners, and behavior to the exclusion of differing standards? Forced to depend largely upon its own resources, as it is, this may be an expected consequence. In any event, family restrictions present another hazard in the child's struggle to grow up. These are found in the nature of the relationships between old and young and the sexes and exhibit emotional correlates. Informed observers agree that not all is well in our family system, and yet what degree of credence should we give to those who see our children as guilt-ridden and hostile? Does the American mother exhibit the black widow spider tendencies as described by Philip Wylie? To what extent have males abdicated their role in the squeeze of demands between wife and job and to what extent are they delinquent in claiming their sons for manhood?

Perhaps these questions really have no answers. Yet they have been repeatedly asked and answered by those with ready replies. The concern should be evidence enough that the child finds himself in a confused and hence difficult position. There seems little doubt, however, that there has been both an increase in pressure upon the child from home and school and at the same time a diminution in his opportunities and hence his ability to act independently. This combination is bound to produce serious trouble. . . .

Questions and Implications for Practice

6.1 CONRAD M. ARENSBERG

1. Arensberg describes clearly the roles young people are made to learn by our family system if they are to create a family that is typical of our culture. He asserts that the roles each must learn to perform are not easy ones. Young people are helped most effectively with their learning of roles by the models they have to understudy. How can they be helped to learn their roles when they come from homes in which their natural role models have themselves been inadequate?

2. As Arensberg obviously believes, it is desirable for all of us to understand why and how small-family independence and diffusion of kinship fits into modern social and economic life. Can the curriculum and guidance do anything to help young people understand not only the role demands of any relationship they may undertake, but also the management of social change?

3. What tends to happen to men in our culture when, as adults, they have not become stable members of conjugal families on which they can reliably depend for their meals, minor nursing services, comfort, and affection, and where they can expect to be known and cherished as persons? Consider other ways that do not require marriage that might ensure that most of the needs of an adult man might satisfactorily be met?

4. Is having and discharging responsibility—with suitable appreciation for doing this—among the more or less important needs of individuals? Why?

5. How can the needs of adult women be met satisfactorily outside of the usual family arrangements that are typical of this country?

6.2 PARSONS AND WHITE

1. Is much of the tradition of the guidance-personnel movement in line with Parsons's idea that the occupational role is the main goal of the socialization process? Should guidance-personnel workers persist in this belief and gear their efforts primarily toward the occupational role? Or, in view of the principle of egalitarianism, which holds that everyone has a right to equal opportunity to develop himself or herself, and since development of self must mean developing competence in all of one's roles, must the guidance-personnel worker adopt a broader goal of helping individuals develop competency in all their roles?

2. What role should the guidance-personnel worker play in elementary school, secondary school, and college in helping students learn independence, achievement, and responsibility?

3. What implications might Parsons's argument for the importance to the adolescent of peer-group relations hold for the role of the guidance-personnel worker throughout the child's experience as a school and college member? Might the concern of the guidance-personnel worker extend to an interest in the quality of the peer-group life that ought to be available in order that members of the group

can find the emotional support they need? If the guidance-personnel worker *must* be concerned with the sort of student society that exists in a classroom, a school, a dormitory, a college, how does this contradict the view that the primary role of the guidance-personnel worker is to limit his efforts to counseling individuals in dyadic relationships?

4. Consider the effectiveness of the student's peer-group experiences (his relationships with his peers, the discussions he has with them, and his opportunity to try out various important roles) versus the help an adult can give him, usually limited to verbal interaction and to a superficial relationship with a friendly adult developed in only a few encounters that last relatively short periods of time. What conclusions do you draw from all this as to the roles and functions guidance-personnel workers should assume?

6.3 SHERIF AND SHERIF

1. What do the Sherifs' findings have to say about the effectiveness with which guidance-personnel workers will be able to work with students from "low-rank" neighborhoods if they limit their efforts primarily to face-to-face counseling? What other approaches might guidance-personnel workers attempt to develop if they hope to make a difference to students who use their peer group as their supreme reference?

2. What implications are there in Prado's findings for differences in the roles of the guidance-personnel worker in elementary school, in high school, and in college?

3. Does the wise guidance-personnel worker attempt:
   a. through counseling with an individual to compete with his peer group for his attention and loyalty;
   b. to transfer an individual out of one reference group, in which he is not finding the satisfaction he should and which is causing him to get into trouble, into another;
   c. to work with a given clique or gang in the approved group-counseling or group therapy manner;
   d. to work sympathetically with groups to guide them in developing group activities, competencies, programs, goals, and standards that will be beneficial to members of these groups as well as to the life and vigor of the group itself?

6.4 MARGARET MEAD

1. Margaret Mead describes sensitively the earliest experiences that go into defining the deepest feelings of males and females about themselves as persons and about each other. She draws on primitive cultures for some of her basic data. Are there any conditions in an industrialized society that call into question conclusions drawn too exclusively from a primitive society? Consider, *e.g.*, the longer life span

of men and women, and the limited span of child-bearing; the widespread knowledge and use of contraceptives in industrialized societies; automation; arrangements for pensions, annuities, and old-age benefits.

2. What are some of the problems our contemporary culture faces in defining the male role so men may know a durable sense of achievement?

3. Is it possible that women in industrialized societies, women having produced two children who typically will be in school by the time their mother is 32, will have also to experience achievements of another order to feel fulfilled as persons?

6.5 SOLON T. KIMBALL

1. Do you agree that the pressures on the child that Kimball describes are as severe as are here set forth?

2. Are modern parents demanding more than did parents 100 years ago that their children grow up fast? Do parents today keep youngsters dependent longer than their grandparents kept their parents? Is this combination of pressure and dependency as destructive as Kimball suggests?

3. Do you think that the school you know best makes demands of individual children such as to diminish their opportunities to learn how to act independently?

4. Apply Kimball's generalizations to children whose home backgrounds are impoverished socially and economically. Can you think of individual children from such backgrounds who seem to carry a heavy burden in terms of their parents' hopes for their future or whose parents impose on them few demands for achievement and who at the same time give them a brief period of dependency? What, if any, differential treatment would it be desirable for these different children to find in school?

5. Are "positive expectations" in general helpful to children as they grow up? Can you qualify and particularize, with illustrations, just how such expectations might be held for individual children in such a way as to be helpful, not harmful, to them?

6. Would the energies and skills of the guidance-personnel worker be more wisely spent in:
   a. interpreting to each student what implications this greater or less degree of measured success in learning in the school or college may hold for his future, or
   b. encouraging each child to make his own decisions and plans, with due regard to his processes of deciding and planning, or
   c. working with groups of teachers and students in a process of critical inquiry that would make more evident the qualities of the societies and cultures that impinge upon them and that irresistibly condition their values, attitudes, desires, and learnings, or
   d. is there some optimum combination of the above, or
   e. should each be used on appropriate occasions, or
   f. can you propose some other better approach?

Chapter 7
Cultural Variations within the Society

In the two preceding chapters we have dealt with the relationship between the traits and behavior of an individual and the characteristics of his sociocultural environment and with some of the processes whereby this relationship becomes established. Taken together, the selections presented the general social science understanding of why this relationship is established and maintained: since individuals and their culture are interdependent elements of a single system, their characteristics must be interrelated and compatible for the system to endure, and this requirement will therefore be reflected in the processes of training and development which individuals undergo. As was suggested at various points, however, this larger sociocultural system does not constitute a simple or homogeneous environment that leads to a small number of relatively similar individual adjustments and adaptations. Particularly when we are considering a society of many millions of people spread out over a large geographic area, culture will be subject to a great deal of variation in pattern and emphasis, and even in basic content, according to the particular combinations of physical, economic, social, political, and individual psychological factors that have come together in one region or group, or in one particular place or family. Certain cultural themes will prevail rather generally, regardless of the society's size and complexity; but they will occur in different patterns and combine with different other elements, and thus contribute to a wide variety of results. Any one individual will therefore absorb and reflect only a segment of the total culture of his society. The selections in this chapter discuss some of the major factors which determine the content of that segment in American society, the manner in which they limit and shape an individual's life experience, and some of the consequences of this process for the individual's relationship to the social system as a whole.

As was made clear in the preceding chapter, an individual becomes part of the culture through his cumulative experience with people, objects, and events. His conceptions of himself, of people, and of the world are distilled out of the consequences of his behavior as he interacts with different features of his social and physical environment, the shape and content of which are limited and defined by the culture. Each individual, however, is directly exposed to a relatively small number of people and situations, and the particular segment, or version, of culture which these will represent is largely determined by the individual's "place" in the society, that is, his position on one or more dimensions which its culture defines as significant. In our society, economic resources, race, religion, and ethnic origin are a few of the major characteristics which accomplish this differentiation. The latter is not primarily a consequence of the characteristics in themselves, but, rather, stems from the way they are perceived and evaluated by the culture, judgments which are in turn derived from varied events and trends in our history. Although they are neither unambiguous nor rigidly unchanging, at any point in time these distinctions and evaluations do constitute a meaningful reality in terms of their tangible effects upon the life experiences of individuals. As the selections in this chapter will show, social categories such as those mentioned are major factors in determining an individual's material surroundings, the people with whom he will come in contact, the nature of the relationships that will develop, and the activities in which he engages. Less directly, but perhaps most crucially, they will also shape what he is, what he wants, what he believes in, and the values and standards by which he judges himself and the rest of the world.

These last statements could be understood to imply that, in effect, each member of our large and diverse society becomes part of a minor and distinct culture, limited and defined by certain crucial social variables. Although this is true in some respects, there are general themes that cut across such segmentation and are part of every American's cultural environment. Certain goals, beliefs, and practices, in other words, are "all-American," and virtually every member of the society comes in contact with them. At the same time, such widespread agreements do not indicate that unity and coherence characterize the society and its culture and minimize the effects of the differentiations we have described. General cultural prescriptions and definitions reach the individual through the filter of his immediate environment and it is in the context of the latter that he must try to assimilate and conform to the strong pressures they exert. The abstract and generalized cultural goals and ideals are thus perceived and interpreted in terms of the realities of the individual's life and experience, and the attitude that he develops toward them depends on how valid and appropriate they are in relation to what he has learned from the people and events in his immediate environment.

Every individual, in other words, is affected both by general and pervasive cultural themes and by the variations, adaptations, and elaborations of these that are specific to the individuals and groups who constitute his everyday world. As a result, the structure of his personality and the nature and extent of his integration with the sociocultural system as a whole will be a product of both sets of forces and will reflect the degree of congruence or conflict between them.

7.1   INTRODUCTION

This first selection serves as an introduction to the rest of the chapter by providing a theoretical context for the phenomena of social class and ethnic group membership discussed in the selections that follow. Its relevance for guidance practice might seem remote, and its contents certainly are several steps removed from the concrete problems and situations faced by a guidance counselor. What this excerpt does, however, is to view the phenomenon of stratification as a general feature of all societies, and it thus offers a perspective which is essential for understanding the specific characteristics and consequences of stratification in America.

One can be aware of many of the phenomena that are a product of a society's system of stratification without any knowledge of the sociological theory by which such facts are integrated and explained. For example, one may recognize that in our society Negroes are treated in a unique way, that how much education a person has tends to be related to how much he earns, that children of wealthy families tend to get more education than children of poor ones. Such observations, however, can be misleading and essentially useless unless they are based on some coherent conception of where the specific phenomena fall on the broad range of social and cultural possibilities. The selection that follows combines two different approaches within social science to the study of social class. One is anthropological and views social class in terms of the cultural and subcultural variations it encompasses. The other is sociological and, because of its historical roots, to some extent reflects European history and culture. Thus it views social class in terms of its economic implications and emphasizes the distinctions between clearly separated groups. To this, Kurt Mayer adds an emphasis on social mobility, reflecting traditional American values with respect to social class.

As has already been noted, a basic premise of this book is that understanding of individual or group phenomena is incomplete unless it includes understanding of the relevant sociocultural environment. Carrying this further, it is also our contention that understanding of this environment will be deepened if its particular features are seen as instances of broad classes of phenomena to which well-established generalizations are known to apply. The ensuing selection should provide the beginnings of such a general perspective with respect to one of the most significant aspects of the social environment, namely the system by which individuals are differentiated and ordered.

7.1 CLASS AND SOCIETY[1]

Kurt B. Mayer

THE STUDY OF SOCIAL CLASSES One of the basic facts which characterizes the nature of human association is the existence of rank differences between individuals and groups in all human societies. We cannot fully understand the social life of human beings unless we take into consideration how these rank differences influence their interactions and pattern their social relationships. Of course, the importance of rank differentiation varies greatly from one society to another and from time to time, but most societies have a well structured and fairly evident rank order. In our own society the ranking system takes the form of a class structure which constitutes an element of cardinal importance in the web of social relationships.

As we shall see, class differences and class factors enter into almost every aspect of our lives. From them stem great variations in health and wealth, knowledge and experience, wisdom and happiness. Class distinctions influence our choice of marriage partners and the number of our children; they largely determine the kind of education we can obtain and the occupations we may enter. The house we live in, how it is furnished, what car we drive, how we dress, our friends and associates, the organizations and clubs we belong to, our hobbies, even the kind of books and magazines we read—all these matters are strongly influenced by our class position.

Class affiliation, moreover, may become the basis for collective behavior and organized action. Sometimes classes struggle with other classes for political and economic ascendancy. Under certain conditions class interests may command the loyalty and result in concerted activity of their members in much the same way as nationality or religious affiliation. Thus classes can be a major factor in social change and play an important role not only in structuring the social relationships of the present but also in molding the social patterns of the future.

To be sure, in the United States many people are only dimly aware of the important role which class factors play in determining the round of their daily activities and in shaping their life experiences. The American dream of equal oppor-

---

tunity, the well publicized rags-to-riches stories all depreciate the importance of rank differences. Our cultural clichés assert that "there are no classes in the United States," or "all Americans are middleclass," or "I'm just as good as anybody else." But the fact that people are prone to confuse the dream with reality and are not fully conscious of the influence of class factors on their behavior and experiences does not mean that social classes do not exist. However, it does mean that the social analyst must investigate not only the objective nature of the class structure and its changes, but also the reasons why class differences are but dimly perceived and not well understood by large segments of the public.

Indeed, the differentials of wealth, income, and occupation, of prestige and deference, of authority and power, which all are manifestations of class structure, represent some of the basic realities of our existence. Many of the political issues and social problems which confront us are intimately connected with the hierarchical structure of our society. Therefore, unless we understand the nature of rank differentiation in general and of our class system in particular, we cannot adequately apprehend our present social life nor can we resolve various issues and problems.

SOCIAL DIFFERENTIATION
AND SOCIAL STRATIFICATION

The nature of social differentiation

Ever since men began to meditate and speculate about the nature of human society thousands of years ago, their attention has been drawn to the manifold differences that can readily be observed among human beings in every society. Some of these differences are biological variations like sex, age, size, mental capacity, and other traits inherent in the human organism. In addition to these inherited differences, the members of every society are further differentiated by many acquired social distinctions. Everywhere individuals differ from one another in occupation and possessions, in prestige and authority, in habits, interests, and cultural accomplishments, in tastes, attitudes, values, beliefs, and other acquired traits. All human societies take note of these individual differences. They necessarily become the bases of different social positions and of different functions in the organization of group activities and the patterns of daily living. This division of distinctive social roles and functions, based upon both inherited and acquired individual differences, is called *social differentiation*.

Social differentiation is a universal characteristic of human societies because it is essential for their maintenance and survival. Some division of functions, some mode of specializing and dividing labor, is necessary in all societies, human or animal. But in the nonhuman world this matter is determined by heredity: the division of labor is accomplished by physiological specialization of individual organisms who react in a fixed, instinctive manner to stimuli provided by other organisms of the same species. Thus the whole intricate structure and detailed functional specialization of such insect societies as those of bees and ants are essentially a consequence of physiological differentiation. This does not hold true on the human level, however, where patterns of social behavior are determined not by heredity but by culture. In human societies the coordination of individual efforts necessary for the preservation of the group is achieved through cultural specialization. The division of labor must be accomplished by cultural means: individual members of the society must be induced to fill the requisite positions and to acquire the skills necessary to perform the corresponding duties. Thus without social differentiation no human society could survive.

The process of ranking

One of the main ways in which human societies distribute their members in the available social positions and induce them to perform the duties of these positions is to give them differential evaluations—positions are *ranked* in importance. The incumbents of different positions are accorded differential rank and receive differential rewards and privileges. Individuals who fill positions of great importance and who perform functions which require exceptional skills and abilities generally enjoy more prestige and deference than those who perform humdrum tasks.

The process of invidious evaluation is thus a necessary characteristic of social differentiation, being inherent in the nature of human social organization itself. If a human society is to function effectively in the pursuit of its daily tasks it is necessary that the qualities, attributes, and characteristics of its members, as well as their behavior and achievements, be judged and evaluated. Since social behavior cannot be random and haphazard but must be purposeful and oriented toward the achievement of definite goals it makes a difference what people are and what they do. We therefore find that every human society, even the most equalitarian and democratic, makes invidious judgments of the characteristics and behavior of its members and treats them accordingly. Differential evaluations are attached to most social differences: males are everywhere treated differently than females, the behavior of the married is judged differently from that of the unmarried, the learned always occupy a different position in society than the ignorant, and so on.

**Stratification as a special type
of social differentiation**

While all social differences contain an invidious element and ranking is universal we find that most, though not all, human societies elaborate the process of ranking further by arranging certain social positions in a graded hierarchy of socially superior or inferior ranks. Whenever a society in this manner displays a *graded series of ranks*, we say that it is stratified. Social stratification is a special type of social differentiation, signifying the existence of a systematic hierarchy of social positions whose occupants are treated as superior, equal, or inferior relative to one another in socially important respects. Social *strata* are collectivities of people who occupy positions of the same or similar rank.

It should be clearly understood, however, that not all social positions form part of a graded series of ranks. All Catholics do not form a social stratum, nor do all grandfathers, all Republicans, or all motorists, but we do consider all aristocrats or all manual laborers as forming social strata because these positions are part of a hierarchical gradation and command differentially graded rewards and privileges.

Prerequisites of stratification

Hierarchical ranking then is but one way in which individuals may be socially differentiated; it does not occur in all human societies. This poses two important questions: first, why do certain positions rather than others become stratified; and second, under what conditions does social stratification arise? The answers to these questions are by no means entirely clear, but there seem to be several factors involved, all of which concern the relationship between social stratification and other elements of social organization.

As has been pointed out by several scholars,[2] one of the differences between stratified and unstratified positions hinges upon the role which the family plays in the social ranking system. In order to fulfill its important functions properly, the family must be a well-integrated, intimate group. It not only procreates and rears children but also places them in the social order. At birth every child acquires the position of his family in the existing rank hierarchy. This placement function could not take place if the family did not form a unit with respect to the rank order, its members sharing the same rank and being treated as social equals. To be sure, sex, age, and kinship differences within the family involve an invidious element—the head of the household has higher prestige than his dependents, and deference is due to elders on the part of children—but these invidious evaluations must not overly interfere with the proper functioning of the family unit. Therefore those positions which are combined in the same family cannot be made the basis of stratification; husbands and wives, parents and children, brothers and sisters must belong to the same social stratum.

While age, sex, and kinship positions are nonstratified, those positions which give access to power over others than members of one's own family tend to become the main bases of stratification. By *power* we understand the ability to control the behavior of others. It is inherent in the nature of all organized human activity that some individuals are in a position to control the behavior of others. No human

---

[2] *Cf.* T. H. Marshall, *Citizenship and Social Class*, Cambridge, Mass.: Cambridge University Press, 1950, pp. 96–97; and Kingsley Davis, *Human Society*, New York: Crowell-Collier and Macmillan, 1949, pp. 364–365.

groups can function effectively unless some individuals perform the functions of coordinating and integrating the efforts of its members, thereby assuming the responsibilities of leadership, guidance, and control. The means by which guidance and control are exercised vary greatly, ranging from subtle influence and suggestion to the use of overt force and compulsion. But the exercise of power in whatever form always commands prestige and reflects the existence of superiority-inferiority relationships.

However, the social positions which give access to power can actually become bases of stratification only if power can be institutionalized and made *permanent*. This is an important prerequisite. The possession of physical prowess, for example, or of the wisdom of old age may entail power and command respect, but such powers and the resulting prestige are necessarily transitory and impermanent and cannot be converted into enduring rank. Permanence is an important characteristic of social stratification. Rank hierarchies, like everything human, are changeable, but they tend to be relatively stable and enduring. Only those positions, therefore, which permit the exercise of power based on durable criteria, such as the possession of valuable material goods or the control of nonmaterial values like magic formulas or religious symbols, can become the bases of permanent social strata.

In turn, the existence of social positions which permit the exercise of permanent power and therefore the development of relatively stable rank hierarchies depends upon two factors: the numerical size of the group and the complexity of its economic organization. In very small primitive tribes who live at a marginal level of subsistence the social organization often rests almost entirely on age, sex, and kinship divisions. They are so small numerically and their culture is so simple that no graded hierarchies of rank appear. There are differences in prestige and social influence, but these distinctions depend upon age, sex, and personal attributes, the exercise of power being casual in nature.[3]

The absence of social stratification among the smallest human societies has been admired by travelers who sometimes reported such cases to be a close approximation to a utopian state of perfect social equality. One must beware, however, of facile misinterpretations. The absence of social strata among the simplest tribes does not reflect the realization of any philosophical ideals of equality but simply the inability of any individual or group to convert personal prestige into permanent social superiority. As Hobhouse put it long ago, "the savage enjoys freedom and equality, not because he has realized the value of these conceptions,

---

[3] *Cf.* Gunnar Landtman, *The Origin of the Inequality of Social Classes*, Chicago: University of Chicago Press, 1938, Chap. 1; and Melville J. Herskovits, *Economic Anthropology*, New York: Alfred A. Knopf, Inc., 1952, Chap. 18. It should be noted that the actual number of unstratified tribes is quite limited. Of the several hundred nonliterate societies discussed by these authors hardly a score are characterized by the complete absence of graded rank hierarchies. All the others exhibit definite evidence either of incipient or of well-developed systems of stratification.

but because neither he nor his fellow is strong enough to put himself above his neighbor."[4]

In addition to sheer size, the institutionalization of power and the establishment of permanent rank hierarchies depends upon the production of an *economic surplus*. By economic surplus we understand the production of goods in a quantity more than sufficient to assure the continuous physical existence of all members of the group. So long as a society remains close to the bare level of subsistence, no individual can control much more than an equal share of its material wealth. The productive resources are the property of all members of the group. But as soon as technological skills become sufficiently advanced to produce more than a subsistence minimum, the economic surplus tends to be allocated unequally: it is claimed by individuals of outstanding abilities in hunting, fishing, or warfare, as well as by those who perform special services with respect to the supernatural. The respect and prestige that special abilities and unusual exploits command among humans provide the necessary social recognition of the claims advanced by specific individuals and groups to a larger share of the economic surplus. This permits the accumulation of individual fortunes and results in the unequal distribution of wealth.

Since wealth is durable and property transmissible, they provide a convenient basis for the institutionalization of personal prestige. The control of wealth makes it possible to perpetuate power and to transform individual differences in prestige and influence into hereditary hierarchies of rank. Consequently, as soon as substantial numerical size and an economic surplus have been attained, rudimentary equality tends to give way to unmistakable social stratification.[5]

**Major types of stratification systems:
caste, estate, class**

Although all societies which have progressed beyond the barest level of subsistence are stratified, concrete forms of rank hierarchy vary greatly from society to society. Cultural variations stimulate different forms of stratification so that ranking systems differ markedly from time to time and from one society to another. In concrete fact then there are as many different forms of stratification as there are human societies.

Despite the manifold variations, there appear to be three general types of stratification: systems of caste, estate, and class. Before depicting each of these types, it should be stressed that they are "pure," that is abstract, types. Concrete systems

---

[4]L. T. Hobhouse, *Morals in Evolution*, New York: Holt, Rinehart and Winston, Vol. 1, 1906, p. 284.

[5]For an excellent recent treatment of interconnections between economic and noneconomic phenomena, see Willard E. Moore, *Economy and Society*, Doubleday Short Studies in Sociology, New York: Doubleday & Company, 1955.

of stratification never occur in "pure" form, merely approximating a given type. Moreover, some systems often represent a mixture of these types.

In a caste system the social strata consist of closed social groups, arranged in a fixed order of superiority and inferiority. An individual is born into a particular caste and must stay there for life. He acquires his social position with its accompanying rights and obligations from his parents and cannot change his rank through personal qualities or achievements. There being no provision for individual social mobility, the individual cannot rise or fall in the caste system, not even through intermarriage for the castes are endogamous. A caste system represents the most rigid type of social stratification. In its fully developed form it has been approximated only in India . . ., but castelike or quasicaste systems have occurred in various societies whenever one or more social strata have tended to evolve into closed, endogamous groups.

The second type of stratification system, that of *estates*, typically occurs in feudal societies where social organization revolves around a specific form of land tenure—land is held on condition of military service and a man's social position depends on his relationship to the land. An estate system consists of a hierarchy of several social strata which are clearly distinguished and rigidly set off from one another by law and custom. Characteristically, estate systems manifest the following general hierarchical arrangements: At the top stands a royal family and a landholding, hereditary military aristocracy, closely followed by an allied priesthood, ranking on a par with the secular nobility. Below them are merchants and craftsmen, while free peasants and unfree serfs form the broad bottom strata. Each estate has clearly defined rights and duties, and social position is usually inherited. However, individuals may legally change their estates under certain circumstances. Thus the king may confer a title of nobility on a commoner, or the daughter of a wealthy merchant may marry into the aristocracy. To be sure, marriages between persons of different estate are rare, but they are not absolutely prohibited as in a caste system. Again, a serf may be freed by his master, or an exceptionally bright peasant lad may advance his rank by entering the priesthood or the military service, both of which function as channels of upward mobility. Estates, then, are less rigid than castes, but since this form of stratification is based upon a stable agricultural economy, estate systems tend to be static and fixed. Hereditary transmission of social position is the rule and social mobility, though possible within the legal definitions of a given system, is difficult and limited. . . .

Finally, in a *class* system, the social hierarchy is based primarily upon differences in monetary wealth and income. Social classes are not sharply marked off from each other nor are they demarcated by tangible boundaries. Unlike estates they have no legal standing, individuals of all classes being in principle equal before the law. Consequently there are no legal restraints on the movement of individuals and families from one class to another. The same is true of intermarriage which, while it may be frowned upon and informally discouraged, is not prevented by law or insuperable social pressures. Unlike castes, social classes are not organized, closed social groups. Rather they are aggregates of persons with similar amounts of wealth and property and similar sources of income.

The differences in wealth and income are expressed in different ways of life: patterns of consumption, types of education, speech, manners, dress, tastes, and other cultural attributes. In turn these differences give rise to the formation of *status groups, informal social groups* whose members view each other as equals because they share common understandings, as expressed in similar attitudes and similar modes of behavior, and who treat or regard outsiders as social superiors or inferiors. Thus in a class society there develops a hierarchy of status groups which is interrelated but not identical with the hierarchy of classes. The reciprocal and changing relationships between classes and status groups result in a highly complex stratification structure. . . .

. . .[A]s a general type class systems are less rigid than estate or caste systems. The different classes, and to a lesser extent the status groups, are highly permeable. There is a considerable amount of movement up and down the class and status hierarchies. Although the individual acquires his initial position by birth, this ascription does not necessarily determine his later social rank, which can be changed through the acquisition or loss of wealth and other attainments. As a result, class societies are apt to be highly competitive and fluid, since individuals and families may compete for wealth and social position on the basis of personal qualities and achievements as well as through inheritance. . . .

DIMENSIONS OF SOCIAL STRATIFICATION IN MODERN SOCIETY

. . . .In preceding stratification systems, despite their many concrete differences, the various social strata were set off from each other by clear-cut lines of demarcation. Members of different strata were distinguished not only by differences in income, wealth, and occupation, but also by distinct styles of life. Each stratum was characterized by patterns of conduct and behavior standards which gave clear recognition to its place in the social hierarchy. Differing sharply in rank, honor, prestige, and political power, the various strata were also separated by severe limits on intermarriage and social intercourse, by a sharp sense of social distance, and by outward symbols of their distinctive ways of life. At the same time, the prevailing ideologies and religious creeds explained and justified the existing hierarchical arrangements. There was thus no difficulty either in recognizing a given individual's social position or in perceiving the system as a whole. . . .

. . .Modern class systems are not characterized by such a close and visible correlation between economic inequality and differences in authority, power, and prestige. In the highly complex and more loosely integrated industrial society, the prestige, authority, and power of the individual is not necessarily matched by his economic position. This is to say that the interrelationship between economic inequality and the differential distribution of power and prestige is considerably more complicated in modern class systems than it was, for example, in the feudal estate hierarchy.

Of fundamental sociological importance are the several *different dimensions* in modern systems of stratification. Each of these dimensions constitutes a separate rank order with respect to specific opportunities by which certain values and advantages may be obtained, though these different rank orders are interrelated. Together they account for the wide range of opportunities in modern societies.[6]

Class, life chances, and class consciousness

First, the *economic* dimension stratifies modern populations according to the amount and source of income, which is usually derived from a set of occupational activities, the ownership of property, or both. Differences in income, property, and occupation divide the members of modern societies into several strata or *classes*. Classes are thus aggregates of individuals and families in similar economic positions. Individuals of the same or similar economic position have identical or similar goods and services to offer in the system of production and distribution and therefore receive identical or similar monetary rewards in the market place. This also means that in modern industrial societies members of the same economic class have similar chances to obtain certain values and opportunities which are of primary importance for life and survival. "Everything from the chance to stay alive during the first year after birth to the chance to view fine arts, the chance to remain healthy and grow tall, and if sick to get well again quickly, the chance to avoid becoming a juvenile delinquent—and very crucially, the chance to complete an intermediary or higher educational grade"[7]—all these *life-chances* are crucially influenced by one's position in the economic class structure.

Note, however, that these classes are neither communities nor organized groups but simply aggregates of people possessing similar economic interests. The members of a class may or may not be aware of the likeness of their economic interests and life chances. And even if such awareness does exist, it may influence their behavior in quite different ways. One consequence of the recognition of a shared class situation is class solidarity and *class consciousness*. In this case the

---

[6] The exposition presented in the next paragraphs is based essentially on an essay by the German sociologist Max Weber, translated by H. H. Gerth and C. Wright Mills: from Max Weber, *Essays in Sociology*, New York: Oxford University Press, 1946, pp. 180–195. For some more recent elaborations of Weber's theory see Milton M. Gordon, "A System of Social Class Analysis," *The Drew University Bulletin*, 39, August 1951; Seymour M. Lipset and Reinhard Bendix, "Social Status and Social Structure: A Re-examination of Data and Interpretations," *British Journal of Sociology*, 2, June and September 1951, pp. 50–68, 230–254; Hans Gerth and C. Wright Mills, *Character and Social Structure*, New York: Harcourt, Brace & World, 1953, Chap. 11; and Kurt Mayer, "The Theory of Social Classes," *Harvard Educational Review*, 23, Summer 1953, pp. 149–167, from which many of the above formulations are taken.

[7] Gerth and Mills, p. 313.

members of a given class come to identify like (individualized) interests as common (shared) interests and, perhaps, to organize in such associations as labor unions and political parties designed in part to pursue these interests, which in turn, may lead to open conflict and struggle with people in other class situations. But this development does not necessarily take place. Class awareness and class consciousness may lead only to diffuse reactions. For example, industrial workers over the world may tend to restrict their production by virtue of a more or less tacit agreement, but whether or not they band together and engage in economic and political class action and class warfare depends on a number of circumstances, primarily, perhaps, on whether they consciously recognize the causal connections between their life chances and the structure of the economic order which determines them. Concerted action also depends on the availability of an articulate leadership and the physical possibilities of organizing and acting in unison. Often one or all of these factors are lacking, and there may be many additional reasons which prevent the rise of class consciousness and class action despite the factual existence of sharp class differentials in the distribution of income and property.

Whether or not class consciousness and class action arise from a given class situation is always a matter to be determined by study of concrete cases. . . .

Status and status groups

A second dimension of stratification in modern societies is the status order. The term *status* as used in this study refers to the *differentiation of prestige and deference* among individuals and groups in a society.

Now prestige rests upon interpersonal recognition, always involving at least one individual who claims deference and another who honors the claim. A person's claim to prestige and his position in the prestige hierarchy generally depend upon the way in which his behavior is evaluated by the members of his own community. Therefore, prestige hierarchies are usually of a local character. Individuals who occupy a similar position in the status hierarchy of a local community tend to form *status groups*; that is, they treat each other as social equals, encouraging the intermarriage of their children, joining the same clubs and associations, and participating together in such informal activities as visiting, dances, dinners, and receptions. However, some status hierarchies may also be nationwide or even international, involving, for example, a person's status as a statesman, a film actor, a sports hero, or a scientist. In fact, there are as many status hierarchies as there are distinguishable patterns of interpersonal relations.[8]

Of paramount sociological importance is the realization that in modern societies the economic order and the status order are closely related but not identical; classes and status groups must be carefully distinguished. However, although the two dimensions are distinct, the status order to a high degree is conditioned by the class structure, and in its turn reacts upon it. The reason for this lies in the fact

---

[8] *Cf.* Lipset and Bendix, p. 249.

that since economic factors necessarily play a primary role in industrial societies, people maintain intimate social relations largely with others in similar economic positions. Social intercourse, intermarriage, and participation in clubs and other organizations tend to be restricted to others in one's own economic bracket. Therefore a close correspondence is often found between class position and rank in the status hierarchy, wealthy people generally possessing high prestige. But no exact correspondence and, in fact, frequent discrepancies exist between an individual's class position and his standing in the prestige hierarchy. Such discrepancies cannot be explained in static terms but should be understood dynamically as the result of an individual's mobility along only some of the stratification dimensions or of an established social distinction between the class and status hierarchies as a whole.

A status group is characterized by specific behavior patterns, a definite "style of life," which must be adhered to by those who wish to belong to it. Linked with this expectation are tendencies toward closure, as manifested in restrictions on intermarriage and social participation of those who "don't act right" and therefore do not belong. When restrictions of this kind result in complete group endogamy and full closure, status groups take on castelike features. But in modern societies this development is confined for the most part to differences which are defined as "ethnic" or "racial."

In general, the effect of status hierarchies seems to be the stabilization of the existing class structure, their function in this instance being the legitimation of class positions. Thus groups which have attained high economic positions usually attempt to solidify these positions by restricting status recognition and excluding others from access to the status symbols which they try to monopolize.[9] The result is that while high status is dependent in the long run upon high class position—the maintenance of a prestigeful style of life costs money—there is no necessary correspondence between them at any given time. A fishmonger, for example, who has acquired wealth through skillful operations in the impersonal market, may not be accepted as a social equal without reservations by the "bluebloods" of Boston's Beacon Hill or Philadelphia's Main Line, however faithfully he imitates their style of life. But they may accept his descendants who have been educated in the conventions of their status groups and who have not dirtied their own hands by manual labor. And the reverse also holds: impoverished descendants of old Southern plantation families, for instance, may retain their high status reputation for several generations after their wealth has been lost and receive more deference from more people than well-to-do newcomers who lack the appropriate grandparents. In the long run, however, the style of life required by high status necessarily depends upon commensurate class position, and in the course of time, the broken-down aristocrat becomes simply broken-down and the son of the nouveau riche fishmonger becomes a man of "clean, old wealth."[10]

---

[9]Lipset and Bendix, pp. 249–250.

[10]Gerth and Mills, p. 317.

The interrelations between the dimensions of class and status are thus dynamic reciprocal, and in constant flux. Status groups tend to grow strong and to hinder and retard the operation of sheer economic forces when economic conditions are relatively stable. By the same token, significant economic changes tend to weaken status restrictions and may even break down existing prestige distinctions altogether. An illuminating example of the operation of cross pressures between class and status systems in American society can be seen in the use of restrictive covenants by which established prestigeful groups sometimes attempt to keep out "undesirable elements" who have risen in the class structure to the point where they can afford to purchase high status symbols in the form of property in the best residential areas. Here class mobility is defined as a threat to the privileged position and stability of the high status groups, who wield the restrictive covenant as a defensive weapon. And where dominant groups are successful in keeping out the "nouveaux riches," these newcomers often form parallel status hierarchies, developing their own exclusive residential sections and organizing their own Junior Leagues, country clubs, and resorts.

Power

A third dimension of social stratification is the *power structure*. We have defined power as the ability to control the behavior of others. Sociologically power refers especially to the control which certain groups and individuals are able to exercise over the life chances of others.

The unequal distribution of power in modern society is linked with both the class and the status hierarchies, the connection between economic position and the ability to exercise power being especially close. Entrepreneurial and property-owning upper classes obviously hold great power over job markets, their investment decisions and market operations affecting the life chances of large numbers of others. But in urban-industrial societies such immense power rarely goes unchallenged. The propertyless wage earners may organize labor unions and farmers may band together in associations in an effort to offset the industrialists power by the exercise of countervailing power.[11]

In the ensuing maneuvering and struggle different classes and interest groups often seek to transform economic power into political power in order to influence or determine the policies or activities of the state. This is accomplished directly through political parties, which may represent the interest of a specific class, a typical situation in many European countries, or more indirectly through the activities of organized pressure groups and lobbies, a common device in the United States. It should be noted, however, that ability to wield economic and political

---

[11]For an analysis of the concept of countervailing power see John K. Galbraith, *American Capitalism*, Boston: Houghton Mifflin Co., 1952.

power is not identical with its actual exercise. Whether or not a given class or interest group transforms its potential power into actual power depends upon a number of factors, including the objective conditions and opportunities, the will and purpose, and finally the skill and judgment of its leaders.[12]

A close connection also exists between power and prestige. Generally the very fact that individuals or groups hold positions in which they can make important decisions that affect the lives of others brings the power-holders a good deal of prestige. This obviously applies to those who hold key economic positions, but prestige is not confined to the economically powerful. A large amount of power today is also exercised by those who head other large-scale hierarchical organizations, such as the government, the armed forces, labor unions, and the church. These are organizations of varying prestige in modern society. A successful military or political career often bestows both power and prestige upon an individual which he can then "cash in" and use to acquire high economic position if he so desires. Thus retired generals and heads of government agencies, though not labor leaders as a rule, may find open doors to the very top levels of the corporate business hierarchy.

Again, the relationship between the distribution of power, class structure, and status hierarchy is highly dynamic. In stable periods most people occupy quite similar positions in all three hierarchies, and the three dimensions overlap closely. But when social change is rapid because of technological or economic shifts or war, this correlation is disturbed and numerous discrepancies occur. A whole class may rise at the expense of another, established status groups may be challenged by new groups who have suddenly acquired wealth and power, and many individuals may find that they have moved along the different dimensions of stratification at unequal rates of speed.

Social mobility

This brings us, finally, to another concept of fundamental importance in the analysis of modern social stratification, *social mobility*. Social mobility refers to the possibility of individuals moving up and down the class, status, and power hierarchies.

. . .[T]he frequency and extent to which individuals move between social strata is one of the crucial criteria used to distinguish the major types of stratification systems: caste, estate, and class. To be sure, some mobility up and down the social ladder exists in every society, including India where, notwithstanding the rigid caste system, whole castes and subcastes, as well as some individuals, rise and fall in the rank hierarchy. As we have seen, social mobility also exists in estate systems, but there it is rigidly circumscribed and limited and usually involves a

---

[12]*Cf.* Gerth and Mills, pp. 328–330; and Lipset and Bendix, pp. 249–254.

change in legal status. Only in modern class systems where formal and legal barriers are absent and where equality of opportunity is an officially acknowledged ideal, is social mobility viewed as commonplace and normal. According to democratic ideology a person's social position should depend solely upon his own qualities and achievements and he should be free to rise above or fall below his parents' class and status groups in accordance with his personal capacities. Correspondingly, social classes should consist merely of temporary aggregates of individuals who happen to have achieved similar social positions at any particular time. In reality, of course, modern class systems deviate considerably from these ideals. The extent to which it is actually possible for individuals to move between classes and status groups is a matter of empirical study in each concrete case. . . .

7.2   INTRODUCTION

The excerpt that follows surveys the existing evidence on the relationship between social class on the one hand and various areas of behavior and experience on the other, underlining the extent to which the former limits and shapes virtually every aspect of the latter. The authors locate the core of this effect in the family and then detail the manner in which the most fundamental elements of life—food clothing, shelter—as well as those more obviously linked to the social environment—values, attitudes, beliefs—are differentiated by the family's social class status.

In addition to the empirical information it conveys, this selection effectively translates "social class" from a static category into a meaningful aspect of psychological as well as social and cultural experience. In the light of the evidence reviewed here, it is clear that the individual's very concept of himself, the way he structures every experience, what he wants and expects from himself and others how he interprets others' behavior—all these processes which we tend to think of as personally unique are, instead, systematically differentiated by the individual's family's social-class standing. Previous chapters have already emphasized the fact that what an individual "is" is very specific to the cultural context in which he lives and develops. This selection goes further, showing that the particular cultural context which is relevant to each individual is one small portion of that encompassed by the entire society, and that its content and boundaries are largely defined in terms of social class.

The necessity for emphasizing the pervasive effect of social class is especially great in American society. Our awareness of this effect tends to be dimmed and even negated by our democratic values and by the belief which commonly follows from them, that social class does not exist in America—or at least that it certainly is not important. Thus it does not come easily to us to interpret another person's behavior partly in terms of his social class or to explain differences between ourselves and others in terms of the different learnings that our different social class environments have produced. As the Indian students, reported on by Lambert and Bressler (Selection 5.3), did with respect to Americans, so are we likely to do with respect to those from another social class, namely, to view their behavior in terms of our own culture, interpreting and evaluating it in terms of our own premises. The cultural gaps between classes are not necessarily any smaller than those between nationalities, but they are less likely to be recognized because we tend to think that they should not exist.

The guidance worker's role is likely to put him in a position quite frequently of interacting across the cultural gap that separates different classes. Given all the combinations of religion, ethnic origin, income, occupation, etc., that occur in American society, he is likely to deal with the products of a variety of other backgrounds, so that the problem will arise whatever his own standing on the social-class scale. At the same time, the objectives of his role make the possible consequences of such cultural gaps particularly serious. The attitudes and intentions attributed to him by those he tries to help will crucially affect the success of his efforts, and the content of these attributions will depend on the class-determined learnings about people that these individuals bring with them. Conversely, the interpretation that the guidance worker places on their behavior—the kinds of reasons he posits to explain their problems, their reactions, their statements—will be the basis of his professional efforts, but, unless it is deliberately disciplined, this interpretation will reflect the guidance worker's own social class learnings. It may thus be as inappropriate to the individuals concerned as their views of him are to him.

No single essay can take note of all the aspects to which social class is relevant nor can it even begin to suggest the full subtlety and complexity of its effects. What the ensuing selection should accomplish, however, is to impress the reader with the importance and pervasiveness of these effects and to sensitize him to the need for making social class a major dimension of the context in terms of which he views other individuals.

7.2   SOCIAL CLASS DIFFERENCES [1]

Robert J. Havighurst and Bernice L. Neugarten

. . .[T]he family acts to teach the child the culture and subculture to which he belongs. In the gross sense, a child born into an American family learns the American culture. He learns to speak English rather than Spanish; to eat with a fork

---

[1]Robert J. Havighurst and Bernice L. Neugarten, "Social Class Differences," *Society and Education*, Boston: Allyn and Bacon, 1962, pp. 103–111, 138–141, 558–559, 562–575, 578–579.

rather than with chopsticks; to dress in a suit rather than a bearskin; to cry when he is sad rather than to smile. He learns how to talk, walk, and think in ways that are distinctively American. He learns not only the overt behaviors; he learns also the social, moral, and economic values of the culture: how children relate to adults, and how men relate to women; how to curb his aggressiveness and yet to cultivate his competitiveness; how to develop loyalties and how to seek for self-achievement. The overall expectancies and way of life of the culture are transmitted to the child through the family; any child raised in an American family emerges as an American.

The family also teaches the child its own variation of the culture, . . .which we [refer to]. . .as the subculture. Thus a child born into a farm family learns to behave in somewhat different ways from the child born into a city family; the child born into a Catholic family learns a somewhat different set of values from the child born into a Protestant family; the child born into a Japanese-American family learns something different from the child born into a Mexican-American family; and the child born into an upper-class family learns a different way of life from the child born into a lower-class family. Ethnic, religious, racial, and social groups maintain their differences through time to the extent to which they provide their offspring with different and distinctive patterns of thought and action.

SOCIAL CLASS DIFFERENCES IN FAMILY LIFE

We have indicated that different social classes in America have somewhat different ways of life: different behavior, values, attitudes, different goals and expectations. Nowhere are social class differences so clearly seen as within the family setting. The family, furthermore, as compared with other social institutions, is most intimately bound up with the social structure. Not only are class differences clearly reflected in family patterns, but the family reinforces and modifies the social-class structure in a direct way. This is true because any given family trains its offspring in its own way of life. While there is much social mobility from one class to another, middle-class families, by and large, train their children in middle-class ways and these children grow up to be adults who lead middle-class lives. Lower-class families train their children in lower-class ways and these children in turn grow up to lead lower-class lives. Thus our social-class system produces wide variations in family life, and these, in turn, maintain the social-class system.

While the differences in family life between various social classes are many, we shall illustrate only a few. It should not be assumed, from the descriptions to follow, that all families at a given social-class level are alike. There is not only a great range of difference from individual family to individual family; there are also group differences within social classes related to ethnic, religious, geographic factors; and, as will be described below, differences related to entrepreneurial or bureaucratic orientations.

The physical setting

The physical setting varies enormously from class to class. One has only to consider the housing typical for lower-class families in a slum area of New York or Chicago, as compared with that of a middle-class family living in a house in a suburban community. Lower-class children in urban areas grow up in living quarters that are not only aesthetically unattractive and unhygienic, but also provide little privacy for the child by day or by night. There is little play space indoors or outdoors. Not only is a single family crowded into a few rooms, but many families are crowded together, allowing little in the way of family privacy or insularity against neighbors.

The basic necessities

Family life differs also from one social class to another as regards the basic necessities of life: food, shelter, heat, light, and clothing. Davis has pointed out:

> One of the most basic differences in motivation between lower-class and middle-class people is their attitude toward eating. Owing to the greater security of their food supply, middle-class people eat more regularly. They therefore have learned to eat more sparingly at any given time, because they know they are certain of their next meal. They have also developed a conscientious taboo upon "overeating"; they feel some guilt about getting fat and about what they call "raiding the icebox."
>
> Slum people, however, have a very uncertain food supply. Their fear that they will not get enough to eat develops soon after the nursing period. Therefore, when the supply is plentiful, they eat as much as they can hold. They "pack food away" in themselves as a protection against the shortage which will develop before the next payday. They wish to get fat as a protection against tuberculosis and physical weakness. Basically, the origin of this attitude toward eating is their deep fear of starvation.
>
> Just as food-anxiety is far more urgent in lower-class than it is in middle-class society, so is the anxiety which is aroused by the danger of eviction from shelter, the danger of having too little sleep, the danger of being cold, and the danger of being in the dark. The middle-class individual is relatively certain that he will have enough coal or light; he buys his coal by the ton or the five tons; he burns five or ten electric lights. But the lower-class person's hold upon fire for heating is on a day-to-day or week-to-week basis. He buys coal by the bushel, or by the five bushels, or by one ton loads. Every week or so, therefore, he has to face the fear of being cold, and of having his children cold (Davis, 1948, pp. 24–26).

While the above description may seem somewhat overstated, since there are very few persons in America today, even at the lowest socioeconomic levels, who lack the basic necessities of life, still it serves to dramatize the point under discussion. . . .

Family relationships

Family relationships also vary at different social levels. There is, generally speaking, less family stability in lower-class groups than in those of the middle or upper class. While divorce rates are high at all levels, they are highest among lower socioeconomic groups; desertion and illegitimacy are more frequent; broken homes are more common; and relationships between adults are often more transitory.

To take another example, attitudes toward children are different in one social class than in another. One author (Bossard, 1954, pp. 330 ff.), in discussing these differences, points out that the attitude of upper-class families toward the child is one of pride and hope; the child is expected to carry on the family name, and there is a good deal of pressure to behave in ways that the extended family will approve. "What would your Grandmother Elson say?" The typical upper-status family strives to produce the best possible care for the child—physical, social, and intellectual—and to be constantly selective about the child's activities and about his associates.

In lower-class families, children may be considered "a sort of inevitable price that fate exacts in payment for sex relations"; children are less often planned for, and after a certain point, the appearance of each additional child may become something of an economic crisis.

There is no evidence, however, that lower-class families love their children less than do higher-status families; nor that they are less concerned about the child's welfare. Yet, while the lower-class family may strive to do its best for the child, it is usually less able, for economic and social reasons, to provide good physical, social, and intellectual conditions. There is less leisure time and less knowledge available for careful rearing; and, with mothers working outside the home, there is likely to be less supervision given to the child's activities and associates.

Regard for authority

To illustrate further, we know that there is variation in the ways children are taught to regard authority. It has been pointed out (Kluckhohn and Kluckhohn, 1947) that lower-class children are taught to fear authority; middle-class children, to respect it.

Discipline

Social-class differences also exist in ways of handling aggressive impulses. The slum child and adolescent learn to be good fighters and to express aggression directly and by physical means. The middle-class child learns that fighting is forbidden and he is encouraged to turn aggressive impulses into more acceptable forms of initiative or competitiveness. Davis and Dollard, in their studies of Negro families in Natchez and New Orleans, say:

In their efforts to teach, lower-class Negro parents punish their children with great energy and frequency and reward them seldom. . . .

A lower-class boy in Natchez, fifteen years old, tells the interviewer that he has failed the fifth grade twice. "Everytime I gits home from school, my papa say I ain't goin' to be nothin' nohow, but he whips me jes' the same." . . .

The source of discipline in a lower-class family changes frequently from mother to father, to aunt, to grandmother, to uncle or to an older child. But whoever the disciplinarian at any given moment may be, he is certain to believe that the way to make a child learn is to beat him. Locking the child in the house or withdrawing his play privileges may be used, but whippings are inevitable no matter what other forms of punishment the child may have to suffer. A lower-class mother in New Orleans says of her son of thirteen, "He went out when I told him not to. I tried to choke his neck off when I got him." Equally typical was the woman who said of her son, "I can't understand why he is so bad. I licks him all the time" (Davis and Dollard, 1940, pp. 267–68).

Not only are lower-class children, white as well as Negro, disciplined through physical punishment, but they are taught to use physical aggression themselves. Here is the comment of a white mother who was called in by a teacher to discuss her boy's behavior difficulties:

Of course, he's a fighter. He'd better be. His dad and all of us would be ashamed of him otherwise. Be better and faster than the next fellow, is what we tell him. Why even my little girl, Ruthie—she's learning to hit and hit hard. A girl has to learn to take care of herself, too, and she'd better learn while she's young.

In a middle-class family, parents tell their children it's wrong to fight—"If anybody hits you, come and tell *me*, but don't be a rowdy."

The differences in the types of punishment used by parents in different social classes and the types of behavior which they punish are reflections of actual differences in values between these two groups. Kohn (1959, I, II), in a study of the values and use of authority by lower- and middle-class parents in Washington, D.C., found that lower-class mothers used physical punishment in an attempt to change behavior which they did not consider respectable and thus to fit their children to the mold of respectability. Middle-class mothers, on the other hand, placing the highest value on internal standards and controls, used a calculated holding-out and withdrawal of affection to create the pressures needed to change the child's behavior. In deciding whether or not to punish a child's misbehavior, middle-class parents tend to consider the child's motives and feelings; while working-class parents focus on the act itself. The middle-class child is likely to be punished for loss of self-control; the working-class child, for disobeying the parent.

CHILD-REARING PRACTICES We have said that, from an overall point of view, the family teaches the child the culture and the subculture to which he belongs. In the learning and teaching that go on within the family, a whole variety of processes of social learning are at work. . . .There is formal and informal teaching; there is the use of rewards and punishments, there is didactic teaching, there is imitation and identification. One way in which the family teaches the child the particular set of behaviors, values, and attitudes that are its own—one way the child becomes socialized—is through the child-training practices that parents use.

For example, Davis and Havighurst (1946) studied the ways in which lower-class and middle-class families in Chicago trained their children in respect to feeding and weaning, toilet-training, sexual modesty, and the control of impulse life in such areas as cleanliness, care of property, and respect for authority. They found that lower-class mothers breast-fed their babies more often than middle-class; they weaned their babies later; they started toilet-training later; they allowed the child greater indulgence of impulse life, such as allowing the child to stop taking naps at an earlier age and to begin to go to movies at night at an earlier age. Middle-class mothers set higher achievement goals for their children: the child was expected to dress himself at an early age, to help with household chores such as washing dishes; to do well in school; and to take on various other responsibilities earlier than the lower-class child. These investigators concluded that the middle class is more rigid than the lower class in its child-training, more achievement-minded, more demanding of the child.

A few years later, Maccoby and Gibbs (1954) undertook a similar study, but upon a sample of Boston mothers. While they used a somewhat different interview form, about half the questions were the same as those asked in the Chicago study. There were some agreements between the Chicago and Boston findings (Havighurst and Davis, 1955); but Maccoby and Gibbs found fewer overall differences between social classes than were found in the earlier study; and they concluded, contrary to Davis and Havighurst, that it is the middle class that is more "permissive" in child-rearing.

A number of recent investigators (Littman, Moore, and Pierce-Jones, 1957; White, 1957; Miller and Swanson, 1958) have attempted to resolve the question raised by the Chicago and Harvard studies as to whether or not there has been an actual change over time in middle-class child-rearing practices. These later studies have all had results which in general support the conclusions reached in the Harvard study. Bronfenbrenner (1958), summarizing some 18 major studies carried out over a 25-year period, concludes that there has been a general shift toward greater permissiveness in infant care in the middle class and that, in relation to child training, there have been changes toward greater permissiveness, more tolerance of the child's impulses and desires, and freer expression of affection by the mother. In addition, middle-class mothers were found to have higher expectations for their children, to rely more on punishment techniques which involve the threat of loss of love, and to be more equalitarian than lower-class mothers.

At the same time, while these differences do exist, Bronfenbrenner also reports that over the past 25 years there has been a narrowing of the differences between the social classes.

At least two factors appear to have played causal roles both in narrowing the gap between the classes and in bringing about major changes in middle-class child-rearing practices. The first is the widespread dissemination of "expert" advice on child rearing through the mass media; the second is the change in American value patterns, often described as the shift from an entrepreneurial to a bureaucratic value orientation. . . .

Social-class factors

The peer group also reflects the social structure of the wider society. Social-class differences not only operate in the adult society but operate also in the society of children and adolescents.

The first study of social-class differences in the child's society was made in Jonesville. There Neugarten found that fifth- and sixth-grade children (all of whom were together in the same school), when asked who were their best friends, most often named children above them in social class, then, second, children from their own social class. Few choices were made downward in the social scale, with the result that most lower-class children were chosen only by others of their own social status. Similarly, as regarded reputation, children ascribed favorable personality traits to children of the higher social classes; and unfavorable personality traits to the children from lower social classes. There was a consistent relationship between social class and reputation: as one moved up the social scale, from lower-lower to upper-middle class, children received consistently higher proportions of mentions on favorable characteristics and consistently lower proportions on unfavorable ones.

Among tenth- and eleventh-graders in Jonesville, social-class differences were also clearly operative, but in somewhat more complex ways. Here, where a large proportion of lower-class children had already dropped out of school, adolescents also chose upward or horizontally on the social scale, but seldom downward, in selecting their friends. Adolescents of upper social status, while less uniformly regarded by their classmates in favorable terms, were nevertheless in the limelight so far as social visibility is concerned. Lower-class adolescents were rarely mentioned, either positively or negatively (Neugarten, 1949).

Subsequent studies showed similar findings as regards the influence of social class upon the child's and the adolescent's social groups. Thus, Hollingshead, studying adolescents in Elmtown, found that clique relationships reflected the social-class position of the adolescents' families. Three out of five clique relationships were within single social classes; and only one out of twenty-five crossed more than one social-class line. Dating patterns also followed social-class lines clearly and consistently (Hollingshead, 1949, pp. 212, 231).

Similarly, Stendler, studying the children of Brasstown, found that while young children crossed social-class lines in choosing their school associates, their general tendency was to choose out-of-school friends from within their own social class (Stendler, 1949).

Social class may, in some instances at least, outweigh skin color as a factor that influences children's perceptions of each other. Weddington (1958) carried out a carefully designed study of the ways in which seven-year-olds and ten-year-olds assigned favorable and unfavorable traits. A picture technique was devised in which white and Negro individuals of obviously middle and lower class were presented in pairs, and the child was asked, "Which of these two people is more honest? Smart? Noisy?" and so on. The children assigned traits more in terms of social class than in terms of color. While this study differs from the others just described in that it focuses not on actual friendship choices, but upon what are probably children's stereotypes, nevertheless such stereotyped perceptions probably play a role in the child's interaction patterns.

The extent to which awareness of social-class differences operates in the minds of children and adolescents may be expected to vary not only with age, but with type of community. Sargent, in studying Ventura, a California community of about 18,000 population, found less class consciousness and fewer class distinctions among adults than in cities in other parts of the country. Correspondingly, among fifth- and sixth-grade children, repeating the same approach as was used in Jonesville, he found less of a trend among children to differentiate along social-class lines. Table 1 shows the differences between Jonesville and Ventura children.

TABLE 1   SOCIAL CLASS AND CHILDREN'S REPUTATIONS

IN TWO COMMUNITIES

	Jonesville, Grades 5-6 (all in one school)		Ventura, Grades 5-6 (three schools)	
	percent of children	*percent of votes received on favorable traits*	*percent of children*	*percent of votes received on favorable traits*
Upper-middle	6	19	16	20
Lower-middle	17	27	45	47
Upper-lower	62	50	34	30
Lower-lower	15	4	5	3

Source: Sargent, 1953 (adapted).

The extent to which social-status differences are reflected within peer groups may also be expected to vary with the school setting. In a school that draws children from a relatively narrow range of social classes, class lines within the school group may be minimal. At the same time, the pupils may feel themselves clearly marked off from other groups in the wider community; as in one school in an all upper-middle-class neighborhood, where a first-grader reported to the visitor, "Well, you see, it's going to be Christmas pretty soon, and our school is making presents for poor kids. Every room is making presents, and then they'll all be put in a big truck, and somebody will drive the truck over to where those people are, and then those poor kids can have these things and have some fun."

In a school whose pupils come from a variety of backgrounds, the so-called heterogeneous school, social-class lines within the school group may be relatively clear-cut, as in Jonesville; or relatively blurred, as in many a school where there is an explicit policy of minimizing social-class factors among pupils, and where the policy is successfully implemented. . . .

BIBLIOGRAPHY

BOSSARD, JAMES H. S., 1954, *The Sociology of Child Development*, revised edition, New York: Harper & Row.

BRONFENBRENNER, URIE, 1958, "Socialization and Social Class Through Time and Space," *Readings in Social Psychology*, Eleanor E. Maccoby, ed., New York: Holt, Rinehart, and Winston.

DAVIS, ALLISON, 1948, *Social-Class Influences Upon Learning*, Cambridge, Mass.: Harvard University Press.

DAVIS, ALLISON, AND JOHN DOLLARD, 1940, *Children of Bondage*, Washington, D. C.: American Council on Education.

DAVIS, ALLISON, AND ROBERT J. HAVIGHURST, 1946, "Social Class and Color Differences in Child-Rearing," *American Sociological Review*, XI, pp. 698–710.

HAVIGHURST, ROBERT J., AND ALLISON DAVIS, 1955, "A Comparison of the Chicago and Harvard Studies of Social-Class Differences in Child Rearing," *American Sociological Review*, 20, pp. 438–442.

HOLLINGSHEAD, AUGUST B., 1949, *Elmtown's Youth*, New York: John Wiley & Sons.

KLUCKHOHN, CLYDE, AND FLORENCE R., 1947, "American Culture: Generalized Orientations and Class Patterns," *Conflicts of Power in Modern Culture*, Lyman Bryson, Louis Finkelstein, and R. M. MacIver, eds., New York: Harper & Row.

KOHN, MELVIN L., 1959, I, "Social Class and the Exercise of Parental Authority," *American Sociological Review*, 1959, 24, pp. 352–366.

KOHN, MELVIN L., 1959, II, "Social Class and Parental Values," *American Journal of Sociology*, LXIV, 1959, pp. 337–351.

LITTMAN, RICHARD A., ROBERT C. A. MOORE, AND JOHN PIERCE-JONES, 1957, "Social Class Differences in Child Rearing: A Third Community for Comparison with Chicago and Newton, Massachusetts," *American Sociological Review*, 22, pp. 694–704.

MACCOBY, ELEANOR E., PATRICIA K. GIBBS, and the Staff of the Laboratory of Human Development, Harvard University, 1954, "Methods of Child-Rearing in Two Social Classes," *Readings in Child Development*, William E. Martin and Celia Burns Stendler, eds., New York: Harcourt, Brace & World.

MILLER, DANIEL R., and GUY E. SWANSON, 1958, *The Changing American Parent*, New York: John Wiley & Sons.

NEUGARTEN, BERNICE L., 1949, "The Democracy of Childhood," *Democracy in Jonesville*, W. Lloyd Warner and Associates.

SARGENT, S. STANSFELD, 1953, "Class and Class-Consciousness in a California Town," *Social Problems*, 1, pp. 22–27.

STENDLER, CELIA BURNS, 1949, *Children of Brasstown*, Urbana, Ill.: Bureau of Research and Service of the College of Education, University of Illinois.

WEDDINGTON, RACHEL, 1958, "The Relative Influence of Social Class and Color on the Stereotypes of Young Children," unpublished Ph.D. dissertation, Committee on Human Development, University of Chicago.

WHITE, MARTHA S., 1957, "Social Class, Child-rearing Practices, and Child Behavior," *American Sociological Review*, 22, pp. 704–712.

7.3   INTRODUCTION

This selection examines one stratum of the American class structure, the working class. The authors' purpose is to dispel what they consider to be some common misconceptions of what workers are like and to replace them with a view that is consistent with the facts and concerns of workers' daily lives. Thus, their discussion conveys the sense that there is a certain logic to the basic themes of working-class life in relation to its physical, social, and economic realities. This is consistent with the authors' belief that "the nature of the conditions of working-class lives (jobs, opportunities, family structure) affects behavior more than has been frequently realized." The analysis in this article is explicitly oriented toward structural and cognitive factors, rather than toward "motivational-psychological-affectual" ones. It is thus especially enlightening to note the extent to which psychological processes are encompassed within the insights produced by this analysis. In each case, however, references to psychological processes link them to the social and cultural context in which they occur, leading to an integrated picture of how the relationship between the individual worker and the working-class environment is produced and sustained.

Many of the characteristics that Miller and Riessman attribute to the worker have important implications for guidance counselors and, indeed, for educators generally. Some of these are clearly obstacles standing between the working-class child and his attainment of formal education. Others, however, if responded to appropriately by the various individuals who make up the child's school environment are just as clearly possible bases for positive outcomes. One of the more obvious obstacles is the worker's negative attitude toward "talk" and abstract ideas and the emphasis on practical results. This is likely to interfere in several ways. Regardless of interest, positive attitude, and high I.Q., a child who is not attuned to exploring ideas for their own sake and to working toward them as goals, rather than using them incidentally as means, may find himself constantly missing the point of what he is supposed to learn even as he senses that he is brighter and more interested than others who have no difficulty. One likely outcome of such a situation is that the child will begin to experience the school and all that is associated with it as part of an alien world to which he cannot gain entry, and thus see as validated his family's initial attitude of remoteness and estrangement from education.

Such a child, however, also has other attitudes which, if tapped, could start a spiral process in quite a different direction. This article suggests, for example, that he is likely, on the one hand, to have an "exaggerated respect for the ability of the learned" and, on the other, that he will probably be especially responsive to personal attention and expressions of personal interest toward him. Together, these two attitudes make it seem quite possible that a skillful teacher, by helping the child through his first frustrations, could establish a warm relationship with him, fostering a sense of personal connection with the new world to which he is exposed, a belief that his own abilities will serve him well in it, and a desire to use and develop these abilities and become "learned" himself.

Such an accomplishment, of course, might create different and even greater problems for the child. If he becomes academically motivated and is successful, he might develop vocational aspirations that his parents might oppose as impractical. The conflict that might thus be engendered could be considerable, the parents seeing the school as leading their child astray and responding with attempts to forcibly impose their own views, and the child torn between his new desires and his well-learned belief that parents must be obeyed. Attempts on the part of teachers and counselors to persuade the parents in such a case that they were harming their child would tend to confirm their attitudes and antagonize them further, accentuating the conflicting pressures on the child.

Although this article deals with only one portion of the class structure, the same kind of analytic description would be possible for any other portion, revealing the many points at which subcultural differences can operate for and against the attainment of educational values. What this one example of such analysis should convey is a sense of the coherent and integrated nature of the many pressures that comprise an individual's social-class culture and of the role of these pressures in determining the consequences of all the individual's experiences.

7.3   THE WORKING CLASS SUBCULTURE: A NEW VIEW [1]

Sutherland M. Miller and Frank Riessman

A decade and a half ago the working class was depicted by Allison Davis and Robert J. Havighurst[2] as permissive and indulgent toward their children and free of

[1]Sutherland M. Miller and Frank Riessman, "The Working Class Subculture: a New View," *Social Problems*, 9, 1961, pp. 86–97.
[2]Allison Davis and Robert J. Havighurst, "Social Class and Color Differences in Child Rearing," *American Sociological Review*, 11, December 1946, pp. 698–710.

the emotional strain of impulse-inhibition which characterized the middle class in the United States. Indeed, it was felt by many that the middle class had much to envy and imitate in the working class.[3] This romantic view of the working class has faded. It is now asserted that the working class (usually termed the "lower class") is incapable of deferring gratification[4] and consequently unable to make major strides in improving their conditions. Frequently accompanying this view is the belief that this lower class is "immoral," "uncivilized," "promiscuous," "lazy," "obscene," "dirty," and "loud."[5] With the rising plane and standard of living of workers has come the argument that workers are middle class in their outlook and desires;[6] the difficulties in attaining full middle-class status lead to juvenile delinquency on the part of those youth who fall back into the working and lower classes[7] and to authoritarianism on the part of those who rise into the middle class.[8] Recently, a further vigorous blow has felled any notions of desirable characteristics of workers: their economic liberalism is not paralleled by political liberalism for workers are said to be more authoritarian in outlook than are members of the middle class.[9] The free, spontaneous worker is now seen as an aggressive, authoritarian, yet fettered person.

The cyclothymic views of workers are more fitting as a topic in the sociology of knowledge than they are in the analysis of what workers actually believe and

---

[3]*Cf.* David Riesman in his introduction to Ely Chinoy's *American Workers and Their Dreams*, New York: Doubleday & Company, 1955.

[4]Louis Schneider and Sverre Lysgaard, "The Deferred Gratification Pattern: A Preliminary Study," *American Sociological Review*, 18, April 1953, pp. 142–149.

[5]These adjectives are taken from Rodman who then goes on to declare: "Lantz, Centers, Warner *et al.*, Hollingshead, Drake and Cayton, West, and David, Gardner and Gardner make it clear that this is the way the lower class is viewed within the United States, the Henriques and Braithwaite studies make it clear that this is the way the lower class is viewed within the West Indies." Hyman Rodman, "On Understanding Lower-Class Behaviour," *Social and Economics Studies*, 8, December, 1959. Other authors state: "One of the most venerable stereotypes has been that applied by middle-class people to lower-class people. The qualities have from time to time included lack of thrift, intellectual inferiority, habitual dirtyness, licentiousness, and many that have derogatory implications." Robert R. Sears, Eleanor E. Maccoby, and Harry Levin, *Patterns of Child Rearing*, New York: Harper & Row, 1957, p. 442. We have isolated five types of stereotypes of workers— anomic, depraved, incapable of deferring gratification, class conscious, and middle-class oriented; these are discussed in S. M. Miller and Frank Riessman, "Images of Workers," a paper presented to the Eastern Sociological Society, New York, 1957.

[6]Daniel Bell, *The End of Ideology*, New York: The Free Press, 1959, and in various issues of *Fortune* magazine. On the other hand, see his path-breaking article, "The Subversion of Collective Bargaining," *Commentary*, March 1960.

[7]Albert Cohen, *Delinquent Boys: The Culture of the Gang*, New York: The Free Press, 1955.

[8]Joseph Greenblum and Leonard I. Pearlin, "Vertical Mobility and Prejudice: A Socio-Psychological Analysis," *Class, Status and Power*, Reinhard Bendix and Seymour Martin Lipset, eds., New York: The Free Press, 1953.

[9]Seymour Martin Lipset, *Political Man: The Social Bases of Politics*, Garden City: Doubleday & Company, 1960, Chap. IV.

practice. In other work, we have criticized in some detail a number of prevailing interpretations of workers—the middle-class image,[10] the nondeferred gratification pattern,[11] the authoritarian view.[12] By the nature of criticism, we have not been able to present our view of what workers are like, for they are not simply the negative or opposite of prevailing views.

For example, because it is demonstrated that workers' behavior is not consistently characterized by an inability to postpone gratifications, we cannot therefore conclude that a major characteristic of the working class is *having* a deferred gratification pattern. It may very well be that the whole issue of deferred gratification does not have special relevance to workers' lives. The concept might seem from a sociocentric point of view, where the middle-class observer, in a sense, says, "If I were in the workers' boots, I wouldn't postpone gratification; I would enjoy myself while I could in the present and not worry about a future which is pretty vague and hopeless anyway." This thinking does not arise out of the context in which workers' behavior takes place, but rather is imposed upon it. In other words, the entire concept of deferred gratification may be inappropriate to understanding the essence of workers' lives.

In this paper, we can only present a few elements of what we believe is a more realistic picture of workers. This analysis is severely compressed and truncated in this presentation and it might be helpful therefore to indicate at the outset an important element of our general orientation. Our stress is much more on cognitive and structural factors than on the more commonly cited affectual and motivational ones. The nature of the conditions of working-class lives (jobs, opportunities, family structure) affects behavior more than has been frequently realized; similarly, modes of understanding the environment can be more important than deep-seated personality factors in behavioral patterns. (For example, workers' low estimates of opportunities and high expectations of risk and loss may be more crucial in the unwillingness to undertake certain long-term actions than personality inadequacies involved in a presumed inability to defer gratification.) This is not to argue that motivational-psychological-affectual variables are unimportant but that they have been overstressed while cognitive and structural variables have been underemphasized. The recognition of the importance of the internal life of man has sometimes overshadowed the significance of the more manifest aspects of his existence. . . .

---

[10]S. M. Miller and Frank Riessman, "Are Workers Middle Class?" *Dissent*, Fall 1961 (forthcoming).

[11]S. M. Miller and Frank Riessman, "The Non-Deferred Gratification Pattern: A Critique," unpublished.

[12]S. M. Miller and Frank Riessman, "Working-Class Authoritarianism: A Critique of Lipset," *British Journal of Sociology*, forthcoming.

BASIC THEMES   Before discussing a few of the themes which we think are basic in working-class life, we present a brief overall picture of what we believe are the essential characteristics of the stable American worker today.

He is traditional, "old fashioned," somewhat religious, and patriarchal.[13] The worker likes discipline, structure, order, organization and directive, definite (strong) leadership, although he does not see such strong leadership in opposition to human, warm, informal, personal qualities.[14] Despite the inadequacy of his education, he is able to build abstractions, but he does so in a slow, physical fashion.[15] He reads ineffectively, is poorly informed in many areas, and is often quite suggestible, although interestingly enough he is frequently suspicious of "talk" and "new fangled ideas."

He is family-centered; most of his relationships take place around the large extended, fairly cooperative family.[16] Cooperation and mutual aid are among his most important characteristics.[17]

While desiring a good standard of living, he is not attracted to the middle-class style of life with its accompanying concern for status and prestige.[18]

He is not class conscious, although aware of class differences. While he is

---

[13]The cross-class F-scale studies uniformly show that workers are more likely than middle-class individuals to support the statement that "the most important thing a child should learn is obedience to his parents." Maccoby and Gibbs have pointed out that workers strongly demand respect and obedience from their children. Eleanor E. Maccoby, Patricia K. Gibbs, *et al.*, "Methods of Child Rearing in Two Social Classes," *Readings in Child Development*, William E. Martin and Celia Burns Stendler, eds., New York: Harcourt Brace & World, 1954, pp. 380–96. Riessman's data indicate that not only parents but older people in general are to be obeyed and respected. See Frank Riessman, "Workers' Attitudes towards Participation and Leadership," unpublished Ph.D. dissertation in social psychology, Columbia University, 1955. Also Evelyn Millis Duval, "Conceptions of Parenthood," *American Journal of Sociology*, LII, November 1946, pp. 193–203.

[14]Frank Riessman, "Workers' Attitudes."

[15]For a review of the relevant literature, see Frank Riessman, *Education and the Culturally Deprived Child*, New York: Harper & Row, 1961, forthcoming.

[16]Floyd Dotson, "Patterns of Voluntary Association Among Urban Working Class Families," *American Sociological Review*, 16, October, 1951, pp. 687–93. "In at least 15 of the 50 families, leisure-time activities of the husbands and wives were completely dominated by the kin group. In another 28 families, regular-visiting patterns with relatives constituted a major, although not exclusive, form of social activity." (p. 691) Also see p. 693.

[17]August B. Hollingshead, "Class Differences in Family Stability," Bendix and Lipset, p. 290. A similar point is made by Allison Davis, Burleigh B. Gardner and Mary R. Gardner, *Deep South*, Chicago: University of Chicago Press, 1941, p. 111. Also see John Useem, Pierre Tangent, and Ruth Useem, "Stratification in a Prairie Town," *American Sociological Review*, 7, June, 1942, p. 334.

[18]The relevant literature is discussed in Miller and Riessman, "Are Workers Middle Class?"

somewhat radical on certain economic issues, he is quite illiberal on numerous matters, particularly civil liberties and foreign policy.[19]

The outstanding weakness of the worker is lack of education. Strongly desiring education for his children, he shows considerable concern about their school work, although he feels estranged and alienated from the teacher and the school, as he similarly feels alienated from many institutions in our society.[20] This alienation is expressed in a ready willingness to believe in the corruptness of leaders and a general negative feeling toward "big shots."

He is stubborn in his ways, concerned with strength and ruggedness, interested in mechanics, materialistic, superstitious, holds an "eye for an eye" psychology, and is largely uninterested in politics.

STABILITY AND SECURITY   We suspect that one of the central determinants in working-class life is the striving for stability and security.[21] External and internal factors promote instability and insecurity. Chief among the external factors is unemployment and layoff. Prosperity has of course barred the anguish of the prolonged depression of the 1930's, but the danger of occasional layoffs of some duration are not remote during the usually shaky prosperity conditions which are interlarded with episodes of recession, plant relocation, industry decline, and strikes.[22]

Chief among the internal factors promoting instability are family discord, including divorce and desertion, intergenerational conflict, and the desire for excitement.

Coping with the instability threats becomes a dominant activity within the working-class family. Many practices, such as mutual aid and cooperation, extended family perspectives, are important as adjustive mechanisms. "Getting by" rather than "getting ahead" in the middle-class self-realization and advancement sense is likely to be dominant.[23] For example, the limited desire to become foremen

---

[19]The Centers' findings can be interposed to support the first sentence of the paragraph despite Centers' mode of analysis. Richard Centers, *The Psychology of Social Classes*, Princeton: Princeton University Press, 1949. *Cf.* Ralf Dahrendorf, *Class and Class Conflict in Industrial Society*, Stanford: Stanford University Press, 1959, pp. 288–289. On civil liberties and foreign policy, see Lipset.

[20]Riessman, *Education and the Culturally Deprived Child*, has a discussion of some of the relevant literature.

[21]Hollingshead, pp. 290–1.

[22]Charles H. Hession, S. M. Miller and Curwen Stoddart, *The Dynamics of the American Economy*, New York: Alfred A. Knopf, 1956, Chap. 11.

[23]Joseph A. Kahl, *The American Class Structure*, New York: Holt, Rinehart and Winston, 1959, pp. 205–210.

is partly a result of the economic insecurity resulting from the loss of job seniority in case of a layoff.[24]

Part of the ambivalence toward obtaining a college education reflects the same emphasis on security. Even a highly talented working-class youth is not sure what he can do with a college diploma, and he may fear the disruption of his familial, community, and peer group security.[25]

The poll data indicating the unwillingness of workers to take economic risks and their greater concern for jobs with security, is part of the same pattern of a striving for stability.[26]

TRADITIONALISM   The American working class is primarily a migrant group; not only have people come from European farms and rural settlements to American factories but they also have migrated from America's rural life to the industrial scene.[27] Traditional practices, once thought to be infrequent in urbanized, industrialized, nuclear-oriented families, are very strong in working-class families.[28] The pattern is patriarchal, extended (with many relevant cousins, grandparents, and aunts and uncles) and delineated by sharply separated sex roles. The family is not child-centered (or child-dominant or dominating), but parent-centered and controlled. Traditional values of automatic obedience by children are expected to be the norm even if not always observed in practice.[29]

One probable consequence of this is that workers seem to be more authoritarian than they probably are. For while on the F-scale type of test, they tend to be "conventional," a characteristic of the authoritarian according to Adorno *et al.*, it is doubtful, as we have tried to argue elsewhere,[30] that this conventionalism means the same in both the middle and working class.

---

[24]Ely Chinoy, *American Workers and Their Dreams*, and Charles R. Walker, *Steeltown*, New York: Harper & Row, 1950, have data showing the considerable reluctance of workers to become foremen.

[25]The initial attraction of many working-class youth to engineering is partly due to the apparently concrete and clear nature of the work and the presumed definiteness of the education for a particular type of job. Motivating working-class youth to go to college may require an expansion and sharpening of working-class children's interpretation of the job market.

[26]Centers, *The Psychology of Social Classes*, p. 62.

[27]Lloyd Reynolds, *Labor Economics and Labor Relations*, Englewood Cliffs, N.J.: Prentice-Hall, Inc., 1949, pp. 7–23.

[28]Recent literature, particularly Weinstein and Axelrad, have pointed out that traditional practices are more widespread than previously thought in the middle class. The lack of differences between middle-class and working-class respondents reported in the studies may be due to the lack of sensitive instruments. While our analysis is not necessarily based on the notion of greater traditional and extended practices in working-class than in middle-class families, we believe that these practices assume a greater importance in the overall activities of the former.

[29]Duvall.

[30]Miller and Riessman, "Working-Class Authoritarianism: A Critique of Lipset." Also, our "Social Class, Education and Authoritarianism," a paper presented to the American Sociological Society, Washington, 1957.

The worker also has a traditional attitude toward discipline which again may be confused with authoritarianism. All the child-rearing data indicate that workers utilize physical punishment as a basic discipline technique. In the eyes of the worker punishment discourages people from wrongdoing whether the punishment is inflicted upon them or upon others who serve as "examples." There is also a "rightness" about punishment for a misdeed, for punishment is the other side of responsibility for one's actions. Thus, for example, acceptance of the death penalty may not be the result of a sado-masochistic character structure but the product of a belief in the efficacy of punishment in deterring others from misdeeds and in the value of attaching responsibility to people's actions.[31] Workers consequently do not easily accept the notion that an individual is not responsible for his crimes because of his emotional state at the time of their occurrence.

INTENSITY We believe that one of the most neglected themes in working-class life and one of the most difficult to understand and interpret is that of intensity. This intensity is expressed in a number of different ways. It is found in the areas in which workers have belief and emotional involvement. While there are numerous areas about which workers are confused, and lacking in opinion (*e.g.*, the high percentage of "no answer" and "don't know" on public opinion polls), there are important spheres in which they have definite convictions, and indeed, are highly stubborn. Their beliefs about religion, morality, superstition, diet, punishment, custom, traditional education, the role of women, intellectuals, are illustrative here. Many of these attitudes are related to their traditional orientation and they are held unquestioningly in the usual traditional manner. They are not readily open to reason and they are not flexible opinions.

Other possible sources of this intensity may be their physical (less symbolic) relation to life,[32] their person centeredness (to be discussed below), and their lack of education.

PERSON-CENTERED Threaded through much of working-class life is a person-centered theme. On one level this theme has an informal, human quality, of easy, comfortable relationship to people where the affectionate bite of humor is appreciated. The factory "horse-play," the ritualistic kidding, is part of this although by no means all of it. It is an expressive component of life.[33]

---

[31] *Cf.* Bordua, David Joseph, "Authoritarianism and Intolerance, A Study of High School Students," unpublished Ph.D. thesis, Department of Social Relations, Harvard University, 1956, pp. 228, 237, 239.

[32] The discussion by Miller and Swanson on the "motoric" orientation of workers is one of the most suggestive in the literature. Daniel R. Miller and Guy E. Swanson, *Inner Conflict and Defense*, New York: Holt, Rinehart and Winston, 1960.

[33] Miller and Swanson.

At another level, it is the importance of personal qualities. One learns more from people than from books, it is said. At a political level, the candidate as a decent, human person is more important than the platform.[34]

In the bureaucratic situation, the worker still tends to think of himself as relating to people, not to roles and invisible organizational structure. This orientation is an aspect of particularism, the reaction to persons and situations in terms of their personal qualities and relations to oneself rather than in terms of some universal characteristics of their social position. The neighbor or workmate who gets ahead is expected "not to put on airs"; he should like the "old gang" and accept them despite his new position. An individual is expected to transcend his office. A foreman is a s.o.b. not because he has stresses and demands on the job which force him to act forcibly and harshly, but because of his personal qualities. Contrariwise, one of the top executives is frequently regarded as one who would help the rank-and-file workers if he had the chance, because *he* is a "nice guy"; putting him in the stresses of a new position would not force him to act as others in that position have acted.[35] It is the man not the job that makes for behavior; this attitude is not a class-conscious one, far from it. Another example of particularism is the juvenile delinquent who reacts positively to the social worker or therapist who seems to be interested in him beyond the call of professional duty.

PRAGMATISM AND ANTI-INTELLECTUALISM   With workers, it is the end-result of action rather than the planning of action or the preoccupation with means that counts. An action that goes astray is not liked for itself; it has to achieve the goal intended to be satisfactory.[36] It is results that pay off. While this orientation has an anti-intellectual dimension, it does somewhat reduce the reliance on personality (person-centered theme) by its emphasis on results. Workers like the specific action, the clear action, the understood result. What can be seen and felt is more likely to be real and true in the workers' perspectives, which are therefore likely to be limited. The pragmatic orientation of workers does not encourage them to see abstract ideas as useful. Education, for what it does for one in terms of opportunities, may be desirable but abstract intellectual speculation, ideas which are not rooted in the realities of the present, are not useful, indeed may be harmful.

On the other hand, workers often have an exaggerated respect for the ability of the learned. A person with intellectual competence in one field is frequently thought to be a "brain" with ability in all fields; partly this is due to the general abstract nature of ideas regardless of field. If a real obstacle comes up, they may

---

[34]*Cf.* Lipset, pp. 285–286.

[35]S. M. Miller, "Union Structure and Industrial Relations: A Case Study of a Local Labor Union," unpublished Ph.D. thesis, Princeton University, 1951.

[36]Melvin L. Kohn, "Social Class and the Exercise of Parental Authority," *American Sociological Review*, 24, June 1959, pp. 364–365.

expect "the brain" to have a ready solution for it, even if they may not be willing to adopt it.

At first glance, the antiwords orientation may appear to be incompatible with the possible appeal of the charismatic. But it is not. For the charismatic are charismatic because they can be emotional and expressive, qualities not usually associated with abstract ideas. Also, the charismatic leader may promise "pie in the sky" but it is a very concrete, specific set of ingredients with a clear distribution of the pie.

EXCITEMENT   Another component in workers' lives is the appreciation of excitement, of moving out of the humdrum. News, gossip, new gadgets, sports, are consequently very attractive to workers. To some extent, the consumership of workers—the desire to have new goods, whether television sets or cars—is part of this excitement dimension. The excitement theme is often in contradiction with the traditional orientation.

It is worth noting that different sub-groups within the working class may favor one theme rather than another. Thus younger groups, and especially juvenile delinquents, are probably much more attracted to the excitement theme, are more alienated and less traditional. On the other hand, workers with a more middle-class orientation are probably less alienated, more traditional, and pragmatic. . . .

7.4, 7.5   INTRODUCTION

The two selections that follow are grouped together under a single introduction to call attention as much to the differences between them as to the similarities. Each of them deals with some of the consequences of the Negro's history in America. In both cases, their conclusions refer to what might loosely, but not unreasonably, be called "personality damage." Taken together, the two selections illustrate the enormous variation that is possible in the long-range effects of a single historical and social fact.

The excerpt by Pettigrew, a social psychologist, surveys the evidence on the effects of family disorganization, a condition that occurs to a disproportionate extent among Negroes, upon personality and social development. The author provides a clear and integrated view of the effects of a major element of family disorganization—the absence of a father. One of the most important casualties of this condition is sex-role identification, in both girls and boys, and it is also one of the mechanisms through which the pattern of female-dominated broken homes is perpetuated.

Frazier, a sociologist and a Negro, undertakes the task of tracing the rise of the "black bourgeoisie" and examining the values, behavior, and self-attitudes that characterize these individuals. As described here, their overriding motivation is toward the external symbols of the dominant cultural goals (*e.g.*, money and material possessions as symbols of success), perceiving these symbols as instrumental for gaining acceptance into white society. Such acceptance, however, does not follow, irrespective of their striving, and they are thus caught in between Negro and white culture, rejecting one and rejected by the other.

Many issues touched on by these two selections seem relevant to guidance-personnel workers in their attempts to help Negro youngsters. Recalling the suggestion by Parsons and White in Chapter 6 (Selection 6.2) that the peer group serves an important function in sex-role clarification, it would seem that the period of late childhood and adolescence, when peer attachments are most salient, should be particularly crucial for Negro boys and girls and should thus be an opportunity for constructive action to counter some of the damage discussed by Pettigrew. Similarly, the interaction between a Negro child and a guidance counselor will tend to reflect the child's sex-role identification and thus the relationship could serve either to aggravate its bias or to push it toward some better balance.

In counseling Negro youth with respect to college and career choices there would also seem to be numerous potentialities and hazards for the guidance counselor. From Frazier's discussion one would guess that, for Negro adolescents from a middle-class background, such choices might be very significant in relation to their status strivings and that other considerations besides their interests and talents might be predominant for them. From Pettigrew we might reasonably suppose that for boys from another kind of background vocational choices would evoke insecurities about their masculinity and they might reject certain alternatives primarily out of fear that choosing them would be a confirmation of their inadequacy.

In introducing some of the earlier selections we pointed to the necessity of recognizing the implications of a person's "social-class" position in order to understand his personality and behavior. The two selections that follow make it clear that what may seem to be similar positions in the system of stratification can differ very significantly in their effects on the individual. Thus, there is serious danger of categorizing individuals too readily in terms of simple differentiations which do not account for the elaborate subtlety of the American class structure.

7.4   FAMILY DISORGANIZATION AND PERSONALITY: A PROFILE OF THE NEGRO AMERICAN [1]

Thomas F. Pettigrew

Both poverty and migration . . . act to maintain the old slave pattern of a mother-centered family. Not only does desperate poverty disturb healthy family

---

[1]Thomas F. Pettigrew, *A Profile of the Negro American*, Princeton N.J.: Van Nostrand, 1964, pp. 15–25, 202–205, 208–219, 222–233.

life through dilapidated housing, crowded living conditions, restricted recreational facilities, and direct contact with the most corrupting elements of urban disorganization, but it makes the ideal American pattern of household economics practically impossible. Employment discrimination has traditionally made it more difficult for the poorly educated Negro male to secure steady employment than the poorly educated Negro female. In many areas of the nation, North as well as South, this is still true, with Negro females always able to obtain jobs as domestics if nothing else is available. When the unskilled Negro male does manage to secure a job, he generally assumes an occupation that pays barely enough to support himself— much less a family. Such conditions obviously limit the ability of lower-class Negroes to follow the typical American pattern—that is, a stable unit with the husband providing a steady income for his family.

The Negro wife in this situation can easily become disgusted with her financially dependent husband, and her rejection of him further alienates the male from family life. Embittered by their experiences with men, many Negro mothers often act to perpetuate the mother-centered pattern by taking a greater interest in their daughters than their sons. For example, more Negro females graduate from college than Negro males, the reverse of the pattern found among white Americans.

Family stability also suffers from the effects of migration, with its tensions over relocation and its release of the migrant from the sanctions of his home community. When all of these factors are considered, the prevalence of divorce, separation, and illegitimacy among poor Negroes should not come as a surprise. For when American society isolates the lower-class Negro from contact with the general norms and prevents him from sharing in the rewards which follow from abiding by these norms, it guarantees the emergence of a ghetto subculture with different standards of conduct, motivation, and family life.

Census data for 1960 illustrate the depth of this family disorganization among Negroes: over a third (34.3 percent) of all nonwhite mothers with children under six years of age hold jobs as compared with less than a fifth (19.5 percent) of white mothers with children under six[2] (U.S. Bureau of the Census, 1962); only three-fourths (74.9 percent) of all nonwhite families have both the husband and the wife present in the household as compared with nine-tenths (89.2 percent) of white families[3] (U.S. Bureau of the Census, 1962); and only two-thirds (66.3 percent) of nonewhites under 18 years of age live with both of their parents as compared with nine-tenths (90.2 percent) of such whites (U.S. Bureau of the Census, 1962).

---

[2]During 1950, 35 percent of all nonwhite mothers under 45 years of age held jobs compared with 19 percent of similarly aged white mothers. (Ginsberg, 1956, p.98)

[3]The vast majority of incomplete Negro households is lacking the husband. Frazier estimated in 1950 that the male parent was missing in roughly 20 percent of Negro households (Frazier, 1950). In addition to divorce and separation, part of this phenomenon is due to a higher Negro male death rate. The percentage of widows among Negro women fifty-four years old or less is roughly twice that of white women (Metropolitan Life, 1962).

These data do not cancel out the effects of social-class differences between the two groups; rough comparisons between the lower classes of each race, however, still reveal a greater prevalence of father-absence among Negroes. The scar of slavery upon Negro family life, perpetuated through poverty and migration, is still evident.

Recent psychological research vividly demonstrates the personality effects upon children of having been raised in a disorganized home without a father. One such study reveals that eight-and-nine-year-old children whose fathers are absent seek immediate gratification far more than children whose fathers are present in the home. For example, when offered their choice of receiving a tiny candy bar immediately or a large bar a week later, fatherless children typically take the small bar while other children prefer to wait for the larger bar (Mischel, 1961 c). This hunger for immediate gratification among fatherless children seems to have serious implications. Regardless of race, children manifesting this trait also tend to be less accurate in judging time, less "socially responsible," less oriented toward achievement, and more prone toward delinquency (Mischel, 1961 a and b). Indeed, two psychologists maintain that the inability to delay gratification is a critical factor in immature, criminal, and neurotic behavior[4] (Mowrer and Ullman, 1945).

Sex-role adoption is a second personality area which distinguishes children from intact homes from those in homes without fathers. One study found that five-to-fourteen-year-old Negro youths without fathers experienced unusual difficulty in differentiating between male and female roles. Thus, boys and girls without fathers described themselves in very similar ways, while boys from whole families described themselves in considerably more masculine terms than girls from whole families (D'Andrade, 1962). Another investigation of high school students reported far sharper differences between the sexes in their values among white than among Negro children. This occurred primarily because the Negro girls revealed interests generally associated with males; compared with the white girls, they valued theoretical and political concerns more and religious and esthetic concerns less. Significantly, these Negro children more often came from families without fathers than did the white children (Lott and Lott, 1963).

Studies of white American boys whose fathers left them during World War II and of Norwegian boys whose sailor-fathers ship out for years at a time report related phenomena. These father-deprived boys are markedly more immature, submissive, dependent, and effeminate than other boys both in their overt behavior and fantasies (Bach, 1946; Lynn and Sawrey, 1959; Pauline Sears, 1951; Sears,

---

[4]Contributing to this situation is the fact that where fathers are not present children more often have the additional stigma of being illegitimate. Although illegitimacy is more naturally accepted in lower-class Negro culture (Knapp and Cambria, 1947), careful research reveals better school and personal "adjustment" among legitimate Negro children (Jenkins, 1958).

Pintler, and Sears, 1946; Stolz, 1954). Eight-and-nine-year-old, father-absent Norwegian boys, for instance, when playing with self-representative dolls, put them in a crib rather than a bed (Lynn and Sawrey, 1959). As they grow older, this passive behavior may continue, but, more typically, it is vigorously overcompensated for by exaggerated masculinity. Juvenile gangs, white and Negro, classically act out this pseudo-masculinity with leather jackets, harsh language, and physical "toughness" (Miller, 1958).

The reasons for these characteristics of father-absent children seem clear. Negro girls in such families model themselves after their mothers and prepare to assume male as well as female responsibilities. And various investigations have demonstrated the crucial importance of the father in the socialization of boys (Bandura and Walters, 1959). Mothers raising their children in homes without fathers are frequently overprotective, sometimes even smothering, in their compensatory attempts to be a combined father and mother. Burton and Whiting persuasively contend that the boys whose fathers are not present have initially identified with their mothers and must later, in America's relatively patrifocal society, develop a conflicting, secondary identification with males (Burton and Whiting, 1961). In other words, they must painfully achieve a masculine self-image late in their childhood after having established an original self-image on the basis of the only parental model they have had—their mother.

Several studies point to the applicability of this sex-identity problem to lower-class Negro males. Two objective test assessments of widely different groups—Alabama jail prisoners and Wisconsin working-class veterans with tuberculosis—found that Negro males scored higher than white males on a measure of femininity (Caldwell, 1959; Hokanson and Calden, 1960). This measure is a part of the Minnesota Multiphasic Inventory (MMPI), a well-known psychological instrument that requires the respondent to judge the applicability to himself of over five hundred simple statements. Thus, Negroes in these samples generally agreed more often with such "feminine" choices as "I would like to be a singer" and "I think that I feel more intensely than most people do."

Psychiatrists have noted the prevalence of pseudo-masculine defenses among neurotic Negro male patients (Sclare, 1953). And an investigation employing the personality-probing Thematic Apperception Test (TAT) with a representative national sample revealed Negro males to be unusually high in their need for social power and dominance. This need is apparently a compensatory reaction to their lowly role, for it, too, grows partly out of the broken home situation. The same study demonstrated that a strongly felt need for power is a typical personality trait among men, Negro and white, raised by only one parent as opposed to men from intact homes (Veroff *et al.*, 1960). Finally, a survey of working-class Negroes in Boston matched 21 adult males whose fathers had been absent during their early childhoods, with 21 men who possessed similar social characteristics (age, income, education, region of birth, etc.), but whose fathers had been present during their early childhoods (Pettigrew). Figure 1 illustrates the differences between these

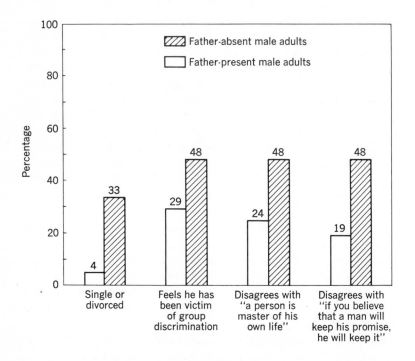

FIGURE 1.   FATHER ABSENCE AND ADULT NEGRO PERSONALITY
(Data from: T. F. Pettigrew, "Father-Absence and Negro Adult
Personality: A Research Note," unpublished paper.)

matched groups. The most critical distinction involves marriage; the first group of men was more likely to be either single or divorced—another manifestation of their disturbed sexual identification. They also felt more victimized, less in control of the environment, and more distrustful of others (Figure 1).

These findings reflect not only the effects of family disorganization but also the effeminate aspects of the "Negro" role many of these men must play in adult life. Servility is often required, and most low-paying service occupations typically open to unskilled Negro males—for example, cook, waiter, orderly, dishwasher—generally carry a connotation in American culture of being "women's work." Thus, the sex-identity problems created by the fatherless home are perpetuated in adulthood.

Personality development of children in families without fathers may also be related to three recurrent problems among Negro Americans: juvenile delinquency, crimes against persons, and schizophrenia. More research is necessary to link definitely these symptoms of social disorganization to impaired family structure, but present data are most suggestive. In predicting juvenile crime, Eleanor and

Sheldon Glueck find that more delinquent boys, when compared with nondelinquents, come from broken homes (Glueck and Glueck, 1950, p. 280). Other researchers, focusing upon the "good" boy in high delinquency neighborhoods, note that such nondelinquents typically come from exceptionally stable, intact families. These boys think of themselves as "good" and score favorably on a personality measure of socialization (Scarpitti *et al.*, 1960). Family disorganization upsets this normal socializing influence of the home and creates the potential for juvenile delinquency. Community institutions such as the school and the church, which sometimes can help deter delinquent acts, simply do not possess the same meaning for unsocialized children from impaired families as they do for other children (Frazier, 1950). In fact, one investigator finds that Negro delinquents tend to come from homes even more unstable than those of comparable white delinquents (Axelrad, 1952).

The findings connecting personal crime and schizophrenia with family structure are more tenuous. One ingenious study of a variety of nonliterate societies throughout the world reveals that those with high rates of crime against persons are characterized by: mother-child households with inadequate opportunity to identify with the father; mother-child sleeping arrangements which foster a strong dependent relationship between the child and his mother; an abrupt and anxiety-producing preparation for independence; and a general distrustfulness of others (as in Figure 1) (Bacon, *et al.*, 1963). Perhaps personal crime is merely one aspect of the masculine façade which mother-raised boys tend to present as they enter "the man's world." Concerned about their sexual identity, they assert their masculinity through person-directed violence. In any event, this suggestive lead deserves further attention in research among Negro Americans. Likewise, a matrifocal situation, particularly a family composed of a strong mother and a present but weak father, seems to be positively related to schizophrenia (Kohn and Clausen, 1956). Since this pattern is common even among intact lower-class Negro families and this particular psychosis is especially prevalent among lower-class Negroes, future research along these lines is also indicated.

These considerations have led social scientists to emphasize the stability and structure of the home as crucial factors in counteracting the effects of racism upon Negro personality. A warm, supportive home can effectively compensate for many of the restrictions the Negro child faces outside of the ghetto; consequently, the type of home life a Negro enjoys as a child may be far more crucial for governing the influence of segregation upon his personality than the form the segregation takes—legal or informal, Southern or Northern (Ausubel, 1958). One psychologist maintains that full awareness of his social devaluation and role as a "Negro" does not usually impinge upon the individual until early adolescence (Jones and Arrington, 1945). Just how the Negro bears up under this severe emotional stress is largely a function of the degree of ego-strength that he has developed in his earlier, family-centered years. The ego-strong Negro, nurtured in a stable and complete family, may come out of this stressful encounter harboring some self-hatred, but he generally manages to dissociate his basic personality from his socially defined role of "Negro." He maintains his self-respect as a unique and worthwhile human being apart from the position of inferior being that the racists insist he assume. As one elderly Negro candidly expressed it, "Being a Negro is no disgrace, but it sure is an inconvenience" (Johnson, 1957).

By contrast, the "psychologically vulnerable" Negro, crippled by weak ego development from earlier family disorganization, is more likely to fall prey to mental illness, drug addiction, or crime, depending on his particular life history. He has few personality resources to withstand the gale winds of discrimination that strike him full force in adolescence. Thus, segregation has its most fundamental influence on Negro personality in the manner in which it affects Negro family functioning (Jones and Arrington, 1965).

Case studies bear out these contentions. In their psychoanalytic investigation of 25 Negroes, *The Mark of Oppression*, Kardiner and Ovesey studied "O. D.," a 29-year-old, lower-class male (Kardiner and Ovesey, 1951, pp. 91–98). Although he was a trained automobile mechanic, O. D. had been forced by the usual pattern of employment discrimination to take a series of poorly paid service jobs with their typically effeminate features—dishwasher, short order cook, and hospital orderly. His mother had been warm yet strict, but he had never known a stable father-figure during his poor, and sometimes hungry, childhood. As an adult, O. D. had substituted an aggressive, educated wife for his mother and had become very dependent upon her. Also consistent with the father-deprived personality pattern were his serious difficulties in adopting a masculine role; he suffered from problems of sexual impotency and an almost complete inability to express anger. The case of O. D. offers an example of a lower-class Negro who, made "psychologically vulnerable" by an impaired family background, expressed his serious personality difficulties in sexual disturbance.

The case studies of New Orleans Negroes conducted by Rohrer and his associates provide further examples (Rohrer and Edmonson, 1960). This research consisted of a re-examination of individuals who, as children nearly two decades earlier, had served as subjects for a pioneer study of Negro personality, published as *Children of Bondage* (Davis and Dollard, 1940). Again the devastating personality scars rendered by the absence of fathers in matrifocal family life were apparent in many of the lower-class Negroes. Girls raised in such households tended as adults to establish similar households for themselves and to live either with or very close to their mothers. Boys from this background evidenced the familiar pattern of conflict over sexual identity. Many of them as youths had joined gangs of older boys and acted out this conflict within the gang in the form of compulsive masculine behavior. "The gang member," conclude the investigators, "rejects this femininity in every form, and he sees it in women and in effeminate men, in laws and morals and religion, in schools and occupational striving" (Rohrer and Edmonson, 1960, p. 163). This blanket rejection by gang members of the values and institutions of society is obviously not likely to lead to an ambitious struggle out of the lower class. In fact, such alienation often leads directly into a life of crime, drug addiction, and deep despair. . . .

BIBLIOGRAPHY

AUSUBEL, D. P., 1958, "Ego Development among Segregated Negro Children," *Mental Hygiene*, 42, pp. 362–369.

AXELRAD, S., 1952, "Negro and White Male Institutionalized Delinquents," *American Journal of Sociology*, 57, pp. 569–574.

BACH, G. R., 1946, "Father-Fantasies and Father-Typing in Father-Separated Children," *Child Development*, 17, pp. 63–79.

BACON, MARGARET K., I. L. CHILD, AND H. BARRY, III, 1963, "A Cross-Cultural Study of Correlates of Crime," *Journal of Abnormal and Social Psychology*, 66, pp. 291–300.

BANDURA, A., AND R. H. WALTERS, 1959, *Adolescent Aggression*, New York: The Ronald Press.

BURTON, R. V., AND J. W. M. WHITING, 1961, "The Absent Father and Cross-Sex Identity," *Merrill-Palmer Quarterly*, 7, pp. 85–95.

CALDWELL, M. G., 1959, "Personality Trends in the Youthful Male Offender," *Journal of Criminal Law, Criminology, and Police Science*, 49, pp. 405–416.

D'ANDRADE, R. G., 1962, "Father Absence and Cross-Sex Identification," unpublished doctoral dissertation, Harvard University.

DAVIS, A., AND J. DOLLARD, 1940, *Children of Bondage*, Washington, D.C.: American Council on Education.

FRAZIER, E. F., 1950, "Problems and Needs of Negro Children and Youth Resulting from Family Disorganization," *Journal of Negro Education*, 19, pp. 269–277.

GINSBERG, E., 1956, *The Negro Potential*, New York: Columbia University Press.

GLUECK, S., AND ELEANOR T. GLUECK, 1950, *Unraveling Juvenile Delinquency*, New York: Commonwealth Fund.

HOKANSON, J. E., AND G. CALDEN, 1960, "Negro-White Differences on the MMPI," *Journal of Clinical Psychology*, 16, pp. 32–33.

JENKINS, W. W., 1958, "An Experimental Study of the Relationship of Legitimate and Illegitimate Birth Status to School and Personal Adjustment of Negro Children," *American Journal of Sociology*, 64, pp. 169–173.

JOHNSON, R., 1957, "Negro Reactions to Minority Group Status," *American Minorities*, M. L. Barron, ed., New York: Alfred A. Knopf, pp. 192–212.

JONES, F. N., AND M. G. ARRINGTON, 1945, "The Explanations of Physical Phenomena Given by White and Negro Children," *Comparative Psychology Monographs*, 18(5), pp. 1–43.

KARDINER, A., AND L. OVESEY, 1951, *The Mark of Oppression*, New York: W. W. Norton.

KNAPP, PATRICIA, AND SOPHIA CAMBRIA, 1947, "The Attitudes of Negro Unmarried Mothers toward Illegitimacy," *Smith College Studies in Social Work*, 17, pp. 185–203.

KOHN, M. L., AND J. A. CLAUSEN, 1956, "Parental Authority Behavior and Schizophrenia," *American Journal of Orthopsychiatry*, 26, pp. 297–313.

LYNN, D. B., AND W. L. SAWREY, 1959, "The Effects of Father-Absence on Norwegian Boys and Girls," *Journal of Abnormal and Social Psychology*, 59, pp. 258–262.

METROPOLITAN LIFE INSURANCE COMPANY, 1962, "The American Widow," *Statistical Bulletin*, 43, November, pp. 1–4.

MILLER, W. B., 1958, "Lower Class Culture as a Generating Milieu of Gang Delinquency," *Journal of Social Issues*, 14(3), pp. 5–19.

MISCHEL, W., 1961a, "Preference for Delayed Reinforcement and Social Responsibility," *Journal of Abnormal and Social Psychology*, 62, pp. 1–7.
MISCHEL, W., 1961b, "Delay of Gratification, Need for Achievement, and Acquiescence in Another Culture," *Journal of Abnormal and Social Psychology*, 62, pp. 543–552.
MISCHEL, W., 1961c, "Father-Absence and Delay of Gratification: Cross-Cultural Comparisons," *Journal of Abnormal and Social Psychology*, 63, pp. 116–124.
MOWRER, O. H., AND A. D. ULLMAN, 1945, "Time as a Determinant in Integrative Learning," *Psychological Review*, 52, pp. 61–90.
MUSSEN, P. H., AND L. DISTLER, 1959, "Masculinity, Identification, and Father-Son Relationships," *Journal of Abnormal and Social Psychology*, 59, pp. 350–356.
PETTIGREW, T. F., "Father-Absence and Negro Adult Personality: A Research Note," unpublished paper.
ROHRER, J. H., AND M. S. EDMONSON, eds., 1960, *The Eighth Generation*, New York: Harper & Row.
SCARPITTI, F. R., ELLEN MURRAY, S. DINITZ, AND W. C. RECKLESS, 1960, "The 'Good' Boy in a High Delinquency Area: Four Years Later," *American Sociological Review*, 25, pp. 555–558.
SCLARE, A., 1953, "Cultural Determinants in the Neurotic Negro," *British Journal of Medical Psychology*, 26, pp. 278–288.
SEARS, PAULINE S., 1951, "Doll Play Aggression in Normal Young Children: Influence of Sex, Age, Sibling Status, Father's Absence," *Psychological Monographs*, 65(6), (Whole no. 323).
SEARS, R. R., M. H. PINTLER, AND PAULINE S. SEARS, 1946, "Effects of Father-Separation on Preschool Children's Doll Play Aggression," *Child Development*, 17, pp. 219–243.
STOLZ, LOIS M., 1954, *Father Relations of Warborn Children*, Palo Alto, Calif.: Stanford University Press.
UNITED STATES BUREAU OF THE CENSUS, 1962, *U.S. Census of Population, General Social and Economic Characteristics, United States Summary*, Final Report PC (1)—1C, Washington, D. C.: U.S. Government Printing Office.
VEROFF, J., J. W. ATKINSON, SHEILA C. FELD, AND G. GURIN, 1960, "The Use of Thematic Apperception to Assess Motivation in a Nationwide Interview Study," *Psychological Monographs*, 4(12), (Whole no. 499).

7.5 BLACK BOURGEOISIE: THE RISE OF A NEW MIDDLE CLASS[1]

E. Franklin Frazier

From the making of men to the making of money-makers

The mass migration of Negroes from the South during and following the first World War affected the education of the Negro as it did other phases of his life.

[1]Reprinted with permission of The Macmillan Company from *Black Bourgeoisie: The Rise of a New Middle Class in the United States*, by E. F. Frazier, Copyright 1957, by The Free Press, a Corporation. Pp. 70–76, 108–111, 121–126, 176–189, 210–211, 214–215.

When hundreds of thousands of Negroes who had migrated to Northern cities gained access to the same education as whites, the controversy concerning the relative merits of industrial education and higher education lost its significance. In the South, where industrialization was making rapid progress, school boards began to show a willingness to have the less expensive classical courses, such as Latin, taught in Negro high schools while instituting technical and vocational courses in white high schools.[2] There was also a change in the attitudes of southern whites toward college education for Negroes, but Negro institutions of higher education continued to receive only a small fraction of the state appropriation for higher education.[3]

The philanthropic foundations in the North responded quickly to the changing situation and began to give millions of dollars to the higher education of Negroes.[4] . . .

While these changes were occurring in the attitude of the South and the philanthropic foundations toward the higher education of the Negro, the Negro was beginning to assume greater control of his education. . . .The election of Negro administrators in Negro colleges represented to a certain extent a revolt against missionary education. But the transformation which was occurring indicated something more fundamental than a change from white to Negro administration.

The entire orientation and aim of higher education of Negroes was changing. It was natural that as the result of the revolt against missionary education, these institutions would lose much of their piety. . . .Then there was less talk about thrift and the dignity of labor. . . .Moreover, in all the institutions, the canons of respectability were undergoing a radical change. Respectability became less a question of morals and manners and more a matter of the external marks of a high standard of living.

As the children of the Negro masses have flooded the colleges, it was inevitable that the traditional standards of morals and manners would have to give way. . . .Many of them, having come from a background of disorganized family life, were strangers to the traditional puritanical morality of these schools. . . .The colleges had to make concessions to their poor educational and social backgrounds.[5] But the children of the Negro masses were not primarily responsible for the change in the character of the Negro college. The outlook and aims of the colleges changed in response to the aspirations and values of the second generation of Negro college students and their Negro teachers who were imbued with middle-class values. . . .

---

[2]Horace Mann Bond, *The Education of the Negro in the American Social Order*, Englewood Cliffs, N.J.: Prentice-Hall, Inc., 1934, p. 362.

[3]See Frazier, *The Negro in the United States*, New York: Macmillan, 1949, pp. 471–473.

[4]Charles S. Johnson, *The Negro College Graduate*, Chapel Hill, N.C.: University of North Carolina Press, 1938, p. 467 ff.

[5]See Ambrose Caliver, *A Background Study of Negro College Student*, Washington, D.C.: U.S. Government Printing Office, 1933, and by the same author, *A Personal Study of Negro College Students*, New York: Teachers College, Columbia University, 1931.

The second and third generations of Negro college students are as listless as the children of peasants. The former are interested primarily in the activities of Greek letter societies and "social" life, while the latter are concerned with gaining social acceptance by the former. Both are less concerned with the history or the understanding of the world about them than with their appearance at the next social affair. The girl with a peasant or working-class background may be irritated by her mother's inability to buy an expensive "party" dress. But what can be expected when the dean of women has instructed her to tell her mother that she must have the dress at any sacrifice? So teachers and students alike are agreed that money and conspicuous consumption are more important than knowledge or the enjoyment of books and art and music. . . .

The majority of the graduates of Negro colleges, including the land-grant colleges and vocational schools, have entered professional occupations.[6] The majority of present-day college students still aspire to the same field of activity. In recent years, however, Negro colleges have increasingly instituted courses in education for business. When a survey of Negro business and education for business was made nearly a decade ago, there were 16 Negro colleges offering courses in business education, and other colleges were planning to institute such courses.[7] Only 5 percent of the fathers of the students who were pursuing courses in business education were engaged in business, while the majority of their fathers were unskilled workers. Many of these students, coming from poor homes and with inadequate academic preparation, have undoubtedly seized upon business education as a means to rise to middle-class status. They have also been told that by becoming money-makers they would help the Negro to achieve economic independence in American life.

Thus it has turned out that Negro higher education has become devoted chiefly to the task of educating the black bourgeoisie. The United Negro College Fund which was started in 1944, provides the small sum of about 2 million dollars for 32 Negro colleges.[8] This is a gesture on the part of white America, expressing its approval of middle-class education for Negroes behind the walls of segregation. Sometimes the appeal to white America is made on the sentimental grounds that the schools receiving financial support are educating the "children of slaves" who are thirsting for "knowledge" which will enable them to become "men." But the present generation of Negro college students (who are not the children but the great grand-children of slaves) do not wish to recall their past. As they ride to school in their automobiles, they prefer to think of the money which they will earn as professional and business men. For they have been taught that money will

---

[6]Johnson, p. 92 ff.

[7]Joseph A. Pierce, *Negro Business and Business Education*, New York: Harper & Row, 1947, pp 239 ff.

[8]Pierce, p. 268.

ring them justice and equality in American life, and they propose to get money. . . .

As the system of rigid racial segregation has broken down, the black bourgeoisie has lost much of its feeling of racial solidarity with the Negro masses. In the metropolitan areas of the North where there are increasing opportunities for employment and earning money, social mobility, which means primarily the attainment of middle-class status, has become a question of the amount of money which one has to spend. When a French sociologist, on a study tour in the United States, saw the emergence of the black bourgeoisie in Northern cities, he observed that they were "really colored Babbitts."[9]

The break with traditional values is seen in the changes in the canons of respectability. Among the older upper-class families in the Negro community, who really stood for a middle-class way of life, the canons of respectability required a stable family life and conventional sex behavior. On the other hand, among the new black bourgeoisie these values are regarded as "old-fashioned" virtues and there is much confusion in thinking and behavior with reference to these values. Divorces and scandals in family and sex behavior do not affect one's social status; rather the notoriety which one acquires in such cases adds to one's prestige. The change in attitudes towards the "old-fashioned" bourgeois values is due largely to the fact that the new bourgeoisie is recruited from those elements in the Negro population among whom these virtues never existed and that money has become the chief requirement for social acceptance.[10]

Among the professional classes in the Negro community, actors and entertainers are relatively numerous and have the largest incomes. The actors and entertainers, who very often have a lower-class background in the social hierarchy of the Negro community, exercise a far greater influence upon the morals and manners in the Negro community than actors and entertainers in the white community. Their prestige is owing partly to the glamor of their personalities, but more especially to their financial success, which is due to their support by the white world. The black bourgeoisie is also being recruited from the successful underworld Negroes, who have gained their money from gambling, prostitution, bootlegging, and the "numbers." The old upper class in the Negro community erected an impenetrable barrier between themselves and Negroes who represented the "sporting" and criminal world. Since such Negroes were generally able to handle more money than the majority of Negroes, they always constituted a threat to the respectable way of life cherished by the old middle classes. As the result of urbanization,

---

[9]George Friedmann, *Où va le travail humain*, Paris: Gallimard, 1950.

[10]See St. Clair Drake and Horace R. Cayton, *Black Metropolis*, New York: Harcourt, Brace, 1945, Chap. 19. The old upper class, like the new upper class, in the Negro community was composed of middle-class Negroes whose position in the Negro community caused them to play the role of an upper class.

which upset the old class structure of the Negro community, the "sporting" an
criminal elements began to acquire a dominant position among Negroes.[11]. . .

The deeper significance of the break with the Negro's traditional background i
revealed in the religious outlook and behavior of the black bourgeoisie. . . .[I]
moving up the social ladder Negroes have tended to leave the Baptist an
Methodist churches and have affiliated with the Episcopal, Congregational, an
Presbyterian churches, and to a less extent with the Catholic Church. In the pa:
this usually meant that Negroes who were rising in the social scale mainly becaus
of education were seeking a form of religious expression more in accord with thei
developed religious sentiments. But with the emergence of the new black bourgeoi
sie, a radical change has occurred in the religious outlook and practices of thos
who have risen to the top of the social pyramid. Religion has become secular an
practical in the sense that it is no longer concerned with the mystery and meanin
of life and that it has become divorced from any real religious sentiment. Th
church of the Negro masses, like the fraternal organizations, is regarded as a
instrument for the advancement of the interests of the black bourgeoisie, while th
churches with which the black bourgeoisie affiliate are regarded as part of th
social paraphernalia of this class. They give money to the churches of the masse
as an expenditure for good "public relations." The contributions which they mak
to the churches with which they themselves are affiliated have become a form c
conspicuous consumption. But they have little time or sympathy for the traditiona
religion of the Negro as expressed in the Spirituals. Such religion, according t
their view, belongs to the past which should be forgotten.

Having abandoned their social heritage and being rejected by the white world
the black bourgeoisie have an intense feeling of inferiority, constantly seek variou
forms of recognition and place great value upon status symbols in order to com
pensate for their inferiority complex. . . .

What has erroneously been called "the rise of the poor whites" in the 1890'
inaugurated a period in the history of the Negro in the United States during whicl
a studied campaign was carried on to prove that the Negro was subhuman, mor
ally degenerate, and incapable of being educated. Although the "Bourbons" ha
achieved political power on the racial issue, they often had as little regard for poo
whites as for poor Negroes. Once in power, they were willing to leave the voteles
and landless Negroes in peace. But the demagogic leaders of the poor white
carried on a ceaseless campaign of terror and vituperation against all persons o
Negro descent for over a quarter of a century. . . .

During this campaign to prove that the Negro was subhuman and unfit fo
human association, the masses of Negroes found a refuge within the isolated worl
of the Negro folk. Their lives revolved principally about their churches, wher
they sang their songs of resignation and looked forward to another world in whicl
they might escape the contempt and disdain of the white man. The Negro wh
migrated to a Northern city discovered that he was only half-a-man in the whit

---

[11]Drake, pp. 546–550.

man's world.[12] The educated middle-class Negroes, who had striven to conform to American ideals and had contacts with a larger social world, could not find a refuge in the world of the Negro folk. In the South they were subject to the same Jim Crow Laws and contempt as the Negro masses, and in the North they were outsiders.[13] The mass migrations of Negroes to Northern cities and the impact of the two world wars upon the United States changed the relation of the Negro to American society. But Negroes have remained outsiders, who still face the problem of being integrated into American society. The black bourgeoisie, who have striven to mold themselves in the image of the white man, have not been able to escape from the mark of racial inferiority.

The struggle for status and recognition

Although the old black bourgeoisie, or Negro upper class, was not able to find a refuge in the world of the Negro folk, nevertheless, they were sheltered to some extent against the contempt and terror of the white man because they lived within the segregated Negro world. Their privileged position at the top of the social pyramid behind the walls of segregation provided some compensation for their hurt self-esteem. But while the Negro folk were exposed to a greater extent to the violence of the whites, the black bourgeoisie was more exposed in a spiritual sense. Except for the economic relations with whites, the Negro folk could retreat within their own world with its peculiar religious life, recreation, and family and sex life. Moreover, since the thinking of the Negro folk was not affected as that of the black bourgeoisie by the books and papers in which the Negro's inferiority was proclaimed, the black bourgeoisie suffered spiritually not only because they were affected by ideas concerning the Negro's inferiority, but perhaps even more because they had adopted the white man's values and patterns of behavior. Consequently, they developed an intense inferiority complex and because of this inferiority complex sought compensations.

A large section of the old middle class sought compensations in their white heritage.[14] They were not merely proud of their white complexion, but they boasted of

---

[12]See Mary White Ovington, *Half a Man*, New York: Longmans, 1911.

[13]In 1908, Charles Francis Adams of the famous Adams family, influential in the history of the United States since the American Revolution, declared that the American theory concerning the assimilation of all races had broken in regard to the Negro since he was "a foreign substance" that could "neither be assimilated nor thrown out." Quoted in Robert E. Park and Ernest W. Burgess, *Introduction to the Science of Sociology*, Chicago: University of Chicago Press, 1924, p. 760.

[14]See Edward B. Reuter, *The Mulatto in the United States*, Boston: Richard G. Badger, Gorham Press, 1918, for a study of the extent of race mixture and the role of the mixed bloods among Negroes in the United States. This book is the most important source of information on the mulatto or Negro of mixed ancestry up to the second decade of the present century, despite the fact that it reflects some of the current prejudices of whites and contains a number of serious errors. For example, the author states on p. 317 that "In the United States almost every Negro of prominence from Frederick Douglass to Jack Johnson has married a white woman or a light-colored mulatto." While it was very likely true that the majority of prominent Negroes, who were themselves mulattoes, married mulattoes, only a negligible number of prominent Negroes married white women.

their kinship with the aristocratic whites of the South. In fact, in some cases their white ancestors had helped them to secure an education or had provided for them economically. They also sought compensations in the standards of puritanical family and sex mores, which set them apart from the black masses. But the chief compensation for their inferior status in American society was found in education. While their racial heritage and conventional standards of morality only gave them a privileged position in the Negro community, education gave them access to a world of ideas that provided an intellectual escape from their physical and social segregation in American life. Therefore, they placed an exaggerated importance upon academic degrees, especially if they were secured from white colleges in the North. If one secured the degree of doctor of philosophy in a northern university, he was regarded as a sort of genius. Consequently, for the relatively small group of educated Negroes, education was an indication of their "superior culture" and a mark of "refinement."

Education was not simply a form of compensation because it set them apart from the Negro masses; it provided a form of compensation as regards their relations with whites. They constantly asserted their educational and "cultural" superiority to the majority of the whites whose education was inferior to theirs. Whenever they had contacts with white men who called them by their first names or insulted them, they would take consolation in the fact that the white man was ignorant and could not appreciate art and literature or the things of the spirit as they could. Was not DuBois expressing this type of compensation when, while a professor of sociology in Atlanta University during the early years of the century, he wrote, "I sit with Shakespeare and he winces not. Across the color line I move arm in arm with Balzac and Dumas, where smiling men and welcoming women glide in gilded hall"?[15]

Despite their solid achievements and the satisfactions which they derived from their way of life, there was always an atmosphere of unreality surrounding the isolated life of the small black middle class. As we have seen, urbanization and the increasing occupational differentiation of the Negro population undermined the privileged position of the old middle class. But more important still, the compensations which ancestry, puritanical morals, and especially education, provided in a hostile white world were inadequate in the life of a new black bourgeoisie. Having become less isolated and thus more exposed to the contempt and hostility of the white world, but at the same time cherishing the values of the white world, the new black bourgeoisie with more money at their disposal, have sought compensations in the things that money can buy. Moreover, their larger incomes have enabled them to propagate false notions about their place in American life and to create a world of make-believe. . . .

---

[15]W. E. Burghardt DuBois, *The Souls of Black Folks*, fifteenth edition, Chicago: A. C. McClurg and Co., 1926, p. 109.

BEHIND THE MASKS Since the black bourgeoisie live largely in a world of make-believe, the masks which they wear to play their sorry roles conceal the feelings of inferiority and of insecurity and the frustrations that haunt their inner lives. Despite their attempt to escape from real identification with the masses of Negroes, they can not escape the mark of oppression any more than their less favored kinsmen. In attempting to escape identification with the black masses, they have developed a self-hatred that reveals itself in their deprecation of the physical and social characteristics of Negroes. Likewise, their feelings of inferiority and insecurity are revealed in their pathological struggle for status within the isolated Negro world and craving for recognition in the white world. Their escape into a world of make-believe with its sham "society" leaves them with a feeling of emptiness and futility which causes them to constantly seek an escape in new delusions.

The mark of oppression

There is an attempt on the part of the parents in middle-class families to shield their children against racial discrimination and the contempt of whites for colored people. Sometimes the parents go to fantastic extremes, such as prohibiting the use of the words "Negro" or "colored" in the presence of their children.[16] They sometimes try to prevent their children from knowing that they can not enter restaurants or other public places because they are Negroes, or even that the schools they attend are segregated schools for Negroes. Despite such efforts to insulate their children against a hostile white world, the children of the black bourgeoisie can not escape the mark of oppression. . . .

Not all middle-class Negroes consciously desire . . . to be white in order to escape from their feelings of inferiority. In fact, the majority of middle-class Negroes would deny having the desire to be white, since this would be an admission of their feeling of inferiority. Within an intimate circle of friends some middle-class Negroes may admit that they desire to be white, but publicly they would deny any such wish. The black bourgeoisie constantly boast of their pride in their identification as Negroes. But when one studies the attitude of this class in regard to the physical traits or the social characteristics of Negroes, it becomes clear that the black bourgeoisie do not really wish to be identified with Negroes.

Insecurities and frustrations

Since the black bourgeoisie cannot escape identification with Negroes, they experience certain feelings of insecurity because of their feeling of inferiority. Their feeling of inferiority is revealed in their fear of competition with whites. . . .

[16]E. Franklin Frazier, *Negro Youth at the Crossways*, Washington, D.C.: American Council on Education, 1940, p. 62.

The fear of competition with whites is probably responsible for the black bour geoisie's fear of competence and first-rate performance within its own ranks When a Negro is competent and insists upon first-rate work it appears to th class that he is trying to be a white man, or that he is insisting that Negroe measure up to white standards. This is especially true where the approval c whites is taken as a mark of competence and first-rate performance. In such case the black bourgeoisie reveal their ambivalent attitudes toward the white worl They slavishly accept the estimate which almost any white man places upon Negro or his work, but at the same time they fear and reject white standards. Fo example, when a group of Negro doctors were being shown the modern equipmen and techniques of a white clinic, one of them remarked to a Negro professor in medical school, "This is the white man's medicine. I never bother with it and sti I make $30,000 a year." Negroes who adopt the standards of the white worl create among the black bourgeoisie a feeling of insecurity and often become th object of both the envy and hatred of this class. . . .

Both men and women among the black bourgeoisie have a feeling of insecurit because of their constant fear of the loss of status. Since they have no status in th larger American society, the intense struggle for status among middle-clas Negroes is, as we have seen, an attempt to compensate for the contempt and lov esteem of the whites. Great value is, therefore, placed upon all kinds of statu symbols. Academic degrees, both real and honorary, are sought in order to secur status. Usually the symbols are of a material nature implying wealth and conspicu ous consumption. Sometimes Negro doctors do not attend what are supposedl scientific meetings because they do not have a Cadillac or some other expensiv automobile. School teachers wear mink coats and maintain homes beyond thei income for fear that they may lose status. The extravagance in "social" life gen erally is due to an effort not to lose status. But in attempting to overcome thei fear of loss of status they are often beset by new feelings of insecurity. In spite o their pretended wealth, they are aware that their incomes are insignificant an that they must struggle to maintain their mortgaged homes and the show o "wealth" in lavish "social" affairs. Moreover, they are beset by a feeling of inse curity because of their struggles to maintain a show of wealth through illega means. From time to time "wealthy" Negro doctors are arrested for selling nar cotics and performing abortions. The life of many a "wealthy" Negro doctor i shortened by the struggle to provide diamonds, minks, and an expensive home fo his wife.

There is much frustration among the black bourgeoisie despite their privilegec position within the segregated Negro world. Their "wealth" and "social" positior can not erase the fact that they are generally segregated and rejected by the white world. Their incomes and occupations may enable them to escape the cruder manifestations of racial prejudice, but they can not insulate themselves against the more subtle forms of racial discrimination. These discriminations cause frustrations in Negro men because they are not allowed to play the "masculine role" as defined by American culture. They can not assert themselves or exercise power as white men do. When they protest against racial discrimination there is always the threat that they will be punished by the white world. In spite of the movement toward the wider integration of the Negro into the general stream of American life, middle-class Negroes are still threatened with the loss of positions and earning power if they insist upon their rights.[17] After the Supreme Court of the United States ruled that segregation in public education was illegal, Negro teachers in some parts of the South were dismissed because they would not sign statements supporting racial segregation in education. . . .

The frustrated lives of the black bourgeoisie are reflected in the attitudes of parents towards their children. Middle-class Negro families as a whole have few children, while among the families that constitute Negro "society" there are many childless couples.[18] One finds today, as an American observed over 40 years ago, that "where the children are few, they are usually spoiled" in middle-class Negro families.[19] There is often not only a deep devotion to their one or two children, but a subservience to them. It is not uncommon for the only son to be called and treated as the "boss" in the family. Parents cater to the transient wishes of their children and often rationalize their behavior towards them on the grounds that children should not be "inhibited." They spend large sums of money on their children for toys and especially for clothes. They provide their children with automobiles when they go to college. All of this is done in order that the children may maintain the status of the parents and be eligible to enter the "social" set in Negro colleges. When they send their children to Northern "white" colleges they often spend more time in preparing them for what they imagine will be their "social" life than in preparing them for the academic requirements of these institutions.

In their fierce devotion to their children, which generally results in spoiling them, middle-class Negro parents are seemingly striving at times to establish a human relationship that will compensate for their own frustrations in the realm of human relationships. Devotion to their children often becomes the one human tie that is sincere and free from the competition and artificiality of the make-believe world in which they live. Sometimes they may project upon their children their own frustrated professional ambitions. But usually, even when they send their children to Northern "white" universities as a part of their "social" striving within the Negro community, they seem to hope that their children will have an acceptance in the white world which has been denied them.

---

[17]See, for example, the article "YMCA Secretary in Virginia Fired for Equality Fight," *Washington Afro-American*, August 1954, p. 20.

[18]See Frazier, *The Negro Family in the United States*, Chicago: University of Chicago Press, 1939, pp. 440–443.

[19]Robert E. Park, "Negro Home Life and Standards of Living," *The Negro's Progress in Fifty Years*, Philadelphia, Pa.: American Academy of Political and Social Science, 1913, p. 163.

Self-hatred and guilt feelings

One of the chief frustrations of the middle-class Negro is that he can not escape identification with the Negro race and consequently is subject to the contempt of whites.[20] Despite his "wealth" in which he has placed so much faith as a solvent of racial discrimination, he is still subject to daily insults and is excluded from participation in white American society. Middle-class Negroes do not express their resentment against discrimination and insults in violent outbreaks, as lower-class Negroes often do. They constantly repress their hostility toward whites and seek to soothe their hurt self-esteem in all kinds of rationalizations. They may boast of their wealth and culture as compared with the condition of the poor whites. Most often they will resort to any kind of subterfuge in order to avoid contact with whites. For example, in the South they often pay their bills by mail rather than risk unpleasant contacts with representatives of white firms.[21] The daily repression of resentment and the constant resort to means of avoiding contacts with whites do not relieve them of their hostility toward whites. Even middle-class Negroes who gain a reputation for exhibiting "objectivity" and a "statesmanlike" attitude on racial discrimination harbor deep-seated hostilities toward whites. A Negro college president who has been considered such an interracial "statesman" once confessed to the writer that some day he was going to "break loose" and tell white people what he really thought. However, it is unlikely that a middle-class Negro of his standing will ever "break loose." Middle-class Negroes generally express their aggressions against whites by other means, such as deceiving whites and utilizing them for their own advantage.

Because middle-class Negroes are unable to indulge in aggressions against whites as such, they will sometimes make other minority groups the object of their hostilities. For example, they may show hostility against Italians, who are also

---

[20]A Middle-class mulatto woman, a former school teacher, who was fearful of the impact of this book on European readers and Southern detractors of "The Race," concluded her review of the original French edition with these words:

"Isn't it about time our sociologists and specialists on the 'race problem' in America, began to discuss and consider middle-class Negroes as middle-class Americans, or better, *all* U.S. Negroes as *Americans* with three hundred unbroken years of American tradition, way of life, cultural and spiritual contacts behind them—influences which have molded them as they have molded all others who are considered, even when not treated completely so, as members of the American community? Isn't it time to stop thinking of and talking about Negroes as a separate and distinct entity in the general scheme of things? And above all, isn't it time to realize that the melting pot has melted truly and fused together all the myriad (albeit conflicting) racial, cultural, educational, spiritual, and social elements which have combined in such peculiar fashion to produce the American Negro of our time?" *Journal of Negro Education*, Vol. XXV, p. 141.

[21]See Charles S. Johnson, *Patterns of Negro Segregation*, New York: Harper & Row, 1943, Chaps. XII, XIII, and XIV which describe the ways in which Negroes in various classes deal with racial discrimination.

subject to discrimination. But more often middle-class Negroes, especially those who are engaged in a mad scramble to accumulate money, will direct their hostilities against Jews. They are constantly expressing their anti-semitism within Negro circles, while pretending publicly to be free from prejudice. They blame the Jew for the poverty of Negroes and for their own failures and inefficiencies in their business undertakings. In expressing their hostility towards Jews, they are attempting at the same time to identify with the white American majority.

The repressed hostilities of middle-class Negroes to whites are not only directed towards other minority groups but inward toward themselves. This results in self-hatred, which may appear from their behavior to be directed towards the Negro masses but which in reality is directed against themselves.[22] While pretending to be proud of being a Negro, they ridicule Negroid physical characteristics and seek to modify or efface them as much as possible. Within their own groups they constantly proclaim that "niggers" make them sick. The very use of the term "nigger," which they claim to resent, indicates that they want to disassociate themselves from the Negro masses. . . .

The self-hatred of middle-class Negroes is often revealed in the keen competition which exists among them for status and recognition. This keen competition is the result of the frustrations which they experience in attempting to obtain acceptance and recognition by whites. Middle-class Negroes are constantly criticizing and belittling Negroes who achieve some recognition or who acquire a status above them. They prefer to submit to the authority of whites than to be subordinate to other Negroes. For example, Negro scholars generally refuse to seek the advice and criticism of competent Negro scholars and prefer to turn to white scholars for such cooperation. In fact, it is difficult for middle-class Negroes to cooperate in any field of endeavor. This failure in social relations is, as indicated in an important study, because "in every Negro he encounters his own self-contempt."[23] It is as if he said, "You are only a Negro like myself; so why should you be in a position above me?"

This self-hatred often results in guilt feelings on the part of the Negro who succeeds in elevating himself above his fellows.[24] He feels unconsciously that in rising above other Negroes he is committing an act of aggression which will result in hatred and revenge on their part. The act of aggression may be imagined, but very often it is real. This is the case when middle-class Negroes oppose the economic and social welfare of Negroes because of their own interests. In some American cities, it has been the black bourgeoisie and not the whites who have opposed the building of low-cost public housing for Negro workers. In one city two wealthy Negro doctors, who have successfully opposed public housing projects

---

[22]See Abram Kardiner and Lionel Ovesey, *The Mark of Oppression*, New York: Norton, 1951, pp. 190, 282, 297.
[23]Kardiner and Ovesey, p. 177.
[24]Kardiner and Ovesey, p. 203.

for Negro workers, own some of the worst slums in the United States. While their wives, who wear mink coats, "drip with diamonds" and are written up in the "society" columns of Negro newspapers, ride in Cadillacs, their Negro tenants sleep on the dirt floors of hovels unfit for human habitation. The guilt feelings of the middle-class Negro are not always unconscious. For example, take the case of the Negro leader who proclaimed over the radio in a national broadcast that the Negro did not want social equity. He was conscious of his guilt feelings and his self-hatred in playing such a role, for he sent word privately to the writer that he never hated so much to do anything in his life, but that it was necessary because of his position as head of a state college which was under white supervision. The self-hatred of the middle-class Negro arises, then, not only from the fact that he does not want to be a Negro but also because of his sorry role in American society. . . .

7.6 INTRODUCTION

The concluding selection in this chapter raises some fundamental questions about the phenomenon of social class and about our understanding of it. The authors suggest that some of the concepts that are generally applied may be inappropriate and inadequate to comprehend the facts of social class in our complex urban society and they offer their own framework as an alternative. Their discussion thus provides a fresh perspective on the earlier materials in this chapter. Its distinctive feature is its emphasis on the necessity of examining the cultural and social system as a whole in order to properly identify what social classes differentiate within it. Doing this leads Arensberg and Kimball to seriously question the simple upper-middle-lower structure which is the usual conception of our system. More basically, they caution against the danger of treating social class as a real aspect of the world rather than as an abstract concept that we use to understand it.

In addition to this broadening perspective, this essay offers the reader some basic analytic tools that should sharpen his understanding of "social class differences." The authors consider one of the unique and most important characteristics of the social system of the metropolis to be the contrast and separation between the two worlds in which individuals live and interact—the private one of family and friends and the public one of work and organizations. They assert (and demonstrate) that the interrelationships between these two worlds are different at different points in the social structure and they consider that it is within the distinctions that thus emerge that are to be found the significant dimensions of social differentiation in urban society.

As one of the authors of this selection stated in an earlier one (Selection 6.5), a major function of educational institutions is to promote the individual's shift from the private to the public world. From the evidence presented here it seems likely hat such a shift will often be incompatible with the attitudes toward the two worlds that the individual child acquired in his family and that, as a result, such a child will be "out of tune" in a number of ways with the expectations and demands in terms of which education is transmitted. He will probably be equally alienated from the attempts of relevant adults—teachers, guidance counselors, administrators—to help him with his difficulties, since such attempts would undoubtedly be based on the same values and attitudes that he cannot accept or even comprehend.

As the ensuing selection underlines, the essence of social class is cultural identity, rather than income level, occupation, or status. It is thus in such basic processes as perception, communication, and interaction that class differences will be most evident and out of which organizational problems are most likely to arise. Either of these points is sufficient to make social class of central relevance to a guidance counselor's theoretical framework and practical concerns.

7.6 METROPOLIS AND SOCIAL CLASS[1]

Solon J. Kimball and Conrad M. Arensberg

BASIC THEORY The widely prevalent misunderstandings that have plagued most discussions about social class analysis force us to restate, initially, some underlying assumptions. Basic to all other considerations is the biocultural nature of man. Its significance is emphasized in the universally present cultural distinctions based upon sex, age, and status. These three distinctions contain the crucial aspects of family structure and function, the process of mate selection, reproduction of the species, care of the young, and transmission of the culture. Within family organization and through its correlative processes the behavior of each individual is ordered in relation to his membership in a group. In this ordering, the biological factors of sex and age become culturally defined. Status, in contrast, may be derived entirely from sociocultural differentiations, although its linkage to biological criteria such as sex, race, or ancestry is not uncommon. Thus, a hierarchy of status distinctions in a society is itself one cultural aspect of the social ordering. When we speak of social

[1]Abridged from *Culture and Community* by Conrad Arensberg and Solon T. Kimball, © 1965 by Harcourt, Brace & World, Inc., and reprinted with their permission.

class we are designating one type of status system. But the primacy of biocultural behavior in mate selection and family structure is a fact to be kept continuously in mind.

The social ordering of individuals is only one of the devices through which the group sustains and perpetuates itself. There are, in addition, what are called the cultural instrumentalities. These include the items and means by which individuals are fed, clothed, and housed—the technology, the customary ways in which persons behave toward each other and organize themselves in cooperative groups and the secular and sacred beliefs that explain and sanction the relations of men to the universe. These instrumentalities are an integral part of all groupings, and their differential distribution and use provide major criteria upon which to base determinations about status and social class. . . .

But there is a further proposition to which we must also give heed, namely, that each cultural system is associated with its own form of community. If this proposition proves valid then we must also accept social class in the metropolis as something other than that which has been described for the mill and Main Street towns, or for the two-class county-town and plantation community of the antebellum South. Each pattern carries its own meaning within the context of a specific cultural and organizational system. . . .

SOCIAL CLASS   . . .We differ most strongly with those who
AND METROPOLIS   attempt to theorize upon class as something apart from community. Our own position is derived from the basic anthropological axiom that data must be examined within their context.

Affirmatively and specifically, we contend that each culture possesses its characteristic community form; hence, the organizational forms through which people order their relations with each other are essential correlates of the culture and of its subcultural variants. Thus theory and empirical delineation of social class must be consonant with comparable concerns about community, and vice versa. Since the metropolis is one of several forms of community, any conceptual formulations about it, usually labeled urban theory, must also include the cultural dimension of social class. Any other procedure leads to an incomplete or even distorted basis from which to comprehend the whole.

The gross outline of the organizational system of the metropolis is relatively obvious. We could begin to construct it from any one of several vantages—time, space, groupings, or activities—and the formulations to which we would come would be essentially similar. Let us arbitrarily begin with activity by differentiating between work and nonwork. . . .

Even casual reflection quickly establishes the extent to which we automatically, and often unconsciously, assign the events in which we act alone or participate with others to either work or nonwork categories. Furthermore, the distinctions are reinforced through association with other variables. For example, eating, sleeping, playing, making love, vacationing, and so forth, follow a rhythmic sequence in specific locales and with designated persons quite distinct from the rhythm, locale, and associations of work. We engage in the latter in the office, factory, store, or field. Even students when they are in the classroom or doing homework are at work in a very special sense. Now the separation of activity into work and nonwork is not peculiar to metropolitan culture, but the degree to which the two are dichotomized and their respective linkage with social groupings and places are distinctive. In fact, the organizational form of the metropolis itself explains the cleavage we observe.

In metropolitan society the production and distribution of goods and the provision of services are relegated to one or more of its great organizational superstructures—government, industry, commerce, transportation, education, health—even recreation and religion. Directly, as in the case of the federal government with its millions of employees, or of General Motors and comparable industrial giants with their hundreds of thousands; or indirectly, in the case of self-employed repairmen, retailers, professional men, or farmers, there exists a vast network of interrelated formal organizational and individual ties. In this social milieu the work of the world gets done, and only special groups, such as children and the aged, are exempt, while escape from contribution to it is limited to the handful who comprise the insane, the criminal, the social derelicts, and the very rich. These organizations and the consequences of the activities of their members are public, not in the old dualism of governmental versus private enterprise, but in the sense that the consequences of the activities of their members have direct relevance for the functioning of the total society.

The sense of public value can hardly be attached to activities carried on within one's family, among friends, or in leisure-time pursuits. Any housewife will stoutly defend her domestic chores as essential to the well-being of her husband and children, and the family head will protest that his devotion to yard and house is both desirable and necessary. But rationally there is no labor requirement on the premises of a family dwelling that cannot be supplied by an organization external to its occupants, a fact that has already been established for those thousands who are occupants of apartment hotels. Even the primacy of the traditional family as a procreating unit was challenged in nineteenth century agrarian America by the radical experiments in communal living at Oneida and similar utopian communities (Nordhoff, 1961). We do not deny the importance and usefulness of the work activity within the family setting but insist that its meaning must be sought within its own context—the distinctive structural form and functional purposes that characterize the family in contemporary America. And further, we must seek the relation between this form of the family and other institutional arrangements.

When the family and the larger units are examined in the framework of their complementary relations, we are impressed with the extent to which they differ in structure and function (Kimball and McClellan, 1962). If the members of the metropolis make their contribution to society and derive their livelihood from participation in the public world of the organizational superstructures, it is within the bosom of family and friends that the intimate, personal, and private world is contained. Those who proclaim that the organization threatens to engulf the total life of its members need to look again at the evidence (Whyte, 1956). It might be argued with equal vigor that only because of organizational membership is it possible to claim a separate, private life. Certainly for the vast majority of people there is little direct intrusion by the organization into their private world. When one's private life, intentionally or fortuitously, becomes intertwined with role performance in organizational structure, the consequences range from simple complications to disaster. The validity of the separation of the two can be seen with great clarity in the ethics that prescribe the relation between practitioner and client in professional circles. Revelation of personal confidences or utilization of position or knowledge for personal gain by a priest, lawyer, or physician is abhorrent and condemned. Although this tradition arose in response to the emergence of public roles once relegated to relatively few, as new occupations become professionalized the tradition has been extended to include them also.

When we contrast the metropolitan system with its massive social groupings in their structural counterpoise with the family and friendship group, and with the internal social arrangements of other community types, we are additionally struck by the uniqueness of the contemporary system. In the New England village, religious, civic, and familial forms were intertwined as community. The accompanying values and sanctioned behavior were neatly joined in a coherent whole which ideally prescribed a single code of conduct in all situations except those involving the deviant or stranger—these by definition being unworthy of full community status. The physically dispersed but blood-bound families of the Appalachian Mountains knew no organizational tie more complex than the equalitarian religious association which, in reality, conjoined extended kindred. Actually, neither "public" nor "private" could be viable categories in a culture in which all events were refracted through a code of individual liberty and family obligation.

When we observe how the far more complex community form of the mill and Main Street towns developed, we note the proliferation of formally organized institutional arrangements in government, religion, commerce, education, health, industry, transportation, and voluntary associations. An elaborate cultural diversity accompanied the new social complexity. Family lineage, manners, morals, wealth, and participation and position within organized groups together contributed to and gave expression to status evaluations and rankings. The grouping of linked traits in configurational patterns was called social class (Warner, 1941; Davis *et al.*, 1941). But distinctions between public and private were still not sharply delineated. The identification of the business and professional class with the town-community never permitted a sharp separation between their personal affairs and the town's economic well-being and institutions. As each town grew and prospered, so did its citizens and all of their enterprises, whether they were religious, educational, or commercial.

Our understanding of social class in America has arisen largely from the empirical studies of mill and Main Street towns. The designations that portrayed the dynamics of such communities are not fully applicable to the older industrial or commerical cities of the Northeast in their new transition, or to the newer ones of the Southwest and Pacific Coast. The latter are forging a community form expressive of a newer America, while the heritage of the others inevitably constricts their current transformation. But for all, the new community form is contained within the counterpoise of the public, organizational superstructures and the nuclear family. If, then, social class is a manifestation of the social system, as we proposed earlier, from what criteria do we erect the categorization to express social class in metropolis?

However useful the categorization of subcultures in town-community into the broad categories of lower, middle, and upper classes (or other euphemistic variations) may have been for that community type, we claim that this division has about the same relevance for the metropolis that the separation of living forms into plants and animals possesses for advanced scientific study among biologists. In some measure there is a correspondence between the complexity of the problem and the techniques and concepts utilized to examine it. Comparatively, the social elaboration of the metropolis is much greater than that of the town-community. As one consequence there exists a greater variety of subcultural divisions. Their significance, however, appears only when we establish their functions and trace their connections with the relevant social forms. As an example, a first series of problems arises from the attempt to relate coordinate positions within the multiple layered hierarchies of the corporate superstructures and cultural behavior. Would such an analysis justify further subdivisions of existing class categories, or should we re-examine our analytic procedures? The logic of the argument also forces us to ask the question: Is it necessary, or possible, to substitute an analytic process for the one that now "stratifies" a society into a series of inferior and superior positions? Basically, we are asking if there might not be another and more scientifically rewarding method of delineating class, other than that leading to the geometric imagery which now prevails. As yet we have no sure alternative to offer, although we believe that social class examined as a function of participation in events provides a new direction.

The problems mentioned above are germane, since the conception of social classes as a vertical arrangement of subcultural systems must in the future also take account of the parallel of public and private social groupings, each with its own cultural identities and its own logic. Only if we recognize this basic structural dichotomy can we handle analytically the institutional culture of large organizations and professionally trained and oriented workers on the one hand, and the culture of the personal world exemplified in kinship and peer group on the other. The degree to which these two cultural systems are interconnected provides a fascinating problem for future researchers. Moreover, the organization of empirical data within this framework offers one key to clearing away much of the confusion that now surrounds urban theory. At the very least, class and urban theory will be examined as complementary. . . .

If the ordering of relationships and behavior in our private lives were the same as that in the world of work, or if the position of individuals in the hierarchical scale of a bureaucracy or institution or in professional ranking could be used as the basis for explaining social class, many of our problems would be solved. If a population could be tabulated by ranked occupational position, the rate and magnitude of mobility could be precisely gauged by compiling changes in grade and salary. In a thoroughly institutionalized setting such as an army post, one finds a nearly precise correspondence between official status, grade, size, and quality of housing, perquisites, deference, and prescribed manner of social behavior. No one believes that such rigid and complete organizational structure exists or could be imposed upon private life in a civilian population, although research to establish the extent to which comparability does exist has yet to be done. Even casual observation, however, easily confirms some degree of correspondence, and we are in the habit of rating urban districts and suburbs on a scale of greater or lesser prestige based upon our perception of their dwellings as expressive of the social ranking of their residents in organizations and professions. But if, as we believe, the organizational system of work impinges only indirectly upon the private lives of its members, then we must turn to criteria other than those which determine organizational status if we are to understand social class, although to deny any connection between them is absurd. It is obvious that the amount of income one derives from his employment or profession potentially has a direct effect upon his level of consumption and hence upon his accessibility to persons and things which are indices of class position. But it has also been established that the way wealth is used is of greater diagnostic value in class determination than the mere facts of its possession or acquisition. . . .

CULTURAL IDENTITY AND SOCIAL CLASS Among the principles that explain the adjustment and survival of plant and animal species, one holds direct analogy and relevance for cultural systems. Survival of individuals and species depends upon adaptation to existing conditions and includes such processes as symbiosis, parasitism, cooperation, competition, and successions; the modification of these conditions; genetic changes in the species through natural selection; or any combination of these. Although we must avoid imputing species consciousness to adjustment behavior, or assuming a natural determinism, it is difficult to express the consequences in other than vitalistic language. Thus, we say that each species strives to create an optimum environment for itself and its descendants. Obviously, the finely balanced tension between life forms stimulates further modification and adjustment as each individual strives for advantage. In this perspective the central business district or the slums have never provided a favorable environment for the middle class. The departure of its members from the older industrial cities for the suburbs may be explained, in part, by the principle of succession of groups based upon environmental changes.

If we view the subcultural variants (social class) of any society as analogous to a species (or subspecies) and accept the general validity of the principles that explain stability and change, then our search for the dynamics of social class carries us to the examination of cultural identity. Cultural identity is derived from the specific behavioral configuration associated with each group. Its possession permits its members to distinguish between themselves and others. The identification is made on the basis of similarities and dissimilarities—the external evidences of cultural variability—and membership through participation. This latter is given expression through family, neighborhood, peer group, and sociability among equals.

We must remember, however, that the perpetuation of a subcultural system is more than the re-enactment, through events, of behavior and values. There must be successors. These may be acquired through recruitment and conversion, but ordinarily cultural and biological inheritances are linked. Cultural transmission comes first through learning by the young from parents and later from cultural peers and others. For this reason the choice of a mate and marriage are so crucial. Through their offspring, those joined in marriage as cultural equivalents provide an environment that ensures the continuation of a cultural line. The cruciality rests upon more, however, than mere perpetuation. Marriage is also a test of the validity of cultural identity, not only for the principals, but in particular for the parents of the newly wedded couple. And if participation is extended to the kin and friends, it is because the event affirms both identity and membership. Note, however, that only incidentally is marriage inclusive of neighborhood, and it is not at all inclusive of community.

Social class, however, is only one of the facets of cultural identity. In fact, in comparison with other identities such as sex, age, race, religion, or ethnic group, it is far more comprehensive and fluid. For these latter dimensions a person is permanently labeled. Microcultural examination of subcultural behavior verifies the minuteness and overlappings of the gradations of cultural identity, which are less exact than a pecking order and testify to the range of variability. Thus there can be no absoluteness in class identity, as there is in sex or race. The social position one inherits must be validated or it is impaired, and change in behavior is a possibility which can carry one up or down the scale.

These observations are abstractions which should be examined against empirical data. For verification we shall rely on the evidence contained in two studies of contrasting subcommunities. The first is a recently published report on a working-class Italian section in the West End of Boston (Gans, 1962). The other describes an upper-middle-class suburb of Toronto populated about equally by Jews and Gentiles (Seeley, Sim, and Loosley, 1956). For each of these we shall summarize and contrast the relevant data in four areas: family organization, transmission of culture, selection of marriage partners, and work and relations with the outside. These are the variables that appear to us to make the greatest contribution to an understanding of social class in the metropolis.

THE WEST END   It is not surprising that the family system congenial to the American-born Italians of Boston's West End resembles that of their immigrant parents. It is a society of intense relationships and deep loyalties to those of the same blood and to the friends with whom one has grown to adulthood. This restrictive grouping of conjoined age mates has led Gans (1962) to refer to this form of organization as a "peer group society," in which "during adulthood, the family is its most important component. Adult West Enders spend almost as much time with siblings, in-laws, and cousins—that is, with relatives of the same sex and age—as with their spouses, and more time than with parents, aunts, and uncles" (Gans, p. 37).

Within this tightly knit group of adults—kin and peers—each child learns the behavior and values which he carries with him as he joins with those whose similar backgrounds provide a familiar environment of personal relationships. Here he builds the ties that persist beyond the time when the young man takes a bride and establishes his own family.

In this adult-centered family system, the child encounters "a continuous barrage of prohibitions and threats, intertwined with words and deeds of reward and affection" (Gans, p. 59). He is viewed as a little adult, for whom it is necessary to prescribe the behavior that is expected of him, but with little evidence of parental concern "about how he receives their messages" (Gans, p. 59). "Impulsive child-rearing is possible because West Enders are not concerned with *developing* their children, that is, with raising them in accordance with a predetermined goal or target which they are expected to achieve. Unlike adult-directed or even child-centered families found in the middle class, West Enders have no clear image of the future social status, occupational level, or life-style that they want their children to reach. And even when they do, they do not know how to build it into the child-rearing process" (Gans, pp. 59–60).

As Gans describes it, the "West Enders want for their children what they want for themselves" (Gans, p. 60). But there is no pressure to push them toward this goal, although there is concern that the child may not equal his peers, and real fear that he may become a "bum."

The social environment that the family circle and peer group builds for its children is also the one to which the adolescent-become-adult turns in his search for a spouse. It should come as no surprise that intermarriage with non-Italians is rare in the second generation and not favored for the third, although if the choice is also a Catholic the disapproval is slight. In those rare instances where out-marriage occurs, there is the usual effort to bring the stranger into the orbit of established peers and the family circle.

The peer group shapes its members' perspectives and organizes their relations with those who differ from themselves and who are found in what is to them the "outside world." The institutions, values, and behavior of the outside are judged by the same rules that govern the peer group. Outside rejection of their norms leads them to expect exploitation (which is often justified) and, in turn, to a calculated exploitation of others. They view those who hold positions in government as uniformly corrupt and guilty of denying the citizen what should be naturally his. The services that reach the peer group from the world beyond are "to be used if they are desirable and to be ignored or fought if they seek to change or injure the individual or the peer group" (Gans, p. 121).

It is in the setting of a potentially hostile, corrupt, and exploitative outside world that most members of the peer group must seek their means of livelihood. It is not surprising to discover that work as an end in itself, as an opportunity for self-development and improvement, or as a contribution to the welfare of the larger society, has little or no meaning. One works in order to make a living and to enjoy and extend the pleasures of life which are found beyond the job. Since work must be endured, the goal is to find employment where one is treated as an equal, or in some small firm that permits expression of relationships comparable to those within the peer group. This is rarely achieved. "What does matter is that identification with work, work success, and job advancement—while not absolutely rejected—are of secondary priority to the life that goes on within the family circle" (Gans, p. 245).

The rejection of the outside contributes to the intense involvement in family and peer group and produces related effects that further preserve and accentuate separation from the remainder of the society. West Enders reject middle-class status and values. In particular, they do not understand nor wish to use the educational ladder as the device for upward social mobility. In fact the "worry about downward mobility is stronger than any desire for upward mobility. Consequently, the major hope is that in education, occupation, and general status, the child will not fall below that of his peers" (Gans, p. 60). Exemplification of this rejection may also be found in the indifference, even hostility, to those cultural missionaries of the middle class found in settlement houses, libraries, and similar transplants from middle-class society.

CRESTWOOD HEIGHTS No yardstick extant can convey any true measure of the cultural gulf that separates the Italian, working-class West Enders from the upper-middle-class residents of Crestwood Heights (Seeley *et al.*, 1956). Our recourse is to let the weight of comparative, empirical description carry the burden of establishing the differences.

The physical contrast alone is impressive enough. In the West End one found the massed tenements of an older American city in association with the small shops and street-corner bars catering to the local population, a setting in which street corner society flourished. In contrast, Crestwood Heights is a community of single family homes, each separated by lawn and shrubbery from those adjoining it, and a community in which "the massive centrality of the schools. . .assert the community as a physically organized entity, as a psychological reality, and as a social fact" (Seeley *et al.,* p. 224).

In the Crestwood Heights family one encounters a pattern that is nearly identical to that found in the upper-middle-class suburbs which stretch across America. It is the family of parents and children, isolated from its kin (often socially as well as geographically), temporarily anchored in its own separate dwelling, and dependent upon the success of the father's career for its status and its future. In the limitation of emotional life to relatively few persons, disharmony in the relations among its members can be shattering to the psychic stability of the individual.

It is a family in which the finely balanced tensions between independence and dependence of its members impose upon children and parents alike a responsibility for its maintenance as a smoothly functioning unit. Within its confines and the adjunct activities of school, church, and community, the woman finds her validation as wife and mother. The man must also validate his roles as father and husband in his relationships with wife and children, but his success in these roles, and that of the others in theirs, is inexorably linked to his success in another realm of life, that of his career. It is "from this base of home and male career, which are almost inseparable, [that] the family can articulate with the community" (Seeley *et al.,* p. 163).

It is a family formed from and held together by "love," in the union of man and woman through marriage and in the care for and attention to its children. This love unites but does not bind, since freedom and individuality are highly prized. Each family member values his independence in relations with the institutions of the community.

It is a family which in its orientation to the future is perpetually poised for mobility. Unattached to the past, which "tends to be obliterated from the collective thinking of the family" (Seeley *et al.,* p. 164), it presents a flexibility that permits change of residence, of job, and of friends, if the new promises to enhance status ranking and economic well-being. When one joins the values of independence, hope in the future, and mobility, it is easy to understand why the successful separation of the child from his family of orientation and his own willful launching upon a career are both possible and necessary. But the potential and recognized consequences extend to the very nature of relations within the family itself. "Consciously, the future is optimistically viewed; and the task of the family is to equip the child as effectively as possible in the present with all available means for his later solitary climb to better and more prosperous worlds lying far ahead of him. . . . But the future nevertheless beckons with sufficient force that the parental generation, if it seriously hinders the child's upward progress, must be virtually abandoned; this is well understood by both parents and children. Only the promise of continuous upward social mobility (or, at the very least, continually validated status at the present level) can nerve the Crestwood Heights family to its obligations; and for its members to feel the full poignancy of the separation to which it, as a family, is dedicated, might well wreck the whole precarious structure" (Seeley *et al.*, p. 164).

As the children move into their teens their participation with their parents lessens as that with their peers increases. Finally, there is an almost complete separation of social life from that of the parents. One consequence of this wide range of activity permitted the teen-ager outside the family is that the older children provide a model of behavior for the younger ones and in fact can open opportunities of participation for them and teach them ways of behavior "which may be new or strange to parents" (Seeley *et al.*, p. 203).

The club or association is the focus of organized social life for the parents; the school serves the same purpose for their children. Here, in extracurricular activities, in planned social affairs, and in the exclusive system of fraternities and sororities, the young join with their peers in reproducing a system of status differentials based upon competitive achievement, family background, and the religious separation of Jews and Gentiles which resembles that of their parents. It is here also that those friendships are formed that may prove so crucial later on in the careers of the males, and that courtships blossom which prepare young people for the social roles of male and female as husband and wife in the adult life of Crestwood Heights or in its suburban counterpart elsewhere.

Only one ideal, that of "love," is accepted as the proper basis for marriage. This concept is surrounded, however, by a series of beliefs which ostensibly supply the greatest possible latitude in the search for a mate but which in reality restrict that choice to a narrow band of persons who closely resemble each other. The belief in equality, in the right of the individual to free choice, and in permissiveness in behavior and the selection of friends, might conceivably lead to an openness of groupings that would extend across class and religious lines (assuming that other groups were equally disposed). In fact, no such thing happens. The children early come to learn of the great disparity between the preachments of their parents and reality. They come to understand that the beliefs can be effected only if one is with those who resemble oneself.

The wall of exclusion that the parents throw around their children is maintained in the selection of a residence, in the summer camps to which their children go, in the arranged participation in adult social activities, and in the social affairs arranged by church or synagogue. If need be, the child may be sent to a private school, further to assure his isolation from unacceptable associates and his inclusion with his own kind, or with those whom his parents hope he will emulate.

Prior to adolescence the necessity to maintain an exclusiveness of participation is not felt as strongly as it is after the child reaches that age. In practice, romantic love does not cross ethnic or class lines. With adolescence begins the subtly enforced guidance that directs the child toward those with whom courtship and marriage is approved. There can be no open rejection of the belief that romantic love recognizes no boundaries, but it is tacitly understood that Gentile boys do not date

Jewish girls, and that Jewish boys do not date Gentile girls. There is set at this stage the barrier to intermarriage and, in turn, the definition of that group from which one seeks his marriage partner. But the system is much more precise and complicated than that based upon obvious designations of religion alone.

The ideology of the middle class in its romantic, liberal version stipulates that only those who also hold the same beliefs as it does are worthy of compatibility and intimacy. It matters not that the disjunction between belief and action is so great, because those who do not hold such beliefs (the other social classes) automatically repel the Crestwooder and hence "tend to render their possessors repugnant or less attractive as possible partners for intimacy or marriage. The very belief, therefore, that 'class is of no consequence' (which is on one side a middle-class view exclusively) becomes a token of compatibility and a basis for intimacy, and in so far as it determines friendship, membership in a clique, and marriage, a potent factor in the maintenance of the class boundaries which 'do not exist!' 'do not matter,' or 'ought not to be considered' " (Seeley *et al.*, p. 400).

Thus the guides to marriage are far more pervasive than the simple prescription of romantic love. If the indoctrination of middle-class values is successful, then there is no necessity to enforce overtly the selection of a suitable marriage partner. The child, turned adult, has already deeply internalized exactly the kind of person with whom he or she is expected to, and will, fall in love with and marry. This, then, is the cultural situation within which mate selection occurs and which led the authors to state that beliefs "in the dignity of the individual and the sacredness of personality, in the valuation of people 'for what they are instead of what they have'. . .come to their ultimate expression and test in the 'romantic' view of how marriages of their children ought to be founded: on 'love,' sympathy, compatibility, and personality characteristics, 'without regard to race, creed or color' or, above all—ugly word—money. Despite these deeply held and pervasive views, the marriages that do occur are not notably different from those that might have been arranged in a caste system based on race, creed, color, and—above all—money. Marriages between Jew and Gentile, Protestant and Catholic, rich and poor, are almost as rare as 'marriages out' in any group that punishes them by formal expulsion (for example, the Quakers until recently)" (Seeley *et al.*, pp. 396–397).

WORK AND THE OUTSIDE Unlike the West Enders, the upper-middle-class people of Crestwood Heights maintain a direct relationship between their way of life and the outside. It is this arena for which the young, especially the males, have been oriented since their childhood and which they enter upon completion of their schooling. It is here that, sometimes in cooperation with and sometimes in competition with others, they work and strive for success in the careers they have chosen. In its economic and status aspects the measure of that success is reflected in the recognition accorded to one's family. But wife and children are no passive recipients of career success. "Besides 'friends,' no partner is more important to the career than the wife; none can help more—and perhaps none can hinder more than she, though this is more difficult to establish" (Seeley *et al.*, p. 135). And in the education and other advantages that he can provide for his children, a man demonstrates his own merits.

The career pattern follows a predictable course. Following the period of preparation, which is also a time of dependency, there begins the long climb. This is the period of renunciation, of "hard work," which is followed "by a relatively brief period of full realization, and a gradual decline shading into retirement" (Seeley *et al.*, p. 133). Within career activity there are two often complementary but possibly antagonistic directions in which ambition may be channeled. Output may bring either monetary reward, or recognition for achievement, or both.

In Crestwood Heights work is highly valued, not as an end in itself, but as the activity through which one proves the validity of the other values of the culture, particularly status achievement and family welfare. In contrast to the West Enders, the parents do know how to build a view of the future, somewhat different from their own, into their child-rearing practices. "The Crestwood child who is reared in an environment of prosperity and success, comes to feel that life's opportunities are limitless, that he can become anything he wishes to become" (Seeley *et al.*, p. 124). But the inability of the father to transmit his own status to his children is largely concealed. The father can help to open the way to his son, but when the chips are down, it is the latter on whom the full burden falls. It is the son who must struggle and strive and he who will reap the rewards. But in a most peculiar way success cannot be a solitary thing. It is closely tied to his wife and intimate friends, and its validation is also linked to the approving judgment of the others. In this sense there are two worlds in which each man orbits: "the exacting work schedules of life downtown" and "the world of leisure and affection uptown" (Seeley *et al.*, p. 155).

CONCLUSION   We are now ready to return to a consideration of the propositions and questions that were raised in the earlier sections of this chapter and to examine them in the comparative light of the empirical data drawn from the studies of the Italians in the West End of Boston and of the upper-middle-class residents of Crestwood Heights. There is a small problem in deciding which facet of the whole should be treated first, but since the various segments seem to reveal systemic interconnections it may be desirable to begin with the most comprehensive subject, the social structure of the metropolis.

It was suggested earlier that institutional arrangements could be divided into those associated with the private world of family and friends and the counterpoised but parallel public world of social superstructures. These latter contain the corporate and professional activities through which the essential goods and services are produced and distributed. It was also suggested that associated with the cultural and social dichotomy of public and private were two social class systems. The immediate problem, then, is to see to what extent the empirical data support this view.

For the West Enders the separation between the private world of family and peer group and the public world of outside is dramatically sharp. The outside includes all those institutions over which the West Enders exert a minimum of control, and which threaten the continued cohesion of the group. The threat is a double one: It arises from attempts to win allegiance from the group's members (and thus to alienate them) and from the fear of exploitation. In consequence, members of the peer group are thrown even closer together as they unite to reject the values of and participation in activities of the outside, but they are ready to exploit such activities when they appear advantageous. Among the values rejected are those of work and self-improvement as ends in themselves or for purposes of social mobility. The rejection even extends to education as a device for social mobility. In fact, aspiration for higher status is recognized as disruptive of the peer group and opposed to the core of values that give it meaning. The West Enders, by adherence to their own values and rejection of those of the middle class and its institutions, clearly demonstrate the separation between private and public worlds and the potential conflict between the two.

The evidence from Crestwood Heights is equally striking in its substantiation of the distinction between the private world of family and friends and the public world of profession and corporate structure. But here the two are related in a vastly different and almost opposite fashion from the West End. Although the activities of either private or public world are distinct in kind and separate in space, their interdependence is of such magnitude that success or failure in one has its repercussions on the other. The male Crestwooder learns early that the goal of his pre-adult training is to prepare him to do battle for the honors that can be won in the arena of profession or business. Only thus does he validate and perhaps improve upon the status to which he was born. The girl learns equally soon the significance of the complementary role that she must play as wife and mother. For both parents and children aspiration in self-development is the psychological counterpart of the achievement of higher social status. For the upper middle class of Crestwood the public world is no threatening "outside"; it is the familiar environment in which its members contest and attempt to control. They call their activities in it "work," and it is for this work that a part of their formal education prepares them. For some, work may become an end in itself, but this is not the social purpose that it serves.

We can extend and deepen our understanding of the dual structure of the metropolis and its relation to social class if at this time we turn to the first of three propositions offered earlier. There we postulated that social class is a manifestation of the social system rather than the system itself. At first glance this statement might appear to be a truism that was hardly worthy of much attention. We could accept this view readily enough if it were not for the fact that all delineations of social class rely almost exclusively upon the determination of cultural configurations. Now the basis for such analyses has been derived from the grouping of attributes or qualities associated with things, activities, and individuals. This approach has yielded some good results, but we would argue that their validation rests upon the relationships of these attributes to interaction between specific individuals in specific events. We contend that such an examination would show that patterns of interaction contain the key to understanding social class systems. Evidence from two different sources may be adduced to illustrate the point. Since we have already discussed the system of status associated with the hierarchical organization of corporate superstructures, we will not elaborate further on demonstrating the relation between corporate organization and social class. Instead, we shall turn to a comparison of forms of family organization associated with the residents of the West End and of Crestwood Heights, respectively. The significant differences in relations with the "outside" have already been commented on. What is needed now is to look at the relations of family members with the nonwork aspects of the community and the process of mate selection. For each of these it will be our purpose to show how the facts may be interpreted within the context of family structure.

Within the relations of parents and children in the peer-based family circle of the West Enders, certain implicit values find expression. Since it is within the family circle that those activities which are most highly valued are found, it seems logical, and is in fact true, that parental concern for children is that they might also experience a comparable style of life. The generational reconstitution of the peer-group type of family can be realized, however, only if there is relatively great stability. Hence it is easy to understand why middle-class values are meaningless and possibly threatening. The intense and frequent activity among peers ensures a commitment to the present rather than to the future, and ensures the avoidance of time-consuming and involving activities with other types of groups. In fact, limited participation beyond the borders of the family circle should not be viewed as a consequence of conscious avoidance but of the incompatibility between a family system of the peer-group type and other forms of institutional activity, including deep religious involvement. This formulation helps us to understand the continued inability of middle-class civic and cultural enterprises to penetrate or take root in this environment. If successful they would destroy the presently constituted family system.

The relations between the parents of Crestwood Heights and their children are almost entirely different. Parental orientation of children for the future must include a sense of autonomy and desire for achievement that leads to mobility. It is the obligation of the male-child-turned-adult to validate the aspirations of his parents through his success in the world of work, and of the female, in partnership with her husband, to shape the environment within which her children come to maturity. Hence the immediate community is of utmost significance. The activities associated with social clubs and the time devoted to civic and school betterment should not be viewed as ends in themselves but as part of the necessary effort to create and preserve an environment compatible with the relations between members of the family and its adjunct values. Thus, as was argued earlier, the interconnections and interdependencies between the relationships of a family system, its values, and the participation pattern in the nonwork extra-familial activities can be made explicit. Further substantiation of this and other points appears when we turn to the processes of courtship and marriage.

Mating, reproduction, and care of the young are biological processes culturally organized among humans. Thus, variations in the processes may be examined as variations in culture. For this part of the analysis the crucial aspect is to examine the relation between the definition of a suitable mate and forms of human grouping. It is obvious from the empirical evidence that mates are chosen from those who are similar in cultural behavior and outlook. Among the West Enders marriage with other than an Italian is disapproved, and only rarely does it occur. In Crestwood Heights the separation of Jews from Gentiles appears in adolescence in dating behavior, a type of activity preliminary to later final mate choice. Both groups resemble each other, however, in the care with which the definition of a proper and improper marriage partner is inculcated in the young. What weight may be given to the several factors that contribute to the success of this effort is not entirely clear and possibly may not be completely determinable. Admonition and precept undoubtedly have an effect, but the relative power of verbal command to direct behavior must still be determined. This problem really belongs in the category of the dynamics of learning. Our own inclination is to give greater priority to patterns of relationships as explanatory.

The marriage partnership is fully intermingled with peer group and family circle in the West End. Between the period of adolescence and marriage the males separate themselves from the family setting to regroup as an all male peer group, congregating on street corners and in other locales. Marriage pulls them once again into the family circle, but in a gathering of their own age mates, and not that of their parents. For their wives they choose girls of similar backgrounds. Thus, through the joining of biological and cultural processes there is ensured a continuity of cultural tradition.

The process of mate selection and family formation for Crestwood Heights varies only in its details. So also is the consequence of cultural perpetuation the same. But the cultural stability, almost inertia, which this analysis suggests must also be examined in the context of the environment of the other institutional arrangements in the society. When these are taken into account we then inject a new dimension, one whose changes bring repercussions elsewhere. For this reason the rise of great social superstructures are relevant to the system of social class and to changes in its definition. For this reason social class, defined as the configuration of cultural elements, should be considered as a manifestation of the social system and not as the system itself. This leads to a further conclusion that each form of civilization has its own kind of social ranking.

Little additional comment seems necessary for the other two propositions presented earlier. The empirical data and their analysis support the proposition that social class should be examined from two perspectives—from the vantage point of those who are participants and from criteria that are external to the system. Finally, the insistence that comparative analysis requires concepts and procedures which are free of substantive particularism was exemplified in the comparisons between the West End and Crestwood Heights. It will be remembered that we utilized the categories of work and nonwork, family organization, transmission of culture, and mate selection. . . .

BIBLIOGRAPHY

DAVIS, ALLISON, BURLEIGH B. GARDNER, AND MARY R. GARDNER, 1941, *Deep South: A Socio-Anthropological Study of Caste and Class*, Chicago: University of Chicago Press.

GANS, HERBERT J., 1962, *The Urban Villagers: Group and Class in the Life of Italian-Americans*, New York: The Free Press.

KIMBALL, SOLON T., AND JAMES E. MCCLELLAN, 1962, *Education and the New America*, New York: Random House.

NORDHOFF, CHARLES, 1961, *The Communistic Societies of the United States*, New York: Humanities Press.

SEELEY, JOHN R., R. ALEXANDER SIM, AND ELIZABETH W. LOOSLEY, 1956, *Crestwood Heights: A Study of the Culture of Suburban Life*, New York: John Wiley & Sons.

WARNER, WILLIAM LLOYD, 1941, "Social Anthropology and the Modern Community," *American Journal of Sociology*, 46, pp. 785–96.

WHYTE, WILLIAM H., 1956, *The Organization Man*, New York: Simon and Schuster.

Questions and Implications for Practice

7.1 KURT B. MAYER

1. Why is it important for counselors and other guidance-personnel workers to understand principles and processes of social differentiation and stratification?

2. Must one's social philosophy be restricted, or is it better that it not be restricted by power, class, prestige, and status as one develops his own ideas of the good society?

3. As one studies the society that exists in a selected elementary or secondary school, college or university, can the trained observer see at work any of the principles and processes that Mayer describes? On what kind of bases does this school society ascribe positions to its members: teachers, administrators, students, and within these groups what other kinds of social differentiations are operating? What are the status groups? On what bases do they form? How does a teacher, an administrator, a student acquire power in this society?

4. Are individuals in the society of the school or college frozen inescapably into ascribed positions or are there kinds of social escalation and de-escalation that can be observed? How does this happen?

5. Many thoughtful people today are maintaining that education is the surest instrument of social mobility that our society possesses. Is this only because of its relationship to the acquisition of economic wealth or are there other reasons why education contributes to social mobility and the insurance of favorable status? As everyone acquires more and more education will the advantage it confers tend to diminish or will those who possess the most education (doctorates, postdoctorates, and high professional degrees) still enjoy favorable status because of their comparatively superior educational advantages? If so, how will this status be evidenced?

7.2 HAVIGHURST AND NEUGARTEN

1. Although Havighurst and Neugarten wrote this piece only in 1962, some remarkable changes in economic conditions and personal expectations have clearly been stirring since then. What trends in your opinion, should the guidance-personnel worker watch in order to keep as nearly abreast of incipient change as possible and to avoid holding expectations and maintaining attitudes that are no longer tenable? What, for instance, is apt to be the situation for young people 10 or 20 years from now with respect to: (a) housing; (b) recreation; (c) work opportunities; (d) sex mores; (e) family life; (f) population control; (g) health; (h) economic security; (i) educational opportunities; (j) race relations; (k) differential role expectations for men and women; (l) widely held values; (m) social class; (n) travel; (o) communication?

2. Since changes in all of these areas are taking place so rapidly, it would be well to think in terms of a sort of slide rule that starts with what is now and then tries to project what will be 5, 10, or 20 years hence for those now 5 years old, 10, 15, 20, respectively, as these persons' lives project on into the changing future.

7.3 MILLER AND RIESSMAN

1. Do you agree that Miller and Riessman are able to present a new view of the values by which the working class lives?

2. How can an understanding of the themes that run through the lives of working-class members of our society help the guidance-personnel worker in the elementary school to better understand (a) children who have a working class background—and (b) the parents of those children?

3. Do the authors' generalizations apply helpfully to junior and senior high school students you have known? In what ways, specifically?

4. Suppose that more young people from working-class backgrounds get to college. What are some of the psychological hazards that, according to Miller and Riessman, might operate rather persistently to increase the possibility of their dropping out of college? What kind of reason would such a student probably give in an exit interview if he did decide to drop out?

5. Could the Hawthorne effect be used, at least temporarily, to lessen the problems that the need for security might create for these students? How, specifically, could this be brought in to play?

6. How much of a chance does an individual brought up in the culture described above have to acquire a whole new set of values? If he were able to, would this mean, in effect, that he would be deserting the class in which he has been reared, and moving into a different class? Is this essentially what must often happen to individuals who move to a foreign country, for instance, as well as into a different class in their own country?

7. Have we already created some post high school institutions (technical institutes of various sorts, for example) that are not so incompatible with the perfectly good values of the working class as those of our liberal arts colleges might be?

8. How compatible would the values of individuals from working-class backgrounds be with the value systems they would find in a large multiversity? In a liberal arts college strongly related to a church which the individual's family (a) did strongly support, or (b) did not support?

7.4 THOMAS F. PETTIGREW

1. Pettigrew describes vividly the plight of the Negro male, the genesis of his problem back in the patterns of slavery and some of the tragic consequence of his condition for Negro family life, and for the roles of Negro women and girls, but especially of Negro boys.

Could the vicious circle here described be altered by introducing strong, understanding male guidance-personnel workers to counsel Negro boys individually and to work with their peer groups throughout their school and college lives? What are some dangers in doing this?

2. Since social reforms are altering the life chances for Negroes, should the school undertake special efforts to help Negro boys experience responsibility, independence, and success in meeting carefully set standards? How might this kind of guided program help change the self-concepts of Negro boys and make it more possible for them to exploit successfully the new role possibilities that are opening up to them?

3. No one has yet represented with so much passion and sensitive concern the conditions of life that limit the development by the Negro girl of all of the roles through which she should legitimately expect to live a satisfying and productive life. What are some of these limiting conditions as you have observed them? What, if any, special conditions and consideration should educational institutions supply to the Negro girl?

4. What difficulties might you expect to encounter in attempting to work with the families of the Negro youngsters whose backgrounds are here described? What methods might be used most successfully?

7.5   E. FRANKLIN FRAZIER

1. This stark and uncompromising description by Frazier of the black bourgeoisie will give the guidance-personnel worker and all educators a more sympathetic understanding of the role middle-class Negro young people are attempting to learn as well as of their problems in learning them. In elementary and secondary schools and in colleges where Negro students come from the various social and economic classes it will be helpful to the guidance-personnel worker to understand the feelings of these individuals toward each other, the lines along which social groups have formed, the importance of these groups to their members, and the feelings of these groups toward each other.

How can the guidance-personnel worker use this more accurate and sensitive understanding to help Negro youth in their struggle to learn new and more rewarding roles?

2. If the guidance-personnel worker has to choose how best to use his time, then his greatest contribution will be made

a. as he helps individuals prepare for and get placed in the most lucrative jobs possible;

b. as he helps individuals and groups clarify what it is they really want out of life;

c. as he guides them in their human relationships, interprets to them the values they are seeing concretized, and helps them understand the social roles each is experimenting with and learning.

3. Discuss the above alternatives. It may be that the effective guidance-personnel worker will use educational and vocational guidance, individual and group counseling, and the skillful guidance of school and college group experience without concentrating exclusively on any one objective.

4. How is the situation today different from that described by Frazier? Why do you think that some of those who used to be designated as "Negroes" now glory in calling themselves "blacks"? Discuss this in relation to Frazier's views.

5. In your view, should middle-class Negroes, or blacks, work for an integrated or a segregated society? Why?

7.6 ARENSBERG AND KIMBALL

1. In their discussion of cultural identity, Arensberg and Kimball cite the family, the neighborhood, peer groups, and sociability among equals as avenues whereby individuals acquire a sense of cultural at-homeness and come to know with what elements they are compatible and with what they are not. How does the human interaction in the school or college community affect the sense of "belonging" that each individual carries with him always?

2. Might it be possible for guided group experience in the school or college to furnish individuals a crude method of social locomotion—movement from one group with which he feels at home to another that will furnish him a surer sense of identity?

3. How might change in behavior be encouraged within a school or a college setting so that an individual or a whole group of students might literally have their social position raised? What means do certain private schools or colleges you know now take to accomplish just this result? May there be other methods, or comparable methods, that could be used in a school in Harlem, for example, to escalate the level of culture with which its students could feel identified?

4. Can this be done by the school, counter to the home and neighborhood, when students do not board at the school or college? Can it be accomplished by involving parents and influential members of the community in the general elevation attempt?

5. Consider specifically what means might be utilized and what kind of program developed in a particular school or college if that institution wanted to experiment along these lines.

Chapter 8

Social
and
Cultural
Conditions
of Learning

The chapters that have so far comprised this part of the book on the individual, the society, and the culture, have examined a variety of interrelationships among the three systems. The cumulative import of all the materials presented can be summed up by the statement that the three levels are separable analytically but thoroughly intermeshed in actuality. At whichever level one may direct one's inquiry, its pursuit will lead to the others as well. Thus an explanation cast in terms of a single class of events—psychological, social, or cultural—of necessity rests on assumptions about the other two types of phenomena, whether such assumptions are made explicit or not.

These statements are neither novel nor startling, and only reassert what has already been noted by a number of the authors quoted in preceding chapters. The necessity to stress the point here stems from the special nature of the subject of this chapter. There is a common tendency to think of learning as an exclusively psychological concern, perhaps because so much activity on the part of psychologists has focused on it. This activity has produced a vast body of knowledge about the relationship between specific causal factors and specific effects on various aspects of the learning process. Thus, we have available to us much information about the consequences of both internal conditions of the individual (*e.g.,* motives, attitudes, previous learning, ability level) and aspects of the external environment (*e.g.,* methods of instruction, incentives, rewards, punishments, order of presentation of material) on rate of learning, degree of retention, persistence of learned behavior, number and type of errors, and a variety of other aspects. Psychological understanding of learning, however, has remained largely detached from other areas of knowledge about human behavior. In itself it is relevant only within a social and cultural vacuum, or at best within unchanging and clearly specified conditions. For it also to be relevant in real situations, the determinants of learning as an individual process must be linked to the social and cultural conditions within which they operate and by which they are in turn shaped.

In other words, to understand learning as it occurs in situations not under the investigator's control, it is not sufficient to know the particular effects of such factors as, say, anxiety or reward. It is also necessary to know both the nature of the events that the culture defines as anxiety-producing or rewarding and the social conditions which make the occurrence of these events more or less probable. A formalized and integrated statement of the relationships between the facts of individual learning and the facts of the sociocultural environment has yet to be worked out. Some of the components of such a conception have been identified, however, and a few of these are dealt with in the articles collected in this chapter. The selections have some themes in common, but primarily this chapter is characterized by variability in approach and content.

There are two reasons for highlighting the topic of learning in this book. One is that the nature of the human organism and its relationship to the environment make learning the core process in every aspect of the individual's development and adaptation. In this sense, all the materials that have been presented so far have dealt with the products of learning and have assumed its occurrence. A broad conception of learning as a psychological, social, and cultural process will thus enhance understanding of all the other topics covered in this book. The second, more obvious and perhaps more important, reason for giving special attention to learning is its centrality for the process of education. We have seen that schools and colleges serve many functions for students, teachers, parents, politicians, and for the society as a whole. Whether we consider education as a value, as an activity, or as a social and political issue, however, the process of learning is at its core. In suggesting some of the relationships between learning and the other classes of phenomena discussed in this book, this chapter thus specifies the link that makes these other topics relevant to the practical problems faced by educators in general and guidance counselors in particular.

8.1 INTRODUCTION

The first selection in this chapter brings together a variety of implications from the materials of earlier chapters and relates them clearly and provocatively to school performance. The author focuses particularly on "disadvantaged" children—from lower-class, slum, and frequently Negro homes—analyzing the extent to which their preschool experience prepares them to meet the demands and expectations that comprise education. His general thesis is that this preparation is grossly inadequate, and he details the specific deficiencies that are produced in many areas of ability, motivation, and attitudes.

Deutsch identifies a number of aspects of the human and nonhuman environment in the preschool years as significant factors relative to the development of the attitudinal and cognitive equipment that adequate academic performance requires. The lower-class child is severely disadvantaged with respect to virtually all of these, with the result that the learning experiences that the school provides are essentially inaccessible to him. Therefore, those differences between children from privileged and deprived backgrounds that reflect the latter's inadequacies are smallest in the first grade and get larger as education progresses.

This selection makes particularly clear that the school reflects a particular set of cultural orientations. It is far from being a neutral environment in which all forms of talent will flourish, but, rather, the school represents a very special configuration of cultural values, which, although widespread, do not prevail at all levels of American society. Between "disadvantaged" children and the school—*i.e.*, teachers, administrators, guidance counselors, and other students—there is, in short, a large cultural gap, and the author of this selection points to the "failure of the school to promote the proper acculturation of these children."

Throughout the essay he also offers many suggestions as to how this failure might be remedied—from increased emphasis on learning to conform to routine at the nursery and kindergarten levels to special training in the use of language for abstract purposes. It is clear that there will be no simple or single measure which will enable all lower-class children to profit from the offerings of a middle-class-oriented school. It seems likely, however, that guidance counselors will be in a position to mediate between the two, interpreting one to the other, and thus possibly restraining the spiral which pulls so many children away from the educational process. The ensuing selection provides fresh insight with respect to the specific problems that such positive intervention would have to overcome.

8.1   THE DISADVANTAGED CHILD AND THE LEARNING PROCESS [1]

Martin P. Deutsch

This paper will discuss the interaction of social and developmental factors and their impact on the intellectual growth and school performance of the child. It will make particular reference to the large number of urban children who come from

[1]From Martin P. Deutsch, "The Disadvantaged Child and the Learning Process," *Education in Depressed Areas*, A. Harry Passow, ed., New York: Bureau of Publications, Teachers College, Columbia University, 1963, pp. 163–179.

marginal social circumstances. While much of the discussion will be speculative, where appropriate it will draw on data from the field, and will suggest particular relationships and avenues for future investigation or demonstration.

Among children who come from lower-class socially impoverished circumstances, there is a high proportion of school failure, school dropouts, reading and learning disabilities, as well as life adjustment problems. This means not only that these children grow up poorly equipped academically, but also that the effectiveness of the school as a major institution for socialization is diminished. The effect of this process is underlined by the fact that this same segment of the population contributes disproportionately to the delinquency and other social deviancy statistics.

The thesis here is that the lower-class child enters the school situation so poorly prepared to produce what the school demands that initial failures are almost inevitable, and the school experience becomes negatively rather than positively reinforced. Thus the child's experience in school does nothing to counteract the invidious influences to which he is exposed in his slum, and sometimes segregated, neighborhood.

We know that children from underprivileged environments tend to come to school with a qualitatively different preparation for the demands of both the learning process and the behavioral requirements of the classroom. These are various differences in the kinds of socializing experiences these children have had, as contrasted with the middle-class child. The culture of their environment is a different one from the culture that has molded the school and its educational techniques and theory.

We know that it is difficult for all peoples to span cultural discontinuities, and yet we make little if any effort to prepare administrative personnel or teachers and guidance staff to assist the child in this transition from one cultural context to another. This transition must have serious psychological consequences for the child, and probably plays a major role in influencing his later perceptions of other social institutions as he is introduced to them.

It must be pointed out that the relationship between social background and school performance is not a simple one. Rather, evidence which is accumulating points more and more to the influence of background variables on the patterns of perceptual, language, and cognitive development of the child and the subsequent diffusion of the effects of such patterns into all areas of the child's academic and psychological performance. To understand these effects requires delineating the underlying skills in which these children are not sufficiently proficient. A related problem is that of defining what aspects of the background are most influential in producing what kinds of deficits in skills.

ENVIRONMENTAL FACTORS Let us begin with the most macroscopic background factors. While it is likely that slum life might have delimited areas that allow for positive growth and that the middle-class community has attributes which might retard healthy development, generally the combination of circumstances in middle-class life is considerably more likely to furnish opportunities for normal growth of the child. At the same time, slum conditions are more likely to have deleterious effects on physical and mental development. This is not to say that middle-class life furnishes a really adequate milieu for the maximum development of individual potential: it doesn't. The fact that we often speak as though it does is a function of viewing the middle-class environment in comparison to the slum. Middle-class people who work and teach across social-class lines often are unable to be aware of the negative aspects of the middle-class background because of its apparent superiority over the less advantageous background provided by lower-class life. We really have no external criterion for evaluating the characteristics of a milieu in terms of how well it is designed to foster development; as a result we might actually be measuring one area of social failure with the yardstick of social catastrophe.

It is true that many leading personalities in twentieth century American life have come from the slums, and this is a fact often pointed out by nativistic pragmatists in an effort to prove that if the individual "has it in him" he can overcome—and even be challenged by—his humble surroundings. This argument, though fundamentally fallacious, might have had more to recommend it in the past. At the turn of the century we were a massively vertical mobile society—that is, with the exception of certain large minority groups such as the Negroes, the Indians, and the Mexican-Americans who were rarely allowed on the social elevator. In the mid-twentieth century, it is now increasingly possible for all groups to get on, but social and economic conditions have changed, and the same elevator more frequently moves in two directions or stands still altogether. When it does move, it goes more slowly, and, most discouragingly, it also provides an observation window on what, at least superficially, appears to be a most affluent society. Television, movies, and other media continually expose the individual from the slum to the explicit assumption that the products of a consumer society are available to all—or, rather, as he sees it, to all but him. In effect, this means that the child from the disadvantaged environment is an outsider and an observer—through his own eyes and those of his parents or neighbors—of the mainstream of American life. At the same time, when the child enters school he is exposing himself directly to the values and anticipations of a participant in that mainstream—his teacher. It is not sufficiently recognized that there is quite a gap between the training of a teacher and the needs, limitations, and unique strengths of the child from a marginal situation. This gap is, of course, maximized when the child belongs to a minority group that until quite recently was not only excluded from the mainstream, but was not even allowed to bathe in the tributaries.

What are some of the special characteristics of these children, and why do they apparently need exceptional social and educational planning? So often, administrators and teachers say, they are children who are "curious," "cute," "affectionate," "warm," and independently dependent in the kindergarten and the first grade, but who so often become "alienated," "withdrawn," "angry," "passive," "apathetic," or just "trouble-makers" by the fifth and sixth grade. In our research at the Institute for Developmental Studies, it is in the first grade that we usually see the smallest differences between socioeconomic or racial groups in intellectual, language, and some conceptual measures, and in the later grades that we find the greatest differences in favor of the more socially privileged groups. From both teacher's observations and the finding of this increasing gap, it appears that there is a failure on some level of society and, more specifically, the educational system. Was the school scientifically prepared to receive these children in the first place? And, in addition, were the children perhaps introduced to the individual demands of the larger culture at too late an age—that is, in first grade?

Before discussing these psychological products of social deprivation, it is appropriate to look more closely at the special circumstances of Negro slum residents. In the core city of most of our large metropolitan areas, 40 to 70 percent of the elementary school population is likely to be Negro. In my observations, through workshops in many of these cities, I have often been surprised to find how little real comprehension of the particular problems of these youngsters exists as part of the consciousness of the Negro or white middle-class teachers. While in middle-class schools there is great sensitivity to emotional climates and pressures and tensions that might be operating on the child in either the home or the school, in lower-class schools the problems of social adaptation are so massive that sensitivity tends to become blunted.

In the lower-class Negro group there still exist the sequelae of the conditions of slavery. While a hundred years have passed, this is a short time in the life of a people. And the extension of tendrils of the effects of slavery into modern life has been effectively discouraged only in the last few decades, when there have been some real attempts to integrate the Negro fully into American life. It is often difficult for teachers and the personnel of other community agencies to understand the Negro lower-class child—particularly the child who has come, or whose parents have come, from the rural South. There is a whole set of implicit and explicit value systems which determine our educational philosophies, and the institutional expectation is that all children participate in these systems. And yet for these expectations to be met, the child must experience some continuity of sociocultural participation in and sharing of these value systems before he comes to school. This is often just not the case for the child who comes from an encapsulated community, particularly when the walls have been built by the dominant social and cultural forces that have also determined the value systems relating to learning.

A recent article in *Fortune* magazine asked why the Negro failed to take full advantage of opportunities open to him in American life. At least part of the answer is that the Negro has not been fully integrated into American life, and that even knowledge about particular occupations and their requirements is not available outside the cultural mainstream. Implications of this for the aspirations and motivations of children will be discussed later.

Another source of misunderstanding on the part of school and social agency people is the difficulty of putting in historical perspective the causal conditions responsible for the high percentage of broken homes in the Negro community. Implications of this for the child's emotional stability are very frequently recognized, but the effects on the child's motivation, self-concept, and achievement orientation are not often understood.

The Negro family was first broken deliberately by the slave traders and the plantation owners for their own purposes. As was pointed out earlier, the hundred years since slavery is not a very long time for a total social metamorphosis even under fostering conditions—and during that period the Negro community has been for the most part economically marginal and isolated from the contacts which would have accelerated change. The 13 depressions and recessions we have had since Emancipation have been devastating to this community. These marginal economic and encapsulated social circumstances have been particularly harsh on the Negro male. The chronic instability has greatly influenced the Negro man's concept of himself and his general motivation to succeed in competitive areas of society where the rewards are greatest. All these circumstances have contributed to the instability of the Negro family, and particularly to the fact that it is most often broken by the absence of the father. As a result, the lower-class Negro child entering school often has had no experience with a "successful" male model or thereby with a psychological framework in which effort can result in at least the possibility of achievement. Yet the value system of the school and of the learning process is predicated on the assumption that effort will result in achievement.

To a large extent, much of this is true not only for the Negro child but for all children who come from impoverished and marginal social and economic conditions. These living conditions are characterized by great overcrowding in substandard housing, often lacking adequate sanitary and other facilities. While we don't know the actual importance, for example, of moments of privacy, we do know that the opportunity frequently does not exist. In addition, there are likely to be large numbers of siblings and half-siblings, again with there being little opportunity for individuation. At the same time, the child tends to be restricted to his immediate environment, with conducted explorations of the "outside" world being infrequent and sometimes nonexistent. In the slums, and to an unfortunately large extent in many other areas of our largest cities, there is little opportunity to observe natural beauty, clean landscapes, or other pleasant and aesthetically pleasing surroundings.

In the child's home, there is a scarcity of objects of all types, but especially of books, toys, puzzles, pencils, and scribbling paper. It is not that the mere presence of such materials would necessarily result in their productive use, but it would increase the child's familiarity with the tools he'll be confronted with in school. Actually, for the most effective utilization of these tools, guidance and explanations are necessary from the earliest time of exposure. Such guidance requires not only the presence of aware and educated adults, but also time—a rare commodity in these marginal circumstances. Though many parents will share in the larger value system of having high aspirations for their children, they are unaware of the operational steps required for the preparation of the child to use optimally the learning opportunities in the school. Individual potential is one of the most unmarketable properties if the child acquires no means for its development, or if no means exist for measuring it objectively. It is here that we must understand the consequences of all these aspects of the slum matrix for the psychological and cognitive development of the child.

PSYCHOLOGICAL FACTORS   A child from any circumstance who has been deprived of a substantial portion of the variety of stimuli which he is maturationally capable of responding to is likely to be deficient in the equipment required for learning.

Support for this is found in Hunt who, in discussing Piaget's developmental theories, points out that, according to Piaget, ". . . the rate of development is in substantial part, but certainly not wholly, a function of environmental circumstances. Change in circumstances is required to force the accommodative modifications of schemata that constitute development. Thus, the greater the variety of situations to which the child must accommodate his behavioral structures, the more differentiated and mobile they become. Thus, the more new things a child has seen and the more he has heard, the more things he is interested in seeing and hearing. Moreover, the more variation in reality with which he has coped, the greater is his capacity for coping." (Hunt, 1961, pp. 258–259)

This emphasis on the importance of variety in the environment implies the detrimental effects of lack of variety. This in turn leads to a concept of "stimulus deprivation." But it is important that it be correctly understood. By this is not necessarily meant any restriction of the quantity of stimulation, but, rather, a restriction to a segment of the spectrum of stimulation potentially available. In addition to the restriction in variety, from what is known of the slum environment, it might be postulated that the segments made available to these children tend to have poorer and less systematic ordering of stimulation sequences, and would thereby be less useful to the growth and activation of cognitive potential.

This deprivation has effects on both the formal and the contentual aspects of cognition. By "formal" is meant the operations—the behavior —by which stimuli are perceived, encouraged, and responded to. By "contentual" is meant the actual content of the child's knowledge and comprehension. "Formal equipment" would include perceptual discrimination skills, the ability to sustain attention, and the ability to use adults as sources of information and for satisfying curiosity. Also included would be the establishment of expectations of reward from accumulation of knowledge, from task completion, and from adult reinforcement, and the ability to delay gratification. Examples of "contentual equipment" would be the language-symbolic system, environmental information, general and environmental orientation, and concepts of comparability and relativity appropriate to the child's age level. The growth of a differentiated attitudinal set toward learning is probably a resultant of the interaction between formal and contentual levels.

Hypothesizing that stimulus deprivation will result in deficiencies in either of these equipments, let us examine the particular stimuli which are available and those which are absent from the environment of the child who comes from the conditions discussed above. This reasoning suggests also certain hypotheses regarding the role of environment in the evolving of the formal and contentual systems.

As was pointed out in the previous section, the disadvantaged environment as well as certain aspects of the middle-class circumstance offers the child, overall, a restricted range of experience. While one does see great individual variability in these children, social conditions reduce the range of this variation; with less variety in input, it would be reasonable to assume a concomitant restriction in the variety of output. This is an important respect in which social poverty may have a leveling effect on the achievement of individual skills and abilities. Concomitantly, in the current problem of extensive underachievement in suburban lower-middle-class areas, the overroutinization of activity with the consequent reduction in variety may well be the major factor.

In individual terms, a child is probably farther away from his maturational ceiling as a result of this experiential poverty. This might well be a crucial factor in the poorer performance of the lower socioeconomic children on standardized tests of intelligence. On such tests, the child is compared with others of his own age. But if his point of development in relation to the maturational ceiling for his age group is influenced by his experience, then the child with restricted experience may actually be developed to a proportionately lower level of his own actual ceiling. If a certain quantum of fostering experience is necessary to activate the achievement of particular maturational levels, then perhaps the child who is deficient in this experience will take longer to achieve these levels, even though his potential may be the same as the more advantaged child. It might be that in order to achieve a realistic appraisal of the ability levels of children, an "experience" age rather than the chronological age should be used to arrive at norms.

This suggests a limitation on the frequent studies comparing Negro and white children. Even when it is possible to control for the formal attributes of social-class membership, the uniqueness of the Negro child's experience would make comparability impossible when limited to these class factors. Perhaps too, if such an interaction exists between experiential and biological determinants of development, it would account for the failure of the culture-free tests, as they too are standardized on an age basis without allowing for the experiential interaction (as distinguished from specific experiential *influence*).

Let us now consider some of the specifics in the child's environment, and their effects on the development of the formal, contentual, and attitudinal systems.

Visually, the urban slum and its overcrowded apartments offer the child a minimal range of stimuli. There are usually few if any pictures on the wall, and the objects in the household, be they toys, furniture, or utensils, tend to be sparse, repetitious, and lacking in form and color variations. The sparsity of objects and lack of diversity of home artifacts which are available and meaningful to the child, in addition to the unavailability of individualized training, gives the child few opportunities to manipulate and organize the visual properties of his environment and thus perceptually to organize and discriminate the nuances of that environment. These would include figure-ground relationships and the spatial organization of the visual field. The sparsity of manipulable objects probably also hampers the development of these functions in the tactile area. For example, while these children have broomsticks and usually a ball, possibly a doll or a discarded kitchen pot to play with, they don't have the different shapes and colors and sizes to manipulate which the middle-class child has in the form of blocks which are bought just for him, or even in the variety of sizes and shapes of cooking utensils which might be available to him as playthings.

It is true, as has been pointed out frequently, that the pioneer child didn't have many playthings either. But he had a more active responsibility toward the environment and a great variety of growing plants and other natural resources as well as a stable family that assumed a primary role for the education and training of the child. In addition, the intellectually normal or superior frontier child could and usually did grow up to be a farmer. Today's child will grow up into a world of automation requiring highly differentiated skills if he and society are to use his intellect.

The effect of sparsity of manipulable objects on visual perception is, of course, quite speculative, as few data now exist. However, it is an important area, as among skills necessary for reading are form discrimination and visual spatial organization. Children from depressed areas, because of inadequate training and stimulation, may not have developed the requisite skills by the time they enter first grade, and the assumption that they do possess these skills may thus add to the frustration these children experience on entering school.

The lower-class home is not a verbally oriented environment. The implications of this for language development will be considered below in the discussion of the contentual systems. Here let us consider its implication for the development of auditory discrimination skills. While the environment is a noisy one, the noise is not, for the most part, meaningful in relation to the child, and for him most of it is background. In the crowded apartments with all the daily living stresses, is a minimum of noninstructional conversation directed toward the child. In actuality, the situation is ideal for the child to learn inattention. Furthermore, he does not get practice in auditory discrimination or feedback from adults correcting his enunciation, pronunciation, and grammar. In studies at the Institute for Developmental Studies at New York Medical College, as yet unreported in the literature, we have found significant differences in auditory discrimination between lower-class and middle-class children in the first grade. These differences seem to diminish markedly as the children get older, though the effects of their early existence on other functioning remain to be investigated. Here again, we are dealing with a skill very important to reading. Our data indicate too that poor readers within social-class groups have significantly more difficulty in auditory discrimination than do good readers. Further, this difference between good and poor readers is greater for the lower-class group.

If the child learns to be inattentive in the preschool environment, as has been postulated, this further diminishes incoming stimulation. Further, if this trained inattention comes about as a result of his being insufficiently called upon to respond to particular stimuli, then his general level of responsiveness will also be diminished. The nature of the total environment and the child-adult interaction is such that reinforcement is too infrequent, and, as a result, the quantity of response is diminished. The implications of this for the structured learning situation in the school are quite obvious.

Related to attentivity is memory. Here also we would postulate the dependence of the child, particularly in the preschool period, on interaction with the parent. It is adults who link the past and the present by calling to mind prior shared experiences. The combination of the constriction in the use of language and in shared activity results, for the lower-class child, in much less stimulation of the early memory function. Although I don't know of any data supporting this thesis, from my observations it would seem that there is a tendency for these children to be proportionately more present-oriented and less aware of the past-present sequences than the middle-class child. This is consistent with anthropological research and thinking. While this could be a function of the poorer time orientation of these children or of their difficulty in verbal expression, both of which will be discussed below, it could also relate to a greater difficulty in seeing themselves in the past or in a different context. Another area which points up the home-school discontinuity is that of time. Anthropologists have pointed out that from culture to culture time concepts differ and that time as life's governor is a relatively modern phenomenon and one which finds most of its slaves in the lower-middle, middle-middle, and upper-middle classes. It might not even be an important factor in learning, but it is an essential feature in the measurement of children's performance by testing and in the adjustment of children to the organizational demands of the school. The middle-class teacher organizes the day by allowing a certain amount of time for each activity. Psychologists have long noticed that American Indian children, mountain children, and children from other nonindustrial groups have great difficulty organizing their response tempo to meet time limitations. In the Orientation Scale developed at the Institute, we have found that lower-class children in the first grade had significantly greater difficulty than did middle-class children in handling items related to time judgments.

Another area in which the lower-class child lacks preschool orientation is the well-inculcated expectation of reward for performance, especially for successful task completion. The lack of such expectation, of course, reduces motivation for beginning a task and, therefore, also makes less likely the self-reinforcement of activity through the gaining of feelings of competence. In these impoverished, broken homes there is very little of the type of interaction seen so commonly in middle-class homes, in which the parent sets a task for the child, observes its performance, and in some way rewards its completion. Neither, for most tasks, is there the disapproval which the middle-class child incurs when he does not perform properly or when he leaves something unfinished. Again, much of the organization of the classroom is based on the assumption that children anticipate rewards for performance and that they will respond in these terms to tasks which are set for them. This is not to imply that the young lower-class child is not given assignments in his home, nor that he is never given approval or punishment. Rather, the assignments tend to be motoric in character, have a short time span, and are more likely to relate to very concrete objects or services for people. The tasks given to preschool children in the middle class are more likely to involve language and conceptual processes, and are thereby more attuned to the later school setting.

Related to the whole issue of the adult-child dynamic in establishing a basis for the later learning process is the ability of the child to use the adult as a source for information, correction, and the reality testing involved in problem solving and the absorption of new knowledge. When free adult time is greatly limited, homes vastly overcrowded, economic stress chronic, and the general educational level very low—and, in addition, when adults in our media culture are aware of the inadequacy of their education—questions from children are not encouraged, as the adults might be embarrassed by their own limitations and anyway are too preoccupied with the business of just living and surviving. In the child's formulation of concepts of the world, the ability to formulate questions is an essential step in data gathering. If questions are not encouraged or if they are not responded to, this is a function which does not mature.

At the Institute, in our observations of children at the kindergarten level and in our discussions with parents, we find that many lower-class children have difficulty here. It follows that this problem, if it is not compensated for by special school efforts, becomes more serious later in the learning process, as more complex subject matter is introduced. It is here that questioning is not only desirable but essential, for if the child is not prepared to demand clarification he again falls farther behind, the process of alienation from school is facilitated, and his inattentiveness becomes further reinforced as he just does not understand what is being presented.

It is generally agreed that the language-symbolic process plays an important role at all levels of learning. It is included here under the "contentual" rubric because language development evolves through the correct labeling of the environment, and through the use of appropriate words for the relating and combining and recombining of the concrete and abstract components in describing, interpreting, and communicating perceptions, experiences, and ideational matter. One can postulate on considerable evidence that language is one of the areas which is most sensitive to the impact of the multiplicity of problems associated with the stimulus deprivation found in the marginal circumstances of lower-class life. There are various dimensions of language, and for each of these it is possible to evaluate the influence of the verbal environment of the home and its immediate neighborhood.

In order for a child to handle multiple attributes of words and to associate words with their proper referents, a great deal of exposure to language is presupposed. Such exposure involves training, experimenting with identifying objects and having corrective feedback, listening to a variety of verbal material, and just observing adult language usage. Exposure of children to this type of experience is one of the great strengths of the middle-class home, and concomitantly represents a weakness in the lower-class home. In a middle-class home also, the availability of a great range of objects to be labeled and verbally related to each other strengthens the overall language fluency of the child and gives him a basis for both understanding the teacher and for being able to communicate with her on various levels. An implicit hypothesis in a recent Institute survey of verbal skills is that verbal fluency is strongly related to reading skills and to other highly organized integrative and conceptual verbal activity.

The acquisition of language facility and fluency and experience with the multiple attributes of words is particularly important in view of the estimate that only 60 to 80 percent of any sustained communication is usually heard. Knowledge of context and of the syntactical regularities of a language make correct completion and comprehension of the speech sequence possible. This completion occurs as a result of the correct anticipation of the sequence of language and thought. The child who has not achieved these anticipatory language skills is greatly handicapped in school. Thus for the child who already is deficient in auditory discrimination and in ability to sustain attention, it becomes increasingly important that he have the very skills he lacks most.

The problem in developing preventive and early remedial programs for these children is in determining the emphasis on the various areas that need remediation. For example, would it be more effective to place the greatest emphasis on the training of auditory discrimination, or on attentional mechanisms, or on anticipatory receptive language functions in order to achieve the primary goal of enabling the child to understand his teacher? In programming special remedial procedures, we do not know how much variation we will find from child to child, or if social-class experiences create a sufficiently homogeneous pattern of deficit so that the fact of any intervention and systematic training may be more important than its sequences. If this is so, the intervention would probably be most valid in the language area, because the large group of lower-class children with the kinds of deficits mentioned are probably maturationally ready for more complex language functioning than they have achieved. Language knowledge, once acquired, can be self-reinforcing in just communicating with peers or talking to oneself.

In observations of lower-class homes, it appears that speech sequences seem to be temporally very limited and poorly structured syntactically. It is thus not surprising to find that a major focus of deficit in the children's language development is syntactical organization and subject continuity. In preliminary analysis of expressive and receptive language data on samples of middle- and lower-class children at the first- and fifth-grade levels, there are indications that the lower-class child has more expressive language ability than is generally recognized or than emerges in the classroom. The main differences between the social classes seem to lie in the level of syntactical organization. If, as is indicated in this research, with proper stimulation a surprisingly high level of expressive language functioning is available to the same children who show syntactical deficits, then we might conclude that the language variables we are dealing with here are by-products of social experience rather than indices of basic ability or intellectual level. This again suggests another possible vital area to be included in an enrichment or a remedial program: training in the use of word sequences to relate and unify cognitions.

Also on the basis of preliminary analysis of data, it appears that retarded readers have the most difficulty with the organization of expressive language.

In another type of social-class-related language analysis, Bernstein (1960), an English sociologist, has pointed out that the lowerclass tends to use informal language and mainly to convey concrete needs and immediate consequences, while the middle-class usage tends to be more formal and to emphasize the relating of concepts. This difference between these two milieus, then, might explain the finding in some of our recent research that the middle-class fifth-grade child has an advantage over the lower-class fifth-grader in tasks where precise and somewhat abstract language is required for solution. Further, Bernstein's reasoning would again emphasize the communication gap which exists between the middle-class teacher and the lower-class child.

Though it might belong more in the formal than in the contentual area, one can postulate that the absence of well-structured routine and activity in the home is reflected in the difficulty that the lower-class child has in structuring language. The implication of this for curriculum in the kindergarten and nursery school would be that these children should be offered a great deal of verbalized routine and regulation so that expectation can be built up in the child and then met.

According to Piaget's theories, later problem-solving and logical abilities are built on the earlier and orderly progression through a series of developmental stages involving the active interaction between the child and his environment. This is considered a maturational process, though highly related to experience and practice. Language development does not occupy a superordinate position.

However, Whorf, Vygotsky, and some contemporary theorists have made language the essential ingredient in concept formation, problem-solving, and in the relating to an interpretation of the environment. Current data at the Institute tend to indicate that class differences in perceptual abilities and in general environmental orientation decrease with chronological age, whereas language differences tend to increase. These might tentatively be interpreted to mean that perceptual development occurs first and that language growth and its importance in problem-solving comes later. If later data and further analysis support this interpretation, then the implication would be that the lower-class child comes to school with major deficits in the perceptual rather than the language area. Perhaps the poverty of his experience has slowed his rate of maturation. Then by requiring, without the antecedent verbal preparation, a relatively high level of language skill, the school may contribute to an increase in the child's deficit in this area, relative to middle-class children. Meanwhile, his increased experience and normal maturational processes stimulate perceptual development, and that deficit is overcome. But the child is left with a language handicap. The remedy for such a situation would be emphasis on perceptual training for these children in the early school, or, better, preschool, years, combined with a more gradual introduction of language training and requirements.

This theory and interpretation are somewhat, but by no means wholly, in conflict with the previous discussion of language. In an area where there is as yet much uncertainty, it is important to consider as many alternatives as possible, in order not to restrict experimentation.

In any event, whether or not we consider language skills as primary mediators in concept formation and problem solving, the lower-class child seems to be at a disadvantage at the point of entry into the formal learning process.

The other contentual factors that so often result in a poorly prepared child being brought to the school situation are closely interrelated with language. Briefly, they revolve around the child's understanding and knowledge of the physical, geographic, and geometric characteristics of the world around him, as well as information about his self-identity and some of the more macroscopic items of general information. It could be reasonably expected, for example, that a kindergarten or first-grade child who is not mentally defective would know both his first and last names, his address or the city he lives in, would have a rudimentary concept of number relationships, and would know something about the differences between near and far, high and low, and similar relational concepts. Much of what happens in school is predicated on the prior availability of this basic information. We know that educational procedures frequently proceed without establishing the actual existence of such a baseline. Again, in the lower-class child it cannot be taken for granted that the home experience has supplied this information or that it has tested the child for this knowledge. In facilitating the learning process in these children, the school must expect frequently to do a portion of the job traditionally assigned to the home, and curriculum must be reorganized to provide for establishing a good base. This type of basic information is essential so that the child can relate the input of new information to some stable core.

From all of the foregoing, it is obvious that the lower-class child when he enters school has as many problems in understanding what it is all about and why he is there as school personnel have in relating traditional curriculum and learning procedures to this child. Some reorientation is really necessary, as discussion of these problems almost always focuses on the problems the school has, rather than on the enormous confusion, hesitations, and frustrations the child experiences and does not have the language to articulate when he meets an essentially rigid set of academic expectations. Again, from all the foregoing, the child, from the time he enters school and is exposed to assumptions about him derived from experience with the middle-class child, has few success experiences and much failure and generalized frustration, and thus begins the alienating process in the direction of the apathetic and disgruntled fifth grader described earlier.

The frustration inherent in not understanding, not succeeding, and not being stimulated in the school—although being regulated by it, creates a basis for the further development of negative self-images and low evaluations of individual competencies. This would be especially true for the Negro child who, as we know from doll-play and other studies, starts reflecting the social bias in his own self-image at very early ages. No matter how the parents might aspire to a higher achievement level for their child, their lack of knowledge as to the operational implementation, combined with the child's early failure experiences in school, can so effectively attenuate confidence in his ability ever to handle competently challenge in the academic area, that the child loses all motivation.

It is important to state that not all the negative factors and deficits discussed here are present in every or even in any one child. Rather, there is a patterning of socially determined school-achievement-related disabilities which tends initially to set artificially low ceilings for these children: initially artificial, because as age increases it becomes more and more difficult for these children to develop compensatory mechanisms, to respond to special programs, or to make the psychological readjustments required to overcome the cumulative effects of their early deficits.

It is also important to state that there are strengths and positive features associated with lower-class life. Unfortunately, they generally tend not to be, at least immediately, congruent with the demands of the school. For example, lack of close supervision or protection fosters the growth of independence in lower-class children. However, this independence—and probably confidence—in regard to the handling of younger siblings, the crossing of streets, self-care, and creating of their own amusements, does not necessarily meaningfully transfer to the unfamiliar world of books, language, and abstract thought.

SCHOOL CONDITIONS Educational factors have of course been interlaced throughout this discussion, but there are some special features that need separate delineation.

The lower-class child probably enters school with a nebulous and essentially neutral attitude. His home rarely, if ever, negatively predisposes him toward the school situation, though it might not offer positive motivation and correct interpretation of the school experience. It is in the school situation that the highly charged negative attitudes toward learning evolve, and the responsibility for such large groups of normal children showing great scholastic retardation, the high dropout rate, and to some extent the delinquency problem, must rest with the failure of the school to promote the proper acculturation of these children. Though some of the responsibility may be shared by the larger society, the school, as the institution of that society, offers the only mechanism by which the job can be done.

It is unfair to imply that the school has all the appropriate methods at its disposal and has somehow chosen not to apply them. On the contrary, what is called for is flexible experimentation in the development of new methods, the clear delineation of the problem, and the training and retraining of administrative and teaching personnel in the educational philosophy and the learning procedures that this problem requires.

In addition, the school should assume responsibility for a systematic plan for the education of the child in the areas that have been delineated here by the time the child reaches kindergarten or first grade. This does not mean that the school will abrogate the family's role with regard to the child, but rather that the school will insure both the intellectual and the attitudinal receptivity of each child to its requirements. Part of a hypothesis now being tested in a new preschool program is based on the assumption that early intervention by well-structured programs will significantly reduce the attenuating influence of the socially marginal environment.

What might be necessary to establish the required base to assure the eventual full participation of these children in the opportunity structure offered by the educational system is an ungraded sequence from age three or four through eight, with a low teacher-pupil ratio. Perhaps, also, the school system should make full use of anthropologists, sociologists, and social psychologists for description and interpretation of the cultural discontinuities which face the individual child when he enters school. In addition, the previously discussed patterning of deficits and strengths should be evaluated for each child and placed in a format which the teacher can use as a guide. In the early years this would enable diagnostic reviews of the intellectual functioning of each child, so that learning procedures, to whatever extent possible, could be appropriate to a particular child's needs. New evaluation techniques must be developed for this purpose, as the standardized procedures generally cannot produce accurate evaluation of the functioning level or achievement potential of these children.

Possibly most important would be the greater utilization by educators in both curriculum development and teacher training of the new and enormous knowledge, techniques, and researches in the social and behavioral sciences. Similarly, social and behavioral scientists have in the school a wonderful laboratory to study the interpenetration and interaction of fundamental social, cognitive, psychological, and developmental processes. Close and continuing collaboration, thus, should be mutually productive and satisfying, and is strongly indicated.

BIBLIOGRAPHY

BERNSTEIN, B., 1960, "Language and Social Class," *British Journal of Psychology*, 11, September, pp. 271-276.
HUNT, J. McV., 1961, *Intelligence and Experience*, New York: The Ronald Press.

8.2 INTRODUCTION

The selection that follows is excerpted from an extensive inquiry into the sources of learning difficulties. The findings about the effects of social class confirm the analysis in the previous selection and specify the particular manner in which these effects are reflected in the classroom. The remainder of the excerpt deals with certain aspects of family structure, extending the insights provided by Pettigrew in an earlier selection (Selection 7.4) on the effects of family disorganization and identifying the child's birth order as an additional factor of significance for his intellectual development.

Although the title of this selection refers to "emotional blocks to learning," it is mainly concerned with aspect of social structure and interaction that underlie psychological difficulties. The author links the data on learning problems to the specific expectations of behavior encountered by the child, depending on the social structure of his family and his particular position within it. Thus, in addition to its educational relevance, this selection probes deeper into the linkage between the individual's psychological make-up and his sociocultural background, specifying some of the intricacies of interpersonal relationships that are the concrete components of the latter. The discussion portrays the emotional blocks to children's learning as not merely reflections but actual reproductions of features of their immediate social environments. Thus the differences in content between the learning problems of first-born and last-born children parallel the differences between the attitudes and expectations that underlay their parents' treatment of them.

This selection contains important implications for the concerns of a guidance counselor. It points, in the first place, to the fact that different kinds of psychological processes can underlie the common symptom of failure to learn, suggesting the need for caution in attributing particular motives and conflicts to particular individuals. Secondly, and more importantly, it shows that different psychological processes can result from a seemingly unitary social environment, such as a single family, depending on the individual's particular role within it.

At the same time, the nature of Harris's interpretation suggests the potential value of social measures as remedies for emotional problems. Thus, for example, a child whose learning difficulties are of the rebellious kind associated here with first-born boys might well improve in response to a situation where his own capacities were emphasized as the standard for evaluating his performance and where comparisons and competitive incentives were minimized. Indeed, improvement might follow much more easily from such conditions than from attempts to directly alter his rebellious attitudes. Moreover, the long-range consequences of such environmental measures might well be that the child learns new ways of responding to requirements and expectations and thus that rebelliousness becomes a less dominant feature of his behavior.

The ensuing excerpt concerns itself with the sources of learning problems and not with their solutions. In doing so, however, it directs attention to a particular range of factors—*i.e.*, aspects of social structure and interaction—which are as relevant to the task of dealing with the problems as to that of understanding them.

8.2   EMOTIONAL BLOCKS TO LEARNING [1]

Irving D. Harris

. . .[T]he study began with an inquiry into those psychological factors which are specific to learning difficulties. One hundred emotionally disturbed boys with learning problems were compared with 100 emotionally disturbed boys without learning problems. We hoped, for example, to find why a boy with an I.Q. of 110 would be failing in all subjects whereas another emotionally disturbed boy with the same I.Q. would have no trouble in school. Our task was complicated by the fact that learning difficulties did not take one particular form. Thus, among the nonlearner boys we saw such different symptoms as lack of motivation, low-average intelligence, difficulties in concentrating, repeating of grades, resistance to the educator, specific difficulty in reading, etc. We turned our attention, then, to finding which emotional or psychological factors are related to the several symptoms of learning difficulties.

SOCIAL CLASS   It has been said that the best method of insuring a long life is to select parents and grandparents who were long-lived. The same may be said of education. The best assurance a boy may have of being properly equipped and motivated to get the most from our educational system is the possession of parents and grandparents of a socioeconomic group which places a high value on education. . . .

---

[1]Reprinted with permission of The Macmillan Company from *Emotional Blocks to Learning: A Study of the Reasons for Failure in School*, by I. D. Harris.©The Free Press, a Corporation, 1961. Pp. 139, 13-27, 53-59, 63, 67-69, 197-199, 203-207.

Differences in social class proved to be one of the few general factors distinguishing the entire learner group from the entire nonlearner group. Taking occupation and education of the father as the prime indicator of social class, we found among the 100 learners a much greater proportion of boys whose fathers had "professional" occupations (teachers, ministers, physicians, lawyers, scientists, etc.) or who had some college education. In contrast, among the 100 nonlearners, there was a greater frequency of boys whose fathers had occupations which could be categorized as "semiskilled" or who had not finished high school. The percentage of fathers who were skilled craftsmen or had a high school education was about the same for the learners and the nonlearners. . . .

Before proceeding further, we must emphasize that a boy coming from an uppermiddle-class family is not guaranteed freedom from learning difficulty. Similarly, lower-class origins do not inevitably coincide with a learning problem. These results merely indicate that, all other things being equal, the uppermiddle-class boy has a better chance of avoiding a learning difficulty than does the lower-class boy.

Specific learning problems, lower-class boys

What, we may ask, are the learning symptoms most often reported by the school about lower-class boys? Three statements are characteristic: (1) low average intelligence; (2) working up to intellectual capacity; (3) has repeated at least one grade. These characteristics may stand out more prominently if we tell what was *not* frequently mentioned by the school. The latter include daydreaming, not working up to capacity, and having a reading problem.

The picture of lower-class boys that emerges from these three characteristics and from reading all of the case histories is one of children whose habits, experiences, and social motivations have kept them from ever having fully exercised their intellects. It is definitely not a picture of boys whose neurotic or emotional conflicts block the constructive use of an easily observable keen intellect. . . .

ATTITUDES TOWARD EDUCATION   Let us now inquire more systematically into the effects of lower-class origin. First, we must call attention to the fact that our findings are much in keeping with the findings of leading educators and sociologists. They have emphasized that each socioeconomic class—from lower-lower to upper-upper (in Lloyd Warner's terms)—views and values education in a somewhat different way. The middleclass, most important numerically, values education more highly than does the lowerclass, the second largest group. It is not surprising that members of the middle classes, as professional or college educated persons, highly skilled craftsmen, etc., should more frequently give their children a valued concept of education than would members of the lowerclass, such as semiskilled workmen and persons with only a grade school education.

Allison Davis, Robert Havighurst (1946), and James Bossard (1948), among others, have been leading investigators of this problem. All agree that middle-class parents place a premium on education because it constitutes a way for the children to rise in the world economically, socially, and professionally. This is not true, however, of the lower-class parents. Not only have they not had firsthand experience with the advantages of education, but they are likely to view anyone who has risen through education with jealous suspicion. Bossard tells of the emotional reaction of the lower-class father whose son had used the word "preference." He said, "Preference, preference, I'll preference you. You with the fancy words. You can't high-hat me as long as I pay the bills" (Bossard, 1948, p. 184).

The middle-class boy, then, would be likely to win the approval of his parents by doing well in school; whereas, a lower-class boy might lose approval in so doing. However, not only the approval of the parents is at stake. Davis and Bossard and Havighurst, separately have indicated that the public school itself is primarily a middle-class institution. The values it emphasizes are middleclass, and the teachers themselves are drawn from this class. The middle-class boy, therefore, has a chance of winning the approval of the middle-class teacher so long as he adheres to his ingrained middle-class attitudes. The lower-class boy has less chance of winning the teacher's approval because she tends not to understand that her values are different from his and to be exasperated with the lower-class boy who is resentful of demands that he learn. Davis and Havighurst say that the teachers, instead of changing teaching methods to accommodate the differences in attitudes which arise from different social class origins, tend more often to increase the pressure on lower-class children by forcing them to comply with existing methods and values. As a result, many children become frustrated and discouraged with school, and are likely to develop problems in learning (Davis and Havighurst, 1946).

DEVELOPMENT OF THE INTELLECT   We should like to go deeper into this matter because we believe an additional factor is working here. It is true that if a child learns because of external rewards, the reward of approval by parent and teacher will constitute an incentive for learning. But a child cannot respond by learning—no matter how attractive the incentive—unless he is equipped to respond. In this respect, we believe that the lower-class boy is at a comparative disadvantage. *His intellectual apparatus has not been exercised.* In order to converse with a parent or other members of his social class, a lower-class child must rise to the level of the discourse. If the discourse requires only a low intellectual level, the child, out of habit and inertia, finds it a needless expenditure of intellectual energy to rise higher.

Interviews with lower-class parents yield the impression that conversing with them would neither stimulate nor exercise the intellect. They are more preoccupied with the "What is it?" and "How can I use it?" aspects of human existence than with the "Why is it?" aspects. The brute necessities of economic survival compel them to be basically practical—not to wonder about the meaning and the interrelatedness of life. When their preschool son goes through the phase of "Why is this?" and "Why is that?" the parents usually do not know how to respond. Often, perhaps, they react impatiently saying, "Never mind 'Why this is?' It is just that way." The son realizes that it does not pay to communicate on this level.

The intellectual powers of most lower-class boys, then, have never been adequately stimulated. To employ a medical term, these powers have been atrophied through disuse. This may account in part for the lower scores that the lower-class boys in our sample received on intelligence tests. Their scores were most frequently in the 90 to 105 range; whereas the scores of middle-class boys were usually above 105. While intelligence tests strive to measure intellectual ability, it is well known that their scores can be raised by stimulation. Children from orphanages who have had minimal discourse with adults have added ten points to their I.Q.'s after placement in foster or adoptive homes where they communicate more frequently with adults. Similarly, it is known that northern Negroes who are exposed to and stimulated by urban middle-class surroundings, score higher on I.Q. tests than do southern Negroes. . . .

Ethnic attitudes toward learning

. . . .Certain ethnic groups emphasize the value of learning regardless of the social class of the particular family. In our study, this was seen in reference to Jewish boys. There were fewer Jewish boys in the nonlearner group than in the learner group; intelligence scores were higher and grade repetition was rare. . . . It is well known that Jewish parents, following their tradition of being the people of the Book, value learning not only as a means of coping with and advancing in the external world, but also as a thing in itself. Within the Jewish family, intellectual failure carries with it certain penalties; love of learning brings great rewards. While this emphasis may have unfavorable reverberations in other areas of learning performance, it does not usually reflect itself in low-average intelligence scores or in grade repetition. . . .

FAMILY DISORGANIZATION It is difficult to determine which is more upsetting for a young boy—chronic arguments between his father and mother, or a mother who is unavailable because she is employed outside of the home. However, when both these elements are present in the home, one can be sure that the effect on the boy is highly disturbing. Such family disorganization—regardless of social class— could only result in the boy's having chronic uncertainty about whether his home would stay intact and about whether he could depend on his mother.

In our study, we found these disturbances to have a crucial impact on learning. One factor differentiating the nonlearners from the learners was the number of *younger* nonlearners who had been exposed to severe family disorganization. That is to say, in boys under ten, the percentage of nonlearners coming from homes where *both* marital discord and a working mother—*double disorganization*—

were present, was almost three times the percentage of young learners coming from such homes.

We may ask what symptoms of learning difficulties are associated with family disorganization. We shall find a picture somewhat different from that of the lower-class nonlearner. The evidence suggested that lower socioeconomic status affected the boy's motivation to learn. With family disorganization, however, influences impinge on the actual thinking processes. In other words, regardless of basic motivation, the inner anxious turmoil aroused in the nonlearning boy by family disorganization appears to take up energy which could have been used for learning.

The characteristic statements made about younger nonlearners coming from such homes were: (1) he has thinking difficulties (daydreaming, inattentiveness, and difficulty in concentrating); (2) he is not working up to capacity; (3) he has repeated a grade; (4) he has reading problems. Except for grade repetition, these symptoms are different from the characteristics noted in the previous chapter. . . .

BIRTH ORDER AND
PARENTAL EXPECTATIONS
OF MATURITY

A subtle but powerful influence on the growing boy arises from his position among the children in the family, *i.e.*, from his being the first-born, a middle-born or the last-born. Parents have different maturity expectations of the first-born and the last-born child. Specifically, they generally expect the first-born to be more mature and permit the last-born to be less mature. How these expectations affect learning and other forms of behavior will be the subject of this chapter.

Expectations arising from family position differ from those stemming from parental ambitiousness. Parental ambitiousness looks toward the future and envisages the boy's status some years hence; maturity expectations are geared more to the present. Thus, while the status-conscious parent may wish the son eventually to enter one of the professions, the maturity-conscious parent may wish that he knew how to tie his shoe laces and keep his room in order today. If maturity expectations are in keeping with the child's actual age, wholesome effects will undoubtedly result. But sometimes the expectations are excessively high or low: unwholesome effects generally result if parents expect that a three-year-old boy consistently behave like a six-year-old, or constantly permit a six-year-old to behave like a three-year-old.

The initial and central finding of this part of the study was discovered when we compared the ordinal positions of the learner and nonlearner boys. We found little difference in the positions of middle and "only" children, but a striking difference in the percentages of the eldest and youngest. Eldest or first-born boys were found almost twice as frequently in the group *without* learning problems. Conversely, youngest or last-born boys were found almost twice as frequently in the group *with* learning problems. . . .

Because we had collateral evidence from another source, we were not prepared to dismiss this trend as of accidental significance. We investigated 1,300 boys and 500 girls who came from comparatively small families (two or three children) and who were clinic admissions to the Institute. We found that first-born children were more frequently described by their mothers as being "bright" and more often obtained high-average to superior scores on intelligence tests than did last-born children. The percentage of first-born boys described by their mothers as "bright" was twice that of last-born boys. For boys, there was no difference in intelligence scores. With the girls, although the maternal descriptions of "bright" were equally frequent for first- and last-born youngsters, their descriptions of "slow" were almost two times more frequent for the last-born girls. Furthermore, the first-born girls had a significantly greater percentage of intelligence test scores ranging from high-average to superior, and the last-born girls obtained a significantly greater percentage of scores ranging from dull to mental defective. . . .

Reasons for differences between first- and last-born children

Disposed, then, to consider this trend seriously, we thought of three possible reasons to explain it. The first was that the mother may be more tired of child-rearing when she is raising the last-born child and may give him less mothering. We were inclined to discount this possibility because this trend was seen even in small families. In any event, we could find no evidence to prove or disprove this hypothesis.

The second possible reason was that the first-born has a head start in learning achievement, and he strives to maintain this ascendency over his younger siblings. The last-born, being at the bottom of the "pecking order," becomes discouraged with trying to compete with his older sibling and selects an area other than learning as his competitive strength. Although we did see situations like this in some cases, we did not find that sufficient consistent data strongly supported this explanation.

The third possible reason was that the parents have a different emotional relationship with their first child than they do with their last. We were eventually able to find the best supporting evidence for this reason. The first hint that learning differences had to do with maturity expectations came from the previously mentioned investigation of 1,300 boys and 500 girls. It revealed that mothers described their children as "immature," or as "acting babyish," more often when speaking of last-born boys and girls than when describing their first-born children. Looking, then, at our 100 learning boys and our 100 nonlearning boys, we found that the teacher's description of boys as "overly serious or sad" was given much more frequently for first-born than for last-born boys. The description "carefree" was more often applied to the last-born.

At this point, we thought the following regarding the psychological situation of the eldest and youngest: The first-born encounter a variety of expectations and stress. The parents, unfamiliar with what children are like, tend to expect them to act like the parents, to be miniature adults. Also, the parents are unsure about their adequacy as parents and measure their competence by how well the first-born thrives. The oldest child, then, has the burden of having to come up to the parents' higher standards of maturity and of maintaining the self-esteem of the parents as parents.

This closeness of the success of the child to the feelings of the parents is further increased by the parents' use of the oldest child as a substitute parent. If the family is under some stress, most often it is the oldest child whom the parents take into their confidence and with whom they share their anxiety. Even when there is no stress, it is more often the oldest who is asked to look after the younger children and to be a proper example for them. Because of these expectations, life, then, tends to be more serious for the eldest or first-born.

In contrast, the youngest is much less likely to have to meet such expectations of responsibility. He is looked after rather than required to look after. The parents tend to be more relaxed in their "do's" and "don't's"—sometimes because they have been too strict with the older children. Thus, the youngest is not as rule-conscious as is the oldest. Moreover, in their relaxation, the parents are more inclined to enjoy the last-born. The oldest child is expected to cope with that half of life concerned with the duties of stern reality. The youngest child is permitted to enjoy that half of life concerned with the pursuit of happiness.

These, then, are the general—though not invariable—considerations which apply to the positions of the eldest and the youngest in the family. Usually the oldest child is the vehicle for the parents' ideas of responsibilities in life, and the youngest is the vehicle for their conceptions of the pleasurable privileges of life. The "grown-up" portion of the parents' personality is more often assigned to the eldest, and the more childlike portion is more often assigned to the youngest. . . .

Another question which interested us was whether the problems the first-born have in learning are different from those experienced by the last-born. Although the oldest children appeared less likely to have learning problems, they certainly were not immune to them. For our investigation, then, we shall focus on the 33 first-born and the 28 last-born nonlearners.

We especially noted a difference between the oldest and youngest in the classroom situation—not in their intelligence test scores, in working up to capacity, in thinking difficulties, nor in proneness to reading difficulties. Rather, the difference was most evident in their resistance reactions to the learning task. The main characteristic of the first-born was a contrariness, an excessive expression of individuality as indicated by the most frequent comment of the teacher, "He resists directions." This sometimes barely disguised "I won't" or "I'll do it my way" of the first-born boys contrasted with a helpless, immature, apparently disorganized, "I can't" frequently characteristic of the last-born youngsters. Thus, the most frequent teacher's comments about the youngest children were: "socially immature," "speaks in an infantile manner," "shows need for affection," "hands in incomplete assignments," "careless."

Learning problems: first-born boys

...We are...led to believe that there are at least two kinds of learning difficulties. One is the pressure-resisting kind seen most often in first-born boys; the other is the disorganized spilling kind seen most often in last-born boys. Phrased in somewhat more technical language, the first kind of problem constitutes an inner rebellion against the internalized demands of the parents. The second kind constitutes a swamping of the psyche with uncontrolled impulses stimulated by the parents. . . .

Mothers of oldest and youngest nonlearners: an analysis

...[W]e...can discover what appears to be a common characteristic of the mothers of first-born nonlearners: *an emphasis on order and conformity.* How the child's impulses and feelings are regulated is more important to the mother than the feelings themselves. Mother expects a high degree of self-regulation not only of the first-born but also of herself.

In contrast is the common denominator of the mothers of last-born nonlearners, which appears to be an emphasis on *impulse gratification and release.* The child's expression of feeling is more important to the mother than how the feeling is regulated or modulated. Again, mother not only allows emotional gratification in the last-born child, but also permits it in herself. . . .

We have . . .combined all these characteristics under the rubric of maturity expectations. Thus, excessively high maturity expectations—as seen in the case of the first-born—mean excessive regulation of impulses. Excessively low maturity expectations—as seen in the case of the last-born—mean excessive stimulation of the impulses. The first-born reacts by exhibiting a persistent open or masked resistance to pressure; whereas the last-born reacts with a disorganized, overstimulated emotional outflow. The first-born is caught up in a battle between conforming to and resisting mother's regulatory pressures; whereas the last-born is involved in a conflict between succumbing to and resisting mother's tantalizing overstimulating tendencies.

The pertinence of these reactions to learning is complex, and we will be satisfied if we have provided only some preliminary insights. It appears, though, that two conditions for successful learning are indicated here. One condition is that the boy not reject the incorporation of new ideas, and not regard the educator's efforts as a pressuring infringement of his autonomy. In the first-born nonlearners, this condition for learning is comparatively lacking. The other condition is that there be sufficient regulation of the child's excitatory impulses; the environment must be consistent, patterned so that the boy can focus his energies on the learning tasks rather than spilling them randomly. This learning condition is comparatively lacking in the environments of the last-born nonlearners.

These conditions for learning and the lack thereof were noted in a study of normal children and mothers carried out by the author. These children were in the age-range of eight to nine, when intellectual mastery is the prime developmental task. The least well-adjusted of these normal children were of two types: those who were overregulated and feared ingesting new ideas, and those who were overstimulated by a chaotic, primitive family atmosphere (Harris, 1959, pp. 101–110). . . .

BIBLIOGRAPHY

BOSSARD, JAMES, 1948, *The Sociology of Child Development*, New York: Harper & Row.
DAVIS, ALLISON, AND HAVIGHURST, ROBERT, 1946, "Social Class and Color Differences in Child Rearing," *American Sociological Review*, XII, pp. 698–710.
HARRIS, IRVING, 1959, *Normal Children and Mothers*, New York: The Free Press.

8.3 INTRODUCTION

The ensuing excerpt deals with a very special child-rearing situation which is quite distinct from anything to be found in our society, that of the Kibbutz in Israel. The author identifies several interrelated features of this form of child-rearing—the separation of children from their parents, the primary role of the peer group in socialization, and the overall depersonalization of the socializing process—as basic to the emotional and intellectual development of the "children of the Kibbutz." His discussion of the consequences of these practices brings out, by contrast, the significance of the nuclear family and of personal relationships—that is, relationships laden with emotion and affect—between adults and children in shaping the individual's most basic intellectual capacities. Indeed, it is precisely because Diamond isolates the relationship within a cultural context different from our own that the implications of his analysis seem so compelling. The detachment that such distance provides, together with the added insights that the comparative perspective permits into the intricacies of cause-and-effect relationships, are, of course, the distinctive strengths of the anthropological approach. Diamond's analysis illustrates the extent to which cross-cultural study can deepen our understanding of individual psychological processes.

Although the particular pattern of child-rearing discussed here is not to be found as a whole anywhere in our society, some of its qualities may be found in very different institutional arrangements, as the author points out. Thus, for example, the degree of emotional and affective intensity in the relationships between children and their socializing agents may be found to vary widely in families from different classes and different cultural backgrounds, even if the extreme described here as typical of the Kibbutz is never reached. The more general import of this analysis of a very special case, in other words, is to link certain intellectual capacities, often considered innate and independent of experience, to the social structure and the consequent nature of the social interaction through which child-rearing is carried out.

For the guidance counselor, it thus points once again to the importance of viewing individual characteristics against the social background in which they arose in order to comprehend their function within the person and their susceptibility to growth and change. Moreover, it suggests that social interaction and deliberately structured social relationships may, if they occur at the right time, serve to remedy the kind of deficiencies discussed in the first selection of this chapter and even to exert more purely positive influences on individual growth.

8.3   KIBBUTZ AND SHTETL: THE HISTORY OF AN IDEA [1]

Stanley Diamond

. . .[T]he collective method of rearing children represents a rejection of the Shtetl family, with particular reference to the parental roles. . . . It was felt that the family itself had to be banished, in order to rear the "new Jew", the "normalized" man, in the Zionist sense of that term. The Vatikim were moved by the desire to create a new generation, a generation that would be "normal", "free", and "manly", unsullied by the Galut (exile), rather than "complex", "insecure", and "parasitic". They did not think themselves worthy of rearing such children within the confines of their own nuclear families, and they dared not trust themselves to the task. Above all, they did not want to reproduce such people as they conceived themselves to be. Thus, beneath the surface of expressed and conscious intent lay an unexpressed and inexpressible rejection of the child, a fear and trembling about the problem of meeting the parental roles, while realizing the ideological ends in sight. This is not to imply that the Vatikim did not or do not "love" their children, or that they were not concerned with the welfare and organization of the children's houses. But it is to imply that they anesthetized themselves against the operation that severed the psychic link between the generations, and converted the *Sabra* into an Israeli as opposed to a Jew, by ideological rationalizations and justifications of every sort. This operation demanded a further abnegation of the Jewish self that the Vatik carried within him to the Kibbutz; it implied a subordination, indeed a denial of his own identity, thus depriving the Kibbutz Sabra of deep identification with the parent who was indirectly nurturing

[1]From Stanley Diamond, "Kibbutz and Shtetl: The History of an Idea," *Social Problems*, 5, 1957, pp. 88–91.

him, providing for his care, and supplying the formal precepts by which he was reared. His relentless rejection of the past dissociated the Vatik from the very future he was so self-absorbedly engaged in building.

The complex and immediate tensions that characterize the relations between the human generations, that provide leverage for emotional growth and the refinement of perception, were, in the Kibbutz, attenuated. Put another way, the concrete relationships between the generations were abstracted, an *institution* was interposed between parent and child. The family no longer served as mediator between society and the child, diffusing, individualizing and synthesizing social imperatives, and affording the possibility of idiosyncratic response. This function of the family, which may well emerge as its indispensable *raison d'être*, as the pressures of public life increase, was, in the Kibbutz, abandoned. Society had become the *direct* socializing agency, the collective *idea* had triumphed over the concrete *person*. For the great majority of Kibbutz Sabras, in the first transitional generation, comprising the sons and daughters of the Vatikim, the result was an inner uniformity of personality; a genuine modal type was created, a rare phenomenon in human history.

Now we emphasize that this was the case for the "great majority," not for all Kibbutz Sabras, since authentic deviants exist, and since the modal characteristics are epitomized among the "classic" Sabras, and more moderately, although powerfully, expressed among the "average"[2] Sabras. Yet the modality is apparent, and we have called it a rare phenomenon in order to distinguish it from that tautological conception of "modal personality" which deduces psychic identity from customary or conventional behavior, and from psychic identity reasons back to customary or conventional behavior (Hart, 1954). Genuine modal personality would seem to stem from the institutionalization, or depersonalization of the rearing process, and *that* has been rare in human history. Of course, modal psychological *processes* occur everywhere, to one degree or another, but these can be expressed by quite different kinds of people, and so should be distinguished from modal personality *types*.

Now it is appropriate to point out here that the Kibbutz is not a folk society, it is not an extended family, or localized clan, nor is it in any way analogous to these.[3] In such primitive structures, the web of personal contacts between the generations is highly ramified, embracing not only the biological parents, but usually a host of parent surrogates, along with classes of relatives, real or fictional, to whom the growing child relates in specific ways. Children reared in primitive villages are thus, often, children of the village. But the Sabra is a "child of the Kibbutz," as he is frequently called, in an entirely different sense. He is a "child

---

[2] The terms "average," "classic," and "deviant" represent categories sorted out from Rorschach results, personal observation, case history materials, and intensive interviewing.

[3] It should be noted that this point contradicts the view expressed by M. E. Spiro in his article on the Kibbutz: "Is the Family Universal?" (Spiro, 1954)

of the Kibbutz" because he has been reared in a peer group world of his own, sheltered, so to speak, from the parental generation. He has been reared, in short, more or less *institutionally*, in distinction to *personal* rearing, and it is in this sense that he is a "child of the Kibbutz."

This primary emphasis on the peer group in the socialization of the Sabra, beginning in the earliest weeks of life, functioned, of course, as the most effective way to break the psychic link between the generations, thus attaining the ideological ends adhered to by the parents. At the same time, however, it substantially deprived the child of profound and complexly ramifying affective-intellectual contact with one or more significant adults, concerned primarily with him, through whom the child first feels his way into the world, and ultimately comes to reflect on it, to think about it, to *conceive* it. Put another way, the conceptual capacity, the capacity to relate things and events, to symbolize, to abstract, and the desire to do so, although a latent, phylogenetically determined, distinctive human capacity, seems to germinate in the soil of personal contacts. That is, the concrete personal relationships, and in the growing psyche these can only be *affectively* apprehended, serve as the prototype for the relational or conceptual capacity in general. This abstractive-conceptual capacity is, apparently, a function of the quality and nature of concrete affective relationships as these accumulate and ramify through the various phases of the culturally determined life-cycle. Learning to think conceptually, then, seems imbedded in learning to relate affectively from the earliest years of life. This, we would contend, is the crucial link, pulling together, indeed fusing, the intellectual and emotional functions, a process clearly implied in the psychotherapeutic act, if obscured in psychoanalytic theory, and a process strongly implied in the work of Sullivan (1953), Goldstein (1940), Piaget (1955), Spitz (1945), and others.

We would state, further, that the split between the intellectual and emotional functions is always a symptom of pathology, no matter where we find it, and despite the cultural sanction of the personalities involved. It is instructive, in this context, to note the typical remark of the Sabras: "If we can think, why must we feel?" However, this dissociation between the intellectual and the emotive, impoverishes both. . . .

. . .[T]he attenuation of the complex linkage between generations has inhibited the development of the conceptual capacities, the imaginative faculties, and affective expression. Thus, the Kibbutz Sabra is widely recognized as a "realistic" ("naturalistic" is a more accurate word), "stolid," "straightforward," "pragmatic" man. However these adjectival descriptions, although true enough, must be seen in sociopsychological depth if we are to grasp their particular character and meaning. . . .

We should also note here that the depersonalization of the rearing process, which we believe is the key to an understanding of the typical Sabra and a "necessary" result of the parental motives, is by no means inevitably associated with nursery systems as such, nor even with overtly structured collective rearing. We mean by this that depersonalization can occur within an ordinary family structure under certain social conditions, while nursery systems can function as genuine family surrogates. In the latter case, the family serves as the example on which the system is patterned. Therefore the collective method of child rearing in the Kibbutz cannot be mechanically compared with nursery systems existing elsewhere; a more germane comparison would seem possible with depersonalized rearing in ordinary family structures in our society (Spitz, 1945). It is, in short, the quality and depth of relationships between the generations with which we are primarily concerned from a sociopsychological standpoint and not the literal form of the institution involved. . . .

BIBLIOGRAPHY

GOLDSTEIN, KURT, 1940, *Human Nature in the Light of Psychopathology*, Cambridge Harvard University Press.
HART, C. W. M., 1954, "The Sons of Turimpi," *American Anthropologist*, 56, pp 242–261.
PIAGET, JEAN, 1955, *The Child's Construction of Reality*, London: Routledge and Kegan Paul.
SPIRO, M. E., 1954, "Is the Family Universal?", *American Anthropologist*, 56, pp 839–846.
SPITZ, RENÉ, 1945, "Hospitalism," etc. *The Psychoanalytic Study of the Child*, International Universities Press.
SULLIVAN, H. S., 1953, *The Interpersonal Theory of Psychiatry*, New York: W. W Norton, especially pp. 38–39, 42–44, 69, 71–72, 75–76, 206, 211, 287, 369.

8.4 INTRODUCTION

This selection carries further the analysis of the relationship between social and cultural factors on the one hand and individual traits on the other, focusing on family structure, the institution of slavery, and occupational status as indirect sources of the need for achievement (*n* Achievement). The latter is a characteristic which individuals have to varying degrees, and it is generally defined as a concern with performing successfully in relation to a standard of excellence. This excerpt thus links some major social phenomena to a psychological process that is directly relevant to learning and education.

Reviewing data from a variety of societies, the author illustrates the extent to which different consequences can follow from the same aspect of the social environment in different cultures. The same family structure, for example, can foster either high or low levels of achievement motivation depending on the types of social interaction and social relationships to which it gives rise in a particular cultural context. Thus, while emphasizing the dependence of this psychological process on the social environment, this excerpt also suggests the necessity for caution in attempting to trace its sources in any given individual.

A different kind of caution which it seems relevant to introduce refers to the broader implications of McClelland's focus and consequent findings. It seems well to ask, as one examines the relationships he finds between high levels of need for achievement and economic productivity in a society, about what other types of 'productivity" are made less possible by strong achievement motivation. In other words, it seems useful to place McClelland's research within a wider context of human phenomena and concerns and to view the relationships he does find in relation to those that have been precluded by the same causal processes in each situation.

Regardless of one's judgment about the value in human terms of high or low achievement motivation, this selection has significant implications for those concerned with maximizing the number of individuals who profit from the American educational system. It suggests some of the limits that an individual's early experiences set on what he brings to the formal learning situation and thus on the nature of his performance within it. As described here, the need for mastering a standard of excellence clearly involves more than a belief in hard work or an interest in specific rewards, although such attitudes may often be associated with it in particular individuals. It refers, rather, to a more basic orientation toward the self and others that gets established very early in life and is not readily susceptible to alteration. Thus, to the extent that our educational system assumes a moderate or high degree of achievement motivation, to that extent children whose backgrounds did not produce such a result will be at a disadvantage.

Many questions follow from this. Is our educational system capable of appealing to other motives and thus enabling a greater number of individuals to learn? Would it be possible to raise the level of achievement motivation in children by introducing the appropriate experience in the early grades? What are the consequences of the emphasis on grades for the development of the inner standards which are a basic component of achievement motivation?

8.4 INDIRECT INFLUENCES ON
n ACHIEVEMENT LEVELS [1]

David C. McClelland

THE FAMILY STRUCTURE   What family setup is most likely to promote the development of *n* Achievement? It is difficult to generalize because family variations mean different things in different cultures. Consider birth order as a typical variable. In the United States Atkinson and Miller (1956) have obtained evidence

---

[1]From David C. McClelland, "Sources of *n* Achievement," *The Achieving Society*, Princeton: Van Nostrand, 1961, pp. 373–383.

showing that first-born children tend to have higher *n* Achievement, presumably because their achievement-oriented parents can set higher standards, be more affectionate, etc., with one child than with several. But in our sample of Indian students from Madras, the correlation between *n* Achievement (verbal) and birth order is actually +.10 (*p* ∽.20), suggesting that younger children may have higher *n* Achievement in India. Furthermore, Abegglen's study of Japan (1958) indicates that there it may also be the younger sons who get more independence and achievement training so that they leave home and go into business in town while the first-born son stays home and responsibly continues the family traditions.

Consider next the question of broken homes. Veroff *et al.* (1960) report for the United States that men more often have low *n* Achievement (*p* < .05) if the family is broken because of divorce, separation, or death of parents. Yet Bradburn (1960) has found that separation from the father in Turkey is associated with higher *n* Achievement in the son, as we shall see below.

Nevertheless, the family variations most likely to influence *n* Achievement in the same way cross-culturally are those in which the father is absent or the son lives with the mother. A check of our data on the family types of the tribes on which we have folk tale *n* Achievement scores shows that mother-child households are associated with low *n* Achievement. Any type of polygyny, for example, favors household units in which a mother lives with her own children. If the 42 cultures on which data exist are classified as to whether they permit or encourage *any* type of polygyny or not, it appears that only 48 percent of the 21 cultures high in *n* Achievement as contrasted with 77 percent of the 21 cultures low in *n* Achievement are characterized by some form of polygyny (chi-square = 4.08, *p* < .05) (Strodtbeck, 1958). Presumably polygyny promotes mother-son households in which the son stays dependent on the mother longer and does not get the strong emphasis on independent achievement needed to develop *n* Achievement. Further evidence in support of this interpretation is provided not only by the data on effects of broken homes in the United States already cited but also by knowledge of family types among lower-class Negroes known to be low in *n* Achievement. . . . In many such families the mothers are the consistent breadwinners, and the fathers may come and go in a fashion which creates a family type sometimes known as "serial monogamy." The young children typically stay with the mother as the more consistent provider of nurturance so that opportunities for strong mother-son ties are present just as in polygynous societies. Again it does not seem far-fetched to infer that *n* Achievement is low in such groups because the institution of serial monogamy tends to favor the creation of mother-son dependency. At any rate Mischel (1960) has reported direct evidence that in Trinidad where serial monogamy is common among lower-class Negroes, father-absence is significantly associated with lower *n* Achievement.

On the other hand, Bradburn has obtained some very striking evidence from Turkey showing that father-absence is associated with higher *n* Achievement. . . .In three separate samples, the Turkish men show higher *n* Achievement

more often if they had escaped their father's influence, as contrasted with continuing to live in the intact family after the age of 14 or 18. Isn't this contradictory
to what has just been argued? Shouldn't "father-absence" tend to create
mother-son families which supposedly inhibit the development of n Achievement?
The paradox nicely illustrates the importance of determining how environmental
conditions work through the factors more directly influencing n Achievement level.
It can be resolved by remembering that low n Achievement can be produced in
several ways—*i.e.*, either by overindulgence (lack of high standards) particularly
early and in the mother or by authoritarianism in the father, particularly later in
the boy's development. The mother-child family follows the first path in which
the son is unlikely to develop high standards of excellence at all. The Turkish
family follows the second path in which the son may be exposed to high standards
but fails to develop high n Achievement because his authoritarian father stands in
the way. Consequently, in Turkey, getting the boy out from under the father's
influence should promote his n Achievement *so long as it does not occur so early
as to promote the development of a mother-child household,* which, of course, may
be unlikely in Turkey for other cultural reasons or because the boy escapes his
father not to live with his mother but to get away from home altogether. Variations in family type are important as they modify the key factors responsible for
the development of n Achievement—*e.g.,* high standards of excellence, warmth,
and low father dominance—and so far, mother-son families and father absence
(perhaps especially from around age 8 on) seem most likely to have consistent
effects in this respect; father absence, because it cuts down father dominance, and
mother-son families, because they tend to lower stress on high standards of excellence for the son.

SLAVERY   Previous theorizing about economic development has tended to stress
the direct influence on men of environmental conditions. The whole thesis of this
book is that the influence is not direct, but is tempered and altered by the
character of the men on whom the external factors operate. The environment may
yet, however, be the final determinant of man's response in that it shaped his
character even earlier. In the present context such a general question becomes:
does the environment, or more particularly the type of economy, determine the n
Achievement level which in turn determines the level of economic activity?

The answer is: "Yes, but not directly, in the sense of opportunity automatically
creating the n Achievement needed to exploit it." Consider the institution of
slavery, to start with. It has been a major way of organizing economic activity for
millennia, in fact up to very recent times, in many if not most nations. Does
slavery promote or inhibit economic development? The question might be hard to
answer from a purely economic point of view, but from the psychological standpoint, the answer is unequivocal both on theoretical and some empirical
grounds. It impedes economic development because it is an economic institution
which indirectly affects child-rearing practices which affect n Achievement level
which affects economic development! Psychologically speaking, slavery is a form of

symbiosis, which should lower n Achievement both in the slave and the slave-holder, though for somewhat different reasons. The slave is by definition put in a position of being more or less completely dependent on his master. He and his children will get the responsibility and obedience training which Child *et al.*, found to be negatively related cross-culturally to n Achievement. All his rewards come, not from individualistic achievement, but from dependent compliance (see Dollard, 1937, for example). Furthermore, slaves are nearly always "decultured" in the sense of being removed from their own culture and thrown with slaves from quite different cultures. This was certainly true among Negro slaves in the South. Thus the economic and social conditions surrounding the institution of slavery became dominant in determining their life adjustment, since they shared no cultural values to oppose or mold the effects of such conditions. Negro slaves should, therefore, have developed child-rearing practices calculated to produce obedience and responsibility not n Achievement, and their descendants, while free, should still show the effects of such training in lower n Achievement—which in fact is exactly the case. . . . The lower-class Negroes in the North, presumably those least removed from southern lower-caste Negroes, have the lowest average n Achievement level of any of the minority groups tested, in fact. The Negroes as a group are significantly lower than practically all the other groups tested, although middle- and upper-class Negroes are conspicuously high in n Achievement level, reflecting once again the fact that individuals who have managed to move out of a low n Achievement group tend to have exceptionally high n Achievement.

The slaveholders should also tend to develop low n Achievement over the generations because they nearly always use slaves as personal servants responsible for the more disagreeable aspects of child-rearing. The child of a white Southern plantation owner normally had several slaves to take care of all his needs. Even though parental standards of achievement for him might be theoretically high, they would tend to be constantly undermined by the empirical fact that there was a slave whom the child could order to his rescue whenever he got into difficulty. Servants are not, strictly speaking, in the same category, since they can always technically leave their employment if too much is demanded of them. Slaves, on the other hand, can "get ahead" best by ingratiating their masters, by doing them favors, or more simply by "spoiling the young master." It is difficult to see how high standards of individualistic achievement for young children could be maintained in families where slaves were used to rear the children. The evidence is all indirect as far as the South is concerned, but it supports the inference that n Achievement level, which may have been high initially among those who founded the plantations in the South, tended to decrease in succeeding generations. Certainly it was the nonslaveholding North which excelled in all forms of business and even nonslaveholding portions of the South, like North Carolina, which took the lead in commercial enterprise.

What is most fascinating about such a possibility is that it suggests a rather simple, if ironic, account of the rise and fall of many great civilizations in the past.

The argument runs as follows: a people with higher level of *n* Achievement tend to pursue business enterprise more vigorously and ultimately to become more wealthy. Nearly always in the past such wealth has been used to support slaves. Certainly this was the case in Ancient Greece. Beginning around 525 B.C. when a much larger proportion of Athenian families were wealthy enough to support slaves, each child of good family was ordinarily assigned two slaves—a nurse and a pedagogue to go to school with him (Glotz, 1925). Furthermore, in our sample of preliterate cultures, 45 percent of twenty cultures with high *n* Achievement versus only 19 percent of 21 low in *n* Achievement had slaves (chi-square = 3.29, *p* < .10) (Strodtbeck, 1958). In short, high *n* Achievement leads to increased wealth, which leads to more household slaves. But in Greece the more general use of such slaves preceded by a generation or two the marked drop in *n* Achievement. . . Is it unreasonable to infer that the slaves undermined the achievement training of their masters' children, although probably not consciously? So, ironically, the masters were undone by the very instrument that demonstrated, they thought, their mastery—namely, their enslavement of those they had conquered. The irony lies in the fact that what happened was certainly not *intentional* on either side. Explanations of the decline of slave civilizations in terms of the "decay of moral fiber," although vague and *ad hoc*, do have at least this kernel of truth in them: the institution of slavery in all probability undermined achievement training, which in turn lowered general *n* Achievement level and made civilizations less enterprising in business and more vulnerable to economic decline and ultimately attack and destruction from without.

OCCUPATIONAL STATUS   What about economic and social conditions less extreme than slavery? Do they have an effect on *n* Achievement level? Clearly, socioeconomic status of the parents is an important determinant of *n* Achievement in children, as Rosen's (1959) data. . .show, at least as far as the United States is concerned. Middle-class children are significantly higher in *n* Achievement than lower-class children. Furthermore businessmen and professionals in several countries tend to have higher *n* Achievement if they come from middle-class families than if they come from upper- or working-class backgrounds.

Some insight into how their family background might condition their motivational level is given in a study by Douvan (1958) in which she found that both failure and possible loss of money were necessary to mobilize the same amount of *n* Achievement in lower-class children that failure alone produced in middle-class children. An explanation runs as follows: several studies have shown that middle-class families work for longer range goals and think in terms of longer time spans (LeShan, 1952). Middle-class children are more willing to work for a delayed reward than working-class children (Mischel, 1960). In behaving in these ways, the children seem to be conditioned by the nature of the occupations in which their fathers are predominantly engaged. Middle-class occupations require more planning ahead, as in the case of small business; they may require a longer period of education before financial rewards begin to be available, as in the minor professions like secondary school teaching; and even the pay for such occupations tends to come only once or twice a month, as compared with weekly for lower-class occupations, so that more planning ahead is required in terms of household expenditures. Consequently, children of middle-class background may find failure sufficient to arouse their achievement striving, because they recognize its long-range significance in terms of deprivation of possible future rewards. For children from the working classes, however, who are used to thinking in terms of a bird in the hand rather than two in the bush, it is only when the "bird-in-hand" or the actual financial reward is threatened that their n Achievement is aroused.

In a wider frame of reference, n Achievement is itself a somewhat irrational concern in that it is not tied to immediate present rewards but has to do with much longer range goals of personal significance. . . . Such "irrational" long-range achievement concerns should appear more often among families whose occupations and economic positions "require" or promote the development of just such concerns.

One must be constantly wary, however, of falling too easily into a Social Darwinist position of arguing that the social environment inevitably tends to produce the character structure or motivational level "best" adapted to it. Consider some results from Japan. . . . They are only vaguely similar to the American results. Among these samples, the boys from the upper-middle and upper classes attending a private school in Osaka have the highest n Achievement level, whereas boys drawn from a middle-class district of small shops, from the working-class district, or from a rural area appear not to differ significantly in n Achievement level. There is a hint in the graphic measure of n Achievement, which has generally been more sensitive than the verbal measure of n Achievement, that the working-class boys in Japan have the second highest level of n Achievement of the four groups tested. Since socioeconomic status is clearly an "extrinsic" factor which is only indirectly connected with n Achievement development in boys, it follows that theoretically it should be quite possible to find situations, particularly in a less mobile society perhaps, where the lower classes might have higher n Achievement than the upper or middle classes. We mentioned this possibility in dealing with the class differences in n Achievement level reflected in different types of literature in English history. Wesleyanism in England appeared to affect primarily the upper-lower and lower-middle classes and, if our general interpretation is correct, it probably raised the n Achievement level there above what it was in the middle classes at the time. Members of these "lower" classes then tended to rise and to become middle and upper-middle class themselves, but if testing had been done before their upward mobility, a result not unlike that suggested by the working-class data for Japan would doubtless have been obtained. The upper-lower classes would have had as high (or higher) n Achievement as those above them. . . .

On the whole, however, one would expect that social-class status would be an imperfect indicator of n Achievement level, since it does not group occupations together in terms of their motivational requirements. . . .

More direct data on the relationship of parental occupation to child's *n* Achievement level is available from rural India. In many ways India provides an ideal test of the connection, because its occupations are more rigidly separated by the caste system than they are in a complex industrialized country like the United States, where a man may actually fill several occupational roles and every man, regardless of his occupation, is expected to be something of an entrepreneur. At any rate, some data collected by Fraser (1961) in India are amazingly clear-cut. He tested a large number of school children for *n* Achievement (graphic) in villages in Orissa Province, with the results as classified by father's occupation (caste). . . . The children whose fathers were members of the Teli or Gaud castes—the only real "entrepreneurial" castes in this section of rural India—had higher *n* Achievement than the children whose fathers were engaged in traditional agriculture. The children from the weaving castes fell somewhere in between, as in fact they should, since the weavers are somewhat entrepreneurial in function—certainly more so than the traditional cultivators but less so than those in the Teli or Gaud castes. One would have to predict, on the basis of our theory, that fathers engaged in the production and sale of commodities would have higher *n* Achievement than those engaged exclusively in traditional agriculture. And the fact that their children have higher *n* Achievement tends to confirm the prediction that the parents do and also the inference that the parents have managed to bring up their children in a way to give them the same higher level of *n* Achievement that they have.

There are also indications in our cross-cultural comparisons of preliterate societies that traditional agriculture is negatively related to *n* Achievement level. Our entire picture of the person with high *n* Achievement. . .would not lead us to expect him to be the kind of person who would stay on the land, raising food in the same traditional ways. . . . The low *n* Achievement cultures are much more often physically located where the soil is at least fair or good, permitting successful agriculture. Barry, Child, and Bacon (1959) report that high food accumulation has a strong negative relationship $(-.60)$ to achievement training and Child, Storm, and Veroff (1958) have reported elsewhere that achievement training is correlated positively $(+.34)$ with *n* Achievement content in folk tales. What is associated with high food accumulation (*e.g.*, herding) is *compliance training*, or training for responsibility and obedience rather than achievement and self-reliance. The results make good sense in terms of the view that a culture adopts the child-rearing practices suited to its economy. "Pressure toward obedience and responsibility should tend to make children into the obedient and responsible adults who can best insure the continuing welfare of a society with a high accumulation economy, whose food supply must be protected and developed gradually throughout the year. Pressure toward self-reliance and achievement should shape children into the venturesome, independent adults who can take initiative in wresting food daily from nature and thus insure survival in societies with a low accumulation economy" (*i.e.*, in societies that live by hunting and fishing).

It would be logical to assume from the very high correlation between food accumulation in the economy and compliance versus assertion training that economies high in food accumulation ought to be significantly lower in *n* Achievement folk tale content. But, oddly enough, there is no relationship that even remotely approaches statistical significance. Thus, of the ten cultures high in food accumulation according to Barry *et al.*, six are below the median in *n* Achievement folk tale content; whereas, of the 13 classified as very low in food accumulation, seven are above the median in *n* Achievement scores. The trend is in the predicted direction but it is nowhere near significant.

Such a finding can mean either one of two things. First, there is plenty of opportunity for sampling error to distort the true picture. The number of cases on which we have both *n* Achievement and food accumulation data is quite small; the number of folk tales was also small and may have been unrepresentative in particular cases. . . .

Second, there is an interesting possibility of much theoretical importance. If, as Barry *et al.* argue, people tend to adjust their child rearing to the social and economic requirements of their life situation, this does not mean they will automatically know how to raise their children to give them the characteristics most adaptive to that life situation. The low food accumulation societies may well realize that they should stress achievement and self-assertion, but they may do it in ways that do not produce high *n* Achievement necessarily. To assume that they would generally know how to produce the qualities in their children that they realize are necessary is to take a Social Darwinist or functionalist point of view that gives parents everywhere the credit for knowing more psychology than even those modern psychologists know who have studied the problem in detail. Moreover, our data suggest that there is a particular error that parents trying to induce *n* Achievement and self-reliance in their children may commit. They may undermine the very characteristic they want to produce by becoming so authoritarian in demanding it (precisely because they realize it is needed) that a boy will not develop his own standards of achievement but continue to rely on those imposed on him by his parents, particularly his father. Previous data have shown that the father must not be too demanding. . .nor the mother either, if the son is to develop high *n* Achievement.

Finally, specific studies by Strodtbeck (1958a) of American families suggest that one of the reasons why parents of upper socioeconomic status do not always produce an overachieving son is precisely because they may stress the importance of achievement too much for him. The father in particular continues to make too many suggestions, so that in the end the son finds it more adaptive to be passive and dependent. Here as elsewhere, we must be very cautious about concluding that the environment automatically produces certain adaptive characteristics in people, or that a society always gets the character structure it deserves. . . .

BIBLIOGRAPHY

ABBLEGEN, J. C., 1958, *The Japanese Factory*, New York: The Free Press.

ATKINSON, J. W., AND MILLER, D. R., 1956, "Parental Experiences in Child Training," unpublished dittoed paper, University of Michigan.

BARRY, H., III., CHILD, I. L., AND BACON, M. K., "Relation of Child Training to Subsistence Economy," *American Anthropologist*, 1959, 61, pp. 51–63.

BRADBURN, N. M., 1960, "The Managerial Role in Turkey: A Psychological Study," unpublished doctoral dissertation, Harvard University.

CHILD, I. L., STORM, T., AND VEROFF, J., 1958, "Achievement Themes in Folk Tales Related to Socialization Practice," *Motives in Fantasy, Action and Society*, J. W. Atkinson, ed., Princeton, N. J.: Van Nostrand, pp. 479–492.

DOLLARD, J., 1937, *Caste and Class in a Southern Town*, New Haven, Conn.: Yale University Press.

DOUVAN, ELIZABETH, 1958, "Social Status and Success Strivings," *Motives in Fantasy, Action, and Society*, J. W. Atkinson, ed., Princeton, N.J.: Van Nostrand, pp. 509–517.

FRASER, T. M., 1961, "Achievement Motivation as a Factor in Rural Development: A Report on Research in Western Orissa," unpublished paper, Haverford, Pa.: Haverford College.

GLOTZ, G., 1925, *Histoire Grecque*, 2 vols., Paris: Les Presses Universitaires de France.

LESHAN, L., 1952, "Time Orientation and Social Class," *Journal of Abnormal and Social Psychology*, 47, pp. 589–592.

MISCHEL, W., 1960, "Delay of Gratification, Need for Achievement and Acquiescence in Another Culture," unpublished paper, Cambridge, Mass.: Harvard University.

ROSEN, B. C., 1959, "Race, Ethnicity and the Achievement Syndrome," *American Sociological Review*, 24, pp. 47–60.

STRODTBECK, F. L., 1958, "Family Interaction, Values, and Achievement," D. C. McClelland, *et al.*, *Talent and Society*, Princeton, N.J.: Van Nostrand, pp. 135–194.

VEROFF, J., ATKINSON, J. W., FELD, S., AND GURIN, G., 1960, "The Use of Thematic Apperception to Assess Motivation in a Nationwide Interview Study," *Psychological Monographs*.

Questions and Implications for Practice

8.1 MARTIN P. DEUTSCH

1. Deutsch's rich and sensitive description of the cultural discontinuities which each child faces as he enters school affords a valuable opportunity to study and evaluate in detail each child's learning situation. Make a complete outline of all of the facets which Deutsch describes and consider the use to which this outline might be put in trying to improve the learning process of any disadvantaged child.

2. It would make life simpler for teachers and guidance-personnel workers if they could continue to believe—as some used to—that ability seeks its own level: that professional people are professional people, for example, because they possess the native ability to learn what is necessary to function in the professions and to meet successfully the competition of others in the professions. Another part of this philosophy is that intelligence is biologically transmitted so that professionals will tend to produce offspring who will have the native capacity to become professionals, whereas others will produce offspring who, by and large, are not so bright. This philosophy permits a guidance-personnel worker to operate confidently in terms of readymade expectations. Do you agree that Deutsch's outlook makes of the guidance-personnel worker an interventionist rather than an educational decision-maker or gate-keeper?

3. In what specific ways would Deutsch encourage intervention?

4. What may be some of the consequences of the guidance worker's becoming an interventionist?

8.2 IRVING D. HARRIS

1. Harris's sensitive description of why some children have difficulty in school leads to suggestive generalizations that of course may not be applicable in some cases. Nevertheless, the guidance-personnel worker may well ask himself in the case of each learner: to what kind of consistent, irresistible cultural pressures has this student been subjected that affect his present ability to learn? How have the conditions of his home tended to support or detract from his learning efforts? Have the expectations extended by his family been negative or positive for his role as a learner?

2. How might the school or college alter its conditions as experienced by the student so as to reinforce his readiness to learn; so as to change his self-concept in desirable directions; so as to encourage more productive habits?

3. What, specifically, might the guidance-personnel worker do to enrich the experience of the individual as a school or college member? How, for instance, might he enrich his experience by interpreting him to key individuals in his environment? In what ways might the student be helped to become a more suc-

cessful learner through engaging in direct verbal interaction with a guidance-personnel worker?

4. Prepare as complete an outline as possible for your use in assessing the cultural pressures that might enhance or cripple a student's ability to learn.

5. Suggest some of the ways in which a particular school or college that you know well might be improved as a context for a student's learning.

8.3 STANLEY DIAMOND

1. Since there are a sizable number of individuals in our schools and colleges who have had an insufficient opportunity for the invaluable learnings that can take place in relationships with their parents, would you recommend that schools and colleges supply individual psychotherapy for all who fall in this classification?

2. Are there other ways than individual psychotherapy by which children deprived by life conditions of participating in profound relationships with adults to whom they feel intimately connected, can have the resulting deficiencies at least partially remedied? Name some of these.

3. Who might most appropriately take leadership within schools and colleges in seeing that some of these ways are implemented?

4. How might this person or these persons become qualified to take this leadership?

8.4 DAVID C. McCLELLAND

1. McClelland's research on the need for achievement has many implications for those who work with young people in schools and colleges. What precisely is the nature of *n* Achievement?

2. Note that all of the research reported by McClelland has to do with the need of boys to achieve. Would you have any hunches about the need of girls to achieve? Would the same factors be apt to operate in the same ways to develop *n* Achievement in boys and in girls?

3. How would a high *n* Achievement make a person behave? Would persons with a very high *n* Achievement necessarily make high marks in school?

4. Can an individual have too great a need for achievement? Explain.

Chapter 9

Roles
and
Role
Conflict

So far in this part of the book we have examined general and specific factors that affect the process by which the human organism becomes a social individual and which account for differences and similarities among members of the same or of different societies. In this chapter we will attempt to understand the individual and his behavior in somewhat different terms, namely, as the occupant and product of the roles through which he participates in social situations and relationships.

The term *role* has been used in many of the selections already presented, so that by now the reader may have some conception of what it denotes. As a word, it is not uncommon in everyday language, where its usage has been extended from meaning an actor's part on the stage to denoting the part played or contributed by any person, object, or event to a situation. In the selections below, the term is used in a more specific and technical sense, but its theatrical and its general everyday meanings are by no means unrelated to the phenomena which the term denotes to social scientists.

The concept of role is primarily an analytic device. It does not refer to anything concrete or tangible, but is useful as a label for certain patterns and regularities discernible in the behavior of individuals. As we will see below, the term is sometimes used to denote behavior and sometimes to describe the psychological processes inferred to underlie it. From the viewpoint of systematic theory in sociology or social psychology, such imprecision is undesirable, but for our purposes here we are concerned with all aspects of what we can broadly call role phenomena—the social, the cultural, and the psychological, both as sources and as consequences.

The analysis of social behavior and interaction in terms of roles is consistent with the general view that we have been developing through our selections to this point—that an individual is largely the product of the social and cultural aspects of his environment. The content of a role derives from the structure of the social context in which it is enacted and reflects what is required for the stability and maintenance of that structure. If we consider any social relationship as constituting a system, then it follows that, in order for it to persist, the behavior of the individuals involved in it must be in accord with its structure. It is this stable pattern of behavior vis-à-vis one or more other individuals in response to the nature of their relationship(s) that we call the individual's role. In terms of definition, one may argue about whether role refers to the way the individual actually behaves or the way he is expected to behave. Both of these, however, as well as any discrepancy that may occur between them, are significant phenomena with respect to social roles. We will be concerned with both sides of this distinction, whether they be called simply role or role expectations and role behavior.

As has already been discussed in various contexts, an individual's response to his environment is the product of both the external factors and his own make-up. A role, or rather an individual's enactment of it, can be understood in the same way. There are, on the one hand, the requirements of the particular social system involved as to what an individual must do in order to maximize the fulfillment of the system's needs. There are also, on the other hand, the individual's own needs, purposes, and capacities, in terms of which he perceives and interprets his position in the system and which determine his performance of the role. This distinction parallels the definitional one referred to in the previous paragraph, but here it calls attention to the two independent sources of what is comprised by an actual role.

It is easiest to think of those roles that are part of certain formalized systems, such as a family, a school, a business firm, or a government. Thus, some of the main requirements, for example, for the role of father, teacher, employer, or mayor are relatively obvious. There are many other roles, however, which impose their requirements on individuals but which are not institutionalized. Indeed, we may define a role as existing for every characteristic which is socially recognized as a basis for distinctive status. Age and sex, for example, are important dimensions in terms of which roles are structured and, in particular contexts, so are such specific characteristics as intelligence, education, special training, marital status, social class, occupation. As a result, every individual actually plays many roles, both in one situation and over a variety of situations. A woman, for example, may have to be mother, wife, household manager, and disciplinarian at the family dinner table, after spending much of her day playing an entirely different set of roles, such as daughter to her own mother, employer to a servant, or, if she works, employee, supervisor, colleague, and expert of some sort.

When we begin to analyze social participation in this manner, it becomes clear that roles vary widely along a number of dimensions. In speaking of the roles of son and school administrator, for example, we are referring to vastly different phenomena, despite the conceptual similarity we attribute to them. The consequences of some of the ways in which roles are distinguished from each other are discussed in the selections below. Among the possible variations are the facts that the requirements can be vague or clear, that the role can apply to one limited situation or to every situation the individual encounters, that the role's prescriptions can be explicit and detailed or relatively implicit and general, that the role can be one which is voluntarily achieved or one into which the individual falls by virtue of factors beyond his control (such as his sex, his family's economic position, his physical appearance, or capacities).

The utility of the concept of role for understanding behavior and interaction is that, whatever the specific character of a given actual role, it focuses and integrates the motives, attitudes, predispositions, and social pressures that are likely to be operative on the individual, and it thus facilitates a coherent explanation of his actions. This is so because, in identifying the individual's role, we identify the system of relationship(s) within which he is responding and which is the source of the pressures he is likely to experience. Take, as a hypothetical example, an instance in which one person is observed hitting another and ask yourself what you would infer to be the causes and consequences of such behavior. It is likely that you would find it difficult to offer much of an interpretation without additional information. Compare then the various ways in which you would view the same action if you were told that the two people involved were mother and child, two children on a playground, two boxers in the ring, or a policeman and a rough-looking man. Each case would evoke an entirely different perspective which would lead to different judgments as to whether the behavior was appropriate or inappropriate, good or bad, effective or ineffective, desirable or undesirable. In arriving at such different evaluations, you would in effect be using your conception of particular roles—what they require, what limits they set on behavior, what motivations and attitudes they imply or necessitate, what the individual's purposes are likely to be.

We are saying, then, that the preponderance of social interaction can be viewed as determined by roles and that the manner in which these shape and limit behavior can be understood in terms of the system of which they are a part. At the same time, the particular characteristics of the individual also contribute to his performance, so that the latter is the product of both the person's and the system's needs and requirements. The individual, in other words, has a range of choice within which he can put his own stamp on the manner in which the role is carried out. There are limits, however, which are different both for each role and for each individual, beyond which the requirements of one cannot be pushed in favor of those of the other. If these limits are exceeded, the person is removed (or removes himself) from the system, or the system either changes or disintegrates.

To describe or explain situations in terms of roles is not to say that roles are the "real" sources of behavior or that they are more relevant than other processes which can also be inferred to be operative. Role is only one of the many units in terms of which social behavior can be analyzed. Its particular value is that it encompasses both social and psychological processes and thus makes possible a fuller understanding of the interrelationship between the individual and his social environment.

9.1   INTRODUCTION

The first selection in this chapter, drawn from two works by the anthropologist Ralph Linton, presents a basic definition of what is encompassed by the concept of role. As was the case with his treatment of culture and personality (Selection 5.1), his discussion constitutes a classic statement of the issue and remains valid and useful in the light of the elaborations and empirical observations which have followed in the ensuing years. This selection thus provides a basic perspective with respect to the more specific materials that make up the remainder of this chapter.

As will be illustrated in several of the subsequent selections, conflicts among roles or among the demands of a single role are the source of phenomena of particular significance for the functioning of individuals, groups, and organizations. Professor Linton suggests the possibility of such conflicts and sees their likelihood as increasing with increased social and technological complexity. His essay, however, deals primarily with the characteristics of single roles, and establishes a background for understanding the consequences of the coincidence of numerous roles in the same individual.

Viewing the relationship between the individual and his sociocultural context in terms of roles can add considerably to our understanding of people's behavior in particular situations. From the viewpoint of a guidance counselor, for example, a student's behavior in two different situations may appear inconsistent and erratic, and perhaps be taken as a symptom of instability and immaturity. A different interpretation would follow, however, if the child or adolescent were viewed as responding to two different, and in some respects discrepant, sets of role requirements in the two cases. This inconsistency would then be at least partly attributable to the differences between the two situations and it would become clear that the individual to some extent "had" to behave as he did in each case.

Consider a student, for example, who is outstanding in the classroom and exhibits signs of real intellectual commitment. Suppose further that, in discussing his vocational plans with the guidance counselor, none of this is evident and his aspirations take a very practical, and in relation to his classroom performance, uninspired, form. It may be enlightening to consider in such a case that, whereas the role of student is a narrow one that specifically evokes whatever intellectual orientations are there, plans for a career involve many different additional roles—in relation to family, ethnic group, out-of-school friends, and the social-class structure in general.

The requirements of these other roles may make, say, an academic career unacceptable and thus for the student there may be a real gap between his student role and his future "real-life" role. The same sets of considerations might lead to just the opposite type of situation, where a poor student from an upwardly mobile middle-class family might view his future in terms of a career that requires extensive schooling for which he does not have the necessary talent. The first student might be viewed as "unmotivated" and the second one as "unrealistic," but an awareness of the different role requirements involved for each of them as students and as adults in the society would account for the inconsistencies in their behaviors and could be of practical value in giving them advice and helping them to integrate the various pressures impinging upon them.

9.1   STATUS AND ROLE[1]

Ralph Linton

. . . [T]he functioning of societies depends upon the presence of patterns for reciprocal behavior between individuals or groups of individuals. The polar positions in such patterns of reciprocal behavior are technically known as *statuses.* The term *status,* like the term *culture,* has come to be used with a double significance. A *status,* in the abstract, is a position in a particular pattern. It is thus quite correct to speak of each individual as having many statuses, since each individual participates in the expression of a number of patterns. However, unless the term is qualified in some way, *the status* of any individual means the sum total of all the statuses which he occupies. It represents his position with relation to the total society. Thus the status of Mr. Jones as a member of his community derives from a combination of all the statuses which he holds as a citizen, as an attorney, as a Mason, as a Methodist, as Mrs. Jones's husband, and so on.

A status, as distinct from the individual who may occupy it, is simply a collection of rights and duties. Since these rights and duties can find expression only through the medium of individuals, it is extremely hard for us to maintain a distinction in our thinking between statuses and the people who hold them and exercise the rights and duties which constitute them. The relation between any individual and any status he holds is somewhat like that between the driver of an automobile and the driver's place in the machine. The driver's seat with its

[1]From *The Study of Man.* Copyright, 1936 By D. Appleton-Century, Inc. Reprinted by permission of Appleton-Century-Crofts. And from Ralph Linton, *The Cultural Background of Personality,* London: Routledge and Kegan Paul Ltd., 1947, pp. 50–53.

steering wheel, accelerator, and other controls is a constant with ever present potentialities for action and control, while the driver may be any member of the family and may exercise these potentialities very well or very badly.

A *role* represents the dynamic aspect of a status. The individual is socially assigned to a status and occupies it with relation to other statuses. When he puts the rights and duties which constitute the status into effect, he is performing a role. Role and status are quite inseparable, and the distinction between them is of only academic interest. There are no roles without statuses or statuses without roles. Just as in the case of *status*, the term *role* is used with a double significance. Every individual has a series of roles deriving from the various patterns in which he participates and at the same time *a role*, general, which represents the sum total of these roles and determines what he does for his society and what he can expect from it.

Although all statuses and roles derive from social patterns and are integral parts of patterns, they have an independent function with relation to the individuals who occupy particular statuses and exercise their roles. To such individuals the combined status and role represent the minimum of attitudes and behavior which he must assume if he is to participate in the overt expression of the pattern. Status and role serve to reduce the ideal patterns for social life to individual terms. They become models for organizing the attitudes and behavior of the individual so that these will be congruous with those of the other individuals participating in the expression of the pattern. Thus if we are studying football teams in the abstract, the position of quarterback is meaningless except in relation to the other positions. From the point of view of the quarterback himself it is a distinct and important entity. It determines where he shall take his place in the line-up and what he shall do in various plays. His assignment to this position at once limits and defines his activities and establishes a minimum of things which he must learn. Similarly, in a social pattern such as that for the employer-employee relationship the statuses of employer and employee define what each has to know and do to put the pattern into operation. The employer does not need to know the techniques involved in the employee's labor, and the employee does not need to know the techniques for marketing or accounting. . . .

A particular status within a social system can be occupied, and its associated role known and exercised, by a number of individuals simultaneously. In fact, this is the normal condition. Thus every society ordinarily includes several persons who occupy the status of adult male and adhere to the adult male role. It similarly includes a number of persons who occupy the status of father in the organizations of the particular family groups to which they belong. Conversely, the same individual can and does occupy simultaneously a series of statuses each of which derives from one of the systems of organization in which he participates. He not only occupies these statuses, but he also knows the roles pertaining to them.

However, he can never exercise all these roles simultaneously. Such roles are a constant element in his participation in the covert culture of his society, but function intermittently with respect to his participation in its overt culture. In other words, although he occupies statuses and knows roles at all times, he operates sometimes in terms of one status and its role, sometimes in those of another. The status in terms of which an individual is operating is his *active status* at that particular point in time. His other statuses are, for the time being, *latent statuses*. The roles associated with such latent statuses are temporarily held in abeyance, but they are integral parts of the individual's culture equipment.

This formulation can be made clearer by an example. Let us suppose that a man spends the day working as assistant in a shop. While he is behind the counter, his active status is that of an assistant, established by his position in our society's system of specialized occupations. The role associated with this status provides him with patterns for his relations with customers. These patterns will be well known both to him and to the customers and will enable them to transact business with a minimum of delay or misunderstanding. When he retires to the rest room for a smoke and meets other employees there, his assistant status becomes latent and he assumes another active status based upon his position in the association group composed of the shop's employees as a whole. In this status his relations with other employees will be governed by a different set of culture patterns from those employed in his relations with customers. Moreover, since he probably knows most of the other employees, his exercise of these culture patterns will be modified by his personal likes and dislikes of certain individuals and by considerations of their and his own relative positions in the prestige series of the shop association's members. When closing time comes he lays aside both his assistant and shop association statuses and, while on the way home, operates simply in terms of his status with respect to the society's age-sex system. Thus if he is a young man he will at least feel that he ought to get up and give his seat to a lady, while if he is an old one he will be quite comfortable about keeping it. As soon as he arrives at his house, a new set of statuses will be activated. These statuses derive from the kinship ties which relate him to various members of the family group. In pursuance of the roles associated with these family statuses he will try to be cordial to his mother-in-law, affectionate to his wife, and a stern disciplinarian to his son, whose report card marks a new low. If it happens to be lodge night, all his familial statuses will become latent at about eight o'clock. As soon as he enters the lodge room and puts on his uniform as Grand Imperial Lizard, in the Ancient Order of Dinosaurs, he assumes a new status, one which has been latent since the last lodge meeting, and performs in terms of its role until it is time for him to take off his uniform and go home.

The fact that the individual's various statuses are activated at different times prevents a head-on collision between the roles associated with them. At most, the overt behavior which is part of the role connected with one status may negate the results of the overt behavior which is part of another role. The behaviors themselves will not conflict because of the time differential. Moreover, the roles associated with the statuses within a single system are usually fairly well adjusted to one another and produce no conflicts as long as the individual is operating within this system. This also holds for statuses within different systems whenever these statuses are of such a sort that they normally converge upon the same individuals. Thus in any society the roles of adult male, of father, of craft specialist, of friend, and so on, will normally be adjusted to one another in spite of the different systems from which they derive. Such adjustments, of course, are not the result of conscious planning. They are developed through the experience of individuals who have occupied such series of statuses simultaneously and have gradually eliminated most of the conflicts through a process of trial and error. Thus if patterns of formal friendship are borrowed from some other society, such patterns will soon be modified in such ways that there will be no conflict between them and the patterns already established by the local system of family organization.

In the rare cases in which, through some accident, statuses whose roles are fundamentally incompatible converge upon the same individual, we have the material of high tragedy. While most societies feel little sympathy for the individual who is trying to escape the performance of certain of his roles, all can sympathize with the dilemma of a person who must choose between statuses and roles which are equally valid. Such dilemmas are a favorite theme in the literature of the more sophisticated or introspective societies. The tragedy of the House of Oedipus and the closing episodes of the *Niebelungenlied* are classical examples, while at the level of simpler folklore we have the Scottish story of the man who finds himself host to his brother's murderer. In each of these cases the individual upon whom the incompatible roles converge meets the problem by the familiar pattern of operating in terms of different statuses at different times, even though recognizing that the associated roles will, in their performance, negate each other's results. Thus in the Scottish story the brother, as host, conducts the murderer safely beyond clan territory, then, as brother to the victim, engages him in combat to the death.

Such conflicts rarely arise in primary societies or even within larger social groupings which have persisted for some time and developed well-integrated cultures. However, they may become fairly frequent under the conditions existing in our current society. Under the necessity of reorganizing our social structure to meet the needs of a new technology and of a spatial mobility unparalleled in human history, our inherited system of statuses and roles is breaking down; while a new system, compatible with the actual conditions of modern life, has not yet emerged. The individual thus finds himself frequently confronted by situations in which he is uncertain both of his own statuses and roles and of those of others. He is not only compelled to make choices but also can feel no certainty that he has chosen correctly and that the reciprocal behavior of others will be that which he anticipates on the basis of the statuses which he has assumed that they occupy. This results in numerous disappointments and frustrations.

9.2   INTRODUCTION

This selection pursues further the implications of analyzing behavior in terms of roles. The authors specify some of the important components of role phenomena, offer some hypotheses about how these aspects affect attitudes and behavior, and report some empirical data to illustrate and support their approach. Their focus is on roles associated with positions in formal organizations and they are interested in the effects of expectations about roles on the manner in which they are performed and on the reactions of others to these role performances. Their findings point to the importance of expectations with respect to both of these and demonstrate the complex interplay among the individual's own expectations, the expectations of others and the expectations that the individual perceives others to have.

One of their most striking findings is that whether others react favorably or unfavorably to an individual's behavior depends more on how it relates to their expectations than on the content of the behavior itself. Thus what is acceptable from one person may not be so from another. This fact seems particularly significant for a guidance counselor who must assess and interpret others' behavior and whose effectiveness is dependent on others' reactions to his behavior. It suggests that how he defines those roles which are important aspects of his social environment—that is, what he expects from teachers, students, parents, principals, other guidance-personnel workers—will be a major factor shaping his interpretation and evaluation of their behavior as well as his own behavior in response. Thus, for example, his judgment of a child's behavior will depend on whether he sees the individual primarily as a student, or as the leader of a clique, or as a 12-year old, or as the school's athletic star, and on his conception of what each role entails.

Role expectations will have consequences for the guidance counselor in yet another way, namely, in determining what his statements and actions communicate to others. In a school where the guidance counselor is most frequently seen dealing with discipline problems, students will develop different expectations of what guidance counselors do than in another school where the guidance counselors deal mostly with learning problems. An attempt in the first school to counsel a student about personal problems might well be interpreted by the student as a reprimand rather than an attempt to help, while in the second school students might not take seriously a guidance counselor's assertion of authority when the necessity for it arises.

This selection deals specifically with some of the major formal roles in a factory, but its analysis seems to have a more general applicability and to be relevant to the whole network of informal and formal roles of educational organizations.

9.2 THE USE OF THE ROLE CONCEPT IN THE STUDY OF COMPLEX ORGANIZATIONS[1]

Eugene Jacobson, W. W. Charters, Jr., and Seymour Lieberman

The search for insights into the functioning of complex organizations has led to the development of a variety of systematic frameworks within which organizations may be described and measured. One of the approaches used stems from the common observation that people in organizations tend to have relatively uniform expectations about the behavior of persons in various positions and that the behavior of these persons is interpreted in terms of such expectations. These observations suggest the usefulness of some of the concepts developed in connection with role theory. . . .

In applying role theory to the study of hierarchical organizations, we have elaborated on a number of role concepts and have developed related concepts, some of which are outlined below. In addition, we have designed and carried out a study in which some of the problems and research techniques were formulated explicitly in terms of role concepts. This study was made in an automobile factory and was designed to investigate some of the determinants of union-management relationships. In outlining our approach to role theory and describing its uses, we shall refer to this study for illustrative and supportive material.[2]

SOME ROLE DEFINITIONS In the automobile company analysis, we have defined role in the following way:

ROLE: A set of expectations which others share of the behavior an individual will exhibit as an occupant of a position, or status category.

When we refer to behavior, rather than to the expectations of behavior, we use the concept of:

---

[1]From Eugene Jacobson, Werrett Charters, Jr., and Seymour Lieberman, "The Use of the Role Concept in the Study of Complex Organizations," *Journal of Social Issues*, 7, No. 3, 1951, pp. 18–27.

[2]A more complete account of research problems in this area is available in: Daniel Katz, *The Attitude-Survey Approach to Labor-Management Relations*, Survey Research Center, University of Michigan, 1949.

ROLE BEHAVIOR: A pattern of behavior exhibited by an individual as the occupant of a position or status category.

These expectations and behaviors have two components which are interdependent but which must be distinguished:

SOCIAL ROLE: A set of expectations which others share of the behavior associated with a position, without respect to the characteristics of the person who occupies the position.

PERSONAL ROLE: A set of expectations which others share of an individual's behavior in a position, without respect to the social role.

In any specific role measurement, the data will reflect both social and personal expectations of behavior, although the two have different degrees of importance in different kinds of situations. In a neighborhood gang, for example, with a relatively unstructured system of social roles, the expectations concerning the behavior of one of the gang members will be based to a large degree upon knowledge of the personality of the gang member, or personal role. In a highly structured hierarchical organization, on the other hand, expectations are more likely to be based upon knowledge of the standard role prescriptions for the office he holds, or his social role.

The value of a definition of role based on shared expectations is that it emphasizes the social consequences of consensus. The system of shared expectations in a formal organization can be looked upon as the basis for the behavior of individuals in the organization and for their interpretations of the behaviors of others. Thus, the degree of integration existing within an organization at any time stems in part from the degree of consensus or sharing of expectations about the behavior of people who occupy various positions. Behavior can be predicted more accurately in an organization where consensus is highly developed than in one where it is relatively undeveloped, even though the formal organization charts may be identical.

The definition of role in terms of shared expectations must take account of the question of whose expectations are relevant. We shall refer to the relevant populations as "criterion" populations. In hierarchical organizations, at least three such groups should receive consideration. One is composed of persons who occupy like positions. Another is composed of persons who have a high degree of functional interdependence with the position in question. A third is composed of persons who do not have direct functionally interdependent relationships with the position, but who nevertheless are related to it through a concern with the formulation and implementation of the broader purposes of the organization.

If we deal with the sets of expectations relevant to the position of the production line foreman in a factory, the three criterion populations would consist, respectively, of: (1) other production line foremen; (2) the union stewards, etc.; and (3) the superordinate persons in the organization, including those who are in a position to initiate or apply sanctions in the event that the foreman's behavior deviates from that required by the purposes of the organization. . . .

SOME USES OF THE SOCIAL ROLE CONCEPT   The meaning of the above concepts is clarified and their uses illustrated in data obtained in the automobile factory study. The study was designed to gather information on some of the determinants of supervisory attitudes and behavior, and on the ways in which supervisors' attitudes and behavior are related to workers' attitudes towards the company, the industrial union, the company foreman, the union steward, and union-management relationships. To meet these ends, interviews were obtained (in the summer of 1948) with all of the company foremen and union stewards (about seven hundred persons) in seven work departments, and a sample of 450 workers in these departments. Among the role concepts that were developed to analyze the data from this study, those that we will discuss briefly are:

1. role distribution
2. role conflict
3. estimation of role expectations
4. impact of role expectations
5. impact of past role experience on attitudes and behavior
6. relationship between role and role behavior.

ROLE DISTRIBUTION   In a complex organization, it might be expected that not all persons in a criterion population will have the same expectations about a given position. One is thus required to introduce a conception of role as the *range* of behaviors which all or nearly all of the criterion population can agree upon as delimiting the expected behavior, or else one must consider the distribution of agreement in the criterion population regarding a more specific expected behavior. This latter alternative and its utility can be illustrated by an examination of the distribution of expectations about the steward position.

Foremen, stewards, and workers were asked, "What would you say are the most important things a steward has to do as a steward?" Responses were categorized as "steward expected to be *active* in promoting the interests of the men," and "stewards expected to be *passive* and act only to protect the rights and welfare of the men." If the expectations of the majority of each criterion group are labeled the "shared" or "modal" expectation, we are then able to identify those respondents whose expectations are modal with respect to the criterion group of which they are a part, and those who are deviant.[3]

---

[3]An implicit assumption here is that the expectations of a majority of a "criterion group" constitutes a meaningful definition of role prescriptions. Operationally defining role prescriptions involves serious problems, and the use of the majority measure should be looked upon only as a first step in laying out a rigorous operational definition. The *extent* of agreement of consensus of expectations constitutes an additional variable: *role clarity or role ambiguity*. An ambiguous role—one where the degree of agreement is slight—presents a condition of particular interest to the social psychologist.

The data indicate that the modal expectation among workers and stewards is that the steward will be active (69 and 70 percent agreement, respectively), while the modal expectation among foremen is that he will be passive (58 percent agreement). The deviants among the stewards are the 26 percent who expect stewards to be passive, and among the foremen the deviants are the 30 percent who expect the steward to be active.[4] The deviant foreman is in agreement with the modal steward, and the deviant steward is in agreement with the modal foreman.

The condition of deviation from the modal expectation permits us to test the proposition that the ease of interpersonal relations (in this case, between foremen and stewards) is a function of mutual agreement on the steward's role. Foremen were asked how they get along with the stewards in their department, and stewards in turn were asked about their relations with their foremen. Although the differences were not great, deviant foremen (who agree with the majority of stewards) are more inclined than modal foremen to report their relations with the stewards are easy; and deviant stewards (who agree with the majority of foremen) are more apt than modal stewards to report easy relations with foremen. . . .

ROLE CONFLICT   We shall designate as social role conflict the situation in which there are differences between criterion groups with respect to social role. An example of such conflict was seen in the case of the steward's role, described above, where the foremen have role expectations with respect to the steward position which are inconsistent with the role expectations of the stewards themselves. Another example is found in the conflict between the "line" and "staff" executives of a factory which sometimes arises because of differing expectations about whose "role" it is to make certain kinds of decisions.

It should be clear that our conception of role conflict refers to cultural discrepancies and does not imply that the subject of the discrepant expectations necessarily perceives them or experiences psychological conflict as a result of them. . . .The significance of identifying situations of role conflict lies in the fact that the situations are *potential* sources of psychological conflict.

One analysis in the study dealt in part with the conditions under which the foremen will feel they are in a conflict situation. It was hypothesized that *past role experience* might, under certain conditions, influence the extent to which a foreman feels that he is in a conflict situation. A comparison of foremen who had once been stewards with foremen who had never been stewards indicates that, in situations where the union and management are seen as incompatible, ex-stewards will more often feel they are in conflict than foremen who had never been stewards.[5]

---

[4]The percentages do not total 100 because some responses could not be categorized as "active" or "passive."

[5]Seymour Lieberman, *An Analysis of Role Change in a Factory Situation*, Survey Research Center, University of Michigan, 1951.

ESTIMATION OF ROLE EXPECTATION   Our definition of role in terms of *shared* expectations raises the question of perceptive accuracy on the part of the occupants of a position as to the role expectations that exist in various criterion populations. If the stewards in the automobile factory are taken as an example, one can ask what role expectations regarding the stewards' position the stewards attribute to, say, the worker population. A substantial majority of the stewards (76 percent) perceive the workers as expecting them to take an *active* rather than a *passive* role. This perception is "accurate" in the sense that these stewards correctly perceive· the expectation of the *majority* of the workers. Eighteen percent of the stewards estimate, incorrectly, that the shared expectation of the workers is *passive*. . . .

Having classified respondents for accuracy of estimation of role expectations, one can then investigate the determinants and consequences of differential accuracy in perception. By way of illustration, our data show that there is a strong relationship between a steward's expectations of his own role and the expectations which he attributes to workers. If a steward expects the behavior of a steward to be active, he is very likely to believe that the workers also expect him to be active; on the other hand, if he expects the steward's behavior to be passive, he is likely to believe that the workers expect him to be passive. From this information, however, we cannot determine whether inaccurate perceptions are a cause of or a consequence of one's own expectations.

IMPACT OF ROLE EXPECTATIONS   The measurement of differential role expectations has little consequence unless it is found to be a factor of importance in the understanding of social psychological events. One way to test the impact of role expectations is to examine the relationship between differential attitudes and differential role expectations. An example of this kind is described below.

One of the basic concerns of the automobile company study was an investigation of the determinants of individual worker identification with the company and with the union.[6] A preliminary analysis of the data showed that foreman and steward participation practices seemed to be related to worker identification. In departments where foremen were more likely to involve workers in joint decision making about company matters, the workers were more likely to have company values. And, in departments where stewards were more likely to involve workers in joint decision making about union matters, workers were more likely to have union values.

---

[6]Relevant data are given in detail in these publications of the Survey Research Center: B. Willerman, *Group Identification in Industry*, doctoral dissertation, Massachusetts Institute of Technology, 1949; Eugene Jacobson, *Foreman-Steward Participation Practices and Worker Attitudes in a Unionized Factory*, doctoral dissertation, University of Michigan, 1951; and Eugene Jacobson, *An Analysis of Foreman-Steward Power Relationships*, 1949.

The most striking relationship was found in shops where the stewards did not involve men in joint participation and the foremen did. In these departments, there was a marked rejection of union values by the workers. This is in sharp contrast with a relative nonrejection of company values in those departments where the foreman-steward participation practices are reversed.

An explanation of these contrasting findings seems possible by taking into account the workers' expectations about steward participation and foreman participation. Almost all of the workers expect stewards to solicit their help actively in settling union affairs, while there is less consensus that foremen should involve them in shop matters. The interpretation might then be made that the workers' rejection of union values is a function of the failure of the stewards to meet the expectations of the workers about joint decision making, while the less strong relations between foreman participation and attitudes toward the company might be attributed to the fact that nonparticipation by foremen does *not* involve a failure to meet the workers' expectations.

IMPACT OF PAST ROLE EXPERIENCE ON ATTITUDES AND BEHAVIOR   Another clue to the understanding of the attitudes and behavior of a person in an organization with a complex system of roles is furnished by a knowledge of positions he has occupied in the past. We have attempted to determine the extent to which past role behavior is reflected in current attitudes and perceptions by an intensive analysis of data about company foremen who previously had been union stewards. Two assumptions that dictated the analysis were: (1) when people change to new positions, the attitudes and perceptions they operate with are in part a "carry-over" from their old role behaviors, and (2) people's experience in earlier positions provides a frame of reference for their adapting to new role expectations.

The foreman population in the automobile factory was divided into two groups. One group, about one out of four foremen, had been rank and file workers and union stewards before becoming foremen. The other group were foremen who had been hired as foremen from the "outside" or had been workers prior to becoming foremen, but had *not* been union stewards. We compared the foremen who had been stewards with those who had not to find out whether the two groups had different perceptions and attitudes and, if they did, in what areas the differences existed.

It was found that foremen who had not been stewards were more likely to take the company's position on union-management relations, while those who had been stewards were more likely to take both the point of view of the men and the company. Neither group took the union side predominantly. Foremen who had been stewards were more likely to report that the goals of union and management were compatible and that there was little conflict between being a "union man" and a "company man." Both groups had essentially the same notion of the steward role. That is, their expectations were comparable.

An interpretation of these findings, after further exploration of the data, indicated that differences between the two groups of foremen reflected differences between stewards and nonstewards among the workers, while similarities reflected homogeneity between stewards and nonstewards in the worker population. . . .

RELATIONSHIP BETWEEN ROLE AND ROLE BEHAVIOR All of these explorations are leading toward increased facility in handling one of the basic problems in the investigation of organizational behavior: how is it possible to account for an individual's internalization of his social role in such a way that his behavior corresponds to the expectations of others?. . .The hypothesis. . .is that discrepancy or congruity between social role and role behavior can be accounted for in terms of accuracy of perceptions and the extent of motivation toward performing the behavior. Both of these can be measured and interpreted in terms of the analysis we have outlined. . . .

9.3 INTRODUCTION

The next selection, based on a study of an academic community, introduces some finer differentiations into the role concept and applies these to an analysis of the role of faculty member. One of its major distinctions, between manifest and latent social roles, relates back to the difference between informal and formal organizational structures discussed in Chapter 3 and refers to whether or not the requirements for a role are institutionalized within the culture of a group or an organization.

Gouldner considers that an individual's performance of a role includes more than his conformity to its explicit requirements and, further, that every manifest role will come to have a few typical configurations of latent roles associated with it. In the case of college faculty members, he posits three factors as important in determining these latent patterns—loyalty to the organization, commitment to a profession or specialized skill, and reference group orientation (whether the individual is oriented to the standards of the organization, of a group within it, or those of an outside group). From his data he derives six different types of faculty-member roles in the college he studied, describing them in terms of these three latent dimensions.

The value of this selection is not to be found exclusively in the particular content of the role types it describes. These seem to have a good deal of general validity, but they are also undoubtedly subject to much variation depending on the history, setting, recruitment policies, etc., of the particular college involved. What is of more general value in this article is its underlying conception of the relationship between a formal role and the full range of behavior relevant to its performance. Thus it is relevant, for example, for the individual guidance-personnel worker to consider the latent roles that are associated with the manifest role of "guidance counselor" or "personnel worker" and to assess his own particular pattern of latent roles. The dimensions used by Gouldner in relation to college faculty seem equally applicable to guidance-personnel workers, and others can be added, such as his approach to the problems of individuals (*e.g.*, clinical or nonclinical), the types of problems he is most inclined to become concerned about (*e.g.*, emotional, social, academic, disciplinary), his relationships with groups of students (of varying patterns and characteristics), his attitude towards the relationships between guidance-personnel workers and the faculty and between guidance-personnel workers and administrators, and so on. These are all aspects that enter into his behavior as a guidance-personnel worker, but there are no formal and specific prescriptions for them. Such an analysis of these aspects, together with a similar one of the latent roles that surround all the other significant manifest roles in the guidance-personnel worker's environment—student, parent, principal, etc.—might contribute significantly to an understanding of the relationships that develop among guidance-personnel workers and individuals in these other roles.

9.3   COSMOPOLITANS AND LOCALS: TOWARD AN ANALYSIS OF LATENT SOCIAL ROLES[1]

Alvin Gouldner

. . .Obviously the people in any one group have a variety of social identities. In a classroom, for example, there are those identified as "students," but these same people are also identified as men, women, young, mature, and so on. In the classroom situation, it is primarily their identity as students that others in the group regard as central and properly salient. It is also the expectations congruent with this salient identity that are most appropriately activated and have the fullest claim to application. But while the expectations congruent with the student identity are most institutionally relevant and legitimately mobilizable, it is clear that in various ways certain of the other identities do "intrude" and affect the group's behavior in sociologically interesting ways. For example, there is usually

[1]From Alvin Gouldner, "Cosmopolitans and Locals: Toward an Analysis of Latent Social Roles," *Administrative Science Quarterly,* I, 2, 1957, pp. 281–306, II, 2, 1958, pp. 444–480.

something happening between the students that is influenced by their sexual identities.

It is necessary to distinguish, then, between those social identities of group members which are consensually regarded as relevant to them in a given setting and those which group members define as being irrelevant, inappropriate to consider, or illegitimate to take into account. The former can be called the *manifest* social identities, the latter, the *latent* social identities. Let us be clear that "social identities," manifest or latent, are not synonymous with the concept of social status. Social identities have to do with the way in which an individual is in fact *perceived* and classified by others in terms of a system of culturally standardized categories. Social statuses, however, refer to the complex of culturally standardized categories to which individuals in a group may be assigned; they are sometimes also defined as the hierarchical "position" of the individual in relation to others, as well as the culturally prescribed expectations directed toward those in this position.

Expectations which are associated with the manifest social identities can be termed the manifest social *roles*, while expectations oriented toward the latent identities can be called the latent social roles. Just as others can be oriented toward an individual's latent identities, so, too, can the individual himself be oriented to his own latent identities. . . .

While it is obvious that a group member may have many social identities, it needs to be stressed that not all of them are regarded as equally relevant or legitimately activated in that group. This is precisely the point to which the concepts of latent identities and roles direct attention.

This implies that when group members orient themselves to the latent identities of others in their group, they are involved in a relationship with them which is not culturally *prescribed* by the group norms governing their manifest roles. It implies, also, that they are utilizing reference persons or groups which are not culturally prescribed for those in their roles. Thus the concepts of latent identities and roles focus research on those patterns of social interaction, and lines of orientation, which are not prescribed by the group under study. It would also seem clear that latent identities and roles are important because they exert pressure upon the manifest roles, often impairing conformity with their requirements and endemically threatening the equilibrium of the manifest role system. In contrast, the concept of manifest roles focuses on the manner in which group norms yield *prescribed* similarities in the behavior and beliefs of those performing the same role. . . .

This distinction between manifest and latent roles directs us to search out and specify the latent identities, and the expectations corresponding to them, which crosscut and underlie those which are culturally prescribed in the group under study. The concept of latent roles suggests that people playing *different* manifest roles may be performing *similar* latent roles and, conversely, that those performing the *same* manifest role may be playing *different* latent roles. The concept of latent role may then aid in accounting for some of the differences (in behavior or belief) among those in the same manifest role or for some of the similarities among those having different manifest roles. Neither the similarities nor the differences mentioned above need be due to the intrusion of "personality" factors or other individual attributes. They may derive from the nature of the latent roles, that is, from the responses to the latent identities of group members, which yield culturally unprescribed yet structured interactions and orientations with others.

The problem that will be explored in the following analysis is whether there are latent identities and roles of general significance for the study of the modern complex organization. That is, can we discern latent identities and roles which are common to a number of different complex organizations? In this connection, we will explore the possibility that, as distinguished from and in addition to their manifest identities, members of formal organizations may have two latent social identities, here called "cosmopolitan" and "local."[2] Development of these concepts may enable organizational analysis to proceed without focusing solely on the relatively visible, culturally differentiated, manifest organizational identities and roles, but without confining analysis to an undifferentiated blob of "bureaucrats." There are of course other latent identities which are of organizational significance, and, in Part II of this paper, we shall consider a more complex structure of latent identities.

CONCERNING COSMOPOLITANS AND LOCALS   A number of prior researches have identified certain role-playing patterns which appear convergent with each other and which, further, seem to be commonly based upon those latent identities which will be called "cosmopolitans." . . .

These. . .suggested the importance of three variables for analyzing latent identities in organizations: (1) loyalty to the employing organization, (2) commitment to specialized or professional skills, and (3) reference group orientations. Considerations of space do not permit this to be developed here, but each of these studies also found role-playing patterns polar to those discussed. This led us to hypothesize that *two* latent organizational identities could be found. These were:

COSMOPOLITANS   Those low on loyalty to the employing organization, high on

---

[2]These terms are taken from Robert K. Merton, "Patterns of Influence, Local and Cosmopolitan Influentials," *Social Theory and Social Structure*, revised edition, New York: The Free Press, 1957, pp. 387–420. Merton's terms are used with respect to types of roles within communities rather than in connection with formal organizations, as they are here. Moreover, Merton's focus is on the conjunction between influence and cosmopolitans-locals, whereas our analysis applies cosmopolitan and local orientations to role players apart from considerations of their influence. Note, also, the similarity between my own discussion of "latent" identities and roles and that of R. Linton, *Readings in Social Psychology*, T. M. Newcomb and E. L. Hartley, eds., New York: Holt, Rinehart and Winston, 1947, p. 368.

commitment to specialized role skills, and likely to use an outer reference group orientation.

LOCALS   Those high on loyalty to the employing organization, low on commitment to specialized role skills, and likely to use an inner reference group orientation.

Cosmopolitans and locals are regarded as *latent* identities because they involve criteria which are not fully institutionalized as bases for classifying people in the modern organization, though they are in fact often used as such. . . .

While organizations are in fact concerned with the loyalty of their personnel, as indicated by the ritual awarding of gold watches for lengthy years of "faithful service," the dominant organizational orientation toward rationality imposes a ban of pathos on the use of loyalty criteria. . . .Despite the devotion to rational criteria in the modern organization, however, considerations of loyalty can never be entirely excluded and loyalty criteria frequently serve as a basis for assigning latent identities. In some measure, loyalty to the organization often implies the other two criteria, (1) a willingness to limit or relinquish the commitment to a specialized professional task and (2) a dominant career orientation to the employing organization as a reference group. This linking of organizational criteria is only barely understood by the group members. Thus cosmopolitans and locals are also latent identities because the *conjunction* of criteria involved is not normatively prescribed by the organization. . . .

While the significance of reference group orientation varies from one type of organization to another, it remains a commonplace if somewhat subtle criterion for assigning latent identities. In colleges, groups distinguish between "insiders" and "outsiders," sometimes using such informal indices as whether or not individuals orient themselves to certain "schools of thought" or people, share familiarity with a prestigious literature, or utilize certain styles of research. . . .Such identities are not fully institutionalized or legitimated, although they may obliquely impinge on promotions, election to office, and evaluation of performance.

COSMOPOLITANS
AND LOCALS
IN "CO-OP COLLEGE"

A new research was undertaken within the framework of the above considerations. . . . in a college setting, . . . a small, private liberal arts college, with about 1,000 students and 130 faculty situated in a town with a population of less than 5,000. I shall refer to it as "Co-op College" because it was conducted on a "cooperative plan," under which students had alternating periods of regular academic instruction and of work experience away from the campus. . . .

. . .[W]e wanted to determine whether organizational personnel did, in fact, manifest the combination of characteristics implied by the notions of cosmopolitan and local. It was therefore assumed that the following variables would be positively correlated: high organizational loyalty, low commitment to specialized skills, and the use of an inner reference group orientation. The finding of such a correlation would be taken to indicate the "locals." The opposite combination, low organizational loyalty, high commitment to specialized skills, and use of an outer reference group orientation, would be taken to indicate the "cosmopolitans." It would seem reasonable to expect that persons manifesting two such different combinations of variables would have differing self-conceptions and identities, as well as being differently perceived and identified by others in their group.

The sample was drawn from the names listed in the college catalogue of 1952–1953, consisting of all those mentioned as teaching and administrative faculty, and was supplemented by a list of new faculty members who had joined the staff that year. . . .One hundred and twenty-five interviews, with teaching, research, and administrative personnel, were secured, providing a nearly complete census of the faculty then on campus. . . .

II

It was realized from the beginning that our initial treatment of cosmopolitans and locals was at best a simplified first approximation which, if it showed any promise, would require refinement. In particular we realized that neither cosmopolitans nor locals were likely to be of one piece; there might be different kinds of cosmopolitans as well as different kinds of locals. . . .

Originally cosmopolitans and locals had been treated as if, to use an astronomical metaphor, they were a binary system of two stars, each revolving around the other and together forming a single system of interdependent elements. The factors produced by our new analysis now leads us to think of a more complex system of six "planets." Four of the factors seem to be types of locals, and the other two appear to be types of cosmopolitans. . . .

THE LOCALS

The dedicated

These are the "true believers" who are identified with and affirm the distinctive ideology of their organization. Here, in particular, they are those who stress the distinctive educational philosophy of the college. They are deeply committed to their organization—and to it as a whole—on the grounds that it embodies unique values which they regard as important. They are concerned that those within the organization support this ideology, believing that community agreement is more important than the acceptance of individual differences. They are also more likely to insist that their colleagues possess certain local value orientations rather than technical competencies.

They reveal themselves as a type of local, having stronger commitments to their organization than to a distinctive professional role within it. In this context they are those who support programs for interdisciplinary education rather than those organized along traditional departmental lines. (These men are likely to be the "deployables," who accept transfer from job to job or department to department and are more likely to think of themselves as members of Co-op College—"Co-opians"—rather than as economists, psychologists, or geologists.) Their focus is on the maintenance of internal organizational cohesion and consensus rather than on the pursuit of occupational specializations, which they may think of as having divisive and dispersive effects on the group. They are likely to be thought of as the loyal and reliable members of the group, as pillars of its ideological purity. Theirs is an inner reference group, focusing on the college and its distinctively embodied values.

The true bureaucrat

These, too, are a type of local. For example, they opposed establishment of an American Association of University Professors chapter on the grounds that it was controlled by "outsiders" or was an outside organization. They did not regard then-current investigations of communism in colleges as having any effect on their own local campus. But their commitment to Co-op College is basically different from that of the dedicated locals in that their loyalties are much more particularistic. They are loyal not so much to the college's distinctive values as to the place itself. They are distinguished, for example, by their orientation to the town in which their organization is located and their sensitiveness to the criticisms that townspeople level at the college. In effect, they are a dissident group of locals who seek to adjust their organization's values to those in the immediate environment. Unlike the dedicated locals, they are not advocates of internal consensus but are willing to engage in internal conflict in order to adjust the group to external pressures. Thus, far from upholding the organization's traditional values, they may actually contribute to their subversion. Their concern about outside criticism leads them to seek changes in the traditional institutions and values of the organization; *e.g.*, they seek greater control over student behavior and call for more supervision of students, they are somewhat critical of conscientious objectors for whom the college had long provided something of a haven, and they express the belief that it is important to remember that they live in a community which believes in segregation, although the college itself has long been firmly antisegregation.

Like other locals, they are committed to Co-op College, as indicated by the fact that they would recommend it as a place for a young teacher to begin his career and that they do not regard their salaries as too low. There is also some indication that they are locals also in that their professional role commitments are not salient for them, as suggested by their beliefs that teachers should *not* have greater influence in the organization as a whole and that they would *not* prefer to have their loads lightened to allow more time for their own research or writing. If the dedicated locals can be said to be concerned about the integrity of the organizational values, the true bureaucrat locals are concerned about the security of the organization. This they seek to accomplish by installing more authoritarian and *formal* regulations to control the behavior of others. It is because of this last propensity that we term them "true bureaucrats."

The homeguard

These locals have the least occupational specialization and commitment; they have little or no advanced college training, write little or nothing, and attend few or no professional conventions. Unlike the dedicated locals, they are not characterized by a commitment to the distinctive values of the local organization; nor, for that matter, are they especially oriented to the local community. There is reason to believe that the organizational subgroup membership of these locals is of distinctive importance in characterizing them. One of the highest factor loadings, for example, is for their department; they tend to be neither full-time researchers nor teachers, but rather administrators.

It is most likely also that they do not occupy the highest administrative positions but the second-rung ones; this is suggested by the loading on the sex factor, which indicates that they are likely to be females. They seem to be bound and loyal to the organization for peculiarly particularistic reasons, especially because they themselves were likely to have studied at the college, or to have married people who had, or both. In short, they are the second-generation "Co-opians," people who came back to live and work at their Alma Mater. They are people whose personal history is intimately interwoven with the organization. There are some indications that they use an inner rather than an outer reference group orientation. However, their inner reference group orientation seems likely to be focused on a distinctive part of the whole organization, namely, the middle administrative echelon.

The elders

These locals are characterized by the fact that they tend to be the oldest people in the group, as well as those who have been with the organization for the longest time. Like other locals, they are characterized by a deep commitment to the organization, intending to remain with it indefinitely. Their commitment to the organization and their older age are likely to be connected. That is, they are likely to be in part constrained to this commitment by their age and imminent retirement; conversely, they may have remained for so long in the group because they were committed to it. They are also probably committed to the organization on the particularistic grounds of their involvement in its informal group structure; they know the largest number of other faculty members.

Their older age may distinctively influence their reference orientations in at least two ways: (1) it is likely that they are oriented to an informal peer group, those as old as themselves and those who came into the organization at about the time they did; (2) having been with the group for a longer time than most others, they are likely to evaluate its present in terms of its past. In other words, their reference orientation may be distinguished not only by a special reference group, other elders, but by a concern about a special or earlier *time period*.

THE COSMOPOLITANS

The outsiders

These cosmopolitans have relatively little integration in either the formal or informal structure of the organization. They are not close to students, nor do they know many faculty members well. They have relatively low participation and influence in the formal structures of the organization, nor do they wish more. In a sense they are "in" but not "of" the organization. They have little loyalty to the organization and do not intend to remain with it permanently. They would not stay if their salary was lowered, and they would leave to take a job at Harvard or Princeton even at a lower salary.

They are cosmopolitans also in that they are more highly committed to their specialized skills; for example, they tend to be against interdisciplinary education. Like cosmopolitans in general, they tend to be oriented toward an outer reference group, feeling, for example, that they do not get adequate intellectual stimulation from their Co-op College colleagues and that they get more intellectual stimulation from colleagues elsewhere. These cosmopolitans tend to define their role in ways more in keeping with traditional academic conceptions than in conformity with the distinctive Co-op College ideology.

The empire builders

These faculty members believe that their employment opportunities outside of the college are good, and thus their college commitment is tempered by a sense of economic independence. There is an indication that they are not entirely satisfied with their career possibilities within the college and are likely to be keeping an eye on outside possibilities. Their commitment to their specialized roles is suggested by their feeling that there is too much demand made on them to participate in extracurricular activities. In short, they manifest cosmopolitan orientations.

But they are cosmopolitans of a distinctive stamp. Above all, they are committed to their specific *academic departments*, particularly in the physical sciences and the creative arts (which were especially strong and cohesive on this college campus). This departmental commitment is suggested, not only by the way in which it turns up on the factor, but also by their expressed feelings that there was too much thoughtless criticism of departments and their members. They seem to have a strong pull toward increased departmental autonomy. For example, they tend to resent the student rating system and to feel that power is too concentrated in the administration's hands. Unlike the outsiders, these men are integrated into the college structure, but primarily into its formal organization. For example, while they will see students fairly frequently concerning their work, they will not invite students to their homes for a class. . . .

9.4 INTRODUCTION

The selection that follows, from a study of the roles of officials in a prison camp, focuses on the interdependence between the expectations associated with organizational roles and the goals toward which organizational activity is directed. In the case of the prison studied here, the organization was committed to two different and largely incompatible goals—custody and treatment—and thus there were two different and incompatible sets of expectations operating on prison officials. The author examines the specific form that this conflict took for the supervisor and for the guards, the different adaptations that these two levels of officials developed to cope with their role conflicts, and the consequences of these modes of adaptation for their role performance and their satisfaction with their tasks.

The differences between the supervisor and the guards are particularly interesting in showing the different ways in which the same aspect of an organization impinges on individuals at different points within it. The supervisor had to somehow manage to pursue both the custodial and the treatment goals without evoking too much opposition from those, within and outside the organization, who exerted pressure for either one of them. For the guards, on the other hand, the necessity to choose between the goals was more urgent, since the two goals had different implications for the most basic aspect of their jobs, namely interaction with the inmates. For the supervisor, an attitude of neutrality toward his conflict increased his effectiveness. For the guards, neutrality was not possible, but a definite choice led to ambivalence and less than complete satisfaction with their jobs.

It is not necessary to view educational institutions as similar to prisons to see many points of relevance in the findings reported here for the organizational problems of schools and colleges, and particularly for the practice of guidance within educational organizations. The discrepancy between the goals of custody and treatment is not entirely remote from some of the discrepancies that are built into the total set of objectives of a dean, a residence counselor in a college, a guidance counselor in a secondary school, or a child guidance consultant in an elementary school. Certainly it is similar to some of the conflicting pressures that the guidance-personnel worker must reconcile in particular situations—between discipline and "understanding," between the exercise of authority and permissiveness, between the enforcement of rules and the encouragement of independence and autonomy. Can he be neutral like the prison's supervisor, or is his position more similar to that of the guards? If he emphasizes, say, discipline one time, will this hinder his effectiveness in being helpful and supportive another time?

The fact of conflicting but simultaneous goals is a more general feature of the role of guidance-personnel workers beyond the custody-treatment parallel, and each individual's performance of the role will reflect his particular adaptation to the specific conflicts inherent in his particular situation. Is his primary responsibility to students or the organization? Can he adhere to both his professional views and the organization's established orientations? One can think of any number of questions of this sort, for none of which there is a clear answer. Given the multiple objectives that make up such goals as "education," "guidance," and "counseling," conflicting role expectations are virtually inevitable. More importantly, whatever the resolution of a given conflict, it will have repercussions for the individual's relationships and interaction with others in the organization and shape what his role will contribute to the total system.

9.4 ROLE CONFLICT IN ORGANIZATION: A STUDY OF PRISON CAMP OFFICIALS[1]

Oscar Grusky

The official goals of an organization determine in large part the types of role expectations associated with the positions that make up the social strueture of the system.[2] If an organization is assigned[3] a new major goal, and if this goal is in conflict with what formerly was the only primary goal of the system, then we would expect that conflict between the goals would create new stresses for many members of the organization. These two or more sets of conflicting role expectations, defined by the organization as legitimate by the fact that they are derived from an official goal, create role conflict.

The increasing emphasis on quasi-environmental, rehabilitation or "milieu" treatment programs in organizations such as prisons and mental hospitals, which formerly have had primarily custodial goals, presents a situation containing the necessary ingredients for such role conflict. In this paper we are primarily concerned with the effect of the conflicting goals of custody and quasi-milieu

---

[1]From Oscar Grusky, "Role Conflict in Organization: A Study of Prison Camp Officials," *Administrative Science Quarterly*, 3, 1959, pp. 452–463.

[2]By role we mean a set of behaviors which are expected of people who occupy a certain position in a social system. The expectations are commonly shared attitudes about what the person in the role ought to or ought not to do.

[3]The decision to adopt a new goal for the organization may occur in the following three ways, or in a combination of them: (1) if the organization is in a hierarchy of organizations, as in this study, the official goal is assigned by a higher level organization (in this case, the State Correction Agency); (2) if the organization is independent, the elite of the system may arbitrarily decide to adopt a new goal; or (3) the members of the organization may consensually make the decision.

treatment in a small midwestern prison camp (Camp Davis) on role conflict among the officers and staff.

Associated with the goal of custody in a prison or mental-hospital setting are staff role expectations that typically involve a general distrust and suspicion of inmate or patient behavior. Consequently in traditional custodial prisons, for example, the officials and inmates are characteristically hostile to one another and show a relatively low level of interaction. On the other hand, associated with the goal of quasi-milieu treatment is a distinctly opposite set of role expectations for officials. The guard or the attendant in a treatment-oriented setting is encouraged to trust the inmate or patient, to interact often with him, and in general to be emotionally supportive.[4] The two goals, then, prescribe conflicting expectations for guard or attendant behavior. The assumption implicit in the custodial goal affirms that the function of the organization is to protect the community by keeping the prisoner in the organization. He is correspondingly labeled as "dangerous," deserving of punishment, and unfit for the "outside world." In contrast, the assumption implicit in the treatment goal affirms that the function of the organization is to protect the community by "rehabilitating" the prisoner. He is correspondingly seen as "mentally ill" or "neurotic" and hence to a considerable extent not really responsible for his past actions. He is deserving of "individual treatment" by which his personal needs can be cared for and his ego healed.[5]

The conventional prison or mental hospital where the custodial goal is the primary objective can be characterized as a formalistically oriented bureaucracy, which like Gouldner's punishment-centered bureaucracy entails continuous enforcement of official regulations resulting in a considerable amount of inmate (or patient) resistance as well as highly formalized relationships between the officials and the inmates.[6] On the other hand, the prison organization or mental hospital where quasi-milieu treatment is a major goal contains the structural elements of a formalistically oriented bureaucracy combined with a pattern of social relationships in the organization which represents a process of a radically different nature. Institutionalization of a highly supportive staff-inmate relationship, which derives from the promulgation of the treatment goals, is characteristic of an indulgency-oriented bureaucratic pattern. Thus from the point of view of the organizational structure as a whole the conflicting goals, *i.e.,* custody and treatment, set in motion conflicting organizational processes.

Although conflict between an organization's basic objectives may create the underlying conditions necessary for role conflict, other factors will be instrumental in determining both the essential nature of the conflict for the role occupant and

---

[4]*Cf.* M. Greenblatt *et al., From Custodial to Therapeutic Patient Care in Mental Hospitals,* New York, 1955, pp. 1–34.

[5]Although this picture is purposely somewhat overdrawn for any *particular* prison setting or mental hospital, it is accurate in its essentials.

[6]*Cf.* Alvin Gouldner, *Patterns of Industrial Bureaucracy,* New York: The Free Press, 1951.

the type of adaptation to the role conflict that is possible. Formal position in the hierarchy of the organization is of fundamental importance in determining the extent of the conflict experienced. The occupants of the elite authority roles in most organizations are expected to demonstrate greater loyalty to the organization's goals (be they incompatible or not) than are other staff members. Moreover, the elite are commonly responsible for maintaining the integration of the organization and hence are likely to be subjected to a greater variety of internal pressures than are the nonelite. Finally, the elite are more likely to be responsible for negotiations with other social systems which impinge on their organization and thus are more exposed to forces from these systems than are the other officials.

With respect to the prison system that was the object of our research, we hypothesized as follows:

(1) Role conflict among the prison camp officials stemmed directly from the conflict between the organization's formal goals of custody and treatment.

(2) The differences in the formal hierarchical position of the supervisor and the other staff members should produce different types of role conflict and correspondingly different types of adaptation to the conflict.

THE SUPERVISOR The chief administrator of a prison organization is traditionally granted extensive independent authority. At Camp Davis the supervisor was at all times the center of a highly centralized authority system. No guard or other officer was permitted to make a policy decision without first consulting him. And in time of an emergency, such as an escape, his immediate notification was required even if he was not on duty.

The formal responsibilities of the supervisor involved policy-making with respect to both of the camp's two major goals—custody (maintaining discipline and control over the inmates) and treatment ("rehabilitating" them). During any given time the supervisor's decisions played a crucial role in creating conditions consistent with one goal or the other. . . .

The mutual interdependence and the contradictions implicit in the camp's goals served both to create and to intensify three major problems confronting the supervisor.[7] First, the guards were differentially committed to the two goals: some preferred emphasizing their custodial duties at the expense of their treatment responsibilities; others preferred emphasizing treatment and neglecting discipline. The problem for the supervisor was to maintain an integrated staff in the face of the divisive pressures generated by the two conflicting goals. . . .

---

[7]Seeman suggests that leadership positions in organizations automatically create contradictory demands and hence predispose role conflict. *Cf.* M. Seeman, "Role Conflict and Ambivalence in Leadership," *American Sociological Review*, 18, August 1953, p. 374.

The two goals, moreover, helped to set the conditions for the creation of an informal system of social relationships among the guards, which in turn reinforced their incompatibility and increased the supervisor's integrative problems.

The second problem was that of reconciling the conflicting demands made by officials of the State Corrections Agency—demands which were often incompatible, though authoritative. . . .

The position of the camp in the formal organizational structure of the State Corrections Agency was such that the supervisor was administratively responsible to separate divisions of the Agency for each of the camp's goals. Thus we see that conflict in the organizational goals, abetted by the organizational structure, created a situation where mutually conflicting demands were continually made on the supervisor on the policy-making level. . . .

Thirdly, the incompatible goals complicated relationships with the nearby community. . . .

The common antagonism of communities to correctional institutions was intensified by the fact that the camp was a minimum security camp where escape was relatively easy and where "treatment" was being attempted. . . .The supervisor's problems in this regard were aggravated by the fact that the camp was defined as experimental and as a result was very much in the limelight. . . .As a result pressures from the representatives of the two major factions in the State Corrections Agency tended to be intensified, so that the supervisor was always "on the spot."

The adaptation of the supervisor to the role conflict generated by the contradictory goals might be labeled "administrative neutrality," to connote an orientation of affective impartiality with respect to the two major policy areas. The supervisor, though a social worker by training, was neither strongly protreatment nor strongly procustody, as this comment suggests: "Another thing I found out is that you can be custodially minded as well as treatment-minded. You don't have to be one or the other."

The administrative neutrality response was effective in several ways. First of all, it enabled the supervisor to maintain at least adequate relations with representatives of both factions of the Corrections Agency. It also facilitated his being accepted by the staff, an acceptance which he could not have achieved if he had been overcommitted to either of the conflicting objectives. Moreover, the administrative neutrality adaptation tended to increase the relative power position of the supervisor in an already highly centralized authority structure. Because he was neutral, both the custodially oriented staff members and the treatment oriented staff members were compelled to operate through him to extend their influence successfully in the camp.

The supervisor's position with regard to the formal treatment program was one of accepting ultimate responsibility, yet manifesting a relative lack of involvement in its day-to-day program. . . .This lack of overcommitment to treatment. . .allowed him to operate impartially and hence to balance the incompatible demands of the goals of custody and those of treatment.

THE GUARDS Associated with role conflict is a lack of consensus in the organization concerning approved behavior in situations that are morally conflicting. In Camp Davis, as we have indicated, this lack of consensus lay in the conflict between the goal of custody and of treatment. For the guards the conflict stemmed principally from the fact that the objectives of quasimilieu treatment required a different set of decision-making criteria than did the custodial objectives. If an inmate in a traditional prison system violates the rules, the guard simply writes up a "ticket" and the inmate is punished by a central disciplinary court or a disciplinary officer. However, if the same violation occurs in a treatment-oriented prison organization, it complicates the guard's response and creates conflict, for he must decide whether he ought to write up a ticket or whether, for treatment reasons, he ought to let the inmate "express his emotions.". . .

Two modes of adaptation to the situation were found among the four guards. Two of the guards (to be called "custodially oriented guards") responded by emphasizing the application of custodial criteria, and two (to be called "treatment-oriented guards") responded by emphasizing the application of treatment criteria. Hence, the opposite goals and the ambiguity of expectations derived from them created a corresponding bifurcation in the orientation of the guards.[8]

Even the terminology of the custodially oriented guards reflected their orientation. The camp was a "penitentiary" and the offenders were labeled "inmates" or "cons." The treatment-oriented guards, in contrast, referred to the inmates as "men," "campers," or occasionally "boys." Both of the custodially oriented guards decried the lack of discipline in the camp. . . .

Not only did they recommend greater discipline in order to decrease the influence of treatment criteria, and thus decrease the ambiguity of their role expectations, but they believed that the inmates agreed with their orientation in this regard. . . .

All of the ambiguity implicit in their role, however, could not be resolved simply by stressing custodial criteria. Although the two guards could and did avoid participating in the formal aspects of the treatment program, and did interact less with the treatment-oriented guards,[9] they could not completely reject

---

[8]Although we are stressing organizational factors in this paper, obviously degree of commitment to one goal or the other is also influenced by personality predispositions. *Cf.* S. A. Stouffer and J. Toby, "Role Conflict and Personality," *Toward a General Theory of Action*, T. Parsons and E. A. Shils, eds., Cambridge, Mass.: 1952.

[9]As suggested earlier, the staff interaction patterns, like the role expectations, were bifurcated along the same custody-treatment dimension. Hence the treatment-oriented guards interacted primarily with each other and the custodially oriented guards did likewise. The supervisor in general maintained his neutral position by interacting with both, although he tended more toward the treatment clique, partly because his middle-class background and college education equipped him with values more consonant with theirs. The custodially oriented guards, unlike the other guards, did not have any college training.

the treatment goals, for to do so would have resulted in sanctions against them. Moreover, although this adaptation involved, at the least, latent resistance to the treatment aims, the very existence in the camp of a treatment program provided them with a distinct source of gratification. Unlike the guards in many prisons, all the guards in the camp had a considerable number of friendly associations with the inmates. Since it was the treatment program that helped facilitate such associations, even the custodially oriented guards experienced these rewards. . . .

Naturally such personally satisfying events only complicated the problem for the custodially oriented guards. Committed as they were to a strong emphasis on discipline, an ambivalent orientation toward the treatment program could serve only to intensify their role conflict.

On the other hand, the treatment-oriented guards were faced with stresses of a different sort. The role of one of them was formally defined as having both counseling and guard functions attached to it. He was responsible for organizing and maintaining the treatment program and for providing individual counseling to the inmates. At the same time he was responsible for performing strictly custodial functions such as making a periodic count of the inmates. The former duties were the most time consuming; hence this role, more than any other, officially represented the treatment goals of the camp.

The counselor guard, being overcommitted to the treatment aspects of his role, saw the other duties as hindering his effectiveness. . . .

The other treatment-oriented guard, though somewhat less committed to the treatment aspects of his role than the counselor guard (he had no formal counseling functions) demonstrated a similar pattern. Only the two treatment-oriented guards on the staff, for example, led any group therapy sessions and, correspondingly, they tended to have much closer relations with the inmates than did the other guards.

The adaptation of the treatment-oriented guards like that of the custodially oriented guards could not entirely alleviate the ambiguity implicit in their role. The former could not fully reject the custodial expectations associated with their role just as the latter could not completely reject the treatment expectations. Thus both were left with strong feelings of ambivalence. . . .

9.5   INTRODUCTION

The final selection in this chapter goes even further than the previous ones in specifying the extent to which roles are integral parts of the social structure in which they occur. Merton analyzes the social structure as it impinges upon the individual performing a role, introducing the concept of role-set to denote the cluster of other roles with whom the individual has relationships as a result of his own role. The focus of the discussion is on some of the facts about social structure and relationships that make social order possible despite the potential for disintegrating conflict inherent in the multiple requirements of a single role. Thus, although the selection refers to the individual's own experience of conflict in response to discrepant pressures, its main emphasis is on the extent to which psychological conflict is dependent in nature and degree on social structural factors.

Merton's analysis suggests a number of interesting questions about the guidance-personnel worker's role and his relationships with the various members of his role-set. The latter may include any or all of the following: school board members; school superintendent; principal; department chairmen; teachers; parents; social workers; psychologists; psychiatrists; other guidance-personnel workers within the school or college; outside members of the profession; outside groups or organizations (church, business, civic groups); students; and many others. It is clear that the expectations of these various other individuals with respect to the guidance worker will not be uniform or constant, nor will they always align themselves in the same ways on different issues. A teacher and a principal in a high school, for example, may make the same demands with respect to how the guidance counselor deals with a child who is a discipline problem and contrary demands with respect to how he deals with a parent who is complaining about his child's grades. Moreover, how the guidance counselor resolves the conflict in the latter case may well affect the pressures that he will be subjected to from these same individuals on a later issue. The ensuing discussion of structural factors that affect the nature of the conflicts among role demands suggests some of the major factors that the individual guidance counselor might consider in such a case in deciding on a course of action that will bring about a desirable balance between favorable and unfavorable consequences.

But the guidance-personnel worker is concerned not only with his particular set of role relationships. The role-sets of all the members of his own role-set are also, in different ways, relevant to his work. It seems clear, for example, that the effectiveness of the guidance worker's interactions with any member of his role-set will be enhanced to the extent that he is aware of the various pressures impinging on the other individuals from their role-sets. His recognition that principals must deal with school boards, teachers with other teachers, students with their peers, etc., will make it more likely that the pressures he exerts on these other individuals, as a member of their role-sets, will be compatible with their other role-demands.

Moreover, as a member of students' role-sets, the guidance-personnel worker would seem to be in an unique position. Unlike all the other roles with whom the individual child or adolescent has relationships—teachers or professors, siblings, friends, parent, other adults—intrinsic in the guidance worker's role is, on the one hand, a responsibility for being concerned with the students' total pattern of relationships and, on the other, unusual access to information about this total pattern. In other words, the guidance-personnel worker is at the same time one part of the student's role-set and a spectator to its totality. Viewed in this way, the potential for exerting influence upon students inherent in his role appears large indeed, and its actual responsibility even greater.

9.5   ON THE ROLE-SET[1]

Robert K. Merton

THE STRUCTURAL CONTEXT OF REFERENCE GROUP BEHAVIOR: ROLE-SETS, STATUS-SETS, AND STATUS-SEQUENCES

. . . .Without engaging in heavier deliberation than the subject deserves, we must note that a particular social status involves, not a single associated role, but an array of associated roles. This is a basic characteristic of social structure. This fact of structure can be registered by a distinctive term, *role-set*, by which I mean that *complement of role relationships which persons have by virtue of occupying a particular social status.* As one example: the single status of medical student entails not only the role of a student in relation to his teachers, but also an array of other roles relating the occupant of that status to other students, nurses, physicians, social workers, medical technicians, etc.[2] Again: the status of public school teacher has its distinctive role-set, relating the teacher to his pupils, to colleagues, the school principal and superintendent, the board of education, and, on frequent occasion, to local patriotic organizations, to professional organizations of teachers, Parent-Teachers Associations, and the like.

It should be plain that the role-set differs from the structural pattern which has long been identified by sociologists as that of "multiple roles." For in the established usage, multiple roles refer to the complex of roles associated, not with a *single* social status, but with the *various* statuses (often, in differing institutional spheres) in which individuals find themselves—the roles, for example, connected with the distinct statuses of teacher, wife, mother, Catholic, Republican, and so on. We designate this complement of social statuses of an individual as his *status-set*, each of the statuses in turn having its distinctive role-set.

The concepts of role-set and of status-set are structural and refer to parts of the social structure *at a particular time.* Considered as changing in the course of time, the succession of statuses occurring with sufficient frequency as to be socially pat-

[1]Reprinted with permission of The Macmillan Company from *Social Theory and Social Structure,* revised edition, by Robert K. Merton.©by The Free Press, a Corporation, 1957. Copyright by The Free Press 1949.

[2]For a preliminary analysis of the role-set of the medical student which is of direct import for reference group theory, see Mary Jean Huntington, "The development of a professional self-image," *The Student-Physician: Introductory Studies in the Sociology of Medical Education,* R. K. Merton, P. L. Kendall and G. G. Reader, eds., Cambridge: Harvard University Press, 1957, this being part of the studies conducted by the Columbia University Bureau of Applied Social Research under a grant from the Commonwealth Fund.

terned will be designated as a *status-sequence*, as in the case, for example, of the statuses successively occupied by a medical student, intern, resident, and independent medical practitioner. In much the same sense, of course, we can observe *sequences of role-sets and status-sets.*

The patterned arrangements of role-sets, status-sets, and status-sequences can be held to comprise the social structure. The concepts remind us, in the unlikely event that we need to be reminded of this insistent and obstinate fact, that even the seemingly simple social structure is extremely complex. For operating social structures must somehow manage to organize these sets and sequences of statuses and roles so that an appreciable degree of social order obtains, sufficient to enable most of the people most of the time to go about their business of social life without having to improvise adjustments anew in each newly confronted situation. . . .

STRUCTURAL SOURCES It would seem that the basic source of disturb-
OF INSTABILITY IN ance in the role-set is the structural circumstance that any one occupying a particular
THE ROLE-SET status has role-partners who are differently
located in the social structure. As a result,
these others have, in some measure, values and moral expectations differing from those held by the occupant of the status in question. The fact, for example, that the members of a school board are often in social and economic strata quite different from that of the public school teacher will mean that, in certain respects, their values and expectations differ from those of the teacher. The individual teacher may thus be readily subject to conflicting role-expectations among his professional colleagues and among the influential members of the school board and, at times, derivatively, of the superintendent of schools. What is an educational frill for the one may be judged as an essential of education by the other. These disparate and inconsistent evaluations complicate the task of coming to terms with them all. What holds conspicuously for the status of the teacher holds, in varying degree, for the occupants of other statuses who are structurally related, in their role-set, to others who themselves occupy diverse statuses.

As things now stand, this appears to be the major structural basis for potential disturbance of a stable role-set. The question does not arise, of course, in those special circumstances in which all those in the role-set have the same values and same role-expectations. But this is a special and, perhaps historically rare, situation. More often, it would seem, and particularly in highly differentiated societies, the role-partners are drawn from diverse social statuses with, to some degree, correspondingly different social values. To the extent that this obtains, the characteristic situation should be one of disorder, rather than of relative order. And yet, although historical societies vary in the extent to which this is true, it seems generally the case that a substantial degree of order rather than of acute disorder prevails. . . .

SOCIAL MECHANISMS FOR THE ARTICULATION OF ROLES IN THE ROLE-SET   . . . .We are concerned, not with a broad historical generalization that social order prevails but with the analytical problem of identifying the social mechanisms which operate to produce a greater degree of social order than would obtain, if these mechanisms were not called into play. . . .

THE MECHANISM OF DIFFERING INTENSITY OF ROLE-INVOLVEMENT AMONG THOSE IN THE ROLE-SET   Role-partners are variously concerned with the behavior of those in a particular social status. This means that the role-expectations of those in the role-set are not maintained with the same degree of intensity. For some, this role-relationship may be of only peripheral concern; for others, it may be central. As an hypothetical example: the parents of children in a public school may be more directly engaged in appraising and controlling the behavior of teachers than, say, the members of a local patriotic organization who have no children in the school. The values of the parents and of the patriotic organization may be at odds in numerous respects and may call for quite different behavior on the part of the teacher. But if the expectations of the one group in the role-set of the teacher are central to their concerns and interests, and the expectations of the other group, only peripheral, this eases the problem of the teacher seeking to come to terms with these disparate expectations. . . .

The teacher, for whom this status holds primary significance, is in this degree better able to withstand the demands for conformity with the differing expectations of those in his role-set for whom this relationship has only peripheral significance. . . . What holds for the particular case of the teacher presumably holds for the occupants of any other status: the impact upon them of diverse expectations of appropriate behavior among those in their role-set can be structurally mitigated by differentials of involvement in the relationship among those constituting their role-set. . . .

THE MECHANISM OF DIFFERENCES IN THE POWER OF THOSE INVOLVED IN A ROLE-SET   A second mechanism which affects the stability of a role-set is potentially provided by the distribution of power. By power, in this connection, is meant nothing more than the observed and predictable capacity for imposing one's own will in a social action, even against the resistance of others taking part in that action.[3]

The members of a role-set are not apt to be equally powerful in shaping the behavior of occupants of a particular status. However, it does not follow that the individual, group, or stratum in the role-set which is *separately* most powerful uniformly succeeds in imposing its expectations upon the status-occupants—say, the teacher. This would be so only in the circumstance when the one member of

---

[3]This will be recognized as Max Weber's conception of power, and one not far removed from other contemporary versions of the concept. From *Max Weber: Essays in Sociology*, pp. 180 ff.

the role-set has an effective monopoly of power, either to the exclusion of all others or outweighing the combined power of the others. Failing this special situation, the individuals subject to conflicting expectations among the members of their role-set can effect, deliberately or unwittingly, *coalitions of power* among them which enable these individuals to go their own way. The conflict is then not so much between the status-occupants and the diverse members of their role-set as between the members of the role-set itself. . . .The familiar pattern of "balance of power" is not confined to power struggles among nations; in less easily visible form, it can be found in the workings of role-sets generally, as the child who succeeds in having his father's decision offset his mother's contrasting decision has ample occasion to know. When conflicting powers in the role-set neutralize one another, the status-occupant has relative freedom to proceed as he intended in the first place.

Thus, even in those potentially unstable structures in which the members of a role-set hold distinct and contrasting expectations of what the status-occupant should do, the latter is not wholly at the mercy of the most powerful among them. Moreover, a high degree of involvement in his status reinforces his relative power. For to the extent that powerful members of his role-set are not primarily concerned with this particular relationship in the same degree as the status-occupant, they will not be motivated to exercise their potential power to the full. Within wide margins of his role-activity, the status-occupant will then be free to act, uncontrolled because unnoticed.

This does not mean, of course, that the status-occupant subject to conflicting expectations among members of his role-set is in fact immune to control by them. It is only to say that the power-structure of role-sets is often such that the status-occupant more nearly has autonomy than would be the case if this structure of competing powers did not obtain.

THE MECHANISM OF INSULATING ROLE-ACTIVITIES FROM OBSERVABILITY BY MEMBERS OF THE ROLE-SET   The occupant of a status does not engage in continuous interaction with all those in his role-set. . . .The interaction with each member (individual or groups) of the role-set is variously limited and intermittent; it is not equally sustained throughout the range of relationships entailed by the social status. This fundamental fact of role-structure allows for role-behavior which is at odds with the expectations of some in the role-set to proceed without undue stress. For. . .effective social control presupposes an appreciable degree of *observability* of role-behavior. To the extent that the role-structure insulates the status-occupant from direct observation by some of his role-set, he is not uniformly subject to competing pressures. It should be emphasized that we are dealing here with a fact of social structure, not with individual adjustments whereby this or that person *happens* to conceal parts of his role-behavior from certain members of his role-set. . . .

. . .[Some] social statuses have a functionally significant insulation from easy observability by some of those in the role-set. The status of the university teacher provides one example. The norm which holds that what is said in the classrooms of universities is privileged, in the sense of being restricted to the professor and his students, has this function of maintaining a degree of autonomy for the teacher. For if this were uniformly made available to all those comprising the role-set of the teacher, he might be driven to teach not what he knows or what the evidence leads him to believe, but what will placate the numerous and diverse expectations of all those concerned with "the education of youth.". . . .

More broadly, the concept of privileged information and confidential communication in the professions—law and medicine, teaching and the ministry—has the same function of insulating clients from ready observability of their behavior and beliefs by others in their role-set. If the physician or priest were free to tell all they have learned about the private lives of their clients, they could not adequately discharge their functions. More, as we have seen in our review of observability, if the facts of all role-behavior and all attitudes were freely available to anyone, social structures could not operate. What is sometimes called "the need for privacy"— that is, insulation of actions and thoughts from surveillance by others—is the individual counterpart to the functional requirement of social structure that some measure of exemption from full observability be provided for. Otherwise, the pressure to live up to the details of all (and often conflicting) social norms would become literally unbearable; in a complex society, schizophrenic behavior would become the rule rather than the formidable exception it already is. "Privacy" is not merely a personal predilection; it is an important functional requirement for the effective operation of social structure. . . .

The mechanism of insulation from observability can, of course, miscarry. . . .The teacher who is fully insulated from observation by peers and superiors may fail to live up to the minimum requirements of his status. The physician in his private practice who is largely exempt from the judgment of competent colleagues may allow his role-performance to sink below tolerable standards. The secret policeman may violate the values of the society, and not be detected.

All this means that some measure of observability of role-performance by members of the role-set is required, if the indispensable social requirement of accountability is to be met. . . .[T]here is some optimum of observability, difficult as yet to identify in measurable terms and doubtless varying for different social statuses, which will simultaneously make for accountability of role-performance and for autonomy of role-performance, rather than for a frightened acquiescence with the distribution of power that happens, at a given moment, to obtain in the role-set. Varying patterns of observability can operate to enable the occupants of social statuses to cope with the conflicting expectations among members of their role-sets.

THE MECHANISM MAKING FOR OBSERVABILITY OF MEMBERS OF THE ROLE-SET OF THEIR CONFLICTING DEMANDS UPON THE OCCUPANTS OF A SOCIAL STATUS. . . . As long as members of the role-set are happily ignorant that their demands upon the occupants of a status are incompatible, each member may press his own case upon the status-occupants. The pattern is then many against one. But when it is made plain that the demands of some members of the role-set are in full contradiction with the demands of other members, it becomes the task of the role-set, rather than the task of the status-occupant, to resolve these contradictions, either by a struggle for exclusive power or by some degree of compromise. As the conflict becomes abundantly manifest, the pressure upon the status-occupant becomes temporarily relieved.

In such cases, the occupant of the status subjected to conflicting demands and expectations can become cast in the role of the *tertius gaudens*, the third (or more often, the nth) party who draws advantage from the conflict of the others. The status-occupant, originally at the focus of the conflict, virtually becomes a more or less influential bystander whose function it is to highlight the conflicting demands by members of his role-set and to make it a problem for them, rather than for him, to resolve *their* contradictory demands. Often enough, this serves to change the structure of the situation. . . .

THE MECHANISM OF SOCIAL SUPPORT BY OTHERS IN SIMILAR SOCIAL STATUSES WITH SIMILAR DIFFICULTIES OF COPING WITH AN UNINTEGRATED ROLE-SET This mechanism presupposes the not unusual structural situation that others occupying the same social status have much the same problems of dealing with their role-sets. Whatever he may believe to the contrary, the occupant of a social status is usually not alone. The very fact that it is a *social status* means that there are others more or less like-circumstanced. The actual and potential experience of confronting conflicting role-expectations among those in one's role-set is to this extent common to occupants of the status. The individual subject to these conflicts need not, therefore, meet them as a wholly private problem which must be handled in a wholly private fashion. Such conflicts of role-expectations become patterned and shared by occupants of the same social status.

These facts of social structure afford a basis for understanding the formation of organizations and normative systems among those occupying the same social status. Occupational and professional associations, for example, constitute a structural response to the problems of coping with the power structure and (potentially or actually) conflicting demands by those in the role-set of the status. They constitute social formations designed to counter the power of the role-set. . . .They provide social support to the individual status-occupant. They minimize the need for his improvising private adjustments to conflict situations.

It is this same function, it might be said, which also constitutes part of the sociological significance of the emergence of professional codes which are designed to state in advance what the socially supported behavior of the status-occupant should be. . . .[S]ocial support is provided by consensus among status-peers as this consensus is recorded in the code. The function of such codes becomes all the more significant in those cases in which status-occupants are vulnerable to pressures from their role-set precisely because they are relatively isolated from one another. . . .This kind of social support for conformity to the requirements of the status when confronted with pressures by the role-set to depart from these requirements serves to counteract the instability of role-performance which would otherwise develop.

ABRIDGING THE ROLE-SET: DISRUPTION OF ROLE-RELATIONSHIPS This is, of course, the limiting case in modes of coping with incompatible demands upon status-occupants by members of the role-set. Certain relationships are broken off, leaving a consensus of role-expectations among those that remain. But this mode of adaptation is possible only under special and limited conditions. It can be effectively utilized only in those circumstances where it is still possible for the status-occupant to perform his other roles, without the support of those with whom he has discontinued relations. Otherwise put, this requires that the remaining relationships in the role-set are not substantially damaged by this device. It presupposes that social structure provides the option to discontinue some relations in the role-set as, for example, in a network of personal friendships. By and large, however, this option is far from unlimited, since the role-set is not so much a matter of personal choice as a matter of the social structure in which the status is embedded. Under these conditions, the option is apt to be that of the status-occupant removing himself from the status rather than that of removing the role-set, or an appreciable part of it, from the status. Typically, the individual goes, and the social structure remains. . . .

Questions and Implications for Practice

9.1 RALPH LINTON

1. Discuss in relation to student and racial unrest Linton's statement that our inherited system of statuses and roles is breaking down. How do you see this evidencing itself in the school or college you know best? What characteristics in terms of statuses and roles would you hope the emerging new system might have? Why?

2. To what extent do you think it might be (a) possible, and (b) desirable to help students even in elementary school to understand the concepts of status and role?

3. Can—and should—students be helped to understand the effects that the statuses and roles others ascribe to them have on their self-concepts?

4. Discuss the pros and cons of teaching students in school and college how to analyze groups in terms of the statuses and roles these groups permit to their members.

9.2 JACOBSON, CHARTERS, AND LIEBERMAN

1. Here is a description of role concept in an automobile factory. Is a school or college as you know it essentially like or unlike this factory? Describe the similarities as you see them, and the differences.

2. Analyze the social organization of some school or college you know (or some well-defined part of that school or college) from the standpoints that Jacobson, Charters, and Lieberman use: (a) role distribution, (b) role conflict, (c) estimation of role expectations, (d) impact of role expectations, (e) impact of past role experience on attitudes and behavior, and (f) relationship between role and role behavior. Is it possible to do this without using the systematic interview and survey approach used by the authors of this article? Outline a study that you could then carry out systematically.

3. Find some research studies that attempt to get at the role expectations of some one certain kind of guidance-personnel worker. How does the approach in these studies differ from that of Jacobson, Charters, and Lieberman?

4. How and in what ways are the approach and the findings of these research studies in the field of education useful to you in understanding better the school or college as a complex organization?

9.3 ALVIN GOULDNER

1. Does Gouldner's analysis of the latent social roles of six types of "locals" and "cosmopolitans" help you to understand better your own role type? Discuss.

2. Think of some school or college situation you know well and write down the names of some of the staff members in that situation whom you know best. Attempt to classify each of these individuals as belonging more to some one of the six types than to the other five.

3. To which of Gouldner's groups would you prefer to belong? If you feel you might be most comfortable being "dedicated," does this have implications as to the kind of institution you had better try to get yourself into?

4. Would you find it fulfilling to be one of the "homeguard"?

5. Is there a possibility that, inevitably, without effort on your part, you will find yourself in the social role of an "elder"?

6. Would you feel safer and have a better self-concept if you could maintain yourself as an "outsider"? If so, what kind of qualifications must you work to develop?

7. Discuss the proposition that students are criticizing today essentially the high proportion of cosmopolitans that colleges tend to have on their faculties. What would you say to a group of students who complained about the predominance of cosmopolitans?

9.4 OSCAR GRUSKY

1. Among guidance-personnel workers is it possible that counselors *qua* counselors deliberately try to shun the elite authority role in order to avoid as much as possible being exposed to forces from social systems that will complicate their lives? Explain your point of view.

2. Does society perhaps award elitism to those who have to endure and deal with antagonistic social forces, both as compensation to them for their ordeals and courage as well as to give them whatever extra power can be derived from the advantages that inhere in a higher position in the hierarchy? Take a position and defend it.

3. To what extent do you think basic personality traits predispose some guidance-personnel workers to work at so-called custodial duties with more commitment than at treatment? And vice-versa?

4. To what extent can/should professional training teach a worker to use "discipline" and "treatment" with versatility rather than teach him to rely exclusively on either one or the other?

5. Could you develop a position that the mission of schools and colleges is neither primarily custodial nor therapeutic, but rather educational? Is there properly a place for both discipline and treatment in a sound educational approach?

Is it necessary—or desirable—for the disciplinary and treatment components of education to be assigned as totally as they sometimes are to guidance-personnel workers viewed as specialists in either discipline or treatment? Or might it be possible for guidance-personnel workers to view themselves as educators with well-defined educational goals that reinforce, supplement, and help students to see relationships among their learnings? What are some of the radical consequences that such a major shift in role would have?

6. Would it perhaps be better to leave the field and its roles very much as they are now with their tensions and ambiguities, but also with some of the comfortable familiarities with which we have learned to live—as have the guards in Camp Davis? Does it look to you as though we shall be permitted to keep most of our "comfortable familiarities"?

9.5 ROBERT MERTON

1. Referring back to Lakeshore High, as described by Cicourel and Kitsuse (in Selection 3.4), describe the status-set (as defined by Merton) of the counselors at Lakeshore High. Describe the role-set of the counselor.

2. Who are the counselors' role-partners in Lakeshore High?

3. If the counselors in Lakeshore High were no longer to behave as though their high school was a kind of factory and they the ones who tested and sorted out individual students and aimed them toward their preordained destinations, what kind of disturbance not only of their own role-sets, but also of those of their role-partners, might occur?

4. How powerfully do the expectations of others in our role-sets control our status-set?

5. Consider the diverse expectations among those in the role-set of some one of the following: high school superintendent; elementary school child development consultant; university president; dean of women; admissions director; a Latin teacher; or a Negro, Mexican-American, Puerto Rican, or Indian child who has a recorded score of 35 to 50 percent on a group aptitude test. How might these various expectations affect the role-behavior of the individual who is the focus of them?

Chapter 10

The
Individual
and
the Group

This part of the book has been devoted to an examination of the relationship between the individual and his social environment. So far, we have elaborated from various viewpoints the notion that what an individual is and does must be understood in terms of his past and current social experiences. The selections have spelled out both the general logic of this conception and many of its specific and empirically based extensions. It remains for us now to examine some of the psychological and social-psychological mechanisms that establish and maintain the interdependence between the individual and his culture.

Stated somewhat differently, up to this point we have dealt with the individual's adaptation to his sociocultural environment in rather general terms, assuming that such adaptation does occur but without examining the process itself. In this chapter, our discussion of the relationship between the individual and his social environment will focus on the processes that give rise to and support the relationship and which account for both its regularities and its variations. In short, having examined many phenomena which demonstrate that the individual is affected by the nature of his social environment, we will now look at how these effects are actually accomplished.

The selections in previous chapters have made it clear that the events through which the individual comes to reflect his culture all involve, to varying degrees and in a more of less direct manner, interaction with others. Social relationships, in other words, are the medium through which cultural factors become part of the individual and direct his behavior. An individual's adaptation to his social environment thus consists of the particular set of needs, wants, expectations, and predispositions which he has acquired, and which he expresses, in interaction with others. It has also become evident that pattern and regularity characterize social interaction, implying that the actions of diverse individuals are determined by at least some common factors. Thus it follows that these underlying, or less visible, psychological and social-psychological processes also fall into patterns that are related in stable ways to those that are evident at the group or societal level.

Even without any training or sophistication in social science, most of us are aware of such facts as that a person acts differently when he is in a group than when he is alone, that we are susceptible to being influenced by the opinions or example of others, that friends and associates usually have many things in common—opinions, beliefs, tastes, habits. Although we may have many such rather clear conceptions of social-psychological processes, we are less likely to be aware of the regulatory and adaptive role they play in our own behavior. Indeed, such phenomena tend to be considered as simply natural—as inherent in something vaguely labeled "human nature." From the broadened perspective that knowledge of differences among cultures and subcultures fosters, it is clear that such uniform patterns are neither innate nor inevitable but that they are the result of complex and consistent learning experiences within a particular context. It is these patterns, in effect, that account for the more general fact that the individual reflects and is a part of his culture. They are in one sense the component elements and in another sense the sources of the characteristic patterns of behavior and interaction that prevail in a given society.

As we have seen, every culture is likely to have dominant patterns, because regularity in the social realm is necessary to social stability and integration. Their contents, however, are neither fixed nor universal and need to be viewed in terms of the dominant cultural themes, which determine the structure, value, and consequences of individual and group behavior. Thus, in some cultures (or subcultures), individual adaptations may typically include a great deal of spontaneity and innovation, whereas in others they may be predominantly uniform and norm-oriented. As some of the following selections will show, this does not necessarily mean that individuals in the first case are less likely to be members of groups than in the second case, or that they are subject to less pressure from the social environment. It means, rather, that environmental pressures can operate in any direction and that individuality as well as uniformity can be culturally valued goals that people are motivated to attain.

Human behavior, in other words, exhibits both variability and regularity. In attempting to understand both, social psychologists and sociologists have been led to translate the overall relationship between the person and his social environment into specific relationships between aspects of the individual and aspects of the situation. They have found that how an individual responds in a particular case depends on the relationships among a number of specifiable factors, some within and some outside of himself. Thus, many stable relationships have been demonstrated to obtain between particular motives, opinions, past experiences, and personality traits and responses to particular stimuli. Such understanding makes it possible to explain both differences among the reactions of different individuals to the same overall situation and differences in the behavior of the same individual in response to different situations. Our knowledge is still far from complete, but there is already emerging an empirically validated understanding of the subtle interdependence between individual phenomena, both overt and covert, and the social situations in which they occur.

10.1   INTRODUCTION

The first selection in this chapter is by an anthropologist and draws on observations made in a number of primitive cultures to show the depth of the interconnections between individual autonomy and social structure. Dorothy Lee describes some typical interactions between adults and children in various cultures that illustrate the manner in which individuals can learn to see themselves and those around them as conforming to their own inner directives rather than to those imposed on them by others. The cumulative picture portrayed by the societies she has selected is one of individuals living predominantly in order and harmony without need for interpersonal demands or coercion. What emerges most clearly from this discussion is that, once the directives that comprise a social structure have been fully internalized by an individual, he is then committed to the structure as an integral part of his world and his conformity to it stems, not from fear of the sanctions that deviation would incur, but from his acceptance and knowledge of the structure as a helpful map in his interaction with his environment.

One of the most significant points in this article is the novel perspective it implies with respect to the concept of autonomy. From the materials presented in earlier chapters it might well seem as if notions of individual spontaneity or initiative are essentially meaningless in relation to the pervasive nature of social and cultural determination. Lee's discussion, however, makes it possible to derive a somewhat different interpretation. Starting from the fact that the individual exists only in a social context and that, by his very nature, he will be deeply affected by this context, Lee suggests that the greatest autonomy is possible in a clear-cut social structure if the latter is experienced as an opportunity, a guide, and even a tool for the satisfaction of individual needs and the attainment of aspirations. A vague set of social pressures, with neither the requirements nor their implications clearly delineated and understood, may be the most inhibiting condition of all, depriving the individual of the opportunity of acting in full awareness of the consequences. This, the author suggests, is the difference between autonomy and permissiveness.

It is interesting to relate Dorothy Lee's conception to the importance and power of peer groups in adolescence when, presumably, the development of individual autonomy is at a crucial stage. It may be that the intricate and clear prescriptions for behavior that peer groups establish, and to which adolescents predominantly conform, are actually a condition that frees them to develop and practice their own individual adaptations to the social environment.

This is only one of the implications of importance for guidance contained in the selection. The guidance counselor is, on the one hand, an important element in the social structure to which students must adapt, and he is concerned with their responses to norms, expectations, and regulations. On the other hand, and at the same time, the fostering of individual autonomy is one of his primary objectives. The relationship that is the focus of the next discussion, between individual autonomy and group structure, is thus one of central and immediate relevance for guidance theory and practice.

10.1 INDIVIDUAL AUTONOMY AND SOCIAL STRUCTURE[1]

Dorothy Lee

Respect for individual integrity, for what we have called human dignity, has long been a tenet in American culture, and it is certainly no novel principle to anyone working in the area of interpersonal relations. However, in a heterogeneous society such as ours, and in an era of induced change and speeded tempo of living, it has been difficult to implement this tenet in the everyday details of living. We have to reconcile principles of conformity and individual initiative, group living and private freedom of choice, social regulation and personal autonomy. I believe that a study of other societies dealing with such issues in different circumstances can furnish us with insights which we can use in understanding our own situation. So I present here scattered material from a number of societies, ending with a brief sketch of the culture of the Navaho Indians, to show how the principle of personal autonomy is supported by the cultural framework.

In every society we find some organized social unit; but not everywhere does the social unit provide freedom to the individual or the opportunity for spontaneous

[1]From Dorothy Lee, "Individual Autonomy and Social Structure," copyright *Personnel and Guidance Journal*, 1956. See also *Freedom and Culture* by Dorothy Lee, Prentice-Hall Inc., Englewood Cliffs, N.J., pp. 5-15

functioning; nor do we find everywhere the value for sheer personal being of which I shall speak below. We often find a hierarchy where women or children or the uninitiated or the commoners are accorded a minority status. In some societies we find what amounts to a dictatorship; in others, the group may demand such sacrifice of individual uniqueness as to make for totalitarianism. On the other hand, in some societies we encounter a conception of individual autonomy and democratic procedures which far outstrip anything we have practiced or even have conceived of as democracy. It is only the latter kind which concerns me here.

It is often difficult for us to decide exactly how much our principle of personal autonomy involves. We find ourselves asking questions such as: to what extent can we allow a child to make his own decisions, to speak and act for himself? And: at what point do we begin to allow him to do so? For example, obviously when the mother first takes her infant to the pediatrician, she has to speak for him. Exactly when does she begin to remain silent, waiting for him to understand and answer the doctor's questions and to express his own likes and opinions and conclusions? And to what extent can she do this, using up the time of her appointment, taking up the valuable time of a busy physician?

Many of us feel that to allow a child to decide for himself and to act according to his own wish, that is, to be permissive, is to show respect for the unique being of the child. Yet for many of the societies we know, it would be presumption for any person to "allow" another to take what is essentially his prerogative—the right to decide for himself. These people do not "permit" others. When their children, as for example the children of the Wintu Indians, ask "Can I?" they are asking for information on the rules of the structure; for instance, they may be seeking clarification about a religious taboo or a social custom. They are saying in effect, "Is it permissible for me to . . .?" and not, "Do you allow me to . . .?" These people do not "give" freedom to their children, because it is not theirs to give. If they do not impose an external time schedule on their infants, but feed them when they are hungry, and put them to bed when they are sleepy, they are not being "permissive"; they are showing their deep-seated respect for individual worth, and their awareness of the unique tempo of the individual.

Ethnographers have presented us with many incidents, apparently commonplace and trivial, which point out for us an amazingly thoroughgoing implementation of respect for personal quality. For instance, Marian Smith tells how, when she was visiting a Sikh household in British Columbia, she noticed that a small child, asked to entertain his baby brother, merely went up to the playpen and put in a toy truck. He did not show the baby how the truck worked, how he could make the wheels go round; he gave the truck silently. This amazed the visitor, since she knew that the Sikhs were people of great empathy and warmth, and with a great love for babies. She knew, also, that the child in question had approached the baby with friendliness and affection. Yet, under similar circumstances an American child would probably have told the baby what to look for. Then she remembered the personal autonomy of the Sikh, and realized that the boy was acting consistently with the cultural values; he was furnishing the baby with the raw material for experience, and leaving him to explore and discover for himself, without any attempt to influence him. He was expressing respect, not noninvolvement.

Such respect for autonomy may appear extreme to us, yet it would be taken for granted in a number of the Indian tribes in this continent. For example, an anthropology student who was observing relations between parents and children was puzzled to see a baby with hair so long that it got in his eyes and seemed to cause him discomfort, though otherwise his mother treated him with care and affection. When she finally asked why the baby's hair had been left so long, the mother answered, "He has not asked to have it cut." The baby was about eighteen months old, and could barely talk; yet the mother would not take it upon herself to act for him without his request or consent.

These instances exemplify a belief so deep that it apparently permeates behavior and decisions, and operates without question or reflection or conscious plan. It is a belief so internalized as to be regarded as almost an organic ingredient of the personality. The individual, shown absolute respect from birth and valued as sheer being for his own uniqueness, apparently learns with every experience to have this same respect and value for others; he is "trained" to be constantly sensitive to the beginnings of others.

An instance of this "training" in sensitivity comes from the culture of the Chinese. American observers had noticed that Chinese babies had learned, by the time they were about six months old, to indicate that they wanted to micturate; yet they seemed to be treated very permissively, with no attempt at toilet training. A Chinese mother explained that there actually is such "training"; only it is the mother who "trains" herself. When the baby wants to urinate, his whole body participates in the preliminary process. The Chinese mother, holding the baby in her arms, learns to be sensitive to the minute details of this process, and to hold her baby away from herself at exactly the critical moment. Eventually, the infant learns to ask to be held out. The mother neither tries to control the baby, nor does she train the infant to control himself according to imposed standards. Instead, she sensitizes herself to his rhythm, and helps him to adopt social discipline with spontaneity, starting from his unique pattern. What is interesting here is that as an end result of this, the baby is "toilet-trained" at a very early age; but it has been an experience of spontaneity for him and his autonomy has remained inviolate, because his mother has had the sensitivity and the patience to "listen" to him.

Among the Wintu Indians of California, the principle of the inviolate integrity of the individual is basic to the very morphology of the language. Many of the verbs which express coercion in our language—such as to take a baby to (the shade), or to change the baby—are formed in such a way that they express a cooperative effort instead. For example, the Wintu would say, "I *went with* the baby," instead of "*I took* the baby." And they say, "The chief *stood with* the people," which they have to translate into English as, "The chief ruled the people." They never say, and in fact they cannot say, as we do, "I have a sister," or a "son," or "husband." Instead, they say, "I am sistered," or "I live with my sister." To *live with* is the usual way in which they express what we call possession, and they use this term for everything that they respect, so that a man will be said to live with his bow and arrows. In our society, when we try to express respect for individual uniqueness, we have to do it in so many words, and even then we have to grapple with an uncooperative language. This is why we have to resort to terms which actually defeat our ends; terms such as *permissiveness*, or phrases such as *to give freedom to the child*. In Wintu, every interpersonal reference is couched in grammar which rests on the principle of individual integrity. Yet, for this people, the emphasis on personal inviolability did not mean that the individual was an isolate. There was such pervasive empathy among them that this, too, was expressed in the grammatical forms; if a boy was sick, the father used a special form of the verb phrase *to be sick*, and thus said, "I-am-sick-in-respect-of-my-son."

A corollary of the principle of individual integrity is that no personal orders can be given or taken without a violation of personal autonomy; we have been familiar with this corollary, particularly in rural areas where the farmer and his wife had "help" but not "servants." In a society such as that of Upper Burma before it was much affected by Western administration, there were no agricultural laborers nor household help at all. In the monasteries, where novices performed menial tasks, the monks did not give orders. Instead, the work was structured throughout the day; and all that the monk said to get the work done was, "Do what is lawful," reminding the novice to act according to the cultural tenet, not ordering him.

This last illustration introduces a further principle: that of structure. Many people in our society have been apprehensive of the implications of personal autonomy, because they have felt that it is apt to lead to lawlessness and chaos. Yet actually it is in connection with the highest personal autonomy that we often find the most intricately developed structure; and it is this structure that makes autonomy possible in a group situation. For example, the Burmese novices could proceed without receiving orders only because the structure clearly indicated what could and could not be done and at what time of the day or month or year.

Margaret Mead and Gregory Bateson have described this combination of autonomy and structure for the Balinese. These people have an exceedingly complex calendrical system, consisting of a permutation of ten weeks of differing lengths; and this system, in combination with an intricately patterned spacial and status system, furnishes the structure according to which an individual behaves. For instance, according to the specific combination of "weeks" on which his birthday falls, and according to his status, an individual has to participate in a special way at a particular temple festival. No one imposes this tribute upon him; and no one asks for his contribution. However, because of the enormous amount of detail involved in the precision of the structure, there are officials known as reminders, who merely remind the people of the exact character of the pending festival. Each person then proceeds to act according to his peculiar position in the temporal structure, acting autonomously, finding guidance in the structure.

When the specific aspects of the structure are not clear, the people in such societies can turn to authority for clarification. And here we often find, as with the Burmese or the Navaho Indians, that the authority of the headman or the chief or the leader is in many ways like the authority of the dictionary, or of Einstein. There is no hint of coercion or command here; the people go to the leader with faith, as we go to a reference book, and the leader answers according to his greater knowledge, or clarifies an obscure point, or amplifies according to his greater experience and wisdom. He does not say: You must do this, because I order you to. Yet, he does use the *must* or its equivalent; he says, so to speak: As I see it, this is what must be done. In a sense, it is like the recipe which says: You must not open the oven door for ten minutes after you put the cake in. No housewife, preparing a cake and going to the cookbook for guidance, feels that her personal integrity is violated by this interdiction. Once she is committed to the cake-making, she finds the recipe, the structure, enabling and guiding; she finds it freeing, not restricting.

If permissiveness at times leads to lawlessness and chaos, and even to immobilization instead of the freedom to be and to act, this happens usually in those cases where "permission" goes from person to person, in a structural vacuum. It happens when the structure is by-passed through the dictatorial permissiveness of the person who takes it upon himself to allow, and by implication to forbid, another person. In the societies which were mentioned above, where we find absolute valuing of unique being, what often takes the form of permissiveness in our society exists as the freedom to be, and to find actualization; and it is found within a clearly delineated structure.

Such is the society of the Navaho Indians of Arizona and New Mexico. How long this picture will last, we cannot predict. The mineral resources of their land are now being developed, and rapid change is being introduced. What I say here draws on the autobiographies of Navaho men, as well as on recent ethnographies.

In these accounts, we find a tightly knit group, depending on mutual responsibility among all its members, a precisely structured universe, and a great respect for individual autonomy and integrity. We find people who maintain an inviolable privacy while living as a family in a one-room house, sharing work and responsibility to such an extent that even a child of six will contribute his share of mutton to the family meal. The family unit is so closely knit that, if a child of five is ill or absent, the family suffers because there is a gap in the cooperative effort; and when a man goes hunting, he can get nothing unless his wife cooperates at home by observing the necessary taboos. The well-being of a Navaho, his health and the health of all his undertakings, depend on the maintenance of harmony with nature. All being is both good and evil; and by walking carefully according to a highly structured map of procedure, within a detailed framework of "do's" and "don'ts," the Navaho can keep the proper balance of good and evil in his life, and thus find health and harmony. The rules according to which he lives originate in the structure, and come to him as guidance from the parents, not as commands.

Within this structured universe and tightly knit society, the Navaho lives in personal autonomy. Adults and children are valued for their sheer being, just because they *are*. There is no urge toward achievement; no one has to strive for success. In fact, neither is there reward for success, nor is success held out as a reward for hard work. Wealth may be the result of hard work and skill, but obviously it is also the blatant result of lack of generosity, lack of responsibility for one's relatives, perhaps even of malicious witchcraft. No good Navaho becomes and remains "wealthy" in our terms.

Hard work is valued in itself, as a personal quality which combines the ability to withstand hardship with the paramount sense of responsibility for the work of the group. Even a young child will be trained to see to it that the whole flock of sheep is safe before he takes shelter during a blizzard. This means a systematic program in developing hardihood. He is waked up at daybreak in winter, so that he may run for miles; and in summer, he runs in the hot sun of noontime. Presently, he intensifies this program by his own decision, perhaps putting sand in his moccasins to make the running more rigorous; that is, he relates himself to this discipline with spontaneity. Children learn responsibility by being given indispensable household tasks; in addition, they are given sheep of their own from the time they are about five. They are responsible for the care and welfare of these animals; thus, they acquire a further opportunity at responsible participation. Now they can take their turn at supplying the meat for the family meal, and they can contribute mutton when this is needed for ceremonials, or to entertain visitors.

Most of all, an individual has to learn to walk safely through life, maintaining his harmony with the universe. This involves learning to observe a large number of taboos and procedures, which are aspects of every act: to learn, for example, what is to be done with the left hand, which direction to have his hogan face, what is to be started in a sunwise direction, or to be taken from the east side of a tree; what to avoid touching, or saying, or looking at. All this could be seen as inhibiting, or negative, or as interfering with the individual; but to the Navaho it is guidance in the acquisition of an essential skill—the freedom to act and to be. The intricate set of regulations is like a map which affords freedom to proceed to a man lost in the jungles.

In Navaho autobiographies we often find the phrase, "I followed the advice of my parents," but rarely, "I obeyed my parents." The good Navaho does not command his child; and a mother who is aggressive toward her children, who "talks rough" to them, is strongly criticized. In teaching her children the tremendous number of taboos they have to learn for their well-being, the good Navaho mother does not say: I will punish you if you do thus-and-thus; but: Such-and-such an unpleasant thing will happen to you. The mother is guiding the child; and if the child takes a wrong turn, if he breaks a taboo, he is not "guilty." He has not committed a sin against the mother and is not in need of forgiveness. He has made a mistake which he must set right.

This attitude is basic to all Navaho relatedness, so that here man is not burdened with guilt, and does not feel apologetic toward human or divine beings. He is neither grateful nor abject to his gods. As a matter of fact, he must never humble himself before them, since the process of healing, of the recovery of harmony with the universe, involves identification with the appropriate god, who would be slighted if the patient humiliated himself. This means that the Navaho has—and indeed must have—as much respect and value for himself as for others; in fact, this is the Navaho version of the principle that we have discovered so recently in our society: that we cannot accept and respect others until we learn to accept and respect ourselves.

In what I have said, I have made no distinction between adults and children, as the Navaho do not differentiate between the two in the respect they show for personal autonomy. There is no minority status for children. For example, a good Navaho will not take it upon himself to speak for another, whether for adult or child. A man, asked by a White what his wife thinks on a certain subject, is likely to answer, "I don't know, I haven't asked her." In the same way, a father, asked to sell his child's bow and arrow, will refer the request to a five-year-old boy, and abide by the child's decision not to sell, even though he knows the child is badly in need of the clothing that can be bought with the price of the toy. A woman, asked whether a certain baby could talk, said "Yes"; and when the ethnographer was puzzled by the "meaningless" sounds the baby was making, she explained that the baby could talk, but she could not understand what the baby said. All that she had the right to do was to speak for herself, to say that she could not understand. She would not presume to speak for the child, and to say—as I think we would have said—that the child was making meaningless sounds.

So the individual remains inviolate. No one coerces another among the Navaho. Traditionally, parents do not force their children to do what they unequivocally do not want to do, such as going to school or to the hospital; children are not coerced even "for their own good." As the mother of two unschooled children put it, "I listen to my children, and I have to take their word." There is no political coercion, and all leadership is traditionally incidental. A man finds himself in a position of leadership when the people seek him out because of the high degree of his inner development; because of his wisdom, his knowledge, his assumption of responsibility, his physical skill and hardihood, the wealth which he is ready to use to help his relatives. Men do not seek leadership; and White employers have found that the Navaho are reluctant to become foremen, however able they may be, and in spite of the higher pay involved. It is "fundamentally indecent" according to Clyde Kluckhohn, "for a single individual to presume to make decisions for the group," and therefore not even a leader will make decisions for others, or give orders to others.

For the Navaho mother, personal autonomy means that her child has the freedom to make his own mistakes, to suffer pain or grief or joy and learn from experience. And the child has his freedom because the mother has faith in him. This does not mean that she has high expectations of him, but that she trusts him.

She knows that he is a mingling of good and evil; she knows that life is unpredictable, and that a mistake may bring disaster. But she is willing to refrain from interfering with her child as he explores, as he takes his steps in life. When the baby starts walking, the mother does not see to it that he is out of reach of the fire, and that all the sharp knives have been put away. The child gets burned a little, and the mother helps him learn from this experience that he has to be careful of fire; he has a small accident, and the mother helps him understand and deal with that particular danger. By taking a chance on her child, the mother teaches him to be ready to meet and deal with danger, instead of warning him away from danger.

This trust means that the child has freedom to move, to act, to undertake responsibility. It means that the child is given significant tasks in the household. A psychiatrist visiting a Navaho family wrote in her diary: "After supper the girl (ten years old) went to water the horses, and the boy (five years old) to take the little flock back to some older members of the family who lived in a hogan a quarter of a mile away." No mention is made here of orders given, nor of any checking on the mother's part to see that the job was done.

COEXISTENCE OF AUTONOMY AND LIMITS   If the societies I have mentioned here present an enviable consistency in the expression of the principle of individual integrity, it is well to keep in mind that there may be no special virtue in this; at the time these societies were studied, they enjoyed great social homogeneity, and were relatively unchanging over time. This means that the children could learn the adult role at home by gradually sharing the life of the father or mother—as a matter of course, expecting and wanting to live the life of the parents, and to hold the same values and principles. However, the fact remains that consistency was there; that the principle was upheld by the various aspects of the culture, even by the very grammar of the language, as among the Wintu.

The practices I have presented here are not for us to copy, but rather food for thought, the basis for new insights. I have tried to show that law and limits and personal autonomy can coexist effectively, that spontaneity is not necessarily killed by group responsibility, that respect for individual integrity is not an end to be achieved by specific means, but that it can exist only if it is supported by deep conviction and by the entire way of life.

BIBLIOGRAPHY

DYK, WALTER, Recorder, 1938, "Son of Old Man Hat", *A Navaho Autobiography*, New York: Harcourt, Brace and World.
KLUCKHOHN, CLYDE, AND DOROTHEA LEIGHTON, 1946, *The Navaho*, Cambridge: Harvard University Press.

LEIGHTON, DOROTHEA, AND CLYDE KLUCKHOHN, 1947, *Children of the People*, Cambridge: Harvard University Press.
REICHARD, GLADYS A., 1944, *Prayer, The Compulsive Word*, Monographs of the American Ethnological Society, New York: J. J. Augustin.

10.2, 10.3   INTRODUCTION

The next two selections are of a different nature than all the others in this book, both being rather technical reports of social-psychological experiments. The purpose of such experiments is to create situations in which the effects of changes in one or a few factors can be observed with some confidence that these effects were not produced by changes in other factors beyond the ones of interest.

As Theodore Newcomb described in Chapter 2 (Selection 2.1), social psychologists are interested in the *relationship* between the individual and the environment: What changes in the individual are due to what changes in the environment? Or, what individual variations are produced by particular variations in the environment? The first selection, by Solomon Asch, reports the findings of a pioneering study in social psychology which reveals some of the aspects of a group situation that will lead individuals to agree with others against their own judgment. By comparing the behavior of individuals in situations that differed in the amount and homogeneity of group pressure, Asch is able to draw some conclusions about a few of the conditions which make individuals more or less vulnerable to such pressure. The Selection 10.3, by Deutsch and Gerard, reports on one of the many studies into the sources of group conformity that have followed Asch's initial inquiry. These authors were interested in qualitative differences in the social pressures operating on the individual. Particularly, they observed the different effects of different degrees of pressures for the individual to conform to his own, rather than to the group's, judgment on the extent to which an individual maintained his own judgment or agreed with the group. In other words, the question they raise is: can the social pressures to which an individual conforms be such as to make the individual more likely to maintain his own judgment in the face of disagreement from other group members? The answer seems to be positive.

Together these two studies shed light on some of the processes that underlie the individual's reactions to social pressures, while at the same time demonstrating that these pressures need not be contrary to, and indeed can foster, independence and autonomy. These two articles thus convey a point very similar to that of the previous selection, arriving at it through very different procedures and observations and thus extending its meaning and validity. The emphasis on the nature of a group's norms and standards as the basic factor determining whether a group is "good" or "bad" for its members is perhaps a novel perspective, but one that would seem to have important and optimistic implications for guidance counselors and all those concerned with the social processes of education and educational organizations. It suggests that it may be possible to foster productive behavior in a large number of individuals if somehow such behavior can be made salient as a goal in the group or groups to which they belong. Not only does this make it unnecessary to deal with individuals separately in attempting to foster positive changes, but it actually suggests that such individual attention is likely to be in vain unless the social pressures on the individual are also taken into account. In this respect, it seems most significant to emphasize two related aspects of Asch's data. The first is the fact that, regardless of the nature of the social pressures, a large majority of the subjects remained independent—true to their own judgments—throughout the experiment. The second fact is the strong effect that even minimal social support had in increasing the size of this independent majority, that is, in making it possible for most individuals to withstand social pressures alien to their own tendencies.

10.2   EFFECTS OF GROUP PRESSURE UPON THE MODIFICATION AND DISTORTION OF JUDGMENTS[1]

Solomon E. Asch

We shall here describe in summary form the conception and first findings of a program of investigation into the conditions of independence and submission to group pressure.[2]

Our immediate object was to study the social and personal conditions that induce individuals to resist or to yield to group pressures when the latter are perceived to be *contrary to fact*. . . .

The problem under investigation requires the direct observation of certain basic processes in the interaction between individuals, and between individuals and groups. . . .

[1]From Solomon E. Asch, "Effects of Group Pressure upon the Modification and Distortion of Judgments," *Readings in Social Psychology*, Theodore M. Newcomb and Eugene Hartley, eds., New York: Holt, Rinehart and Winston, 1958, pp. 174–183; prepared by the author from data previously reported in an article by the same title in *Groups, Leadership and Men*, Harold Guetzkow, ed., Pittsburgh: Carnegie Press, 1951. Some portions reprinted by permission of Carnegie-Mellon University.

[2]The earlier experiments out of which the present work developed and the theoretical issues which prompted it are discussed in S. E. Asch, *Social Psychology*, Englewood Cliffs, N. J.: Prentice-Hall, Inc., 1952, Chap. 16.

A full account of the procedures and data on which the present report is based will be published shortly.

Basic to the current approach has been the axiom that group pressures characteristically induce psychological changes *arbitrarily*, in far-reaching disregard of the material properties of the given conditions. This mode of thinking has almost exclusively stressed the slavish submission of individuals to group forces, has neglected to inquire into their possibilities for independence and for productive relations with the human environment, and has virtually denied the capacity of men under certain conditions to rise above group passion and prejudice. It was our aim to contribute to a clarification of these questions, important both for theory and for their human implications, by means of direct observation of the effects of groups upon the decisions and evaluations of individuals.

THE EXPERIMENT AND FIRST RESULTS To this end we developed an experimental technique which has served as the basis for the present series of studies. We employed the procedure of placing an individual in a relation of radical conflict with all the other members of a group, of measuring its effect upon him in quantitative terms, and of describing its psychological consequences. A group of eight individuals was instructed to judge a series of simple, clearly structured perceptual relations—to match the length of a given line with one of three unequal lines. Each member of the group announced his judgments publicly. In the midst of this monotonous "test" one individual found himself suddenly contradicted by the entire group, and this contradiction was repeated again and again in the course of the experiment. The group in question had, with the exception of one member, previously met with the experimenter and received instructions to respond at certain points with wrong—and unanimous—judgments. The errors of the majority were large (ranging between $1/2''$ and $1 3/4''$) and of an order not encountered under control conditions. The outstanding person—the critical subject—whom we had placed in the position of a *minority of one* in the midst of a *unanimous majority*—was the object of investigation. He faced, possibly for the first time in his life, a situation in which a group unanimously contradicted the evidence of his senses.

This procedure was the starting point of the investigation and the point of departure for the study of further problems. Its main features were the following: (1) The critical subject was submitted to two contradictory and irreconcilable forces— the evidence of his own experience of a clearly perceived relation, and the unanimous evidence of a group of equals. (2) Both forces were part of the immediate situation; the majority was concretely present, surrounding the subject physically. (3) The critical subject, who was requested together with all others to state his judgments publicly, was obliged to declare himself and to take a definite stand *vis-à-vis* the group. (4) The situation possessed a self-contained character. The critical subject could not avoid or evade the dilemma by reference to conditions external to the experimental situation. (It may be mentioned at this point that the forces generated by the given conditions acted so quickly upon the critical subjects that instances of suspicion were infrequent.)

The technique employed permitted a simple quantitative measure of the "majority effect" in terms of the frequency of errors in the direction of the distorted estimates of the majority. At the same time we were concerned to obtain evidence of the ways in which the subjects perceived the group, to establish whether they became doubtful, whether they were tempted to join the majority. Most important, it was our object to establish the grounds of the subject's independence or yielding—whether, for example, the yielding subject was aware of the effect of the majority upon him, whether he abandoned his judgment deliberately or compulsively. To this end we constructed a comprehensive set of questions which served as the basis of an individual interview immediately following the experimental period. Toward the conclusion of the interview each subject was informed fully of the purpose of the experiment, of his role and of that of the majority. The reactions to the disclosure of the purpose of the experiment became in fact an integral part of the procedure. The information derived from the interview became an indispensable source of evidence and insight into the psychological structure of the experimental situation, and in particular, of the nature of the individual differences. . . .

Both the members of the majority and the critical subjects were male college students. We shall report the results for a total of fifty critical subjects in this experiment. . . .[O]n certain trials the majority responded correctly; these were the "neutral" trials. There were twelve critical trials on which the responses of the majority responded incorrectly.

The quantitative results are clear and unambiguous.

(1) There was a marked movement toward the majority. One third of all the estimates in the critical group were errors identical with or in the direction of the distorted estimates of the majority. The significance of this finding becomes clear in the light of the virtual absence of errors in the control group, the members of which recorded their estimates in writing. The relevant data of the critical and control groups are summarized in Table 1.

(2) At the same time the effect of the majority was far from complete. The preponderance of estimates in the critical group (68 percent) was correct despite the pressure of the majority.

(3) We found evidence of extreme individual differences. There were in the critical group subjects who remained independent without exception, and there were those who went nearly all the time with the majority. (The maximum possible number of errors was 12, while the actual range of errors was 0–11.) One fourth of the critical subjects was completely independent; at the other extreme, one third of the group displaced the estimates toward the majority in one half or more of the trials.

The differences between the critical subjects in their reactions to the given conditions were equally striking. There were subjects who remained completely confident throughout. At the other extreme were those who became disoriented, doubt-ridden, and experienced a powerful impulse not to appear different from the majority. . . .

TABLE 1 DISTRIBUTION OF ERRORS IN EXPERIMENTAL
AND CONTROL GROUPS

Number of Critical Errors	Critical Group* (N = 50)	Control Group (N = 37)
	F	F
0	13	35
1	4	1
2	5	1
3	6	
4	3	
5	4	
6	1	
7	2	
8	5	
9	3	
10	3	
11	1	
12	0	
Total	50	37
Mean	3.84	0.08

* All errors in the critical group were in the direction of the majority estimates.

A FIRST ANALYSIS OF INDIVIDUAL DIFFERENCES On the basis of the interview data described earlier, we undertook to differentiate and describe the major forms of reaction to the experimental situation, which we shall now briefly summarize.

Among the *independent* subjects we distinguished the following main categories:

(1) Independence based on *confidence* in one's perception and experience. The most striking characteristic of these subjects is the vigor with which they withstand the group opposition. Though they are sensitive to the group, and experience the conflict, they show a resilience in coping with it, which is expressed in their continuing reliance on their perception and the effectiveness with which they shake off the oppressive group opposition.

(2) Quite different are those subjects who are independent and *withdrawn*. These do not react in a spontaneously emotional way, but rather on the basis of explicit principles concerning the necessity of being an individual.

(3) A third group of independent subjects manifests considerable tension and doubt, but adhere to their judgment on the basis of a felt necessity to deal adequately with the task.

The following were the main categories of reaction among the *yielding* subjects, or those who went with the majority during one half or more of the trials.

(1) *Distortion of perception* under the stress of group pressure. In this category belong a very few subjects who yield completely, but are not aware that their estimates have been displaced or distorted by the majority. These subjects report that they came to perceive the majority estimates as correct.

(2) *Distortion of judgment.* Most submitting subjects belong to this category. The factor of greatest importance in this group is a decision the subjects reach that their perceptions are inaccurate, and that those of the majority are correct. These subjects suffer from primary doubt and lack of confidence; on this basis they feel a strong tendency to join the majority.

(3) *Distortion of action.* The subjects in this group do not suffer a modification of perception nor do they conclude that they are wrong. They yield because of an overmastering need not to appear different from or inferior to others, because of an inability to tolerate the appearance of defectiveness in the eyes of the group. These subjects suppress their observations and voice the majority position with awareness of what they are doing.

The results are sufficient to establish that independence and yielding are not psychologically homogeneous, that submission to group pressure and freedom from pressure can be the result of different psychological conditions. It should also be noted that the categories described above, being based exclusively on the subjects' reactions to the experimental conditions, are descriptive, not presuming to explain why a given individual responded in one way rather than another. The further exploration of the basis for the individual differences is a separate task.

EXPERIMENTAL VARIATIONS   The results described are clearly a joint function of two broadly different sets of conditions. They are determined first by the specific external conditions, by the particular character of the relation between social evidence and one's own experience. Second, the presence of pronounced individual differences points to the important role of personal factors, or factors connected with the individual's character structure. We reasoned that there are group conditions which would produce independence in all subjects, and that there probably are group conditions which would induce intensified yielding in many, though not in all. Secondly, we deemed it reasonable to assume that behavior under the experimental social pressure is significantly related to certain characteristics of the individual. The present account will be limited to the effect of the surrounding conditions upon independence and submission. To this end we followed the procedure of experimental variation, systematically altering the quality of social evidence by means of systematic variation of the group conditions and of the task.

The effect of nonunanimous majorities

Evidence obtained from the basic experiment suggested that the condition of being exposed *alone* to the opposition of a "compact majority" may have played a decisive role in determining the course and strength of the effects observed. Accordingly we undertook to investigate in a series of successive variations the effects of *nonunanimous* majorities. The technical problem of altering the uniformity of a majority is, in terms of our procedure, relatively simple. In most instances we merely directed one or more members of the instructed group to deviate from the majority in prescribed ways. It is obvious that we cannot hope to compare the performance of the same individual in two situations on the assumption that they remain independent of one another; at best we can investigate the effect of an earlier upon a later experimental condition. The comparison of different experimental situations therefore requires the use of different but comparable groups of critical subjects. This is the procedure we have followed. In the variations to be described we have maintained the conditions of the basic experiment (*e.g.,* the sex of the subjects, the size of the majority, the content of the task, and so on) save for the specific factor that was varied. The following were some of the variations studied:

THE PRESENCE OF A "TRUE PARTNER"   (*a*) In the midst of the majority were *two* naïve, critical subjects. The subjects were separated spatially, being seated in the fourth and eighth positions, respectively. Each therefore heard his judgments confirmed by one other person (provided the other person remain independent), one prior to, the other after announcing his own judgment. In addition, each experienced a break in the unanimity of the majority. There were six pairs of critical subjects. (*b*) In a further variation the "partner" to the critical subject was a member of the group who had been instructed to respond correctly throughout. This procedure permits the exact control of the partner's responses. The partner was always seated in the fourth position; he therefore announced his estimates in each case before the critical subject.

The results clearly demonstrate that a disturbance of the unanimity of the majority markedly increased the independence of the critical subjects. The frequency of promajority errors dropped to 10.4 percent of the total number of estimates in variation (*a*), and to 5.5 percent in variation (*b*). These results are to be compared with the frequency of yielding to the unanimous majorities in the basic experiment, which was 32 percent of the total number of estimates. It is clear that the presence in the field of *one other* individual who responded correctly was sufficient to deplete the power of the majority, and in some cases to destroy it. This finding is all the more sriking in the light of other variations which demonstrate the effect of even small minorities provided they are unanimous. Indeed, we have been able to show that a unanimous majority of 3 is, under the given conditions, far more effective than a majority of 8 containing 1 dissenter. That critical subjects will under these conditions free themselves of a majority of 7 and join forces with one other person in the minority is, we believe, a result significant for theory. It points to a fundamental psychological difference between the condition of being alone and having a minimum of human support. It further demonstrates that the effects obtained are not the result of a summation of influences proceeding from each member of the group; it is necessary to conceive the results as being relationally determined.

WITHDRAWAL OF A "TRUE PARTNER"   What will be the effect of providing the critical subject with a partner who responds correctly and then withdrawing him? The critical subject started with a partner who responded correctly. The partner was a member of the majority who had been instructed to respond correctly and to "desert" to the majority in the middle of the experiment. This procedure permits the observation of the same subject in the course of the transition from one condition to another. The withdrawal of the partner produced a powerful and unexpected result. We had assumed that the critical subject, having gone through the experience of opposing the majority with a minimum of support, would maintain his independence when alone. Contrary to this expectation, we found that the experience of having had and then lost a partner restored the majority effect to its full force, the proportion of errors rising to 28.5 percent of all judgments, in contrast to the preceding level of 5.5 percent. Further experimentation is needed to establish whether the critical subjects were responding to the sheer fact of being alone, or to the fact that the partner abandoned them.

LATE ARRIVAL OF A "TRUE PARTNER"   The critical subject started as a minority of 1 in the midst of a unanimous majority. Toward the conclusion of the experiment one member of the majority "broke" away and began announcing correct estimates. This procedure, which reverses the order of conditions of the preceding experiment, permits the observation of the transition from being alone to being a member of a pair against a majority. It is obvious that those critical subjects who were independent when alone would continue to be so when joined by a partner. The variation is therefore of significance primarily for those subjects who yielded during the first phase of the experiment. The appearance of the late partner exerts a freeing effect, reducing the level of yielding to 8.7 percent. Those who had previously yielded also became markedly more independent, but not completely so, continuing to yield more than previously independent subjects. The reports of the subjects do not cast much light on the factors responsible for the result. It is our impression that some subjects, having once committed themselves to yielding, find it difficult to change their direction completely. To do so is tantamount to a public admission that they had not acted rightly. They therefore follow to an extent the precarious course they had chosen in order to maintain an outward semblance of consistency and conviction.

THE PRESENCE OF A "COMPROMISE PARTNER"   The majority was consistently extremist, always matching the standard with the most unequal line. One instructed subject (who, as in the other variations, preceded the critical subject) also responded incorrectly, but his estimates were always intermediate between the truth and the majority position. The critical subject therefore faced an extremist majority whose unanimity was broken by one more moderately erring person. Under these conditions the frequency of errors was reduced but not significantly. However, the lack of unanimity determined in a strikingly consistent way the *direction* of the errors. The preponderance of the errors, 75.7 percent of the total, was moderate, whereas in a parallel experiment in which the majority was unanimously extremist (*i.e.*, with the "compromise" partner excluded), the incidence of moderate errors was 42 percent of the total. As might be expected, in a unanimously moderate majority, the errors of the critical subjects were without exception moderate.

The Role of Majority Size

To gain further understanding of the majority effect, we varied the size of the majority in several different variations. The majorities, which were in each case unanimous, consisted of 2, 3, 4, 8, and 10–15 persons, respectively. In addition, we studied the limiting case in which the critical subject was opposed by one instructed subject. Table 2 contains the mean and the range of errors under each condition.

With the opposition reduced to 1, the majority effect all but disappeared. When the opposition proceeded from a group of 2, it produced a measurable though small distortion, the errors being 12.8 percent of the total number of estimates. The effect appeared in full force with a majority of 3. Larger majorities did not produce effects greater than a majority of 3.

The effect of a majority is often silent, revealing little of its operation to the subject, and often hiding it from the experimenter. To examine the range of effects it is capable of inducing, decisive variations of conditions are necessary. An indication of one effect is furnished by the following variation in which the conditions of the basic experiment were simply reversed. Here the majority, consisting of a group of 16, was naïve; in the midst of it we placed a single individual who responded wrongly according to instructions. Under these conditions the members of

TABLE 2   ERRORS OF CRITICAL SUBJECTS WITH UNANIMOUS
MAJORITIES OF DIFFERENT SIZE

Size of Majority	Control	1	2	3	4	8	10–15
N	37	10	15	10	10	50	12
Mean number of errors	0.08	0.33	1.53	4.0	4.20	3.84	3.75
Range of errors	0–2	0–1	0–5	1–12	0–11	0–11	0–10

the naïve majority reacted to the lone dissenter with amusement. Contagious laughter spread through the group at the droll minority of 1. Of significance is the fact that the members lacked awareness that they drew their strength from the majority, and that their reactions would change radically if they faced the dissenter individually. These observations demonstrate the role of social support as a source of power and stability, in contrast to the preceding investigations which stressed the effects of social opposition. Both aspects must be explicitly considered in a unified formulation of the effects of group conditions on the formation and change of judgments.

The role of the stimulus-situation

It is obviously not possible to divorce the quality and course of the group forces which act upon the individual from the specific stimulus-conditions. Of necessity the structure of the situation molds the group forces and determines their direction as well as their strength. Indeed, this was the reason that we took pains in the investigations described above to center the issue between the individual and the group around an elementary matter of fact. And there can be no doubt that the resulting reactions were directly a function of the contradiction between the observed relations and the majority position. These general considerations are sufficient to establish the need to vary the stimulus-conditions and to observe their effect on the resulting group forces.

Accordingly we have studied the effect of increasing and decreasing the discrepancy between the correct relation and the position of the majority, going beyond the basic experiment which contained discrepancies of a relatively moderate order. Our technique permits the easy variation of this factor, since we can vary at will the deviation of the majority from the correct relation. At this point we can only summarize the trend of the results which is entirely clear. The degree of independence increases with the distance of the majority from correctness. However, even glaring discrepancies (of the order of 3–6″) did not produce independence in all. While independence increases with the magnitude of contradiction, a certain proportion of individuals continues to yield under extreme conditions.

We have also varied systematically the structural clarity of the task, employing judgments based on mental standards. In agreement with other investigators, we find that the majority effect grows stronger as the situation diminishes in clarity. Concurrently, however, the disturbance of the subjects and the conflict-quality of the situation decrease markedly. We consider it of significance that the majority achieves its most pronounced effect when it acts most painlessly.

SUMMARY   We have investigated the effects upon individuals of majority opinions when the latter were seen to be in a direction contrary to fact. By means of a simple technique we produced a radical divergence between a majority and a minority, and observed the ways in which individuals coped with the resulting difficulty. Despite the stress of the given conditions, a substantial proportion of individuals retained their independence throughout. At the same time a substantial minority yielded, modifying their judgments in accordance with the majority. Independence and yielding are a joint function of the following major factors: (1) The character of the stimulus situation. Variations in structural clarity have a decisive effect: with diminishing clarity of the stimulus-conditions the majority effect increases. (2) The character of the group forces. Individuals are highly sensitive to the structural qualities of group opposition. In particular, we demonstrated the great importance of the factor of unanimity. Also, the majority effect is a function of the size of group opposition. (3) The character of the individual. There were wide and, indeed, striking differences among individuals within the same experimental situation.

10.3 A STUDY OF NORMATIVE AND INFORMATIONAL SOCIAL INFLUENCES UPON INDIVIDUAL JUDGMENT[1]

Morton Deutsch and Harold B. Gerard

By now, many experimental studies (*e.g.*, Asch, 1951; Bovard, 1951; Sherif, 1935) have demonstrated that individual psychological processes are subject to social influences. Most investigators, however, have not distinguished among different kinds of social influences; rather, they have carelessly used the term "group" influence to characterize the impact of many different kinds of social factors. In fact, a review of the major experiments in this area—*e.g.*, those by Sherif (1935), Asch (1951), Bovard (1951)—would indicate that the subjects (*S*s) in these experiments as they made their judgments were *not* functioning as *members* of a group in any simple or obvious manner. The *S*, in the usual experiment in this area, made perceptual judgments in the physical presence of others after hearing their judgments. Typically, the *S* was *not* given experimental instructions which made him feel that he was a member of a group faced with a common task requiring cooperative effort for its most effective solution. If "group" influences were at work in the foregoing experiments, they were subtly and indirectly created rather than purposefully created by the experimenter.

[1]From Morton Deutsch and Harold B. Gerard, "A Study of Normative and Informational Social Influences Upon Individual Judgment," *Journal of Abnormal and Social Psychology*, 51, 1955, pp. 629–636. This research was conducted under a grant from the Office of Naval Research, Contract No. NONR 285(10).

HYPOTHESES The purpose of this paper is to consider two types of social influence, "normative" and "informational," which we believe were operative in the experiments mentioned above, and to report the results of an experiment bearing upon hypotheses that are particularly relevant to the former influence. We shall define a *normative social influence* as an influence to conform with the positive expectations[2] of another.[3] An *informational social influence* may be defined as an influence to accept information obtained from another as *evidence* about reality. Commonly these two types of influence are found together. However, it is possible to conform behaviorally with the expectations of others and say things which one disbelieves but which agree with the beliefs of others. Also, it is possible that one will accept an opponent's beliefs as evidence about reality even though one has no motivation to agree with him, per se.

Our hypotheses are particularly relevant to normative social influence upon individual judgement. We shall not elaborate the theoretical rationales for the hypotheses, since they are for the most part obvious and they follow from other theoretical writings (*e.g.*, Deutsch, 1949; Festinger, 1950).

HYPOTHESIS I   Normative social influence upon individual judgments will be greater among individuals forming a group than among an aggregation of individuals who do not compose a group.[4]

That is, even when susceptibility to informational social influence is equated, we would predict that the greater susceptibility to normative social influence among group members would be reflected in the greater group influence upon individual judgment. This is not to say that individuals, even when they are not group members, may not have some motivation to conform to the expectations of others—*e.g.*, so as to ingratiate themselves or so as to avoid ridicule.

HYPOTHESIS II   Normative social influence upon individual judgment will be reduced when the individual perceives that his judgment cannot be identified or,

---

[2]By positive expectations we mean to refer to those expectations whose fulfillment by another leads to or reinforces positive rather than negative feelings, and whose nonfulfillment leads to the opposite, to alienation rather than solidarity; conformity to negative expectations, on the other hand, leads to or reinforces negative rather than positive feelings.

[3]The term *another* is being used inclusively to refer to "another person," to a "group," or to one's "self." Thus, a normative social influence can result from the expectations of oneself, or of a group, or of another person.

[4]Generally one would also expect that group members would be more likely to take the judgments of other group members as trustworthy evidence for forming judgments about reality and, hence, they would be more susceptible to informational social influence than would nongroup members. The greater trustworthiness usually reflects more experience of the reliability of the judgments of other members and more confidence in the benevolence of their motivations. However, when group members have had no prior experience together and when it is apparent in both the group and nongroup situations that the others are motivated and in a position to report correct judgments, there is no reason to expect differential susceptibility to informational social influence among group and nongroup members.

more generally, when the individual perceives no pressure to conform directed at him from others.

HYPOTHESIS III   Normative social influence to conform to one's own judgment will reduce the impact of the normative social influence to conform to the judgment of others.

HYPOTHESIS IV   Normative social influence to conform to one's own judgment from another as well as from oneself will be stronger than normative social influence from oneself.

Normative social influence from oneself to conform to one's own judgment may be thought of as an internalized social process in which the individual holds expectations with regard to his own behavior; conforming to positive self-expectations leads to feelings of self-esteem or self-approval while nonconformity leads to feelings of anxiety or guilt. In general, one would expect that the strength of these internalized self-expectations would reflect the individual's prior experiences with them as sources of need satisfaction—*e.g.*, by conforming to his own judgments or by self-reliance he has won approval from such significant others as his parents. As Hypothesis IV indicates, we believe that contemporaneous social pressure to conform to one's own judgment may supplement, and perhaps be even stronger than, the individual's internalized pressure to conform to his own judgment. . . .

HYPOTHESIS V   The more uncertain the individual is about the correctness of his judgment, the more likely he is to be susceptible to both normative and informational social influences in making his judgment. . . .

METHOD

SUBJECTS   One hundred and one college students from psychology courses at New York University were employed as *S*s. The study was defined for the *S*s as an experimental study of perception.

PROCEDURE   We employed the experimental situation developed by Asch (1951) with certain modifications and variations which are specified below. For detailed description of the procedures utilized by Asch and replicated in this experiment, Asch's publication should be consulted. The basic features of the Asch situation are: (*a*) the *S*s are instructed that they are participating in a perceptual experiment, wherein they have to match accurately the length of a given line with one of three lines; (*b*) correct judgments are easy to make; (*c*) in each experimental session there is only one *naïve S*, the other participants, while ostensibly *S*s, are in fact "stooges" who carry out the experimenter's instructions; (*d*) each participant (*i.e.*, the naïve *S* and the stooges) has to indicate his judgments publicly; (*e*) on 12 of the 18 perceptual judgments the stooges announce wrong and unanimous judgments, the errors of the stooges are large and clearly in error; (*f*) the naïve *S* and the stooges are in a face-to-face relationship and have been previously acquainted with one another.[5]

---

[5]Inspection of the Asch situation would suggest that informational social influence would be strongly operative. As Asch has put it (1952, p. 461):

To test the hypotheses set forth in the foregoing section, the following experimental variations upon Asch's situation were employed:

1. THE FACE-TO-FACE SITUATION   This was an exact replication of Asch's situation except for the following minor modifications: (a) Only three stooges, rather than eight, were employed;[6] (b) the S and the stooges were unacquainted prior to the experiment; and (c) two series of 18 judgments were employed. In one series (the visual series), the lines were physically present when the S and the stooges announced their judgments; in the other series (the memory series), the lines were removed before any one announced his judgment. In the memory series, approximately three seconds after the lines were removed the first stooge was asked to announce his judgment. The sequences of visual and memory series were alternated so that approximately half the Ss had the memory series first and half had the visual series first.

2. THE ANONYMOUS SITUATION   This situation was identical with the face-to-face situation except for the following differences: (a) Instead of sitting in the visual presence of each other, the Ss were separated by partitions which prevented them from talking to each other or seeing one another; (b) Instead of announcing their judgments by voice, the Ss indicated their judgments by pressing a button; (c) No stooges were employed. Each S was led to believe he was Subject No. 3, and the others were No. 1, No. 2, and No. 4. He was told that when the experimenter called out "Subject No. 3" he was to indicate his judgment by pressing one of three buttons (A, B, or C) which corresponded to what he thought the correct line was. When an S pressed a given button, a corresponding bulb lit on his own panel and on a hidden master panel. Presumably the appropriate bulb also lit on the panels of each of the other Ss, but, in fact, the bulbs on any S's panel were not connected to the buttons of the other Ss. When the experimenter called for the judgments of Subject No. 1, of Subject No. 2, and of Subject No. 4, a concealed accomplice manipulated master switches which lit bulbs on each of the S's panels

---

The subject knows (a) that the issue is one of fact; (b) that a correct result is possible; (c) that only one result is correct; (d) that the others and he are oriented to and reporting about the same objectively given relations; (e) that the group is in unanimous opposition at certain points with him.

He further, perceives that the others are motivated to report a correct judgment. In such a situation, the subject's accumulated past experience would lead him to expect that he could rely on the judgments of others, especially if they all agreed. . . .This is a strong informational social influence and one would expect it to be overriding except for the fact that the subject. . .receives information from a source which he also feels to be completely trustworthy—*i.e.*, from his own perceptual apparatus. The subject is placed in strong conflict because the evidences from two sources of trustworthy information are in opposition.

In the Asch situation, it is apparent that, in addition to informational social influence, normative social influence is likely to be operating. The naïve S is in a face-to-face situation with acquaintances and he may be motivated to conform to their judgments in order to avoid being ridiculed, or being negatively evaluated, or even possibly out of a sense of obligation. . . .

[6]Asch found that three stooges were about as effective in influencing the Ss as eight.

that corresponded to judgments presumably being made by these respective Ss. Subjects No. 1, No. 2, and No. 4 were, in effect, "electrical stooges" whose judgments were indicated on the panels of the four naïve Ss (all of whom were Subject No. 3) by an accomplice of the experimenter who manipulated master switches controlling the lights on the panels of the naïve Ss. The pattern of judgments followed by the "electrical stooges" was the same as that followed by the "live stooges" in the face-to-face situation. (*d*) In providing rationale for being labeled Subject No. 3 for each of the naïve Ss, we explained that due to the complicated wiring setup, the S's number had no relation to his seating position. . . .

3. THE GROUP SITUATION   This situation was identical to the anonymous situation except that the subjects were instructed as follows:

This group is one of 20 similar groups who are participating in this experiment. We want to see how accurately you can make judgments. We are going to give a reward to the five best groups—the five groups that make the fewest errors on the series of judgments that you are given. The reward will be a pair of tickets to a Broadway play of your own choosing for each member of the winning group. An error will be counted any time one of you makes an incorrect judgment. That is, on any given card the group can make as many as four errors if you each judge incorrectly or you can make no errors if you each judge correctly. The five groups that make the best scores will be rewarded.

4. THE SELF-COMMITMENT VARIATION   This variation was employed in both the face-to-face and anonymous situations. In it, each S was given a sheet of paper on which to write down his judgment before he was exposed to the judgments of the others. He was told not to sign the sheet of paper and that it would not be collected at the end of the experiment. After the first series of 18 judgments, the Ss threw away their sheets. The Ss did not erase their recorded judgments after each trial as they did in the Magic Pad self-commitment variation.

4A. THE MAGIC PAD SELF-COMMITMENT VARIATION   This variation was employed in the anonymous situation. In it, each S was given a Magic Writing Pad on which to write down his judgment before he was exposed to the judgments of the others. After each S had been exposed to the judgment of the others and had indicated his own judgment, he erased his judgment on the Magic Writing Pad by lifting up the plastic covering. It was made convincingly clear to the S that only he would ever know what he had written down on the pad.

5. THE PUBLIC COMMITMENT VARIATION   This variation was employed in both the face-to-face situation and in the anonymous situation. In it, the Ss followed the same procedure as in the self-commitment variation except that they wrote down their initial judgments on sheets of paper which they signed and which they knew were to be handed to the experimenter after each series of 18 judgments.

RESULTS   The primary data used in the analysis of the results are the errors made by the Ss which were in the direction of the errors made by the stooges. . . .

HYPOTHESIS I   . . . The data provide strong support for the prediction that the normative social influence upon individual judgments will be greater among individuals forming a group than among individuals who do not compose a group. The average member of the group made more than twice as many errors as the comparable individual who did not participate in the task as a member of a group. . . .

HYPOTHESIS II   To test the second hypothesis, it is necessary to compare the data from the face-to-face and anonymous situations among the individuals who were otherwise exposed to similar experimental treatments. . . . It is apparent that there was less social influence upon individual judgment in the anonymous as compared with the face-to-face situation. . . . [T]he differences between the face-to-face and the anonymous situations are most strongly brought out when there is no commitment. Similarly, if we compare the anonymous and face-to-face situations, employing the memory rather than the visual series, the effect of the normative influence upon judgments in the face-to-face situation is increased somewhat, but not significantly. That is, as we eliminate counternormative influences (*i.e.,* the "commitment") and as we weaken reality restraints (*i.e.,* employ the "memory" rather than "visual" series), the normative influences in the face-to-face situation operate more freely. . . .

HYPOTHESES III AND IV   . . .The public and the self-commitment variations markedly reduce the socially influenced errors in both the face-to-face and anonymous situations. In other words, the data provide strong support for Hypothesis III which asserts that normative social influence to conform to one's own judgment will reduce the impact of the normative influence to conform to the judgment of others.

The data with regard to the influence of self-commitment are ambiguous in implication since the results of the two self-commitment variations—*i.e.,* the "Magic Pad self-commitment" and the "self-commitment"—are not the same. The first self-commitment variation produced results which are essentially the same as the public commitment variation, markedly reducing socially influenced errors. The Magic Pad self-commitment variation produced results which were different from the no commitment variation, reducing the errors to an extent which is statistically significant; however, unlike the first self-commitment variation, the Magic Pad self-commitment was significantly less effective than the public commitment in reducing socially influenced errors.

Our hunch is that the *S*s in the first self-commitment variation perceived the commitment situation as though it were a public commitment and that this is the explanation of the lack of differences between these two variations. That is, writing their judgments indelibly supported the belief that "others can see what I have written." The *S*s in the Magic Pad self-commitment variation, on the other hand, were literally wiping their initial judgments away in such a manner that they would be inaccessible to anyone. Hence, in the Magic Pad variation, the normative influences to conform to one's own judgment had to be sustained by the *S* himself. Normative influences from the *S*'s self (to be, in a sense, true to himself) were undoubtedly also operating in the noncommitment variation. What the Magic Pad did was to prevent the *S* from distorting his recollection of his independent judgment after being exposed to the judgments of the others. Further, there is a theoretical basis for assuming that the commitment to a judgment or decision is increased following the occurrence of behavior based upon it. Hence, the behavior of writing one's judgment down on the Magic Pad makes the original decision less tentative and less subject to change. However, it is apparent that this internally sustained influence to conform with one's own judgment was not as strong as the combination of external and self-motivated influences. These results support our fourth hypothesis.

HYPOTHESIS V . . .[T]he *S*s were less influenced by the judgments of others when the judgments were made on a visual rather than on a memory basis. It is also evident . . . that the differences between the visual and memory series were reduced or disappeared when the *S*s wrote down their initial, independent judgments. These results support our fifth hypothesis which asserts that the more uncertain the individual is about the correctness of his judgment, the more likely he is to be susceptible to social influences in making his judgment. . . .

Being exposed first to the memory series rather than the visual series had the effect of making the *S*s more susceptible to social influence upon their judgments throughout both series of judgments. In other words, an *S* was more likely to make socially influenced errors on the memory series and, having allowed himself to be influenced by the others on this first series of judgments, he was more likely to be influenced on the visual series than if he had not previously participated in the memory series. It is as though once having given in to the social influence (and it is easier to give in when one is less certain about one's judgment), the *S* is more susceptible to further social influences.

DISCUSSION   A central thesis of this experiment has been that prior experiments which have been concerned with "group" influence upon individual judgment have, in fact, only incidentally been concerned with the type of social influence most specifically associated with groups, namely "normative social influence." Our results indicate that, even when normative social influence in the direction of an incorrect judgment is largely removed (as in the anonymous situation), more errors are made by our *S*s than by a control group of *S*s making their judgments when alone.[7] It seems reasonable to conclude that the *S*, even if not normatively influenced, may be influenced by the others in the sense that the judgments of others are taken to be a more or less trustworthy source of information about the objective reality with which he and the others are confronted.

---

[7]Asch (1952) reports that his control group of *S*s made an average of considerably less than one error per *S*.

It is not surprising that the judgments of others (particularly when they are perceived to be motivated and competent to judge accurately) should be taken as evidence to be weighed in coming to one's own judgment. From birth on, we learn that the perceptions and judgments of others are frequently reliable sources of evidence about reality. Hence, it is to be expected that if the perceptions by two or more people of the same objective situation are discrepant, each will tend to re-examine his own view and that of the others to see if they can be reconciled. This process of mutual influence does not necessarily indicate the operation of normative social influence as distinct from informational social influence. Essentially the same process (except that the influence is likely to be unilateral) can go on in interaction with a measuring or computing machine. For example, suppose one were to judge which of two lines is longer (as in the Müller-Lyer illusion) and then were given information that a measuring instrument (which past experience had led one to believe was infallible) came up with a different answer; certainly one might be influenced by this information. This influence could hardly be called a normative influence except in the most indirect sense.

While the results of prior experiments of "group" influence upon perception can be largely explained in terms of nonnormative social influence, there is little doubt that normative influences were incidentally operative. However, these were the casual normative influences which can not be completely eliminated from any human situation, rather than normative influences deriving from specific group membership. Our experimental results indicate that when a group situation is created, even when the group situation is as trivial and artificial as it was in our groups, the normative social influences are grossly increased, producing considerably more errors in individual judgment.

The implications of the foregoing result are not particularly optimistic for those who place a high value on the ability of an individual to resist group pressures which run counter to his individual judgment. In the experimental situation we employed, the *S*, by allowing himself to be influenced by the others, in effect acquiesced in the distortion of his judgment and denied the authenticity of his own immediate experience. The strength of the normative social influences that were generated in the course of our experiment was small; had it been stronger, one would have expected even more distortion and submission.

Our findings, with regard to the commitment variations, do, however, suggest that normative social influences can be utilized to buttress as well as to undermine individual integrity. In other words, normative social influence can be exerted to help make an individual be an individual and not merely a mirror or puppet of the group. Groups can demand of their members that they have self-respect, that they value their own experience, that they be capable of acting without slavish regard for popularity. Unless groups encourage their members to express their own, independent judgments, group consensus is likely to be an empty achievement. Group process which rests on the distortion of individual experience undermines its own potential for creativity and productiveness.

SUMMARY AND CONCLUSIONS   Employing modifications of the Asch situation, an experiment was carried out to test hypotheses concerning the effects of normative and informational social influences upon individual judgment. The hypotheses received strong support from the experimental data.

In discussion of our results, the thesis was advanced that prior studies of "group" influence upon individual judgment were only incidentally studies of the type of social influence most specifically associated with groups—*i.e.*, of normative social influence. The role of normative social influence in buttressing as well as undermining individual experience was considered.

BIBLIOGRAPHY

ASCH, S. E., 1951, "Effects of Group Pressure upon the Modification and Distortion of Judgments," *Groups, Leadership and Men*, H. Guetzkow, ed., Pittsburgh: Carnegie Press, pp. 177–190.

ASCH, S. E., 1952, *Social Psychology*, Englewood Cliffs, N.J.: Prentice-Hall.

BOVARD, E. W., 1951, "Group Structure and Perception," *Journal of Abnormal and Social Psychology*, 46, pp. 398–405.

DEUTSCH, M., 1949, "A Theory of Cooperation and Competition," *Human Relations*, 2, pp. 129–152.

FESTINGER, L., 1950, "Informal Social Communication," *Psychological Review*, 57, pp. 271–282.

SHERIF, M., 1935, "A study of Some Social Factors in Perception," *Archives of Psychology*, 27, No. 187.

10.4 INTRODUCTION

The next selection focuses on the effects of belonging to a group for the attitudes of group members toward other individuals not in their group. The results of the author's imaginative experiment with adolescent boys demonstrate the significance of a group's goals for the attitudes and behavior of its members. Specifically, this study reveals, first, the effects of the relationship between the goals of two different groups (in this case whether achievement of the goals implies competition or cooperation between the groups) on the nature of the interaction among the groups' members. Secondly, the results show the effect that the content of intergroup interaction in turn has upon the attitudes of the interacting individuals toward each other. Thus this selection again emphasizes both the importance of group membership for individual attitudes and, more generally, the major role played by the structure of a social situation in shaping the reactions of individuals.

The relevance of findings about intergroup relations is so evident and general that it seems almost unnecessary to call attention to them. Thus they readily suggest applications to a variety of social issues—prejudice, race relations, labor-management conflicts, and even international relations. For the guidance-personnel worker concerned with children and youth in educational settings, which often involve attempting to get groups to work together, there are similarly extensive implications. Of particular significance is one of the major findings of this study, namely, the important role played by superordinate goals, shared by groups, in transforming conflict into cooperation. The importance of groups and of group membership was dealt with in earlier chapters in relation to such varied topics, among others, as the role of peer groups in development, the consequences of organizational membership for behavior, and the significance of social class and other subcultural groupings for individual values. The findings of the study reported here add further insight into these issues, showing the important effects of group membership on the manner in which individuals relate to the rest of their environment.

Even more specifically, it seems relevant to consider the relationships between such groups as students and faculty, or students and the administration, or faculty and the guidance staff, or children and adults generally, from the perspective provided by the ensuing selection. Do students and teachers, for example, perceive themselves as pursuing common or contrary goals? What are the implications for the educational process of the different types of interaction and interpersonal attitudes that these two forms of perception foster? What about faculty members and guidance counselors? Do they perceive their goals as competitive or cooperative? What are the consequences of these views for the pressures that each group exerts on students?

10.4   INTERGROUP CONFLICT AND COOPERATION[1]

Muzafer Sherif, et al.

APPROACH, HYPOTHESES, AND GENERAL DESIGN OF THE STUDY[2]   The focal concern of this study is intergroup relations. As an experiment in social psychology, it undertakes to trace over a time period the formation and functioning of negative and positive attitudes of members of one group toward another group and its members as a consequence of experimentally introduced situations. Therefore, the main hypotheses relate to attitudinal and

[1]From Muzafer Sherif, O.J. Harvey, B. Jack White, William R. Hood, and Carolyn W. Sherif, *Intergroup Conflict and Cooperation: the Robbers Cave Experiment*, Norman, Okla.: Institute of Group Relations, The University of Oklahoma, 1961, pp. 27–33, 151–153, 158–161, 164–167, 170–179, 182–183.
[2]This chapter is an outline of the study prepared and distributed prior to the experiment in mimeographed form to staff members of the study and a number of colleagues interested in this problem area

behavioral trends predicted as a result of controlled alterations of the conditions in which experimentally formed in-groups interact.

The general trend of findings from the sociology of small in-groups and their intergroup relations and relevent findings from the work of experimental psychologists led us to the experimental study of the problem of intergroup relations in successive stages. In the present undertaking (Summer, 1954) it will be carried out in three successive stages. The main features of these three successive stages are the following:

STAGE 1 Experimental production of in-groups with a hierarchical structure and set of norms (intragroup relations). In line with our 1949 and 1953 studies, this will be done, not through discussion methods or through lecture or exhortation by resource persons or experts, but through *the introduction of goals which arise as integral parts in the situations, which have common appeal value, and which necessitate facing a common problem, discussion, planning and execution in a mutually cooperative way.*

STAGE 2 Bringing the two experimentally formed groups into functional relations in situations in which the groups find themselves in competition for given goals and in conditions which imply some frustration in relation to one another (*intergroup tension*).

STAGE 3 Introduction of goals which cannot be easily ignored by members of the two antagonistic groups, but the attainment of which is beyond the resources and efforts of one group alone. Such goals will be referred to as *superordinate goals* throughout this report. Superordinate goals are to be introduced with the aim of studying the reduction of intergroup tension in order to derive realistic leads for the integration of hostile groups. Considerations which led to the selection of this approach rather than other possible alternatives (such as a common enemy, leadership technique, or discussion techniques) are stated briefly in the discussion of Stage 3 [on page 542ff]. . . .[3]

It should be emphasized at the outset that individuals brought into an experimental situation to function as small groups are already members of actual groups in their social settings and thus have internalized values or norms (*i.e.*, attitudes) which are necessarily brought to the situation. With this consideration in mind and in order to give greater weight to experimentally introduced factors in the situation, a special effort will be made in this study not to appeal to internalized values or to prestige symbols coming from the larger setting in the formation and change of positive or negative attitudes in relation to respective in-groups and out-groups.

---

throughout the country. Since this paper gave the high points of the theoretical rationale and the blueprint to guide the actual experiment, it is presented here in substantially the same form, including the use of the future tense in referring to various procedures.

[3] [In the excerpts selected for the present volume, the detailed discussions of Stage 1 and Stage 2 will be deleted as less important to the purpose of this book than Stage 3. Eds.]

Background of the above summary

The rationale that underlies the above formulation of our approach to the study of intergroup relations stems from relevant findings in both sociology and psychology. . . .

Empirical observations by social scientists and inferences made by psychologists without direct experimental verification present a rather confusing picture at the present time. Therefore it is necessary to state precisely the sense in which the concept "group" and the issue of relations between them (intergroup relations) are used here:

A group may be defined as a social unit (1) which consists of a number of individuals who, at a given time, stand in more or less definite interdependent status and role relationships to one another and (2) which explicitly or implicitly possesses a set of values or norms of its own regulating the behavior of individual members, at least in matters of consequence to the group.

In order that this definition not be unwieldy, common attitudes, common aspirations, and goals are omitted. Such shared attitudes, aspirations, and goals are related to and, in fact, are implicit in the concept of common values or norms of a group. From the point of view of the members within the group, these social units may be referred to as *in-groups*. Again from the point of view of a member within the group, those social units of which he is not a part psychologically or to which he does not relate himself may be referred to as *out-groups*. It follows that the term *intergroup relations* refers to the relations between two or more in-groups and their respective members. Whenever individuals belonging to one in-group interact, collectively or individually, with another group or its members in terms of their group identification, we have an instance of intergroup relations.

From a survey of empirical literature it can be stated that intergroup attitudes and behavior regulated by them are produced in the form of social distances and standardized stereotypes as a consequence of functional relations between in-groups. Once these intergroup attitudes and stereotypes are standardized they take their place in the cultural repertory of the group and in many cases, through the vehicle of language, outlast the very functional relations which were responsible for their rise.

These functional relations between groups and their consequences, rather than the study of the deviate individual, constitute the central problem of intergroup relations. Of course, this does not imply a denial of various unique influences in the life history of the individual member (such as personal frustrations, special hardships in the family or other situations). Such personal influences in the life history may have a great deal to do with the individual becoming a nonconformist or deviate in terms of the prevailing scales of attitudes of his group. But such unique or personal influences *do not determine the scale themselves*. Rather they come in an important way to determine the particular place the individual will occupy within these scales or, in the case of nonconformists or deviates, the acceptance of a position outside of the scale. . . .

[T]he conception of the present study differs markedly from existing theories which posit one factor or a few factors as sole or primary determinants of the course of intergroup relations. (1) Inherent superiority or inferiority of human groups, (2) national character ("warlike people," "peaceful people"), (3) deep-seated innate instincts of aggression or destruction, (4) frustrations suffered individually, (5) direct economic gain, (6) the character of leadership—are variously advanced as sole or primary determinants of intergroup relations. Each of these theories still has its strong supporters. . . .

One primary point of departure in our approach. . .is the principle that various factors are functionally interrelated. In this respect the present approach is opposed to theories which make this or that factor sovereign in its own right; it attempts rather to ascertain the relative weights of all the possible factors that may be operative at the time.

The functional relatedness of various factors leads us to the cardinal psychological principle of our whole plan of study:

In the study of (intra- and inter-) group relations the relative contribution of given external stimulus factors and internal factors pertaining to participating individuals (hunger, sex, status desire, complexes, etc.) have to be analyzed within the framework of the on-going interaction process among the members in question.

The relative contribution of an external stimulus factor, or an attitude, a drive, or other internal factors, cannot be simply extrapolated from individual situations to interaction situations. Interaction processes are not voids. Whatever drives, motives, or attitudes the individual brings into the situation operate as deflected, modified, and, at times, transformed in the interaction process among the several individuals (who stand or come to stand in time in definite role relations toward one another).

The application of this cardinal principle to the study of group relations is derived from more basic findings in the field of judgment and perception. The judgment of a given weight is not determined solely by its absolute value, but also, within limits, by its relative position in the scale of which it is a part and by the presence or absence of other functionally related anchoring stimuli with values within and without the scale. Likewise placement of attitudinal items on a scale with categories specified by the experimenter or with categories chosen by the subject is determined not only by whatever intrinsic value these items may have when considered singly, but also by their relation to one another and their relation to the stand that the individual has taken on the issue.

Following the implications of this general psychological principle, it may be plausible to state that behavior revealing discriminations, perceptions, evaluations of individuals participating in the interaction process as group members will be determined *not* only by whatever motivational components and personality characteristics each member brings with him, *not* only by the properties of stimulus conditions specified in an unrelated way, but as influenced, modified, and even *transformed* interdependently by these and the special properties of the interaction process, in which a developing or established *state of reciprocities* (roles, statuses) plays no small part. The developing state of reciprocities between individual members can be measured in various differentiated dimensions (*e.g.*, status, popularity, initiative, etc.).

In short, one cannot directly extrapolate from the knowledge of stimulus conditions alone, or motivational components of participating individuals alone, but one has to study behavior in the framework of the actual interaction process with its developing reciprocities.

Carrying this line of conceptualization to the area of intergroup relations, one should start with the recognition that *the area of interaction between groups* cannot be directly extrapolated from the nature of relations within groups or prevailing practices within them, even though a careful analysis of intragroup relations is an essential prerequisite in any approach to intergroup relations. Numerous instances of intergroup relations in which the pattern (positive or negative) is different from the pattern prevailing within the respective in-groups might be mentioned.

The interaction process between groups and its consequences have to be studied in their own right in addition to studying relations prevailing within the in-groups in question. . . .

INTERGROUP RELATIONS: REDUCING FRICTION

(STAGE 3)

Approach to reducing friction

At this stage of the experiment, the main objective of our study could be undertaken, namely the reduction of intergroup friction. There are now two distinct groups in an unmistakable state of friction with one another. The groups exhibited in word and deed repeated hostility toward one another; they standardized unflattering attitudes and stereotypes toward one another.

The derogatory attitudes toward one another are not the consequence of pre-existing feelings or attitudes which the subjects had when they came to the experimental site. They are not the consequence of ethnic, religious, educational, or other background differentiation among the subjects. Nor are they the result of any extraordinary personal frustration in the particular life histories of the subjects, or of marked differentiation in physical, intellectual, or other psychological abilities or characteristics of the subjects. Possible effects of such differences were carefully ruled out in the laborious procedures used in subject selection. . . .

The state of friction was produced systematically through the introduction of conditions of rivalry and frustration perceived by the subjects as stemming from the other group. By the end of Stage 2, . . .the intergroup friction was crystallized in some unfavorable stereotypes and in the repeatedly expressed desire to have nothing more to do with the other group. To be sure, the words and deeds of hostility, the unflattering stereotypes towards the out-group, the self-righteousness of the in-group were not expressed with the same determination, the same vehemence, the same degree of feeling by any two group members. But, whatever the differentiating degree or intensity in the unique personal manifestation of hostility, the general trend of negative attitude toward the out-group was a common property of all group members. The intergroup hostility was prevalent despite the occurrence of occasional interpersonal rivalry, bickering and friction in the relations within each group. Two boys who engaged in some interpersonal exchange of unfavorable reactions toward one another, at a given time, would join hands a few minutes later in a concerted, common front in carrying out the developing intergroup trend in relation to the out-group. It should also be remembered that the in-group identification and solidarity in in-group and intergroup relations exhibited by in-group members did not stem from pre-existing interpersonal ties. The boys were not even personally acquainted with one another prior to the study. The two in-groups themselves were experimentally produced from scratch. . . .

It would have been a relatively easy task to bring about positive relations or harmony between groups right after the formation of the two in-groups. We deliberately postponed this positive step in intergroup relations until after the unpleasant task of producing a state of friction, because the vital issue of intergroup relations in the present-day world is the reduction of existing intergroup friction. . . .

[T]he alternative of appeal to a common enemy, which was effectively used in our 1949 study because of expediency at the time, was not used. The unification of groups against a "common enemy" necessarily implies widening the area of conflict.

The alternative of reducing tension by disintegrating the groups as units through devices which make individual "shining" and rivalry supreme without concern for the other fellow was rejected. By following such an approach, we would be destroying the property of intergroup relations which makes its study so crucial today, namely, the relations between group units.

Likewise, the alternative which emphasizes exclusively the role of leaders in change misses the mark, because the effectiveness of leaders, even though weighty, is not unlimited. Leaders are not immune to influences coming from the rank-and-file, once a group trend starts rolling, even though initially the leaders might have been largely responsible for starting the trend.

With such considerations in mind we chose the alternative of introducing common, superordinate goals of sufficient appeal value. But before doing this, we studied the possible effect of mere intergroup *contact* situations as *equals*, because there are adherents of this approach both in academic and practitioner circles.

At this point a word of clarification concerning the concept "contact" will be helpful. The word "contact" has flexible denotations which allow it to become a blanket term. It could be used to refer to any kind of interpersonal or intergroup interaction which is within the actual perceptual range. In customary usage, the word "contact" in intergroup relations refers to having individuals from different social, ethnic, or national backgrounds come together on some specific occasion, such as a tea party, lecture, dinner, or dancing party. We are using the term "contact" in this customary sense and reserving the concept "interaction" for broader generic reference. . . .

Intergroup relations: contacts introduced to reduce friction

The first part of Stage 3 was devoted to a series of contact situations varying in duration from about 15 minutes to an hour or so, and differing in the character, such as (a) participating together in a psychological experiment with opportunity to interact before and after the experiment, (b) attending a movie together, (c) having meals together in the same mess hall with utmost freedom to choose seats and interact with anyone in any way desired.

Essentially the same general procedure was followed in each of the contact situations. The two groups were taken to the place of contact (for example, the recreation hall or mess hall), both groups arriving at the same time or one shortly after the other, and then they were left to their own devices. Once the groups were in the contact situation, the staff walked away from the immediate contact range and pretended to be engaged in some activity, such as sitting under a tree in conversation. In no contact situations did the Eagle and Rattler staff members associate with one another during the period while the contact situations were being initiated and carried out. . . .

The intergroup events accompanying and following the series of contact situations. . .confirm the following hypothesis:

It is predicted that contact in itself will not produce marked decrease in the existing state of tension between groups.

Accordingly, it was decided to start introducing interaction situations involving common superordinate goals, instead of situations involving mere contact. In spite of the fact that the activity engaged in during contacts (such as eating, shooting fire-crackers) was gratifying or pleasing for each individual member within the in-group bounds, the mere fact of contact had no positive effect toward reducing existing hostility.

Intergroup interaction involving superordinate goals

Thus, contacts which did not involve superordinate goals, in the sense defined at the outset, were far from effective in reducing intergroup friction. If anything such contacts served as occasions for further irritation and for expressing unflattering attitudes of group against group.

At this point we turned to procedures suitable for testing the main hypothesis concerning the reduction of intergroup conflict:

When groups in a state of friction are brought into contact under conditions embodying superordinate goals, the attainment of which is compelling but which cannot be achieved by the efforts of one group alone, they will tend to cooperate toward the common goal.

Superordinate goals and interaction episodes related to them

THE DRINKING-WATER PROBLEM   The first superordinate goal to be introduced pertained to drinking-water at a time when both groups faced the prospect of thirst and became progressively thirstier with the successive steps of activities directed toward solution of the problem. In general outline, the plan consisted of having members of both groups perceive common deprivation which could be alleviated (so it appeared to them) by the cooperation of members of both groups. Thus a situation of functional interdependence involving a common goal was produced. . . .

It cannot be said that the negative attitudes toward the out-groups, the standardized unfavorable stereotypes were disappearing as a consequence of the introduction of this single superordinate goal of high appeal value, even though there was cooperation and friendly mingling at the time of the activities related to it. The carryover effects of the negative intergroup attitudes were observed at supper that very evening, and on subsequent occasions as well. . . .

THE PROBLEM OF SECURING A MOVIE   The next superordinate goal to be introduced was a feature-length movie which has been a favorite for boys of this age level. Two films had been chosen after consulting experts on films and brought to camp along with other stimulus materials. The plan was to ascertain the appeal value of the film for the boys and then to make securing it (supposedly from the neighboring town) dependent on both groups contributing a sum of money which would appear rather prohibitive for one group to contribute alone.

In the afternoon, the boys were called together and the staff suggested the possibility of securing either "Treasure Island" or "Kidnapped." Both groups yelled approval of these films. After some discussion, one Rattler said, "Everyone that wants 'Treasure Island' raise their hands." The majority of members in both groups gave enthusiastic approval to "Treasure Island" even though a few dissensions were expressed to this choice.

Then the staff announced that securing the film would cost $15 and the camp could not pay the whole sum. Members of both groups began to make all kinds of suggestions. . . .[T]here was heated discussion in both groups concerning who would do the figuring for each group to find out how much each member of the respective groups would have to pay. While the groups were figuring this out, there was a great deal of horseplay and intermixing of the groups.

At last, each group came up with its solution. The Rattlers figured that each of the 11 Rattlers would have to contribute 31 cents. Each of the 9 Eagles would have to contribute 39 cents toward securing the common goal. The Rattlers asked their staff members to contribute so that their total would come to $3.50. McGraw and Myers (E's) told the Eagle staff members that they would have to pay too, and gave the reason that the staff would get to see the movie too. Both staff members agreed to do so. Martin read the list of contributions from the Rattlers, and McGraw those of the Eagles.

It is worth noting that in individual terms this scheme of contribution was not equitable. But it was an equitable solution between the two groups. The cooperation needed to secure the movie was cooperation *between groups*, and it was perceived as such by individual members. Therefore, the solution was seen as an equitable one by individual members of both groups.

At supper there were no objections to eating together. Some scuffling and play at sticking chewing gum around occurred between members of the two groups, but it involved fewer boys on both sides than were usually involved in such encounters. . . .

After supper, "Treasure Island" was shown in the mess hall. Five rows of benches were placed in the hall with an aisle in between. Both groups were waiting to enter, and were told to come in. There was some confusion momentarily as to where to sit. When the milling about stopped, the seating arrangement was pretty much along group lines with a few exceptions. The boys were absorbed in the film, and there was very little conversation. . . .

[A] serious concern arose for further planning of superordinate goals. It became evident that in a camp situation like this one, isolated from a city or town and from outside influences, the facilities for daily activities were by this time acquiring decidedly routine aspects. Since the subjects had come to know the facilities afforded by the camp and in the general surroundings, it became increasingly difficult to introduce superordinate goals that would arouse high motivational appeal but were also inherent in the situations. Therefore, an attempt was made during the day to secure additional transportation facilities to take both groups to Cedar Lake, which is 60 miles southeast of the camp and affords complete detachment from the accustomed camp facilities in many respects. . . .

On arrival at Cedar Lake each group was taken first to a level place over the concrete dock by the lake. The swimming place was about one-fifth of a mile from the main camping area and separated from it by a little valley and trees so that it was not visible. When the Rattlers arrived the Eagles were already in the water. The Rattlers went in the water also. There was about a half-hour overlap when both groups were in the water together. There was some intermingling between groups, but most conversation was directed to fellow group members. . . .

TUG-OF-WAR AGAINST THE TRUCK   The staff member who drove the truck announced, so that everyone could hear, that he would go down the road a piece to get the food. Both groups (about 15 yards apart now) watched with interest as the driver got into the truck. The driver struggled and perspired, the truck made all sorts of noises, but it just would not start (as planned). The boys became more and more interested. Several Rattlers suggested, "Let's push it," but they abandoned the idea because the truck was parked facing uphill. The tug-of-war rope was in plain sight of both groups. Mills (R) said, "Let's get 'our' tug-of-war rope and have a tug-of-war against the truck." Someone said, "Yeah, we can't push it." Swift (R) said, "20 of us can." Several boys agreed loudly with this, Mills adding, "20 of us can pull it for sure." The idea of having a tug-of-war against the truck was repeated by several boys in both groups. . . .

The line-up pulling on the two ends of the rope was Eagles on one side and Rattlers on the other, with the exception that Swift (big R) joined the Eagle side as anchor-man and Craig (E) was next to Brown (R), the anchor-man on the Rattler side.

The first pull did not "start" the truck, and it was allowed to roll back down the hill for another pull. (The truck was, of course in running order, but the performance was completely convincing.) On the second pull, the members of both groups were thoroughly intermixed on both ropes. Some members of both groups began chanting "Heave, heave" in rhythm, something the Eagles had started during the tug-of-wars in Stage 2. Finally, the truck started, and the boys all jumped and cheered. Allen (R) shouted: "We won the tug-of-war against the truck!" Bryan (E) repeated, "Yeah! We won the tug-of-war against the truck." This cry was echoed with satisfaction by others from both groups.

Immediately following this success, there was much intermingling of groups, friendly talk, and backslapping. Four boys went to the pump and pumped water for each other: Mills (R), Hill (R), Craig (E), and Bryan (E). Thus the successful, interdependent efforts of both groups in pulling the truck, which was to get their food, had an immediate effect similar to that of superordinate goals introduced on previous days at the camp—intermingling of members of the two groups and friendly interaction between them.

SEPARATE VERSUS INTEGRATED MEAL PREPARATION   The driver went to get the food in the truck. While waiting for it to arrive, the participant observer of each group brought up the problem of whether his group wanted to alternate preparing meals with the other group or prepare them separately for themselves. In the Rattler group, Mills (leader) suggested that the Rattlers prepare one meal that day and the Eagles the other. This was discussed at some length and agreed upon by the Rattlers. There were no derisive comments about the Eagles during this discussion, and no objections made to eating with them, although prior to the trip, several Rattlers had objected to the idea of coming to the same place the Eagles were.

The discussion on this topic in the Eagle group took a different turn: At the outset, Craig and McGraw objected to an alternating arrangement in preparing meals, saying they wanted to cook for themselves. Low status Eagles (Clark, Cutler, Lane) were in favor of alternating with the Rattlers. After some discussion the decision was crystallized by Mason (E leader) who stated his opposition to alternating food preparation, and other high status members supported his position, one after another.

These discussions and the decisions reached are particularly enlightening in view of what actually took place immediately thereafter. The lunch materials had been selected so that if the groups decided to eat separately, they would have to divide the ingredients before doing so. For example, the main item was an 8 pound can of uncut luncheon meat. These situational factors, including the location of the food, took the upper hand in determining how the meal would be prepared. Here curtailment of effort involved in division of the supplies became dominant.

When the truck arrived with the food, both groups rushed from their respective camp areas and started carrying the food to the centrally located picnic table. At the table, they gathered around discussing across group lines whether they would alternate in meal preparation, the Rattlers favoring it and the Eagles opposing it. But in the midst of this discussion, food preparation *together* actually began. . . .

The first Eagles through the line went to a centrally located picnic shed nearby and sat down at the tables. The first five or six Rattlers went to tables near their own camp area. Allen (R) asked a staff member where he should sit, and was told to sit any place he wanted. He then went to the shed and sat down with the Eagles. Neither at this time nor later was he criticized for his action. After eating, Mills (R) and Barton (R) also drifted over to the Eagle table for a short time. Shortly both groups went to their respective camp areas for a rest period.

After separate rests, the two groups were taken to swim, one shortly after the other. This time the Rattlers were in first, but got out of the water on seeing a water moccasin darting about. When the Eagles arrived, the Rattlers told them in excited tones of a snake moving around in the vicinity, describing it in detail. For about 15 minutes, all of the boys stood together at the pier and discussed this common threat coming from nature. Then they swam together at another spot for a short period, both groups mixing together in the water. . . .

THE TRUCK STALLS AGAIN   Before supper, the truck going to get food stalled again, as planned. This time, discussion was practically unnecessary. The pattern for cooperation was established. The first effort, initiated by Rattlers, was to push the truck. . . .When the truck rolled into a hanging tree limb, Mills (R) got the tug-of-war rope again. The rope was pulled through the bumper, and two bunches of boys lined up to pull. However, these two lines on each side were not the Eagle and Rattler groups. Members of both groups were thoroughly mixed together in the pulling, which was accompanied by concerted rhythmic chants of "Heave, heave."

Again there was pride in the joint accomplishment. Thus the same tool which had served first in a competitive situation during group conflict, and which was later used by one group in their efforts to fell a tree, now became the standard means for interdependent efforts by both groups toward a common, superordinate goal (starting the truck which brought food for all). . . .

THE TRIP TO THE BORDER   The following morning (Day 6, Stage 3), the Rattlers awoke first and started talking about the trip to Arkansas, exchanging notes on the states they had visited. The Rattlers' attention was concentrated on the Eagle camp. Martin (R) asked if the Eagles were going to Arkansas too. When the counselor answered affirmatively, there was no objection or comment. Simpson, Newman, Harrison, and Allen (all R's) went to the Eagle camp to see the lizards Mason (E) had caught and frogs that Cutler (E) and Clark (E) had collected. The Rattlers were anxious to start on the trip to Arkansas before breakfast, and they kept getting in and out of their truck, which they had loaded even before breakfast. A short time later both groups were asked to come to a central location for an announcement.

It was announced that, as they well knew from experiences of the previous day, the older truck was not in good shape for the trip to Arkansas and back to the camp. (The truck referred to happened to be the Eagle truck. Of course it was in running condition. But it had been demonstrated to be liable to break down on the previous day as a part of the plans for producing problem situations embodying superordinate goals. This build-up of a poor reputation for the truck was also appropriate for the introduction of the problem situation now being described.) It was added that in view of the condition of the truck, it might be preferable to give up the idea of going to Arkansas, since there was only one truck. General disappointment was voiced, especially by the Eagles.

McGraw (E) suggested that the Rattlers go to Arkansas first, and then that the Eagles would go in the Rattler truck when they returned. But Craig (E) objected that the Eagles didn't want to wait around all morning; and when Mason (erstwhile E leader) started chanting "Let's go home, let's go home. . ." (meaning camp), Craig joined him.

At one point, Clark (E) said, "We could all go together" but Simpson (R) said, "No"—that the Rattlers would go to Arkansas and the Eagles could go back to the camp. This discussion illustrates well the state of flux which prevailed at this time in intergroup affairs. At times, as at supper the previous evening, the group lines seemed to disappear; at others the group demarcations would reappear. Whether or not group lines would be followed was coming to depend more and more on factors in the immediate situation (*situational factors*).

In this instance, the problem at hand was discussed for a short time. Then Mills (R leader) proposed that they all go in the Rattler truck: "We can move some of the mattresses into the other truck, and then we can all get in our truck." Allen (low status R) repeated this suggestion and several Eagles expressed approval. Simpson (R) agreed that would be possible, but added, "Let's don't."

Mills (R) now moved out of his group and paced up and down between the groups, explaining his ideas to both of them. When staff asked what they were going to do, there was a general hubbub which was resolved when Mills (R) and Clark (E) said "Let's go!" and headed for the Rattler truck. All the other boys, both Rattlers and Eagles, ran after them, piled in the truck, and yelled out to staff to "Hurry up!," "Let's go!" This is another striking instance of action taking precedence over verbal discussion, although the latter played an important part even in this decision. . . .

During the entire trip from Cedar Lake into Arkansas and back across the line into Oklahoma, there were very few signs of group demarcations or identifications. However, when the truck arrived at camp and the Eagles were dropped off at their cabin, the Rattlers started yelling "Goodbye, Eagles," and the Eagles reciprocated.

THE LAST EVENING IN CAMP   In order to check the influence of situational factors at this rather fluid state of intergroup relations, the staff rearranged the camp dining room while the two groups were at their cabins cleaning up from the trip. Four tables smaller than the usual mess hall tables were brought from various parts of the camp. They were square and could conveniently seat eight people, two to a side. This change was made so that the habitual spacing and size of tables in the mess hall situation would be entirely different. The influence of situational factors has been noted previously. It was thought that if the mess hall situation were different than it had been previously, the present state of relationship between the two groups would be revealed more clearly through a new seating arrangement.

The wisdom of this plan was confirmed even outside of the mess hall. There the two groups formed two lines, just as they had done prior to the Cedar Lake campout, even though they had been mixing up at meals as well as in other situations during the past 24 hours. The groups began discussing who would go in first, the trip away from camp having upset their "taking turns" arrangement. There was discussion on both sides as to whose "turn" it was. When Simpson (R) finally said, "O.K., let them go ahead," the Eagles entered the mess hall first without further objections by the Rattlers.

Once inside the two groups went through the line to get their food separately, but there was friendly conversation between members of the two groups. The reactions to the new table arrangement were as anticipated. In spite of the fact that the groups had lined up separately in habitual fashion to get food, the seating at the newly arranged tables cut across the in-group demarcations. The two tables in the middle were occupied by Eagles and Rattlers, sitting together. The few Rattlers left over occupied one or the other of the two end tables. . . .

THE TRIP HOME   The majority of subjects had agreed by the last day that it would be a good thing to return to Oklahoma City all together on one bus. When they asked if this might be done and received an affirmative answer from the staff, some of them actually cheered. When the bus pulled out, the seating arrangement did not follow group lines. . . .

Summary of observations in Stage 3

On the basis of the above observations reported by participant observers and independent observations by other staff members, it can be concluded that:

When groups in a state of friction are brought into contact under conditions embodying superordinate goals the attainment of which is compelling but which cannot be achieved by the efforts of one group alone, they cooperate toward the common goal.

On the basis of the above observational data it can also be concluded that:

Cooperation between groups necessitated by a series of situations embodying superordinate goals will have a cumulative effect in the direction of reduction of existing tensions between groups.

10.5 INTRODUCTION

In the final selection of this chapter, Theodore Newcomb expands upon, and at the same time ties together, some of the phenomena discussed in the preceding selections. His hypotheses and supporting findings about the relationship between interpersonal similarity and interpersonal attraction are relevant to understanding the tendency toward agreement among members of the same group (as in the Asch and the Deutsch and Gerard experiments) and the effects of compatibility or opposition between goals on individuals' attitudes toward each other (as in the Sherif, *et al.*, study). As Newcomb states, most of his findings are not surprising and they coincide with many common-sense ideas about interpersonal relations. The special value of his formulation lies in the fact that it integrates seemingly diverse notions and successfully predicts certain facts that might be thought of as contrary to common sense—such as the finding that individuals are attracted to those who accurately perceive their faults as well as to those who recognize their strengths.

There are many implications for education and guidance inherent in the basic phenomena explored in this selection. For example, they would seem to imply quite directly that good interpersonal relations between students and teachers will increase the extent to which students internalize intellectual values and become motivated academically. More generally, Newcomb's findings tend to negate the validity of viewing the transmission of intellectual content as independent of the social interaction within and outside of the classroom, and they suggest that interaction among students, as well as between students and faculty, will be a significant determinant of students' academic orientations. Friends will tend to reinforce each other's attitudes toward, among other things, learning and education, and it is obvious that this process may operate in either a positive *or* a negative direction. This points once again to the importance of peer groups, and specifically of the *content* of their norms, for individual growth and change. It suggests, for example, that if educational goals were salient in informal peer situations, such as in extracurricular activities, then commitment to such goals would be extended and enhanced through the mechanisms that link interpersonal similarity and interpersonal attraction.

10.5   THE PREDICTION OF INTERPERSONAL ATTRACTION[1]

Theodore M. Newcomb

. . .Perhaps the simplest. . .of the notions concerning determinants of positive attraction is that of *propinquity*. In its baldest form, the proposition of propinquity reads as follows: other things equal, people are most likely to be attracted toward those in closest contact with them. Everyday illustrations readily leap to mind. Adults generally have strongest attraction toward those children, and children toward those adults, with whom they are in most immediate contact— which is to say, their own children and their own parents. And this commonly occurs, let me remind you, in spite of the fact that neither parents nor children choose each other. Or, if we are willing to accept the fact of selection of marriage partners as an index of positive attraction, then the available data are strongly in support of a theory of propinquity. If we use an adequate range of distance— miles, or city blocks rather than yards, or within-block distances—there is a neat, monotonic relationship between residential propinquity and probability of marriage, other criteria of eligibility being held constant (*e.g.,* Bossard, 1932; Campbel, 1939; Davie, 1939).

It is, of course, a truism that distance per se will have no consequences for attraction; what we are concerned with is something that is made possible, or more likely, with decreasing distance. I think we may also consider it a truism that that something is behavior. Further, it is behavior on the part of one person that is observed and responded to by another: it is interaction. So widespread and so compelling is the evidence for the relationship between frequency of interaction and positive attraction that Homans (1950) has ventured to hypothesize that "If the frequency of interaction between two or more persons increases, the degree of their liking for one another will increase." Actuarially speaking, the evidence is altogether overwhelming that, *ignoring other variables*, the proposition is correct in a wide range of situations.

Why should this be so? Accepting the proposition only in an actuarial sense, and ignoring for the moment the other variables obviously involved, what theoretical considerations will enable us to make psychological sense out of it? The principle which comes first to mind is that of *reward and reinforcement*. Two simple assumptions will enable us to make direct use of this principle: first, that when

[1]From Theodore M. Newcomb, "The Prediction of Interpersonal Attraction," *American Psychologist*, 11, 1956, pp. 575–586; the article has been abridged considerably.

persons interact, the reward-punishment ratio is more often such as to be reinforcing than extinguishing; and second, that the on-the-whole rewarding effects of interaction are most apt to be obtained from those with whom one interacts most frequently. These assumptions, together with the principles of reward and reinforcement and canalization, would account for the general association of frequency of interaction with positive attraction; they would not, of course, account for the many observed exceptions to the generalization.

To return to my earlier illustrations, this set of assumptions and principles would not apply in exactly the same way to the facts of attraction between parents and children and to the facts of marital selection. One difference, of course, is that selection is possible in the latter but not in the former case. As applied to the facts of parent-child attraction, the principle of propinquity asserts, in effect, that we are attracted to those whom "fate" has made rewarding. As applied to the facts of marital selection, the principle of propinquity says little more, in addition to this, than that the likelihood of being rewarded by interaction varies with opportunity for interaction. The problem of selection, among those with whom opportunity for interaction is the same, still remains. . . .

There is an interesting consequence of the proposition that attraction toward others varies with the frequency of being rewarded by them. Opportunities for being rewarded by others vary not only with propinquity, as determined by irrelevant considerations like birth and residence, but also with the motivations of the potentially rewarding persons. This suggests that the likelihood of being continually rewarded by a given person varies with the frequency with which that person is in turn rewarded, and thus we have a proposition of *reciprocal reward:* the likelihood of receiving rewards from a given person, over time, varies with the frequency of rewarding him. This proposition is significant for my problem in various ways, especially because it forces further consideration of the conditions under which continued interaction between the same persons is most likely, and under which, therefore, the possibilities of continued reciprocal reward are greatest.

The first of these may be most simply described as the possession by two or more persons of common interests, apart from themselves, that require interdependent behavior. If you like to play piano duets, or tennis, you are apt to be rewarded by those who make it possible for you to do so, and at the same time you are apt to reward your partner. Insofar as both partners are rewarded, another evening of duets or another set of tennis is likely to ensue, together with still further opportunities for reciprocal reward. Thus attraction breeds attraction.

The second condition favorable to continued reciprocal rewards has to do with complementary interests (rather than with similar ones) that require interdependent behavior. These are symbiotic relationships, like that in which cow and cowbird become attracted to each other: the cow provides sustenance for the bird in the form of parasitic insects, the removal of which is rewarding to both. Or, at the human level, consider the exchange of gratifications between a pair of lovers.

Here, too, under conditions of complementary rather than of similar motivations, the general rule is that attraction breeds attraction. . . .

Up to this point I have noted that we acquire favorable or unfavorable attitudes toward persons as we are rewarded or punished by them, and that the principles of contiguity, of reciprocal reward, and of complementarity have to do with the conditions under which rewards are most probable. From now on I shall be primarily concerned with a special subclass of reciprocal rewards—those associated with communicative behavior.

The interaction processes through which reciprocal reward occurs have to do not with the exchange of energy but with the exchange of information, and are therefore communicative. I prefer the term "communicative behavior" to "social interaction" because it calls attention to certain consequences that are characteristic of information exchange, but not of energy exchange, among symbol-using humans. The use of symbols, needless to say, involves the expenditure of energy, but—even in so obvious an example as that of receiving a slap in the face—it is the consequences of the information exchange rather than the energy exchange which interest us, as psychologists.

I shall note two of these consequences, in the form of very general propositions—though each of them is in fact subject to very specific limitations. The first is this: Communicators tend to become more similar to each other, at least momentarily, in one or more respects, than they were before the communication. At the very least (assuming more or less accurate receipt of a message that has been intentionally sent), both sender and receiver now have the information that the sender wishes to call the attention of the receiver to the object of communication— *i.e.,* that which the symbols symbolize. If we stipulate still further conditions, the proposition will apply to a wider range of similarity. Suppose, for example, that a person has just expressed an opinion about something—say the United Nations; to the degree that he is sincere, and insofar as the receiver trusts his sincerity, the communication (if accurately received) will be followed by increased cognitive similarity, to the effect that the transmitter holds the stated opinion. Now suppose we add a further stipulation—that the receiver not only trusts the sender's sincerity but also respects his knowledgeability; under these conditions the opinions of sender and receiver are likely to be more similar than they were before.

It is this last kind of similarity—*i.e.,* that of attitudes—that has a special importance for the problem of interpersonal attraction. In fact, the proposition, as applied to similarity of attitudes toward objects of communication, has already introduced, as independent variables, certain dimensions of attraction—namely, trust and respect. Change toward similarity in one kind of attitude following communication, I have asserted, varies with another kind of attitude—*i.e.,* attraction.

My second proposition reverses this relationship: Attraction toward a co-communicator (actual or potential) varies with perceived similarity of attitudes toward the object of communication. Before specifying the limited conditions under which this proposition applies, let me briefly present its rationale.

While there are, of course, many exceptions, it is a highly dependable generalization that the life history of every human has made accurate communication rewarding far more often than punishing. Such is our dependence upon one another, from the very beginnings of communicative experience, and such is our indebtedness to culture, which is transmitted via communication, that success in the enterprise of becoming socialized depends upon success in transmitting and receiving messages. Insofar as accurate communication is in fact rewarding, reward value will attach to the co-communicator—which is to say that positive attraction toward him will increase (other things equal) with frequency of accurate communication with him. Please note the qualification: "insofar as accurate communication is in fact rewarding"; there are many messages—*e.g.*, "I hate you"—the accurate receipt of which is not in fact rewarding.

If, as I have maintained, increased similarity in some degree and manner is the regular accompaniment of accurate communication, it would be no surprise to discover that increased similarity becomes a goal of communication, and that its achievement is rewarding. And if, as I have also maintained, the reward value of successful communication attaches to the co-communicator, then it follows that the two kinds of reward effects—perception of increased similarity as rewarding, and perception of the co-communicator as rewarding—should vary together. This, in brief, is the rationale of my second proposition.

It is, however, a very general statement, and its usefulness can be enhanced by a further specification of conditions. I shall mention only two of them. First, the discovery of increased similarity is rewarding to the degree that the object with regard to which there is similarity of attitudes is valued (either negatively or positively). The discovery of agreement between oneself and a new acquaintance regarding some matter of only casual interest will probably be less rewarding than the discovery of agreement concerning one's own pet prejudices. The reward value of increased similarity increases, secondly, with the common relevance of the attitude object to the communicators. The success of a certain presidential candidate, for example, is likely to be seen as having consequences for both, whereas matters regarded as belonging in the area of personal taste—like taking cream in one's coffee—are viewed as devoid of common consequences. The discovery of similarity of the latter kind is not very likely to have much reward value. . . .

As the foregoing implies, and as I have elsewhere suggested (Newcomb, 1953), attraction and perceived similarity of attitude tend to maintain a constant relationship because each of them is sensitive to changes in the other. If newly received information about another person leads to increased or decreased attraction toward him, appropriate changes in perceived similarity readily ensue—often at the cost of accuracy. And if new information—either about the object or about another person's attitudes toward it—leads to perceptions of increased or decreased similarity with him, then the direction or the degree of attraction toward him easily accommodates itself to the situation as newly perceived. Change in attraction is one, but only one, of the devices by which some sort of tension state, associated with perceived discrepancy about important and relevant objects, is kept at a minimum. . . .

The remainder of this paper is devoted to some tests of specific predictions derived from the two propositions already presented, which may be telescoped as follows: Insofar as communication results in the perception of increased similarity of attitude toward important and relevant objects, it will also be followed by an increase in positive attraction. I shall therefore consider perceived similarity of attitude as a predictor of attraction. I shall also, for obvious reasons, be interested in actual, or objective, similarity.

Since the findings which I shall present were obtained in a single research setting, I shall stop briefly to note the nature of that setting. I started with the research objective of observing the changing interrelationships, over time, between attraction and similarity of attitudes. Since it seemed important to start with a base line of zero, as far as attraction was concerned, it was necessary to find a population of persons who were complete strangers to each other. It also seemed desirable to provide a setting in which it would be possible for a high degree of positive attraction to develop, and in which regular and repeated observations could be made. All of these requirements seemed to be met by the following arrangements. A student house was rented; male transfer students, all strangers to the University of Michigan, were offered the opportunity (several weeks before their planned arrival at the University) of receiving free room rent for a full semester; in return they were to spend four or five hours a week in responding to questionnaires and interviews, and in participating in experiments. Among those who submitted applications to live in the house under these conditions, 17 (the capacity of the house) were selected, no two of whom had ever lived in the same city, nor attended the same school. All 17 men arrived within a 24-hour period, and all responded to a questionnaire within a very few hours thereafter. The men were given no voice in the selection of roommates, but (within the limits of University regulations) they were given complete freedom to conduct the house, including the cooking and eating arrangements, as they chose. . . .

In this setting, data were obtained by questionnaire and interview, at semi-weekly intervals. A wide range of attitude responses was obtained, as well as rather complete data concerning interpersonal attraction. Measures of the latter were derived both from responses to direct questions about how favorably each house member felt toward each of the others, and from reports by each about informal, freely associating subgroups of two or more. . . .

I turn now to some specific predictions. First, if the basic generalization is correct, it should follow that, regardless of the content of communication, positive attraction will increase with opportunity for communication, other things equal. The only additional assumption involved in this prediction is that the likelihood of being rewarded by a co-communicator increases with opportunity for communication. . . .

The remainder of my predictions, unlike the first, take into account the content of communication. They are of the following general form: If and when increased attraction between pairs of persons does occur with opportunity for communication, it will be associated with increased similarity of attitude toward important and relevant objects.

The first of these predictions is based upon the additional assumption that one's self is a valued object to oneself. If so, then attraction should vary closely with self-other agreement about oneself. More specifically, insofar as a person's presumably ambivalent self-orientations are predominantly positive, his attraction toward others will vary directly with their attraction toward him. . . .

. . .[O]ur data show that an individual's distribution of General Liking among his associates is related to their liking for him. The relationship is almost as close on the fourth day as at the end of the fourth month, and as a general tendency is highly significant, though there are individual exceptions. One can predict an individual's liking for another individual with much better than chance accuracy if one knows the latter's liking for the former, at any time after the fourth day.

The prediction will be a good deal more accurate, however, if it is made from an individual's *estimate* of how well he is liked by the other. At any time from the second week on (when such estimates were first made), about three of every four estimates of another person's liking for oneself were in the same half of the distribution as own liking for that other person. Median rank-order correlations were .86 at the end, and .75 at the beginning, between each man's liking for each other man and his estimate of the reciprocals. As might be expected, this relationship was especially close at the extremes; five out of six predictions of liking for other persons would be in the correct quarter of the distribution, if based only upon subjects' estimates that they are in the highest or lowest quarter of reciprocated liking. Such findings correspond closely to those previously reported by Tagiuri (1952).

Apparently the close relationship between General Liking and its estimated reciprocal is but slightly influenced by communication. At any rate, the relationship does not increase significantly from near-strangership to close acquaintance, nor is the relationship significantly closer for roommates, at the end of the four-month period, than for nonroommates. Neither, as a matter of fact, does accuracy in estimating reciprocal liking increase with further acquaintance, for most subjects. Estimates of others' liking for oneself are so closely correlated with own liking for those same persons (the relationship approaches the self-correlation of either measure, at any given time), that most of the variance of either can be accounted for by the other. Whatever influences either of them influences both in about the same way.

These facts—that perceived reciprocation remains closely tied to own liking without increasing in accuracy over time—do not mean that estimated reciprocation is purely autistic. On the contrary, it tends to be quite accurate, differing from chance distributions at beyond the .001 level. Two of every three estimates, at all times, are in the correct half. What these facts do mean, apparently, is that both attraction toward others and its estimated reciprocal are jointly determined by autistic and by "realistic" factors, in such manner as to remain closely bound together in a relationship that does not change over time. I believe that a clue to the manner of interaction between autistic and "realistic" influences is provided by the following additional fact. Without exception, the men whose liking status rose with time either became more accurate in their estimates of reciprocation or maintained the earlier degree of accuracy, while those whose status declined tended to become less accurate. Our subjects had no difficulty in adapting, realistically, to the fact of rising sociometric status, but acceptance of declining status was only partial. All subjects distributed about the same range of liking scores, but each tended to receive a distinctive distribution. Estimated reciprocals represent a compromise between own liking for the individual in question and *amour propre*.

The proposition that perceived similarity in valuing the self contributes heavily to variance in attraction, together with the assumption that self-valuation tends to remain high at all times, is thus well supported. All persons, at all times, are liked according as they are judged to agree with oneself about oneself. These judgments become more accurate over time to the degree that one's actual changes in status make it possible to judge them accurately and at the same time continue to believe that one's own likings are reciprocated. For those who are discovering that their actual status is relatively low, the conflict—or, more specifically, the strain of perceived discrepancy—thus aroused is reduced at the cost of accuracy.

I have already implied that attraction is hypothetically predictable from cognitive as well as from cathectic similarity regarding objects of importance. I shall present findings concerning cognitive similarity regarding only one kind of object—persons. Each subject was asked to describe himself as well as the other house members by checking adjectives drawn from a list prepared by Professor Harrison Gough (1955). Each was also asked to describe his "ideal self," by using the same list, and to describe himself as he thought other house members would describe him. By comparing these responses with self-descriptions, we obtained measures of perceived similarity regarding the self. (This work closely parallels that by Fiedler (1954) concerning "assumed similarity.")

Attraction turns out to be closely related to perceived agreement (at considerably less than the .001 level). When the same data are analyzed individually, only two of 17 subjects fail to show the relationship in the predicted direction, and only one of these reverses it. This finding is more impressive than it would be if it resulted from attributing only favorable judgments of oneself to high-liked others, and only unfavorable judgments to low-liked others. Actually, eight of the ten subjects who accepted unfavorable adjectives as describing themselves, and who indicated that one or more others agreed with them, showed more agreement in these unfavorable descriptions with high-liked than with low-liked others. The relationship between attraction and perceived agreement on favorable items is, not surprisingly, a good deal closer. At any rate, the finding that attraction varies with perceived cognitive agreement about the self is not merely an artifactual result of the common-sense assumption that one is attracted toward those who are believed to think well of one. Judging from our data, it is also true—and perhaps contrary to common sense—that we are attracted to those whom we perceive as seeing both our foibles and our virtues as we ourselves see them. Many psychotherapists, I am told,[2] can readily confirm this observation. I believe, by the way, that the patient's perception of converging attitudes toward himself, by himself and therapist, has much to do with the phenomena of positive attraction in "transference."[3]

My next prediction deals not with the self as object of attitudes but with other house members. Of all the objects about which we obtained responses, nothing compared in importance or in group relevance with the house members themselves. Very early they became differentiated in attraction status, so that it was easy to measure similarity, on the part of any pair of persons, in attraction toward the remaining members. Correlations were calculated between the attraction scores of each member and those of each other member (there were 136 such pairs, each year) toward all of the other 15 members; this was done for each of the 16 weeks that the group lived together. Thus the proposition could be tested that the greater the similarity between any two members in assigning General Liking scores to the other 15 members, the higher their attraction for each other. A related prediction is that this relationship will increase with communication—that is, with time.

Both propositions receive clear support, according to both criteria of attraction. On the fourth day the relationship between within-pair General Liking and within-pair correlation of General Liking for remaining members is barely significant, and only slightly higher a week later. It increases fairly steadily till, at the end of four months, two-thirds of all within-pair attractions would be correctly placed in the upper or lower half of the distribution, judging only from the fact of being in the upper or the lower half of the distribution of correlations. . . .

Individuals in high agreement with each other about the other 15 house members clearly tend to be attracted to each other. The opposite tendency is much less pronounced; none of the categories involving subjects in the lower eight ranks has a mean correlation much below the average of the total set of pairs. The lowest of all the mean correlations. . .is that of all pairs of which one member—and only one—is in the lowest quarter of attraction (ranks 13–16). For these 44 pairs the mean correlation is .35—not significantly different from zero. Thus, the correlations predict not only to within-pair attraction but also (particularly at the extremes) to interpersonal mutuality, regardless of level of attraction; the relationship between them, as calculated by X^2, is in fact significant at the .001 level. . . .

---

[2] Dr. Keith Sward, in particular, has called this to my attention.

[3] *Cf.* Rogers (1951, pp. 66–96) for empirical evidence to the effect that, in at least one case of successful psychotherapy, the correlation between the patient's self-sort and the therapist's description of the patient, by a sorting of the same items, increased over time. I do not know of other data on this point.

At a theoretical level, I consider it highly significant that these two predictors, the combined effects of which are more successful than either alone, include one subjective index (estimates of reciprocal attraction) and one that is objective, in the sense of describing a relationship between a pair of persons and not referring to either person alone. Theoretically speaking, this is as it should be. Doubtless most forms of social behavior, like attraction, are jointly determined by individual characteristics and by relationships to others—relationships which pertain to the recipient of behavior quite as much as to the behaver himself. . . .

You are doubtless wondering about the generality of the proposition that attraction is predictable from similarity of attitude toward important and relevant objects, since the only objects that I have mentioned, so far, are persons. Although our analyses are far from complete, they indicate that the proposition also applies to objects other than persons, though at lower levels of confidence. But it is already clear that, in this research setting, there were no objects which compared in relevance, *for all members*, to house members themselves. We sampled a range of attitudes that extended virtually from cabbages to kings; there were several pairs of subjects for whom kings (or at least presidents) were highly relevant, and there may have been some whose within-pair attraction was influenced by attitudes toward cole slaw. There were, however, no *single* nonperson objects of sufficient relevance for *all* members to account for very much variance in the attraction level among all pairs. . . .

I have two brief and final comments concerning the significance of findings such as I have been presenting. First, as to the very limited setting in which they were obtained, there is no reason to believe that the particular students whom we happen to have studied differed very greatly from other groups of young-adult peers, in the kinds of relationships here reported, at comparable stages of acquaintance. Indeed, it is likely that the very fact of their homogeneity in regard to age and sex and student status tended to reduce the variance of many of their attitudes; if so, at least some of the predictors here reported would prove still more satisfactory with more varied groups. I feel, therefore, that I am not grossly overextending the application of my own findings when I report, with considerable confidence, that the conditions under which attraction develops and changes or remains stable are orderly ones. It is possible, moreover, to formulate statements of these conditions into a consistent body of propositions.

Secondly, as to the common-sense nature of much that I have reported, none of you has been overcome with astonishment on learning, for example, that our subjects tended to like those by whom they thought they were liked, or by those who, they thought, would describe them in most favorable terms. My concern is not so much to point out that some of our findings are *un*expected—*e.g.*, that perceived agreement with others concerning one's own *un*favorable traits is a reasonably good predictor of positive attraction. Nor is it to repeat the ancient truism that no one knows whether what every one knows is true is really true until it has been properly tested. Rather, I want to note that several different propositions (some conforming to common sense and some not), which superficially have nothing to do with one another, are derivable from the same set of assumptions.

The fact seems to be that one can predict to interpersonal attraction, under specified conditions, from frequency of interaction, from the perception of reciprocated attraction, from certain combinations of personality characteristics, and from attitudinal agreement. There is no self-evident reason why such diverse variables, viewed common-sensewise, should belong together; one might almost suspect that they had been drawn out of a hatful of miscellaneous variables. But predictive propositions about those variables all flow, as I have tried to show, from a very few psychological assumptions. I believe the confluence to be both theoretically required and empirically supported. These considerations seem to me to lend confidence to the point of view that a limited theory about a limited class of objects— namely, persons—can profit by taking account of the significant properties of those objects, and in particular those properties closely related to the fact of human dependence upon communication.

You may remember an old story whose punch line is "Vive la différence"— Thank God for the little difference. If we are inclined to take a favorable view of positive interpersonal attraction, perhaps we should also be grateful for similarities: Vive la similarité!

BIBLIOGRAPHY

BOSSARD, J. H. S., 1932, "Residential propinquity as a Factor in Marriage Selection," *American Journal of Sociology*, 38, pp. 219–224.

CAMPBEL, W. D., 1939, "The Importance of Occupation, as Compared with Age and Residence, in Marital Selection," unpublished master's thesis, Ann Arbor: University of Michigan.

DAVIE, M. R., AND R. J. REEVES, 1939, "Propinquity of Residence before Marriage," *American Journal of Sociology*, 44, pp. 510–517.

FESTINGER, L., S. SCHACHTER, AND K. BACK, 1950, *Social Pressures in Informal Groups*, New York: Harper & Row.

FIEDLER, F., 1954, "Assumed Similarity Measures as Predictors of Team Effectiveness," *Journal of Abnormal and Social Psychology*, 49, pp. 381–388.

GOUGH, H., 1955, *Reference Handbook for the Gough Adjective Checklist*, mimeographed, Berkeley, Calif.: Institute for Personality Assessment and Research, University of California.

HOMANS, G. C., 1950, *The Human Group*, New York: Harcourt, Brace & World.

NEWCOMB, T. M., 1953, "An Approach to the Study of Communicative Acts," *Psychological Review*, 60, pp. 393–404.

ROGERS, C. R., 1951, "The Case of Mrs. Oak," *Studies in Client-centered Psychotherapy*, Washington: Psychological Service Center Press, Chap. III.

TAGIURI, R., 1952, "Relational Analysis: An Extension of Sociometric Method with Emphasis upon Social Perception," *Sociometry*, 15, pp. 91–104.

Questions and Implications for Practice

10.1 DOROTHY LEE

1. In her wisdom Dorothy Lee advises that we should not feel we must copy the practices of the Wiutu or the Navahoes. We are profoundly interested, however, in how to reconcile principles of conformity and individual initiative, group living and freedom of choice, social regulation and personal autonomy, within the context of our national and regional culture and within the school or college subculture.

Is it possible and desirable for the guidance-personnel worker to attempt to interpret—to mediate—the norms and taboos of the culture to individuals? Can this be done in such a way as not to inhibit or be negative, but rather, to help the individual acquire more freedom to act and to be? Of what must the guidance-personnel worker beware if he or she is not to inhibit or be negative?

2. Is it possible, as Dorothy Lee suggests, for regulations to be guidelines for individuals who otherwise might get hopelessly lost in the intricacies of their culture and subculture? What role can the guidance-personnel worker most appropriately play in making these real to students?

3. Can guidance-personnel workers work in such a way that the individual's integrity is not violated even though limits are maintained? What are some of the principles and conditions that must be observed if law and limits and personal autonomy are to coexist optimally?

10.2 SOLOMON ASCH

1. What social situations can you cite in history where majority opinion has induced individuals to profess beliefs or positions which they may actually have perceived as false?

2. Can you describe a situation in an elementary or a secondary school or in a college where individuals found themselves in a non-contrived situation similar to the contrived situation that Asch describes? Speculate about the effect that such a situation may have on the personality of the individual.

3. Asch reports on experiments with male college students. At least two other experimenters—Robert Blake and Harry Hawkins—have reported that while Asch found that 68 percent of the male college students retained their independence in the face of the kind of social pressure that Asch contrived, only 40 percent of female college students maintained their independence when subjected to similar laboratory conditions.* Why do you think this is so? Do you think this is a reflection on inherent feminine characteristics? Do you think it may be desirable that, on the whole, women tend to be "yielding?" Why?

---

*Esther Lloyd-Jones, *Educational Record*, 1955.

4. What would be the characteristics of a group that would permit and encourage independent judgment by its members and the development of their maximum integrity? Where might leadership come from to help such groups develop? What knowledge, skills and other qualifications would such leadership need?

10.3 DEUTSCH AND GERARD

1. Can you see a direct relationship between the kind of student government that is practiced in an elementary school, secondary school, or college and the personalities of the students? What would be some of the characteristic modes of operation of a student government that would contribute beneficially to the students who participated in it?

2. Should a guidance-personnel worker or teachers, interested in the personality development of students, assess periodically the nature of the normative influence that specific groups are exercising on their members? Can groups themselves try to understand their own natures and potential effects on members? How might this be done?

3. Would some guidance-personnel workers consider it prudent and more appropriate to spend their full time counseling with individuals who seek their help in handling the effects that groups have had on their sense of self-respect and integrity? What do you think?

10.4 MUZAFER SHERIF, *ET AL.*

1. Any school or college is rife with intergroup tensions, many of which prove disruptive to other activities that are essential to the on-going life of the institution.

Describe an incident you have observed in your school or college experience that had some similarities to the Rattler-Eagle affair described in Selection 10.4.

2. What was the outcome in the situation you observed? Could superordinate goals have been introduced by a guidance-personnel worker? Describe, specifically, how this might have been done?

3. The professional education of guidance-personnel workers tends to make them rely upon verbal methods to resolve conflicts within or between groups. Should guidance-personnel workers be competent to work with groups on an action level as well as a verbal one? Consider the relative merits of situation manipulation, the guided acting out of problems, and the introduction of superordinate goals, versus individual counseling, group counseling, and discussion in relation to the following:

a. elementary school children from middle-class homes
b. high school students from middle-class homes
c. students in a complex multiversity
d. students in a big urban school from homes where spoken language is sparsely used
e. students from a small church related college who come from middle-class homes

In your considerations use any research that seems pertinent.

4. Over and beyond the "management" aspects of a situation, might it be possible for a guidance-personnel worker as an educator to help the groups concerned to learn something about the nature of in-groups, intergroup tensions, and the constructive use of conflict and superordinate goals by throwing the light of social science on their own personal experience *ex post facto*?

10.5 THEODORE M. NEWCOMB

1. List ways in which the guidance-personnel worker might make practical use of Newcomb's theories of interpersonal attraction.

2. Apply Newcomb's discussion of communication specifically to the "situation" that exists:

a. between a teacher and a student;
b. between a counselor and a student in a dyadic relationship;
c. between an employee and his supervisor or his employer or the administrator of his work area;
d. a professor and a class of 30;
e. a dean and his faculty of 45;
f. a residence head and students in his or her dormitory;
g. a dean and the parents of the students in his school.

Chapter 11

Social Change

Previous chapters have dealt with social systems of various kinds from a variety of different viewpoints. We have seen that a formal organization, a friendship group, a family, an artificially created aggregate, and an entire society can each be viewed as a social system and that doing so provides us with fresh understanding of some of the events and qualities that characterize social groupings. Our selections have touched both on their structural aspects and on some of the processes that keep them going, and through these treatments it has become apparent that social systems are not static entities but that they undergo growth and change even as they maintain some of their basic characteristics. In this chapter we deal more directly with the process of change itself—its sources, the actions and events that actually constitute it, and its direct and indirect consequences.

Our reason for focusing on change as such is twofold. If change is a characteristic feature of social systems, then comprehending it should deepen and extend our understanding of the nature of the systems themselves. We should gain new insight into the way systems operate and maintain themselves by viewing social systems through different stages of their existence and attempting to discern the factors that determine the nature of their progress. In addition, change is an aspect of social systems, which is of particular relevance to guidance-personnel workers, whose goals and concerns often lead them to initiate, direct, or restrict social changes. Thus, knowledge of the relevant variables and greater understanding of the nature of the change process should enable a guidance-personnel worker to act more effectively.

Perhaps the first point to emphasize is that social change is essentially inevitable and, in itself, neither desirable nor undesirable. Whatever abstract models one might construct, no real social system can be unchanging, since for that to be true a system would have to be impervious to any influence from its surrounding environment and be in a state of perfect balance internally—two conditions which are improbable if not impossible when human beings are the elements. Let us examine these two general conditions more specifically.

Considering the various social systems dealt with previously, we realize that they represent, at any point in time, some sort of equilibrium among a number of different and even incompatible elements and pressures. For example, if we view a classroom as a functioning social system, we can see that for it to remain so requires that a number of mutual adjustments be made by the individuals who make it up—the teacher and the students. Ideally, the students must temporarily give up some of their independence and submit to certain rules of conduct and procedure. The teacher must restrain any personal preferences he may develop among his students and treat them with equal fairness and he must not try to extend his authority indiscriminately into areas where it is not legitimate. The mutual reconciliation of all such pressures (and the ones just mentioned are only some of the most superficial among the multitude actually existing in such a situation) at any point can be equally well described as a state of tension or of equilibrium, since it is clear that there is always present the possibility that some member of the system will act independently rather than in terms of the system's requirements and that disorganization will result. "Deviations," of course, can be expressions of any kind of individual tendency and thus may, in a larger sense, be either creative or destructive, worthwhile or worthless. The essential point here is only that the likelihood is constant and not inconsiderable that the strict requirements which are necessary for a system to maintain itself static and intact will not be met precisely or completely. Therefore, an on-going social system will always contain areas of both balance and disorganization to different degrees and will be continuously engaged in readjusting its elements and neutralizing its internal inconsistencies. Every social system is thus at all times, and for intrinsic reasons, changing.

Moreover, what a social system is at any time is the product not only of its internal conditions but also of the conditions in the environment in which it exists and of the relationship between these two sets of conditions. What goes on in a classroom is not the result only of the personal characteristics and tendencies of the teacher and the students and of the mutual adjustments among them. The classroom exists within the larger system of the school and the students and the teacher have a number of official and unofficial responsibilities and attachments to other social systems (the faculty, peer groups, families, social clubs, etc.). To varying degrees, the requirements of these outside systems exert pressure on the individuals *when they are acting as members of the social system of the classroom* and are thus an integral part of what that social system is. But these outside systems are themselves not necessarily unchanging and their demands are thus also variable. As a result, what goes on in the classroom—and, more generally, in any given social system—is constantly subject to change for this reason too, namely the fact that it is part of a larger—complex and dynamic—environment.

In pointing out the reasons why a social system is continually and inevitably subject to change we have indicated that there are two possible sources for such change—internal and external. This, of course, is true not only of the inherent process of change but also of change that is more deliberately initiated and directed. When we speak of social change we refer both to those "natural" processes of growth and development that occur in a social system and to events and actions that an individual or a group, inside or outside the system, plans and calculates to bring about certain desired alterations. These two extreme types actually differ less than one might think and they are more usefully viewed as falling along a continuum with many gradual differentiations.

However change arises—internally or externally, deliberately or spontaneously— many of the processes it comprises and the consequences it sets off will be the same. Suppose, for example, that in a classroom one can observe over time that a change has occurred in the pattern of interaction between the teacher and the students so that instead of allowing discussion to flow on its own without imposing order or structure the teacher now calls on students to recite in a definite sequence, giving more opportunity to some and none to others. Such a change could come about in at least two quite different ways. The teacher might decide that the undirected style of discussion was proving ineffective as a teaching technique because it led too often to domination by the most talkative rather than by those who had the most to contribute or those who could profit most from active participation. He might then further decide to call on those students he wanted to hear from and ignore others, thus curbing and directing the free flow of discussion. Or, instead of the change occurring in this way, it might gradually develop that fewer and fewer students participated in the undirected discussions and the teacher had to call on particular students simply in order to keep the class going. In doing so, the pattern he followed would actually, though not necessarily due to deliberate calculations, express his judgments about the relative worth of what the various students had to offer or their relative susceptibilities to learning from participation. The resulting alteration in the teacher's behavior and in the pattern of participation would therefore be the same as in the case where it stemmed from a deliberate attempt to change the situation.

In many respects, of course, these would be two very different phenomena. Arising from different sets of motives, perceptions, and intentions on the part of those involved, they would be likely to evoke different subsequent reactions. Their effects on the feelings of the teacher and the students toward each other would undoubtedly be quite different and this would inevitably lead to different sets of additional changes in their patterns of interaction. Through all of this, the effects of the two sets of events on the learning process would be far from the same and would lead to different evaluations on the part of individuals outside the classroom about the quality of both the teacher and the students. On the other hand, there are a number of respects in which the two change processes would be quite similar. In both cases, the same students would now participate most and the same ones least or not at all. This would have similar effects on the way the students perceived each other and judged each other's abilities, which would be likely to have similar repercussions for the relative status and prestige of various individuals within the students' friendship structure. In both cases the teacher would have the same basis for evaluating the students—their new pattern of classroom performance—and he might thus be led to similar reassessments of their aptitude and achievement. In sum, the two change processes that arose in rather different ways would overlap perhaps as much as they differed from each other and whether one stressed the similarities or the distinctions would be dictated by one's purpose in analyzing the two cases rather than by their intrinsic features.

As has been variously implied in the preceding paragraphs, social change encompasses processes at all levels of a social system—cultural, social, and psychological. It may start primarily at one level, but this will soon and inevitably necessitate change at the other levels too if an actual alteration in the system is to come about. For example, a change in the leadership structure of a clique will not take hold unless habits and norms are altered to adjust to the demands of the new social hierarchy and unless the individual members can accept and fulfill new role expectations. In order to understand the total phenomenon of change it is necessary to understand the various types of changes separately and to assess their role and relative importance. It is also and equally necessary to understand the manner in which changes at different levels can produce, influence, or prevent each other: how individual discontent can generate changes in the status hierarchy of a clique; how one member's idiosyncratic attitudes or values can promote changes in a group's norms; how the introduction of new practices or techniques can lead to the deterioration of individual attachments and loyalties to an organization; how changes in the formal status system of an institution can facilitate the acceptance of new values, norms, or policies; how an atmosphere of increased tolerance for a certain practice can alter the patterns of interaction and relationships that focus on it.

Such interrelationships among the different aspects, or levels, of the total process of social change are particularly crucial with respect to planned change. In any particular situation, one kind of alteration may be easier to accomplish directly than another, but the easier one may be an effective first step to initiate the process that will eventuate in the desired change. For example, it would undoubtedly be easier to reassign the members of a troublesome high school clique to different sections of their classes than it would be to lessen their commitment to each other or their involvement in those joint activities that are creating a problem. Reassignment, however, will mean that they will be together less often and it may lead them to develop other friendships and loyalties. As a result, the bonds that have held the clique together will be weakened. Further and more direct steps to prevent trouble-making will then be less likely to arouse strong resistance and, indeed, the problem behavior may well diminish on its own.

The planning of social change is made both more difficult and more possible by the complexity of the process. On the positive side, the individual or group interested in initiating a change can select from a variety of possible approaches and, when appropriate, he may use several mutually reinforcing techniques simultaneously. In trying to break up a delinquent clique as above, for example, the effects of reassignment could be bolstered in the following ways: by concurrent attempts to influence the key members of the clique toward more worthwhile attitudes through individual counseling; by actively encouraging and rewarding any evidence of interest in more desirable activities on the part of the clique members; by facilitating their becoming involved in such activities whenever the usual rules and procedures are in the way; by persuading teachers and other personnel not to treat these particular individuals with suspicion even though it may seem justified at the outset; and by attempting to introduce and develop a broader and less subjective view of their situation among the clique members themselves. Any one of these approaches alone might not be enough to produce substantial or lasting change, but attacking a number of interrelated aspects of the total situation simultaneously might give the process the momentum needed for change to be accomplished.

The planning of change is, however, also made difficult by the complexity of what it encompasses. For a change to actually become a reality within a social system, all those aspects which are affected must be compatible with the final situation that is envisioned or must be made so as part of bringing that situation about. Success thus implies a much more thorough and detailed understanding than that probably available to the change agent. Except in very limited situations where a narrow change is being attempted, it is not possible to be aware of every personal involvement among the individuals in a situation or to know the particular intensity and significance of all those that are evident. Nor is it possible to know enough about each individual personality to fully anticipate all the reactions that the change will evoke, or to recognize all the subtleties of the informal status systems in terms of which relationships and interaction are structured. Yet a great many factors such as these will be relevant to a sequence of changes as it unfolds, and they will contribute to it and affect its course whether they are recognized or not. Moreover, even if many of the complexities are identified, it is not always possible to manipulate all the relevant aspects, either for practical reasons or because doing so would be culturally, socially, or psychologically unacceptable. As a result, the chain of consequences set off by any deliberately instituted change will include unanticipated as well as anticipated ones, and the overall effect of the process will depend on how these events are taken advantage of, limited, shaped, and directed as they occur, as well as on the initial steps that set the process in motion.

With respect to any social change one can think of, it is obvious that it can occur at different rates, but, essentially, change is a gradual process with identifiable stages. Even when a change can be said to have occurred suddenly, closer analysis would reveal that it had been preceded by a period or set of events that could now be seen as leading up to and preparing for it, and which were thus an integral part of it. A more detailed examination might also show that although major aspects of the social system in question did undergo rapid transformation, there were others that lagged, so that there was a period of transition during which different parts of the system were out of step with each other. For example, a change in the status structure of a group subsumes changes in individual attitudes and values and in group practices and norms, but not all of these changes occur simultaneously or in a smoothly integrated manner. More probably, individuals experience considerable frustration and disorientation and the group exists in a state of partial social disorganization until its norms and goals, its status hierarchy and interaction patterns, and the needs, attitudes, and expectations of its members gradually readjust into a new pattern.

It must be emphasized, however, that, although change is gradual and can be broken down into successive stages for purposes of analysis, its beginning and its end are not in actuality as clear and distinct from the on-going life of a social system as an observer's account might suggest. Indeed, it would be misleading to view stability and change as opposites or even as primarily incompatible with each other. As we emphasized at the outset, change is continual and inevitable in all human systems and it is an inherent part of whatever stability they achieve. We do not understand a social system fully until we understand how it changes and can be changed, and we cannot understand social change except in terms of the psychological, social, and cultural events of which social systems consist.

11.1 INTRODUCTION

The first selection in this chapter deals with a primitive culture and with an instance of change that may seem rather remote from modern organizational settings and not very clearly related to the reader's concerns. The value of this initial discussion is that it exposes, more clearly than it is possible to do with respect to a more complex social system, the concrete changes in behavior and interaction that a "social change" actually comprises. It thus points to some of the general issues and principles that it will be important to consider in attempting to understand the situations that are examined later.

Focusing on the single fact of the displacement of stone axes by steel axes in a primitive society, where social relations and interaction can be traced rather fully, the author shows how extensive can be the total network of practices and relations that are contingent on a single item and that will be affected by changes that involve that item. Particularly worthy of note in the case discussed here is the lack of relationship between the obvious and expected consequences of the technological change and its indirect social effects. The introduction of the steel axe did not, as might seem likely, lead to greater technological efficiency and did not improve the material aspects of the society's way of life. It did, however, have deep and widespread effects on some of the most basic aspects of social relations: familiar status relationships were disrupted, privileges that had been unique to certain roles no longer held, new relationships developed for which there were no expectations or norms, traditional practices and occasions lost their function. Thus this selection suggests at least two important distinctions with respect to the effects of change that are relevant to the discussions that follow in the rest of the chapter—between direct and indirect and between anticipated and unanticipated consequences.

11.1   STEEL AXES FOR STONE AGE AUSTRALIANS[1]

Lauriston Sharp

THE PROBLEM   Like other Australian aboriginals, the Yir Yoront group at the mouth of the Coleman River on the west coast of tropical Cape York Peninsula originally had no knowledge of metals. Technologically their culture was of the old stone age or paleolithic type; they supported themselves by hunting and fishing, obtaining vegetable foods and needed materials from the bush by simple gathering techniques. Their only domesticated animal was the dog, and they had no domesticated plants of any kind. Unlike some other aboriginal groups, however, the Yir Yoront did have polished stone axes hafted in short handles, and these implements were most important in their economy.

Toward the end of the nineteenth century metal tools and other European artifacts began to filter into the Yir Yoront territory. The flow increased with the gradual expansion of the white frontier outward from southern and eastern Queensland. Of all the items of western technology thus made available, none was more acceptable, none more highly valued by aboriginals of all conditions than the hatchet or short-handled steel axe.

[1]Lauriston Sharp, "Steel Axes for Stone Age Australians," *Human Problems in Technological Change: A Casebook*, Edward H. Spicer, ed., New York: Russell Sage Foundation, 1952, pp. 69, 72-79, 82-87.

In the mid-1930s an American anthropologist was able to live alone in the bush among the Yir Yoront for 13 months without seeing another white man. They were thus still relatively isolated and they continued an essentially independent economic life, supporting themselves entirely by means of their old stoneage techniques. Yet their polished stone axes were fast disappearing and were being replaced by steel axes, which came to them in considerable numbers directly or indirectly from various European sources to the south.

What changes in the life of the Yir Yoront still living under aboriginal conditions in the Australian bush could be expected as a result of their increasing possession and use of the steel axe?. . .

RELEVANT FACTORS   If we concentrate our attention on Yir Yoront behavior centering about the original stone axe, rather than on the axe—the thing—we should get some conception of the role this implement played in aboriginal culture. This conception, in turn, should permit us to foresee with considerable accuracy some of the results of the displacement of stone axes by steel axes acquired directly or indirectly from Europeans by the Yir Yoront.

The production of a stone axe required a number of simple skills. With the idea of the axe in its various details well in mind, the adult men—and only the adult men—could set about producing it, a task not considered appropriate for women or children. First of all, a man had to know the location and properties of several natural resources found in his immediate environment: pliable wood, which could be doubled or bent over the axe head and bound tightly to form a handle; bark, which could be rolled into cord for the binding; and gum, with which the stone head could be firmly fixed in the haft. These materials had to be correctly gathered, stored, prepared, cut to size, and applied or manipulated. They were plentifully supplied by nature, and could be taken by a man from anyone's property without special permission. Postponing consideration of the stone head of the axe, we see that simple knowledge of nature and of the technological skills involved, together with the possession of fire (for heating the gum) and a few simple cutting tools, which might be nothing more than the sharp shells of plentiful bivalves, all of which were available to everyone, were sufficient to enable any normal man to make a stone axe.

The use of the stone axe as a piece of capital equipment for the production of other goods indicates its very great importance in the subsistence economy of the aboriginal. Anyone—man, woman, or child—could use the axe; indeed, it was used more by women, for theirs was the onerous, daily task of obtaining sufficient wood to keep the campfire of each family burning all day for cooking or other purposes and all night against mosquitoes and cold (in July, winter temperature might drop below 40 degrees). In a normal lifetime any woman would use the axe to cut or knock down literally tons of firewood. Men and women, and sometimes children, needed the axe to make other tools, or weapons, or a variety of material equipment required by the aboriginal in his daily life. The stone axe was essential in making the wet-season domed huts, which keep out some rain and some insects; or platforms, which provide dry storage; or shelters, which give shade when days are bright and hot. In hunting and fishing and in gathering vegetable or animal food the axe was also a necessary tool; and in this tropical culture without preservatives or other means of storage, the native spends more time obtaining food than in any other occupation except sleeping.

In only two instances was the use of the stone axe strictly limited to adult men: Wild honey, the most prized food known to the Yir Yoront, was gathered only by men who usually used the axe to get it; and only men could make the secret paraphernalia for ceremonies, an activity often requiring use of the axe. From this brief listing of some of the activities in which the axe was used, it is easy to understand why there was at least one stone axe in every camp, in every hunting or fighting party, in every group out on a "walk-about" in the bush.

While the stone axe helped relate men and women and often children to nature in technological behavior, in the transformation of natural into cultural equipment, it also was prominent in that aspect of behavior which may be called conduct, primarily directed toward persons. Yir Yoront men were dependent upon interpersonal relations for their stone axe heads, since the flat, geologically recent alluvial country over which they range, provides no stone from which axe heads can be made. The stone they used comes from known quarries four hundred miles to the south. It reached the Yir Yoront through long lines of male trading partners, some of these chains terminating with the Yir Yoront men, while others extended on farther north to other groups, having utilized Yir Yoront men as links. Almost every older adult man had one or more regular trading partners, some to the north and some to the south. His partner or partners in the south he provided with surplus spears, and particularly fighting spears tipped with the human flesh. For a dozen spears, some of which he may have obtained from a partner to the north, he would receive from a southern partner one stone axe head. Studies have shown that the sting ray spears become more and more valuable as they move south farther from the sea, being passed on in recent times from a native on one cattle station to a native on another where they are used during the wet season, when almost all aboriginal employees are thrust into the bush to shift for themselves until the next cattle-working dry season is at hand. A hundred and fifty miles south of the Yir Yoront one such spear may be exchanged for one stone axe head. Although actual investigations could not be made, presumably still farther south and nearer the quarries, one sting ray spear would bring several stone axe heads. It is apparent that links in the middle of the chain who make neither spears nor axe heads receive both as a middleman's profit simply for passing them back and forth. While many other objects may move along these chains of trading partners, they are still characterized by both bush and station aboriginals as lines along which spears move south and axes move north. Thus trading relations, which may extend the individual's personal relationships out beyond the boundaries of his own group, are associated with two of the most important items in a man's equipment, spears and axes, whether the latter are of stone or steel. Finally, most of the exchanges between partners take place during the dry season at times when the great aboriginal fiestas occur, which center about initiation rites or other totemic ceremonials that attract hundreds and are the occasion for much exciting activity besides trading.

Returning to the Yir Yoront, we find that not only was it adult men alone who obtained axe heads and produced finished axes, but it was adult males who retained the axes, keeping them with other parts of their equipment in camp, or carrying them at the back slipped through a human hair belt when traveling. Thus, every woman or child who wanted to use an axe—and this might be frequently during the day—must get one from some man, use it promptly, and return it to the man in good condition. While a man might speak of "my axe," a woman or child could not; for them it was always "your axe," addressing a male, or "his axe."

This necessary and constant borrowing of axes from older men by women and children was done according to regular patterns of kinship behavior. A woman on good terms with her husband would expect to use his axe unless he were using it; a husband on good terms with his wives would let any one of them use his axe without question. If a woman was unmarried or her husband was absent, she would go first to her older brother or to her father for an axe. Only in extraordinary circumstances would she seek a stone axe from a mother's brother or certain other male kin with whom she had to be most circumspect. A girl, a boy, or a young man would look to a father or an older brother to provide an axe for her or his use, but would never approach a mother's brother, who would be at the same time a potential father-in-law, with such a request. Older men, too, would follow similar rules if they had to borrow an axe.

It will be noted that these social relationships in which the stone axe had a place are all pair relationships and that the use of the axe helped define and maintain the character of the relationships and the roles of the two individual participants: Every active relationship among the Yir Yoront involved a definite and accepted status of superordination or subordination. A person could have no dealings with any other on exactly equal terms. Women and children were dependent on, or subordinate to, older males in every action in which the axe entered. Among the men, the younger was dependent on the older or on certain kinds of kin. The nearest approach to equality was between brothers, although the older was always superordinate to the younger. Since the exchange of goods in a trading relationship involved a mutual reciprocity, trading partners were usually a kind of brother to each other or stood in a brotherly type of relationship, although one was always classified as older than the other and would have some advantage in case of dispute. It can be seen that repeated and widespread conduct centering on the axe helped to generalize and standardize throughout the society these sex, age, and kinship roles, both in their normal benevolent and in exceptional malevolent aspects, and helped to build up expectancies regarding the conduct of others defined as having a particular status.

The status of any individual Yir Yoront was determined not only by sex, age, and extended kin relationships, but also by membership in one of two dozen patrilineal totemic clans into which the entire community was divided. A person's names, rights in particular areas of land, and, in the case of a man, his roles in the totemic ceremonies (from which women are excluded) were all a function of belonging to one clan rather than another. Each clan had literally hundreds of totems, one or two of which gave the clan its name, and from any of which the personal names of clan members were derived. These totems included not only natural species or phenomena like the sun, stars, and daybreak, but also cultural "species": imagined ghosts, rainbow serpents, heroic ancestors; such eternal cultural verities as fires, spears, huts; and such human activities, conditions, or attributes as eating, vomiting, swimming, fighting, babies and corpses, milk and blood, lips and loins. While individual members of such totemic classes or species might disappear or be destroyed, the class itself was obviously ever present and indestructible. The totems therefore lent permanence and stability to the clans, to the groupings of human individuals who generation after generation were each associated with one set of totems that distinguished one clan from another.

Among the many totems of the Sunlit Cloud Iguana clan, and important among them, was the stone axe. The names of many members of this clan referred to the axe itself, or to activities like trading or wild honey gathering in which the axe played a vital part, or to the clan's mythical ancestors with whom the axe was prominently associated. When it was necessary to represent the stone axe in totemic ceremonies, it was only men of this clan who exhibited it or pantomimed its use. In secular life the axe could be made by any man and used by all; but in the sacred realm of the totems it belonged exclusively to the Sunlit Cloud Iguana people.

Supporting those aspects of cultural behavior which we have called technology and conduct is a third area of culture, including ideas, sentiments, and values. These are most difficult to deal with, for they are latent and covert or even unconscious and must be deduced from overt actions and language or other communicating behavior. In this aspect of the culture lies the "meaning" of the stone axe, its significance to the Yir Yoront and to their cultural way of life. The ideal conception of the axe, the knowledge of how to produce it (apart from the purely muscular habits used in its production) are part of the Yir Yoront adult masculine role, just as ideas regarding its technical use are included in the feminine role. These technical ideas constitute a kind of "science" regarding the axe which may be more important in relation to behavioral change than are the neurophysiological patterns drilled into the body by years of practice. Similarly there are normative ideas regarding the part played by the axe in conduct which constitute a kind of "morality" of the axe, and which again may be more important than the overt habits of social interaction in determining the role of the axe in social relationships. More than ideas regarding technology, ideas regarding conduct are likely to be closely associated, or "charged," with sentiment or value. Ideas and sentiments help guide and inform overt behavior; in turn, overt behavior helps support and validate ideas and sentiments.

The stone axe was an important symbol of masculinity among the Yir Yoront (just as pants or pipes are among ourselves). By a complicated set of ideas which we would label "ownership" the axe was defined as "belonging" to males. Everyone in the society (except untrained infants) accepted these ideas. Similarly spears, spear throwers, and fire-making sticks were associated with males, were owned only by them, and were symbols of masculinity. But the masculine values represented by the stone axe were constantly being impressed on all members of society by the fact that nonmales had to use the axe and had to go to males for it, whereas they never borrowed other masculine artifacts. Thus, the axe stood for an important theme that ran all through Yir Yoront culture: the superiority and rightful dominance of the male, and the greater value of his concerns and of all things associated with him. We should call this androcentrism rather than patriarchy, or paternal rule. It is the recognition by all that the values of the man (*andros*) take precedence over feminine values, an idea backed by very strong sentiments among the Yir Yoront. Since the axe had to be borrowed also by the younger from the older, it also represented the prestige of age, another important theme running all through Yir Yoront behavior. . . .

ANALYSIS The introduction of the steel axe indiscriminately and in large numbers into the Yir Yoront technology was only one of many changes occurring at the same time. It is therefore impossible to factor out all the results of this single innovation alone. Nevertheless, a number of specific effects of the change from stone axes to steel axes may be noted; and the steel axe may be used as an epitome of the European goods and implements received by the aboriginals in increasing quantity and of their general influence on the native culture. The use of the steel axe to illustrate such influences would seem to be justified, for it was one of the first European artifacts to be adopted for regular use by the Yir Yoront; and the axe, whether of stone or steel, was clearly one of the most important items of cultural equipment they possessed.

The shift from stone to steel axes provided no major technological difficulties. While the aboriginals themselves could not manufacture steel axe heads, a steady supply from outside continued; and broken wooden axe handles could easily be replaced from bush timbers with aboriginal tools. Among the Yir Yoront the new axe never acquired all the uses it had on mission or cattle stations (carpentry work, pounding tent pegs, use as a hammer, and so on); and, indeed, it was used for little more than the stone axe had been, so that it had no practical effect in improving the native standard of living. It did some jobs better, and could be used longer without breakage; and these factors were sufficient to make it of value to the native. But the assumption of the white man (based in part on a realization that a shift from steel to stone axe in his case would be a definite regression) that his axe was much more efficient, that its use would save time, and that it therefore represented technical "progress" toward goals which he had set for the native was hardly borne out in aboriginal practice. Any leisure time the Yir Yoront might gain by using steel axes or other western tools was invested, not in "improving the conditions of life," and certainly not in developing aesthetic activities, but in sleep, an art they had thoroughly mastered.

Having acquired an axe head through regular trading partners of whom he knew what to expect, a man wanting a stone axe was then dependent solely upon a known and an adequate nature and upon his own skills or easily acquired techniques. A man wanting a steel axe, however, was in no such self-reliant position. While he might acquire one through trade, he now had the new alternative of dispensing with technological behavior in relation with a predictable nature and conduct in relation with a predictable trading partner and of turning instead to conduct alone in relation with a highly erratic missionary. If he attended one of the mission festivals when steel axes were handed out as gifts, he might receive one simply by chance or if he had happened somehow to impress upon the mission staff that he was one of the "better" bush aboriginals (their definition of "better" being quite different from that of his bush fellows). Or he might—but again almost by pure chance—be given some brief job in connection with the mission which would enable him to earn a steel axe. In either case, for older men a preference for the steel axe helped create a situation of dependence in place of a situation of self-reliance and a behavior shift from situations in technology or conduct which were well structured or defined to situations in conduct alone which were ill defined. It was particularly the older ones among the men, whose earlier experience or knowledge of the white man's harshness in any event made them suspicious, who would avoid having any relations with the mission at all, and who thus excluded themselves from acquiring steel axes directly from that source.

The steel axe was the root of psychological stress among the Yir Yoront even more significantly in other aspects of social relations. This was the result of new factors which the missionary considered all to the good: the simple numerical increase in axes per capita as a result of mission distribution; and distribution from the mission directly to younger men, women, and even children. By winning the favor of the mission staff, a woman might be given a steel axe. This was clearly intended to be hers. The situation was quite different from that involved in borrowing an axe from a male relative, with the result that a woman called such an axe "my" steel axe, a possessive form she never used for a stone axe. (Lexically, the steel axe was differentiated from the stone by an adjectival suffix signifying "metal," the element "axe" remaining identical.) Furthermore, young men or even boys might also obtain steel axes directly from the mission. A result was that older men no longer had a complete monopoly of all the axes in the bush community. Indeed, an old man might have only a stone axe, while his wives and sons had steel axes which they considered their own and which he might even desire to borrow. All this led to a revolutionary confusion of sex, age, and kinship roles, with a major gain in independence and loss of subordination on the part of those able now to acquire steel axes when they had been unable to possess stone axes before.

The trading partner relationship was also affected by the new situation. A Yir Yoront might have a trading partner in a tribe to the south whom he defined as a younger brother, and on whom as an older brother he would therefore have an edge. But if the partner were in contact with the mission or had other easier access to steel axes, his subordination to his bush colleague was obviously decreased. Indeed, under the new dispensation he might prefer to give his axe to a bush "sweetheart" in return for favors or otherwise dispose of it outside regular trade channels, since many steel axes were so distributed between natives in new ways. Among other things, this took some of the excitement away from the fiestalike tribal gatherings centering around initiations during the dry season. These had traditionally been the climactic annual occasions for exchanges between trading partners, when a man might seek to acquire a whole year's supply of stone axe heads. Now he might find himself prostituting his wife to almost total strangers in return for steel axes or other white men's goods. With trading partnerships weakened, there was less reason to attend the fiestas, and less fun for those who did. A decline in one of the important social activities which had symbolized these great gatherings created a lessening of interest in the other social aspects of these events.

Not only did an increase in steel axes and their distribution to women change the character of the relations between individual and individual, the paired relationships that have been noted, but a new type of relationship, hitherto practically unknown among the Yir Yoront, was created in their axe-acquiring conduct with whites. In the aboriginal society there were almost no occasions outside the immediate family when one individual would initiate action to several other people at once. For in any average group, while a person in accordance with the kinship system might be superordinate to several people to whom he could suggest or command action, at the same time he was also subordinate to several others, in relation with whom such behavior would be taboo. There was thus no overall chieftainship or authoritarian leadership of any kind. Such complicated operations as grass-burning, animal drives, or totemic ceremonies could be carried out smoothly because each person knew his roles both in technology and conduct.

On both mission and cattle stations, however, the whites imposed upon the aboriginals their conception of leadership roles, with one person in a controlling relationship with a subordinate group. Aboriginals called together to receive gifts, including axes, at a mission Christmas party found themselves facing one or two whites who sought to control their behavior for the occasion, who disregarded the age, sex, and kinship variables among them of which they were so conscious, and who considered them all at one subordinate level. Or the white might impose similar patterns on a working party. (But if he placed an aboriginal in charge of a mixed group of post hole diggers, for example, half of the group, those subordinate to the "boss," would work while the other half, who were superordinate to him, would sleep.) The steel axe, together, of course, with other European goods, came to symbolize for the aboriginal this new and uncomfortable form of social organization, the leader-group relationship.

The most disturbing effects of the steel axe, operating in conjunction with other elements also being introduced from the white man's several subcultures, developed in the realm of traditional ideas, sentiments, and values. These were undermined at a rapidly mounting rate, without new conceptions being defined to replace them. The result was a mental and moral void which foreshadowed the collapse and destruction of all Yir Yoront culture, if not, indeed, the extinction of the biological group itself.

From what has been said it should be clear how changes in overt behavior, in technology and conduct, weakened the values inherent in a reliance on nature, in androcentrism or the prestige of masculinity, in age prestige, and in the various kinship relations. A scene was set in which a wife or young son, his initiation perhaps not even yet completed, need no longer bow to the husband or father, who was left confused and insecure as he asked to borrow a steel axe from them. For the woman and boy the steel axe helped establish a new degree of freedom which was accepted readily as an escape from the unconscious stress of the old patterns, but which left them also confused and insecure. Ownership became less well defined, so that stealing and trespass were introduced into technology and conduct. Some of the excitement surrounding the great ceremonies evaporated, so that the only fiestas the people had became less festive, less interesting. Indeed, life itself became less interesting, although this did not lead the Yir Yoront to invent suicide, a concept foreign to them. . . .

11.2   INTRODUCTION

A theme that has been built up from a variety of approaches throughout this book is asserted most unambiguously in this selection.

Dorwin Cartwright makes clear and explicit the point of view that individuals can be understood only in relation to the groups to which they belong, and goes even further to state that individual characteristics are "in a real sense . . . properties of groups and of the relationships between people." In these terms, it follows that changes in individuals necessarily imply changes in groups.

The author documents and elaborates this point of view, stressing the crucial role of group support in determining whether individual change will occur and endure. In its emphasis on this point, this selection goes right to the core of a guidance counselor's concerns and has a number of implications about the relative value of different practices and approaches. It suggests, for example, that in dealing with a delinquent adolescent, individual counseling directed at the emotional sources of his deviance would be less likely to produce a lasting improvement than would attempts to alter his group affiliations and his exposure to deviant-group norms.

With respect to the general problem of fostering changes in children and adolescents, it would seem important to include the family as one of the major groups that is likely to affect the extent and nature of any changes that occur. On the whole an individual's family will operate as a limiting factor with respect to the changes that are possible for him, but, in certain cases, the family may, in Cartwright's terms, also serve as an important medium of change. Thus, parents can sometimes be enlisted to provide pressure and support without which it may be impossible for a child or adolescent to carry through in some new direction.

As has already been noted at a number of points throughout the book, the fact that a major key to individual change is to be found in groups would seem to have primarily optimistic implications. It seems much more possible, for example, to alter situations, introduce new information into a group, or influence patterns of interaction among individuals than to alter directly an individual's dominant motives or to help him resolve deep-seated ambivalences and insecurities. This selection clearly suggests, moreover, that such individual changes might well follow from alterations in the group environment, and thus the view that it presents makes change a much more accessible goal than it might seem on the basis of a different set of premises.

11.2   ACHIEVING CHANGE IN PEOPLE: SOME APPLICATIONS OF GROUP DYNAMICS THEORY[1]

Dorwin Cartwright

I

. . .The word "change" produces emotional reactions. It is not a neutral word. To many people it is threatening. It conjures up visions of a revolutionary, a dissatisfied idealist, a trouble-maker, a malcontent. Nicer words referring to the

[1]From Dorwin Cartwright, "Achieving Change in People: Some Applications of Group Dynamics Theory," *Human Relations*, 4, 1951, pp. 381–392. Reprinted by permission of Plenum Publishing Company Limited, Wembley, England.

This paper is based on a lecture delivered at Wayne University, Detroit, in the Leo M. Franklin Lecture Series, 1950–1951.

process of changing people are education, training, orientation, guidance, indoctrination, therapy. We are more ready to have others "educate" us than to have them "change" us. We, ourselves, feel less guilty in "training" others than in "changing" them. Why this emotional response? What makes the two kinds of words have such different meanings? I believe that a large part of the difference lies in the fact that the safer words (like education or therapy) carry the implicit assurance that the only changes produced will be good ones, acceptable within a currently held value system. The cold, unmodified word "change," on the contrary, promises no respect for values; it might even tamper with values themselves. Perhaps for this very reason it will foster straight thinking if we use the word "change" and thus force ourselves to struggle directly and self-consciously with the problems of value that are involved. Words like education, training, or therapy, by the very fact that they are not so disturbing, may close our eyes to the fact that they too inevitably involve values.

Another advantage of using the word "change" rather than other related words is that it does not restrict our thinking to a limited set of aspects of people that are legitimate targets of change. Anyone familiar with the history of education knows that there has been endless controversy over what it is about people that "education" properly attempts to modify. Some educators have viewed education simply as imparting knowedge, others mainly as providing skills for doing things, still others as producing healthy "attitudes," and some have aspired to instill a way of life. Or if we choose to use a word like "therapy," we can hardly claim that we refer to a more clearly defined realm of change. Furthermore, one can become inextricably entangled in distinctions and vested interests by attempting to distinguish sharply between, let us say, the domain of education and that of therapy. If we are to try to take a broader view and to develop some basic principles that promise to apply to all types of modifications in people, we had better use a word like "change" to keep our thinking general enough. . . .

II

For various reasons we have found that much of our work has been devoted to an attempt to gain a better understanding of the ways in which people change their behavior or resist efforts by others to have them do so. Whether we set for ourselves the practical goal of improving behavior or whether we take on the intellectual task of understanding why people do what they do, we have to investigate processes of communication, influence, social pressure—in short, problems of change.

In this work we have encountered great frustration. The problems have been most difficult to solve. Looking back over our experience, I have become convinced that no small part of the trouble has resulted from an irresistible tendency to conceive of our problems in terms of the individual. We live in an individualistic culture. We value the individual highly, and rightly so. But I am inclined to believe that our political and social concern for the individual has narrowed our thinking as social scientists so much that we have not been able to state our research problems properly. Perhaps we have taken the individual as the unit of observation and study when some larger unit would have been more appropriate. Let us look at a few examples.

Consider first some matters having to do with the mental health of an individual. We can all agree, I believe, that an important mark of a healthy personality is that the individual's self-esteem has not been undermined. But on what does self-esteem depend? From research on this problem we have discovered that, among other things, repeated experiences of failure or traumatic failures on matters of central importance serve to undermine one's self-esteem. We also know that whether a person experiences success or failure as a result of some undertaking depends upon the level of aspiration which he has set for himself. Now, if we try to discover how the level of aspiration gets set, we are immediately involved in the person's relationships to groups. The groups to which he belongs set standards for his behavior which he must accept if he is to remain in the group. If his capacities do not allow him to reach these standards, he experiences failure, he withdraws or is rejected by the group and his self-esteem suffers a shock.

Suppose, then, that we accept a task of therapy, of rebuilding his self-esteem. It would appear plausible from our analysis of the problem that we should attempt to work with variables of the same sort that produced the difficulty, that is to work with him either in the groups to which he now belongs or to introduce him into new groups which are selected for the purpose and to work upon his relationships to groups as such. From the point of view of preventive mental health, we might even attempt to train the groups in our communities—classes in schools, work groups in business, families, unions, religious and cultural groups—to make use of practices better designed to protect the self-esteem of their members.

Consider a second example. A teacher finds that in her class she has a number of trouble-makers, full of aggression. She wants to know why these children are so aggressive and what can be done about it. A foreman in a factory has the same kind of problem with some of his workers. He wants the same kind of help. The solution most tempting to both the teacher and the foreman often is to transfer the worst trouble-makers to someone else, or if facilities are available, to refer them for counseling. But is the problem really of such a nature that it can be solved by removing the trouble-maker from the situation or by working on his individual motivations and emotional life? What leads does research give us? The evidence indicates, of course, that there are many causes of aggressiveness in people, but one aspect of the problem has become increasingly clear in recent years. If we observe carefully the amount of aggressive behavior and the number of trouble-makers to be found in a large collection of groups, we find that these characteristics can vary tremendously from group to group even when the different groups are composed essentially of the same kinds of people. In the now classic experiments of Lewin, Lippitt, and White (1939) on the effects of different styles of leadership, it was found that the same group of children displayed markedly different levels of aggressive behavior when under different styles of leadership. Moreover, when individual children were transferred from one group to another, their levels of aggressiveness shifted to conform to the atmosphere of the new group. Efforts to account for one child's aggressiveness under one style of leadership merely in terms of his personality traits could hardly succeed under these conditions. This is not to say that a person's behavior is entirely to be accounted for by the atmosphere and structure of the immediate group, but it is remarkable to what an extent a strong, cohesive group can control aspects of a member's behavior traditionally thought to be expressive of enduring personality traits. Recognition of this fact rephrases the problem of how to change such behavior. It directs us to a study of the sources of the influence of the group on its members.

Let us take an example from a different field. What can we learn from efforts to change people by mass media and mass persuasion? In those rare instances when educators, propagandists, advertisers, and others who want to influence large numbers of people, have bothered to make an objective evaluation of the enduring changes produced by their efforts, they have been able to demonstrate only the most negligible effects (Cartwright, 1949). The inefficiency of attempts to influence the public by mass media would be scandalous if there were agreement that it was important or even desirable to have such influences strongly exerted. In fact, it is no exaggeration to say that all of the research and experience of generations has not improved the efficiency of lectures or other means of mass influence to any noticeable degree. Something must be wrong with our theories of learning, motivation, and social psychology.

Within very recent years some research data have been accumulating which may give us a clue to the solution of our problem. In one series of experiments directed by Lewin, it was found that a method of group decision, in which the group as a whole made a decision to have its members change their behavior, was from two to ten times as effective in producing actual change as was a lecture presenting exhortation to change (1951). We have yet to learn precisely what produces these differences of effectiveness, but it is clear that by introducing group forces into the situation a whole new level of influence has been achieved.

The experience has been essentially the same when people have attempted to increase the productivity of individuals in work settings. Traditional conceptions of how to increase the output of workers have stressed the individual: select the right man for the job; simplify the job for him; train him in the skills required; motivate him by economic incentives; make it clear to whom he reports; keep the lines of authority and responsibility simple and straight. But even when all these conditions are fully met we are finding that productivity is far below full potential. There is even good reason to conclude that this individualistic conception of the determinants of productivity actually fosters negative consequences. The individual, now isolated and subjected to the demands of the organization through the commands of his boss, finds that he must create with his fellow employees informal groups, not shown on any table of organization, in order to protect himself from arbitrary control of his life, from the boredom produced by the endless repetition of mechanically sanitary and routine operations, and from the impoverishment of his emotional and social life brought about by the frustration of his basic needs for social interaction, participation, and acceptance in a stable group. Recent experiments have demonstrated clearly that the productivity of work groups can be greatly increased by methods of work organization and supervision which give more responsibility to work groups, which allow for fuller participation in important decisions, and which make stable groups the firm basis for support of the individual's social needs (Coch and French, 1948). I am convinced that future research will also demonstrate that people working under such conditions become more mature and creative individuals in their homes, in community life, and as citizens.

As a final example, let us examine the experience of efforts to train people in workshops, institutes, and special training courses. Such efforts are common in various areas of social welfare, intergroup relations, political affairs, industry, and adult education generally. It is an unfortunate fact that objective evaluation of the effects of such training efforts has only rarely been undertaken, but there is evidence for those who will look that the actual change in behavior produced is most disappointing. A workshop not infrequently develops keen interest among the participants, high morale and enthusiasm, and a firm resolve on the part of many to apply all the wonderful insights back home. But what happens back home? The trainee discovers that his colleagues don't share his enthusiasm. He learns that the task of changing others' expectations and ways of doing things is discouragingly difficult. He senses, perhaps not very clearly, that it would make all the difference in the world if only there were a few other people sharing his enthusiasm and insights with whom he cold plan activities, evaluate consequences of efforts, and from whom he could gain emotional and motivational support. The approach to training which conceives of its task as being merely that of changing the individual probably produces frustration, demoralization, and disillusionment in as large a measure as it accomplishes more positive results.

A few years ago the Research Center for Group Dynamics undertook to shed light on this problem by investigating the operation of a workship for training leaders in intercultural relations (Lippitt, 1949). In a project, directed by Lippitt, we set out to compare systematically the different effects of the workshop upon trainees who came as isolated individuals in contrast to those who came as teams. Since one of the problems in the field of intercultural relations is that of getting people of good will to be more active in community efforts to improve intergroup relations, one goal of the training workshop was to increase the activity of the trainees in such community affairs. We found that before the workshop there was no difference in the activity level of the people who were to be trained as isolates and of those who were to be trained as teams. Six months after the workshop, however, those who had been trained as isolates were only slightly more active than before the workshop whereas those who had been members of strong training teams were now much more active. We do not have clear evidence on the point, but we would be quite certain that the maintenance of heightened activity over a long period of time would also be much better for members of teams. For the isolates the effect of the workshop had the characteristic of a "shot in the arm" while for the team member it produced a more enduring change because the team provided continuous support and reinforcement for its members.

III

What conclusions may we draw from these examples? What principles of achieving change in people can we see emerging? To begin with the most general proposition, we may state that the behavior, attitudes, beliefs, and values of the individual are all firmly grounded in the groups to which he belongs. How aggressive or cooperative a person is, how much self-respect and self-confidence he has, how energetic and productive his work is, what he aspires to, what he believes to be true and good, whom he loves or hates, and what beliefs and prejudices he holds—all these characteristics are highly determined by the individual's group memberships. In a real sense, they are properties of groups and of the relationships between people. Whether they change or resist change will, therefore, be greatly influenced by the nature of these groups. Attempts to change them must be concerned with the dynamics of groups.

In examining more specifically how groups enter into the process of change, we find it useful to view groups in at least three different ways. In the first view, the group is seen as a source of influence over its members. Efforts to change behavior can be supported or blocked by pressures on members stemming from the group. To make constructive use of these pressures the group must be used *as a medium of change*. In the second view, the group itself becomes the *target of change*. To change the behavior of individuals it may be necessary to change the standards of the group, its style of leadership, its emotional atmosphere, or its stratification into cliques and hierarchies. Even though the goal may be to change the behavior of *individuals*, the target of change becomes the group. In the third view, it is recognized that many changes of behavior can be brought about only by the organized efforts of groups *as agents of change*. A committee to combat intolerance, a labor union, an employers association, a citizens group to increase the pay of teachers—any action group will be more or less effective depending upon the way it is organized, the satisfactions it provides to its members, the degree to which its goals are clear, and a host of other properties of the group.

An adequate social technology of change, then, requires at the very least a scientific understanding of groups viewed in each of these ways. We shall consider here only the first two aspects of the problem: the group as a medium of change and as a target of change.

The group as a medium of change

PRINCIPLE NO. 1   If the group is to be used effectively as a medium of change, those people who are to be changed and those who are to exert influence for change must have a strong sense of belonging to the same group.

Kurt Lewin described this principle well: "The normal gap between teacher and student, doctor and patient, social worker and public, can . . . be a real obstacle to acceptance of the advocated conduct." In other words, in spite of whatever status differences there might be between them, the teacher and the student have to feel as members of one group in matters involving their sense of values. The chances for re-education seem to be increased whenever a strong we-feeling is created (1948). Recent experiments by Preston and Heintz have demonstrated greater changes of opinions among members of discussion groups operating with participatory leadership than among those with supervisory leadership (1949). The implications of this principle for classroom teaching are far-reaching. The same may be said of supervision in the factory, army, or hospital.

PRINCIPLE NO. 2   The more attractive the group is to its members the greater is the influence that the group can exert on its members.

This principle has been extensively documented by Festinger and his co-workers (1950). They have been able to show in a variety of settings that in more cohesive groups there is a greater readiness of members to attempt to influence others, a greater readiness to be influenced by others, and stronger pressures toward conformity when conformity is a relevant matter for the group. Important for the practitioner wanting to make use of this principle is, of course, the question of how to increase the attractiveness of groups. This is a question with many answers. Suffice it to say that a group is more attractive the more it satisfies the needs of its members. We have been able to demonstrate experimentally an increase in group cohesiveness by increasing the liking of members for each other as persons, by increasing the perceived importance of the group goal, and by increasing the prestige of the group among other groups. Experienced group workers could add many other ways to this list.

PRINCIPLE NO. 3   In attempts to change attitudes, values, or behavior, the more relevant they are to the basis of attraction to the group, the greater will be the influence that the group can exert upon them.

I believe this principle gives a clue to some otherwise puzzling phenomena. How does it happen that a group, like a labor union, seems to be able to exert such strong discipline over its members in some matters (let us say in dealings with management), while it seems unable to exert nearly the same influence in other matters (let us say in political action)? If we examine why it is that members are attracted to the group, I believe we will find that a particular reason for belonging seems more related to some of the group's activities than to others. If a man joins a union mainly to keep his job and to improve his working conditions, he may be largely uninfluenced by the union's attempt to modify his attitudes toward national and international affairs. Groups differ tremendously in the range of matters that are relevant to them and hence over which they have influence. Much of the inefficiency of adult education could be reduced if more attention were paid to the need that influence attempts be appropriate to the groups in which they are made.

PRINCIPLE NO. 4   The greater the prestige of a group member in the eyes of the other members, the greater the influence he can exert.

Polansky, Lippitt, and Redl (1950) have demonstrated this principle with great care and methodological ingenuity in a series of studies in children's summer camps. From a practical point of view it must be emphasized that the things giving prestige to a member may not be those characteristics most prized by the official management of the group. The most prestige-carrying member of a Sunday School class may not possess the characteristics most similar to the minister of the church. The teacher's pet may be a poor source of influence within a class. This principle is the basis for the common observation that the official leader and the actual leader of a group are often not the same individual.

PRINCIPLE NO. 5   Efforts to change individuals or subparts of a group which, if successful, would have the result of making them deviate from the norms of the group will encounter strong resistance.

During the past few years a great deal of evidence has been accumulated showing the tremendous pressures which groups can exert upon members to conform to the group's norms. The price of deviation in most groups is rejection or even expulsion. If the member really wants to belong and be accepted, he cannot withstand this type of pressure. It is for this reason that efforts to change people by taking them from the group and giving them special training so often have disappointing results. This principle also accounts for the finding that people thus trained sometimes display increased tension, aggressiveness toward the group, or a tendency to form cults or cliques with others who have shared their training.

These five principles concerning the group as a medium of change would appear to have readiest application to groups created for the purpose of producing changes in people. They provide certain specifications for building effective training or therapy groups. They also point, however, to a difficulty in producing change in people in that they show how resistant an individual is to changing in any way contrary to group pressures and expectations. In order to achieve many kinds of changes in people, therefore, it is necessary to deal with the group as a target of change.

The group as a target of change

PRINCIPLE NO. 6   Strong pressure for changes in the group can be established by creating a shared perception by members of the need for change, thus making the source of pressure for change lie within the group.

Marrow and French (1945) report a dramatic case-study which illustrates this principle quite well. A manufacturing concern had a policy against hiring women over thirty because it was believed that they were slower, more difficult to train, and more likely to be absent. The staff psychologist was able to present to management evidence that this belief was clearly unwarranted at least within their own company. The psychologist's facts, however, were rejected and ignored as a basis for action because they violated accepted beliefs. It was claimed that they went against the direct experience of the foremen. Then the psychologist hit upon a plan for achieving change which differed drastically from the usual one of argument, persuasion, and pressure. He proposed that management conduct its own analysis of the situation. With his help management collected all the facts which they believed were relevant to the problem. When the results were in they were now their own facts rather than those of some "outside" expert. Policy was immediately changed without further resistance. The important point here is that facts are not enough. The facts must be the accepted property of the group if they are to become an effective basis for change. There seems to be all the difference in the world in changes actually carried out between those cases in which a consulting firm is hired to do a study and present a report and those in which technical experts are asked to collaborate with the group in doing its own study.

PRINCIPLE NO. 7   Information relating to the need for change, plans for change, and consequences of change must be shared by all relevant people in the group.

Another way of stating this principle is to say that change of a group ordinarily requires the opening of communication channels. Newcomb (1947) has shown how one of the first consequences of mistrust and hostility is the avoidance of communicating openly and freely about the things producing the tension. If you look closely at a pathological group (that is, one that has trouble making decisions or effecting coordinated efforts of its members), you will certainly find strong restraints in that group against communicating vital information among its members. Until these restraints are removed there can be little hope for any real and lasting changes in the group's functioning. In passing it should be pointed out that the removal of barriers to communication will ordinarily be accompanied by a sudden increase in the communication of hostility. The group may appear to be falling apart, and it will certainly be a painful experience to many of the members. This pain and the fear that things are getting out of hand often stop the process of change once begun.

PRINCIPLE NO. 8 Changes in one part of a group produce strain in other related parts which can be reduced only by eliminating the change or by bringing about readjustments in the related parts.

It is a common practice to undertake improvements in group functioning by providing training programs for certain classes of people in the organization. A training program for foremen, for nurses, for teachers, or for group workers is established. If the content of the training is relevant for organizational change, it must of necessity deal with the relationships these people have with other subgroups. If nurses in a hospital change their behavior significantly, it will affect their relations both with the patients and with the doctors. It is unrealistic to assume that both these groups will remain indifferent to any significant changes in this respect. In hierarchical structures this process is most clear. Lippitt has proposed on the basis of research and experience that in such organizations attempts at change should always involve three levels, one being the major target of change and the other two being the one above and the one below.

IV

These eight principles represent a few of the basic propositions emerging from research in group dynamics. Since research is constantly going on and since it is the very nature of research to revise and reformulate our conceptions, we may be sure that these principles will have to be modified and improved as time goes by. In the meantime they may serve as guides in our endeavors to develop a scientifically based technology of social management. . . .

BIBLIOGRAPHY

CARTWRIGHT, D., 1949, "Some Principles of Mass Persuasion: Selected Findings of Research on the Sale of United States War Bonds," *Human Relations*, Vol. II, No. 3, pp. 253–267.

CARTWRIGHT, D., 1950, *The Research Center for Group Dynamics: A Report of Five Years' Activities and a View of Future Needs*, Ann Arbor, Mich.: Institute for Social Research.

COCH, L., AND FRENCH, J. R. P., JR., 1948, "Overcoming Resistance to Change," *Human Relations*, Vol. I, No. 4, pp. 512–532.

FESTINGER, L., *et al.*, 1950, *Theory and Experiment in Social Communication*, collected papers, Ann Arbor: Institute for Social Research.

LEWIN, K., 1948, *Resolving Social Conflicts*, New York: Harper & Row, p. 67.

LEWIN, K., 1951, *Field Theory in Social Science*, New York: Harper & Row, pp. 229–236.

LEWIN, K., LIPPITT, R., AND WHITE, R. K., 1939, "Patterns of Aggressive Behavior in Experimentally Created 'Social Climates'," *Journal of Social Psychology*, 10, pp. 271–299.

LIPPITT, R., 1949, *Training in Community Relations*, New York: Harper & Row.

MARROW, A. J., AND FRENCH, J. R. P., JR., 1945, "Changing a Stereotype in Industry," *Journal of Social Issues*, 1, 3, pp. 33–37.
NEWCOMB, T. M., 1947, "Autistic Hostility and Social Reality," *Human Relations*, Vol. I, No. 1, pp. 69–86.
POLANSKY, N., LIPPITT, R., AND REDL, F., 1950, "An Investigation of Behavioral Contagion in Groups," *Human Relations*, Vol. III, No. 4, pp. 319–348.
PRESTON, M. G., AND HEINTZ, R. K., 1949, "Effects of Participatory vs. Supervisory Leadership on Group Judgment," *Journal of Abnormal and Social Psychology*, 44, pp. 345–355.

11.3 INTRODUCTION

This selection is a case study of an attempt to institute a change in a peasant village and an analysis of the factors that prevented its success. The author, an anthropologist, shows how certain features of the change and of the manner in which it was introduced were inconsistent with, and in some cases directly contrary to, the social structure and the cultural values of the community. Thus, enactment of the change required that people accept and adjust to situations and relationships in which the expectations were incompatible with their orientations to life and society and, indeed, with their personal motivations and self-conceptions.

Some of the reasons that precluded success are quite specific to this particular case, such as the fact that marriage was a prerequisite for full adult status in the society. Every social system, however, has some bases for ascribing status to individuals that are analogous to this, so that such specific features are really instances of more general principles that apply to virtually any group, organization, or society. Age; sex; athletic prowess; body build; specific past experience; seniority; ethnic, social class, or geographic background—any or several of these might serve as criteria for status differentiation.

As in the case described in this selection, the existence of criteria of this sort raises a special and serious problem for the expert—for example, for the guidance-personnel worker. Being a member of the group, he will be subject to evaluation in terms of these ascriptive standards. The particular contribution that defines his job and that his training prepares him to make, however, will not necessarily fit with these expectations and a number of conflicts are likely to follow. For example, a young counselor may be led by his professional judgment and from the perspective of the purposes of a guidance program to suggest changes in a school's grading system. In such a case he would in effect be recommending changes in the roles of others in the system, many of whom would perceive his behavior as inappropriate to his status and to his relationship to them, and would be thus likely to oppose his efforts quite independently of the latter's merits.

This does not mean that the expert is therefore inevitably paralyzed in introducing changes. In the example above, one of the resistant individuals might be a teacher who felt that his competence was being challenged because the change was presented to him as an accomplished fact, originating elsewhere and implying that there was need for improvement in what he felt was his realm of special responsibility. The same individual might respond quite differently, however, if his opinion were sought at the outset and if he was appealed to as being particularly crucial to the success of the planned change. Not all cases will yield to such simple alternatives for solution, but the point of this example is that, as the author of the ensuing selection suggests, in order for an attempt at change or innovation to be effective it must take account of the system's social structure and work in terms of it.

11.3 SOCIAL STRUCTURES AND PLANNED CHANGE: A CASE STUDY FROM THE PHILIPPINES[1]

Willis E. Sibley

This article reports a case in which governmentally planned changes in activities related to economic life and sanitation in a Philippine peasant agricultural village failed to meet the expectations of the initiators of the village improvement program. The failure of the initiators of change to recognize the internal structure and culture of the village seemed to contribute to the program's collapse.

Established by the Philippine Department of Education after the second World War, the Community School program of adult education and community development was designed to ameliorate levels of living in the thousands of small, rural Philippine villages.[2] The program was instituted in response to a rural population steadily increasing in size, the serious effects of inflation in the period following the Second World War, and declining agricultural productivity, all of which had, by the mid-1950s, intensified forces already leading to noticeably lowered levels of living even before the Second World War. Field data utilized in this article were

---

[1]From Willis E. Sibley, "Social Structures and Planned Change: A Case Study from the Philippines," *Human Organization*, 19, 1960, pp. 209–211.

[2]See Jose V. Aguilar, *This Is Your Community School*, Manila, Philippines: Bookman, Inc., 1951; Bureau of Public Schools, Department of Education, Republic of the Philippines, *The Community School of the Philippines*, 1954; Bureau of Public Schools, Manila, *Philippine Community School Bulletin*; Paul C. Fawley, ed., *Operation of the Philippine Community School*, Baguio Summer Institute, University of the Philippines, 1957; Human Relations Area Files, Inc., *The Philippines*, New Haven, Conn.: 1955, Chapter X, "Education."

gathered in a village in southwestern Negros Island, central Philippines, during 1954 and 1955.[3] The village shall be called Ma-ayo.[4]

THE VILLAGE Ma-ayo, a village of about 400 persons, is the principal village in a *barrio*[5] bearing the same name. Culturally, the village is placed in the Bisayan zone of the Philippines. The population of Ma-ayo is quite homogeneous, nearly all nominally Catholic, and it subsists mainly upon piece-work wage labor in neighboring absentee-owned sugar fields and in tenant rice farming in nearby rainfall-watered paddies.

Kinship is reckoned bilaterally. In work teams,[6] and in power groupings associated with community affairs, kin-based structures with some continuity in time are observable. Village endogamy is marked. A 1954 census showed that in fifty percent of all marriages, both partners claimed Ma-ayo as their natal village. The necessity for approval by a large number of kinsmen of spouses brought in from other villages in cases of exogamous unions tends strongly to preserve basic beliefs and values shared in the community.[7] Residence patterns tend toward bilocality at marriage, with neolocality as an ultimate goal. Initial residence choices for newly married couples are influenced strongly by the locus of available living space, and by the fact that most newly married couples cannot afford to fulfill the ideal neolocal pattern by building a house.

As in many nucleated Philippine villages in areas characterized by absentee land ownership and high tenancy rates, the raised bamboo and thatch houses in Ma-ayo are crowded cheek-by-jowl in the limited space which can be kept from agricultural use. Immediately around the houses are small groves of banana and coconut trees which provide important dietary supplements to the daily fare of fish and rice, but which are not important as cash crops. A few families possess small kitchen gardens. The village is neatly quartered by a village street running north and south, and by a narrow-gauge railway (connecting the village with the sugar milling center twenty miles distant) running east and west. This undoubtedly for-

[3]Ten months of the fieldwork was accomplished during 1954 and 1955 with the aid of the United States Educational Foundation in the Philippines (Fulbright Program) and of the Philippine Studies Program, University of Chicago.

[4]Ma-ayo is a pseudonym. The village is nonetheless real and our data are not altered except for village identification.

[5]In the Philippines, the term *barrio* designates a political-geographical zone, which is a constituent part of a municipality. There may be one or more villages in a *barrio*, the largest of which ordinarily bears the same name as the *barrio*.

[6]A discussion of bilaterally organized work teams is offered in Willis E. Sibley, "Work Partner Choice in a Philippine Village," *Silliman Journal*, IV, No. 3, 1957, Dumaguete, Philippines: Silliman University.

[7]See Willis E. Sibley, "The Maintenance of Unity and Distinctiveness in a Philippine Village," *Men in Cultures*, A. F. C. Wallace, ed., Proceedings of the Fifth International Congress of Anthropological and Ethnological Sciences, Philadelphia: University of Pennsylvania Press, 1960.

tuitous, unplanned geographical subdividing of the village by the street and the railway assumes considerable significance in later sections of this report.

ESTABLISHMENT OF THE COMMUNITY SCHOOL PROGRAM

During 1953, the year immediately preceding my fieldwork in Ma-ayo, the six teachers of the elementary school established Community School development sections, or zones. These zones, called by the Tagalog term *purok*, or "little hamlet," were established not only in the main village of Ma-ayo, but also in the satellite hamlets or *sitios* within the geographical area of the *barrio*. Emphasis was placed upon the cleaning of paths and yards, the building of sanitary privies, and a reduction in the use of surface water for drinking and cooking purposes. The 1953 attempt at village improvement appears to have been a total failure, with the teachers suggesting that their efforts had been spread too thinly over too large an area to achieve satisfactory results.

In the latter months of 1954, the Community School program was reinstituted, this time only in the village of Ma-ayo itself. Apparently at the behest of higher officials of the program (I have been unable to find documentary evidence to prove the preceding surmise), an attempt was made to encourage competition in village improvement activities through the setting up of four named zones, or *puroks*,[8] each with an elected President, Vice President, and Secretary-Treasurer.

These zone officers were promptly elected under the supervision of the teachers although, significantly, none of the officers chosen were of the established, observable leadership group in the village.[9] In general, those chosen for zone officers were younger, had had more formal education, and were closer to the teachers socially than were the older established leaders in the village. A majority of the 12 zone officers were, in fact, unmarried, in a village in which marriage clearly is a mark of sociological maturity and a necessary condition for consideration as a fully adult member of the group. They may well be persons who will ultimately assume leadership roles in the community, but they had not gained such status in 1954.

Following the pattern of quadrangles already established by the existence of the village street and the sugar-mill railway mentioned above, the teachers designated these areas as the named zones for village improvement.

As in 1953, but limiting the scope of their activities to the village of Ma-ayo itself, the teachers initiated programs of street cleaning, yard maintenance and fence building, privy construction, well digging, house repair, animal inoculation,

---

[8] In free translation, these names were such exhortatory ones as "long live zone," "cooperative zone," and "advancing zone."

[9] Criteria for leadership choice in Ma-ayo are discussed in Willis E. Sibley, "Leadership in a Philippine Barrio," *Philippine Journal of Public Administration*, I, 1957, Quezon City, P.I.: University of the Philippines.

kitchen gardening, and agricultural improvement. Almost daily, the elementary school children could be seen pulling weeds from the street, carefully aligning rocks as street borders, and informing their parents that their yards should look neater. Periodic inspections of residences were conducted by the teachers, to count new water and privy facilities which were supposedly under construction, but which actually were rarely completed.

Despite a lack of noticeable progress on projects which might ultimately improve levels of living (such as better gardening or the inoculation of animals, vaccines for which were provided free of charge by the government), certain changes could be observed during the weeks immediately following the initiation of Community School programs. The village street was handsome indeed, with its neat borders and lack of weeds. Some houses were repaired, and their tiny yards put in order. Rarely, however, could substantial activity be observed in the absence of a teacher supervisor. Perhaps it was partly because of local disappointment at the failure of a widely heralded official inspection committee from the provincial capital to arrive for an evaluation inspection which led to the rapid loss of interest in community improvement, and to its virtual abandonment within about two months after the initial designation of improvement zones. Yet still more important reasons for the failure seem to exist, and attention is turned next to these.

THE STATUS AND ROLES OF TEACHERS
How do we account for the failure of the Community School program? Let us consider first the status and roles of the teacher group in this peasant village, since the teachers were the primary initiators of change.[10]

Teachers are assigned a high status position in the village by virtue, at least in part, of their education and *relatively* high, steady incomes. They are accorded respect and deference behavior. The villagers do not, however, consider the teachers able to render competent advice concerning agriculture and animal husbandry because they do not plant rice or gardens, nor do they raise pigs and chickens. To some extent, the teachers behave as if they do not know the mechanics of rice planting or pig feeding. This "not knowing" role appears to be a part of their perception of themselves as teachers; for, with the acquisition of formal education and a college degree in this culture, very frequently manual labor is felt to be inappropriate, both by the formally educated person and by his associates and manual laboring acquaintances. Yet most of the teachers in Ma-ayo come from agricultural village backgrounds in which husbandry and planting techniques are learned by all growing youngsters. The villagers' perception that the teachers know nothing about agriculture or animal husbandry is an important

---

[10]For suggestions concerning the analysis of the role of teachers I am indebted to Homer Barnett of the University of Oregon. [W.E.S.]

part of their contribution to the maintenance of the role of teacher. It should be added here that reinforcing the villagers' reluctance to alter techniques of animal husbandry and rice planting are the facts of scarcity and risk. An ensured, although inadequate, rice crop, or a slender pig, are more highly valued than an uncertain but potentially larger harvest or product.

Socially, the teachers do not participate in gossip and joking sessions at the coconut wine stands after the day's work is finished. Thus, the teachers stand apart. It is not unlikely that the teachers' relatively more frequent interaction with the younger members of the community at least indirectly influenced the election of younger persons rather than established village leaders as improvement zone officers.

More important even than the role of the agents of change in the outcome of this experiment are social structural considerations of a different nature. Work in Ma-ayo is often accomplished in parties of two or more persons, this pattern being strongly marked in the traditional practice of rice culture. Through actual counting and tabulation, it was found that the leaders of such parties for work in the paddies, in the sugar fields, in house building, and in other operations, tend strongly to choose kinsmen in preference to nonkinsmen as work partners. It has already been noted that residence in Ma-ayo is either bilocal or neolocal, with the choice of locale dependent largely upon the availability of space in or near the household of either the bride's or groom's parents. The net result of the juxtaposition of desire for working together, along with contemporary residence patterns, is that groups of persons (kinsmen) accustomed to working together often do not reside in contiguous living sites, or even in sites within the same sector of the village as marked by the street and the railway. By designating as operational zones the quarters of the village neatly arranged by the position of the street and railway, the teachers unknowingly ignored a more important principle of organization, namely, accustomed working partnerships.

The fact that the teachers did not tap the internal leadership group provides another possible reason for the failure of the program. Positions of leadership in Ma-ayo traditionally are not actively sought, but are rather imposed upon persons with qualifications, including pleasing personality characteristics, the existence in the village of a sizable kin group of potential followers, relative economic well-being, and seniority in age. In addition, the prospective leader must make at least a nominal show of religious participation, preferably Catholic. The latter statements express the general proposition that the leader must know and conform to existing systems of values and tradition. During 1954–1955, there existed about six such leaders, each of whom had a consistent following in local affairs. The teachers did not succeed in convincing these men of the merits of the Community School program. The role of the "follower" is well developed in Ma-ayo, and in our stay in the village few instances could be recorded of collective action not preceded by the approval of one or more of these leaders. Those actually selected as officers in the improvement zones had the further serious disadvantage of youth, for the population of Ma-ayo forms a subsociety in which the principle of age respect provides a key to the understanding of many habitual patterns of behavior, authority, and decision-making.

In closing this brief analysis, certain relevant features of the local culture are to be stressed. In the rural Philippines, and in Ma-ayo, there is a general lack of awareness of the relationships between sanitation and health. Thus, the sanitary privy and safe water programs seemed to many informants to be additional burdens involving extra work, the value of the projects not being clearly perceived. Similarly, there was little acceptance of the need for improvements in the traditional modes of agricultural practice and animal husbandry, despite patent and recognized inadequacies in the food supply. It should be added in defense of the rational powers of residents of Ma-ayo that drastic changes in rice growing were avoided because of the potential risk as they saw it. One lost crop is to them far more disastrous than the insufficiency of an inadequate but sure crop. To be advised on rice growing and animal husbandry by teachers, who did not themselves participate in such activities, was clearly laughable to a sizable proportion of the adult population. To be directed in village improvement by juniors in age, the elected zone officers, was improper and often insulting, for such direction necessarily ignored or seriously modified traditional beliefs concerning age respect. The importance of age respect cannot safely be ignored in such cases, and it is not uncommon to find young people trained in government agricultural schools who are subsequently deeply discouraged when they return to their natal villages and are prevented from putting their new knowledge into practice. The young people are diffident in putting their new knowledge forward, and their elders are reluctant to accept their advice. It might be possible in such a situation for a young person to convince an elder leader of the value of his new skills and techniques, thus gaining the backing necessary for the initiation of changes. Such behavior was not, however, observed in Ma-ayo.

CONCLUSION This case provides an example from a non-Western area to demonstrate the proposition that, for planned changes to be successful, they must be congruous with existing cultural beliefs (or at least not be in direct conflict with them) and must be presented in a manner which makes full use of existing social structural arrangements. It might have been better for the Community School authorities to initiate their programs by working on problems which were perceived as problems by the villagers themselves, even if they were of little interest to the initiators. That the villagers in Ma-ayo could, on occasion, organize themselves for collective action was amply demonstrated late in 1955 when several local leaders organized a large group of men who labored mightily for several weeks to rebuild the village street so that it would not be muddy during the rainy season and at fiesta time.

Since 1956, the Philippine government has developed a new program for rural community development, separate from the school system, which may eliminate some of the problems reflected in this paper. An attempt is being made to recruit, select, and train as local agents of change high status individuals who, after a period of training in a national center on Luzon Island, will return to their natal villages to initiate changes of various kinds. While it seems clear that structural features of local village organization are being given much more attention in the new program of training, the problem of age may remain a serious one. High status in the village ordinarily means that a man must be adult, preferably married, and reasonably well-to-do, at least in comparison with his village mates. Such men, of course, have the least motivation and interest in taking the risks involved in engaging in a new and little-tried venture. It is, however, still too early to assess the result of the new community development program.

11.4   INTRODUCTION

This selection deals with problems of change that are of direct relevance to guidance specialists and at the same time it integrates some of the main themes that have emerged in this chapter so far. The author describes the introduction of a guidance program in a high school and the resistance it encountered, tracing the sources of the latter through an analysis of the specific ways in which different individuals in the system were affected by the innovation. As a result, Atwood is able to account for the full range of individual reactions in terms of a few factors, these having to do with the nature of the changes in the patterns of interaction among teachers and administrators that the new program brought about.

This article has obvious importance for guidance-personnel workers because of its concern with the reactions of teachers and others to guidance notions and with many concrete features of the life of an educational organization. Its significance and relevance are no less at a general level, however. It clearly translates into patterns of behavior and interaction the basic notion that "social change" consists of many specific alterations affecting specific individuals in particular ways. In doing this, it both adds reality to an abstract principle and elaborates the latter's meaning.

In addition, the underlying theoretical rationale that this selection makes explicit provides the practitioner with a useful framework for thinking about change and about organizational processes in general. It emphasizes and validates the relationship between individual feelings and attitudes and the context of social interaction in which they occur. Although the author does not assert that differences in interaction were the *cause* of differences in attitudes, the relationship is such that the latter could have been predicted from knowledge of the former. Thus the results of the study strongly suggest that each individual's perspective on the introduction of the guidance program depended on its effect on his role in the organization and that this effect can be understood primarily in terms of the content and meaning of his relationships and interaction with others. For this reason, the principal's assessment that the faculty was "guidance-minded" was essentially irrelevant to an accurate anticipation of the reactions to his innovation. Involved was not guidance in general or in the abstract but, rather, specific changes in the structure of statuses, authority, and interaction within which individuals functioned. An analysis of the full complexity of these changes would have led to a much more specific plan than that of "going slow" and would have, instead, taken account of the specific resistances that would be likely at each point in the process and from each part of the system.

11.4 SMALL-SCALE ADMINISTRATIVE CHANGE: RESISTANCE TO THE INTRODUCTION OF A HIGH SCHOOL GUIDANCE PROGRAM[1]*

M. S. Atwood

The major aim of this [article] . . . is to describe in detail and analyze the steps by which the principal of a large city high school, in trying to improve the guidance services offered the students, changed the way his faculty performed guidance activities and by so doing aroused unexpected resistance. . . . In generalizing from . . . case studies about the importance of differences in the size of a change, its duration, or its content for the processes and consequences of innovation, certain problems inherent in the process of comparison must be dealt with first.

If one is to compare large and small, long and short innovations, one needs a common language to describe the cases in terms that are reasonably free of the particular instances, but accurately reflect the specific cases. In addition, one needs to decide on a minimum set of common data to be described for each case. If a particular phenomenon is absent from the description, one must be assured that it is absent in reality. One must also decide how much of the context of an inno-

[1]From M. S. Atwood, "Small-Scale Administrative Change: Resistance to the Introduction of a High School Guidance Program," *Innovation in Education*, Matthew Miles, ed. New York: Bureau of Publications, Teachers College, Columbia University, pp. 49–77.

*The research on which this case is based was supported in part by the Cooperative Center for Educational Administration, a project of the Kellogg Foundation, and by the Advanced School of Education, both of Teachers College, Columbia University. The full study is reported in Atwood (1960).

vation is to be described. This context can be thought of as the conditions in which the innovation was introduced, and succeeded or failed. The immediately prior situation is often given as an adequate statement of these conditions. If it is adequate, one must still decide how much of the situation is "immediate." These are decisions that have usually been made from common sense. However important common sense may be to other aspects of research, it does not guarantee common data for precise comparison.

The second aim of the article. . . .is to explore the usefulness of one set of answers to these problems of comparison, that offered by anthropological interaction theory. . . .The data of the case to be presented were collected and analyzed in line with the assumptions of this theory. A short statement of the theory will help in understanding the choices made in selecting the elements of the case and in judging the usefulness of the method.

INTERACTION THEORY AND METHOD Anthropological interaction theory (Chapple and Arensberg, 1940; and its restatement and elaboration in Arensberg and McGregor, 1942; Arensberg, 1951, 1957; Arensberg and Tootell, 1957; Chapple and Coon, 1942; Chapple, 1953, 1962; Chapple and Sayles, 1961; Homans, 1950; Kimball and Pearsall, 1955; Kimball, 1958; Whyte, 1951) starts with the widely held assumption that society and culture are products of social action. Social action consists of events in time and space in which people stimulate one another and respond to stimulation. Out of the recurrence of such interactional events emerge symbols, attitudes, values, beliefs, norms, and the like. These emergents have meaning primarily in the events of interaction in which they occur. They must therefore be referred back to the events as a first step in describing and interpreting them. This first step may be thought of as placing the phenomenon in its primary or *internal context*. Second, the connection between the phenomenon under study and the other elements of the events is made by observing the order of occurrence in time of each of the elements. Any new phenomenon or change is treated as an emergent from prior changes in the events in which it first appears. This procedure helps to reveal unsuspected causal relations. It represents observable reality more closely than static correlational approaches. This second step may be thought of as placing the phenomenon in a process in *time*. The internal contextualization is thus extended to include prior states of events.

Events take place and recur in a particular *environment* of physical possibilities and limitations. The connection between the events and their physical environment must be described. The environment consists also of other sequences of recurrent events. The connection of these other events to the events under observation must likewise be made. But not all the other events taking place in adjacent spaces and times need to be included in this examination. One distinguishes linked or tangent events occurring before and during the appearance of the events under observation. The linked events are those which share some of the same people interacting in the focal sequence of events. This physical and social environment forms the secondary or *external context*. This third step places the phenomenon under study in it.

So far, the features of the interactional approach which have been brought out are (1) its empirical bias—it deals mainly with observable happenings in space and time; (2) its processual nature—it regards reality as sequences of happenings which must be placed in the order of their occurrence; (3) its contextual emphasis—it makes the first task of the researcher that of looking for connections among the elements in space and time, placing a phenomenon in its primary context of events; and (4) its answers to the question of a sufficient secondary context—the physical context is described when the events are placed in space, the social context is adequately described by the linked events in which some of the same people interact, and the temporal context by the prior state of both of these.

The result of this approach is a number of cases of social action described in their natural setting. The next step imposed by interaction theory is to compare these cases. The classification of similarities and differences is based on the common properties exhibited by the events of interaction. These properties yield universal operations, the simplest of which are (1) enumerating the people taking part in an event, (2) identifying the actors, (3) specifying the order in which they act, (4) measuring the duration of each act in an event, and of events, (5) counting the frequency of occurrence of these orders of action or events, and (6) noting the regularity in time of their occurrence.

Whether or not the patterns of interaction are in fact prior to values and attitudes, and whether or not they are the significant feature of social life and changes in it, the operations that can be performed make interaction the empirical basis for comparative analysis and generalization. These operations give a description of events that is relatively free of the particular and yet more concrete than such nominal descriptions as "high morale" and "tight authority," or than definitions of an innovation as "new" or "representing a qualitative shift in an existing situation."

The way of applying interaction theory to the study of educational innovation is already clear. Educational innovations are to be treated as changes in patterns of social action, and as the emergence of new patterns of events. Educational innovations become processes described operationally as changes from prior states in the number and identity of the people involved, in the direction of action between them, in the frequencies of the specifiable kinds of events involving them, and in the duration and regularity of these events. They also become statements of changes in the spatial distribution of people and actions, and of changes in the preceding and concurrent sequences of linked events. Since the validity of this approach for education remains to be established, additional data on values, sentiments, behavior, and changes in these have to be included for examination against the operationally described patterns of interaction. Interaction thus defined offers a precise and objective framework within which to categorize and compare the observed facts of innovation.

THE CASE STUDY The example of a small-scale educational change to be presented in this manner concerns the efforts of a new principal of a high school to introduce a centralized guidance program. Since the faculty of the high school were noted in the city for being "guidance-minded," he expected no resistance to his plans. And, since he had decided nevertheless to "go slow," the opposition that developed to the program was all the more difficult for him to understand.

The prior situation

The John Quincy Adams High School was started in a large eastern city during the 1920s with two aims: to provide a high school education for difficult students and the apparently uneducable, or "motor-minded," and to give them an opportunity for technical training in a major industry of the area. The first principal and founder of the school, Mr. Doyle, persuaded the industry to donate expensive equipment. He also persuaded the board of education to hire technically trained men from the industry who were licensed to teach only at Adams. He asked the principals of the other city schools to send him their difficult students, those who would otherwise be recommended for discharge. His concern for these students continued within Adams. He went to see his teachers frequently to inquire about a student's progress, or to ask one of them to reconsider a grade or a demand for severe disciplinary action.

The school grew rapidly in the 1930s and then began to decline because of competition from another high school, decreasing high school enrollments throughout the city, and the start of World War II. In 1944 Mr. Doyle became ill and died. The assistant principal, Mr. Fall, became acting principal until 1946, when a second permanent principal, Mr. Lehrer, was appointed. Many of the faculty were sorry that Mr. Fall was not appointed permanently. They were disturbed by Mr. Lehrer's appointment because his major interest was audiovisual aids, not the industry around which the school had developed. They believed that this change in the goals of the school was but temporary until the board could find a technically qualified man like Doyle.

The faculty under Doyle had thought of themselves as "special" and superior in training and experience to the faculties of the other high schools in the city. Even those of the faculty who disliked some of Mr. Doyle's methods shared this feeling. And even these people agreed that Doyle was wholeheartedly devoted to the welfare of his students, a goal that they accepted for themselves. Several talked with pride of the extra time spent after school hours to help students, and of the occasional teacher who had helped finance a college education for a promising student.

In addition to this change in principals and in the aims of the school, certain other changes took place at this time which disturbed the faculty considerably. First, Mr. Lehrer reversed Doyle's policy of acting directly on students' problems. He believed that the responsibility for handling students' problems delegated to the deans and others should carry with it the authority to make decisions. As a result, he saw teachers much less frequently about the students than had Doyle. Many teachers interpreted this decrease in interaction to mean that Lehrer was "not interested in students."

A second change affected not only Adams but the whole school system. In 1947 the salary scale for elementary school teachers in the city was made the same as that for high school teachers. The high school teachers objected to the board of education's setting the same maximum salary for both. High school teachers had to have more training, they said, and pass more difficult examinations than the elementary teachers. These differences should be recognized by different maximum salaries. Discontent with the single-salary scale reached its climax in 1950. The high school teachers in the city went on "strike": they refused to continue their extracurricular school activities without additional pay.

The teachers at Adams also complained of a change in the students during the period "after the War." They said that the students decreased in intelligence, became more difficult to teach, and caused more and more disciplinary problems. They believed that the disciplinary problems began to become serious "before 1952." There are no records to support these beliefs, but there is some indirect evidence. In support of their statements about difficulties in teaching, one may note that the ethnic composition of the students had begun to change. In 1946, it had been mainly Irish, Italian, Jewish, and others, with about 5 percent Negro. By 1952 it was about 20 percent Negro and about 1 percent Puerto Rican. The spatial segregation of the Negroes and Puerto Ricans in their earlier schooling may well have resulted in a different response to learning from that to which the Adams teachers were accustomed. This difference may also have contributed to the teachers' belief that the students were less intelligent.

As for the increasing disciplinary problems, the lenient policy in dealing with students under Doyle was reversed by Lehrer. Though there may not have been any more problems than before, after 1946 increasingly more students were being chastised by the school authorities and transferred (or, if of age, discharged). In addition, the proportion of substitute teachers increased sharply in the fall of 1950 and 1951 from about 4 percent of the faculty to 12 percent and then 16 percent. When a similar situation occurred in the academic year 1956–1957, the older teachers pointed out that the inability of the substitutes to control the students made more work for the experienced teachers, who had to re-establish discipline before their own classes could go on. If the increased number of substitutes had a similar effect in 1950 and 1951, this may have contributed to the belief, in recollection, that students were becoming more difficult at about that time.

In 1952 Mr. Lehrer was transferred to another school. The new principal of Adams, Mr. Daubner, was appointed to his first position. Daubner announced an "open door" policy: all teachers were encouraged to come to see him about any problems. Although this was a change from Lehrer's relations with many of the teachers, it was not a return to Doyle's pattern of seeking out the teachers. But many teachers described the difference between Daubner and Lehrer as the difference "between night and day." Daubner also reversed Lehrer's policy of dealing with disciplinary problems. In Doyle's tradition, he tried wherever possible to give students a "second chance." But now, many of the teachers regarded this as the "easy approach" to discipline. They saw it as his attempt to alleviate the worsening disciplinary situation. When the problems did not get better, but were aggravated by an influx of strangers wandering through the halls of the school (a problem affecting other schools at this time as well), and when complaints came in from people in the neighborhood that the students were blocking their doorways, some of the teachers asked Daubner to have a policeman stationed in the school. He refused, and recommended instead that the faculty be more vigilant themselves in patrolling the halls. He did arrange to have a policeman stationed outside the building to clear the students away from the houses in the vicinity.

During the following academic year, 1952–1953, when Daubner took the first steps in introducing a centralized guidance program, a number of teachers thought that the new program was his alternative both to the failure of his "easy approach" and to their proposed solution of a policeman to keep order. (They judged the program accordingly for its success in lessening disciplinary problems, a much narrower criterion than the aims and scope of the program.) Actually, the decision to introduce a guidance program was made before Daubner became principal. The board of education wanted such programs installed, but left the initiative to the individual principals. Daubner came from a school that had had one of the first pilot programs. From his own experiences, he was convinced of the need for a systematic and expanded handling of the various guidance activities provided by the high schools. He came to Adams prepared to start such a program without knowing of its immediate problems. Some teachers had surmised this, because of the pilot program in the school that Daubner had come from, and because of the comments of their acquaintances who had been Daubner's colleagues in that school.

Some teachers were apprehensive about the new program. They wondered if it would mean a change in their teaching. Still others, those who disliked the "easy approach" shown in the handling of discharges, worried that the new program meant the dominance of "the permissive philosophy of education." On the other side, some worried lest any guidance program be thought adequate to do what they believed only a psychiatrist could accomplish.

THE ADMINISTRATIVE ORGANIZATION OF THE SCHOOL   In addition to this sketch of some of the major changes in personnel, aims, and behavior, and of some of the

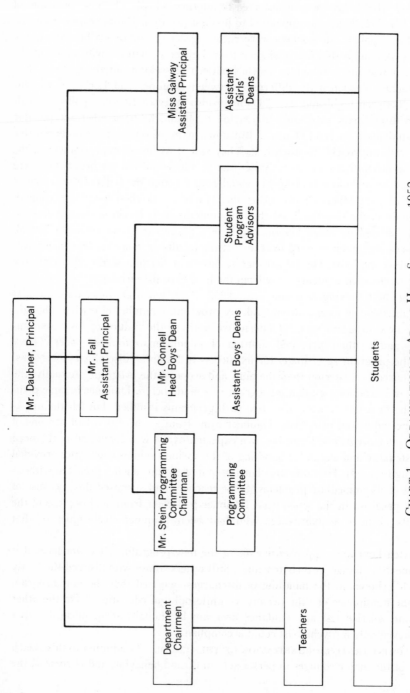

CHART 1. ORGANIZATION OF ADAMS HIGH SCHOOL IN 1952, BEFORE THE GUIDANCE PROGRAM (POSITION OF BOXES INDICATES RELATIVE POWER AND PRESTIGE)

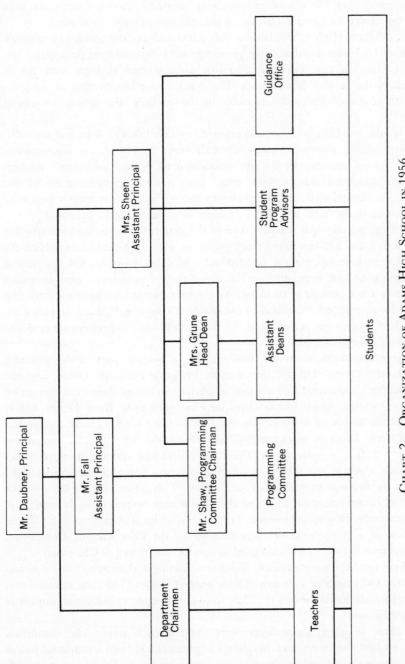

CHART 2.   ORGANIZATION OF ADAMS HIGH SCHOOL IN 1956,
WITH THE GUIDANCE PROGRAM
(POSITION OF BOXES INDICATES RELATIVE POWER AND PRESTIGE)

major values, beliefs, and sentiments of the faculty, it will be necessary to outline the organization of the school and the way in which guidance activities were carried out before the program began, so that changes in both can be seen.

In 1952 Adams High School had roughly 2300 students and about 115 teachers. (See Chart 1.) Under Daubner, the principal, were two assistant principals, Mr. Fall and Miss Galway. Formally equal in pay and rank to them were the 14 chairmen of the subject departments. The regular monthly meeting of the principal with people of this rank was called by the teachers "the principal's cabinet meeting."

The regular teaching staff were appointed from civil service lists, and were distinguished among themselves only by differences in pay based on academic training and on seniority in the city school system. Some "substitute" teachers were also appointed during each term. Each month, representatives of the teachers, the clerical staff, and the chairmen met to discuss grievances which were then taken up in the latter half of the "cabinet meeting" with the principal.

TEACHERS' DUTIES   All teachers, except the department chairmen, taught five periods a day and had one home-room period in which the clerical records on the students were kept up, notices handed out, etc. The chairman did not have a home-room class and, depending on the size of their departments, were exempted from one or more periods of teaching. All teachers except the chairmen were also assigned for one period a day, called the building assignment period, to police the four student lunchroom periods and the study halls, and to perform other duties decided on by the principal.

Among other duties were the activities which became part of the guidance program—the Deans' Offices, the Student Program Advisors' Office, and the Programming Committee. The number of teachers in any of these activities varied from term to term. About five teachers were assigned to be Boys' Deans, one as Dean and the others as Assistant Deans. Two to three teachers were assigned as assistant Girls' Deans to work under Miss Galway, the assistant principal, whose main role was that of Girls' Dean. These two offices took care of cutting of classes by students, absence, and other disciplinary problems. Some 11 teachers were assigned to the Student Program Advisors' Office. This office handled the intricate problem of counseling students about the 13 different courses of study leading to 13 diplomas which the school offered. The actual placement of students in a particular section of a class, however, was handled by the Programming Committee, which had four to five teachers assigned to it, with one named as Chairman.

All these teachers were excused, like the department chairmen, from a home-room class and from one or more of their subject classes. The time released was spent on their duties in the offices. They were assigned for an indefinite number of terms to their jobs.

The other building assignments were rotated each term. The distinction between rotated and nonrotated building assignments had been a continual source of irritation to the rotated teachers. They complained periodically about the difference because, they said, the nonrotated jobs were easier. Since all teachers were formally equal, all should have access to the nonrotated "plums." The teachers in the nonrotated positions agreed with the other teachers that teaching five classes is the hardest job there is, and that time off from teaching is very desirable. But, they added that the other teachers did not recognize just how much work the nonrotated positions required. They often had to take work home at night, and to spend any free periods during the day on these duties.

DEANS' OFFICES   The guidance activities in 1952 were carried out in the following way. When a student cut a subject class or was absent from a home-room class, the teacher had to send a card noting the offense to one of the Deans' Offices. When the student acted in ways that were unacceptable to the teacher (*e.g.*, cheating, insubordination, refusing to work, etc.), the teacher attempted to restore the pattern of acceptable classroom behavior. If he was unsuccessful or believed that the offense required a more formal punishment, he sent a card to the Deans. They in turn sent a notice to the student through his home-room teacher, telling him to report to the Deans' Office at a particular time. The time at which the notice was sent varied from a few days to a week after the offense, depending on the seriousness of the case and on the amount of work the Dean who was handling the student's class had. Whatever action was taken, the Dean made a note of it on the original referral card and sent the card back to the initiating teacher. Instead of waiting for this notice, however, the teacher often stopped a Dean in the halls or in the cafeteria or came into the Deans' Offices to ask what had been done about a case.

The head Boys' Dean, Mr. Connell, had made contact with various city, religious, and welfare agencies and called on them as needed in dealing with a particular case. He took up any problems he could not handle with the assistant principal, Mr. Fall. Mr. Fall reported that he kept a daily eye on the working of the office, dropping in for a few minutes each day to sense the atmosphere and to look at the cards received from the teachers. Mr. Connell thought of himself as responsible directly to the principal.

The sentiments of the faculty about the Deans' Offices in 1952 cannot be reported. In retrospect from 1956, they all spoke well of Connell, often calling attention to his law degree as a mark of his qualities. He, however, in discussing (in 1956) the complaints of the faculty about the office under his successor, said that he saw little difference in the way the two offices were run, and that the teachers had always complained about him also.

PROGRAM ADVISORS' OFFICE   The students talked to their Program Advisors each term in making up their program for the following term. The Advisors sent notices to the home-room teachers, who passed them on to the students whom the Advisors wanted to see. When the Advisors had a problem they went next door to Mr. Fall, the assistant principal, who "always knew the answers." They also advised the students about colleges, consulting Mr. Fall who kept the catalogues of various colleges in his office. The Advisors believed they were autonomous, and that they had no immediate superior: they went to Mr. Fall about problems because of his superior knowledge. Mr. Fall said they were directly under him but, because of his own many duties, he did not supervise them as closely as he would have liked to. He used their questions as a gauge of what they were doing, and interfered only when he thought that the direction of their activities was "getting out of line."

PROGRAMMING COMMITTEE   After the programs for each student had been made up, they were sent to Mr. Stein, the Chairman of the Programming Committee. Mr. Fall worked out with him a master plan of the class hours and the number of sections for each subject and grade. Then, Stein with his group of assistants worked out the specific assignment of students to sections. At the beginning of each term, the size of classes had to be "equalized," made as nearly equal again as possible, because mistakes and changes requested by the students often led to imbalances. If this were not done quickly the teachers complained that they could not begin their work. Stein thought he was directly responsible to the principal, but according to Fall was directly under the latter.

Many of the teachers, as well as the Advisors and Deans, felt free to take the initiative in discovering emotional, financial, or other difficulties of their students and attempting to do something about them. They usually called these to the attention of Mr. Connell, the Boys' Dean, for action. If they did not like his response or did not think it was sufficient, they took the matter up with Mr. Fall. Though they could no longer go to the principal as they had done with Mr. Doyle, they were proud of their "guidance" activities, and of their competence to continue them even without the support of Doyle's successor.

The start of the guidance program

Mr. Daubner became principal in February, 1952. Because of his belief in moving slowly in administrative changes, he "did nothing" about the program in his first term. In one matter alone—the treatment of disciplinary transfers or discharges—he acted immediately by reversing Mr. Lehrer's policy (in the direction of more leniency).

He took every opportunity, however, to discuss the value of guidance in particular instances with faculty members, and arranged to have some films on guidance shown at the faculty meetings. Meanwhile he looked about for someone to head the program. The obvious person was Miss Galway, the assistant principal, who was already acting as Girls' Dean. But she declined the job. There is some doubt as to her reasons. Daubner said that she was elegible for retirement and did not want to take the additional courses necessary to qualify herself as guidance head. Some teachers said that she did not approve of guidance. Whatever the reason, she agreed that he should prepare someone else for the position.

After observing the faculty in the spring term of 1952, he selected Mrs. Sheen, a Student Program Advisor, as a possible candidate, but did not tell her of his choice. She knew the complex courses of study of the school; she was interested in guidance; she always volunteered to do extra jobs; and she was willing to take the additional courses to qualify herself to work in guidance.

Mr. Daubner began to give her small jobs at first in 1952–1953, and had her attend some conferences on guidance. At the same time, he took the handling of girls' cutting offenses away from Miss Galway and added them to the work of the Boys' Deans. In their place, Miss Galway was given some of Mr. Fall's administrative duties in order to even the load of duties between them. One informant reported that Miss Galway began to complain about the amount of work. Some teachers who regarded themselves as especially friendly with Miss Galway were also upset. They said that "all the glamor [of her position] was being taken from Miss Galway and she was left with only the mechanics [the administrative work]."

The following term, the fall of 1953, Miss Galway resigned. To replace her, Mr. Daubner appointed Mrs. Sheen as acting assistant principal and relieved her of all teaching duties. The rest of the duties of the Girls' Deans' Office were transferred to the Boys' Deans' Office, the title of which was changed to the Deans' Office.

DEVELOPMENT OF THE GUIDANCE OFFICE   During the rest of 1953–1954, Mrs. Sheen gave her full time to developing a new activity that was called the Guidance Office. The office took over the handling of all cases of emotional difficulties, welfare problems, college counseling; the honor and various achievement rolls; and the development of a testing program. It also became the official office for making contacts with agencies outside the school. Mrs. Sheen began to address the faculty at the monthly faculty meetings to tell them about her work, explaining which cases were to be sent to her office and which to the Deans, how to fill out the new referral forms, how to compute the various honor rolls, and so on. With succeeding terms, the number of periods of building assignment time for her use and the number of teachers working under her increased.

She was nominated in the fall of 1954 by Daubner to become the assistant principal in charge of guidance. She prepared to take the first part of a "closed" examination in February, 1955, for the position. (The "closed" examination is administered by the city civil service, but is not competitive. This kind of examination was resented by some of the teachers because it prevented them from competing for the position.) She received her formal appointment in the spring of 1956.

Mrs. Sheen was then officially in charge of her Guidance Office, and the Deans' Office and Student Program Advisors' Office were under her direct supervision, the three divisions together forming the Guidance Program. (See Chart 2.)

In addition, she now began to take part in the development of new classes, and to work with department chairmen in the modification of existing classes and curriculum. In the fall of 1956, for example, as the result of a poor showing in mathematics on a school-wide testing program for scholastic achievement which she had instituted, she arranged for more remedial sections to be given the following year in that subject.

CHANGES IN THE PROGRAM ADVISORS' OFFICE   Next after the development of the Guidance Office section of the program, the Students' Program Advisors' Office received Mrs. Sheen's major attention. Beginning with the fall of 1955, they were placed under her direct supervision. The attention she gave to them may in part be attributed to the immediate problem at this time of cutting down the number of classes that had to be "equalized." Two sources of the uneven class enrollments were the errors in the Program Advisors' work, and the changes they made at the students' request. In addition, with the Advisors there was no problem as there would have been with the Deans of placing her, a former subordinate, over a head Advisor. Putting the Deans under Mrs. Sheen's supervision was delayed until she became formally an assistant principal.

Mrs. Sheen began to codify the procedures of the Advisors and put them into writing. The Advisors received a continuing stream of directives telling them what to do and informing them of changes required by the Superintendent's Office. They complained to Mr. Fall. He pointed out that these directives merely stated in large part what they were already doing. But some of the directives contained errors, and new directives followed with corrections and further instructions. Further, they were forbidden to make decisions on problems that occurred without consulting Mrs. Sheen for a ruling. Because she often did not know what to answer at the beginning and had to consult Mr. Fall or Mr. Daubner, and because her other duties occupied her full time, she frequently delayed a few days before making decisions. In addition, she called a number of meetings with the Program Advisors, which they described as "lectures."

The Advisors disliked the delays and the meetings as well as the directives, and during 1955–1956 they continued to go to Mr. Fall for advice. At the beginning he accepted this, for he believed it would take time for the Advisors to become accustomed to the change. Toward the end of the year, he saw that they had no intention of making the change. He began with increasing frequency to refuse to answer their questions until by June, 1956, he was insisting that all problems be taken to Mrs. Sheen. By the spring of 1957 the number of circulars and meetings decreased considerably (which some of the Advisors had not recognized, until the interviews of the present study brought this out).

CHANGES IN THE PROGRAMMING COMMITTEE   In the period after 1952, the efforts of the Programming Committee in making classes nearly equal in size appear to have been less successful than before. Complaints appeared in the minutes of the Teachers' Council, the formal grievance body, about the disruption of classes at the beginning of the term because of this. In the fall of 1955, the term in which Mrs. Sheen completed her examination for assistant principal and the term before she expected to receive her formal appointment, the Chairman of the Committee, Mr. Stein, asked to be relieved of his duties and returned to full classroom teaching. Mr. Daubner agreed, but persuaded him to continue on as a Program Advisor. One of the assistant Deans, Mr. Shaw, agreed to take over the job of

Committee Chairman. In the last half of the fall of 1955, he left his work in the Deans' Office to be trained in the new job. He became the new Chairman in the spring of 1956.

Although the Committee's work was still formally under Mr. Fall, the consequences of the work brought it to Mrs. Sheen's attention. In an effort to cut down the inequalities in class size, she insisted that all requests from Program Advisors and department chairmen for special placement of students, or for changes in their placement, be sent to her first for approval before going on to the Programming Committee Chairman. By the spring of 1957, the following year, teachers reported that there were fewer changes in programs and fewer disruptions of their classes than before. They attributed the decrease to Mrs. Sheen's work and were pleased about it.

CHANGES IN THE DEANS' OFFICE   The first consequences of the start of the program for the Deans' Office have already been described. In the spring of 1953, the Boys' Deans' Office was assigned all cases of girls' cutting, so that Miss Galway in turn could be given some of Mr. Fall's administrative duties. The Boys' Deans did not receive additional time for taking over girls' cutting offenses. The administrators said that adding duties to an already operating office did not require adding an amount of time comparable to that originally assigned to perform them. Further, the steadily decreasing enrollment in the school, a trend throughout the city which continued until the end of the next year, decreased the number of teachers in the school and thus the number of building assignment periods available. In the following term, the fall of 1953, during which Mrs. Sheen became acting assistant principal, the number of periods was cut from 17 to 10. Some teachers believed this time was taken from the Boys' Deans for Mrs. Sheen's use.

In the next term—spring, 1954—all the girls' cases were assigned to the Boys' Deans, who then became the Deans. Mr. Connell, the Head Dean, was unhappy about the amount of time allowed him for his work and repeatedly asked for more time, only some of which he got. In the fall of 1955, the term before Mrs. Sheen's appointment was formally made, the Deans' Office lost one man through sickness for most of the term. For the last two months of the term, Connell also lost the man who was to become the new Programming Committee Chairman to replace Mr. Stein, who had announced his resignation effective in the spring of 1956. After Stein announced his resignation, Mr. Connell asked to be relieved of his job.

In the next term, the spring of 1956, one of the assistant Deans, Mrs. Grune, was named to be Head Dean, and the Deans' Office was formally placed under Mrs. Sheen's supervision. All cases that required contact with outside agencies were now turned over to Mrs. Sheen. Otherwise the office functioned as it had before. However, by 1956–1957 the results of Mrs. Sheen's efforts to cut down the amount of change in class size at the beginning of the term began to affect the Deans' Office. Her interposing herself among the department chairmen, the

Program Advisors, and the Programming Committee forced the students to get her approval for a requested change of class section. She rarely gave this. The students responded in two ways. They began to ask the Deans to intercede for them with Mrs. Sheen. And an increased number of them stopped registering for any classes, and thus became additional disciplinary problems for the Deans.

SUMMARY OF CHANGES   In short, the introduction of a guidance program led to the consolidation of punitive activities in one Deans' Office, and to the coordination of the Deans' Office, some of the Programming Committee's work, and the Program Advisors' Office under one person, the new assistant principal (Mrs. Sheen). It led further to the development of another division, the Guidance Office, which took over college advising and approval of program changes from the Advisors, and the out-of-school contacts formerly made by the Dean. In addition, the Guidance Office took over the treatment of emotional and financial problems which formerly had been handled by the faculty and by the Deans' and Advisors' Offices. The Guidance Office also began a testing program and began to participate in curriculum planning. As a result of the consolidation and coordination of these activities, the teachers lost much of their former control over them.

Associated with the overall program were the resignation of one of the assistant principals (Miss Galway), the appointment of a former teacher and Program Advisor in the school (Mrs. Sheen) to the position, and the resignations of both the Dean (Mr. Connell) and the Chairman of the Programming Committee (Mr. Stein) in the term before the new assistant principal was formally appointed.

Response to the changes

ACTIONS   After the program began in 1952–1953, five major types of action characterized the response of many faculty members to the program. In the "first year" of the operation of the Guidance Office, the teachers "flooded" the office with cases, including "many things that any teacher could handle." Then this stopped, and the teachers had as little to do with the office as they could. Third, they began to make nasty comments about Mrs. Sheen to others, and directly to her. Fourth, they were slow in sending back forms, etc., which she had requested. (This refusal to respond on time to her orders continued until the spring of 1956, when she became the formal assistant principal. Then, they said, she had "the right" to make such requests.) Somewhat after these initial responses, about 1954–1955, Mr. Fall reported that the teachers began increasingly to ridicule the program to him. This action continued to the time of the study (1956–1957). The responses of the teachers upset Mrs. Sheen. Mr. Daubner had foreseen this and arranged for her to "let off steam," not by responding to the teachers' actions but by complaining periodically to him.

SENTIMENTS   At the time of the study in 1956–1957, the sentiments expressed by the faculty about the programs revealed a divided faculty, the division following the length of experience in the school. About 55 percent of the faculty had been in the school before 1952, and about 45 percent had been hired after 1952. Of the teachers in Adams before 1952, almost 90 percent had been there from 1944 or before. They made up the "experienced" teachers. Of the teachers hired after 1952, 86 percent came to the school in 1954 or after. Thus, between most of these "newcomers" and most of the experienced teachers there was at least a ten-year gap. Although most of the newcomers were young and inexperienced, some were not. They had transferred to the school from others in the system. The term *experienced* thus refers primarily to the length of service in Adams.

The sentiments expressed (in interviews) during 1956–1957 by a sample of 45 of the 111 teachers and department chairmen were treated for the *tone* of the comments. Tone refers to the liking or disliking, the approval or disapproval, expressed or implied by a comment. For example, those who criticized the Dean for being too lenient with the offenders and those who criticized her for being too harsh were both considered unfavorable in the tone of their sentiments. This treatment by tone revealed the following differences in sentiments about the guidance program:

	For	Against	Totals
Experienced teachers	8	22	30
Newcomers	12	3	15
	20	25	45

The *content* of the sentiments expressed will be summarized for the two major groups of teachers. The favorable newcomers knew little of the details of the program, but thought that "guidance was a good idea." The sentiments of the unfavorable experienced teachers covered several areas of content. They complained, first of all, about the "philosophy of guidance." By this some referred to the questionable need for a program, since they were already doing the job. For some, the program signified a "permissive" approach which would be interpreted by the students as a sign of "weakness." Second, for many the time spent on the guidance program was time "taken" by the principal from them. Without this program, there would have been more people to handle the clerical tasks, etc., and thus lessen each person's load. Third, for some the interest of "the board" in guidance was "reason enough to be against it." It was, they said, "a fad."

Fourth, if there was to be a program, they disagreed about who should get the time to do guidance. Some believed the time ought to be given to the classroom teachers, as the ones best able to deal with guidance. Others thought that more time should be given to the Deans. Both Deans and Program Advisors thought that more time should be allocated to themselves. Fifth, the teachers complained about who received the attention of the program. Some resented the time spent on "the 5 percent [the trouble-makers] at the expense of the 95 percent." Others resented the attention given to "the 20 percent" [the academically minded], since the school had originally been for the "motor-minded," the apparently uneducables. Sixth, they complained about the lack of results obtained from the program. They saw no improvement in class cutting, absence, or disciplinary problems. Further, they did not know what was going on "down there" (in the Deans' and Guidance Offices): the cards they received reporting on the action taken had inadequate notes on them, and were returned at irregular intervals. Seventh, the teachers complained about their relations with the people in the program, particularly the Head Dean and Mrs. Sheen. The people in the program were accused of being abrupt, and of "acting as if guidance were the answer to everything and as if the teachers knew nothing." People in the program, the teachers said, did not consult them.

Eighth, the teachers criticized the choice of personnel for the program. This sentiment was intimately bound up with their long-standing criticism of nonrotated assignments. These jobs were easier than others, they believed, because they carried "time off," and it was unfair not to rotate the jobs. Since the jobs were not rotated, this implied a special merit among the people selected for the guidance program. But young, inexperienced people had been given some of these jobs. Further, the head of the program was a woman "who had not been such a hot teacher in the classroom that she could now tell everyone else what to do." The new Dean, Mrs. Grune, would have been "all right" as an assistant Dean but not as Dean. Some men said she was "too harsh"; others, "too lenient." The men who made these criticisms believed that the heads of the program and of the Deans' Office should have been men. None of the experienced teachers could understand the appointment of the new people. The lack of special merit demonstrated by the appointment of people they saw as new, inexperienced and not particularly qualified was support, the teachers believed, for their contention that the jobs could be and should be rotated. And it supported their belief that the principal had shown "favoritism"; some of his choices would be incomprehensible otherwise.

CONCLUSION   Despite considerable differences in the content of the responses by various segments of the faculty to the guidance program, the major distinctions followed the length of experience of faculty members at Adams. The majority of newcomers to the school were favorable to guidance, and said that they used the program whenever necessary. The majority of the experienced faculty were unfavorable to the program, and said that they used it as little as they could.

ANALYSIS   The course of events by which a guidance program was introduced in a high school, and the actions and opinions of the faculty relevant to the program have been outlined. The favorable sentiments of the newcomers were in accord with the sentiments which the experienced faculty had expressed toward guidance earlier. But the unfavorable sentiments expressed by the latter in 1956–1957 represented a marked shift from their earlier sentiments. In this section an explanation of the differences in the tone of the sentiments of the faculty will be presented.[2]

The explanation of the differences between the sentiments of the experienced teachers and the newcomers, and between the later and earlier sentiments of the experienced teachers was based on the assumptions of interaction theory. The significant feature of the innovation process was assumed to be the changes in operationally described interaction patterns. These changes were assumed to precede changes in sentiments and individual behavior.

Effects on the interaction of experienced teachers

Examining the introduction of the guidance program as to its consequences for the interaction of the pre-1952 teachers revealed the following changes. Each interaction change is summarized first, and then followed by illustrations of the happenings from which it is derived.

DECREASED INITIATION   The pre-1952 teachers experienced a decrease in the frequency with which they initiated action for others, and initiated action successfully (that is, got the response they wanted). By centralizing the program, the principal inadvertently took away the initiative in some of the guidance events from them. Because the program was set up under a formal superior, they lost control of a case once it had been turned over to the program. Further, they did not know what happened in a case until they received a report from the office. If they did not approve of the action taken, or of the time interval between their action and the response to it, they could now do little about either.

INCREASED RESPONSE REQUIRED   The teachers experienced an increase in the frequency of events in which they had to respond to someone else. Mrs. Sheen issued instructions which they had to follow; she sent around notices which they had to fill in and return; she addressed them at the faculty meetings for longer periods of time than had Miss Galway.

IRREGULAR RESPONSE FROM OTHERS   The teachers experienced more irregularity in the time between their initiating action on a case and the report to them of what had been done.

VALUE VIOLATION   The teachers experienced violations of valued characteristics of their interaction which had become part of their identity. They had been used to going to a man, and to a colleague or older person. Now they had to go to women, which bothered the men particularly, and to younger people in the program, which distressed the older people. The values the men brought into the school from their society—about men rather than women taking the initiative—may account for part of their resentment. Their view had been reinforced by Miss Galway's position in the school. Although formally their superior, she did little to

---

[2]For the complete analysis, including data on the major types of action as well as sentiments, see Atwood, 1960, Chaps. 5ff.

make that position felt, initiating relatively little action for them. In addition, though, the jobs of Dean and Programming Chairman had always been held by men in Adams and were stepping stones in the system to assistant principalships. The appointment to the assistant principalship of a woman, a person who had held neither position, violated both expectations (held particularly by the older men teachers) about the jobs. The appointment of the young violated the expectations of all the older teachers about jobs with "time off." These jobs had come to be looked on both as the perquisite of seniority and as the symbol of competence to deal with children. The older teachers saw the jobs go to those who had not earned the right to the "plums" by their years of service, or by their ability to deal with children, which came only with the years.

Of more importance, the characteristic pattern of the teachers' daily interaction in the classroom had itself become valued. They valued taking the initiative and being responsible for everything that happened in the classroom. They said, "A good teacher handles his own problems." The Deans supported this view in different language: "Only the weak sisters come down here [to the Deans' Office] all the time." The consequences of setting up the program, especially the first two described above, violated the values of independent and self-dependent action, values which had become part of their notion of themselves as teachers.

The operation of the program continued these violations, by requiring the teachers to go outside the classroom more frequently than before, to turn over all cases and potential cases not only to the Deans but now also to Mrs. Sheen, and to give up control over the disposition of a case. The continuing complaints against the Deans' Office before the program began, reported by the former head Dean, may have partly expressed the inherent contradiction between its operation—requiring the teachers to go outside the classroom for help—and the values of independent and self-dependent action of the faculty.

Effects on newcomers

The change in the sentiments toward guidance shown by the majority of the experienced faculty can be correlated, as we have seen, with preceding changes in properties of their interaction patterns. This approach also accounts for the favorable sentiments of the majority of the new faculty. The latter had not been in Adams long enough to develop a pattern of interaction sufficiently stable to suffer change. (It must be assumed that they brought in their generally favorable attitude toward guidance from the outside.) Although they said they used the services of the program as often as necessary—the unfavorable people said they used it as little as possible—the newcomers to Adams did not actually use it significantly more than the other group. It is unlikely that they developed their favorable sentiments from interaction with the personnel of the program. But this explanation, based on change or its absence in interaction patterns, still leaves unaccounted for the eight experienced faculty members who were favorable and the three new people who were *un*favorable to the program.

The exceptions to the explanation

Six of the eight favorable experienced teachers were found to be working in the guidance program. But two of the three unfavorable new people were also in it. Neither a position in the program, nor the relative change in status from getting such a position, was able to account for the sentiments of these people. It was found, however, that the six experienced people were in the Deans' or the Guidance Offices, and the two new people were in the Program Advisors' Office. Examining the interaction patterns of the positions in the Deans' and Guidance Offices revealed that these appointments *reversed* the changes in interaction which the experienced faculty had undergone. Such positions (1) increased the frequency of events in which teachers took the initiative and took it successfully, (2) decreased the frequency with which they had to respond to others, and (3) reinforced their identifying characteristics as people who took the initiative and were competent to deal with students' problems. Because of the very rough quantitative measures used, it was not possible to tell whether the difference in their sentiments was connected to the reversal, to the degree of reversal, or mainly to the stabilization of their interaction patterns in these positions.

The Program Advisors, on the other hand, went through still another set of changes which, nonetheless, had the same interaction consequences as those undergone by the experienced faculty. Mrs. Sheen's action in tightening her supervision of the office resulted in a rapid decrease in the frequency of events in which the Advisors could and did take the initiative (making of decisions about problems). Her supervision increased the frequency of events in which they had to respond to her (continually revised instructions to them, and meetings). It resulted in longer and more irregular time intervals between their initiations to her and her responses. It changed the identity of their superior from a man to a woman, from one who had only been nominally a superior to one who was formally and actually their superior. The Advisors were denied access to the confidential files of the Guidance Office; they believed their competence to counsel the students was impugned, and their own identity was consequently affected. Thus, although the content of the changes affecting the Advisors was different from that experienced by the faculty, the changes had similar consequences in interaction, and the Program Advisors expressed sentiments whose tone was unfavorable, like the rest of the experienced faculty. Since there is no reason to believe that the two new Advisors differed at the start from the other new teachers in their generally favorable sentiments about guidance, their agreement with the unfavorable older group can be attributed to the similarity of their preceding social experiences, just described as changes in interaction.

The difference between these two segments of the guidance program suggests that change alone is not sufficient to account for the resistance and unfavorable sentiments of the experienced faculty. Only when the innovation resulted in the changes in interaction specified above (decreased initiative, increased response to others, etc.) did their sentiments change. The difference in the *content* of the changes affecting the general faculty and the Program Advisors was shown to be misleading. The resultant *interaction* changes experienced by both were similar, and were followed by similar changes to unfavorable sentiments. Where other changes nullified the changes in interaction, as in the Deans' and Guidance Offices, the sentiments of these people remained favorable or became so.

LINKED CHANGES The limits on the size of this [article] . . . do not permit a detailed examination of the changes in the preceding or concurrent linked events. Most of the changes have already been described in the section on the prior situation. The changes preceding the program were: (1) the death in 1944 of the first principal and founder of Adams; (2) the decision of the board after his death to change the goals of the school and thus the special status of the school and its faculty; (3) the equalization in the school system of high school and elementary school salaries; (4) changes in the ethnic composition of the student body beginning about 1946; (5) a general "strike" in 1950, the refusal of the high school teachers in the city to carry out extracurricular activities without pay; and (6) the increasing discipline problems. Concurrent with the development of the program were: (7) a continuation of the change in the composition of the student body; (8) a continuation of the discipline problems, and (9) a steady increase in the number of clerical demands on the teachers. All these changes have been shown (Atwood, 1960, Ch. 6) to have had consequences in interaction for the faculty similar to those described above as the results of the introduction of the guidance program.

Since most of these linked changes having similar interaction consequences for the faculty occurred before the program began, the guidance program may be seen as an intensification and a reinforcement of the changes already occurring in the school and continuing during its development. In judging the strength of the correlation in this case between the changes in sentiments and behavior about guidance and the interaction changes resulting from the program, this state of the external context must be considered. How important such conditions are for the course of events in an innovation remains to be discovered from comparative study. In this instance, the development of the program appears to have exacerbated the feelings of the faculty. Their complaints about guidance served in part as a channel for expressing the feelings of "pressure" resulting from the other changes in the system.

SUMMARY The unexpected resistance that a high-school principal met from his faculty when he introduced a centralized guidance program was examined with the help of anthropological interaction theory. The theory offered a set of answers to some of the problems of describing this small-scale administrative change for comparison with other instances of educational innovation. The theory prescribed the significant elements in the process of innovation as operationally defined interaction and changes in it. The theory also specified the amount of context in space and time to be included. It provided further a scheme for analyzing and interpreting what happened. Interaction analysis revealed the similarities in the structure as well as the results of overt differences in changes. It enabled the diverse changes in the course of events in the case to be compared and added or subtracted from one another.

Resistance to the innovation was shown to be preceded by changes in the properties of interaction. The experienced teachers and the newcomers who became unfavorable to the innovation underwent a decrease in the frequency with which they took the initiative in guidance activities, an increase in the frequency with which they had to respond to others in the school, and an increase in the irregularity of the time lapse between their initiations and responses to them from others. They also suffered a series of changes diminishing valued characteristics of their identity as teachers. On the other hand, where other changes stabilized the interaction of some faculty members and partly restored their earlier pattern, the innovation was accepted by them.

It must, of course, be kept in mind that the connections noted here among the elements in the course of events occurred in an innovation still in progress. Further, the innovation took place in a social context already undergoing interaction changes. Whether or not the sentiments of the experienced faculty will change after the program as a whole stabilizes cannot be determined. Last, the usefulness of the approach for a comparison of innovations has not been attempted, and remains to be examined.

Bibliography

Arensberg, C. M., 1951, "Behavior and Organization: Industrial Studies," *Social Psychology at the Crossroads*, J. Rohrer and M. Sherif, eds., New York: Harper & Row, pp. 324–352.

Arensberg, C. M., 1957, "Anthropology as History," *Trade and Market in the Early Empires*, K. Polanyi, C. M. Arensberg, and H. W. Pearson, New York: The Free Press, pp. vii–ix, 97–113.

Arensberg, C. M., and D. McGregor, 1942, "Determination of Morale in an Industrial Company," *Applied Anthropology*, 1 (2), pp. 12–32.

Arensberg, C. M., and G. Tootell, 1957, "Plant Sociology: Real Discoveries and New Problems," *Common Frontiers of the Social Sciences*, M. Komarovsky, ed., New York: The Free Press, pp. 320–337.

Atwood, M. S., 1960, "An Anthropological Approach to Administrative Change," unpublished doctoral dissertation, Columbia University.

Chapple, E. D., 1953, "Applied Anthropology in Industry," *Anthropology Today*, A. Kroeber, ed., Chicago: University of Chicago Press, pp. 819–830.

CHAPPLE, E. D., 1962, "Quantitative Analysis of Complex Organizational Systems," *Human Organization*, 21 (2), pp. 67-87.

CHAPPLE, E. D., with the collaboration of C. M. Arensberg, 1940, "Measuring Human Relations," *Genetic Psychology Monographs*, 22, No. 1.

CHAPPLE, E. D., AND C. COON, 1942, *Principles of Anthropology*, New York: Holt, Rinehart and Winston.

CHAPPLE, E. D., AND L. R. SAYLES, 1961, *The Measure of Management*, New York: Crowell-Collier and Macmillan.

HOMANS, G. C., 1950, *The Human Group*, New York: Harcourt, Brace & World.

KIMBALL, S. T., 1958, "Problems of Studying American Culture," *American Anthropology*, 57, pp. 1131-1143.

KIMBALL, S. T., AND M. PEARSALL, 1955, "Event Analysis as an Approach to Community Study," *Social Forces*, 34, pp. 58-63.

WHYTE, W. F., 1951, *Pattern for Industrial Peace*, New York: Harper & Row.

11.5 INTRODUCTION

Having examined all the facts, concepts, theories, and insights contained in the selections that comprise this book, what is the reader to do with them? How is his performance of his role and pursuit of his objectives to be affected by all that he has been exposed to here?

This final selection should serve as the grain of salt that the student and future practitioner adds in assimilating all the preceding materials. As the authors suggest, no amount of knowledge will in itself solve real problems and make critical decisions for the practitioner. Knowledge can be useful, but the task of defining problems and evaluating alternatives still rests with the individual. He must select, among all the facts and concepts available, those which are most relevant and practical in his particular situation.

In order to use concepts and findings, the guidance-personnel worker must have more than a superficial acquaintance with them and must understand their background and limitations. At the same time, he must retain a flexible and skeptical attitude, not equating reality with the abstractions used to understand it and remembering the tentative and relative nature of these abstractions even at their best.

Thus, the final excerpt in this book conveys a word of caution to the reader and a plea that the proper perspective be maintained on all that has gone before. The problems that each professional worker faces and the situations in which he must act are specific and unique and cannot be molded to fit the particular bits of knowledge that social scientists may provide. Such knowledge must be translated and adapted and its utility will always be contingent on the intelligence and imagination with which it is applied. Concepts and theories are tools and, as such, their usefulness is ultimately determined by how they are used.

11.5   CONCEPTUAL TOOLS FOR THE CHANGE AGENT: SOCIAL SYSTEM AND CHANGE MODELS[1]

Warren G. Bennis, Kenneth D. Benne, and Robert Chin

SELECTION OF CONCEPTUAL TOOLS   Contributing to the difficulty of the change agent in making use of the knowledge of man contributed by social scientists is the sheer volume of clamorous and conflicting claims to primacy issuing from those in various scientific specializations. Shall he diagnose "role" difficulties? Or are personality mechanisms of the individuals concerned at the root of human difficulties? Or should the change agent concentrate upon the power structure of the organization? How does the practitioner guide his selection from among the competing wares offered by various social sciences?

Two interrelated ideas are useful in sorting out and evaluating the conceptual tools that are of use to the change agent. First, he needs to look at the functions and limitations of a "concept," "conceptual framework," or "model"; second, he must examine the size of human units and the level of analysis which are of central relevance to a particular change agent.

Change agents, accustomed to dealing with "facts," often find hard sledding in dealing with "theory." But, we reiterate, facts are always, in truth, observations made within some conceptual framework. Concepts are invented in order to fix a particular slant on reality and to guide the production of new facts. The preoccupation of behavioral scientists with new concepts unintelligible to present common sense is based on this supposition. The resistance by practitioners to "jargon" may be understandable but is pushed to the extreme would deny the cornerstone of the scientist's contributions to knowledge.

Change agents themselves make use of concepts and conceptual schemas, even while they are most vociferously attacking unfamiliar concepts in the name of naïve realism or common sense. Common sense itself is a loose collection of conceptual schemas, and is the end product of cultural accretions, of folk wisdom,

---

[1]From *The Planning of Change: Readings in the Applied Behavioral Sciences* edited by Warren G. Bennis, Kenneth D. Benne, and Robert Chin. Copyright © 1961 by Holt, Rinehart and Winston, Inc. Reprinted by permission of Holt, Rinehart and Winston, Inc.

habitual modes of thought and hidden assumptions about human nature, and the social arrangements of man. An explicit formulation of concepts into a conceptual schema to be used by the change agent allows him to reveal, examine, and refine his "common-sense" diagnostic orientations. Conceding the fact that there are very many possible conceptual schemas, what underlying unity operates among all of them? Unity can be sought, and at the same time, valid groupings of particular conceptual schemas can be found by examining the thought model lying behind assorted conceptual schemas. The thought models of "system" and of "development" can, we believe, fulfill the function of sorting out and evaluating various concepts for use by change agents.

But which is the correct model, the most useful conceptual schema, the most relevant and powerful concept for a particular change agent? Again, as we have insisted in preceding sections, the artistic skills of the change agent must be used in making such selective judgments. No cook book can tell him exactly what idea to use. He must select and combine from the available tools at hand and must create new tools when the existing stock is shown to be inadequate. He must in the last analysis create his own role and role relationships. But valid knowledge *will* be useful both in the process of creation and in evaluating its products.

Another assumption made by contemporary behavioral scientists is that when change agents are dealing with an individual, a small group, an organization, or a community or nation, there are some similarities and some differences among these clients, regardless of size. All client systems are assumed to be like all others in some ways, like some others in certain other ways, and like no others in still other ways. For example, an individual, a small group, an organization, or a community or nation all are analyzable in terms of the interdependent nature of a social system.

The discussion of *levels* of analysis may best be approached by an anecdotal illustration. A group of spectators sat watching a football game. They saw two groups of eleven men facing each other, heard a whistle blow, then suddenly action erupted, followed by another blast of the whistle, whereupon everyone stopped. One of the spectators said, "That was a good draw play, we gained eight yards." When questioned about his jargon, he said, "Well, the quarterback handed the ball to the fullback, who counted off several seconds, waiting for the opposition to be drawn in, and then crashed into the middle of the line and advanced eight yards before being tackled and stopped. That's what is called a 'draw play'." Someone asked a second spectator, "What did you see?" "Well," he replied, "I saw the acting out in different degrees of the needs for aggression and achievement in the players and the effects of how each views himself in relation to the other 21 men." A third spectator said, "I saw 11 men on either side engage in a pattern of coordinated behavior with very well worked out expectations of action for each position in regard to other positions, until these patterns were disrupted by the other side." A fourth spectator said, "I also saw your role relationship and integrations. But additionally, I saw a leadership structure, which included a man in one position calling signals during the play and a captain exercising some limited authority. I saw a social system of 11 men opposing another social system, each of which was composed of many subsystems and structures like leadership, conflict, plus a coach attached to each system." A fifth spectator said, "I saw two kinds of traditions: the ritualistic and emotional meaning of a game of this sort and the heightened excitement and tension of this particular game due to the traditional rivalry between these two teams. Both traditions reflect the competitive and peer values of our young adult culture."

Here we have a football fan's description and analysis of his "jargon." He has learned the concepts and conceptual schemas of football, and finds that it is a useful shorthand for describing a set of events. Also, we find an analysis of motives and self by the second spectator (perhaps an individual psychologist); a role analysis of expectations in a small task group by the third spectator (perhaps a small-group man); a portrayal of social structures and social systems by the fourth (no doubt a sociologist); and a statement of how the traditions and values of the culture affect behavior by the fifth (a cultural anthropologist). The statements and analyses are pitched at different levels of analysis, each using a different set of concepts and terms. The point is that no one level of analysis is the "real" one. Each is applicable for pointing up a different aspect of the behavior being observed and analyzed. It is conceivable that a football coach or a football player might find interpretations from any of these levels of analysis useful, depending upon the difficulty his team is encountering and the goals of improvement that have been agreed upon by coach and team.

Change agents may not, in relation to the confronting case, be able to select their conceptual tools of diagnosis at one level alone. They may be forced to become multidisciplinary. Furthermore, the change agent must select his tools of analysis on the basis of his preferred intervention strategy, his diagnosis of what he has power to do, the degree of accessibility of various variables to his influence, and the nature of his influence on and relationship to various parts of the client-system.

Questions and Implications for Practice

11.1 LAURISTON SHARP

1. After considering the revolution brought about in the lives of the Yir Yoront by the introduction of steel axe heads, try to imagine some of the changes that the introduction of automation could mean for our culture, specifically in terms of our concepts, values, and habits with respect to : (a) work, (b) masculine and feminine roles, (c) leisure, (d) the prerogatives of youth and age, (e) education.

11.2 DORWIN CARTWRIGHT

Guidance-personnel workers—and educators generally—are committed to trying to achieve change in people. Their unwillingness, sometimes, to acknowledge that this is their purpose leads at times to conscious attempts to be permissive; to "believe" in a wide-open, uncritical way in the essential goodness of human nature; not to coerce or to impose; to be nondirective.

1. Cartwright expresses an interesting point of view in this paper. Might it be possible, however, to lay less stress than he seems to do on the "training" of groups? Might more effort be given to systematic attempts to develop and keep going a continuous critical and rational review by groups of the human relationships that are being practiced, and the norms and values implicit in groups to which individuals are responding? Then, out of the greater understanding and sensitivity of the groups of which they are members, do you think individuals might be helped to realize fuller development? Discuss this proposed modification of Cartwright's ideas.

2. Danilo Dolci has said: "The explosions of nuclear weapons have had their share in making us see how wrong it is to concentrate solely on the individual, or solely on a closed collectivity, or even solely on the human race as a whole; in other words, how essential it is to look for and discover, step by step, the best and most suitable forms of relations among individuals, among groups, and within the entire human community."*

Are Dolci and Cartwright saying the same thing? Do you agree with them? How do you think elementary, secondary, higher, and adult education could implement these ideas more effectively than they are now doing?

3. Who is qualified to give leadership in this endeavor? What kind of qualifications would be necessary in order to provide competent leadership?

11.3 WILLIS E. SIBLEY

1. Sibley's report on an attempt to improve life for the citizens of Ma-ayo has implications for the many attempts that are being made throughout the world to involve residents in improving their own neighborhoods and living conditions.

---

*"Tools for a New World," *Saturday Review*, July 29, 1967, p. 13.

In what ways has the Peace Corps or the Domestic Peace Corps—or some other group you may know better—tried to avoid the mistakes of the Community School program, as described above? Has it succeeded? Has it made other kinds of mistakes?

2. Describe a case you know where some school or college, or some group within some school or college, has attempted to bring about improvements for some community group or neighborhood. How did they go about it? What did they accomplish? What were the reasons they succeeded as well as they did? What mistakes did they make?

3. What do you think of the position which many educators take that schools and colleges were set up to teach subject matter to students—that that is a big enough job—and they should leave to other institutions and other groups the responsibility for community improvement?

4. Would you hold that this position of nonresponsibility is particularly valid for guidance-personnel workers? Or could you justify a guidance-personnel worker's giving some leadership to a program of community betterment by helping students with their efforts, or working directly with parents or community leaders? Be specific about your justification. Give an actual example and be as specific as possible to show why and how the efforts of the guidance-personnel worker paid off for the individuals in that situation—or why they were unsuccessful.

11.4 M. S. ATWOOD

1. We have very few instances thus far of the application of the natural history research method and of interaction theory and method to educational problems. Almost all of the most respected research has consisted of counting and correlating according to various more or less ingenious designs. The very rarity of its method, therefore, makes Atwood's research of special interest.

Can you define some aspect of student life or some other aspects of education to which interaction theory and research method might profitably be applied?

2. The reasons—excuses—for opposing the guidance program in the school Atwood studied are not all uncommon: the head was a woman; the head was not old enough to deserve their confidence, or to deserve such a "plum"; the program robbed them of some of their autonomy. Each of these reasons has back of it threats to the invisible social structure of the school made up of statuses, authority, role-sets, and interaction patterns.

What significance do you see, in terms of statuses, role-sets, and interaction patterns, in the fact that the experienced teachers so overwhelmingly oppose the guidance program while the newcomers favor it four to one?

3. In what ways does this research add new dimensions of caution and wisdom to the development of a successful guidance program?

11.5 BENNIS, BENNE, AND CHIN

1. The analogy of the football game illustrates aptly the complexity of the situation faced by a change agent in an educational institution when his responsibility is to understand what is going on in the school or college and how each individual's particular situation in relation to the total situation is contributing to or retarding his development as a person. The basic problem will not soon or readily be solved.

How is the guidance-personnel worker to learn enough from the several behavioral sciences—how is knowledge from the behavioral sciences to be brought over and made accessible to the practitioner—so that the practitioner can be more adequate to the problems and opportunities that confront him in his work? Outline some specific methods that might be tried.

INDEXES

INDEX OF NAMES

INDEX OF SUBJECTS